Designing, Managing, and Improving Operations

David M. Upton

Harvard Business School

Prentice Hall, Upper Saddle River, New Jersey 07458

Acquisitions Editor: Tom Tucker
Editorial Assistant: Melissa Back
Editor-in-Chief: Natalie E. Anderson
Marketing Manager: Debbie Clare
Senior Production Editor: Cynthia Regan
Production Coordinator: Carol Samet
Managing Editor: Dee Josephson
Manufacturing Buyer: Diane Peirano
Manufacturing Supervisor: Arnold Vila
Manufacturing Manager: Vincent Scelta
Senior Designer: Cheryl Asherman
Art Director/Cover Designer: Jayne Conte
Composition/Illustration (Interior): Omegatype Typography, Inc.

Case material of the Harvard Graduate School of Business Administration is made possible by the cooperation of business firms and other organizations which may wish to remain anonymous by having names, quantities, and other identifying details disguised while maintaining basic relationships. Cases are prepared as the basis for class discussion rather than to illustrate either effective or ineffective handling of an administrative situation.

Library of Congress Cataloging-in-Publication Data

Upton, David M.
    Designing, managing, and improving operations / David M. Upton.
        p.   cm.
    Includes bibliographical references.
    ISBN 0-13-904509-0
    1. Operations research.   2. Management science.   3. Production management.   I. Title.
    T57.6.U693   1998
    658.4'034—dc21   97-48833
                                                           CIP

Prentice-Hall International (UK) Limited, London
Prentice-Hall of Australia Pty. Limited, Sydney
Prentice-Hall Canada, Inc., Toronto
Prentice-Hall Hispanoamericaña, S. A., Mexico
Prentice-Hall of India Private Limited, New Delhi
Prentice-Hall of Japan, Inc., Tokyo
Pearson Education Asia Pte. Ltd., Singapore
Editora Prentice-Hall do Brasil, Ltda., Rio de Janeiro

Printed in the United States of America

10   9   8   7   6   5   4   3

Contents

Preface

The course described in this book has a number of antecedents at the Harvard Business School (HBS). In the mid-1960s, Wickham Skinner at the Harvard Business School became troubled by the increasingly common view among senior executives that manufacturing had become a deadweight in American industry, in spite of its rich history as the original source of much of the nation's economic power. Skinner saw the prospect of a lengthy and damaging decline in manufacturing in the United States. In response to the growing view that the problem of production had been "solved" and that manufacturing was an unnecessary activity in an advanced nation, Skinner set about swimming against the tide. He developed a framework that showed not only why manufacturing was so often seen only as a source of problems, but also how it could become a competitive strength.[1] His work laid the foundation for the concept of a Manufacturing Strategy. The bases of his argument were that (a) companies, even those in the same industry, compete in different ways, (b) that different operations systems had different characteristics and tradeoffs, and (c) that a company was therefore unlikely to succeed by simply adopting the same industry-standard operations system as its competitors. Skinner concluded that the manufacturing task was to mold the manufacturing resource—through a series of interrelated choices—to match the competitive strategy that the firm was pursuing.

With this work as a foundation, Hayes and Wheelwright,[2] and later Hayes, Wheelwright and Clark[3] pursued Skinner's idea of manufacturing as a competitive weapon[4] still further. The key to strengthening the power of that weapon, in their view, lay in the development and renewal of distinctive operating capabilities. To do this, companies needed to build operations that relentlessly pursued customer value and that saw continual learning and improvement as a central part of their task. The dominant source of operational capabilities was the plant itself rather than central corporate staff, and the primary determinant of those capabilities was the effectiveness of the operations manager. Empirical research supported this view, showing large differences in the effectiveness of operations managers across plants in the same industry and even within the same company. These findings alluded to the enormous potential that existed for well-trained operations managers to make a difference to the overall competitiveness of the company. The course on which this book is based was designed to help graduating students make such a difference.

At HBS, the most notable predecessor of this course was "The Operating Manager," launched by Skinner in the mid-seventies. Earl Sasser and Steve Wheelwright each developed material for the course, which broadened its scope over time to include sales functions and service organizations. In 1980, Bob Hayes created a new course, "The Management of Operations" (MOPS), which sought to help students understand the issues associated with operations at all levels in an organization. It achieved this using a model that

---

[1]Skinner, C. W. (1969). "Manufacturing—Missing Link in Corporate Strategy." *Harvard Business Review* May-June.

[2]Hayes, R. H. and S. C. Wheelwright (1984). *Restoring Our Competitive Edge: Competing through Manufacturing.* John Wiley and Sons, New York.

[3]Hayes, R. H., S. C. Wheelwright and K. B. Clark (1988). *Dynamic Manufacturing: Creating the Learning Organization.* The Free Press, New York.

[4]Skinner, C. W. (1985). *Manufacturing: The Formidable Competitive Weapon.* John Wiley and Sons, New York.

resembled peeling and re-assembling an onion: first, the issues, challenges, constraints and performance evaluation of a first-level supervisor were examined; next came the viewpoint of the department manager, then the plant manager and finally, the vice-president of operations. At a time when most manufacturing companies were relatively stable and hierarchical, this was a powerful pedagogical structure. About two-thirds of the way through the course, students were challenged to develop practical action plans for improving various dimensions of operating performance, such as productivity or defect rates, using the insights they had developed in the first part of the course. They would move back down the various levels to see how each was impacted by their plans for action. In 1985, after being developed further by Kim Clark and David Garvin, the course was split into two parts.

Garvin saw that the field of Operations Strategy had grown in importance to the point where it warranted a course of its own, and set about developing some of the material from MOPS as well as fresh material and new frameworks to build a new and successful course.[5] Meanwhile, the MOPS course progressively focused more and more on shop floor human resource issues. With the incorporation of much of its material into the first-year MBA course, it slowly dwindled.

During this time, Hayes, Pisano and Upton[6] developed a new Operations Strategy course. This course focused less on Skinner's initial model that matched operations decisions to a comparatively stable set of competitive priorities, and more on the dynamic development of operating capabilities in response to changing competitive requirements. Operations Strategy provided important insight about how the development and exploitation of operating capabilities can build lasting competitive advantage, but many of the decisions informed by the course were deliberately aimed at a comparatively high level in the organization.

In the 1990s more and more students were becoming interested in operations and manufac-

turing as a first job, either as line/staff managers or consultants, and many returned to talk about their experiences in those functions. In addition, the Harvard Business School was running a summer executive course (Building Competitive Advantage through Operations) that focused on the managers responsible for service and manufacturing operations. The issues they were dealing with were not simply a subset of the issues addressed by Operations Strategy. It became apparent that, to be effective, managers still needed the kind of practical knowledge that the original MOPS provided. Even MOPS, however, would not have addressed many of their concerns.

There were two principal reasons for this. First, the explosion in the application of information technology (IT) in operations often left students without an understanding of IT at a severe disadvantage. Knowing that IT needed to be used strategically in an operation was no substitute for knowing how to select computer hardware and software, how to build systems that would not be obsolete as soon as they were installed, and how to forge the power of information systems into the heart of the operation. Second, the torrent of operations improvement techniques and philosophies—re-engineering, lean production, agile manufacturing, mass customization, and total quality management to name a few—often left managers not knowing where to begin as they sought to improve their operations. Methods for operations improvement, it seemed, were almost randomly applied. The particular combination of methods employed could result from a persuasive consultant, the latest improvement fashion, or the philosophy to which higher levels of the organization subscribed. It became clear that our focus on the power of strategic capabilities in operations had deflected attention from the management of the very source of many of those operating capabilities: the individual operating unit. Designing, Managing, and Improving Operations (DMIO) was developed to address some of these issues.

DMIO explores the management of the individual operating unit, concentrating on the design of improvement paths that allow that unit to become a source of lasting competitive advantage, either in its own right, or as part of a larger network. The book is based on the premise that young operations managers can have a significant impact on

[5]Garvin, D. A. (1992). *Operations Strategy: Text and Cases.* Prentice-Hall, Englewood Cliffs, NJ.
[6]Hayes, R. H., G. P. Pisano and D. M. Upton (1996). *Strategic Operations: Competing through Capabilities.* Free Press, New York.

the effectiveness, improvement rate, and competitiveness of their organization if they have the tools, knowledge, and inspiration to do so.

ACKNOWLEDGMENTS

A large number of people have contributed to this course over the past four years, many of whom are unaware of the importance of their contributions. They include managers, colleagues, and—most of all—the Designing, Managing, and Improving Operations (DMIO) students who have tested the material in its various incarnations.

My thanks go to Bob Hayes, Gary Pisano, Kim Clark, Uday Karmarkar, Steve Wheelwright, David Garvin, Bob Kaplan, Jonathan West, Helen Han, Roger Bohn, Dorothy Leonard, Jai Jaikumar, and Kent Bowen for their material and the ideas they have contributed over the years. Bob and Gary, in particular, spurred me to develop many of the ideas in DMIO when we worked together on our previous coursebook. Part of this course, as you will see, spans from both operations and information technology. Warren McFarlan and Kim Clark have both been important sounding boards for the concepts developed in this part of the course. At other schools, Gary Scudder at Vanderbilt, Morris Cohen at Wharton, and John Ettlie at the University of Michigan have been important contributors and "testers." Their viewpoints have been critical in ensuring a balanced book.

Andrew McAfee, a doctoral student at the Harvard Business School, has been a primary contributor to both the course and the book. Andrew's combined knowledge of both operations management and information technology is rare, and this book embodies much of his own work in the field. He has read countless drafts, attended the course religiously, contributed much of the material and has tested out teaching plans.

Christine Steinman, also a doctoral student at HBS, helped write many of the cases and teaching notes and has been both creative and patient as the various drafts were developed. Susan Rogers has also been an important aid, not least by helping to implement some of the ideas concerning information technology developed in DMIO at the Harvard Business School.

Thanks finally to Daniele Levine who assembled the artwork and to Sally Markham, my assistant. The experiment to cure her anglophilia by assigning her to work with me may now have succeeded.

David Upton
Boston, Massachusetts
April, 1997

Introduction

Over the past decade, operations management has changed in some fundamental and exciting ways. First, the old view of operations management as the task of running and maintaining a comparatively static production or service facility has given way to one characterized by a need for renewed flexibility, relentless improvement, and the development of new capabilities at the operating unit level. As the global curtain draws back to expose more, and more kinds of, operations to the mounting pressures of worldwide competition, there are fewer places for laggard operations to hide. The *context* in which the operations manager now works has changed to one that emphasizes *improving* an operation over simply *administering* it.

Second, as a result of this changing environment, the *skills* required of operations managers have begun to change. The tools of control are now overshadowed by the tools of operations improvement. The ability to involve a workforce as a central part of creating new capabilities has become more important than the ability to *control* them as part of a static process. There are also few operations today in which information technology (IT) does not play a central role. Operations managers now require an intimate understanding of IT and how to mold it into an operation to build superior performance and new ways of competing.

Third, the *scope* of the operating manager's job is broadening. Progressive waves of "rightsizing" and more plants that must compete directly on the open market rather than as protected feeder-plants in larger networks now mean that the unit manager must often be a strategist for the plant while still acting as the steward of its diverse community, building a deep understanding of how the operation and its technology work, and developing an improvement path to keep it ahead of its competition.

As compensation for these new challenges, the power of operations to create competitive advantage is now becoming broadly understood. Operations is seldom now seen as the "tail on the dog," whose job is simply to avoid messing up too badly. In a growing number of companies, operations has become an equal partner whose potential to create difficult-to-imitate and competitively significant capabilities is appreciated and exploited.

This course provides the tools, conceptual frameworks, and technological understanding necessary to manage operations in this increasingly challenging world.

FOCUS

Designing, Managing, and Improving Operations (DMIO) is aimed at students who intend either to manage or consult for operations in the manufacturing and service industries. While many of the cases are informative for senior managers, the primary objective is to prepare more junior operations managers and consultants to take effective action early in their careers, primarily in their first five years after graduation. A substantial part of the book is devoted to exploring issues at the intersection of Information Systems and Operations Management. While DMIO was designed for MBA students, much of the material is useful for students in industrial and manufacturing engineering, as well as students of operations-based information technology.

The focus of the book is primarily on the individual operating unit, in both manufacturing and services. The cases are biased towards action and implementation, but nevertheless rest on a common, conceptual premise: that striving to create a "world-class" operation is not enough to guarantee long-term success. Even "continuous improvement" is insufficient if competitors are improving more rapidly, on more important dimensions of performance, over a longer period of time. DMIO stresses that the key to success lies in *designing* operations to provide a foundation for subsequent improvement, *managing* them in a way that directs, fuels and sustains that improvement path, and *improving* the operating unit with an explicit and effective strategy. Traditional courses in operations management have typically focused on one or the other of these activities. DMIO aims to integrate them.

It does this at three, ascending levels of analysis, which constitute the three modules of the course. These, again, have traditionally been considered in separate advanced courses.[1] Module 1 addresses the design, management and improvement of the fundamental building blocks of operations: operations *processes*. Module 2 looks at the *systems* used to coordinate processes, focusing on the use and management of information technology as part of such systems. Module 3 addresses the *operating unit* as a whole and looks at how the various processes and systems are designed and managed within a human community in a way the builds superior and rapidly improving performance. This final module also introduces the concept of an improvement strategy, which integrates the themes of improvement that run through the previous modules. The overarching message of the course is: operations must be designed for im-

provement, and that improvement must itself be designed.

CONTENT AND STRUCTURE

DMIO is organized into thirty sessions. Approximately 40% of the cases are non-US based. Many of the cases concern protagonists who are comparatively young, addressing the kinds of issues likely to be faced by operations managers early on in their careers.

The course is divided into three modules, which are described in detail in the associated overviews:

- Module 1: Designing, Managing and Improving Operations Processes
- Module 2: Operations Systems and Information Technology
- Module 3: Designing and Implementing Operations Improvement Strategies

The following provides an outline of the modules, as well as some of the driving issues in each of them.

MODULE 1: DESIGNING, MANAGING, AND IMPROVING OPERATIONS PROCESSES

The first module of the course looks at the mechanisms by which the performance of operations processes can be improved. It introduces the competitive importance of rapid process improvement, and shows how operations managers make a difference to the rate of that improvement. The module begins by considering processes designed for single products or services, then turns to multi-product processes and the management of flexibility.

A key concept in this module is that actions taken to change and improve existing processes fall into four progressive categories: *repositioning*, *exploration*, *reconfiguration*, and *radical redesign*. It looks at cases in which each of these levels of action are used and explores how these various process improvement actions combine to build an ongoing path for process improvement. The latter part of the module focuses on the issue of process

[1]See, for example, at the process level, DeGarmo (1997) or Schey (1987). At the systems level, the courses described by Vollman et al. (1997) and Hopp and Spearman (1996) examine coordinative issues. More recently, the course described by Cohen and Apte (1997) explores new technologies associated with manufacturing systems. Klein (1990) provides a case-based course focused at the operating unit (plant) level.

DeGarmo, E. P., R. A. Kohser and J. T. Black (1997). *Materials and Processes in Manufacturing.* Prentice Hall, Englewood Cliffs, NJ.

Schey, J. A. (1987). *Introduction to Manufacturing Processes.* McGraw Hill, New York.

Vollman, T. E., W. L. Berry and D. C. Whybark (1997). *Manufacturing Planning and Control Systems.* Irwin/McGraw-Hill, New York.

Hopp, W. J. and M. L. Spearman (1996). *Factory Physics: Foundations of Operations Management.* Irwin, Chicago.

Cohen, M. A. and U. M. Apte (1997). *Manufacturing Automation.* Irwin, Chicago.

Klein, J. A. (1990). *Revitalizing Manufacturing: Text and Cases.* Irwin, Chicago.

flexibility. It looks at the multi-faceted nature of flexibility, and provides a framework that allows managers to identify precisely the kind of flexibility required by a process or operation, and the action they can take to develop it.

This first module develops some important principles for the rest of the course. First is the idea that the design of a process or system affects its subsequent improvement, and that specific characteristics of a design facilitate or inhibit improvement over time. Second is how incremental improvement can be managed to build knowledge that provides a foundation for more radical change. Finally, it introduces the practical challenges of implementing improvement as an operations manager. Even though there might be a clear best "technical" answer for how the performance of a process should be improved, the approach needs to be shaped to fit the competitive situation of the operation and the human community in which it exists.

Driving Questions in Module 1

- What actions should managers take to foster rapid and ongoing process improvement?
- How should managers balance the need for a stable process with the need to improve it?
- How can manufacturing-based process improvement techniques be applied to service industries? What special considerations are there when doing so?
- How should one respond to a process crash, in which output and quality deteriorate dramatically?
- How should an operation learn about a process and how to improve it over time? How can knowledge be transferred between processes and across generations of processes?
- What is a "flexible" process? What kinds of flexibility are there, and how should one select among them? What mechanisms can be used to develop the various forms of flexibility?

MODULE 2: OPERATIONS SYSTEMS AND INFORMATION TECHNOLOGY

The second module of the course looks at the integration of processes into *systems*. Its focus is primarily on the role of information technology (IT) in building operations systems, rather than the more traditional systems-level issues such as production control and scheduling. This module is important for two reasons. First, it explores an important set of technologies that often appear difficult and unfamiliar. Second, it proposes a radically different approach to the management of those technologies in operations.

The fundamental question posed in the module is: "Can the principles of continuous improvement developed in the first module be applied to Information Systems?" The short answer, in general, is "not very easily". Operations managers frequently cite information technology as the source of their biggest headaches. Part of the reason is that the architecture of the systems, and the principles on which they are designed, constrain their subsequent improvement. Information systems tend to be "installed" in operations (often by "experts"), rather than built progressively as part of an overall improvement path. Cost and time overruns are common, and very often the system delivered is no longer suitable or adaptable to a changed competitive environment.

This module introduces the concept of a *dynamic architecture* for information systems, and explores principles that facilitate the change and improvement of information systems over time. It distinguishes between two very different approaches to information systems management. One focuses on the management of installation projects, while the other relies on the ongoing management and stewardship of a constantly changing system. This latter "path-based" approach demands much more ongoing attention and expertise on the part of the operations managers; but its rewards are increased flexibility, much greater potential for improvement, and an information system that can be shaped as part of the operation to build new forms of competitive advantage.

The module is designed with two additional goals in mind. As well as the broader conceptual ideas outlined above, and in more detail in the module overview, it also aims to teach what the technologies are and how they are used, based on the premise that it is not possible to manage a technology at this level without knowing what it is and what it does. The module begins at the lowest levels of the operation, looking at the role of information technology in process automation. It progressively moves up in level, looking at systems for shop-floor coordination, MRP (Manufacturing Resource Planning) systems, and ERP (Enterprise Resource Planning) systems such as SAP's R/3. Finally, it looks at the use of information systems to connect operations to the outside world, and explores the management of systems for inter-plant coordination and connection with customers and suppliers.

Driving Questions in Module 2

- Why do so many operations spend large sums of money on IT and realize no apparent benefit?

- Why have so many fully-automated, "lights-out" operations been failures?

- How should an operations manager introduce information technology that automates tasks and possibly eliminates jobs?

- How should a manager address a situation in which the operation develops an information technology that is valuable externally? How should she decide whether to sell it?

- What is the value of computer integration? By what mechanisms does it deliver that value?

- How should the transition from push to pull-based manufacturing be managed?

- Why have Enterprise Resource Planning (ERP) systems been adopted so widely and so quickly by large organizations? What are the advantages and pitfalls of their use? Why are they proving so difficult and costly to implement?

- What is an open system? What considerations should be made when choosing between open and closed technologies and systems?

- When should information technology be shaped to fit an improvement path, and when should an improvement path be built around a particular information technology?

MODULE 3: DESIGNING AND IMPLEMENTING OPERATIONS IMPROVEMENT STRATEGIES

Having explored the improvement of processes and systems, Module 3 looks at the management and improvement of the operating unit as a whole. This integrative module uses many of the ideas and approaches seen in earlier classes to examine the challenges of designing and managing the improvement path of the operating unit. This third module develops the idea of an improvement strategy for an operating unit, that integrates the processes within an operation, the systems that control and coordinate it, and the community in which they exist.

The fundamental premise of this module is that there is no "one right way" to improve, just as there is no single way to compete. There are, however, some common decisions that need to be made. Together, this set of decisions characterizes the improvement strategy for the operating unit. Designing an improvement strategy includes such activities as setting a direction for improvement (rather than trying to improve on all performance dimensions at once). It means deciding which parts of the operation to focus on, whether at the level of basic processes, systems used for coordination within the plant, or the links with outside the operation. It involves selecting from the range of tools and methodologies for operations improvement. It means organizing the various subprojects, deciding which people should be involved, who will lead them, and how the projects will be phased over time. Finally, it requires careful consideration of how the operation will learn from the experience of others, and how it will capture the learning it generates to fuel future improvement.

While there is no one right way to improve, some improvement strategies are certainly better than others. A number of the cases in this book describe operations whose improvement paths have been ineffective or have become difficult to sustain. These cases allude to some common principles that inform the design of an operations improvement strategy. First, the improvement strategy should support the competitive mission of the firm. It should aim to develop capabilities that increase the performance of the operation on competitively valuable dimensions. While this might seem obvious, it is surprisingly often forgotten, as a number of the cases show. In the scramble to implement world-class practices or technology, the question "how will this improvement path help us compete?" is commonly unasked.

Second, the improvement path should fit the operations strategy of the company. It should consider, for example, the role of the plant in the broader network, the nature and history of the workforce at the plant, the kind of process technology employed, the sourcing arrangements used, and how these factors work in concert to excel on the chosen competitive dimensions. This is important because managers will often change and "improve" one facet of their operation yet compromise a strength in another area, or be detrimental to how the operations system works as a whole. In addition, improvement in one area often requires a change in another part of the overall operations strategy to have any beneficial effect.

Third, the improvement strategy should be coherent, in the sense that each of its elements should fit together and complement one another. The tools and methods selected, for example, should be appropriate to the desired improvement goals. Finally, the improvement strategy should be efficient and deliver results over an appropriate timeframe: Will it achieve the desired improvement in performance quickly enough (and without Herculean effort)? Will the outcome be worth the resources that are required?

The latter part of this module looks at the challenges of implementing and sustaining operations improvement in a range of environments—for example, in developing countries, in mature, stagnant plants, and in operations that are already improving rapidly and effectively. A number of the implementation cases address the problem of an operations manager being the "person in the middle" who often has to deal with torn loyalties—between the plant in which he works every day and the needs of the corporation as a whole. It also explores how outsiders, such as consultants and customers can foster performance improvement. Finally, as a result of their improvement activities, operations will often generate unintended new capabilities; the last two sessions look at whether and how to exploit the new capabilities of an operating unit.

Driving Questions in Module 3

- How does a manager translate higher-level directives into an actionable strategy for the local operation?
- What are the keys to the successful management of operations crises (such as a chemical spill)?
- If I take charge of a low-performing operation, how do I decide what to tackle first?

- How should I keep an operations improvement initiative from burning out or backsliding? Why do some initiatives fizzle out while others provide the foundation for ongoing performance improvement?
- What are the key decisions that need to be made when developing an improvement strategy for an operating unit?
- How should the operations manager address the tensions that often arise as she tries to balance the demands from above (such as the corporate parent) with those from below (plant personnel)? What kinds of conflict arise, and how can they be resolved?
- What are the practical considerations of "empowerment?" How much authority should operators have over the jobs they do?
- What particular challenges are faced when managing a plant in an unfamiliar country?

THEMES

The themes developed in each part of the book are described in the associated overviews. There are, however, some important themes that run across modules, and bind the course together as a whole.

1. An Integrated View of Operations

Operations can be viewed at three highly interdependent levels. At the lowest level, an operating unit or plant is a collection of machinery and buildings. These physical investments combine with labor and materials to build *processes* that change the form of material and information, in a way to add value for customers. At the next level, an operation is an orchestra of *systems* and routines, which coordinate processes and marshal the flow of work, resources and knowledge in the operation. At a third level, an operation is a community of people. It can have all manner of processes, routines and systems, yet if a sense of common purpose and *community* is absent, it can fail to improve and flounder against competitors. Effective operations managers are constantly balancing these different levels as they manage the operations they lead, and strive to develop principles that integrate them. Managers with technical educations will often focus too heavily on first two levels. Others emphasize "the people side" of operations, in the absence of a technical understanding of how the operation works, and more importantly how it *might* work in the future. The dangers of these biases are illustrated by a number of cases in the book.[2]

Leading the community formed by an operation is one of the operations manager's most important roles. While the technical challenges of operations management have increased, so have the human ones. Plants increasingly comprise a diverse community of people with a wide range of educational backgrounds: People with graduate degrees will frequently work side-by-side those who may not have a high-school education. Managing operations in international environments brings the additional challenges of a different dominant language and culture. Formal, stable, organizational forms have become less common, being replaced with more fluid structures that can be a source of great stress as well as opportunity for those working in them. Aligning such communities around common objectives is difficult: The range of motivations and aspirations is broad. While incentive systems can play an important role, there are still large numbers of people for whom pride in a craft or sense of community overwhelm any financial incentives that might be constructed.

Throughout the course, the challenge is to integrate understanding of these levels at which operations are managed. This means integrating knowledge of the operation's financial circumstances, with a technical and strategic understanding of the operation's role and a social understanding of the community in which it exists. Cases are drawn from a range of social contexts to provide a broad-based exploration of these issues: an aging Midwestern plant with a dispirited workforce; an angry, strike-prone Korean plant; a proud high-technology plant in the Caribbean; and a struggling joint venture in mainland China. These cases stress that an understanding of systems and processes alone is never sufficient to guide effective operations improvement. An effective improvement strategy is founded on a deep understanding of the community and people that will make it work.

2. Designing Operations for Improvement

While the importance of an integrated view of operations management runs throughout the course, one fundamental question dominates the first two modules: "How should an operation be *designed for improvement*"? This theme concerns what appears to be a set of fairly detailed matters related to process design and selection. However, this practical theme is the manifestation of a much broader conceptual issue: that the role of the operations manager is no longer simply to be a caretaker of installed equipment and processes, but is instead to build new operational capabilities through a process of experimentation and invention. Many engineers and information-systems specialists, however, are still working under the assumptions of the former model. The processes and systems they build are designed to be administered rather than improved. This can have a significant detrimental effect on the operation's ability to generate new capabilities over time. While technical specialists may develop a particular piece of equipment or part of a process, the *overall* design of an operation is within the control of the operations manager. She is responsible for the periodic selection and development of new equipment and processes, and decides how they fit together to build a functional whole. In carrying out these tasks, she is also a designer. The potential for ongoing improvement needs to be a primary criterion in developing that design.

Processes and systems that are designed to work flawlessly as soon as they are installed or commissioned can often, paradoxically, be the most difficult to improve. There are a number of reasons for this. The engineers who design a process often aim to optimize the performance of their design *at the time it is designed*. This is not an unreasonable objective, but it has some profound consequences for the operation's improvement path. First, engineers will often view process modularity (or the ability to change some elements of the process without significant impact on others) as secondary to the goal of short-term optimization. This may constrain the ability to make subse-

[2]For example, the *Cybertech* case illustrates the hazards of a processes/systems bias, while the *Corning Z-Glass* case describes a manager who has become ineffective because of an over-concentration on "his people", and his lack of understanding of the technology of process improvement.

quent changes in parts of the process to mold it progressively to match changing requirements. Second, the last few percentage points of yield or microns of precision frequently demand the addition of considerable technical complexity. This can mean that the only people capable of changing a process significantly are the original vendors, or a select group of people within the operation. Finally, engineers will often see the line workers who operate the process as a hazard to its immediate functionality rather than as a potential source of long-term improvement. They will therefore design a process to lock out as much human intervention as possible, partly to avoid unnecessary work on the operators' part, but also to avoid having inexperienced operators (which all are at the outset) upset the way the process works.

Although this approach makes some sense in the short term, in the longer term, circumstances change. The process may need to be adapted for another purpose, and there may be powerful ongoing learning opportunities that derive from operators interacting with the equipment. The operators may even invent ways of using it that the engineers had not anticipated. In reality, this happens all the time. Managers can reflect the imperative for ongoing improvement by selecting equipment and processes whose designs facilitate their subsequent improvement and change. Fortunately, there are some specific principles that can be applied to make it much easier to build the potential for ongoing improvement into processes, systems, and whole operations. The course explores these principles in all three modules.

3. Developing Operations Improvement Strategies

The "design for improvement" theme concerns the creation of the *potential* for improvement and change rather than the improvement itself. If only this theme was emphasized, one might be left with the notion that all that is needed for competitive success through operations is then random 'continuous improvement' until the operation reaches 'world-class.' This is far from the truth.

The idea of world-class operations has been helpful to a large number of mediocre operations: The concept has provided them with a sense of what is achievable and has introduced many effective operations practices ("best practices") to ailing plants and service operations. At its heart, however, "world-class" characterizes a replicative, lagging strategy. First, as Hayes and Pisano[3] point out, it does not address a fundamental question: What should the operation be world class *at*? A fundamental tenet of Skinner's work[4] is that different operations exist to address different competitive needs, even within an industry. "World-class" denies the fundamental trade-offs that exist between, say, flexibility and cost, or responsiveness and degree of customization. It implies that an operation can have it all, and need not configure itself for a primary competitive role.

Second, it suggests that—to be effective—all one needs to do is adopt the operations practices of a group of key leaders in the field. But "world-class" does not address invention and innovation in operations. Innovation in operations means more than developing new products or processes: it means inventing new practices that go beyond the industry norms at many levels. Australian Paper Manufacturers[5] (APM), for example, a firm in the packaging business, saw its business in brown-bag papers evaporate and so needed to look for new uses for its papermaking expertise. To do so, it transformed its existing paper machines to make high-quality fine paper (primarily Xerox paper), and completely reinvented the way paper was made and delivered in the Australian market. It built new methods of scheduling its paper machines, allowing customers to "book time" on the machine to make exactly the kind of paper that they needed. This kind of innovation allowed it, over a period of three years, to attack the incumbent's existing 75% market share until, in 1993, the incumbent's holding company capitulated, and sold its remaining paper-making assets to APM at a steep discount. APM's goal was not mere parity; its assault was fundamentally a process of invention,

[3]Hayes, R. H. and G. P. Pisano (1994). "Beyond World-Class: The New Manufacturing Strategy." *Harvard Business Review* (January-February, 1994) 77–86.

[4]Skinner, C. W. (1969). "Manufacturing—Missing Link in Corporate Strategy." *Harvard Business Review* (May-June), Skinner, C. W. (1978). *Manufacturing in the Corporate Strategy.* John Wiley and Sons, New York.

[5]Upton, D. M. and J. Margolis (1991), *Australian Paper Manufacturers (A).* HBS Case (9–691–041).

and of using operations-based innovation to fuel competitive success.

Finally, bundled with *world-class* is often the idea of world-class *improvement* practices as well as world-class operating practices. With a panoply of such improvement methods available in the operations arena, managers are often hard-pressed to select between them. For example, the recent tide of reengineering and ISO 9000 initiatives has set many operations on a much more productive and appropriate improvement path than they might otherwise have followed. For others, however, they have been expensive and ill-conceived distractions serving, at best, to improve operations on unimportant dimensions of performance while diverting attention from other more valuable and appropriate improvement paths. The solution is to apply Skinner's basic idea that different operations need to do different things, but now in the dynamic sense: Operations must design an improvement path that is appropriate for the operation. Throughout the course, choices must be made between various improvement paths for the operating units. The idea of an improvement strategy for the operating unit is introduced, which provides a framework for developing an actionable improvement path that fits the competitive strategy of the company, meshes well with its operations strategy, and provides a coherent and effective basis for the development of new operating capabilities.

4. Managing Information Technology as an Integral Part of the Operation

The volume of information required to run modern operations has exploded so dramatically that operations without effective information systems are at a severe disadvantage. The information needed to build a Boeing 747 airplane, for example, would fill the aircraft it describes many times over if printed onto paper. In addition, manufacturers are following the lead of many service companies by combining information systems with their operations expertise to build new competitive weapons. This has brought new challenges and new opportunities. But only with sufficient knowledge of the technology and how to harness it as part of an operation is it possible to take advantage of those opportunities. To address this need, General Electric has begun an aggressive program to build IT literacy in operations. This initiative has already

begun to pay off. New innovations in Web-based purchasing, for example, have cut GE Lighting's average purchasing lead time in half (to seven days) while cutting costs by 15%.[6]

In addition to playing an increasingly central role in operations management, the *nature* of the information technologies employed is also changing dramatically and more rapidly than ever before. Client-server architectures are now commonplace, and over the next five years, operations managers will begin to see broad intranet and even internet connectivity on the shop-floor itself. In GE Lighting's case, electronic blueprints are now posted electronically directly from the factory floor by this mechanism, to ensure that suppliers know exactly what current requirements are. Open systems, which facilitate rapidly built "mix-and-match" architectures, allow best-of-breed technologies to be brought together to build systems that are closely tailored to the operation's prevailing needs. While these modular systems allow for ongoing change as part of their design, they demand greater vigilance and stewardship on the part of the operations manager. Without careful, well-informed, and ongoing attention, such architectures can degenerate rapidly into the polyglot mish-mash of systems that have paralyzed so many operations in the past.

The problem of "design for short-term optimality" described earlier is especially severe in IT-based systems. The complexity of modern information systems and the typical operations manager's scant knowledge of the field mean that the IT "problem" is often handed wholesale to a software vendor or consultant. The systems they develop are usually completed late, over budget and match requirements that may have existed when the project was launched, but no longer prevail. This "installation" world-view can leave operations managers watching helplessly as the performance of their systems subsequently falls behind that of competitors. Their lack of knowledge about their IT resources, combined with the complexity and architectural constraints of the systems, precludes improvement without replacement. Their only solution is to leap to install an entirely new system.

---

[6]Wilder, C. and M. McGee (1997), *GE: The Net Pays Off.* Information Week, January 27, 1997.

A better solution is for operations managers to take more responsibility for their IT systems by designing and managing the *path* that IT investments place an operation on, rather than periodically looking for the next replacement system to solve the problem. This means answering questions like "how easy will it be to adapt this system to new requirements?" and "by what mechanisms will we improve it over time?"

This book views the management of information technology as an essential and central part of the operations manager's job, rather than an ancillary activity. It explores how information technology can be used to strengthen or change an operation's primary competitive objectives, and looks at the primary decisions that must be made to build an effective path for the development of IT as a part of an operation. It also introduces a new concept in the management of information technology for operations: the idea of a *dynamic architecture,* which allows the operations manager to mold information systems to the changing requirements of the operation over time.

Designing, Managing, and Improving Operations

MODULE I

Designing, Managing and Improving Operations Processes

OVERVIEW

This module focuses on the management of the fundamental building blocks of an operations system—operations processes—and explores the managerial issues associated with rapid change, and improving process performance and flexibility at the operating unit level.

Process management is changing in some important and fundamental ways. First, just as product life cycles have become much shorter in recent years,[1] so have *process* life cycles.[2,3] A process that has run unchanged for many years is a rarity today. Today—driven by increased product introduction rates and fragmenting markets—processes come, change, and go much more rapidly. Stable, monotonic production is disappearing even in "process-based" industries like chemicals, steel,[4] and paper,[5] where economies of scale are no longer enough to guarantee success. Process innovation, in pursuit of greater efficiency, new capabilities, or new revenue streams, is becoming increasingly common.

Second, the "caretaker" view of processes, which often reduced operators to "machine-tenders," is waning. Process management, in that model, was characterized by acquiring the appropriate equipment for the task at hand, then devising foolproof methods for its operation. Today, however, operations are characterized by a widespread effort to involve operators in the management and development of the processes such equipment is a part of. Rather than subduing inventiveness and initiative in the name of control and standardization, new ways are being found to encourage and capture the knowledge of those who work most closely with the processes. Konosuke Matsushita, founder and executive director of Matsushita Electric, outlined the principal driving force behind this shift: " . . . The survival of firms . . . their continuous existence . . . depends on the day-to-day mobilization of every ounce of intelligence. . . .Only by drawing on the combined brain power of all its employees can a firm face up to the turbulence and constraints of today's environment."[6] While this principle is now well established in some countries, such as Japan and the United States, in others—such as China and parts of Latin America—it is a relatively new idea that often encounters considerable cultural barriers, as seen in a number of cases in the book.

Third, while companies have traditionally developed their operations strategies—and therefore their process capabilities—from the top down, many companies are looking for new ways to exploit and leverage their existing operations

[1]Wheelwright, S. C. and K. B. Clark (1992). *Revolutionizing Product Development.* New York, Free Press: 3–4.

[2]Pine, J. (1993). *Mass Customization: The New Frontier in Business Competition.* Boston, MA, Harvard Business School Press.

[3]Pisano, G. P. (1997). *The Development Factory: Unlocking the Potential of Process Innovation.* Boston, MA, Harvard Business School.

[4]The success of mini mills in the US steel industry demonstrated the extraordinary prevailing power of rapid process innovation and introduction, see, for example, Leonard-Barton, D. and G. Preuss (1992), *Chaparral Steel: Rapid Product and Process Development.* Harvard Business School case (9-692-018).

[5]Upton, D. M. (1995). "Flexibility as process mobility: The management of plant capabilities for quick response manufacturing." *Journal of Operations Management* 12: 205–224.

[6]Steudel, H. J. and P. Desruelle (1992), *Manufacturing in the Nineties.* New York, Van Nostrand Reinhold.

capabilities. For the operations manager, this manifests itself as a need to adapt existing processes to new products, to make processes amenable to different inputs and environments, and to find new applications and markets for existing processes. In addition, it is the operations manager who is in the best position to know what the capabilities of processes are and what they might be able to do. An understanding of process *flexibility,* then, has become a critical element of managing operations processes. As illustrated by a number of cases in this module, the ongoing ability to adapt and improve processes in line with new competitive foci can provide an operation with a powerful long-term advantage.

With the passing of the heyday of the static process, honing a process so that it eventually becomes foolproof (and can therefore be forgotten about) is no longer the primary goal in most industries. Instead, the primary challenges are accumulating knowledge rapidly, developing the ability to use that knowledge to speed the development and improvement of processes, and then learning to leverage that knowledge when introducing subsequent changes. This module examines the management of operations processes in light of these new imperatives.

Module Scope

Processes in manufacturing and service companies exist at four levels. At the first level are *elemental* processes. These are usually carried out by a single machine or workstation, such as a press, a lathe, or a data-entry station, and they carry out material or information transformation at the most basic level. At the next level are *compound* processes: a compound process comprises a collection of elemental processes connected together, often using material handling or communications equipment, to build an overall sequence of actions that change the form of either material or information. A compound process might span a single group of machines, a department, or a whole plant. This module focuses on operations processes at these two levels.

There are, however, two additional levels where processes occur in operations, which are not examined in this module. First are business processes: a business process is a collection of compound processes that are coordinated into an

overall sequence that delivers value to the customer.[7] This would include, for example, the overall process that takes an order as its input and results in the delivery of the ordered goods. The management of these business processes is primarily examined in the second section of the book, "Operations Systems and Information Technology," though two cases (Massachusetts General Hospital (MGH) and Deutsche Allgemeinversicherung (DAV)) included here do address issues at this level. At the highest level are managerial and organizational processes used to make decisions, such as whether or not to approve a new capital investment.[8] Processes at this level are most relevant to the third section of the book "Operations Improvement," which examines the management and improvement of the operating unit as a whole.

In this context, the focus of this module is on the management and improvement of *existing* processes rather than the development of new processes,[9] though several of the cases involve the post-installation management of such processes. Second, the module primarily addresses process management in the single operating unit rather than at the network level, where other issues such as cross-plant learning and multi-site process strategy are more relevant. Finally, throughout this module, as in the book as a whole, the emphasis is on determining the *action* an operating manager should take in the context of the case. The difficult issues are usually problems of implementation. While there is often a clear "theoretical" answer to what should be done to address the problem being faced, the challenge lies in translating that theoretical understanding into a realistic implementation plan which takes into account the complexity and often "messy" realities faced in an operation. Many case protagonists in this module are comparatively young, and carry out the kinds of assignments that might be expected of people early in their careers.

---

[7]Hammer, M. and J. Champy (1993). *Reengineering the Corporation.* New York, HarperCollins: 85.

[8]See Garvin, D. A. (1994). "The Processes of Organization and Management." Harvard Business School Working Paper (94-084).

[9]The development of new processes is described in detail in Wheelwright, S. C. and K. B. Clark (1993). *Managing New Product and Process Development.* New York, Free Press, and Garvin, D. A. (1990), *Operations Strategy: Module Overview, Competing on New Products and Processes.* HBS Module Note (5-690-058).

Module Structure

The module comprises nine class sessions, with eight cases and one lecture session on operations flexibility. The first six sessions look at the management of process design and improvement for a *single* product or service. They examine the actions available to an operations manager and the issues that arise in designing, managing, and improving processes in that context. The last three sessions examine the production processes for multiple products, and the increasingly important issue of process flexibility.

A. Single-Product Processes

The six cases in the first part of the module focus on process change and improvement for single products and services. As the module progresses, the degree of process change being managed increases. So, for example, Display Technologies (DTI) is concerned with the issues that arise when "tuning" a new process to increase its yield, and looks at how one might increase the rate of that improvement. Solagen describes the possibility of wholesale replacement of an existing process with an entirely new one. The framework for analyzing process improvement described below characterizes process improvement in terms of "levels" of action related to process change that the operations manager can undertake. This progression provides the opportunity to identify the conditions under which one would switch from one level of process change to the next.

B. Multi-Product Processes and Process Flexibility

The second part of the module explores the management and improvement of flexibility in operations processes, and situations in which processes must deliver multiple products. Flexible processes add significant complexity to the discussion of process improvement, since the designer/manager must now be concerned not only with the ability to make and improve individual products, but also the ability to manufacture multiple products concurrently and the ability to make transitions between them. In addition, the manager is often concerned with improving the "flexibility" of the process across products, rather than its perfor-

mance on any individual product. The framework used for analyzing process flexibility is also described in the themes below.

THEMES

1. Designing Processes for Improvement

Among the central tenets of Taylor's "Principles of Scientific Management" was the idea of "one right way" to perform a given task. His work and the principles it was founded on have formed the bedrock upon which much of current operations management rests. Much has been said in recent years about the demise of Taylorism. As Schonberger points out, however, rumors of the death of scientific management have been greatly exaggerated.[10] Many of the principles Taylor espoused still apply today, and should not be discarded entirely. The McDonald's case illustrates how Taylor's principles can be applied with great success, and how they have become even more important as the firm globalizes its operations. There are, however, some important implicit assumptions of scientific management that have been progressively eroded over time[11]:

- that production technology is known and predictable;
- that the role of labor is solely to perform procedures;
- that there is a known and stationary environment;
- that there is a known and constant goal for which operations should be designed.

Throughout the cases in this module, one or more of these assumptions are violated. The DTI case explores a world in which the production process is so new and its performance so difficult to predict that very different principles must be applied in its management. While Taylor might have advocated the gradual development of standard operating procedures for this process, this principle is not very helpful to DTI. By the time the process has been proceduralized, the technology

[10]Schonberger, R. J. (1996). *World Class Manufacturing: The Next Decade.* New York, The Free Press.
[11]Jaikumar, R. and R. Bohn (1992). "A dynamic approach to operations management: An alternative to static optimization." *International Journal of Production Economics* 27. 265–282.

will have moved on. In DAV, we see operators move from a role of mechanistic data entry to one of involvement in design and improvement of their processes. Stermon Mills is experiencing a dramatic change in its competitive role, from competing on low cost to competing on flexibility. The processes that Stermon originally installed for a stationary, cost-based competitive world now need quick but careful adaptation to fit with the new goals of the business. Even at McDonald's, a case situation where Taylor's principles have been particularly powerful, the company is seeing the breakdown of proceduralization in the face of too much complexity and change.

If Taylor's principles are not sufficient to manage the situations described in so many cases, one might well ask, is there another perspective that binds processes together and informs their management? Part of the answer comes from the fact that two of the most important capabilities for a modern operation are the rapid accumulation of knowledge and the ability to *improve* existing processes. In each of the cases in this module, the ability to learn rapidly is critically important. In Taylor's more static world, companies had time to allow such expertise to accumulate slowly, over time. The traditional "learning curve,"[12] for example, assumes that knowledge about processes is gradually and autonomously accumulated as a byproduct of production. Today, however, the roles that managers and operators can play in *creating* their operations' learning curves are increasingly emphasized.[13] Many processes, however, are designed in a way that militates against ongoing improvement and learning. Process engineering has been strongly influenced by Taylor, and many process engineers still see their primary role as designing a process that delivers a product or service in a foolproof way once the ramp-up period is over. "Continuous improvement," if it exists at all, is an afterthought. Key questions for today's operations managers considering a re-design of an existing process or the development of a new process are, "How will we improve this process *after* it has been installed?" and "Are there principles that can

be applied in designing the new process that will facilitate its subsequent improvement?"

There are at least three broad principles that can guide operations managers concerned with long-term improvement efforts.

First is *accessibility:* processes that run as "black boxes" are extremely difficult to improve. For example, in many types of advanced manufacturing technology (AMT), the mechanisms for changing a process are buried in layers of software, and the ability to change and experiment is usually confined to a small group of software engineers. To make matters worse, these programmers are often former vendors or consultants, instead of current employees. And even when they are available, these engineers are often wary of disturbing a complex process that is running "well enough." This effect can be extreme. At the PPG Windshield plant (described in Module 3 of this book), the engineers who originally programmed the heat-treatment furnace are long gone, and the language in which the process control software was developed has been forgotten. It was thus extraordinarily difficult to improve the furnace's operation, because it had become inaccessible. In the Stermon case, one improvement project involved a new, sophisticated control system for the paper machine. While this may well deliver the required improvement initially, it is not at all clear what mechanisms are available for the subsequent improvement of the process. An alternative project under consideration would deliver less significant results initially, but it would accommodate ongoing improvement by ensuring that the changeover process would be accessible and not frozen by automation.

A second design principle that fosters ongoing improvement is *inclusiveness.* This principle stresses involvement of operators during design and implementation, awareness of the impact that the changes will have on the existing social system and on the skills of the workforce, and the dangers of treating new process technologies as means to remove the need for people and their skills. Adler[14] calls the combination of these principles "usability," or designing advanced manufacturing technology with primary consideration for how it will fit into the human system of the operation, and

[12]Arrow, K. J. (1962). "The economic implications of learning by doing." *Review of Economic Studies* 29: 155–173.

[13]Adler, P. S. and T. A. Winograd, Eds. (1992). *Usability: Turning Technologies into Tools.* New York, Oxford University Press.

[14]Adler, P. S. and T. A. Winograd, Eds. (1992). "The Usability Challenge," *Usability: Turning Technologies into Tools.* New York, Oxford University Press.

how operators will employ and improve it over time. This principle can be used to inform the design of all operations processes, not just automated ones. Including operators in the design of a process not only provides valuable input to the design; it also builds an understanding of why the process works the way it does, and—most important—fosters a sense of ownership and involvement that provides a platform for ongoing improvement. Annette Kluck explicitly employs this principle in the DAV case.

A final broad principle in designing processes for improvement is *modularity:* building a process so that, as far as possible, a change in one element does not demand change throughout the whole process. If a process manager is solely concerned with "initial" performance, the advantages of modularity may be minimal. However, in the long term, modularity facilitates the rapid adoption of new process elements because it allows a process to be adapted to changing circumstances, makes it much easier to address production problems, and permits local experimentation with one element of a process without disrupting the process as a whole.[15] The processes that McDonald's employs to assemble a meal, for example, are highly modular. They have been integrated tightly, but refined individually.

2. Managing Processes: Building an Integrated View

Many of the problems managers face in the initial six cases of this module are a result of different managerial perspectives on the same operational issues. Hayes and Wheelwright[16] have proposed three general categories for these: the technologist's view, the operations manager's view, and the general manager's view (which we will call the operations strategist's view). An understanding of these different perspectives, each of which is valid and useful, is extremely powerful in understanding how individual situations can be interpreted in very different and sometimes incompatible ways.

The Technologist's View

The technologist's, or engineer's, view of operations processes is driven by problems of material or information conversion. People educated in engineering will often see processes from this viewpoint. A number of engineering texts describe processes and their detailed analysis from this perspective.[17] Its hallmarks are a confidence that operations problems result from technical shortcomings, and an optimism that those problems will yield to measurement, analysis, and implementation of technical fixes. Human issues are considered "technical" process elements to be shaped through training, incentives, or "empowerment." Eric Davidson in the Corning Z-Glass case is a good example of a technologist with this view.

This view and the approach it typically implies have led to numerous successes: robotic assembly, for example, springs directly from the work of technologists. However, given the detailed nature of the analysis required to make the process work, technical specialists often have difficulty abstracting themselves from the specific process so as to consider the broader issues of how it will actually be used. In addition, the engineering mindset encourages building a process that will be "correct" from the outset, rather than one designed to be improved by the people running it. In the Stermon Mills case, for example, one of the options—installing systems that would allow a greater range of paper to be manufactured—would be heavily favored by those with this engineer's viewpoint: it requires the design of a new system, which—provided it is designed well—will be certain to work. The option of decreasing changeover times between products, meanwhile, is much less engineering-intensive but offers much greater opportunity for subsequent improvement by the people working on the line.

The Operations Manager's View

The operations manager's view is shaped by the demands of managing and improving processes, rather than by the challenges of designing them. Such managers are most concerned with a process' ability to function as a part of the

---

[15]A detailed discussion of the advantages of modular processes for improvement, adaptation and customization is included in Fetzinger, E. and H. Lee (1997). "Mass customization at Hewlett-Packard: The power of postponement." *Harvard Business Review.* January–February: 116–121.

[16]Hayes, R. H. and S. C. Wheelwright (1984). *Restoring Our Competitive Edge: Competing through Manufacturing.* New York, John Wiley and Sons.

[17]See, for example, Amstead, B. H., Ostwald, P. F. and M. L. Begeman (1987). *Manufacturing Processes.* New York, John Wiley and Sons; DeGarmo, E. P., Black, J. T., and R. A Kohser (1988). *Materials and Processes in Manufacturing,* Macmillan; and Schey, J. A. (1987). *Introduction to Manufacturing Processes,* McGraw Hill.

operations system as a whole, and with its ability to meet targets in cost, quality, or output. While a technical specialist might consider a process that fails occasionally to be an intriguing intellectual problem, the operations manager may be much less curious—and much more concerned with keeping it up and running. The operations manager's primary concerns are *control* and *coordination*. Can the process deliver to target day after day, and how consistently and robustly will it fit into the manufacturing system as a whole?

Andrew MacTavish in Corning Z-Glass embodies the operations manager's perspective. He wants his organization to function smoothly and has little patience for any disturbances, especially those imposed by outsiders.

The Operations Strategist's View

The operations strategist is concerned much less with either the technical details or the day-to-day control of an operation and much more with the longer-term consequences of employing a particular process technology. Two primary issues are important from this point of view:

- How does the process technology meet the market's competitive requirements and how well does it fit with other elements of the operations strategy (such as plant size and location)?

- What capabilities will the process technology exploit or develop? What learning will be created by employing this particular process, how will the pool of knowledge associated with the process grow over time, and how will that knowledge be transferred to and used in the rest of the organization?

In the MGH—CABG case, Drs. Bohmer and Torchiana are clearly managing from this viewpoint as they attempt to implement a care path process for clinical procedures. They believe that this change will allow them to meet cost reduction pressures imposed by the market for health care while giving their hospital the advantage of shorter stays and higher quality care.

In the past, these three views were often embodied in different individuals. Today, however, managers of operating units need to incorporate all these views into their decision making. As business becomes more volatile and changeable, thereby requiring faster decision making, and as layers of supporting management have been re-

moved by progressive waves of restructuring, neither time nor resources exist to split the various views among different people.

DTI and Stermon illustrate the need for one individual to balance all three perspectives. In DTI, Shima must make decisions about which process technologies to exploit while facing constantly increasing output targets. He also knows that the market will shift to new products soon, as it has done so many times in the past, and he must build an operation capable of surviving this transition. In Stermon, Kiefner must understand not only what is feasible from an engineering point of view, and how this might affect delivery targets, but also how any process changes fit with the competitive environment the plant finds itself in.

If today's operations need to function more like guerrilla units than Roman legions, they cannot maintain separate strategists, tacticians, and commanders; their leaders must possess all of these skills. The operations manager must have a deep technical understanding of the equipment; know how to manage, control, and coordinate it; and how to use it to generate the greatest strategic impact. Table 1 indicates the primary questions suggested by each viewpoint for the cases in this module.

3. Managing Processes: Building Operator Involvement

"The factory is a human phenomenon. Every step from conception to eventual destruction is for, by and because of people."
—NADLER AND ROBINSON, 1983.[18]

The importance of the human community in operations has been powerfully acknowledged over the last several years. In the past, the "caretaker" model of processes implied that the operator's job was primarily to carry out the physical and informational process associated with the operation. Taylor's ideas were the source of an influential framework that justified this approach. Over time, however, many firms have increased the level of responsibility of line workers (or have "empowered" them), and encouraged them to use their minds as well as their hands in the work they perform. Whether or not this shift involves altruism,

---

[18]Nadler, G. and G. H. Robinson (1983). "Design of the automated factory: More than robots." *Annals of the American Academy of Political and Social Science* 470 (November).

TABLE I   Module I Cases and the Three Views of Operations

Case	Technical Specialist (feasibility/design)	Operations Manager (control/reliability)	Operations Strategist (competitive role/learning)
Cummins Engine San Luis Potosí	Is the machine physically capable of manufacturing the part?	Will we be able to satisfy customer needs with the new machine?	What effect will the introduction of a statistically incapable process have on the plant's improvement strategy?
Display Technologies Inc.	How might we design a process that has an inherently higher yield?	How can the quality of the existing process be improved most rapidly?	What will be the consequences for the plant's learning of replicating the line to improve yields, rather than continuing to focus on the existing line?
Corning Glass Works: the Z-Glass Project	(Blackburn/Davidson) What data should we collect about the process to discover the reasons for the low yield?	(MacTavish) How can I ensure that the process is given time to stabilize so that new operators can learn to control it themselves?	(Leibson) When should the M&E group be called into a plant? What should be the role of the group in distributing learning across the plants in the network?
DAV	How might we use optical character recognition to design people out of the process?	How can we ensure that the number of mistakes made is minimized? Will posting the SPC charts publicly lead to inappropriate pressure from management for zero defects?	How will the introduction of SPC affect DAV's approach to quality across the organization? What will we learn from it? Will it allow us to stay ahead of the competition?
MGH CABG Surgery	(surgeon) How should a cardiac bypass operation be performed?	(patient path manager) How might the total process undergone by a patient be improved to increase the number of successful grafts?	(Torchiana/Bohmer) How can the learning made in the Cardiac Arterial Bypass Graft process be spread to other doctors and applied to other surgical procedures?
Solagen	Can the manual process for making gelatin be replaced by a more automated chemical process? How can yields of the new process be improved?	How should the new, automated process be introduced into a plant used to the previous method? How reliable will the new process be?	Can gelatin production ever become a source of competitive advantage for a rival film manufacturer? If so, how will Kodak respond?
McDonald's	How might we design a process to make McPizza as well as our Big Macs?	Can the process be replicated reliably to produce adequate quality across all the franchisees?	Is the addition of the new processes going to blur our focus so much that our current products and services will decline in quality?
Stermon Mills	Can computerization increase the range of the plant? Should we solve the problem of increasing the range of the machine by installing new computerized equipment?	How can we speed up changeovers without sacrificing uptime?	Which option will allow us to best develop valuable capabilities? Which is best matched to our competitive strategy?

competitive requirements certainly have been important; firms not utilizing their people's knowledge and enthusiasm were, in many cases, outpaced by companies that were so doing.

Operators are now much more likely to be involved not only in executing processes but also in improving them and developing new ones.[19] In such circumstances, the atmosphere in which people work and the way they perceive the quality of their working life become much more important. Walton[20] describes a number of difficulties in moving from a "control" model of workforce management to a "commitment" model; and a number of these are particularly relevant to how operations processes are selected and designed, and the subsequent prospects for their adaptation and improvement. Table 2 lists important differences between the two models (which will be revisited in Part 3 of the book).

In situations where the *commitment* model is desirable,[21] the design and selection of new processes requires careful thought about the consequences of a new process or system in bringing the organization towards that goal. The MGH case demonstrates how difficult it can be to move away from a control model. There, the consequences of individualistic behavior have been recognized by Torchiana and Bohmer, who are redesigning the process and hope to change how surgeons see their jobs. The options in the Stermon case are also not neutral with regard to their ability to move the plant towards a commitment model of management. The range-enhancement project relies on investing in computer automation, whereas the increased-mobility option will require that the workforce become much more engaged in upgrading the system's performance. In addition, the complexity of a paper machine will demand that the crew improve as a team rather than as individuals if they are to improve changeover times.

DAV is the most useful case, however, for showing how a process that was originally characterized by individual responsibility can migrate to one in which the team as a whole is responsible for output and able to see the broader consequences of its work. In addition, DAV has changed the nature of work structurally by introducing Statistical Process Control: quality improvement is now part of the job, which not only encourages improvement but also makes for a much richer, more interesting environment in which people can be genuinely engaged in the overall process rather than simply in data entry.

An operation may have a first-rate collection of intellectual and physical capital, yet if a sense of common purpose is absent, it can fail to improve and flounder when confronted with competitor attacks. It is critical for operations managers to keep in mind that changing a process can have a strong impact on the community, both positively and negatively. This is a particularly important element in the Cummins Engine case. San Luis Potosi had grown from a low-cost (and low-importance) manufacturing unit where people were paid for their

---

[19]Adler, P. S. and T. A. Winograd, Eds. (1992). "The Usability Challenge," *Usability: Turning Technologies into Tools.* New York, Oxford University Press.

[20]Walton, R. E. (1985). From Control to Commitment: Transforming Work Force Management in the United States. In *The Uneasy Alliance: Managing the Productivity-Technology Dilemma.* K. B. Clark, R. H. Hayes and C. Lorenz. Boston, MA, Harvard Business School Press: 237–265.

[21]*McDonald's* raises some interesting questions here: would you want to develop a "commitment" model of workforce management in this case?

TABLE 2 Traditional Control and Commitment Models for Job Design (Source: Walton, 1985)

Traditional Control Model	*Commitment Model*
Individual attention limited to performing individual job	Individual responsibility extended to improving system performance
Job design deskills and fragments work and separates doing and thinking	Job design • enhances content of work, • emphasizes whole task • combines doing and thinking
Accountability focused on the individual	Frequent use of teams as basic accountable unit
Fixed job definition	Flexible definition of duties, contingent on changing conditions

manual labor, to a community of people who had begun to take tremendous pride in their work and the quality of the products they produced. The spirit of this community is threatened by the introduction of a below-par manufacturing process, and Joe Panella must balance and mitigate these effects against the immediate requirements of the corporation.

In the Corning Z-Glass case, Eric Davidson has ignored (or at least put at the back of his mind) the fact that the development team he was bringing in would be seen as outsiders in the plant. This oversight has severely limited his ability to improve the ailing process. While at the outset he tried to involve MacTavish and the rest of the plant in his process improvement activities, they saw his efforts as mere tokenism, unsupported by a sincere respect for their views and achievements. One of the first outcomes of DAV's quality improvement efforts was a recognition that error rates were much higher for operators whose desks were situated on the main corridor of the large open-plan office. Why? Because these people were interrupted by passers-by in the corridor, who would stop to chat. It was difficult for the operators to turn people away without appearing unfriendly; they also welcomed the intrusions because they found their jobs boring. Annette Kluck corrected this problem by rearranging the layout and broadening the content of her people's jobs.

While process design and implementation must take into account the changes required in the way people perform their work and the development of a "committed" workforce, it is increasingly important to consider, as well, the effect of the process and its implementation on the spirit of the community in which it is installed. It is this community, after all, whose pride and commitment are increasingly called upon to provide the learning engine that drives competitive success through operations.

4. Improving Processes: The Stages of Knowledge

The stages of knowledge framework developed by Bohn and Jaikumar[22] describes a company's degree of knowledge about a process. Though some

may have seen this framework before, it is a powerful tool for the cases in this module because a diagnosis of the stage of knowledge can inform managerial action for the processes in question. The framework, slightly modified, is shown in Table 3. The Stages of Knowledge are most useful in describing the knowledge embedded in an existing operation.

Why does it matter how much is "known" about a process? The most obvious reason is that a low stage of knowledge (not being able to tell bad output from good, or knowing but not being able to do anything about it) means that the operation is unable to deliver consistent quality or yield, and hence is at a competitive disadvantage compared to better-informed rivals. There are, however, several other reasons why a lack of deep process knowledge can lead to long-term disadvantages on other competitive dimensions.

Unpredictable Effects of Variation in Inputs and Environment

Without a high level of understanding of the factors influencing the output of a process, and how they do so, an operation can be adversely and unpredictably affected by changes in the environment or in input materials. A high stage of knowledge enables managers running the process to predict the consequences of such changes. In the heat treatment of metals, for example, materials scientists can use phase diagrams to predict the likely effects of a change in alloy composition, and compensate for any change by altering other process parameters. But many processes are much less well understood. Processes in biotechnology, for instance, are often at a very low stage of knowledge because of their novelty. These processes are fragile, and are often the result of inspired guesswork about what may or may not work. Mammalian cell cultures, for example, are notoriously capricious—and minute changes in temperature, pressure, or even vibration can take the yield of a process down to zero.[23] This lack of deep process understanding has generated folklore in some plants—processes should be left alone while they are working. The Scotch whisky industry, for which there is a low level of process understanding, has developed such a "lore." When

---

[22]Bohn, R. and R. Jaikumar (1992). "The Structure of Technological Knowledge in Manufacturing." *Harvard Business School Working Paper.* 93035.

[23]Pisano, G. P. (1997). *The Development Factory: Unlocking the Potential of Process Innovation.* Boston, MA, Harvard Business School.

TABLE 3   The Stages of Knowledge (adapted from Bohn and Jaikumar)

Stage of Knowledge	Description	Example
Stage 0	Cannot distinguish good output from bad	Trying to detect blowholes in castings by surface inspection
Stage 1	Extremes of good and bad output can be distinguished but don't know how to obtain it	British Wine
Stage 2	Can identify primary variables that may influence the output (but don't know which are relevant)	Some mammalian-cell biotech processes Solagen (existing process)
Stage 3	Know the primary variables that affect the output of the process	Corning Z-Glass (after Davidson) DAV after *output* measurement initiative
Stage 4	Can *measure* the primary variables affecting process output	Electronic circuit board assembly (final product defect rate determined by component defect rates) Display Technologies' process
Stage 5	Can control the output via these primary variables over a local region	Autoclaving (pressure cooking) of composite materials Paper-making process in Stermon (within the existing range) Cummins SLP on most machines
Stage 6	Can recognize and discriminate secondary variables (which have an indirect or less significant impact on the output)	Auto-body painting; humidity has a secondary effect
Stage 7	Can control the effect of secondary variables on the output	Control of particulates in integrated-circuit manufacturing
Stage 8	Know the complete functional relationship between the output of the process and all variables, over any region. Can predict process output perfectly. Stage 8 is unattainable, but is a useful benchmark stage.	

corrosion finally eats through copper distilling vessels after 15 years or so, operators will often replicate the old vessel's dents in the new one, in case the dents have some undetermined effect on the quality of the output! The problem with this approach, of course, is that competitive requirements often require a more informed response than folklore can provide. Kodak was caught flat-footed when its rival was able to make clearer gelatin, and when consumers demonstrated a preference for it. The company was forced to revive the dormant Solagen process and to re-create the learning it had lost.

Limits to Strategic Flexibility

One consequence of "competing through capabilities" is that processes are often challenged to perform functions different from those they were originally designed for. Stermon's paper-making process was originally designed around one optimal grade to be produced in large quantities. As the market shifted, Stermon's managers needed to "nudge" machines around in the grade range to make new types of paper. At the same time, other paper plants adapted their processes to use waste pulp rather than new fiber to accommodate environmental concerns, and to tap into new markets for "green" products. Neither of these forms of strategic flexibility, however, is possible without a deep understanding of the associated manufacturing processes. Absent such knowledge, it is difficult for a process to be used to do things it was not designed for originally.

Slow Response to Process Shocks

A number of cases in the book describe a "quality crash." Corning Z-Glass and Micom Caribe (the last case in Module 3) both describe process crises in which yields plummet or defect rates soar unexpectedly. Operations managers involved in such crises often recount their frustration that every change they made to correct an increasingly urgent problem either had no effect or actually made the process worse. In these circumstances, a deep understanding of the process is critical to link cause with effect so that the problem can be resolved rapidly and effectively.

5. Improving Processes: Four Levels of Process Change

The term "continuous improvement" has come to embrace a wide range of tools and concepts that can be used in process improvement. TQM or SPC, experimentation on the shop floor and in labs, investment in new capital equipment or information systems, and the adoption of lean production techniques: all can lead to continuous improvement, even though they are often very different in scope and objectives. To provide a richer understanding of "improvement," the following describes a simple model of process improvement in terms of increasing degrees of process change. This taxonomy provides an understanding of the options available for improving the performance of a process according to the mechanisms of change available to the operating manager.

A Model of Process Improvement

The combination of elemental processes and the way those elements are connected together to form a particular compound process is called the process *configuration*. The performance of a process configuration in terms of, for example, output rate, conformance quality, output variability, yield, process uptime or safety may be characterized as a function of the parameters that characterize the process settings, such as the speeds and feeds of a cutting process, the temperature and pressure at which an injection molding is formed, or the metallurgical condition of the steel used in a forming process.

The performance characteristics associated with the production of a particular product with a particular process configuration are **p**, where **p** is a vector of performance measures $(p_1, p_2, \ldots, p_m, p_n, \ldots)$.

$\mathbf{p} = f(s_1, s_2, s_3 \ldots)$ where s_k are process parameters.

The boundary that defines maximal joint performance for a particular process configuration is termed the *process boundary*, **p***. While processes may be operated (sub-optimally) within the region defined by the boundary, the boundary defines the ultimate limit to the combined performance that can be achieved with a particular process configuration.

A two-dimensional depiction of a process boundary is shown in Figure 1.

- The boundary applies to a particular process configuration, rather than a broad set of technologies. In general, only managers of processes at Stage 8 of the stages of knowledge know exactly where the boundary is, and how to set process parameters to achieve any point on the boundary.

- The boundary of a process configuration is multi-dimensional; if there are six relevant aspects of performance, for example, then the process boundary surface will be five-dimensional. The combination of process parameters, **s**, required to access much of the existing boundary may not be known; managers of a process, for example, might not be aware of the exact nature of the tradeoff between output rate and process reliability on the boundary, even though this tradeoff certainly exists.

Four Levels of Managerial Action in Improving Process Performance

This simple model of operations processes allows us to begin to categorize the actions available to managers as they seek to improve process performance. There are four "levels" of process change, which characterize progressively more radical actions that can be taken.

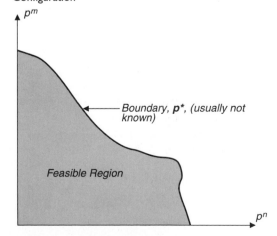

FIGURE 1 Process Boundary for a Particular Process Configuration

The four levels of action are:

1. *repositioning* a process in a local region
2. *exploring and pursuing* the boundary of an existing process configuration
3. *progressive reconfiguration* of the process
4. *radical redesign* to replace the process

I. Level One: Repositioning—Moving in a Local, Known Region by Changing Parameters

Many operations processes are operated far from the frontier of what is possible, even within their existing configuration. However, there is always some knowledge of how to achieve various combinations of performance within a local region. The combination of performance characteristics originally selected for a process can progressively become inappropriate, providing an opportunity to "improve" the process by simply moving it within the currently known region, without exploration or learning. This involves changing the process parameters to provide a new combination of performance characteristics. It might involve, for example, lowering the speed of a machine to increase process stability or increasing the amount of adhesive used to join two components.

This approach is often merely a matter of selecting a more appropriate operating point for the process, given what the operation already knows, and demands little or no additional "discovery" or learning (see Figure 2). There is often considerable opportunity for improvement when repositioning processes, however. A process may have been op-

erated for so long at one point that the assumptions about whether that is the right place to operate it have gone unchallenged for many years. The competitive environment may then have changed (e.g., to favor higher quality over lower cost) so that the repositioning of the process is justified.

As an example of this form of process improvement, Witherington Chemical, a manufacturer of plastic moldings used in the food packaging industry, was plagued by customer complaints about "flashing" around the edges of the components produced. Flashing is a result of excess raw material being extruded between the mating parts of a die, and manifests itself as wafer-thin sheets of extraneous material on a finished component. To address the problem, Witherington's operations manager, Mike Findlay, asked operators to reduce the pressure at which viscous polymer was forced into the die by 10%, knowing that doing so would prevent excess material from being squeezed where it was not needed. Operators, who were paid on piece-rate, were reluctant to do this since a reduced cavity filling rate meant a decrease in the rate at which the injection molding machines could produce parts. By changing how operators were paid, and instituting an across-the-board reduction in injection pressure, Findlay was able to address the growing customer requirement for no-flash components, and in doing so, "improved" the process. However, little experimentation was necessary, since everyone in the plant knew that flashing would be eliminated if the pressure was decreased. Findlay's problem was in tackling the ingrained "custom-and-practice" that cemented the molding processes to an increasingly inappropriate operating point.

2. Level Two: Exploration—Probing the Process Boundary and Repositioning Closer to It

The next level of action applies primarily to processes operating at a point more distant from the boundary, and hence that have considerable potential for improvement. Processes at a low stage of learning, for example, will often be operated at points comparatively distant from the process boundary. Moving closer to the process boundary involves generating new knowledge about the existing process through experimentation (see Figure 3). Experimentation might involve changing temperature settings on a furnace, the feed rate on a milling machine, or decreasing

FIGURE 2 Process Repositioning

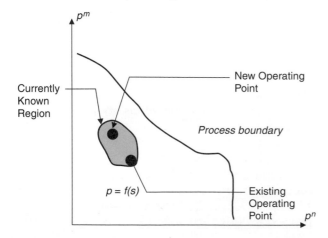

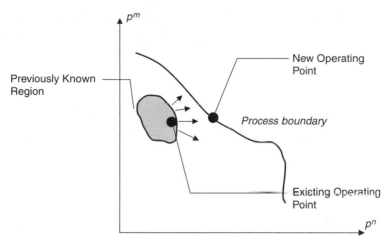

FIGURE 3 Probing and Approaching the Process Boundary

the noise level in the shop that houses the process. The practical development and design of such experiments, resting primarily on the work of Taguchi,[24] is described in detail by Bhote.[25] There are four primary challenges in testing the limits of an existing process configuration and moving towards them. First is to identify the improvement direction: what performance dimension(s) need to be improved? Second is to ensure that the significant parameters affecting the output of the process have been identified. It is here that methods such as fishbone diagrams are useful. Third is to separate controllable factors from factors currently outside the control of the operation, and where possible, to find ways to broaden the set of controllable factors. Fourth is to determine the combination of those factors that move the process' performance in the desired direction. By carrying out experiments in this way, the operation increases its "Stage of Knowledge" of the process and is able to approach advantageous regions of the boundary—and, just as important, to develop insight into how the process might later be reconfigured to access a new boundary. Both Corning and Display Technologies are carrying out improvement at this level: they both suspect that their existing process configuration is performing well below its potential, and are scrambling to bring the processes closer to their frontiers.

As an additional example of this level of improvement, TI Raleigh Limited (a bicycle manufacturer) assembled bicycles by connecting steel tubes together using "lugs"—steel cages formed from sheet metal. As part of the frame assembly process, tubes were inserted into recesses in the lugs, and the assembly was made solid by melting a brass charge in the joint (brazing). A new model of bicycle had a recurring problem, however: the brazed joints would crack apart after a few weeks of use. The problem was addressed by considering all the factors likely to affect the strength of the joint: these included the size of the brass charge, the hardness of the lugs, the braze temperature, and the amount of borax (flux) used. The effect of these process parameters on joint strength was unknown, so Raleigh carried out experiments to explore their impact. The most significant parameters turned out to be lug hardness and the size of the brass charge used. Large brass charges also caused unsightly cosmetic problems, however, since brass would pour out around the joint. Therefore, softer lugs were used in the process to increase the strength of the joint. In carrying out this experiment, Raleigh was able not only to solve the problem, but also to understand the existing process better. It had moved closer to the boundary of performance of the existing process, and repositioned its process to that point. This generated knowledge that was not only useful in the process for this particular model, but also for other

[24]Byrne, D. M. and S. Taguchi (1987). "The Taguchi Approach to Parameter Design." American Society for Quality Control.

[25]Bhote, K. R. (1991). *World Class Quality: Using Design of Experiments to Make It Happen.* New York, American Management Association.

models in which similar problems occurred. It also provided clues about how process reconfiguration (e.g., using lugless joints) might improve the process still further.

Complete knowledge of the boundary of an existing process configuration corresponds to a high stage of knowledge in Jaikumar and Bohn's terms. At Stage 8, all parameters affecting the process have been identified, and can be controlled to position the process at any point on the boundary. However, even a process at the mythical Stage 8 will not provide ongoing improvement. To improve performance beyond the existing boundary, the process must be reconfigured to provide access to a new boundary.

3. Level Three: Reconfiguration—Accessing a New Operating Boundary through Incremental Process Reconfiguration

At the next level, the process can be progressively reconfigured so that the existing process boundary is correspondingly reconfigured (see Figure 4). This again involves experimentation. Reconfiguration might involve changing the order in which elemental processes are carried out; it may add steps to a compound process, and combine process elements or replace elemental process with alternatives. Even though the change may be incremental, and the result of small experiments, the operation is gradually changing the

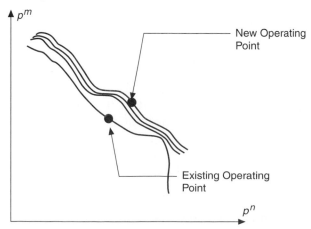

FIGURE 4 Accessing New Boundaries Through Progressive Reconfiguration

process *itself* over time, rather than simply altering the parameters of an existing process. The experimentation carried out to access the existing boundary often provides important clues about how a process might be reconfigured to access a new boundary. In addition, simple concepts such as the 5-Why's[26] and Plan-Do-Check-Act[27] cycles help uncover the roots of existing process configuration limitations. The process of experimentation, which tests and pushes on the boundary of an existing process, simultaneously generating knowledge used to progressively reconfigure the process, is at the heart of "continuous improvement." An operation that *only* carried out experiments to approach and explore the boundary of an existing process would eventually find an optimum place on the boundary, but would then stop improving. The operation can continue to improve, however, if the knowledge generated is used to inform progressive process reconfiguration. DAV's efforts to improve its new policy set-up process are ultimately aimed at progressively reconfiguring the process—to find new ways of combining and re-ordering the various elemental tasks associated with the process so that the overall conformance quality is improved.

Thus, Raleigh was able to use its knowledge of the brazing process to determine that brazing might not always be the best elemental process for building bicycle frames. As the "mountain bike" became more popular, increased needs for lightness and joint strength combined with more profound knowledge of the limitations of the brazing process, which inspired Raleigh's engineers to look at tube welding as an alternative for certain models. While this change in the frame-building process was not without its initial problems, a series of experiments and parameter changes (Level 2) eventually allowed welding to substitute for brazing in frame-assembly. By doing so, Raleigh was able to access a new level of performance. Lug production was dispensed with, and pre-assembly could now be combined with the welding process,

[26]Robinson, A., Ed. (1991). *Continuous Improvement in Operations: A Systematic Approach to Waste Reduction*. Cambridge, MA, Productivity Press.

[27]Latzko, W. J. and D. M. Saunders (1995). *Four Days with Dr. Deming*. Reading, MA, Addison-Wesley.

by assembling the frames on the jig used to steady the tubes as they were welded together.

4. Level Four: Radical Redesign— Replacement of the Entire Process with an Alternative Technology

Instead of carrying out progressive reconfigurations of a process, an operation might decide to develop completely different process architecture, such that it achieves its objectives in an entirely different way (see Figure 5). In the Raleigh frame-building example, this might have included the production of carbon-fiber composite frames, which would use no elements of the existing frame-building process, and would therefore constitute a wholly novel process. A new process might use entirely different material transformations (substituting cast-metal connecting rods in engines for forged rods, for example) or rely on very different physics to achieve the same end.

Kodak's Solagen process illustrates a radically redesigned process; it had almost nothing in common with the company's previous method for making gelatin. Yet the project was canceled because a static comparison of its yields showed them to be inferior to those of the manual process; but this calculation may have been shortsighted. The Solagen process clearly had improvement potential, while its predecessor did not. The radical redesign was an appropriate step, but the company did not persevere to bring it closer to its performance boundary.

FIGURE 5 Accessing a New, Superior Boundary by Radical Redesign

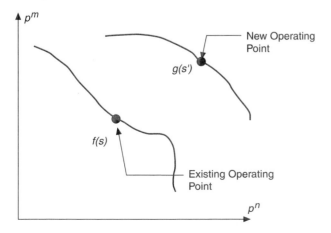

The Progression of Improvement

Levels 1, 2, 3, and 4 provide a sequential picture of how continuous improvement of extant processes takes place in many operations. First, the process is adjusted within a known region. The combination of dissatisfaction with performance, an appreciation of the lack of process knowledge that exists, and a belief that the existing configuration can still deliver better performance all fuel process experimentation to build new knowledge and to bring the existing configuration closer to the boundary.

Eventually, there is a limit to the combined performance that can be achieved with a particular process configuration. The search, however, will often have provided clues about how the boundary might be shifted outwards by reconfiguring the process. The newly reconfigured process will shift the boundary, and further Level 2 experimentation will usually be required to find the best operating point on this new, unknown boundary. Rapidly improving operations carry out improvement actions of Levels 2 and 3 in a tight loop, probing the boundary of a particular configuration through experimentation, then using the "know-why" from those experiments to inform a new process configuration. Eventually, the limits of the existing process *architecture* are reached, and the operation looks to a completely new process to provide it with a superior combination of performance characteristics. This new process can then be improved using much the same techniques as before.

This, of course, is a comparatively simplistic model of process improvement. In reality, the progression is not so sequential, and managers will often consider each available improvement mechanism in parallel. The model, however, does shed some light on the process improvement activities taking place in the cases, as well as raise some important questions. For example, how should a manager decide when to move to the next level of action in improving a process? Each level involves the growth of knowledge, and this knowledge is often used to build a theoretical understanding of the potential of the next level, as well as the reasons for the limitations of the existing level of change.

The cases in the first part of this module are arranged by the levels at which process change occurs, as summarized in Table 4, and can be used to address these questions. In Corning, managers are scrambling with Level 2 type actions: experimenting to find combinations of parameters that provide a satisfactory yield within an existing process configuration. Davidson is going about this task "scientifically," while MacTavish much prefers a "gut feel" approach. Nevertheless, both believe that the existing configuration can—in theory—deliver much better yield and are not yet considering reconfiguring the process. At MGH, Torchiana and Bohmer have recognized that the existing process configuration is close to its limits, and also understand the *reasons* for those limitations (individualistic action, no overall view of the process). They have therefore taken the same basic process elements, and reconfigured them (Level 3). This new configuration not only appears better in its own right, but also may provide a better platform for future Level 2 experimentation since process performance characteristics are now much easier to track. The Solagen case looks at a process architecture which has reached the limits of improvement by the Level 2/Level 3 mechanism. Kodak has carried out many years of reconfiguration and ad hoc experimentation, but it seems likely that the existing process *architecture* has reached its limits. Kodak is therefore developing a totally new process to provide it with an acceptable combination of gelatin clarity and output.

For the operations manager the first step is to decide what level of action is appropriate in improving a particular process. Have the limits of what the process can achieve by "tweaking" and experimenting with parameters been reached? How might the process be reconfigured to provide access to a new performance boundary? Is it possible to develop a wholly different process to achieve the same task? Companies often develop a bias towards one particular approach over another. Many operations will abandon a process for which progressive experimentation and reconfiguration still hold great potential, in favor of a new (and often expensive) process. At the same time, other operations will fight too long to improve an existing process, even though a new process innovation offers overwhelming advantages.

6. Improving Process Flexibility

Most managers are aware that tradeoffs between flexibility and cost[28] usually exist in operations processes. Flexibility, however, is a complex characteristic of an operations process and is not simply one dimensional.[29,30,31] A process can be characterized as "flexible" in a number of different ways, and the benefits and costs of each of the different forms of flexibility are likewise different.[32] How should flexibility be defined, and how does one decide what kind of flexibility is needed from a process?

---

[28]For example, the Product-Process matrix, Hayes, R. H. and S. C. Wheelwright (1979). "The dynamics of product-process life cycles." *Harvard Business Review:* 127–136.

[29]Hyun, J.-H. and B.-H. Ahn (December 1992). "A unifying framework for manufacturing flexibility." *Manufacturing Review* 5(4): 251–260.

[30]Sethi, A. K. and S. P. Sethi (1990). "Flexibility in manufacturing: A survey." *The International Journal of Flexible Manufacturing Systems* 2: 289–328.

[31]Upton, D. M. (1994). "The management of manufacturing flexibility." *California Management Review* (Winter 1994): 72–89.

[32]See, for example, Jordan, W. C. and S. C. Graves (1995). "Principles on the benefits of manufacturing process flexibility." *Management Science* 41(4): 557–594. for a discussion of the benefits of process flexibility.

TABLE 4 Levels of Process Change

Type of Change	Level 1 *Repositioning* *Process Parameters in a known local region*	Level 2 *Exploration* *Process Parameters in an unknown region*	Level 3 *Reconfiguration* *Process Configuration*	Level 4 *Radical Redesign* *Entire Process*
Cummins Engine	⊗	⊗		
Corning Glassworks		⊗		
Display Technologies		⊗	⊗	
DAV		⊗	⊗	
MGH: CABG Surgery			⊗	
Solagen				⊗

Flexibility is the ability to change or react with little penalty in time, effort, cost, or performance. This definition covers a very broad range of capabilities and sources of competitive advantage in operations. Flexibility is an inherently vague quality that has come to be used for a wide range of purposes; it is used both as a precise, analytical term and as a broad, "cheerleading" term meaning anything good about operations! To introduce the conceptual framework for analysis, it is useful to examine why the meaning of flexibility is so difficult to pin down.

Sources of Ambiguity and Confusion

The need to clarify and quantify abstract competitive capabilities has arisen in many operations situations. Garvin's work on quality[33] clearly identifies the multidimensional nature of quality and presents solutions to the measurement of quality on these dimensions. There is a useful parallel between the development of the management of flexibility and the management of quality. Both are "positive" attributes, and difficult to argue against; one would apparently always want more flexibility or quality rather than less. Both exhibit multiple, broad dimensions common across industries yet have some sub-features peculiar to a given situation. They can be understood, measured, and managed better when their vagueness is removed and when managers have a framework that clarifies the issues and provides a path for improvement.

Taxonomies of Flexibility. One common way to approach the subject of flexibility is to develop prescribed "taxonomies" that organize the topic into boxes, each separate from the next. Unfortunately, this can become confusing since predetermined taxonomies tend not to distinguish clearly between important kinds of flexibility. For example, the ability of a process to manufacture a wide range of products concurrently and the ability to adapt to a new product every five years might both be categorized as process flexibility, yet each type of flexibility is supported by a very different set of operational capabilities.

Potential Flexibility or Demonstrated Flexibility? One feature of flexibility distinguishing it from "quality" is that the term is often used to describe an organization's potential to perform a set of hypothetical tasks. It is used to describe the ability of a process to provide customized products, for instance, even though these products may not have yet been produced. The term is also used, however, to describe *demonstrated* abilities such as the provision of a broad product range.

Having an understanding of these and other factors that make flexibility a complex topic is a great advantage when dealing with issues arising in the McDonald's, Stermon, and later cases in the book. The following section provides one way to organize and define the particular types of flexibility observed in each of the cases.

A Framework for the Analysis of Manufacturing Flexibility

This section describes one method for characterizing particular forms of flexibility. The framework is divided into three parts, and is described in the form of questions one must ask in order to clearly identify the type of flexibility at issue in each case. This framework is covered in detail in "The Management of Manufacturing Flexibility."[34]

Characterizing Flexibility: A Summary. In order to characterize the flexibility(s) that is important in a case, three aspects of the situation should be analyzed:

1. Dimension: What exactly is it that flexibility is required over—what needs to change or be adapted to?

2. Time Horizon: What is the general time interval over which changes will occur? Will the process need to respond minute-by-minute, or over periods of hours, days, weeks, or years?

3. Elements: Which element(s) of flexibility is/are most important? Which of the following are we trying to manage or improve:

- Range?
- Uniformity across the range?
- Mobility?

Dimension of Change. Flexibility is the ability of a process to change or react with little penalty in time, cost, or effort of performance. On what dimension is change or adaptation required? What product or process attributes are to be flexible?

[33]Garvin, D. A. (1988). *Managing Quality.* New York, The Free Press.

[34]Upton, D. M. (1994). "The management of manufacturing flexibility." *California Management Review* (Winter 1994): 72–89.

In a given operations situation, this may necessarily be vague but should be identified as precisely as possible. As examples:

- A rolling process may need to produce multiple thicknesses of steel slab.
- A chemical process may need to tolerate changes in input materials and yield, yet still function adequately.
- A refrigerator assembly line may need to be able to switch easily among models within an existing product family.
- The same refrigerator assembly line may need to produce a different family of models each year without extensive retooling.

The dimension may be continuous (output rate, for example) or discrete (steel versus aluminum castings). Even though the nature of the dimension of change will vary considerably from case to case, and be more or less abstract, the first step in identifying the flexibility concerned is the identification of exactly *what it is that changes.*

Time Horizon. The next question that must be answered is: How frequently will the process need to change or adapt? Categorizing change requirements as operational, tactical, and strategic is helpful here. *Operational flexibility* is the ability to change day to day, or within a day as a matter of course; the best example of this is a routine changeover from one product to another. Over this time horizon, a single minute exchange of dies (SMED) program is one process-level initiative that can provide the required flexibility. *Tactical flexibility* is the ability to occasionally change or adapt, perhaps every quarter, and to make changes that typically demand some effort, commitment, and/or investment. An example here is the change from cane sugar to corn syrup as a food sweetener in response to price changes. In this situation the basic process remains unchanged, but it must be flexible enough to accommodate the substitution. *Strategic flexibility* is the ability to make one-way, long-term changes which, in general, involve significant commitment, and which occur infrequently, say, every few years or so. The ability of Cummins Engine to change from forged to cast connecting rods or move production of a given component to a different plant illustrate this type of flexibility.

The Elements of Flexibility: Range, Mobility, and Uniformity. If the time horizon characterizes the context in which flexibility is required, the next step is to determine which elements of flexibility are required over the horizon, and to what degree they are already available or need to be developed. There are three distinct "elements" or *ways of being flexible* in a given context: range, mobility, and uniformity.

Range. The first element of flexibility concerns the ability to effect or accommodate a large range on the dimension of change. This range may be represented as the number of viable positions, or some metric of the "distance" between extremes of the range. For example, flexibility increases with the range of sizes of holes that can be made by a milling machine, the range of basis weights that a paper machine can produce without experiencing too many breaks, or the number of different bottle geometries that a bottling line can handle. In any event, this form of flexibility increases with the size of the set of options or alternatives that can be accommodated.

Mobility. The second way processes are seen as "flexible" is in their ability to move rapidly or with low cost within the selected range. Flexible processes are those in which the transition penalties for these moves are small. In order to operate at a different point on the dimension of change, there will be some transition penalty in time or cost. Low values of transition penalties mean high mobility. For example, a car assembly process that can switch from one model to another with very little time lost is usually considered flexible, even if it only manufactures two models; this is because of its mobility, not its range. A production network that can increase or shed capacity easily is also flexible; it is mobile on the dimension of capacity.

Uniformity. The third way processes are viewed as flexible is in the uniformity of some performance measure (such as yield or quality) within the range. A process is flexible in terms of uniformity of performance when the important performance measure changes very little across the range. A milling machine making different sized parts with the same output rate is flexible in this sense, as is a translator who speaks French, German, and English equally well. This element of flexibility represents the "indifference" to where, within the range, the system is operating. In many situations, managers prefer uniform processes over those that have a definite "peak" and consider them more flexible. Uniformity is very different from mobility, however. Mobility concerns the *transition* penalty for moving to a different point in the range. Uniformity is concerned with the disparity in performance at different points in the range *in stasis*.

These three different ways of being flexible within the context of a particular dimension and time period are conceptually distinct.

Multiple Flexibilities. This procedure has allowed us to identify the characteristics of one type of flexibility. However, operations usually exhibit multiple types of flexibility at the same time—making things a little more complicated. McDonald's and Stermon both explore the management and improvement of flexibility. McDonald's looks at the challenges that an increased range can place on a set of processes that has hitherto been easily capable of delivering good quality and efficiency. Stermon examines the mechanisms by which different types of flexibility can be improved, as well as the differences between improving flexibility and improving other aspects of process performance.

DESCRIPTION OF CASES

Cummins Engine San Luis Potosi focuses on decisions and actions to be taken by an operations manager, Joe Panella, who is in exactly the kind of position people might find themselves in soon after they take operations jobs. Cummins has discovered that the demand for crankshafts for its "B" series engine has begun to outstrip manufacturing capacity. To meet demand and lower costs, Cummins is looking to transfer production from its Fostoria plant in the US to its operation in San Luis Potosi (SLP) in Mexico. SLP has grown from one of the worst performing plants in the Cummins network to one of the best. This has been achieved through a strong focus on processes and process control, as well as a determined effort to build new understanding of the importance of quality throughout the plant community. Panella is charged with trans-

ferring production from Fostoria to SLP. In doing so, he faces a dilemma. Among the machine tools necessary for manufacturing the crankshafts are some old center-drive lathes which can barely hold the tolerances required by the initial machining process. While economic analysis suggests that the best solution is for SLP to accept the existing machines, the plant has built an improvement strategy around ensuring that all its processes are easily capable of producing to specification. The strategy is to develop processes with a process capability index, or C_{pk}, of 1.3 or higher. The C_{pk} of the rough machining process would be less than 1.0 with the proposed equipment. Panella's dilemma, then, is whether to transfer the old equipment to the SLP operation, or whether and how to request additional financing for alternative options, given that Cummins as a whole is short of cash and has many more attractive investment opportunities for the additional funds.

The Cummins case announces a theme that runs throughout the course as a whole: the need to translate theory and frameworks into practical action that might be taken by comparatively junior operations professionals. The machining process problem puts Joe Panella in a difficult organizational situation. Like many operations managers, he is torn between an understanding of the plant's predicament and an appreciation of the corporations' broader needs. While it might be possible to improve the performance of the old equipment, if he brings it into the plant he risks the possibility of pushing the improvement strategy off-track—and more important, of reinforcing the plant's old view of itself: as a poor cousin in a rich family, routinely taking cast-offs.

Display Technologies Inc. also looks at the issue of installing a new process versus improving an existing one, though in this case, time is of the essence. In May 1993, Toru Shima, president of DTI (a joint-venture between IBM and Toshiba) faces explosive demand growth for their new 9.5 inch active matrix Liquid Crystal Displays (LCDs). After an aggressive startup, yields on the panels had risen from 10% to 45%, to bring monthly production from 10,000 per month to 50,000 per month. In order to press home the advantage of its first-to-market position, DTI needs to expand output to 100,000 units. Shima has three choices: replicate the existing line, continue to improve yields on the existing line, or invest in a new line using a promising new technology. Industry history shows that competition in such devices is fierce and directly changes from one based on innovation, i.e., being first with new technologies or screen sizes, to one based on cost as competitors arrive with "me-too" products. This shift occurs in a matter of months, and repeats itself with each new wave of products that hits the market.

Shima's dilemma is profound. On the one hand, the immediate need is for output—so replication of the current process would seem to be the answer. However, this might distract effort from improving yields on the existing process in favor of debugging the cloned line. DTI emphasizes the growing strategic importance of rapid learning in manufacturing processes and implicitly rejects the idea that learning is "something that happens if you make enough of something." This theme of *active* operations learning is revisited throughout the course, from DTI, to the loss-of-learning in the Cybertech case in Module 2, to the quality crash faced by Micom Caribe in Module 3.

Corning Glass Works: the Z-Glass Project looks at the practical problems of improving the performance of a process caught in a downward spiral. This case, however, involves the additional complexity of a conflict of approaches to improvement. Corning's Harrisburg plant has seen the yields of its process for manufacturing Z-Glass, a new industrial product, slump badly over several months. Eric Davidson, a 32-year-old engineer working with a corporate manufacturing development group, has been assigned to the plant to "fix" the problem. With an impressive track record for solving manufacturing problems, Davidson is being groomed for larger roles at Corning. Davidson's approach to the problems he faces is familiar and uncontroversial: he begins by building measurement systems for data collection so he can monitor process performance and parameters correctly before he begins to experiment with changes in the process.

The first three months of the project are a disaster. The plant resists almost all of the changes his group suggests, and Davidson has allowed a deep, personal conflict to develop with the plant manager, who predictably feels his territory has been invaded. This personal conflict is also fueled by disagreements about the cause of the problems and philosophical differences about how to tackle

them. The plant manager, Andrew MacTavish, a gruff 54-year-old Scotsman, is a hands-on, "shoot-from-the-hip" manager who has built tremendous loyalty among his subordinates. MacTavish believes he knows what is wrong with the process and that "his people" will eventually make it work. As the interpersonal situation within the plant worsens, MacTavish becomes overtly obstructive to the improvement group as they try to collect more information; he believes the process just needs to be left alone to stabilize. Davidson must decide whether to go to his superiors and ask for MacTavish to be replaced.

From an engineering point of view, Davidson is faultless; from an operations manager's standpoint, he is a disaster. Despite a wealth of knowledge and skill in improving processes, he seems oblivious to the social context he is working in, and so finds himself in a difficult and precarious professional situation.

Deutsche Allgemeinversicherung (DAV) looks at the application of manufacturing-based process improvement techniques in a service environment. DAV's prominent position in the insurance business is threatened by competitors who are attempting to replicate DAV's traditional sources of success: the quality of service it provides to customers. As it looks for ways to stay ahead of them, DAV has found that its process for entering new customer accounts has, for many years, been troubled by errors in transcription from the handwritten applications customers send in. To attack the problem, DAV had used a process called "Tastenbestätigung," or double-keying. However, as cost pressures mounted, it became clear that this process was unacceptably inefficient. The company undertook a benchmarking effort and developed sampling plans to determine actual error rates. Area manager Annette Kluck and her colleagues realized, however, that knowing these numbers would not necessarily help DAV improve the process, so she decided to build an improvement process that combined periodic sampling with ongoing identification of improvement opportunities. After discussion with a number of manufacturing-based operations specialists, they focused their attention on Statistical Process Control (SPC) as the basic technique for both of these efforts. As such, the DAV case looks at the problems and opportunities associated with using manufacturing-based tools like SPC in a service environment.

Manufacturing and service processes have traditionally been viewed much more separately than is warranted for the purposes of operations management. This distinction is partly due to the influence of previous taxonomies of industries, but it is also a result of obsolete characterizations of the two types of operation. Factories are no longer monolithic mills from which an unchanging stream of products emerges. Many modern manufacturing operations look like service operations; a factory producing quick-response spare parts has many of the characteristics traditionally associated with a service company.[35] McDonald's, normally classified as a service operation, can likewise be seen as an enormous distributed factory designed to make products perfectly in any location around the world. DAV's backroom is a high-volume factory that processes information. It concentrates on the processing of bits rather than atoms (to use Negroponte's words[36]), but is nevertheless a factory.

There are, however, some peculiar features of information-based operations that cause Kluck some difficulties as she begins to roll out SPC across DAV. Her methodology involves periodic sampling and charting the proportion of good items, i.e., correctly transcribed application forms. Sampling is the responsibility of team members themselves, who display their charts in their areas. Paradoxically, the better-performing teams need to do more sampling than did the poorer performers, because errors by the top teams are rarer events. This causes Kluck some considerable organizational problems; it appears that the poor performers are "getting off easy." Second, teams have had difficulty in deciding what constituted good and bad output: Did it matter if the mistake was an "unimportant" one, such as having a postal code wrong? Third, to build some unity around the improvement effort, Kluck has tried to involve every department in the new "Measurement and Improvement" process. However, the performance of some departments, like the legal department, is difficult to measure using SPC. Finally, she has to deal with the problem of senior managers who are confronted with the "truth" about process accuracies on a daily basis as they walk past the charts. Their disapproval of the various error rates threat-ens operators' comfort about being honest on their charts, and therefore Kluck's ability to build improvement grounded on real information.

MGH CABG Surgery looks at the implementation of process standardization in the health-care industry. In December 1994, Drs. Richard Bohmer and David Torchiana were planning the implementation of a new health-care "path" for patients undergoing Coronary Artery Bypass Graft (CABG) surgery. The project's objectives were to improve the quality of care and, secondarily, to reduce cost and length-of-stay. In the early 1990s, knee surgeons had pioneered a standard path for their patients; evidence from their experiments suggested that 20%–30% reductions in length of stay were possible when the hospital followed this standard path. In addition, the knee surgeons found that deviations from the path, e.g., a patient who took longer than expected to begin to feel well, made early identification of complications considerably easier, and thus improved the quality of care. Bohmer and Torchiana hope to replicate these results in CABG surgery.

Solagen examines an effort by Kodak to completely replace its gelatin manufacturing process. Kodak has for many years relied on a very manual process: ossein from bones is mixed with lime, and a single operator relies on his experience to judge whether or not a batch is good by putting his hand into the vat and squeezing and smelling the contents. There are a number of problems with this process (beyond the fact that contact with the lime causes severe skin conditions in some people). First, the process is slow. It takes several months for a batch of gelatin to emerge from the process. Second, it is unpredictable: as one of Kodak's managers notes in the case, "A batch either works or doesn't work with a given film or paper, and there are no reliable techniques for telling in advance which is which." Third, while the gelatin process contributed a small amount to the overall cost of film, it was an essential process whose fragility had become increasingly unacceptable. Finally, there is a potential competitive advantage to be gained from a clearer, less-yellow gelatin.

A new process, Solagen, has been invented at Kodak. This process manufactures gelatin by a very different chemical path, much better understood from a scientific point of view than the manual process. It produces gelatin in a matter of hours, and has the potential to realize much higher

[35]Chase, R. B. and D. A. Garvin (1989). "The service factory." *Harvard Business Review.* July-August.

[36]Negroponte, N. (1995). *Being Digital.* London, Coronet Books.

yields. William Bolten, a young plant superintendent, has to decide whether to spend $41 million to build a full-scale Solagen plant. Unfortunately, the prototype of the new process has generated only meager quality improvements (though the engineers promise ongoing improvement), and the latest predictions of demand for gelatin are much lower than they were when the project began.

McDonald's Corporation introduces the topic of process flexibility and looks at the challenges that a need for increased flexibility places on an operation. The case begins by underscoring the importance of good process selection and improvement to competitive success, and examines the advantages of a very traditional, Tayloristic approach to operations management in a service context. McDonald's has grown from a small, roadside restaurant to become the world's largest global food service retailer. It has done so largely by paying meticulous attention to its processes for preparing its products. McDonald's french fries, for example, are to be exactly 9/32" in width, and are deemed "cooked" when the oil temperature in a standard vat rises by three degrees above the low point. Over the years, thorough process documentation has allowed McDonald's to transfer its excellence to its growing pool of franchisees, in turn allowing the company to guarantee consistent quality across a very rapidly growing organization. By 1992, however, McDonald's was facing new challenges, as other fast food chains (e.g., Taco Bell) encroached on the low-cost end of the business and table service restaurants (e.g., Olive Garden) offered lower prices. These pressures had pushed McDonald's to expand its product range dramatically in order to maintain its growth.

This product proliferation, however, was threatening the simplicity and tight process control upon which McDonald's success had been founded. The simple recipe of doing a few things very well was slowly being replaced by the more complex task of doing many things very well.

Stermon Mills explores the improvement of process flexibility. Stermon is faced with a competitive crisis. Its paper-making processes have become relatively small-scale and out-of-date when compared to the new, gargantuan processes being installed by its rivals. Faced with this competition, and unable to invest at a comparable level, Stermon's managers decide that the plant must compete by becoming more flexible. Flexibility, however, is a complex capability, and there are many different kinds of flexibility that might be developed. Stermon has four plans available to it. It can improve the *range* of its process, so that it is able to make a broader range of products; it can work on *uniformity of performance* across its existing process range, so that changes in product mix are less damaging to overall efficiency; and it can improve the *mobility* of its process, and make changes between products more quickly. Finally, it can work on the flexibility of its workforce, and build more flexible work practices among the operators.

The Cummins Engine Company: Starting Up "B" Crankshaft Manufacturing at the San Luis Potosi Plant

INTRODUCTION

In mid-1992, after several months of rather routine activities and decisions, Joe Panella's job suddenly started getting more difficult. He and his "B-crankshaft Start-Up Team" were responsible for coordinating the installation of a manufacturing line to make crankshafts for Cummins Engine Company's "B-series" engines at its facility in San Luis Potosi, Mexico. In addition to designing the new crankshaft machining line, procuring and installing the appropriate equipment, recruiting and training workers and engineers, and designing new logistics flows and procedures, the team found itself increasingly caught in the crossfire of competing interests and priorities within the far-flung and complex Cummins organization. Mused Panella,

The thing that makes the kind of issues we're encountering now so difficult is that they don't involve determining who's (or what's) right and who's wrong. Both sides have valid points, and are probably each "right" in their terms. But the different "right" answers lead us in different directions. So we have to choose among different degrees of rightness, and balance the needs of different parties—all of whom are good, experienced, and well-meaning people—against the needs of the company as a whole. But since our team is drawn from a number of different organizational units within Cummins, we often find ourselves disagreeing about what those needs are and which are the most important.

Right now, for example, we're trying to mediate the issue of machine capabilities, which has led to a conflict between the original budget developed by the manufacturing engineers at our U.S. crankshaft manufacturing plant and the stringent performance standards that the San Luis plant has embraced. The company as a whole has been losing money for the

past several years, and is therefore taking a very cautious approach to investments in new equipment. On the other hand, not only has the Mexican plant been very profitable, but by enthusiastically adopting and implementing our new Cummins Production System (CPS), which incorporates many of the latest manufacturing philosophies and approaches, it has achieved one of the best productivity and quality records within the company. But some of the used equipment that we are being asked to adapt to B crankshaft machining isn't capable of achieving the precision demanded by the CPS.

There's also the issue of which measurement gauges to use in inspecting crankshaft dimensions, which have to be extremely precise. The obvious approach would be to use the same air-gauging system that is used at our Fostoria plant, where the crankshaft is currently being produced. Doing that would permit similar procedures and facilitate comparisons when we start producing the crankshafts here. On the other hand, that system is quite sophisticated, and requires both a high degree of skill and very tight control over environmental factors. Moreover, the supplier of that equipment doesn't have an office in Mexico. The alternative is to use a contact-gauging system, but some people are concerned that its use might compromise the quality of the crankshaft. What are you supposed to do when the "experts" disagree?

THE SAN LUIS POTOSI PLANT

Mexico had long been Cummins' largest market outside the United States. About a third of the automotive diesel engines operating in the country bore its nameplate, and Cummins' share of the market for electrical generators was about 60%. In 1980 the company entered into a joint venture with Diesel Nacional (DINA), Mexico's state-owned producer of trucks, buses, and diesel engines, to build a new diesel engine assembly and components machining plant. DINA owned 60% of the joint venture and took an active role in its management.

This case was prepared by Robert H. Hayes. Copyright © 1993 by the President and Fellows of Harvard College. Harvard Business School case 693-121.

The new plant was built in San Luis Potosi (often referred to within the company by its initials: S.L.P.), a 400-year-old but fast-growing colonial city of about one million people located on the high plain (elevation 6000 feet) roughly halfway between Mexico City, 250 miles to the south, and Monterrey. S.L.P. had the advantage of being on the main north-south road (along the route of the old Pan-Am highway) connecting Mexico City with the United States at Laredo, Texas. The plant began operations in 1984, initially assembling engines at a rate of two per day.

In the protected Mexican market of the mid-1980s, the joint venture had only one domestic competitor and supplied virtually 100% of the engines installed by Mexican assemblers of heavy duty trucks. Although the company made a profit each year—largely because of aggressive pricing— the plant was plagued with quality and other operating problems. Morale was low, turnover was high, and a status quo mentality prevailed; people were afraid to try anything new. Moreover, the plant was regarded as a poor supplier by other Cummins entities.

By late 1986, the administration of President De la Madrid had signalled its interest in selling off government-owned enterprises, and Cummins had decided that achieving its quality and performance standards was unlikely to happen within the joint venture arrangement. Therefore, Cummins began negotiating the purchase of DINA's share, reaching its objective in September 1987. The new wholly owned subsidiary was renamed Cummins, S.A. de C.V. (CUMMSA).

Freed of the severe budget limitations and bureaucratic requirements of the former government joint venture, and now able to pay salaries competitive with other private sector companies, CUMMSA's top management immediately began to implement new approaches for dealing with its quality, productivity, and delivery problems. Many of the activities performed at CUMMSA's headquarters in Mexico City, including engineering, purchasing, supplier development, human resources, and finance were moved to the plant to improve cross-functional communication and put these people close to where the products were made. Working conditions at the plant were improved, salaries were increased, teamwork was encouraged, hierarchical barriers were knocked down, and attempts were made to increase union involvement and cooperation in the new focus on quality and delivery.

Improvements were quickly obtained; within two years, for example, the rejection rate for cylinder heads shipped to the Cummins plants in Indiana dropped from 40% to less than 1%. But the rate of improvement increased markedly after 1990 when, under the leadership of Plant Manager Norman Brown, the plant began implementing the new Cummins Production System, which emphasized cleanliness and orderliness, involvement of people, functional excellence, synchronized production flows, shortened leadtimes, and visual controls. "The three core concepts behind CPS," commented Brown, "are teamwork, setting high standards for quality and customer service and not compromising them under pressure, and pushing for continuous improvement in all activities."

Material flows were reorganized to reduce distance travelled and time required, a Just-In-Time "pull" production control system was implemented, and employee teams were organized to identify and propose solutions to problems. Internal education programs were also expanded; in 1989 CUMMSA's top management set a goal of 12 training days per employee per year—about five times more than had been carried out in 1987. This target was achieved in 1991.

The plant's steady improvement led Cummins to decide to manufacture additional parts at S.L.P.; for example, in 1989 the production of cylinder heads for the K series engines was moved from Komatsu in Japan without problems or disruption in shipping schedules. As a result, CUMMSA's annual sales had more than tripled between 1987 and 1991, to over $180 million, as heavy duty engine sales grew to nearly 10,000 units a year and exports of engine parts also increased. In 1991, CUMMSA produced and sold 44% more engines than in the previous year, while adding only three people to its payroll (to a total of 604). Its profit after tax was more than 11 times higher than in 1987, even though engine prices (in U.S. dollars) had been reduced an average of 20%. The "teardown quality" index for the engines assembled at the plant rose from under 92% in 1987 to 99.8%, production throughput time was cut in half, to just over three days, and on-time delivery rose from 51.4% in 1989 to almost 93%. Moreover, compressing material flows and reducing inventories (for example, the assembly area for the big NT engine was reduced by almost 50%) freed up several thousand square meters of floor space that were available for the production of additional products.

In mid-1992 the spotless plant employed 363 shop floor workers and 99 engineers, technicians, and administrative people. Most of the workers had at least a high school education or had graduated from a government-sponsored training program for mechanics. In addition to assembling NT and C series engines for domestic consumption (none of these engines were exported), the plant machined and assembled water pumps, machined cylinder heads for the NT and K engines, and manufactured vibration dampers. The plant was surrounded by attractive landscaping, which included a grassy soccer field. In addition to paying the highest wages in the area (equivalent to about $1.50 per hour in 1992), the plant offered a number of fringe benefits whose cost was equivalent to about 70% of the average wage. In addition to the usual retirement and health benefits, for example, most of the workers commuted to work on company buses and paid only 25% of the cost of the 500 hot meals served each day in the plant's modern cafeteria. The normal workweek was 45 hours (five nine-hour days).

Each quarter the plant management shared with its employees the sales, production, and financial information that had just been sent to Cummins headquarters. Employee turnover was about 1.2% per year, and the plant had never had a layoff. Relations with the union (the Confederation of Mexican Workers, or CTM in Spanish) were excellent. The union was primarily interested in insuring job stability and growth—although it pushed hard in wage negotiations to keep CUMMSA's wages among the very highest in the S.L.P. area. The union seldom initiated disputes about work issues, nor did its leadership show concern about jurisdictional matters or about people being moved from job to job. In fact, it supported activities that increased the skills and responsibilities of its members. Contracts were negotiated every other year, and a wage adjustment was agreed to in the off year. CUMMSA's financial success had resulted in its San Luis Potosi employees being among the highest compensated factory workers in Mexico during 1992. Under Mexican law, each legal entity had to distribute 10% of its profits before tax among all its employees in proportion to their wages and hours worked. In 1992

this distribution, based on the company's 1991 results, amounted to over twice the annual salary of the average factory worker.

Rakesh Sachdev, CUMMSA's chief financial officer, was optimistic about both the Mexican economy and the future of his own organization.

Mexico's industrial expansion is bound to continue, due more to the fundamental changes that have been made in its manufacturing sector than to its current low labor and engineering costs. The Mexican workforce is steadily becoming more productive. Quality is increasingly being emphasized in the workplace, and workers are being trained to master highly complex engineering and manufacturing tasks. One of the most significant factors that impact us is the cost of purchasing raw and semi-finished materials—which, in our case, are primarily imported from the U.S. While material costs in Mexico historically have been high, they are coming down as more production moves here.

Depending on the part to be manufactured and the volumes involved, Mexico may or may not be the low-cost source today. Mexico will probably continue to be dependent on the United States and other countries for many components, such as steel forgings and castings, for the foreseeable future. This interdependence will create opportunities for both Mexico and the United States. As far as capital costs are concerned, they're high within Mexico, but a company like Cummins is able to source capital from anywhere in the world.

To promote exports, the Mexican government permits companies to import materials and equipment without paying import duties (normally 22%), provided those materials and equipment are used to produce exported products. This is accomplished through the PITEX (Program permitting Temporary Importation for Export) system. The customs officials carefully record each imported item and check it off when it is exported, and you have to specify in advance roughly when this will occur. All this requires meticulous records and lots of paperwork, and errors (even corrections to the original) are not permitted. Training people in the United States to understand why this is so important has taken more time than we expected.

One of the ironies associated with this system is that it can penalize suppliers that have distribution centers in Mexico. You won't be eligible for the PITEX savings, for example, unless you arrange to purchase the parts from a point across the border!

Another benefit that is available to a company like Cummins is the ability to sell Export Credits, called "DIVISAS." Car companies in Mexico have to maintain a certain ratio of exports to imports, roughly 1.7 to 1. If they can't meet that requirement they can buy export credits from other companies—like Cummins—that are not required to meet the same export-to-import ratio as they do. This has resulted in an active market in DIVISAs, which has made it possible for us to reduce our cost of purchased material for exported products by up to 4%. The benefits from the sale of DIVISAs and programs such as PITEX are constantly changing, however, so it is probably not advisable for a company to count on them when making business decisions regarding Mexico.

As far as the future is concerned, we still have some unoccupied space in the plant and our rate of productivity improvement continues to free up workers. So we've entered into discussions with Cummins headquarters to move a rebuild operation for B and C series engines here from the States. That's a highly labor intensive job, where used engines are completely disassembled, each part is thoroughly checked out and remachined or replaced if necessary, and then the engine is reassembled and tested. As it reaches mature volume levels in about five years, this operation would require more than 300 workers. And we've also had some very tentative discussion with a couple of the automobile assembly plants here in Mexico about supplying them with machined parts that they're currently importing from the United States.

Problems threatened on the horizon, however. The opening of the Mexican market had encouraged imports from Caterpillar, Navistar, and the recently-reinvigorated Detroit Diesel. As a result, Cummins engines faced stiff competition in Mexico. The signing of the NAFTA (North American Free Trade Agreement) was expected to lead to additional reductions in tariffs and encourage these and other competitors to both increase their exports to Mexico and consider establishing manufacturing operations there.

COMPANY BACKGROUND

Cummins Engine, with annual sales of about $3.5 billion, was one of the premier producers of heavy duty diesel engines in the world (see Exhibit 1 for financial background). Its engines were offered as either standard or optional equipment by every major North American truck manufacturer, as well as by the major producers of construction, mining, and farming equipment.

Together with other diesel engine producers, Cummins had experienced turbulent times since the late 1970s growing out of two shifts in the competitive environment. First, the growth of the total market for diesel engines had slowed and emphasis had shifted away from Cummins' most popular engines to smaller, lighter weight, and more fuel efficient designs. Second, competition intensified as both existing and new (largely Asian) competitors fought for a share of this market. Cummins reacted with a series of manufacturing improvement efforts, new product development programs, and financial restructurings.

In the early 1980s, for example, it instituted programs to improve delivery times and achieve world quality standards while cutting manufacturing costs by 30% through a combination of plant rationalizations, outsourcing of components, and personnel and floorspace reductions. In 1984, as this program was still being implemented, Japanese producers attempted to increase their share of the U.S. market for medium-sized truck engines by quoting prices 40% below Cummins'. Refusing to allow itself to be undersold, the company dropped its own prices to competitive levels while maintaining heavy investments in R&D; at the same time it redoubled its efforts to improve its manufacturing competitiveness and introduce lower cost, more fuel efficient models. During the battle for share—and survival—that ensued, Cummins (like most of its competitors) experienced a series of operating losses. In 1992 it hoped to show a profit for the first time in five years.

By then the company was able to boast that its product line, consisting of both redesigned models and three new engine families, offered the most advanced diesel engine technology in the world. As a result of their superior operating performance (as measured by reliability, durability, and fuel economy), they not only held share in Cummins' traditional markets but gained share in those where the company had not had a significant presence in the past.

Each mountain climbed, however, revealed new mountains ahead. The toughened emissions requirements that went into effect in 1991 had been met, but the more stringent ones that would be required in 1994 were widely regarded to be "10 times more difficult" to achieve. The company gritted its teeth and committed itself to continuing heavy expenditures on R&D and efforts to im-

EXHIBIT I Summary of Consolidated Financial Information for 10 Years ($ millions, except per share amounts)

	1991	1990	1989
Results of operations:			
Net sales	$3,405.5	$3,461.8	$3,519.5
Cost of goods sold	2,776.7	2,857.1	2,856.9
Gross profit	628.8	604.7	662.6
Selling, administrative, research and engineering expenses	619.3	631.7	607.4
Interest expense	42.5	43.9	51.8
Other expense (income), net	12.7	8.4	(17.2)
Unusual charges	—	—	—
Earnings (loss) before income taxes	(45.7)	(142.2)	20.6
Provision (credit) for income taxes	16.9	25.0	22.2
Minority interest	3.0	(2.1)	4.5
Earnings (loss) before extraordinary credit and cumulative effect of accounting changes	(65.6)	(165.1)	(6.1)
Extraordinary credit	—	27.4	—
Cumulative effect of accounting changes	51.5	—	—
Net earnings (loss)	(14.1)	(137.7)	(6.1)
Preferred and preference stock dividends	8.0	13.7	
Earnings (loss) available for common shares	$(22.1)	$(151.4)	$(15.9)
Per common share:			
Earnings (loss) before extraordinary credit and cumulative effect of accounting changes:			
Primary	$(4.96)	$(14.47)	$(1.52)
Fully diluted	(4.96)	(14.47)	(1.52)
Net earnings (loss):			
Primary	(1.49)	(12.25)	(1.52)
Fully diluted	(1.49)	(12.25)	(1.52)
Cash dividends	.70	2.20	2.20
Common shareholders' investment	34.29	37.37	39.77
Average number of common shares (millions):			
Primary	14.8	12.4	10.5
Fully diluted	14.8	12.4	10.5
Operating percentages:			
Gross profit	1.85%	17.5%	18.8%
Return on net sales	(.4)	(4.0)	(.2)
Financial data:			
Working capital	$219.2	$263.4	$224.2
Property, plant and equipment, net	953.0	921.2	890.1
Total assets	2,041.2	2,086.3	2,030.8
Long-term debt and redeemable preferred stock	443.2	411.4	473.7
Shareholders' investment	623.8	669.3	559.2
Supplemental data:			
Property, plant and equipment expenditures	$123.9	$147.0	$137.9
Depreciation and amortization	127.2	143.4	135.0
Number of common shareholders of record	5,900	5,900	5,700
Number of employees	22,900	24,900	25,100

Notes: Effective January 1, 1991, the company changed its accounting to include in inventory certain production-related costs previously charged directly to expense. The company also changed its method of depreciation for substantially all engine production equipment to a modified units-of-production depreciation method.

In 1990, the company purchased a portion of its outstanding zero coupon notes resulting in an extraordinary credit of $27.4 million.

Source: 1991 Annual Report.

prove manufacturing efficiency and quality. Both Cummins' top management and capital market observers were concerned about the impact such expenditures were likely to have on the company's ability to meet its financial goals.

MANUFACTURING ORGANIZATION

Cummins assembled diesel engines at six major facilities (one of them a joint venture with another company) in North America. Each facility produced a limited range of engines and was supplied through a central purchasing office at its Columbus, Indiana headquarters. A major in-house producer of mechanical components for these plants was its Atlas subsidiary, which had two plants in the United States and one in Brazil. More and more components were being outsourced from a global network of suppliers. Supplying each assembly plant with all the components and materials it required, therefore, necessitated complex administrative and logistics processes.

Until recently, for example, Atlas had produced the bulk of the crankshafts used in Cummins engines. During the 1980s, however, it had turned to external suppliers from as far away as India. Outsourcing decisions required a careful balance of competing concerns. On the one hand, the main Atlas factory in Fostoria, Ohio, was regarded as having higher costs than other Cummins facilities. On the other, past experience had taught Cummins that unless it established strong partnerships with single source suppliers, it risked being exploited by price increases.

THE B CRANKSHAFT DECISION

In 1991 Cummins forecast that worldwide demand for its six cylinder B (5.9 liter) and C (8.3 liter) engines would almost double over the following five years. Most of this increased demand would take place in the United States, as both Ford and Chrysler had decided to switch to Cummins engines from their current source. The crankshafts for these engines were produced primarily at Atlas's Fostoria plant. Smaller amounts were purchased, at delivered prices that were generally about the same as Fostoria's, from two other external suppliers—one in Brazil and the other in the United Kingdom. The capacity of all these facilities, however, was not expected to keep pace with the increasing demand.

In particular, the crankshafts for its B engines represented a potential bottleneck. The capacity of all current suppliers was estimated to be only 400 to 460 per day—not much more than current requirements and far less than the 800 crankshafts per day (200,000 per year) that were expected to be needed by 1995. Moreover, it was unclear whether Cummins' external suppliers would be willing to commit the funds required to expand capacity. Three alternatives for breaking this bottleneck were considered: 1) expand capacity at the existing Fostoria plant; 2) build a new facility near the CDC engine manufacturing plant, Cummins' joint venture with J.I. Case in North Carolina; or 3) begin production at a new Atlas-CUMMSA joint venture to be housed in the area freed up when the S.L.P. plant's NT engine assembly line had been compressed.

Adding capacity at the Fostoria plant would not provide the required return on investment, while the investment required to build a new crankshaft production facility near CDC in North Carolina was considered prohibitive. The last alternative promised the lowest investment and operating costs (see Exhibit 2). In addition, it would offer Cummins the potential opportunity to displace local crankshaft manufacturers who were selling crankshafts to Mexico's fast growing vehicle manufacturing sector. Potential customers included Chrysler, Ford, G.M., Nissan, and Volkswagen.

But the Mexican alternative also would take the longest time to implement because of the problems associated with equipping a production line from scratch and training workers to produce a

EXHIBIT 2 Crankshaft Manufacturing Cost Comparisons

Manufacturing Cost per Unit at:

	S.L.P		Fostoria
	@ 150/da	@ 300/da	
Materials	$141.2	$141.2	$139.3
Direct Labor	9.9	8.8	102.8
Overhead	39.9	22.3	38.9
Freight	22.5	22.5	0
Depreciation	19.9	15.1	5.5
Total	**$233.4**	**$209.9**	**$286.5**

Source: Company records (disguised).

component that was much more complex and precise than any they had ever made before. It was anticipated that the earliest date production could begin there would be the first quarter of 1993, and that it would take at least another year to ramp up to 250 per day. Therefore, in order to make up the production shortfall that would be experienced during the transition, an investment of almost $1.0 million would be required at the Fostoria plant in order to increase its capacity temporarily from 275 to 325 per day.

After considering many factors, Cummins decided to add a new crankshaft production line in Mexico that would be able to produce 375 B crankshafts per day by 1995. It would be located in a 40,000 square foot area of the S.L.P. plant and, at capacity, would employ about 110 factory workers on three shifts, supported by 31 salaried workers in Mexico. An additional five people would be required in the United States to coordinate the materials flows required. Setting up the facility would require the installation of 45 pieces of equipment, of which two would be transferred from Fostoria to S.L.P. and the remainder would be a mix of purchased new and used machines. Fourteen million dollars were budgeted for these purchases, and another $2.5 million was provided for the costs associated with coordinating the installation and managing the start-up. The manufacturing cost of a crankshaft produced at S.L.P. depended somewhat on the rate of production, but was anticipated to be about $210 when the line was at full capacity—almost $80 less than Fostoria's manufacturing cost.

In addition to these cost savings, adding the B Crankshaft line produced tax savings, according to Rakesh Sachdev.

> The line's investment and start-up costs, which are substantial during the first two years of the start-up, will be offset somewhat by lowering our Mexican income tax and profit sharing obligations—totalling 45% of the start-up expenses. If we'd made the same investment in the United States, on the other hand, we would not have benefitted from that tax shield because Cummins' U.S. operations have not been in a tax-paying situation for the past several years.

CRANKSHAFT MANUFACTURING

The crankshaft (see Exhibit 3 for a schematic) of a modern diesel truck engine was one of its most intricately shaped and technically demanding com-

ponents, requiring both careful handling and extremely high precision throughout a series of tightly specified and linked steps. Constant monitoring of dimensions was required during all these steps. A deviation anywhere along the line could have repercussions that reverberated throughout the remainder of the process.

The process began with a forged steel blank costing about $100, which was imported from a U.S. supplier (the same company that currently supplied the Fostoria plant). Although Mexican suppliers existed for the cast steel blanks that were used as the basis for manufacturing automobile engine crankshafts, there was no domestic source for forged blanks (castings did not have the strength or durability needed for long-running and heavily loaded truck engines). After cleaning, the crankshaft's main bearings (the load-bearing round surfaces that rotated around its central axis) and pins (the surfaces that transferred the reciprocating power of the pistons to the rotating crankshaft) were rough machined, first on a center drive lathe and then a rough milling machine to +/-10 thousandths of an inch. Then they were individually hardened using electrical induction heating. The heat and stresses created during this operation were then relieved through heat treating, in which the whole crankshaft passed through a furnace.

These induction hardening and heat treating processes served to toughen the crankshaft's surface and relieve its internal stresses; on the other hand, they also caused the shaft to "bow" (bend, and therefore lose its rotational symmetry) slightly and its length to grow by about 0.06 inch. Therefore, the ensuing milling and grinding steps not only had to achieve tolerances of 0.001 inch, they also had to correct those distortions. In addition, precise holes that permitted engine oil to circulate through a variety of locations on the crankshaft had to be drilled to specified depths at complex angles.

After the basic dimensions and rotational integrity of the crankshaft had been achieved, it went through a series of delicate grinding (on grinding wheels) and lapping (polishing with an abrasive tape) steps that achieved tolerances of +/-3 millionths of an inch. Prior to lapping, the crankshaft also had to be "balanced," just as the tires of a car had to be balanced to prevent wobbling at high rotational speeds. Instead of adding weights, as on an automobile wheel, however, the crankshaft was balanced by drilling out precise amounts

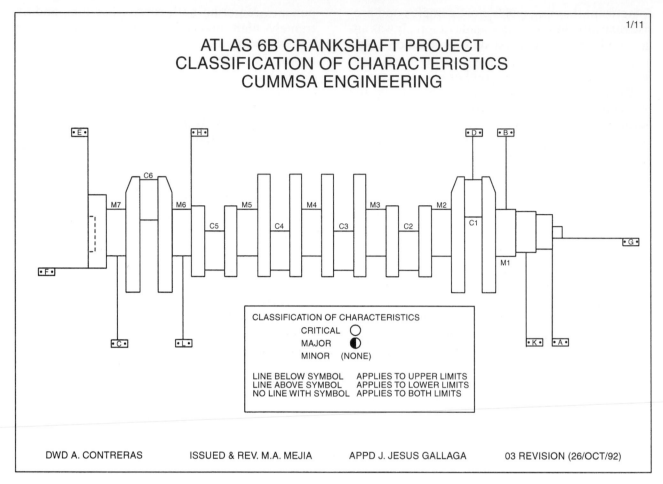

EXHIBIT 3 Crankshaft Schematic

of metal from non-critical surfaces. Finally, the crankshaft was subjected to a thorough cleaning and inspection process before being carefully packed for shipment.

The whole machining process required such precision, control, and discipline that many within Cummins were concerned that it might be too difficult for the S.L.P. plant to master at this stage of its development. Only one other crankshaft manufacturing facility was located in Mexico, but it was producing automobile crankshafts, which required far less demanding tolerances.

THE B CRANKSHAFT START-UP TEAM

Joe Panella, a young engineer who had recently rounded out his education by graduating from a well-known Eastern business school, was made the project manager for the start-up of B Crankshaft production. In early 1991 he acquired a team made up of people from both the S.L.P. and the Atlas Fostoria plants. A senior engineer from Fostoria, Karen Forster, was appointed U.S. engineering manager. Also from Fostoria came Ken Reynolds, as senior manufacturing engineer, and manufacturing engineers Dick Johnson and Jim Heyman. Bert Hand, a Cummins engineer from the United Kingdom who had more than 25 years experience in quality assurance and supplier development, and who had been in charge of the S.L.P. plant's machining businesses since 1984, was named the on-site project director. CUMMSA's top management, recognizing that the crankshaft project was more sophisticated and complex than any that had been attempted before at the S.L.P. plant, also agreed to move three of its best engineers to the start-up team. Jose Contraras was named on-site manufacturing engineering manager; Manuel Zacarias was put in charge of on-site quality management; and Juan Jose Hernandes was made head of maintenance. Representatives of the corporate purchasing department and the Cummins plants that would become the customers of the new crankshaft line were also associated with the team.

Looking back on their early experience with the transfer, various team members commented:

Karen Forster

The main problems we've encountered here are the obvious ones: the different language and culture. Even though we all speak and understand a little Spanish now, and many of our Mexican colleagues speak some English, we're never really sure if we and they understand each other—even when we phrase things very simply. We think something has been decided, or somebody is going to do something, and later we find it has fallen through the cracks. Then, the next time, in order to make sure that they understand what we are trying to communicate, we tend to ask lots of questions. But sometimes this leads to a different kind of misunderstanding, because it appears that we don't trust them.

Also, we tend to be rather direct, and like to get right to the point when dealing with some issue. But Mexicans tend to approach issues in a more roundabout way and feel more comfortable about talking business with someone once they've established a personal relationship with that person. It's important not only that you know the person you're dealing with well, but you also should know about their family and the various other activities they're involved in.

But in many respects they are more flexible than our Atlas-Fostoria workforce. It is generally much more difficult, for example, to persuade workers in the States to give management the flexibility to change work assignments and adjust jobs that we have in Mexico. And in Mexico the use of videotaping people at work for training purposes is common practice, while in the States it is not easily done.

Basically, we can get product to or from Fostoria in from five to 10 days: two days from S.L.P. to the U.S. border, two days from the border to Fostoria, and one to five days getting across the border, depending on whether the paperwork is right and the customs gods are smiling. Our regular weekly ship-

ments tend to go through pretty quickly; it's the irregular shipments that experience delays. In general, Mexican customs officials assume you're doing something illegal and it's up to you to prove you're not. You have to be extremely precise, and sometimes the language difference trips you up (all documents have to be in Spanish). For example, one time we imported a bunch of highly polished carbide inserts; the customs officials insisted they were mirrors!

Ken Reynolds

The skill level and work ethic of our Mexican employees are excellent. They are also a very proud people. You can be very demanding, and can count on them to respond with enthusiasm, as long as you enlist their involvement in getting the job done. They also like to celebrate accomplishments—more so than in the States—with parties. Taking the time to show appreciation, even for little things, really pays off.

On the other hand, their cultural heritage is one in which hierarchical position is quite important; bosses are typically treated with great deference and their orders are seldom questioned. As a result, it was sometimes hard at first to get them to participate in solving a problem or making a decision. And, whereas in the U. S. we tend to choose group leaders who are decisive, "take charge" kind of people, here we have to be careful that they not become too autocratic.

THE CENTER DRIVE LATHE

According to Joe Panella: "One of the main problems we've encountered so far with transferring this technology to Mexico was created during the formulation of the Project Authorization Document (PAD). Essentially, the manufacturing engineers who prepared the PAD kept cutting and cutting until the investment required was reduced to a level that could be approved in the context of the company's financial situation. To get the investment down they assumed we could make use of—or rehabilitate—a lot of used equipment from existing plants. But much of this equipment was simply too old to provide the precision required by the B crankshaft.

For example, the center drive turning equipment that had been identified for us was over 30 years old. It can't hold the in-process tolerances required. The Atlas-Fostoria people say, "So what. This is the rough machining stage, so you don't need close tolerances. You can machine the parts to the correct tolerances in later stages.

On the other hand, under the CPS system that the S.L.P. plant has adopted, every machine in the place is supposed to be "Cpk capable." The Cp refers to the ratio of the tolerance range required by a part to the range of the precision that the machine is capable of. That ratio reflects the machine's "capability," and naturally we want it to be as large as possible. The k refers to the percentage of the product's tolerance range that the process mean is off center. You would like that always to be zero, of course, but machines do wander off center. Cpk, then, is a combined measure that indicates roughly how far the process can wander off center without causing an unacceptable level of rejects; the higher the Cpk, the better (see Exhibit 4). The goal of our CPS is to have all machines operating at a capability level of 1.33 Cpk or better. That means that if the process is carefully monitored there's almost no chance that we will generate a part that doesn't fall within the required tolerances. Every piece of equipment in the plant has a color-coded sticker on it that specifies its Cpk, so it's pretty obvious if a machine doesn't meet the required level of capability.

Of course you can sometimes compensate for an error early in a process by exercising extra care later on, but this adds complexity and possible sources of errors. Insisting that each machine be Cpk capable is therefore a form of discipline—like insisting on zero defects. If you allow deviations, you get caught up in endless negotiations. S.L.P. has trained their workers that this is bad. Now, because of budget constraints, we're asking them to compromise their values.

Fostoria had used old center drive equipment for many years, and their highly trained workforce had learned how to produce acceptable parts by "tweaking" the equipment, so it was felt that using far more sophisticated and expensive equipment could be avoided. It was estimated that the scrap caused by the old center drives would be higher in S.L.P. than in Fostoria because S.L.P.'s operators were less experienced. But since the cost of this additional scrap could not be substantiated, the decision was made to stay with the old center drives. Therefore, the PAD budgeted $300,000 to refurbish, ship, and install them. But no matter how much we work on them, we probably won't be able to hold a Cpk over 1.0. On the other hand, buying new equipment that does meet our requirements will cost almost $2 million. It's a budget buster.

THE DIMENSION GAUGING SYSTEM

The issue of the gauging system presented a much different problem. "Given today's technology, there are basically only two approaches to measuring the dimensions of parts with the kind of accuracy we demand," commented Ken Reynolds. "One approach is 'contact' gauging, where you use metal calipers to measure the dimension. This is a relatively straightforward and natural approach, and doesn't require special environmental controls, but it can lead to tiny scratches on the metal surface being gauged. These scratches are too small to affect the appearance or performance of most parts, but when you're dealing with dimensions that have to be controlled to a couple of microns it could conceivably cause problems (such as fatigue cracks) over time. The question is, where is the B crankshaft in that grey area?

The other major approach to measurement is based on an air gauging system: you expel some air out of a small orifice and measure how long it takes to bounce back from the surface. The latest versions of this kind of system translate the dimension indicated by the time delay into an electrical signal that can be automatically recorded. Air, of course, can't damage the surface of the part, but it presents its own series of problems. To begin with, a complete air-gauging system costs about half again as much as a contact system. Second, it requires very clean conditions; if it gets contaminated with dust it has to be torn down and cleaned out. Finally, the response of the system to different dimensions isn't exactly linear, so it is only accurate within a rather narrow range and has to be calibrated very carefully. Partly as a result of this, you will get slightly different readings from an air-gauging system than you will from a contact system. If we went to air gauging, therefore, we would need a workforce and support staff that were very well trained and experienced in this particular process.

At our Fostoria plant they use an air-gauging system, which they got from the Dearborn Gauge Company (which makes by far the best system) and with which they've been very satisfied. In fact, our Jamestown plant is now in the process of switching over from contact to air gauging. The problem is, not only is there concern that an air-gauging system may be too difficult for our S.L.P. organization to maintain—at least, at this early stage of its experience with crankshaft manufacturing, but Dearborn Gauge doesn't have a facility in Mexico. If we start having problems, it may take some time to get their service

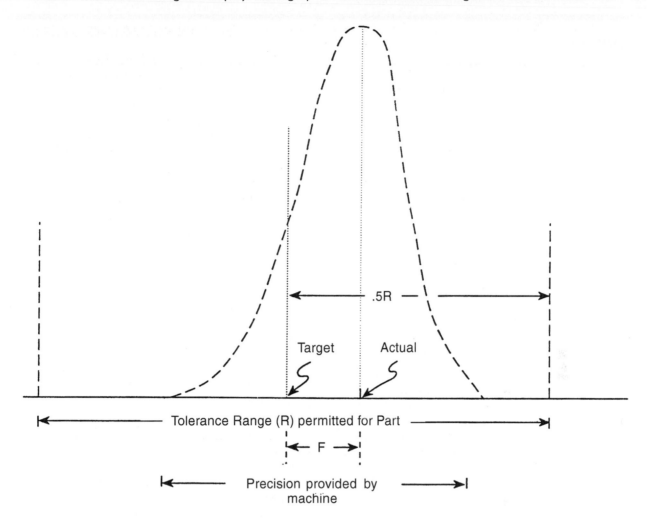

$$C_p = \frac{\text{Product Tolerance Range Required}}{\text{Machine Precision}}$$

k = the percentage of the product tolerance half-range that the process mean is off center ($=F/.5R$)

$$= \frac{|\,\text{Actual} - \text{Target}\,|}{1/2\ \text{Tolerance Range}}$$

$$C_{pk} = C_p\,(1-k) \geq \text{Desired level}$$

EXHIBIT 4 Calculating C_{pk}

people down here, and when they come they probably won't be able to speak Spanish.

The alternative is to use a $70,000 contact gauging system from Marposs, a company that Cummins has lots of experience with and that does have a plant in Mexico City. But this will lead to somewhat different measurements being generated by our new B crankshaft line, and will complicate the transfer process. We'll continually have to determine whether the differences we see between the dimensions Fostoria obtains and those we get here are due to process differences or measurement differences.

Display Technologies Incorporated

In late May 1993, Toru Shima, president of Display Technologies Incorporated (DTI), confronted a choice many managers would envy. His success at manufacturing color Thin Film Transistor-Liquid Crystal Displays (TFT-LCDs)—bright-color screens built into notebook computers—had precipitated mounting calls from his customers for a substantial increase in output. Color LCDs had become hot sellers, as buyers demanded ever-increasing performance and less weight from their portable machines.

Since Shima's main customers were also his company's owners, he could hardly refuse their request. DTI was a joint venture of Toshiba and IBM Japan, 50% owned by each side. Toshiba and IBM could sell every screen Shima's plant produced. Both were amassing a growing backlog of orders. Shima's workforce had already raised output from the original 10,000 units per month to the current 50,000 per month. His people, machines, and systems were stretched. Now he was being pressed to raise production to 100,000 per month. Shima was not sure how to meet these expectations. He knew the task would be tough. TFT-LCDs were fiendishly difficult to make. They required hundreds of delicate steps, each performed on some of the most expensive, cutting-edge manufacturing technology in the electronics business. Few plants yet had substantial experience with color LCDs, but every company building them was racing to supply spiraling demand. None had figured out all the manufacturing process complexities, the main obstacle to increased output.

Shima wanted to weigh his options carefully before deciding. His choice seemed to be among three possibilities: try to drive up yields and reduce cycle time on his existing production line, build a

second line similar to the existing one, or shift to new production technology with larger substrates, which could build twice as many screens in the same time. Each promised to meet the projected needs of his customers, but Shima's past experience and instincts told him that the answer to this problem would have strategic ramifications well into the future.

BACKGROUND

Both IBM and Toshiba had long been leaders in the world computer and electronics industries (Exhibit 1). In the 1980s, they were in the forefront of an industry-wide shift to smaller and more portable personal computers. Following its launch of the personal computer in 1981, IBM introduced its first notebook computer (designed to be as portable as a small book) in 1988. Toshiba had pioneered its own highly successful notebook PC in 1985. These innovative products relied upon advances in component technologies: more-durable batteries, miniaturized disk drives, tiny printed circuit boards, and, finally, flat panel displays (Exhibit 2 is a photo of a Toshiba portable personal computer).

Smaller screens had been a critical bottleneck in the move to portability. Conventional cathode ray tubes (CRTs) offered quick response and high resolution but were far too power consuming, heavy, and bulky for truly portable computers. The alternative was the flat panel display. Several technologies had been proposed to meet the need for a thin, light screen with acceptable resolution in color. Most companies chose some form of Liquid Crystal Display (LCD) (see Exhibit 3 for a description of LCD technology).

Toshiba and IBM in turn had chosen the Thin Film Transistor (TFT) active-matrix version of the LCD. Active-Matrix LCDs (AM-LCD) sandwiched a layer of special liquid-crystal material between sheets of glass to create a full-color display. When voltage was applied to the liquid crystal by

This case was prepared by Ryota Matsui under the direction of Jonathan West and H. Kent Bowen. Copyright © 1997 by the President and Fellows of Harvard College. Harvard Business School case 697-117.

Company	Sales Country	Assets ($1,000)	Stockholders' ($1,000)	Equity ($1,000)	Employees
International Business Machines	USA	65,096,000	86,705,000	27,624,000	308,010
General Electric	USA	62,202,000	192,876,000	23,459,000	268,000
Hitachi	Japan	61,465,000	76,667,600	25,768,300	331,505
Matshushita Electric Industrial	Japan	57,480,000	75,645,100	30,057,600	252,075
Siemens	Germany	51,401,900	50,752,800	13,505,300	413,000
Samsung Group	S Korea	49,559,600	48,030,800	6,430,800	188,558
Toshiba Corporation	Japan	37,471,600	49,341,600	10,068,500	173,000
Philips Electronics	Netherlands	33,269,700	26,853,200	4,968,800	252,200
Sony	Japan	31,451,900	39,700,500	12,517,300	126,000
ABB Asea Brown Boveri	Switzerland	30,536,000	25,949,000	4,095,000	213,407
Alcatel Alsthom	France	30,529,100	44,207,700	9,027,500	203,000
NEC	Japan	28,376,500	34,872,000	7,062,500	140,969
Daewoo	S Korea	28,333,900	39,250,900	5,126,100	78,727
Fujitsu	Japan	27,910,700	33,092,300	9,651,300	161,974
Mitsubishi Electric	Japan	26,502,300	30,747,500	7,146,700	107,859
Hewlett-Packard	USA	16,427,000	13,700,000	7,499,000	92,600
Canon	Japan	15,348,900	17,226,800	5,668,800	67,227
Electrolux	Sweden	14,048,700	10,436,800	2,011,000	119,200
Digital Equipment	USA	14,027,000	11,284,300	4,930,900	113,800
Thomson	France	13,404,700	18,004,900	1,402,600	100,800

EXHIBIT 1 The World's 20 Largest Computer and Electronics Companies (1993, by sales)
Source: Fortune, 26 July 1993.

an intricate matrix of transparent electrodes, hundreds of thousands of separate points of light, or "pixels," were turned on or off. Each pixel was activated by a pair of electrodes. The voltage altered the transmission of a micro-beam of polarized light through the liquid crystal medium and then through a color filter. To create a coherent image, each pixel had to be controlled by separate transistors on an intricate grid, instructing the pixel when and how to turn on. In the TFT version of this technology selected by Toshiba and IBM, the transistors were processed into a very thin film on the surface of special glass substrates. The addition of this large sheet of transistors, while critical to the performance of the product itself, presented complex manufacturing challenges. The TFT-process was the first of three manufacturing processes necessary to fabricate and assemble LCD panels.

EXHIBIT 2 Toshiba's Portable Personal Computer, with 10.4-Inch Active Matrix Display

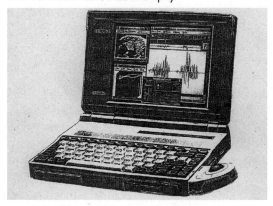

The Joint Venture Decision

In the early 1980s, both IBM and Toshiba pursued independent research projects to develop flat panel displays. IBM's effort had been concentrated at its central research laboratory in Yorktown Heights, New York. By the mid-1980s, IBM had developed an advanced TFT-LCD but did not yet

Workstation Requirements	LCD/TFT	LCD/STN	Plasma	EL	CRT
256 Color	Yes	—	—	—	—
16 Grey Mono (4096 colors)	Yes	—	Yes	Yes	Yes
640 × 480 × 3 10"–12" (limited color)	Yes	Yes	—	—	Yes
1204 × 768 Mono/10"-12" Color	Yes/Yes	Yes	Yes	Yes	Yes/Yes
Broad View Angle	Yes	—	Yes	Yes	Yes
High Contrast (> 30:1)	Yes	—	Yes	Yes	Yes
Fast Response (≤ 30 ms)	Yes	150 ms	Yes	Yes	Yes
High Brightness (≥ 32 NIT)	Yes	—	Yes	Yes	—
Low Voltage	Yes (30 V)	Yes (30 V)	150 V	120 V	10 KV
Low Power	Yes	Yes			
Panel	3 W	3 W	27 W	25W	60–100 W
Back Light	15 W	15 W			
IC Compatible	Yes	—	—	—	—

EXHIBIT 3A Comparisons of Display Technologies

Notes:

STN = Super-twisted nematic (liquid crystals) used with passive matrix

EL = Electroluminescent

CRT = Cathode ray tube

have a economically viable high-volume manufacturing process. When Toshiba's central research and development center announced a 9.5-inch active matrix TFT-LCD in December 1985, Kiyoji Ishida, director of IBM's Yamato Laboratory in Japan, approached Toshiba for discussions about a joint venture. He was impressed by Toshiba's experience with semiconductor manufacturing and believed Toshiba could be the partner IBM needed to develop an effective manufacturing process quickly. Ishida later recalled his motivation in seeking to collaborate with Toshiba:

> IBM's research laboratory in Yorktown Heights is dedicated to fundamental research and is not designed for work on commercial products. IBM wanted to gain access to Toshiba's knowledge and experience with high-volume manufacturing. We did not have the [glass] cell process technology for TFT-LCD, for example. Our strength lay in application technology. Each company's capabilities complemented the other.

For Toshiba, IBM offered fundamental technologies and the possibility of sharing the enormous anticipated cost of the facilities required to manufacture LCDs in volume. Tsuyoshi Kawanishi, Toshiba's senior executive vice president for partnerships and alliances, explained Toshiba's motivation for seeking an alliance with IBM:

> The key was to establish a win-win situation for two competent partners. IBM could offer its brand equity in the PC world, its PC interface applications, and the depth of its research. Toshiba could offer semiconductor process technologies that were applicable to LCD production and close relationships with equipment vendors. It is also necessary to mitigate long-term trade friction with foreign countries. By joining forces with partners who also have world-class competitive core skills, Toshiba has focused on transnational, strategic alliances.

In the late 1980s, electronics industry engineers disagreed about which technology offered the most promising road to a successful—and manufacturable—color LCD. Several technologies competed for attention. After examining the available options, IBM and Toshiba decided that, although TFT-LCD threatened to be the most expensive option, its picture quality was best and it promised the overall highest-quality product. Kawanishi remembered:

> It was my firm conviction that customers would not compromise once they saw the superior quality of our new TFT-LCD product. From my ex-

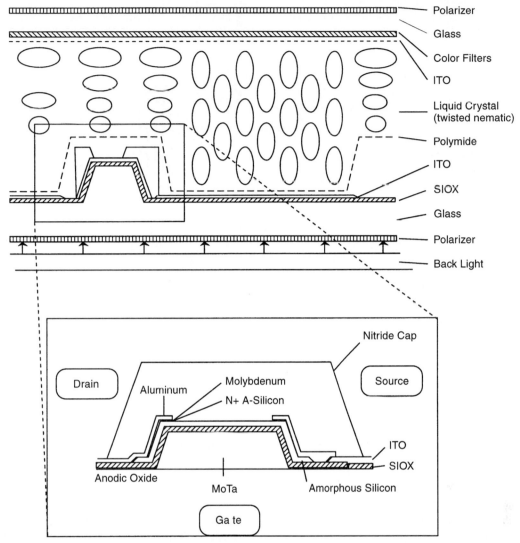

EXHIBIT 3B Thin-Film Transistor LCD Panel Cross-Section (in the region of a single pixel)
Notes:
ITO = indium-tin oxide, an optically transparent electrical conductor
SIOX = a form of silica (silicon oxide), an electrical insulator

perience in the semiconductor industry, I believed the production cost problems could be overcome by increasing productivity. We had achieved a 20% annual improvement in DRAMs [dynamic random access memory].

In the highly capital-intensive LCD industry, where technology evolves day by day, it is very important to be one of the pioneers. The empirical rule says that the top three vendors can make money; numbers four and five will break even; and the other entrants and followers will lose money. The sooner

you invest, the sooner you can finish with depreciation, hopefully during the period when the product's market price is still relatively high.

The two companies signed an initial two-year joint development agreement in August 1986. They established a joint research effort, with a 50-person team of IBM and Toshiba engineers based at IBM's Yamato Laboratory. The engineers shared results from previous research and their experience with process technologies. By May 1988 they

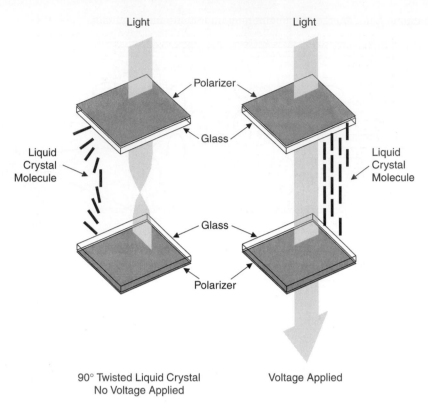

EXHIBIT 3C The Optical Switch Using Twisted Nematic (TN) Liquid Crystals for AM-LCD (schematic represents a single pixel on LCD-panel)

were able to announce a prototype 14-inch TFT-LCD (display screens are measured diagonally).

At the conclusion of their first two-year agreement, the two companies signed a further contract to begin manufacturing. They established Display Technologies Incorporated in August 1988 as an equally owned joint venture to manufacture large, color LCDs. By May of 1993, each parent company had invested more than $125M in DTI. A new production facility was completed in May 1991 next to Toshiba's conventional LCD manufacturing facilities at Himeji City, 600 kilometers west of Tokyo. By the time production got underway four months later, the company employed 130 people and was committed to produce more than 10 varieties of TFT-LCD panels. Each parent company contracted to buy 50% of the output. Each sought somewhat different versions. Toshiba wanted several 9.5-inch as well as 10.4-inch versions, whereas IBM sought mainly 10.4-inch models. To continue to meet the demands for new models, facilities for the product development group would be fully functional in a year.

Sales Growth and Competition

Sales of LCD screens accelerated in the late 1980s (see Exhibit 4). Microelectronics industry analysts estimated that by the year 2000 demand for LCD screens would grow to at least $20 billion and perhaps as high as $40 billion. Some saw the LCD market as "a second semiconductor business" for Japanese industry. Japanese producers supplied 95% of the world market for passive-matrix LCDs in 1993, 29% of electroluminescent displays, and nearly 100% of the new AM-LCDs.

Many in the industry believed, however, that the speed with which the market could expand would depend on how fast the price of LCDs declined. Sakae Arai, senior manager of Toshiba's LCD Device Marketing and Engineering Department, agreed:

Cost is key. A color LCD costs more than five times as much as a CRT. In 1991, the factory production cost for a 14-inch CRT was $200-$300. If LCD prices could be cut so that they were only two or three times as much as those of CRTs, the LCD mar-

Business Growth

Revenue ($ billions)	1992	1995
LCD Total	4.1	8.0
TFT	1.1	4.3
(Large TFT)	(0.9)	(3.6)

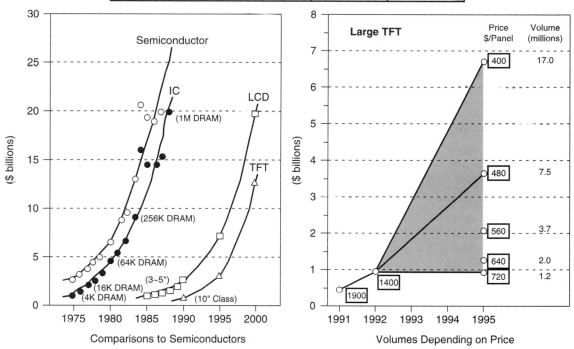

EXHIBIT 4 Industry Growth: Sales Projections and Expected Growth
Source: Data from 9/92 Nikkei Microdevices.

ket could really take off—especially in areas such as workstations and PCs, which look particularly promising. Offices in Japan are often very small. There is little room for desktop equipment. The use of notebook-type word processors and notebook PCs should continue to increase. And along with the growing use of office automation equipment, demands for downsizing are getting stronger.

The potential size of the market was attractive to many microelectronic companies. Several Japanese firms had already begun production and others planned to enter (see Exhibit 5): **Sharp Corporation** had emerged as the early leader and largest TFT-LCD manufacturer. With the industry's largest LCD volumes, Sharp enjoyed economies of scale in production. As an early entrant, it had accumulated considerable manufacturing skill. It pro-

duced small color LCDs, used in audio/visual products such as VCRs and hand-held video cameras, and was essentially a consumer electronics company. As well as supplying its own divisions, however, Sharp also sold LCDs to PC vendors, including Compaq, Apple, Toshiba, and IBM. Sharp's 1992 TFT sales amounted to $615 million.

NEC was the next-biggest LCD manufacturer. NEC was the largest PC maker in Japan, with 50% domestic market share. Most of NEC's LCD production had so far been dedicated to meeting its own needs. It had been aggressively expanding production at its Kagoshima plant. NEC's 1992 TFT external sales were $80 million, but internal production was believed to be much higher.

Hoshiden, the third-largest TFT manufacturer, was a small components manufacturer. Its

Production Plans (May 1993)

Company Name	PlantLocation	Start-Up of New Lines	Current Monthly Production	Planned Capacity (1995)	Planned Investment ($US millions)
Sharp	Tenri	June 1994	150K	250K	$950
	Mie	2nd half 1995		150K	(1993–1995)
NEC	Kagoshima	December 1993	80K	100K	$760
	Akita	December 1994		50K	(1993–1996)
Hitachi	Mobara	Winter 1994	5K	30K	$285
Hoshiden	Kobe	Spring 1994	0K	60K	$95
Fujitsu	Yonago	Spring 1994	0K	15K	$257
					(through 1997)
Matsushita	Ishikawa	April 1994	10K	30K	(undisclosed)
Advanced Display	Kumamoto	February 1994	2K	40K	$127.5
(ADI)		Summer 1996		100K (1996)	

Production Capacity versus Computer-Use Demand

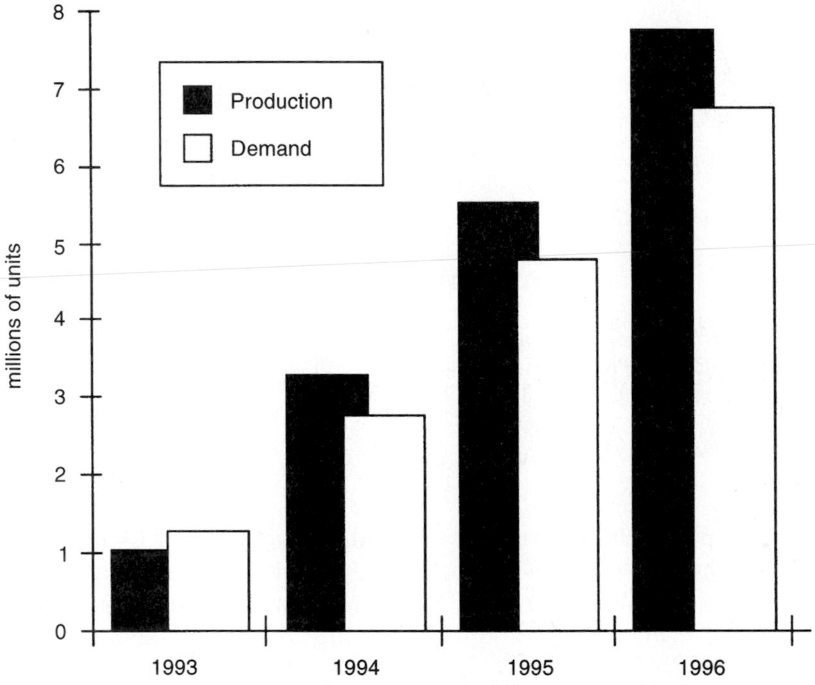

EXHIBIT 5 Large Format (8-Inch to 10-Inch) Color TFT-LCD Production Plans and Demand Forecast
Source: IDC Japan, 1994.

strategy had been to minimize investment risk by starting with the relatively simpler monochrome-TFT manufacturing in 1988. Only after that process had been established did it initiate production of the more-demanding color TFTs. In 1992, its TFT sales were $145 million.

While relatively few companies were yet in full production, at the end of 1992 world-wide pro-duction of color LCDs suitable for computers was poised to expand rapidly. At least three other major Japanese electronics companies—**Hitachi, Matsushita,** and **Sanyo**—planned to begin producing computer-sized color LCDs (most had produced smaller LCDs for several years). Three Korean manufacturers with extensive experience in semi-conductors—**Samsung, Goldstar,** and **Hyundai**—

were also ready to begin production. In addition, a half-billion dollar consortium sponsored by the US Advanced Research Projects Agency (ARPA) was investigating ways to stimulate US firms to enter the business with leap-frog technology.

THE MANUFACTURING PROCESS

While TFT-LCDs posed many of the same manufacturing challenges as other integrated-circuit-based components (such as memories and microprocessors), LCDs were characterized by several unique features that resulted in especially tricky problems for manufacturing managers and engineers. Gaining an acceptable yield (proportion of good output) was particularly difficult. For example, during DRAM or microprocessor production, many defect-free chips could usually be selected from the processed wafer (typically an 8-inch diameter silicon disk), even if some were damaged. By contrast, in display manufacture, the total panel area—itself often larger than the whole microchip wafer—had to be kept defect free to obtain a single good product. Even tiny blemishes on the large glass substrates needed by LCDs could therefore disable the entire product. In addition, the failure rate from each step cumulated, so that the final yield from the entire process was only the proportion remaining after many steps, any one of which could introduce a defect.

Manufacture of TFT-LCDs called for three types of production processes (see Exhibit 6). These were: **array process,** to produce the sheet of transistors that controlled the light pixels; **cell process,** to construct the layer of liquid crystal that created the image; and **module process,** to assemble the finished product. Major testing was carried out at the end of each of the three types of processes.

The **array** was constructed by depositing millions of transistors on a 300 mm × 400 mm (about 11.8 inches by 15.7 inches) glass substrate which produced two 10.4 inch LCD panels. The production process used for this step was similar to that employed by large-scale integrated circuit manufacture: deposition of conducting and insulating materials on a substrate, using photolithography and etching. These steps had to be repeated six to nine times. DTI's yield from the array process was about 75% in 1993.

The **cell** process injected liquid-crystal material into a narrow space between the coated surfaces of two glass substrates. One had the TFT array and the other had an array of similarly small color filter dots (red, blue and green). Each glass substrate was coated with a thin film of polyimide resin which was then rubbed with a cotton roller to create tiny grooves. The glass plates were fitted with a thin film of sealant at the edges and aligned with spacers to create a 0.5 micron gap between the glass layers. Next, a color filter was attached to the glass. Finally, liquid crystal was injected into the resulting space using a vacuum to suck the liquid crystal fluid from a bath. Light polarizers were attached to the cell after completion. DTI's yield from the cell process was about 70% in 1993.

The **module** process assembled a complete TFT-LCD unit. The glass-and-liquid-crystal cell was linked to a printed circuit board (each of the individual transistors had to be connected to the board to allow control of the pixels), drive circuit, and back-light assembly. DTI's yield from this assembly process was about 85% in 1993.

The single largest cause of defects was tiny particles of dust. Akihiro Fukatsu, of Toshiba's Material and Liquid Crystal Display Group, explained:

> If a single, even minute, dust particle remains in the LCD panel, the corrupted spot will ruin an entire LCD panel. The human eye is extremely sensitive to color. It can detect even a slight variance or change in color density.
>
> Every production step contains the hidden possibility of contamination from air-borne dust, people's sweat, skin flakes, or hair. Ideally, automation should be used to minimize the number of people in the clean room.
>
> Equipment control is also key. The debris in the deposition/sputter steps can attach itself to equipment, as can flakes from the resist process, or chipped glass during handling. The particles can remain in the machine.

Much of the challenge in manufacturing LCDs arose from the need to overcome these problems. Toshiba's semiconductor-process experience was valuable in this task, especially in building the transistor array. As was the case for AM-LCDs, successful semiconductor manufacture called for meticulous attention to detail on the part of all equipment operators and precise discipline

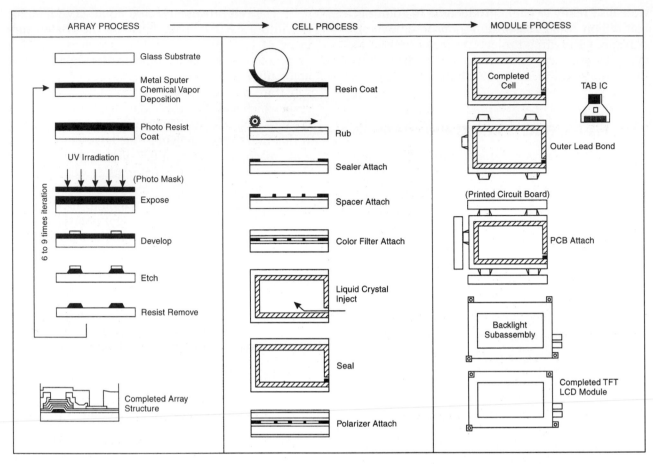

EXHIBIT 6A Process Flow—TFT-LCD Panels

of clean-room practice. This was particularly true when producing such high-volume products as DRAMs.

As a market leader in DRAMs, Toshiba had developed considerable expertise in this field. Much of this know-how could be transferred to AM-LCD manufacture. Shima himself was widely regarded as an industry leader in this task. Although dust-control management in TFT-LCD production was not as "numerically severe" as that in advanced semiconductor manufacture—it called for removal only of particles larger than 0.5 microns, whereas semiconductor manufacture was demanding removal of particles as small as 0.18 microns—the much larger size of TFT substrates made dust control demands particularly stringent. Semiconductor chips were produced in batches of

hundreds per 5"–8" wafer, allowing the vast majority of the chips to be of acceptable quality, even if a given wafer became contaminated with several dust particles. In TFT-LCD production, however, even a single particle on the much larger wafer could destroy an entire unit.

The glass required for the panels was also a very sensitive and difficult material to handle. It easily became electrostatically charged (in which case it actually attracted particles) and was inherently brittle. To ensure the necessary near-perfect transparency, it had to be kept impeccably clean throughout the entire process. Toshiba's nearby LCD manufacturing facility had accumulated considerable experience in overcoming production problems with this material, upon which Shima was able to call.

EXHIBIT 6B DTI Himeji Plant and Clean Room

Early Production Success

Production at the new site began slowly, but soon improved. DTI engineering director Hidenori Akiyoshi revealed later:

> We actually started from nothing. Nobody, us included, had any experience with large-scale TFT-LCD mass production. Although a test production run had been carried out by Toshiba's laboratory, a lot of unexpected problems were waiting for us as we ramped up. When we started production, the overall line yield was far below 10%, primarily due to equipment problems.

> First, we decided that we should work with equipment vendors. This helped us raise the yield to 25%. Then, we faced electrostatic and particle-defect problems. It turned out these had been introduced by previous steps, but became apparent only later. We had to alter steps in the process repeatedly.

Eventually, yields stabilized around 45%. Management focused next on raising throughput. This meant reducing the time taken for a display to move through all the production-process steps. Overcoming problems with throughput was achieved by meticulously examining each step, first to identify and then to remove all, even tiny, unnecessary actions. One such improvement, for example, reduced robot arm movements by two seconds. According to Akiyoshi:

> This accumulation of time-reducing activities eventually made improvements of a minute, and even an hour, in the long run. DTI management also shortened the idle time between each step by 10% to 20%. This kind of activity would have been meaningless until the yield reached a certain level, since workers and equipment would be idle in the subsequent steps under the low-yield production line.

> In this "semi-batch" production style, for instance, each cassette contained 25 pieces of glass substrate. Among them, one piece was a dummy substrate to prevent dust attachment, and another was used for sampling inspection. This meant that two panels were lost from output. After the yield stabilized, I decided to eliminate sampling inspection to increase throughput to 24 pieces per batch.

SHIMA'S CHALLENGE

As Akiyoshi and his engineering group sweated to raise output at DTI, Toshiba and IBM sought a new leader for the fledgling company. On 25 May 1992, they appointed Toru Shima as DTI's president.

Shima began his career with Toshiba in 1961 as a semiconductor engineer. In 1976, he was promoted to senior manager in the MOS (metallic oxide semiconductor) Large Scale Integration Engineering Department, and in 1987 he was appointed president of Tohuku Semiconductor Incorporated, a strategic joint venture between Toshiba and Motorola. In 1989, he became general manager of Toshiba's Memory Division, which produced the world's largest-selling 1 megabit DRAM. This was a blockbuster product for Toshiba, and was regarded by many industry observers as the single most successful semiconductor development program ever. Since 1985, Shima had taught part-time at Osaka University, helping master's degree students grasp the intricacies of semiconductor manufacture. Now he would be confronted by large, color LCDs, perhaps the most difficult electronics-manufacturing challenge of his career. Shima stressed what he called the "four Ms" of manufacturing: machines, materials, methods, and man. He sought improvements in all four to raise DTI's output.

Machines. Shima believed that one key to raising throughput was the total elimination of "doka-tei" (significant breakdowns) in equipment. He developed a 24-hour, on-site support system, in which equipment vendors stayed at the plant round-the-clock for the first three to six months to support the newly installed equipment. The plan succeeded. Equipment failures were prevented and utilization rates improved dramatically.

Another key was to prevent "choko-tei" (minor breakdowns). Attacking this problem, Shima implemented "visual control" of processes and improved operator training. Under the new system, all operators could monitor the process themselves and undertake routine maintenance of their own equipment.

Further pushing machine usage, Shima moved the plant to three-shift, 24-hour operation, with one shift dedicated to maintenance and repair. With the exception of meeting and rest time, the plant was in operation during the two shifts 85% of the time. Taken together, these measures increased the mean time between equipment failure by 300%.

Materials. Shima found that material costs in LCD manufacturing, at about 35% to 40% of manufacturing cost, were considerably higher than in semiconductor manufacturing, where they were about 20% of cost (Exhibit 7). He therefore placed special stress on working with materials suppliers to reduce the cost of all major materials: color filters, backlight units, and driver integrated circuits. Toshiba's research division established joint efforts with several suppliers to tackle this task. The rapid growth in color LCDs had created the color filter materials supply problem which could be resolved with added capacity from the two Japanese producers.

Methods. Shima scrutinized the entire production process to optimize line balance and locate bottlenecks between various process steps. His goal, again, was throughput maximization. He sought the assistance of two groups: Toshiba's semiconductor engineers, to transplant methodologies established in DRAM manufacturing—particularly helpful in improving the transistor-array steps—and Toshiba's passive-matrix LCD engineers, located next door, who were valuable in streamlining the cell processes. Through hard and tedious work and based on deep understanding, each process had to be brought under control and made capable.

EXHIBIT 7 Thin-Film Transistor Active Matrix LCD Cost Breakdown (1993, at 45% Yield)

TFT Array	$23
Cell Assembly	$253
Including:	
Polarizer	$10
Glass	$30
Liquid Crystal	$2
Color Filter	$210
Spacer & Miscellaneous Materials	$1
Module Assembly	
Including: TAB Connector, Backlight Unit, Printed Circuit Board, Anisotrophic Conductive Film, Flexible Printed Circuit, Cable, Shield Cable, Frame, Silicon, Rubber	$400
Total Materials	$676
Depreciation and Overhead	$390
Labor	$240
Scrap	$300
Total Cost (at 45% yield)	**$1,606**
Selling Price	$2,000

Man. To heighten each employee's sense of responsibility for the process, especially of dust reduction, Shima established what he termed the "Doctor Particle" system. Dozens of operators were appointed as a "Doctor Particle," charged with investigating all root causes of particle/dust formation and developing countermeasures. The resulting reduction of contamination was credited with raising yield in key steps by a further 30%. Shima's aim was to ensure that, after yield reached a basically acceptable level, responsibility for further improvement would move entirely to the operators.

Production management was not, however, Shima's only challenge. He also needed to blend two disparate corporate cultures. To help meld his employees into a single culture, he established a tongue-in-cheek rule that prevented employees from invoking the names of their parent companies. If employees mentioned their originating firm during a meeting, they were required to place a 10-yen coin into a big jar in the meeting room. Eventually, Shima said, it became difficult to determine from which firm any particular employee came.

THE CHOICES IN MAY 1993[1]

By the end of 1992, DTI had attained a monthly production target of 40,000 panels. DTI's market share had grown to 18.2% of the total, and revenues stood at approximately $220 million. IBM's newly introduced Think Pad notebook PC, using DTI's 10.4" panel, was a huge success. DTI led the notebook PC display industry, and the 10.4" size became standard.

But success bred further challenge. Toshiba and IBM now wanted DTI to raise production to 100,000. Further increases were in the offing. Toshiba sold almost 600,000 notebook computers in 1992, giving it the single largest share of the world market. IBM ranked fifth. For the future, Toshiba and IBM believed that at least 50% of notebook PCs would use a TFT-LCD by 1997, meaning that very substantial increases in output would soon be needed. Shima had to plan to meet these demands, but he also had to watch—and

[1]By May 1993 DTI had about 600 total employees of which 120 were engineers, 30 managers, and 80 manufacturing /maintenance engineers.

further reduce—current production costs. Toshiba's Sakae Arai projected sharply increased cost and price competition within a few years:

> By 1996, if each manufacturer implements their proposed investment plans (see Exhibit 5), the demand-supply conditions will reverse. Price erosion will surely follow. We need to prepare for this by achieving cost competitiveness for the longer term.

Shima's experience with DRAM production also told him that he could soon be subject—simultaneously—to the need for both rapid volume increases and steep cost reductions, as competitors gained experience. (Typical DRAM volume and cost curves are shown in Exhibit 8.) His plan would therefore have to meet current production demands, but also take into account future volume-increase and cost-reduction needs.

A second major new production site would not be available until March 1995. As he consid-ered his options, Shima believed that, in the short term at least, he had to choose between three pos-sible solutions (Exhibit 9):

1. Continue to focus on improving output in the existing line. Shima was not content with the pre-sent yield and throughput of the existing process. He believed that even though considerable im-provement had been achieved so far and much of the technology was novel, the operators with addi-tional help from 30 engineers and technicans could probably double the monthly output by signifi-cantly increasing yield and throughput. Achieving such improvement, however, would certainly ab-sorb considerable energy and time from the work-force and management. The most optimistic timing would require 6-months and the necessary experi-mentation would also result in some lost produc-tion (10% of the monthly production), which could potentially be costly.

EXHIBIT 8A DRAM Worldwide Shipments (Millions of Units)

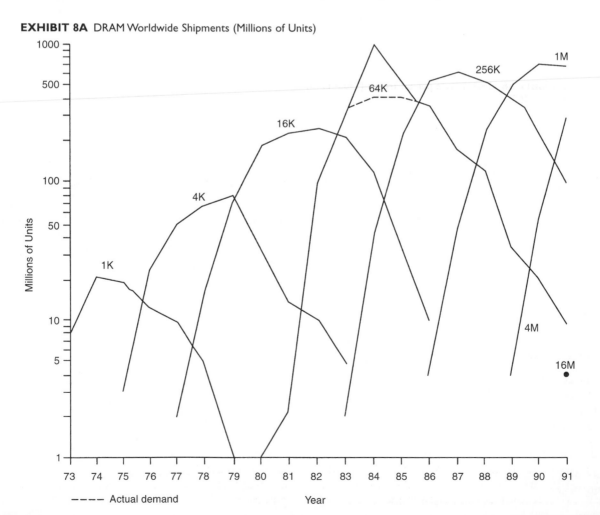

- - - - Actual demand   Year

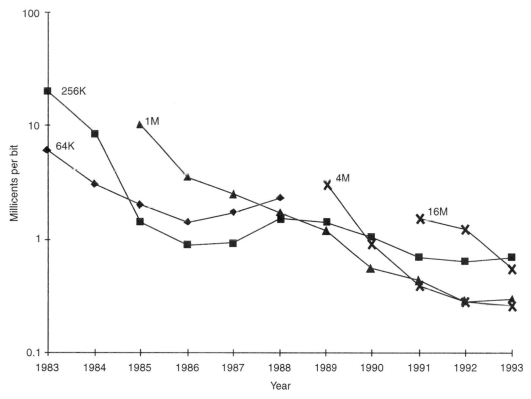

EXHIBIT 8B DRAM Price per Bit Trends (1983–1993)
Source: ICE.

Shima also felt that reductions could be obtained in other aspects of cost. In 1993, it was estimated that a 10-inch TFT-LCD cost $1,600 to build. Of this, materials accounted for about 45%, depreciation 15–20%, and labor 15–20%. Improvements in throughput would reduce the per-unit burden of depreciation and labor; yield increases would lower the unit cost of materials.

2. Duplicate the existing production line. Under this option, DTI could simply replicate its existing technology. It could utilize all that had been learned from experience with the current production line and could anticipate accurately what would be the output of the new line. Importantly, the new line could be ramped up quickly. Shima estimated that within a month of acquiring the equipment for the new line, it could be installed in additional cleanroom space that had been originally designed into the plant. Within a short time thereafter the new line could be functioning at the same level of output as the existing line. Choosing this approach, however, might mean tacit acceptance of a ceiling on current throughput improvement. Shima knew that it would be difficult for his workforce to concentrate on improving the old line while they were installing the new one. The cost implications of such a choice would need to be weighed carefully; estimates were for about $200 million for the second production line and adaptation of the current facilities and shared infrastructure.

3. Invest in a radically new line employing new technologies. Several new production technologies had been developed in Toshiba's Fukaya plant pilot-production line and could be applied to TFT-LCD production. The two most important employed larger substrates and a more advanced handling system. By using larger 360 mm × 465 mm (about 14-inch × 18-inch) substrates, the new system could potentially produce four 10.4-inch panels from each substrate, as opposed to the two panels possible from the existing substrate size.

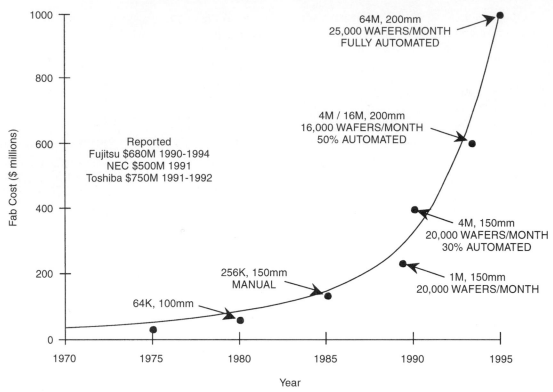

EXHIBIT 8C DRAM Wafer Fab Costs
Source: ICE.

This required different versions of the expensive equipment used for the original line and the design of new jigs, fixtures, and handling equipment.

The new handling system, dubbed "multifunctional substrate handling," would allow a shift from the current batch system to more of a flow process. Dozens of substrates were processed as a batch under the current system. The large substrate size required for LCDs, however, made it difficult to maintain conformity. Quality varied between individual substrates. In addition, under the existing batch system, processing equipment had to be sufficiently large to handle dozens of substrates at once. Robots were needed to load and unload the trays between processing steps, at which time the fragile glass edges of the substrates occasionally became damaged.

The multifunctional substrate handling system was devised to overcome these problems. Shima thought they would have become impossible to resolve under the old system coupled with the even-larger substrates needed by the new line. The

proposed new system moved to a single-piece flow process. In the resist coating step, for example, a substrate would flow from resist coating to baking without loading and unloading. This removed the risk of damage and loss of time during the changeover from one machine to another. But the throughput time of the new system would be determined by the cycle time of the equipment and the number of substrates processed in one cycle. The new system cycle time when Shima had to make his choice was 120 seconds, which would need to be cut to 12 seconds to enable the needed 100% productivity increase if he achieved the same overall 45% yield. While together the elements of this shift in process technology promised a 100% increase in output, the new system had not yet been tested in actual production. Shima knew the new system would require considerable unproven equipment and substantial experimentation before it met the yield and throughput goals of his current line.

The technology did promise, however, to make DTI a pioneer in the next generation pro-

*Option 1: Improve Existing Production Process
(significantly improve yields and cycle time)*

Estimated Time to Completion:	6–24 months
Capital Expenditure:	$5 million
Engineering Resources Required:	30 engineers
Production Disruption Estimate:	10% ($10m per month)

Option 2: Duplicate Existing Line

Estimated Time to Completion:	9 months
Capital Expenditure:	$200 million
Engineering Resources Required:	50 engineers
Production Disruption Estimate:	0

*Option 3: Introduce New Production Technology
(larger substrates, continuous flow)*

Estimated Time to Completion:	9–30 months
Capital Expenditure:	$300 million
Engineering Resources Required:	120 engineers
Production Disruption Estimate:	0%

EXHIBIT 9 Three Options to Raise Output to 100,000 Units/Month

duction technology. With the new technology, DTI could potentially preempt its competitors in the race to establish standards. By establishing his equipment as the industry standard, Shima hoped to encourage equipment suppliers to lock into DTI's technology, reducing the cost of future expansion and allowing more-rapid depreciation of current equipment. One rumor predicted, however, that Sharp would soon move to 450 mm × 370 mm (17.7-inch × 14.6-inch) substrates, each yielding six 8.4-inch panels; another suggested that NEC planned to produce 370mm × 470mm (14.6 inch × 18.5-inch) substrates, each yielding four 10.4-inch panels. If the biggest equipment vendors adopted these as industry standards, DTI's specifications would become a costly, customized one-off line. The option of moving to the new process technology was predicted to cost at least $300 million for a 100,000-per-month line running at about 45% yield.

Shima was not sure how to weigh all the short- and long-term implications of his choice. One thing, however, was certain. Both his company's competitors and owners would maintain their pressure. As significant and costly as this decision was, there was the added dimension of urgency to capture the future rather than just react to the present problem.

Corning Glass Works: The Z-Glass Project

After several highly successful years, 1977 had been difficult at Corning Glass Works' Harrisburg plant. In July 1977, the yields and productivity of the Z-Glass process began a long decline, and the entire plant organization was working overtime trying to correct the problem. Morale plummeted as yields continued to decline throughout the summer and fall. In December 1977, a team of engineers from the corporate manufacturing and engineering (M&E) staff were assigned to the plant; the group's charter was to focus on long-term process improvement while the line organization concentrated on day-to-day operations.

On the morning of March 24, 1978, Eric Davidson, leader of the M&E project team at Harrisburg, sat in his office and reflected on the group's first three months at the plant. The project had not gone well, and Davidson knew that his team members were discouraged. The technical problems they faced were difficult enough, but apparently the line organization had resisted almost everything the M&E team had attempted. In addition to conflicts over responsibility and authority, deep disagreements arose concerning the sources of the problems and how best to solve them. Cooperation was almost nonexistent, and tense relationships developed in some departments between team and line personnel. Davidson favored an immediate change in the project's direction.

Sifting through the comments and memos from his team, he recalled David Leibson, vice president of manufacturing and engineering, saying to him shortly after he accepted the Harrisburg assignment: "Eric, this is the M&E group's first major turnaround project, and the first real project of any kind in the Industrial Products Division. I picked you for this job, because you're the kind of guy who gets things done. This is a key one for our

group and I think a big one for the company. In situations like this, either you win big, or you lose big. There's very little middle ground."

CORNING GLASS WORKS IN THE 1970S

During the late 1960s and early 1970s, Corning Glass Works was a corporation in transition. Long a leader in the development of glass and ceramic products for industrial and commercial uses, Corning had entered several consumer goods markets during the 1960s. Under the direction of Lee Waterman, president from 1962 to 1971, Corning developed a strong marketing emphasis to accompany several new consumer products.

Although the public's perception of Corning in the 1960s was no doubt dominated by its well-known Pyrex and Ovenware cooking products and Pyroceram dinnerware, its most successful consumer product was actually TV tube casings. Utilizing an innovative glass-forming process, Corning entered the market for TV tube funnels and front plates in 1958 and so attained a strong market position. Throughout the mid- to late 1960s, growth in TV at Corning was rapid, and the profits at the TV Division constituted the backbone of the income statement.

During the heyday of TV, Corning's organization was decentralized. The operating divisions had considerable control over marketing and manufacturing decisions, and corporate staffs in these areas were relatively small. Only in research and development did corporate staff personnel influence the company's direction. The Technical Staffs Division was responsible for all research and development activities, well as for manufacturing engineering. New products were regarded as the lifeblood of the corporation, and the director of new product development, Harvey Blackburn, had built a creative and energetic staff. This staff developed the glass-forming process that made TV tube production possible, and the corporation looked to this group when growth in the TV Division and other consumer products began slow in the late 1960s.

CHANGES IN TV AND CORPORATE REORGANIZATION

The critical year for the TV Division was 1968. Until then, sales and profits had grown rapidly and Corning had carved out a substantial share of the market. In 1968, however, RCA (a major Corning customer) opened a plant in Ohio to produce glass funnels and front plates. Several of the engineering and management personnel at the new RCA plant were former Corning employees. RCA's decision to integrate backward into glass production had a noticeable effect on the performance of Corning's TV Division. Although the business remained profitable, growth over the next three years slowed, and Corning's market share declined.

Slower growth in TV in the 1969–1972 period coincided with reduced profitability in other consumer products as costs for labor and basic materials escalated sharply. These developments resulted in weaker corporate financial performance and prompted a reevaluation of the company's basic direction.

These deliberations created a reemphasis on the technical competence of the company in new product development and a focus on process excellence and productivity. A major step in the new approach to operations and production was the establishment of M&E at the corporate level. This reorganization brought together staff specialists in processes, systems, and equipment under the direction of Leibson, who was promoted from director of manufacturing at the TV Division to a corporate vice president.

Shortly after the M&E Division was formed, Thomas MacAvoy, the general manager of the Electronics Division and the former director of Physical Research on Corning's technical staff, was named president of the company. MacAvoy was the first Corning president in recent times with a technical background; he had a Ph.D. in chemistry and a strong record in research and development. An internal staff memorandum summed up the issues facing Corning under MacAvoy:

> Our analysis of productivity growth at Corning from 1960–1970 shows that we performed no better than the average for other glass products manufacturers (2%–4% per year) and in the last two years have actually been below average. With prices on the increase, improved productivity growth is imperative. At the same time, we have to improve our ability to exploit new products. It appears that research output has, if anything, increased in the last few years (Z-Glass is a prime example), but we have to do a much better job of transferring products from the lab into production.

MANUFACTURING AND ENGINEERING DIVISION

Much of the responsibility for improved productivity and the transfer of technology (either product or process) from research to production fell to the new and untried M&E Division. Because of the company's historical preference for a small, relatively inactive manufacturing staff, building the M&E group into a strong and effective organization was a considerable challenge. Remembering the early days, Leibson reflected on his approach:

> I tried to do two things in the first year: (1) attract people with very strong technical skills in the basic processes and disciplines in use at Corning; and (2) establish a working relationship with the manufacturing people in the operating divisions. I think the thing that made the difference in that first year was the solid support we got from Tom MacAvoy. It was made clear to all of the division general managers that productivity growth and cost reduction were top priorities.

From 1972 to 1977, engineers from the M&E Division participated in numerous projects throughout Corning involving the installation of new equipment and process changes. A typical project might require four or five M&E engineers to work with a plant organization to install an innovative conveyor system, possibly designed by the M&E Division. The installation project might last three to four months, and the M&E team would normally serve as consultants thereafter.

In addition to equipment projects and internal consulting, the M&E group participated in the transfer of products from R&D to production. After laboratory development and prototype testing, new products were assigned to an M&E product team that designed any new equipment required, and engineered and implemented the new process. Leibson believed that successful transfer required people who appreciated both the development process and problems of production. In many respects, M&E product teams served as mediators and translators; especially in the first few projects, their primary task was to establish credibility with the R&D group and with the manufacturing people in the operating divisions.

By 1976, M&E had conducted projects and helped to transfer new products in most of Corning's divisions, although its role in Industrial Products remained limited. The manufacturing organization in that division had been relatively strong and independent, but Leibson felt that the reputation and expertise of his staff was increasing and that opportunities for collaboration were not far off. He also felt that M&E was ready to take on a completely new responsibility—a turnaround project. Occasionally parts of a production process, even whole plants, would experience a deterioration in performance, sometimes lasting for several months, with serious competitive consequences. Leibson maintained that a concentrated applica-

tion of engineering expertise could significantly shorten the turnaround time and could have a measurable impact on overall corporate productivity.

THE Z-GLASS PROJECT

The opportunity for M&E involvement in a major turnaround effort and for collaboration with the Industrial Products Division came in late 1977. Since June of that year, yields on the Z-Glass process at the division's Harrisburg plant had declined sharply (see Figure A). Substantial effort by the plant organization failed to change the downward plunge in yields, and in October, Oliver Williams, director of manufacturing for Industrial Products, met with Leibson to establish an M&E project at Harrisburg.

Williams, a chemical engineer with an MBA from New York University, had been named director of manufacturing in November 1976, after 18 years in various engineering and operations positions at Corning. He felt that the product's impor-

FIGURE A Overall Yield

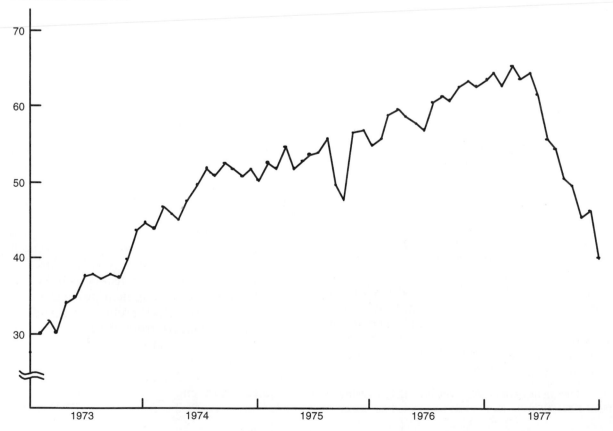

tance (corporate expectations for Z-Glass were great) coupled with the seriousness of the problem warranted strong measures. Williams and Leibson agreed that an M&E project team would work in the plant under the general supervision of a review board composed of Leibson, Williams, Martin Abramson, head of process engineering in the M&E Division, and Bill Chenevert, head of M&E's equipment development group (see Figure B for an organization chart). The team's charter was to increase yields, define and document the process, and train the operating people (see Exhibit 1). A budget, the team's size, specific goals, and a timetable were to be developed in the first month of the team's operation.

Although the plant manager and his staff had not participated in the decision to bring in the M&E team, Williams and Leibson agreed that their involvement and support were essential. A decision was made to allocate all M&E charges to the Industrial Products Division to relieve the plant of the extra overhead. Moreover, M&E specialists assigned to the project would be at the plant full time.

Since this was M&E's first turnaround project, Leibson personally selected the team leader and key project engineers. He easily found people willing to work on the project. Everyone in the M&E group realized that turnarounds were the next major activity for the group and that those working on the first team would be breaking new ground. Leibson chose Eric Davidson to lead the Harrisburg project. He was 32 years old with a master's degree in mechanical engineering from Cornell and six years of experience at Corning. Davidson had completed several projects in the M&E Division, including one in France, and had also worked as an assistant plant manager. A close friend and colleague commented on Davidson's reputation: "To say that Eric is on the fast track is a bit of an understatement. He has been give one challenging assignment after another and has been very successful. The word around M&E is that if you have a tough problem you want solved, just give it to Eric and get out of the way."

Working under Leibson's direction, Davidson spent the first two weeks meeting with the plant management and selecting members of the

FIGURE B Organization Chart

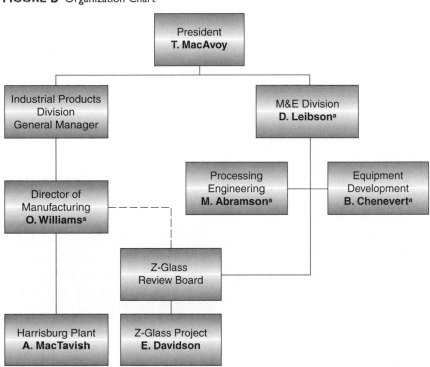

[a]Members of review board

To: Harrisburg Project Team
From: E. Davidson
Date: November 24, 1977
Re: Team Charter

The charter of the project team is yield improvement as top priority, definition and documentation of the process, and operator training. Enclosed is a copy of the proposed Process Definition and Documentation Program; it will serve as the framework for process diagnosis and control. Its main elements are as follows:

Priority

1	Define best known *operating setpoint* for each major variable.
2	Establish auditing system to track variables daily with built-in feedback loop.
3	Develop and implement *process troubleshooting* guides.
4	Write and implement *Operating Procedures*
5	*Train* operating personnel in procedure usage.
6	*Audit* operating procedures on random frequency.
7	Write and implement *Machine Specification* Procedures.

Your comments on the program are encouraged.

EXHIBIT I Memorandum on Team Charter

M&E team. At the outset, he chose four specialists to work on the first phase of the project—data collection and problem definition:

Richard Grebwell—35 years old, an expert in statistical process analysis with 10 years at Corning. Although Grebwell was considered a bit eccentric by some, his characteristically brilliant use of statistical analysis was vital to the project.

Jennifer Rigby—28 years old, with a master's degree in industrial engineering from the University of Texas. She had worked in the Harrisburg plant for six months on her first assignment at Corning.

Arthur Hopkins—40 years old, a mechanical engineer with 12 years at Corning. Hopkins had worked with Davidson on the French project and was, in Davidson's words, "a wizard with equipment."

Frank Arnoldus—37 years old, a chemist with Corning for six years. He also had worked on the French project and had earned Davidson's admiration for his ability to solve processing problems.

For the first two or three weeks, Davidson planned to use the small group to identify problems and then expand the team as specific tasks and subprojects were established. Focusing his objectives on the long term, he explained:

I'm after increases in yields as soon as we can get them, but what I'm really shooting for is permanent improvements in the process. To do that we've got to define the process and document its operation. My whole approach is based on the idea of *receivership:* whatever solutions we come up with have to be received, or accepted, by the plant organization. And I mean really accepted; they have to *own* the changes. That's why I will be taking a team approach—each project we do will have two co-leaders, one from M&E (the transferrer) and one from the plant (the receiver).

After a brief period to get acquainted and develop a plan, Davidson and his M&E team began working in the plant on December 10, 1977.

Z-GLASS: PRODUCT AND PROCESS

Z-Glass was Corning's code name for a multilayered, compression-molded glass product that was exceptionally strong and impact-resistant for its weight. Its durability and hardness, combined with its low weight and competitive cost, made it an attractive substitute for ceramic and plastic products used in the construction and auto industries. Introduced in 1973, Z-Glass products were an immediate success. From 1973 to 1977, production capacity grew 35% to 40% annually yet failed to meet demand (see Exhibit 2). Many people thought that the array of products was only the beginning of Z-Glass applications.

To Corning's knowledge, no other company in the world had yet developed the capability to make a product like Z-Glass, and if one did, presumably it would have to license the technology from Corning. In fact, much of this technology was still an art form because numerous characteristics of most Z-Glass products were not completely explainable in known glass technology: people knew what it could do and roughly why it could do it, but were still using trial-and-error methods to perfect existing products and develop new ones.

Blackburn and his staff developed Z-Glass during the early 1970s. The product was literally Blackburn's baby. He not only conceived the idea but, typical of the way Corning operated before the M&E Division was created, he and his staff solved numerous technical problems, built all the machinery and equipment needed for prototype production, and even worked in the plant during start-up. Furthermore, Blackburn had championed the product in discussions with top management. Several times when the project faltered, his reputation and skills of persuasion obtained the necessary funding. When yields began to fall in 1977, engineers at Harrisburg had consulted Blackburn when necessary; he still felt responsible for the product and knew intimately its nuances and subtleties.

THE PROCESS

Making Z-Glass products consisted of three main steps—melting, molding, and finishing—which were linked and had to be carried out in a fixed time sequence. The process required precise control over the composition and thicknesses of the various glass layers, as well as careful timing and monitoring during the molding and finishing operations. Maintaining precision in a high-volume environment required continuous, tight controls as well as a feel for the process.

Melting. The first step was the preparation of the different types of molten glass that constituted the various layers. These mixtures were prepared in separate electrically heated vats, designed and built by Corning. Each vat was carefully monitored to ensure that the ingredients of the glass were in correct proportion, evenly distributed throughout the vat, and at the appropriate temperature.

The base layer was poured continuously onto a narrow (two to three feet) moving strip. The other layers were poured on top of each other at precisely controlled intervals so that when the layered strip arrived at the molding stage, each layer of the multilayered glass sandwich was at the proper temperature and thickness for molding. Minor (and, at the beginning of process development, almost unmeasurable) deviations from the recipe could lead to major problems, often requiring ad hoc solutions using the unprogrammable skill of the operators and technicians.

EXHIBIT 2 Harrisburg Plant—Sales by Product Line, 1973–1978 (numbers in thousands)

	Z1		Z4[a]		Z10		Z35		Z12[b]		Total	
	Pieces	*$*	*Pieces*	*$*	*Pieces*	*$*	*Pieces*	*$*	*Pieces*	*$*	*Pieces*	*$*
1973	—	—	—	—	119	$2,220.1	495	$5,217.8	—	—	614	$7,437.9
1974	—	—	—	—	232	4,315.2	549	6,313.5	—	—	781	10,628.7
1975	384	$5,161.5	—	—	239	4,983.2	552	6,513.6	—	—	1,175	16,658.3
1976	784	11,514.2	45	$552.3	268	5,831.9	591	7,541.7	82	$1,213.2	1,770	26,653.3
1977	803	12,005.0	407	5,372.4	264	6,087.6	671	8,689.5	534	8,410.5	2,679	40,565.0
1978[c]	171	2,565.1	35	493.5	145	1,957.5	250	2,975.2	61	988.3	662	8,979.6

[a]Introduced in early 1975.

[b]Introduced in late 1976.

[c]Data for 1978 cover reporting periods 1–3 (i.e., first 12 weeks of 1978). Note that, because of seasonal factors, it is not possible to arrive at an accurate indication of annual output of a particular product by multiplying the 1978 (1–3) results by 13/3.

Some problems were clearly identifiable with the melting operation. For example, the existence of blisters (tiny bubbles in one or more of the glass layers), stones (unmelted bits of sand), and streaks (imperfectly melted or mixed ingredients) were visible and obvious indicators of problems. Separation of the different layers, either after the molding or after the finishing operations, often could also be traced to improper execution during melting. But when the glass sandwich did not mold properly, there was usually some question as to which operation was at fault.

A process engineer explained the difficulty of melting control:

> The secret to avoiding problems at the melting stage is maintaining its stability. Sometimes it's easy to tell when something has gone wrong there, but more often you don't find out until something goes wrong at a later stage. And usually it takes a long time to determine whether you've really solved the problem or are simply treating a symptom of a larger problem. It's tough to keep on top of what is going on in each of those melting vats because it's largely a chemical operation.

Despite the difficulty of maintaining control over the melting operation and of correcting it when problems developed, Corning had been able to achieve yields as high as 95% at this stage of the process.

Molding. In contrast to melting, molding was basically a physical operation: rectangles of the soft glass sandwich were cut off the moving strip and moved onto a series of separated conveyor belts. Each slab was inserted between the jaws of a compression-molding device that contained several molds for the particular parts being produced. After the parts were stamped out, they continued down the conveyor line while the glass trim was discarded. Depending on the product mix, several conveyors might pool their contents before the parts entered the finishing stage.

Despite the apparent simplicity of this process (problems could be detected quickly and usually corrected quickly), so many different problems arose and so many different variables could be manipulated that it was generally considered to be even more difficult to control this stage than the melting stage. Typical problems included the basic dimensional specifications of the product, its edge configuration, and buckling and flattening after molding. These problems, together with machine downtime associated both with correcting problems and changing the product mix, made it difficult to achieve more than 80% efficiency (good output to rated machine capacity) during this stage.

Finishing. The finishing operation consisted of heat treating the molded objects, then applying one of several possible coatings. Heat treating stabilized the internal tensions generated by the molding operation and appeared to improve the lamination between the various layers of the glass sandwich. Since it required a precise sequence of temperatures and their duration, this operation occurred as the objects passed on conveyor belts through long ovens. Cracks or lay separation occurred infrequently, sometimes caused by the heat-treating operation. The application of coatings, however, was more of a job-shop operation and could be done off-line. There were numerous coatings that could be applied, from the practical (improving the reflective, insulating, or electrical conducting properties of the surface) to the ornamental.

Sometimes, decals were also applied, either in place of or in addition to a coating. The selection of coatings was steadily increasing, and one process engineer characterized the operation as "a continual bother: lots of new processes and equipment, lots of short runs but a necessity to maintain high speeds." The seldom-attained target yield was 95%.

The unique characteristics of the three stages made overall control and fine-tuning of the total process quite difficult. The backgrounds and skills of the hot-end workers varied considerably from those at the cold end, and involved entirely separate branches of engineering. When problems arose, many went undetected for some time, and often appeared only during destructive testing of parts after they had completed the process. Then it was often difficult to isolate which part of the process was at fault, because there appeared to be a high degree of interrelation among them. And, finally, once a problem and its cause were identified, it sometimes took a long period of trial-and-error fiddling until people could be convinced that it was indeed corrected.

THE HARRISBURG PLANT

The decision to put Z-Glass into the Harrisburg plant had been based on its availability. Built in 1958 and long devoted to the production of headlights and other auto products, the plant had operated at excess capacity for several years in the late 1960s. In 1972, headlight production was consolidated in the Farwell, Ohio, plant while Harrisburg was set up for Z-Glass production. Several of the production foremen and manufacturing staff members were transferred to Farwell and replaced by individuals who had been involved in Z-Glass prototype production. (Table A contains a profit and loss statement for the Harrisburg plant in 1975 and 1976.)

The Harrisburg plant manager was Andrew MacTavish, a 54-year-old Scotsman. He came to the United States shortly after World War II and began working at Corning as a helper on a shipping crew at the old main plant. Over the years, MacTavish had worked his way up through various supervisory positions to production superintendent and finally to plant manager. He was a large man with a ruddy complexion and a booming voice. Although his temper was notorious, most people who had worked with him felt that some of his tirades were more than a little calculated. Whatever people's perceptions of his personality might be, there was no question who was in charge at Harrisburg.

In mid-1977, MacTavish had been at Harrisburg for six years. From the beginning he had developed a reputation as a champion of little people, as he called them. He wore what the workers wore, and spent two to three hours each day on the factory floor talking with foremen, supervisors, and production workers. If he had a philosophy of plant operations, it was to keep management as close to the people as possible and to rely on the experience, judgment, and skill of his workers in solving problems.

The Harrisburg plant was organized along department lines, with a production superintendent responsible for three general foremen who managed the melting, forming, and finishing departments. Ron Lewis, production superintendent, had come to the plant in 1975 after eight years at Corning. He was quietly efficient and had a good rapport with the foremen and supervisors. Besides Lewis, three other managers reported to MacTavish: Al Midgely, director of maintenance and engineering, Arnie Haggstrom, director of production planning and inventory control, and Royce Ferguson, head of personnel.

By June 1977, the management group at Harrisburg plant had worked together for two years and had established what MacTavish thought was a solid organization. He commented to a visitor in May 1977:

> I've seen a lot of plant organizations in my time, but this one has worked better than any of them. When we sit down in staff meetings every morning, everyone is on top of their situation, and we've learned to get to the heart of our problems quickly. With the different personalities around here, you'd think it would be a dog fight, but these people really work together.

Of all the managers on his staff, MacTavish worked most closely with Midgely. Midgely, 46 years old, came to the plant with MacTavish, had a B.S. in mechanical engineering, and was regarded as a genius when it came to equipment. "He can build or fix anything," MacTavish claimed. Midgely was devoted to MacTavish: "Ten years ago, Andy MacTavish saved my life. I had some family problems after I lost my job at Bausch and Lomb, but Andy gave me a chance and helped me pick up the pieces. Everything I have I owe to him." Several

TABLE A	Harrisburg Plant—Profit and Loss Statement, 1976–1977 ($ thousands)	
	1976	*1977*
Sales[a]	$26,653.3	$40,565.0
Direct expenses		
Materials	9,947.2	16,214.2
Labor	3,714.3	6,194.7
Gross profit	12,991.8	18,156.1
Manufacturing overhead		
Fixed[b]	6,582.6	11,106.9
Variable[c]	1,429.3	2,114.4
Plant administrative expenses	1,784.5	2,715.2
Plant profit	3,195.4	2,219.6

[a]Capacity utilization (on a normal sales basis) was 92% in 1976 and 84% in 1977.

[b]Includes depreciation, insurance, taxes, maintenance, utilities, and supervision.

[c]Includes fringe benefits, indirect labor, tools, and supplies.

people in the Harrisburg plant gratefully acknowledged MacTavish's willingness to help his people.

M&E PROJECT AT HARRISBURG

Davidson's top priority in the first two weeks of the project was to define the problem. Overall yields had declined, but no one had analyzed available information to identify the major causes. The M&E group believed that the plant organization had spent its time on fire fighting during the past six months, with little overall direction. Grebwell analyzed the historical data collected by the production control department. Other team members spent this time familiarizing themselves with the process, meeting with their counterparts in the plant organization, and meeting together to compare notes and develop hypotheses about what was going on.

One problem surfaced immediately: the relative inexperience of the department supervisors. As MacTavish explained to them, four of the six supervisors had been in the plant less than nine months. The people they replaced had been with the Z-Glass process since its prototype days. MacTavish felt that part of the explanation for the decline in yields was the departure of experts. He expressed confidence in the new people and indicated that they were rapidly becoming quite knowledgeable.

Grebwell's preliminary statistical work (see Exhibit 3) pointed to the molding department as the primary source of defects, with melting the sec-

EXHIBIT 3 Grebwell's Memorandum of Preliminary Statistics

To: M&E Project Team
From: R. Grebwell
Re: Yield Report for December 1977

Below are data on yields in period 13 (provided by the production control department) along with notes based on preliminary observations. Rejects are based on 100% inspection. Note that selecting a reason for rejection is based on the concept of "principal cause"; if more than one defect is present, the inspector must designate one as the primary reason for rejection.
Harrisburg Plant—Yield Report Period 13, 1977

I. Melting	Good Output as a % of Scheduled Capacity[a]					Downtime[b] as a % of Total Scheduled Time
	Z1	Z4	Z10	Z35	Z12	
Glass	70.4	65.4	72.3	73.5	66.9	—
Equipment downtime	—	—	—	—	—	10.3

II. Molding and Finishing	% Rejected by Product, Reason and Department[c]					Downtime[b] as a % of Total Scheduled Time
	Z1	Z4	Z10	Z35	Z12	
A. *Molding*						
Trim[d]	6.4	12.8	4.1	3.4	10.2	—
Structural	3.7	6.2	1.7	2.8	5.7	—
Adhesion	4.5	8.3	2.5	3.1	8.5	—
Downtime	—	—	—	—	24.4	15.2
B. *Finishing*						
Cracks	0.8	4.2	0.3	1.2	3.6	—
Separation	2.6	3.8	1.5	2.2	4.4	—
Coatings	1.9	2.4	0.6	1.7	2.1	—
Downtime	—	—	—	—	—	12.6

(continued)

III. Summary[e]	Good Output as a % of Scheduled Capacity					
	Z1	Z4	Z10	Z35	Z12	Total
Melting	70.4	65.4	72.3	73.5	66.9	—
Molding	72.4	61.6	77.8	76.9	64.1	—
Finishing	82.8	78.3	85.3	82.9	78.6	—
Overall	42.2	31.5	48.0	46.9	33.7	40.7

[a]This is overall yield and includes the effects of glass defects as well as downtime.

[b]No data are available on equipment downtime by product; the overall figure is applied to each product.

[c]The data are presented by department. They indicate the percentage of department output rejected and the principal reason for rejection. Total overall process yield (good output as a % of rated capacity) depends on both product defects and downtime.

[d]The reasons for rejection breakdown are as follows:

Molding

Trim: This is basically two things—dimensions and edge configuration. It looks to me like the biggest problem is with the edges. The most common cause of defects in the runs I have watched is that the settings drift out of line. Apparently this depends on where the settings are established, how they are adjusted and the quality of the glass.

Structural: Pieces are rejected if they buckle or if the surface has indentations. This one is a real mystery—it could be a problem with the equipment (not right specs) or the operating procedures. Without some testing it's hard to tell. One possibility we need to check is whether the temperature of the incoming glass is a factor.

Adhesion: If compression ratios are too low or if the glass temperature is not "just right" or the glass has stones, then the glass adheres to the surface of the molds. The operators check the ratios, but the ideal range is marked on the gauges with little bits of tape, and I suspect the margin of error is pretty large.

Finishing

Cracks: Pieces sometimes develop cracks after heat treating. The principal suspect is consistency of temperature and flame zone. It is very hard to tell whether this is due to poor initial settings or changes in flames once the process starts. Inconsistencies in the material may be another source of cracks.

Layer Separation: Layer separation seems to be caused by same factors as cracks.

Coatings: This is almost entirely a problem of operator error—handling damage, poor settings on equipment, inattention to equipment going out of spec, and so forth.

[e]There are four steps to calculating overall yield:
1. For a given product in a given department, add up reject rates by reason and subtract from 1;
2. Then multiply by (1 − % downtime) to get department yield for that product (e.g., molding yield for Z12 = $(1 - .244)(1 - .152) = .641$);
3. Multiply department yields to get overall yield by product (e.g., yield for Z12 = $.669 \times .641 \times .786 = .337$);
4. To get overall yield, take a weighted average of product yields, with share in total output (on a total pieces basis) as weights; in period 13 these weights were Z1 = .3, Z4 = .15, Z10 = .10, Z35 = .25, and Z12 = .2.

EXHIBIT 3 (Continued)

ond major source. The team identified four areas for immediate attention: overall downtime, trim settings, glass adhesion, and layer separation. As Grebwell's work proceeded, other projects in other departments were identified, and staff members were added to the team. By mid-January, it was evident that the overall project would have to encompass activities throughout the plant. It was decided that the only way to measure performance equitably was to use overall yield improvement. A timetable for improved yields was established and approved by the review board in late January 1978.

Davidson commented on the first six weeks of the project:

> Our initial reception in the plant was lukewarm. People were a little wary of us at first, but we did establish a pretty good relationship with Ron Lewis and some of the people in the production control group. I was confident that, with time, we could work together with MacTavish and people in other departments, but I wasn't as confident that the problems themselves could be solved. My objective was to obtain long-term improvements by defining and documenting the process, but when I arrived I found an inadequate data base and a process more complex than anyone had imagined.

Davidson encountered resistance to the very idea of process documentation. The view of MacTavish and others in the plant was aptly summarized by Blackburn, who appeared in Harrisburg off and on throughout the first three months of the M&E project. On one such visit, he took Davidson into a conference room to converse:

> BLACKBURN: [after drawing on the blackboard]: Do you know what this is? This is a corral and inside the corral is a bucking bronco. Now what do you suppose this is?
>
> DAVIDSON: It looks like a cowboy with a book in his hand.
>
> BLACKBURN: That's right, sonny, it's a greenhorn cowboy trying to learn how to ride a bucking bronco by reading a book. And that's just what you are trying to do with all your talk about documentation. And you'll end right where that greenhorn is going to end up—flat on your face.

CONFLICT EMERGES

Following the review board's acceptance of the proposed timetable, Davidson intended to create subproject teams, with an M&E specialist and a plant representative as co-leaders. Despite Blackburn's lecture, Davidson pressed ahead with plans for process definition and documentation. A key element of the program was the development of instrumentation to collect information on the critical operating variables (glass temperature, machine speeds, timing and so forth). Beginning in early January, Arnoldus had spent three weeks quietly observing the process, asking questions of the operators, and working on the development of instruments. He had decided to debug and confirm the systems on one production line (there were five separate lines in the plant) before transferring the instruments to other lines.

The instrumentation project was scheduled to begin on February 1, with the installation of sensors to monitor glass temperature in the molding process. No plant representative for the project had been designated by that time, however, and Davidson postponed the installation. A series of meetings between Davidson and MacTavish followed, but not until two days before the next review board meeting, on February 23, were plant representatives for each subproject chosen. Even then, things did not go smoothly. Arnoldus described his experience:

> I didn't want to impose the instrumentation program on the people; I wanted them to understand that it was a tool to help them do their jobs better. But I had a terrible time getting Hank Gordel (the co-leader of the project team) to even talk to me. He claimed he was swamped with other things. The thing of it is, he *was* busy. The plant engineering group had several projects of their own going, and those people were working 15 hours a day. But I knew there was more to it than that when I started hearing people refer to the M&E team as *spies*. After a while, people stopped talking to me and even avoided me in elevators and the cafeteria.

The other subprojects suffered a similar fate. The only team to make any progress was the group working on materials control. Ron Lewis thought the program was a good one and supported it; he had appointed one of his better supervisors to be co-leader. In the other areas of the plant, however, little was accomplished. Attempts to deal informally (lunch, drinks after work) with people in the plant organization failed, and Davidson's meetings with MacTavish and his requests for support were fruitless. Indeed, MacTavish viewed the M&E team as part of the problem. He forcefully expressed himself in a meeting with Davidson in late March 1978:

> I've said right from the beginning that this yield problem is basically a people problem. My experienced production people were promoted out from under me, and it has taken a few months for the new people to get up to speed. But this kind of thing is not

going to happen again. I've been working on a supervisor backup training program that will give me some bench strength. I'm not saying we don't have problems. I know there are problems with the process but the way to solve them is to get good people and give them some room. What this process needs now is some stability. Last year two new products were introduced, and this year I've got you and your engineers out there with your experiments and your projects, fiddling around with my equipment and bothering my people.

And then there's Blackburn. He blows here with some crazy idea and goes right out there on the floor, and gets the operators to let him try out his latest scheme. The best thing for this plant right now would be for all of you to just get out and let us get this place turned around.

I am convinced we can do it. In fact, we've already been doing it. You've seen the data for the last 12 weeks. Yields have been increasing steadily, and we're now above the average for last year. While you people have been making plans and writing memos, we've been solving the problem. [Data from the preliminary yield report are presented in Figure C and Table B.]

FIGURE C Yields and Downtime, 1976–1978

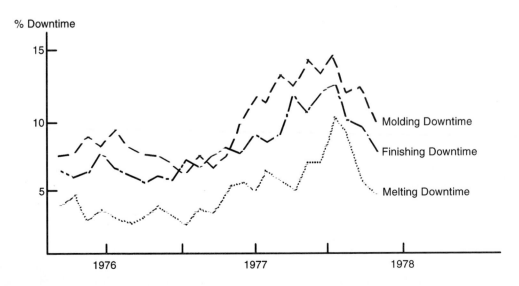

TABLE B Harrisburg Plant—Summary of Yields, Period 3, 1978

| Department | Product Lines | | | | | |
	Z1	Z4	Z10	Z35	Z12	Total
Melting	74.6	69.3	76.6	77.9	70.9	—
Molding	79.7	71.3	83.5	83.8	72.4	—
Finishing	85.8	83.7	88.7	87.6	84.9	—
Overall	51.0	41.4	56.7	57.2	43.6	53.4

RESOLVING THE CRISIS

Davidson sat at his desk in the Harrisburg plant on March 24, 1978, and reviewed the events of the last three months. He realized that he also had been guilty of excessive fire fighting, and had not taken the time to step back from the situation and plot out a course of action. The situation demanded careful thought.

He was genuinely puzzled by the recent improvement in yield performance; since the M&E team had done very little beyond data analysis, the improvement must have come from elsewhere. All his training and experience supported the concept of definition and documentation, but he had never encountered such a complex process. Perhaps MacTavish was right, but he just couldn't bring himself to believe that.

Several options came to mind as he thought of ways to resolve the crisis; none of them were appealing. He could go to Leibson and Williams and ask, perhaps demand, that MacTavish be replaced with someone more supportive. He could continue to try to build alliances with supporters in the plant (there were a few such people) and get a foothold in the organization. Or he could develop a new approach to the problem (perhaps new people) and attempt to win over MacTavish. Davidson knew that his handling of this situation could have important consequences for the M&E Division, for the company, and for the careers of several people, his included.

Deutsche Allgemeinversicherung

Annette Kluck parked her chin on the heel of her hand as she watched her electronic fishbowl, late on a Friday afternoon in January 1996. Frank Schoeck, the head of operations at DAV Kunden dienstgruppe[1] (DAKG), had just made a surprise visit. "So," he had said, in his famously blunt style, "when do you think we'll start seeing some visible results from all this operations improvement work you've got everyone doing?" Kluck was a little chagrined. She was convinced that the performance of the DAKG customer service operation *had* improved, but that the evidence might take a little time to appear.

Kluck, the architect behind Prozessmessung und Verbesserung[2] (PMV), was head of Operations Development at Deutsche Allgemeinversicherung (DAV), one of the largest insurance companies in Europe. The PMV project was a revolutionary effort to use manufacturing-style improvement techniques in insurance services. It had begun six months earlier as part of a broad initiative to improve information accuracy and quality throughout DAV. The project had, as its name suggested, been broken into two phases. In the first phase, methods were developed for measuring the quality of a number of process steps at DAV (such as the process for transcribing information from a customer application form onto the computer). In the second phase, these new measurement methods would be used as the basis for performance improvement. DAV had now completed the measurement phase, and was tracking the performance measures over time. It was now time to begin *improving* the performance of the various processes. Kluck, however, was facing a number of difficult problems with the improvement phase of the project.

[1]Customer Service Group
[2]Process Measurement and Improvement

This case was prepared by David M. Upton. Copyright © 1996 by the President and Fellows of Harvard College. Harvard Business School case 696-084.

DEUTSCHE ALLGEMEINVERSICHERUNG

Founded in 1966 by Andreas Steininger, Deutsche Allgemeinversicherung was one of the world's largest insurance companies, writing nearly DM 48 billion in premiums in 1996 in over 32 countries. Roughly 51% of DAV's business was in Germany. Sixty percent of DAV's business in Germany was in retail insurance (including, for example, health and property insurance). In addition, its retail offerings included life insurance and disability income protection.

Along with companies like Allianz, Credit Lyonnais and Aetna, DAV was one of the giants of the industry. As the second largest firm in Germany, DAV was acutely aware of its prominent position, and had begun to think carefully about how to maintain that position as smaller insurance companies armed themselves to attack its primary markets. While its dominant advantage remained the breadth of its offerings and an excellent group of insurance risk managers, DAV was also aware that individual managers were movable assets and that it needed to develop capabilities that were not only valued by customers, but were also distributed throughout DAV. Kluck commented on the hazards of being a successful firm:

> "We see firms killed by success all the time: they don't know how to use the fat years to prepare for the lean ones. They get so used to their success that they let their operations go, and don't learn to do things better. We are determined not to replicate their mistakes."

Managers in other firms throughout the industry attributed DAV's success to two key factors: sound, traditional insurance management; and outstanding customer service. Though few managers liked to hear it, insurance was becoming more and more of a commodity. In these circumstances, customer service was becoming an important tool for differentiating one firm from another. Quality in customer service had progressively become a critical element in DAV's strategy. As Frank Schoeck pointed out:

"Exceeding customer expectations for the quality of service is an important way to maintain current customers and attract new ones. Customers don't particularly care how the company is organized and where its offices are located. All they care about when they call someone on the phone or write a letter is that the person is nice, and does what they want done correctly and quickly without any hassles."

An important part of delivering this responsive, "hassle-free" service was the ability to process information and data without mistakes, and the ability to retrieve it in a timely manner. Delivering consistent, outstanding quality was complicated by the fact that DAV ran operations in numerous divisions in different locations. In DAV's case, its size and the sheer diversity of its operations meant unusually daunting challenges for its customer service group (*Kundendienstgruppe*).

DAV KUNDENDIENSTGRUPPE

The DAV Kundendienstgruppe (DAKG) was the back-office part of the operation, focusing on the retail side of the business (with the other side servicing institutional insurance, such as environmental insurance). DAKG processed applications from new customers for policies, changed policy information, carried out various legal registrations, and kept track of an customer's personal information. While DAV aimed to provide the highest standards in customer service to the individual, everyone with the group understood the real challenge of running such an operation. "DAKG is a high volume-production environment," remarked Kluck.

DAKG employed over 2,000 people at three primary sites: München; Köln; and Hamburg. Divisions within DAKG included:

- Systems (München, Köln and Hamburg)
- Retail Processing Support (München)
- Life Insurance Operations (Köln)
- Retail Transaction Processing (*Verarbeitung eines Geschäftsabschlüsses*) (München and Hamburg, but in the near future all in Hamburg)
- Customer Communications Division (Hamburg) and
- Customer Problem Resolution (München, Köln)

Because of increased business volatility and the rising costs of permanent employees, DAV managers had recently increased the proportion of temporary employees to be more flexible during business downturns. Business volumes were exposed to seasonal fluctuations, (business being heaviest between September 1 and December 31) and longer-term cyclical changes in the economy. Though overtime could meet some of the up-side fluctuation, it was becoming increasingly important to be able to respond to business downturns by shedding labor.

One of the complicating factors in running this large, distributed operation was a corporate mandate for "same-day" processing. DAV had, for

EXHIBIT I DAV Kudendienstgruppe (DAKG): Organization Chart

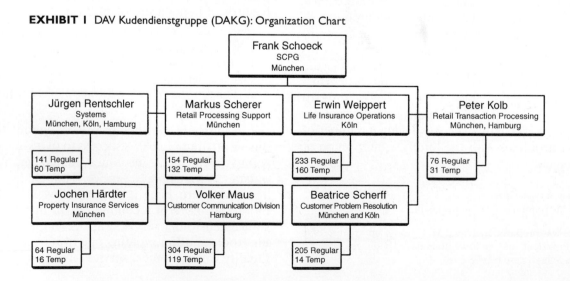

many years, ensured that certain transactions were performed by the end of the working day in which customers requested them. This meant a very difficult capacity management problem—heavy days (for example, during tax-planning season) could result in twice the transaction volume of lighter days. This surge capacity was provided with overtime and, increasingly, by the temporary labor described above. Associates responsible for transcribing information from hand-written forms would often need to work until 8:00 p.m. to clear the day's volume. The technology DAV used in the various processes was generally considered to be on the leading edge—with state-of-the-art image capture technologies being used to store customers' handwritten forms. In spite of the high level of technology employed, manual tasks such as the set-up of new customers and policies remained stubbornly human.

Though DAV had put great effort into designing forms with clear instructions, customers were astonishingly ingenious in finding ways to fill out forms with critical information missing, with illegible handwriting or even without an address. Such forms (deemed "*nicht in ordnung*" [not in good order]) were put aside for expert rework.

A Typical Process Flow: New Policy Set-up

Individual customers who wanted to set-up a new policy would visit one of DAV's eighty Zweigstellen (branch offices) or make contact with an agent. They would then fill out an application and sometimes attach a check. The branch office then sent the application package through company mail to the Verarbeitung eines Geschäftsabschlüsses[3] (VEG) division in Hamburg. In addition, a customer might also fill out the application at home and send it directly to a number of DAV locations, which would then transfer it to the Hamburg operation.

Once received, VEG separated the various parts of the application, then scanned it and digitized it. The electronic image was then retrieved from a server and delivered to associates' desktop client computers. An associate in the Hamburg VEG division typically processed about 70 policy applications during a 7.5 hour shift. The associate was responsible for entering the information on the

form into the appropriate database. If the information supplied was complete, a confirmation notice was automatically printed and sent to the customer. If the information was incomplete, then another associate, trained to deal with customers on the phone, would call the customer to obtain the additional information. Associates cost DM 14.50/hour and about 12% of policy application forms were not-in-good-order, and such forms required an additional 20 minutes processing, on average.

If the customer noticed something wrong on the confirmation notice she received, she would either call a toll-free number or send in a letter describing the problem. The Customer Problem Resolution division dealt with problems arising at this point. Problems at this stage were often a result of mistakes made by associates entering information into the system, and caused considerable dissatisfaction among customers. While it might take only five minutes of the customer's time, it would often take an associate over an hour to rectify it in the information system. In addition, customers were becoming increasingly intolerant of such errors.

Quality at DAV

While accuracy and quality had always been important at DAV, the looming competition and increasingly demanding customers meant that they had recently become even more important. A large number of processes similar to the New Policy Set-up process took place at DAV. Prior to 1994, correct transcription from forms had been assured using a method called "Tastenbestätigung" (Double-key entry). This involved a second associate retyping the transaction in order to cross-check the accuracy of the initial entry. A less laborious alternative (roughly translated as "sight verification") was also used, in which a second associate visually inspected the transaction. In both cases, the second associate would correct any mistakes he or she discovered. There were two problems with this method of assuring accuracy. First, it was very expensive, since it essentially demanded that work be done twice. Second, it was found that first-pass quality actually *deteriorated* over time when the double-key method was used.

Schoeck, Kolb and Kluck were all troubled by the way quality was being delivered at DAV. They often used the services of an industry benchmarking firm to judge their delivered accuracy

[3] Retail Transaction Processing

against competitors but doubted the information was correct:

> "I know we are the best in the industry at this," said Kolb, "but when I see *our* first-time accuracy numbers quoted at 99%, I *know* there's something wrong with these people's data. We're nowhere near that good—I'm sure that, say, in New Policy Setup, closer to 10% of the forms are entered into the system with *some* kind of mistake. But we need to get real accuracy numbers before we can begin to improve.

NEW POLICY SET-UP AS A MODEL

To begin to find out what accuracy levels were like throughout DAV, Kolb and Kluck selected New Policy Set-up as a pilot measurement project. The plan was to take a sample of the work carried out by the associates, and use that sample to infer what the general accuracy rate was in the New Policy Set-up process. However, neither Kolb nor Kluck had experience with statistical sampling, so to ensure that they developed the right kind of sampling plan, Kolb and Kluck deployed the ultimate weapon—an academic consultant.

The Consultant

Hans-Jörg Schoss was a graying professor at a famous local Technische Hochschule, famed for its engineering prowess and nerdy atmosphere. Kluck called to ask him how she should go about sampling to get an accurate measure of process quality—Schoss was not very helpful.

> "But what will you *do* with the number when you get it," responded the socially-challenged Schoss—rather too bluntly—in the first phone call.

> "What do you mean?"

> "Well, let's say your accuracy turns out to be 72.8%, what will you do?" Kluck didn't know.

> "Hmmm—thanks," said Kluck as she hung up the phone.

Links to Manufacturing

The phone call to Schoss had started Kluck thinking. She wondered what would happen if they did know the actual accuracy rate of the process. There would probably be a lot of concerned people, but she wasn't sure what she and the other DAV managers would do with the number once

they had it. As luck would have it, Kluck's husband owned a small auto-spares manufacturing shop in Augsburg, and she explained the problem to him:

> "It seems to me that you are much more interested in *improving* the accuracy number than knowing exactly what it is. Why don't you use Statistical Process Control [SPC] like we do in the plant? That way you'll be working on giving people the right tools to improve the quality themselves, rather than just posting a number every six months. Why not call Schoss, and see if he can help?"

The following morning, Kluck called Schoss and was barraged by an idea he had after their previous call. "Why can't you use SPC?" spluttered the bumbling Schoss.

The next week Schoss gave a presentation to DAV's senior managers to introduce them to the central ideas behind SPC, and to determine how it might be used at DAV. Schoss stressed the importance of using SPC to measure the *process* rather than the *people* who were involved in it. Second, he emphasized the need to have people use a tool which would become part of their everyday job, so that quality management would also be part of that job. Finally, he stressed the need to protect people and teams (who would at last be recording honest numbers) from the wrath of senior managers. Such managers might—in their surprise at the real numbers—resort to the age-old practice of finding the individuals involved and subjecting them to significant emotional events. The New Policy Set-up process was chosen as the pilot process, and Schoss and Kluck set about working out what would be needed for the experiment.

SPC AND RIGHT/WRONG DATA

SPC had traditionally been used for continuous variables such as the diameter of a piston. In such a process, a person would measure five components every few hours, and mark the sample average (*x-bar*) and range (*R*) of the measurement on the chart. In the case of New-Policy Set-up at DAV, however, things were not quite so straightforward.

A new policy request had either been entered correctly or incorrectly by an associate. Items were not on a 'sliding-scale.' According to SPC practice in manufacturing, a "right-wrong" (go/no-go) characteristic demanded the use of a different kind of chart, called a *p*-chart. Rather like an x-bar and an R-chart, a *p*-chart also tracked the sampled performance of key measures over time, but instead of representing continuous variables, it tracked the proportion right and wrong in each sample. An associate would take, say, 60 items, and chart the proportion correct on a chart. *P*-charts also used control limits and action limits set-up on either side of the mean of the process. Crossing the action line (or even being on the same side of the mean for five estimates in a row) would mean that something extraordinary had happened to the process (good or bad!) and that action should be taken to find out *why* (see Exhibit 2).

Technical Issues at DAV

To carry out the experiment, Kluck decided that the New Policy Set-up group should sample each other's work at the end of every day. The sampler on each team of six to ten people was picked from a hat at the start of each day.

"How many items should we sample each day," Kluck asked Schoss.

"Well, that depends on roughly how accurate the process is in the first place," replied the professor, with his usual academic equivocation. "If you have a large proportion correct, you have to gather many more samples in order to get a good estimate of how many wrong items there are."

"Well, let's say the benchmark is correct and we are about 99% accurate—we'd like to be able to

sample enough that we'll find at least three wrong items in each sample—otherwise there will be nothing to chart."

"We have to remember, though, that it takes about five minutes to check each form."

Process Measurement and Improvement

PMV BACKGROUND

After mulling over Schoss's advice, Kluck made the following decisions before the experiment began. First, she brought in an organizational consultant, Kerstin Kober, who would help with training and with the human issues that arose during the course of the experiment. She was confident that the experiment would succeed and was anxious that the lessons learned be captured and leveraged for broader deployment across DAV.

As word got out in the organization that a new quality experiment would be taking place in New Policy Set-up, many other groups asked to be involved immediately. These included a range of processes and departments, from the sorting of mail to the resolution of legal problems. Kluck decided to include these groups, and to use the New Policy Set-up process as a demonstration tool. Each group would learn about the New Policy Set-up process, decide how *they* would measure it, then apply the general principles from the New Policy Set-up case to their own processes. In all, this meant that there were now 15 processes and departments involved in the experiment.

EXHIBIT 2 Example *p*-chart for the New Policy Entry Process

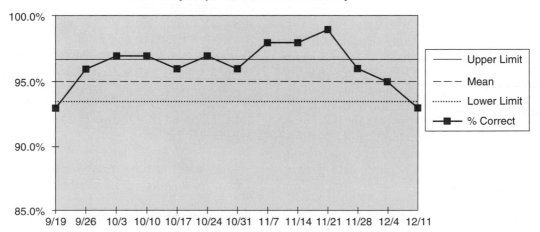

% of Policy Requests Processed Accurately

Ground Rules

Kluck's second decision was to set up some ground rules for these various groups:

- Each process within the DAV was unique and would therefore need to apply SPC principles in an appropriate way for that process.
- There should be no "process inspector" jobs. Sampling should be done by the team itself.
- There should be no "punitive" elements in the process, sampling should be done so that the specific operators who carried out the task (and possibly made a mistake) would remain anonymous (as far as was practicable).

Management Team

A cross-level team of a dozen first-line and middle managers had been brought together from München and Köln to discuss the PMV project, and to set the "ground rules" described above. Erwin Weippert and Annette Kluck (DAV) and Hans-Jörg Schoss and Kerstin Kober (consultants) formed the core management team. The development process for the experiment took approximately eight weeks. As part of this process, the management team developed the New Policy Set-up process as a case-study example for training. Presentations of the process were made to all senior managers, a video-tape was developed and rough scripts were written for managers to introduce associates to PMV. The management team then split into two, with Schoss and Weippert developing a prototype measurement template, and Kluck and Kober working on communications and training.

PMV ROLL-OUT

PMV was rolled out in May 1995 and managers were given a month to get their department together, develop the initial set of measures, and build a sampling checklist. In all, 15 processes/departments volunteered to be included in the pilot (including New Policy Set-up). Initially (and in accordance with the plan), each process checklist was very different. The launch included introductory training sessions for first-level supervisors, along with a question and answer session with senior managers. Kluck was acutely aware that many questions remained unanswered and that the program felt "unfinished."

"But it's much better to get started than to sit around waiting for perfection," remarked Kluck. "Besides, there is a lot of excitement around the place—now is the time to try it."

Some problems arose immediately. For example, sample sizes were set across the board at 200/week (chart points were entered each week to smooth out day-to-day idiosyncracies). However, this had been set based on a very high accuracy process, New Policy Set-up. Less accurate processes did not need to sample as much, yet were still required to do so to maintain some consistency across processes. This meant excessive sampling by some groups.

Making It Happen

The first two months of each team's project had been devoted to charting data, so that the natural variance of each of the processes could be estimated (from this, action lines could be developed). This phase also allowed people to practice keeping SPC charts. The next phase would involve *improving* the processes.

Measurement Challenges

The two months went by very quickly. The measurement phase had been started by different teams at different times, but almost all the groups quickly grasped the idea and began to make it work. "People learned a lot about their business because they were at least all beginning to operate and evaluate using the same tools," said Annette Kluck.

1. Better teams do more sampling. A few problems had surfaced in the measurement phase. First, some groups had to increase their sample sizes so much that the sampling process had started to become burdensome. One associate was dismayed by all the extra work. "We are the best group around—our accuracy is running at 98% yet *we* have to increase our sample size, just so we can find enough errors to measure them! It's just not right. I don't see why we can't all use the same sample size."

2. When is a mistake not a mistake? When it's not important. Second, the definition of right and wrong had started to become a little hazy as the plans were implemented. One senior manager expressed his view that getting a customer's phone number entered wrong should not count in making a form "bad" when sampling. "I know it sounds bad, but the reality is that we rarely use that phone number. It's much more serious if we get the address details wrong. It doesn't make any sense to put these on the same level, so we've started counting forms as bad only when they have critical things wrong. I think we need to use a little bit of judgment with this quality business. If it doesn't matter—it shouldn't count. I'd much rather the associates pay attention to the important things, rather than worry about trivia."

3. Measuring lawyers.   Third, some groups had had trouble measuring themselves. The legal group, for example, who were very keen to be involved in PMV, had had great difficulty deciding what to measure. It seemed to be very difficult to define what was good and bad work in a legal department. It was also difficult to measure even on a sliding scale. Since their job was to resolve customers' legal issues, the sampling process would mean one lawyer rechecking another's work, and making a judgment about its quality. The lawyers were frustrated—they were very keen to be involved in the experiment, but couldn't seem to find a way of measuring "good" legal work.

4. Automatic charting.   Fourth, one group had suggested that their process could be charted automatically. As a problem resolution group, their primary measure was timeliness, and since problems were logged in and out, one associate had suggested that the Information Technology department develop a system for putting the process-control charts on-line automatically, and avoid the burden of manual charting.

5. On the prowl.   Finally, some very senior managers had raised eyebrows when passing the charts for some of the more modestly performing processes. "What the heck is that?" growled one as he passed out a chart showing a 75% accuracy rate. The associates began to worry that it might be better to select things to measure on which performance was better, so that the charts would be less likely to provoke such reactions when such senior managers came to visit.

Everyone looked to Kluck to provide solutions to these problems.

Motivation for Change

Frank Schoeck described the motivation behind the new quality improvement initiative:

"The reason I really like PMV is that I can't do it for them. They have got to figure out what is important to measure, then measure it, and then figure out if there is a better way of doing things. We've had phone representatives taking calls here whom we've watched like assembly workers. We can't do that anymore—they hate it and so do we."

"If you get 2,000 people thinking about how they can make their job better *and* they are empowered to do it *and* they believe in that—that's an awfully powerful tool. The role of management is to make people believe. If a steamroller is coming down the street towards you, you have three options: one, don't move and get flattened; two, step out of the way; three, get on board and control it. PMV is about convincing people to jump on board, management just has to provide the resources to do it."

Monika Volz was an associate in the New Policy Set-up Group, who had previously worked as a telephone representative. She was less enthusiastic about PMV than Schoeck:

"I've seen these things come and go. There's always some new fad that management wants to try out. There are a few people in our area that are really excited about it all, but it's just more of the same. Every so often, management gets some consultant in who sells them the latest idea and we all have to go along with it. This PMV thing is just a way of getting more work out of us: now we have to spend time making all these stupid charts. The way I look at it, if we wait long enough, it'll go away, just like all the other schemes. It's a waste of time."

"I'm worried about where this is going," said Werner Steimle, also an associate in the New Policy Set-up Group, "first, they'll have us measuring each other, then maybe they'll use these charts to decide who to get rid of. Who knows?"

Kluck had heard some of these sentiments around the company, but was confident that they would be heard less and less as time went on.

BUILDING IMPROVEMENT

Now was the time to start using the power of SPC to improve the performance of the processes involved in the PMV initiative. Kluck mused over the problems as a particularly life-like flounder drifted past a piece of electronic coral on her screen. What should she do to consolidate the measurement phase of PMV, and what steps should she take to start the next phase of improvement?

Second, how should she ensure that the improvement gains made were not just part of an initial flurry of success, but would be sustained over time? Schoeck would want to know how she would do this too. Maybe that was the reason he had done so well, she thought. He always knew how to ask the difficult questions.

EXHIBIT 3 Policy Set-up Associates in Hamburg

EXHIBIT 4 Sample Data for Policy Extension Group

Week	Sample Size	Errors	Week	Sample Size	Errors
1	300	18	16	300	13
2	300	15	17	300	17
3	300	18	18	300	17
4	300	6	19	300	21
5	300	20	20	300	18
6	300	16	21	300	16
7	300	16	22	300	14
8	300	19	23	300	33
9	300	20	24	300	46
10	300	16	25	300	10
11	300	10	26	300	12
12	300	14	27	300	13
13	300	21	28	300	18
14	300	13	29	300	19
15	300	13	30	300	14

A Note on Constructing and Using Process Control Charts

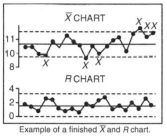

$\overline{X}$ CHART

R CHART

Example of a finished $\overline{X}$ and R chart.

EXHIBIT A

Statistical process control (SPC) is a philosophy, a system, and a set of specific techniques for controlling and improving production and service processes. Developed in the United States in the 1930s and 1940s by W. A. Shewhart, W. E. Deming, J. M. Juran, and many others, SPC has been used effectively in some American industries and many Japanese industries for decades. The use of SPC is on the upsurge in the United States and other countries, both among industries discovering it for the first time and those industries that are rediscovering it.

One of the most important tools of statistical process control is the *process control chart.* Control charts are easy to construct and can be done on the shop floor using only paper and pencil. The charts provide a common language for people from many functions and at many levels of a company. They apply to a diversity of industries and situations, ranging from lathes to restaurants to white-collar operations.

Control charts are graphs that show how a process is performing over time. They can be used to

- detect when something is wrong with the process;
- establish what the process is inherently capable of achieving;
- help diagnose the causes of abnormal behavior of a process;
- monitor and control the process;
- tell when apparent abnormal behavior is, in fact, normal so that no remedial action is needed and the process should be left alone.

Control charts are not a panacea. This note closes with a caution on their limitations.

PROCESSES

A *process* is any set of people, equipment, procedures, and conditions that work together to produce a result. This might be one person at a keypunch or many people and machines preparing an aircraft for departure.

The results of a process vary over time. Each succeeding product or service will be slightly different due to variations in materials, equipment, environmental conditions, and the physical and mental actions of the people who are a part of the process. If these variations are minor, they are not of concern. For example, if 99.8% of all airplanes left the gate within 30 seconds of the scheduled departure time, then on-time departure would probably not be a concern to airline managers. More often in modern operations, however, some processes are not performing up to par. Because competitors are continually improving their products and processes, companies must constantly look for ways to improve. In these situations, control charts often help to diagnose, control, and improve the process.

Processes can be measured by many attributes, and control charts can be constructed for virtually any such attribute. Control charts are commonly used to manage product quality. Any important quality attribute of the product could have its own control chart. For example, a restaurant's "product" would be an enjoyable and delicious meal. Managers can construct control charts for various product attributes such as the following:

- Time the customer waited in line before being seated;
- Time between seating and when the order was taken;
- Time between ordering and arrival of the meal;

- How often food is sent back to the kitchen by a dissatisfied customer;
- Temperature of the hot food when it leaves the kitchen.

These attributes will fluctuate due to various causes—large or small, chronic or intermittent. For example, one oven may heat food differently than another; one chef may prepare the recipe differently than another; sometimes the food may sit on a counter before being served. Part of the management process is to identify and, where necessary, correct these variations.

DEFINITION OF CONTROL CHARTS

A *control chart* is a graph of the performance of a process over time, arranged to emphasize the variation of the process. For example, the chart might show the temperatures of successive meals during one night. Superimposed on each graph are lines called the upper and lower *control limits* (UCL and LCL) for the process. The control limits are drawn so that if the process ever performs outside the control limits, something unusual has almost certainly happened. A centerline (usually the mean of the process performance) is also drawn on the graph. If values are consistently above or below the centerline, something has happened. Thus, the control chart quickly gives a visual answer to the question: Is this process behaving the way it usually does or has something changed? There are also various specific problems that the chart can visually highlight.

A control chart is a neutral tool that acts to identify and describe a situation objectively. Avoid using it to blame someone for a problem. In fact, companies find that putting control charts on the shop floor, where the work is being done and the measurements are being made, serves to make everyone aware of how the process is doing and gives them quick feedback about the effects of changes. This leads workers and managers alike to be much more alert to problems and more responsive to fixing and eliminating them, whether the problem is caused by a faulty machine, bad materials, or human error. Management often becomes more sensitive to providing whatever assistance is needed to keep the process in control.

The simplest use of control charts is probably to tell when a process is in or out of *statistical control*. When a process is *in (statistical) control,* it does not mean that variation in the process is zero; that would be impossible. Instead, it means that the variation is due to a multitude of small, purely random fluctuations. Conversely, when a process is out of control, it means that some of the process variation is due to a few large, irregular causes of variation. Out-of-control processes are hard to manage since on any given day anything can happen. Such processes also tend to perform erratically, reducing their effectiveness. Much of SPC consists of tools to detect, diagnose, and fix the causes of out-of-control situations.

It is easy to detect when a process is out of control on a control chart. Any measurement that falls outside the upper or lower control limits signals an out-of-control situation. The control limits are drawn so that such a measurement would only happen 2.5 times in 1,000 by chance, *if* the only sources of variation were small, random fluctuations. Therefore, if a measurement falls outside these limits, something else must be going on.

CONSTRUCTING CONTROL CHARTS

Control charts measure what a process produces over time. Because many processes produce hundreds or even thousands of parts in a day, it would be time consuming and expensive to plot every single part on a control chart. Fortunately, this is not necessary. Instead, choose a sample size, and periodically collect data in samples of that size. A typical sample size is five, so the data are collected by measuring five consecutive parts every few minutes. These five parts are then aggregated, as described below, to produce a single point on the control chart. The next five-part sample would be the next point on the control chart.[1] A sample size between two and ten is usually chosen and is referred to as *n*.

---

[1] Managers should choose an appropriate sampling plan. For example, one option is to measure the first five parts made each hour. What sampling plan is best will depend on what kind of problems you expect the process to have. It might be best to sample more intensively just before and just after a shift change, to quickly determine whether anything has changed due to the shift change. At other times of day, one sample of five each hour may be adequate. This subtlety is easily overlooked and may require a mix of judgment and experimenting with different sampling plans. Effective control-charting programs should evolve over time as the process evolves and the needs of management change.

Two different control charts are usually constructed:

- The $\bar{X}$ (X-bar) control chart measures the mean of each sample. It reveals any tendency for the process mean to drift or jump around over time.
- The R (range) chart measures the range of each sample (i.e., the largest member of the sample minus the smallest). It reveals any tendency of the process to behave more randomly or less randomly over time. (The standard deviation of the samples in some ways better measures variability than does their range. However, the range is easy to calculate by eye, while the standard deviation requires a calculator.)

The mechanics of constructing control charts are as follows:

1. First, choose the sampling plan and sample size (n). Then, collect several sets of samples of size n.
2. Calculate the range (R) and mean $(\bar{X})$ of each sample. The range is simply the highest value in the sample minus the lowest value.
3. Calculate the average range $(\bar{R})$ of all the samples: This will be the centerline of the R chart. Do the same for the average mean of the values. (This is called $\bar{\bar{X}}$ or X double-bar: the mean of the means.) This will be the centerline of the $\bar{X}$ chart.
4. Now, using the factors and formulas given in Exhibit 1, calculate the upper and lower control limits for the R chart. See Exhibit 2 for an example.
5. Calculate the upper and lower control limits for the $\bar{X}$ chart, again using Exhibit 1 factors and formulas.

EXHIBIT 1 Factors for Setting Control Chart Limits

R Chart Factors

Sample Size n	Lower Limit D_3	Upper Limit D_4	Factor to Estimate σ d_2
2	0	3.27	1.128
3	0	2.57	1.693
4	0	2.28	2.059
5	0	2.11	2.326
6	0	2.00	2.534
7	0.08	1.92	2.704
8	0.14	1.86	2.847
9	0.18	1.82	2.970
10	0.22	1.78	3.078

Source: J. M. Juran, *Quality Control Handbook* (New York: McGraw-Hill, 1974, 3rd edition) Appendix 2, Tables Y and A. These numbers are based on three standard deviations, assuming a normal distribution.

Note: Formulas for larger sample sizes are available.

Definitions:

n = Sample size
$\bar{X}$ = Mean of each sample; $\bar{\bar{X}}$ = mean of the $\bar{X}$'s
R = Range of each sample (largest – smallest)
$\bar{R}$ = Average of all the samples' ranges
σ = Estimate of the standard deviation = $\bar{R}/d_2$

Upper Control Limits (UCL)
$= D_4 \bar{R}$ for R chart
$= \bar{\bar{X}} + \dfrac{3\sigma}{\sqrt{n}} = \bar{\bar{X}} + \dfrac{3\bar{R}}{d_2\sqrt{n}}$ for $\bar{X}$ chart

Lower Control Limits (LCL)
$= D_3 \bar{R}$ for R chart
$= \bar{\bar{X}} + \dfrac{3\sigma}{\sqrt{n}} = \bar{\bar{X}} + \dfrac{3\bar{R}}{d_2\sqrt{n}}$ for $\bar{X}$ chart

EXHIBIT 2 Example of Initial Capability Study Using $\bar{X}$ and R Charts

A restaurant's manager is concerned about the temperature of a food item being served. The manager never wanted the dish to be cooler than 147°F or warmer than 160°F when it left the kitchen to be served. The manager decided to do a capability study over 10 days. Each day, she randomly picked three servings and tested the temperature just as the dish was being served. The following are the data that she collected.

Day	Reading, °F			Range, °F	$\bar{X}$, °F
1	150	160	155	10	155.0
2	140	150	155	15	148.3
3	145	150	150	5	148.3
4	150	150	155	5	151.0
5	130	155	150	25	145.0
6	140	140	145	5	141.6
7	150	150	150	0	150.0
8	155	155	160	5	156.7
9	160	160	160	0	160.0
10	150	160	165	15	158.3
				$\bar{R} = 8.5°F$	$\bar{\bar{X}} = 151.5°F$

Notes:

$n = 3$

R Chart Limits

Lower control limit = $(D_3) \bar{R} = 0(8.5°F) = 0°F$

Upper control limit = $(D_4) \bar{R} = 2.57(8.5°F) = 21.8°F$

Center control line = $R = 8.5°F$

$\bar{X}$ Chart Limits

Lower control limit = $\bar{\bar{X}} + \dfrac{3\bar{R}}{d_2\sqrt{n}} = 151.5 - \dfrac{3(8.5°\text{ F})}{1.693(1.732)} = 142.8°F$

Upper control limit = $\bar{\bar{X}} + \dfrac{3\bar{R}}{d_2\sqrt{n}} = 151.5 + \dfrac{3(8.5°\text{ F})}{1.693(1.732)} = 160.2°F$

Center control line = $\bar{\bar{X}} = 151.5°F$

Typically, the following graphical conventions are used:

- The $\overline{X}$ chart is drawn directly above the R chart.
- The centerlines of the two charts are shown as solid lines, and the upper and lower limits are shown as dashed lines.
- The physical distances between the upper and lower limits of both charts are nearly the same.

Exhibit 3 shows the $\overline{X}$ and R charts for the example in Exhibit 2.

The appendix shows how to construct $\overline{X}$ and R charts using a personal computer.

USING THE CHARTS

The next step is to determine if the process is in a state of statistical control. Examine each chart separately. The simple visual tests for out-of-control conditions are as follows:

1. Any points above the upper control limit or below the lower control limit or
2. Eight points in a row above the centerline or eight points in a row below the centerline

Applying these conditions or "tests" to Exhibit 3, we see that both the $\overline{X}$ and R charts indicate process instability. Clearly the process is not in a state of process control. When the manager checked the records, she remembered that on day eight a new chef took over. The new chef seems to have tighter control (small range on the R chart) but tends to overheat the food.

The manager met with the new chef to stress the importance of delivering the food consistently and not overheating it. Exhibit 4 shows the data collected for the next 10 days. Applying the tests to charts based on this data, we observe that the process now seems to be in statistical control. Setting up control with the new values and tracking performance with the new limits should indicate the occurrence of any unnatural patterns in the future.

PRODUCT TOLERANCES

Just because a process is *in control* does not necessarily mean that it is *within tolerances*. Tolerances refer to how the part must be made to be usable later in the process or by customers. Tolerances are a characteristic of the *design* for the part while control limits are characteristic of the *manufacturing* process. If the design tolerances are too tight, then a particular process may be physically incapable of meeting the tolerances 100% of the time, even if the process is statistically under control.

For the restaurant example in Exhibit 2, suppose that the manager sets the tolerances at 150 to 155 degrees. Any meal outside that range is "unacceptable." Exhibit 4 clearly shows that many of the meals are outside this limit. The process will have to be fundamentally modified to meet the tolerances. Until this is done, some of the meals will be outside the tolerance band or *out of specification*. Of course, if the process were not under statistical control, the problem would be much worse since even more of the meals would be out of specification.

Note that it is not enough to have the $\overline{X}$ control limits and the tolerances coincide. The control limits refer to the mean value of a sample of parts. Even if the mean is within the tolerance on the $\overline{X}$ chart, some members of the sample may not be within tolerance. Simple statistical rules are available to show how far the control limits must be inside the tolerances.

The way tolerances are set is controversial in American manufacturing. Many observers believe that some engineers routinely overspecify the tolerances, that is, they call for tighter tolerances on a part than are really needed, hoping that the actual process variability will be acceptable. This encourages the manufacturing organization to be less diligent about ensuring that *all* parts meet the tolerance and that all processes are capable of meeting them. Some companies have no formal procedures for specifying tolerances during design, and some tolerances may be underspecified while others are overspecified.

An early step in a quality-improvement situation, therefore, is to make specifications meaningful again. They should be no looser and no tighter than what is actually needed. (This may take some experimentation to determine because setting tolerances is an art.) Suppose that after this some parts are still outside of specification. Then the choices available to the manufacturing operation are as follows:

1. Bring the process under statistical control.
2. If this is insufficient, modify the process to have a tighter range.
3. Assign the part to a different machine.
4. As a last resort, use inspection and sorting to cull parts that are out of specification, and either rework or discard them.

EXHIBIT 3 Initial Capability Study and R Charts

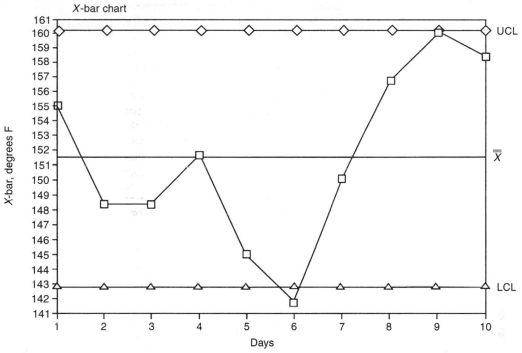

X-bar chart

Note: ◇ signifies UCL   △ signifies LCL

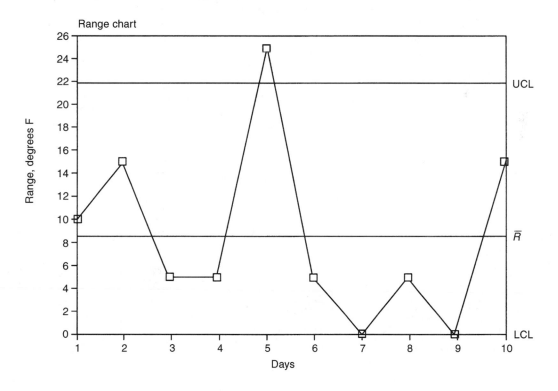

Range chart

EXHIBIT 4 Capability Study of Improved Process

Day	Reading, °F			Range, °F	X, °F
11	151	147	150	4	149.3
12	151	150	147	4	149.3
13	150	152	151	2	151.0
14	150	156	151	6	152.3
15	150	148	152	4	150.0
16	148	151	155	7	151.3
17	152	157	149	8	152.6
18	147	151	150	4	149.3
19	150	150	156	6	152.0
20	150	155	151	5	152.0
				$\overline{R} = 5.0°F$	$\overline{X} = 150.9°F$

Notes:

R Chart Limits: UCL = 12.9°F = 0°F

X Chart Limits: UCL = 159.0°F = 145.8°

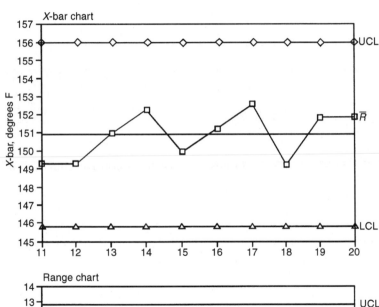

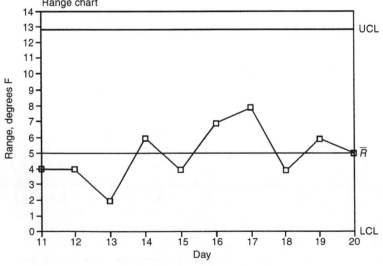

R bar = 5.0   UCL = 12.9

USING CONTROL CHARTS FOR DIAGNOSING PROCESS PROBLEMS

We have shown how to use control charts to detect when a process is not under statistical control. When looked at for the first time, most processes will not be under statistical control. Even after they are brought under control, new factors may intrude and disturb the process.

Control charts can also help in isolating and diagnosing process problems. Exhibit 5 shows several control chart patterns and their related diagnoses. Exhibit 5-A shows an abrupt upward shift in $\bar{X}$. If there is no associated change in R, this is probably due to a systematic change in the process. This might result from an altered machine setting or the introduction of a skilled employee who has an upward bias. If $\bar{X}$ and R move together, as in Exhibits 5-A and 5-B combined, it is more likely due to an untrained employee or a breakdown in the equipment. Exhibit 5 provides various patterns that deserve study.

EXAMPLES OF CONTROL CHARTS

Most repetitive processes can be tracked by control charts. However, considerable management judgment is needed to decide what to track since it is easy to be buried in too many control charts. When examining a process for the first time, look at several characteristics of potential interest. Eventually you will find out which ones are most indicative of the proper functioning of the overall process.

Control charts and other tools of SPC have been developed more fully in manufacturing than in services. With the growth, diversity, and increasing competitiveness of the service sector, however, opportunities abound in services also. A few companies in each industry are leading the way. Examples of what to track with control charts are as follows:

1. The size of a part being machined is a candidate for charting. Individual workers and work centers may track various critical dimensions while higher management just audits the process.

2. Labor time or elapsed time per part can be charted. An out-of-control situation here might signal problems with incoming materials or with machines, requiring more time to do a proper job. It might also signal operator fatigue.

3. Quality measures for mass-service organizations such as restaurants (already discussed) and banks lend themselves to charting. Both front-room operations, such as waiting times for tellers, and back-room operations can be charted. Speed and accuracy of information processing are often useful targets for control charting. Examples include lockbox operations for banks, handling telephone orders and inquiries for WATS line order-taking systems, and data-entry operations in any large information processing company.

4. For airlines, various measurements can be control-charted. The entire maintenance function of some airlines is subject to sophisticated statistical process control. Late departures, lost baggage, overbooking, underbooking, and other measures of customer service can also be charted.

5. Personalized services are more challenging. Control charts may or may not be directly applicable. To use a control chart, the operation or some portions of it must follow a recurrent pattern. In some instances an out-of-control signal on a control chart is due to a shift in the environment rather than in the internal operation. However, even early warning of this can be valuable.

A WARNING

Besides control charts, many other SPC tools are useful to diagnose and solve process problems. These include process-flow diagrams, scatter plots, and fishbone diagrams, as well as more sophisticated methods such as designed experiments. The unique virtue of the control chart is as an attention-signaling device. It gives unambiguous evidence that something has gone wrong. The managers and workers must then use various tools and their common sense to isolate and fix the problem.

Other types of control charts exist as well. The so-called np chart is used to track defectives. The "cusum" chart measures cumulative deviations and is more useful in some situations than standard charts.

Control charts are often not the most important part of an SPC program, and they should never be the only part.

Companies that are starting out with SPC sometimes interpret SPC to mean maximizing the number of control charts. This is unfortunate.

See the references for further information. See also "Statistical Quality Control for Process Improvement" HBS Case No. 9–684–068 for an introduction to other tools of SPC.

EXHIBIT 5 Diagnosis of Patterns of Process Instability

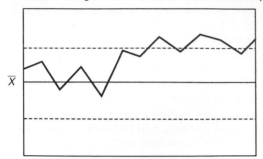

A. This abrupt upswing in $\overline{X}$ suggests a changed machine setting or a new employee unfamiliar with the specification. Also, perhaps a new material was introduced.

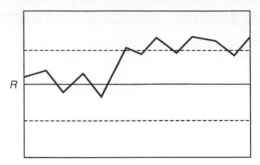

B. This abrupt change in R suggests an untrained employee, a machine needing maintenance, or a new material supplier.

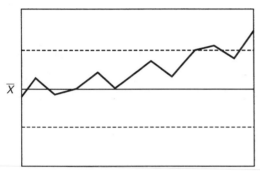

C. This gradual upward drift in $\overline{X}$ indicates a tool being gradually worn down or a gradual slippage in machine settings.

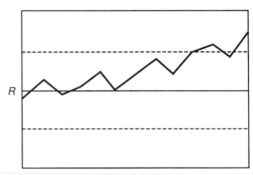

D. This gradual rise in R means greater randomness. It might be the deterioration of a machine, but it can also indicate a decline in operator discipline.

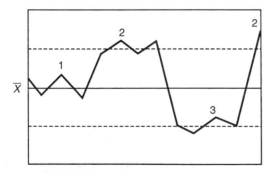

E. One might suspect that we have three different operators who set up and operate at different levels. Also, this might indicate a "sticky" setting in the process.

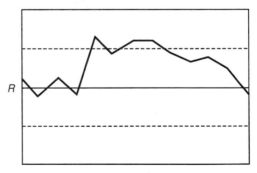

F. This looks like an example of a raw worker who eventually learns the job and approaches normal results. But, it might be the same worker who is distracted and is coming into control.

(continued)

EXHIBIT 5 *(Continued)*

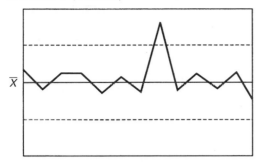

G. This looks like an example of a "freak" point. One might check into the causes of the freak, but be cautious about overreaction.

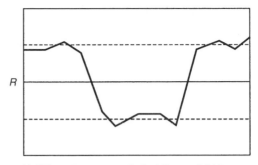

H. This pattern suggests that there might be different employees with different skills and training levels.

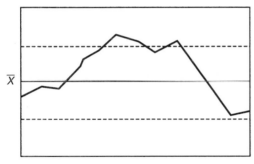

I. This suggests that a cycle interferes with the process. This might be seasonal or monthly. Watch to see if it repeats.

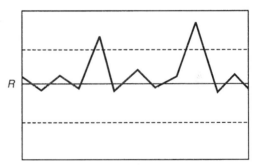

J. This is the chart of a process that shows failures every five days. The problems all occurred on Monday after a weekend shutdown, so they are probably not truly freaks.

REFERENCES

This note gives the basics of control charts. Considerable experience about them exists and has been collected by various authors. These references also discuss other equally important topics in quality control and SPC.

1. Kaoru Ishakawa. *Guide to Quality Control.* Second Revised Edition 1982, copyright Asian Productivity Organization, 1982. Available in the United States from UNIPUB (800) 274-4888. This book is a brief and clear introductory text for non-technical audiences.

2. J. M. Juran, *Quality Control Handbook,* Third Edition, New York: McGraw-Hill Book Company, 1974. Huge, comprehensive, and clearly written. Chapter 23 is specifically about control charts.

3. *Statistical Quality Control Handbook,* Second Edition, Indianapolis: Western Electric Company, 1956. Ref: Select code 700–444. This classic book is available only through AT&T (800) 432-6600. It is a down-to-earth guide on the use of control charts.

APPENDIX

Constructing Control Charts Using Microsoft Excel

Control charts are designed to be simple enough for operators on the factory floor to construct by hand. However, with the ease and availability of spreadsheet software and personal computers, it is often more convenient to construct them utilizing a spreadsheet program. This is particularly useful when data will be collected repeatedly: once the spreadsheet is set up the first time, analysis of data can be automated.

Assume that you have already entered the data into a table where each row represents a sample of size n (sample size = 5 in our example) and each of x columns represents a lot that has been sampled (lots sampled = 20 in our example). Two additional columns can then be created: one to calculate $\overline{X}$ (the mean of each sample) and the other to calculate R (the range of each sample). Using these results, one can calculate $\overline{\overline{X}}$ (mean of the means), $\overline{R}$ (mean of the ranges) and the upper and lower control limits for the chart.

In the following example, 20 samples (rows 3 through 22) of 5 observations each (columns B through F) have been entered. In column H, the mean of the observations has been calculated in row 3 by entering the formula **=AVERAGE(B3:F3),** then copying the formula on through row 22. In the next column, the range of the observations has been calculated by entering the formula **=MAX(B3:F3)-MIN(B3:F3),** and again copying the formula down through row 22. [Note: Instead of using the copy command, in Excel version 4.0

you can take the **Autofill** handle (the plus sign at the bottom right hand corner of the box that highlights the active cell) and drag it down the column: Excel will automatically copy the formula down.]

Next, the mean of the sample means ($\overline{\overline{X}}$) can be calculated and also the mean of the ranges ($\overline{R}$): **= AVERAGE(H3:H22)** gives $\overline{\overline{X}}$ and **=AVERAGE(H3:H22)** gives $\overline{R}$. Below these values are the calculations for the upper control limits (UCL) and lower control limits (LCL). For the example below, the following equations can be used:

For $\overline{\overline{X}}$, the UCL is: $\overline{\overline{X}} + 3(\overline{R} / d_2)/\sqrt{n}$

or = **H24 + 3*(I24/2.326)/SQRT(5)**

and the LCL is: $\overline{\overline{X}} - 3(\overline{R} / d_2)/\sqrt{n}$

or = **H24 - 3*(I24/2.326)/SQRT(5)**

For R, the UCL is: $D_4 * \overline{R}$

or = **2.11*I24**

and the LCL is: $D_3 * \overline{R}$

or = **0.00*I24**

EXHIBIT B Example Spreadsheet: Formulas

	A	B	C	D	E	F	G	H	I
1				Piece					
2	Lot #	1	2	3	4	5		Mean	Range
3	1	7.7251	7.7254	7.7252	7.7254	7.7253		=AVERAGE(B3:F3)	=MAX(B3:F3)-MIN(B3:F3)
4	2	7.7249	7.7247	7.7242	7.724	7.7242		=AVERAGE(B4:F4)	=MAX(B4:F4)-MIN(B4:F4)
5	3	7.7252	7.7254	7.7253	7.7252	7.725		=AVERAGE(B5:F5)	=MAX(B5:F5)-MIN(B5:F5)
6	4	7.7245	7.7246	7.7245	7.7242	7.7245		=AVERAGE(B6:F6)	=MAX(B6:F6)-MIN(B6:F6)
7	5	7.7251	7.7254	7.7244	7.7242	7.7246		=AVERAGE(B7:F7)	=MAX(B7:F7)-MIN(B7:F7)
8	6	7.7248	7.7238	7.7253	7.7252	7.7247		=AVERAGE(B8:F8)	=MAX(B8:F8)-MIN(B8:F8)
9	7	7.7251	7.725	7.7256	7.7262	7.7261		=AVERAGE(B9:F9)	=MAX(B9:F9)-MIN(B9:F9)
10	8	7.7254	7.7253	7.7252	7.7247	7.7245		=AVERAGE(B10:F10)	=MAX(B10:F10)-MIN(B10:F10)
11	9	7.7247	7.7253	7.725	7.725	7.725		=AVERAGE(B11:F11)	=MAX(B11:F11)-MIN(B11:F11)
12	10	7.7249	7.7246	7.7248	7.7255	7.7248		=AVERAGE(B12:F12)	=MAX(B12:F12)-MIN(B12:F12)
13	11	7.7243	7.7241	7.7243	7.7241	7.724		=AVERAGE(B13:F13)	=MAX(B13:F13)-MIN(B13:F13)
14	12	7.7246	7.7242	7.7249	7.7253	7.7249		=AVERAGE(B14:F14)	=MAX(B14:F14)-MIN(B14:F14)
15	13	7.7249	7.7247	7.725	7.7247	7.7248		=AVERAGE(B15:F15)	=MAX(B15:F15)-MIN(B15:F15)
16	14	7.7248	7.7247	7.7246	7.7248	7.7242		=AVERAGE(B16:F16)	=MAX(B16:F16)-MIN(B16:F16)
17	15	7.7252	7.7254	7.7252	7.7253	7.7258		=AVERAGE(B17:F17)	=MAX(B17:F17)-MIN(B17:F17)
18	16	7.7261	7.7261	7.7262	7.7263	7.7262		=AVERAGE(B18:F18)	=MAX(B18:F18)-MIN(B18:F18)
19	17	7.7254	7.7252	7.7256	7.7252	7.7255		=AVERAGE(B19:F19)	=MAX(B19:F19)-MIN(B19:F19)
20	18	7.7259	7.7251	7.7251	7.7249	7.7251		=AVERAGE(B20:F20)	=MAX(B20:F20)-MIN(B20:F20)
21	19	7.7254	7.7251	7.7251	7.7252	7.7252		=AVERAGE(B21:F21)	=MAX(B21:F21)-MIN(B21:F21)
22	20	7.7253	7.7252	7.725	7.725	7.7247		=AVERAGE(B22:F22)	=MAX(B22:F22)-MIN(822 F22)
23									
24								Mean:	=AVERAGE(H3:H22)	=AVERAGE(13:I22)
25								UCL:	=H24+3*(I24/2.326)/SQRT(5)	=2.11*I24
26								LCL:	=H24-3*(I24/2.326)1SQRT(5)	=0*I24

Using the results from above, the Mean and Range Charts can be created. There are two basic options for creating the charts: you can have Excel draw the Means ($\bar{X}$, $\bar{R}$), UCL and LCL lines (the control lines) or you can draw them by hand. In this example, Excel has drawn the control lines—if you choose to draw them yourself, simply graph the mean and range lines.

To have Excel draw the lines, make one column for each of the UCL's, LCL's and Means (see below). Then **Copy** the $\bar{\bar{X}}$, $\bar{R}$, UCL's, and LCL's into the columns. Using **Paste Special** and selecting the **Values** option will place just the number (not the formula) in the chosen column. For example, to make the UCL column for the Mean Chart, highlight cell H25, then select **Edit, Copy;** next highlight cells K3 through K22 and select **Edit,** then **Paste Special,** then **Values.** Once you have columns for UCL, LCL and $\bar{\bar{X}}$, copy the column of sample means ($\bar{X}$), calculated earlier. (Be sure to check that the numbers match your original results whenever you copy a number or column of numbers.) Follow the same procedure to create four columns for the Range Chart data. Lines for upper and lower design tolerances can be drawn by adding two more columns.

EXHIBIT C Example Spreadsheet: Chart Data

	F	G	H	I	J	K	L	M	N	O	P	Q	R	S
1						Mean Chart					Range Chart			
2			Mean	Range		UCL	Average	LCL	Sample Mean		UCL	Average	LCL	Sample Range
3			7.7253	0.0003	1	7.7254	7.7250	7.7246	7.7253	1	0.0014	0.0007	0.0000	0.0003
4			7.7244	0.0009	2	7.7254	7.7250	7.7246	7.7244	2	0.0014	0.0007	0.0000	0.0009
5			7.7252	0.0004	3	7.7254	7.7250	7.7246	7.7252	3	0.0014	0.0007	0.0000	0.0004
6			7.7245	0.0004	4	7.7254	7.7250	7.7246	7.7245	4	0.0014	0.0007	0.0000	0.0004
7			7.7247	0.0012	5	7.7254	7.7250	7.7246	7.7247	5	0.0014	0.0007	0.0000	00012
8			7.7248	0.0015	6	7.7254	7.7250	7.7246	7.7248	6	0.0014	0.0007	0.0000	0.0015
9			7.7256	0.0012	7	7.7254	7.7250	7.7246	7.7256	7	0.0014	0.0007	0.0000	0.0012
10			7.7250	0.0000	8	7.7254	7.7250	7 7246	7.7250	8	0.0014	0.0007	0.0000	0.0009
11			7.7250	0.0006	9	7.7254	7.7250	7.7246	7 7250	9	0.0014	0.0007	0.0000	0.0006
12			7.7249	0.0000	10	7.7254	7.7250	7.7246	7.7249	10	0.0014	0.0007	0.0000	0.0009
13			7.7242	0.0003	11	7.7254	7.7250	7.7246	7.7242	11	0.0014	0.0007	0.0000	0.0003
14			7.7248	0.0011	12	7.7254	7.7250	7.7246	7.7248	12	0.0014	0.0007	0.0000	0.0011
15			7.7248	0.0003	13	7.7254	7.7250	7.7246	7.7248	13	0.0014	0.0007	0.0000	0.0003
16			7.7246	0.0006	14	7.7254	7.7250	7.7246	7.7246	14	0.0014	0.0007	0.0000	0.0006
17			7.7254	0.0006	15	7.7254	7.7250	7.7246	7.7254	15	0.0014	0.0007	0.0000	0.0006
18			7.7262	0.0000	16	7.7254	7.7250	7.7246	7.7262	16	0.0014	0.0007	0.0000	0.0002
19			7.7254	0.0004	17	7.7254	7.7250	7.7246	7.7254	17	0.0014	0.0007	0.0000	0.0004
20			7.7252	0.0010	18	7.7254	7.7250	7.7246	7.7252	18	0.0014	0.0007	0.0000	0.0010
21			7.7252	0.0003	19	7.7254	7.7250	7.7246	7.7252	19	0.0014	0.0007	0.0000	0.0003
22			7.7250	0.0006	20	7.7254	7.7250	7.7246	7.7250	20	0.0014	0.0007	0.0000	0.0006
23														
24	Mean		7.7250	0.0007										
25	UCL		7.725404	0.001445										
26	LCL		7.724614	0										

Next, select the entire area of data you want to graph (along with labels, which are especially helpful for differentiating between data series). In this case, highlight the area J2 through N22. Choose **Edit, Copy,** then **File, New, Chart.** Once you have the blank chart screen, select **Edit, Paste Special** and hit return. Paste Special allows you to tell Excel how your data are arranged: in columns or rows, with or without labels. Also note that in Excel versions 3.0 and 4.0 you can highlight the data you wish to graph, press the **Graph** key on the toolbar and select an area in which Excel can draw the graph.

At this point, all that remains is formatting. If you have used the **Graph** toolbar button, double click on the chart to expand it to fill the screen. Select **Gallery, Line** and choose a type of line graph (#2 in the graphs below), then **Chart, Add Legend** to label your lines. At this point the chart is ready to print: lines that are displayed in color are printed with different symbols on a black and white printer. See Exhibit D for examples of the charts printed using the commands.

EXHIBIT D

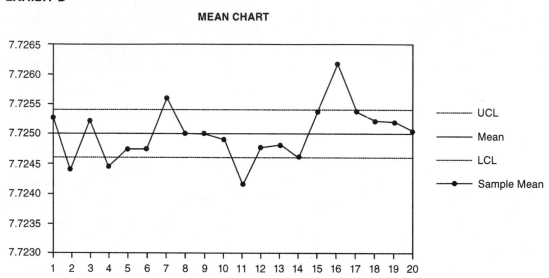

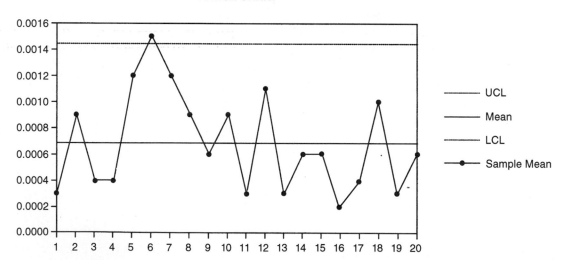

Massachusetts General Hospital: CABG Surgery

In December 1994, Dr. David Torchiana and Dr. Richard Bohmer, cardiac surgeon and quality improvement administrator, respectively, at Massachusetts General Hospital (MGH), were planning the implementation of the newly created care path for CABG surgery.[1] The care path, the result of a year long effort, described expected goals and events before, during, and after CABG surgery, until the patient was discharged from the hospital. The primary goal of the care path was to standardize procedures as far as possible without adversely affecting—and hopefully improving—the quality of the outcome of the CABG surgery. A secondary goal, although nearly as important, was the reduction of costs and length of stay. Cost pressures had become a fact of life throughout the health care industry and increasingly were affecting prestigious, but expensive, academic hospitals such as MGH. Although the care path itself would not dictate the medical treatment of a given patient, the use of a standardized treatment procedure represented a major philosophical shift for physicians accustomed to making independent medical decisions on a case-by-case basis.

Because the care path developed for the CABG area was the first of many such paths planned for use throughout the hospital, its successful implementation was critical to the hospital's overall cost reduction program. Bohmer, the care path team facilitator, believed that a key factor in the success of the path would be its acceptance by the hospital staff. No insurmountable employee concerns were encountered during the path's development; however, implementation could be hindered by the belief that the use of pathways would hasten the ongoing reduction of the hospital bed count or lead to a loss of jobs as a result of more efficient practices. Nor was it clear whether the six cardiac surgeons would be equally willing to put their patients on the pathway and the hospital was in no position to mandate its use.

Torchiana, as the team leader, was instrumental in the creation of the care path and would continue to drive its implementation. He understood the need for controlling costs and believed that the care path had merits. His primary concern, however, was for the CABG patients. Torchiana stated, "If push comes to shove, costs will be secondary before they affect the outcome for the patient."

MGH HISTORY

MGH began treating patients, training practitioners, and conducting medical research in the 1820s. By 1994 it had grown to become one of the largest hospitals in the United States with a nearly $1 billion budget, 10,000 employees, and nearly 1,000 beds, as well as more than 37,000 admissions, 75,000 emergency room visits, and 500,000 ambulatory clinic visits per year. (See Exhibit 1 for financial information.) In addition to being a general hospital for the Boston area, MGH tended to care for the most seriously ill or difficult to treat patients, many of whom were referred from out of state and from throughout the world. As a leading research institution, MGH physicians and researchers had earned six Nobel Prize awards in the last 60 years.

MGH was a pioneer of open heart surgery in the 1950s and had since developed many of the heart surgery techniques in use throughout the world. By 1994, the cardiac surgery department performed some 1,400 cardiovascular operations, including more than 800 CABG operations. CABG surgeries were performed by one of seven surgeons with the assistance of surgical residents.

---

[1] A critical path, called a care path at MGH, was described as "an optimal sequencing and timing of interventions by physicians, nurses, and other staff for a particular diagnosis or procedure, designed to minimize delays and resource utilization and at the same time maximize the quality of care."

	Year Ending September 30,		
	1994	1993	1992
Revenues			
Net patient service revenues	$530,557	$525,463	$498,458
Other Operating Revenues			
Research and other specific purposes	179,042	177,409	164,347
Other	24,253	29,762	29,160
Total operating revenues	$733,852	$732,634	$691,965
Expenditures			
For Operating Expenses			
Salaries and related compensation	$325,526	$342,033	$332,055
Supplies and other expenses	200,435	188,762	172,725
Depreciation	50,397	45,821	41,253
Interest	13,484	14,756	16,872
Provision for doubtful accounts	14,617	12,264	12,666
	604,459	604,636	575,571
Research and other specific expenses	123,479	119,203	111,304
Total operating expenditures	$727,938	$723,839	$686,875
Surplus (Loss) from operations before adjustments	5,914	8,795	5,090
Adjustments for third party payors, estimated settlements, effect of a change in accounting method and loss on bond refinancing	8,260	(8,273)	3,500
Surplus (loss)	**$14,174**	**$522**	**$8,590**

EXHIBIT I Financial Summary ($000)

Source: "Report of the General Hospital," Massachusetts General Hospital.

The CABG Surgical Procedure

Coronary artery bypass graft surgery, commonly known as bypass surgery or CABG (pronounced "cabbage"), was used to restore blood flow to the heart after arterial blockages had reduced flow enough to cause either angina (chest pains) or heart damage. It involved removing a portion of a healthy vessel from one part of the body, usually the leg, and using it to replace (bypass) a blocked artery near the heart. Often three or more coronary arteries were bypassed during a single procedure. During the procedure, the patient's own heart was stopped, which necessitated the use of a heart–lung machine (a device that pumped blood, introduced oxygen into the blood, and removed carbon dioxide). (See Exhibit 2 for an illustration of a heart following the CABG procedure.)

The standard practice for CABG surgery was to perform a number of preoperative medical tests on the patient the day before the surgery. Following the four to eight hour surgical procedure, the patient then spent one to three days in an intensive care unit (ICU) and four to ten days on a recovery floor before being released. Patients with significant complications could stay much longer in the hospital. At MGH, enough coronary surgeries were performed that a medical staff, three operating rooms, a surgical intensive care unit (SICU), and a recovery floor (Ellison 8) were dedicated to these patients.

The CABG Care Path

The care path created at MGH did not introduce new treatment technologies or dramatically alter how the procedure was performed; rather, it attempted to standardize procedures, compress the time-line, and reduce the variability between individual surgeons. However, implementation of the care path required changing behaviors, processes, and practices across departments. In particular, greater coordination and communication would be required between various medical disciplines accustomed to working more independently. A care path manager would monitor patients' progress

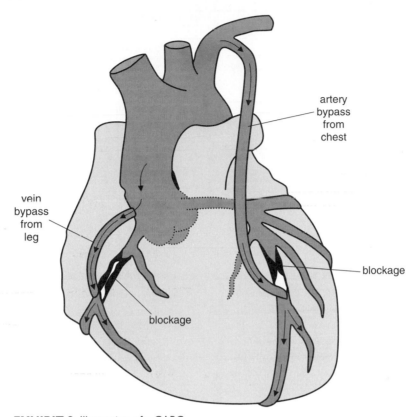

artery
bypass
from
chest

vein
bypass
from
leg

blockage

blockage

EXHIBIT 2 Illustration of a CABG

and ensure that there was an overall coordinated effort of care from the different departments.

The care path existed as a paper checklist of what should happen with a patient the day before surgery, the day of the surgery, and on the post surgical days (called Day 1 through Day 5). (See Exhibit 3 for the standard care path and Exhibit 4 for the patient education version.) A patient "on the path" was one who met all the expected goals of the path and each item listed on the care path sheet was completed on time. Such a patient would be discharged on Day 5. A patient "off the path" was one who had not completed at least one item on the path sheet. The reasons patients could move off the path fell into three categories: systemic, medical, and social. For example, patients could not leave the SICU by the end of the operative day because there was no bed available on Ellison 8 (a systemic problem); they may have had a medical complication that required a longer stay in the hospital (a medical problem); or they may not have had someone to be with them at home until Day 6 (a social problem).

Health Care Payment Methods

Since the early 1980s, rising health care costs had been a growing concern in both the industry and society. Insurers and providers were reexamining payment and service delivery methods in an attempt to reduce costs or at least limit their growth. Hospitals and other health care providers were reimbursed for their services by several different methods. While the payment methods focused on financial issues, for all payment methods quality issues were considered the top priority for reasons which included ethical standards, the need to attract patients, and malpractice concerns.

Fee-for-Service.   Under fee-for-service plans, health care providers simply billed for their services and the payers, usually private insurance companies, were obligated to pay. Patients chose which hospitals and doctors to use, often without looking at costs. While this system provided the physician extensive freedom in evaluating and treating the patient, critics charged that it also provided financial incentives to do perhaps more than

EXHIBIT 3 The CABG Care Path

	Patient's Name (Last, First):		Unit No.:	Date:
	Operative Day			*Prior to Discharge from*
	Pre-Operative Phase	*Operation*	*Surgical Intensive Care Unit*	
GOALS	Patient evaluation complete Preoperative data set complete Patient medically ready for surgery Patient and family understand hosp. process and discharge plan SF-36 completed	Warm Dry Hermodynamically stable	Patient awake, extubated, and vasoactive drugs weaned Lines removed	Performs breathing exercises Coughs and clears secretions Temp. < 100° Initiate oral fluids
CARD	Vital signs and weight Blood pressure both arms		Vital signs (per SICU flow sheet)	❏ D/C Art line ❏ D/C PA line
PULMONARY	○ *Pre-op cardiopulmonary triggers* *1. 70 yrs. old or older* *2. Obese* *3 History of COPD* *4. History of recent pulmonary infection* *5. Recurrent pneumonias* *6. Abn. sputum production and ineffect. cough* *7. Smoking history within 2 mons.* *8. Oxygen dependent* *9. IABP* *10. Pre-op CO2 > 45 mmHG*		Wean from ventilator & extubate when awake and stable	❏ Routine pulmonary care (bed mobility/DB exs/coughing) ○ *Post-op triggers for chest PT* *1. Air space disease on CXR* *2. Positive sputum cultures* *3 Excessive secretion w/ineff. cough* *4. PaO2 < 80 mmHg w/FiO2 > 40%* *5. O2 SAT < 90% w/FiO2 > 40%* *6. Temperature > 100°*
FLUID BLOOD	Type and crossmatch 4 units PRBC	○ Blood products given	○ Blood products given ○ Low total protein ○ High Aa gradient	
MEDS	Fleets enema hs Sedative at HS Review current meds ○ *Anti-platelet med taken within last 7 days*	Anesthesia Premed (on call) Chlorhexidine Cefazolin (Vancomycin if allergic) Current meds as indicated ○ *Steroids* ○ *Antihistamine* ○ *If Diabetic* *Hold oral hypoglycemics* *Stop regular insulin* *1/2 NPH insulin* *D5W at 50 cc/hr to begin at 7 AM*	Lidocaine TNG Cefazolin Rectal ASA within 6 hrs. of admission if not bleeding D/C Fentanyl/Midazolam @ 97° Chlorhexidine while intubated Sucralfate ○ *Hydrocortisone @ 97°* KCL prn	❏ Beta blocker Review pre-op medications ○ *Procainamide* ○ *Digoxin* Prochlorperazine prn Acetaminophen prn Perocet prn Tylenol # 3 prn
TESTS	BB specimen 24 hrs CBC 24 hrs Lytes/Creat/Bun/FBS 24 hrs PT/PTT/Plts. 24 hrs Amylase w/in 1 wk Ca/PO4/Mg w/in 1 wk AlkPhos/T&D Bili/LFTs w/in 1 wk Urinalysis w/in 1 wk ECG w/in 1 wk CRX w/in 1 wk if fever/cough w/sputum or CHF repeat CXR Cardiac Cath Lab Report	Pt/PTT/plts (after protamine) CXR (on leaving OR)	On arrival: CBC Lytes/Creat/Bun CK-MB ECG 2:00:00 AM: CBC Lytes/Creat /Bun CK-MB LFTs PT/PTT/Plts. Amylase 4:00:00 AM: CRX	ECG (prior to discharge) CXR (post chest tube removal)
WOUND	Shower Shave & Betadine Paint	Skin integrity check Dressings per OR	Skin integrity check Epicardial wire care D/C chest tube when < 10cc drainage per tube for 2 hrs. Redress sternal wound	Leg wound dressing
ACTIVITIES	Activity as tolerated Rehab triggers: *1. Lack of home supports* *2. Physical barriers* *3. Recent prior need for home services* *4. Use of assistive devices* *5. Neuro/ortho deficits* *6. Impaired cognition* *7. Prolonged hosp. & bed rest* *8. Pre-op MI/decreased activity*			❏ Routine bed/chair mobility ○ *Physical therapy for patients with rehab triggers*
DIET	NPO after midnight Nutrition screening in Nursing assessment	NPO	NPO	Clear liquid diet, 1500cc fluid restriction
DISCHARGE & PLAN SS	Require social service consult if ○ *Home alone and/or* ○ *> 70 yrs of age and/or* ○ *Caregivers/taker and/or* ○ *Assistive device*			
EDUCATE	Pre-op education Introduce pathway Funcional Status Assessment Informed consent (anesthesia & surgery			
COM	Admitting called to confirm insurance status Advance directives	❏ Family contacted post-op ❏ Op note dictated ❏ Fax to referring MD		

EXHIBIT 3 The CABG Care Path *(continued)*

	Ellison 8—Day 1	Ellison 8—Day 2	Ellison 8—Day 3	Ellison 8—Day 4	Ellison 8—Day 5
GOALS	Transfers OOB to chair with legs elevated under supervision Ambulates in room as tolerated Tolerates food and fluid Continue discharge planning	OOB to chair with legs elevated under supervision TID Ambulates in hall 100' B/TID Breathing/coughing/AROM Enhance oral intake Identify appropriate rehab contact	Independent OOB to chair with legs elevated Ambulate in hall 250' QID	Up/down 10 stairs Shower Patient & family understand discharge instructions Evaluate nutrition care goals	Independent in all functional activities, or rehab planned Understands activity & exercise parameters Complete pt. ed./disch. plan Education re: meds Disch. meds reviewed and communicated to refer MD
CARD	Vital signs & weight Telemetry	Vital signs & weight Telemetry	Vital signs & weight Telemetry	Vital signs & weight Telemetry	Vital signs & weight Telemetry
PULMONARY	Wean O2 via SpO2 IS/DBTC Tech. IS q 1 hour awake	D/C O2 if SpO2 > 92			
FLUID BLOOD	Saline lock Record intake & output Fluid restriction: 1500cc	❏ D/C Foley Monitoring voiding pattern Unrestricted fluids when wt. w/in 2 lb. of pre-op wt.	Unrestricted fluids when wt. w/in 2 lb. of pre-op wt	Unrestricted fluids when wt. w/in 2 lb. of pre-op wt.	
MEDS	❏ Beta blocker Cefazolin or Vanco Ecotrin Moduretic to w/in 2 lbs. of pre-op weight Omeprazole Review usual meds ○ Procainamide ○ Digoxin Prochlorperazine prn Acetaminophen prn Benadryl prn KCl 20 mEq po bid per protocol	_____ _____ ❏ Review diuretics _____ _____ Folate _____ FeSO4 _____ _____ _____ _____ _____	_____ ❏ Review diuretics → _____ _____ _____ _____ _____ _____ _____	_____ _____ ❏ Review diuretics _____ _____ _____ _____ ❏ Discharge meds written	————→ ————→ ❏ Review diuretics ————→ ————→ ————→ ————→ ————→ ————→ ❏ Review discharge meds
TESTS		CBC Lytes/Creat/BUN in AM	CBC Lytes/Creat/BUN in AM	❏ Disch. ECG ❏ Disch. CXR: PA & lat.	
WOUND	Leg and sternal dressing per protocol	D/C sternal dressing if no O2 mask	D/C CT dressing after 48 hrs if no drainage D/C Pacing Wires		
ACTIVITIES		Assess need for: ❏ Gait/mobility training ❏ Independence w/AROM ❏ Pulmonary status & need for further CPT ❏ Inpatient rehab/ SNF/VNA referral	Independent OOB to chair Ambulates in hall 250' QID	Up/down 10 stairs Shower	❏ Develop indiv. home exercise program ○ Provide pt. w/info on cardiac rehab programs
DIET	2 gm Na diet/1500cc restriction Cholesterol < 300 mg fat < 30% of total calories ○ If diabetic: modified carb diet	❏ When pre-op wt. 4 gm Na _____	❏ Nutrition assessment _____	Determine counseling needs _____	○ Individual diet counseling ————→ ————→
DISCHARGE & PLAN SS	○ Refer to SS: patients not seen pre-op in need of assistance ○ Evaluate CVA patients	_____ ○ Continuing care evals complete if applicable ○ Initiate early rehab referral ○ Insurance approval initiated	_____ ❏ Finalize D/C disposition	❏ Disch. summary complete ○ Referral forms completed ○ Community agencies notified	————→
EDUCATE	Disch. info given pt. Initiate med teaching if pt. ready Review activity & chest PT guidelines & expectations Reassess pt./family needs	Disch. info given to pt. Assess patient's readiness for teaching Reinforce or begin medication teaching	Disch. info given to pt. Review wound meeting with patient ○ If diabetic: foot care Patient names medication, purpose, & doses	Review disch. info Disch. class/diet class Pt. & RN est. med. times Complete med. books Assess 10 steps to disch. Physical therapy disch. teaching	
COM				Surgeon indicates Disch. readiness	❏ Fax to referring MD ○ Discharge note written

EXHIBIT 4   Patient Education Pathway

	Day Before Surgery	Day of Operation	Surgical Intensive Care Unit (SICU)	Post-op Day 1	Post-op Day 2
Patient Goals	Arrive at Admitting Dept. at designated time Complete Pre-operative tests Understand hospitalization process, patient responsibilities, post-operative routines, activities, and exercise after surgery, and likely discharge plans	Patient brought to operating room an hour before surgery Reminder: The operating room schedule sometimes changes due to emergencies	You will wake up and have endotracheal (breathing) tube, monitoring lines, and chest tubes removed as soon as you are ready	Transfer from SICU to Ellison 8 (post-operative floor) Get out of bed and walk in room with assistance Start to eat and drink as instructed	Increase activity Discontinue supplemental oxygen Independently perform breathing and coughing exercises
Tests	EKG, chest X-ray, blood tests		EKG, chest X-ray, blood tests		Blood tests
Meds	Take usual medications at home unless specifically instructed to bring them with you to the hospital	All medications will be given to you by the nursing staff (do not take your own) You will receive sedatives before leaving room Antibiotics are started	Pain medications Intravenous IV medications as needed Antibiotics via IV	Pain medications Aspirin Vitamins and iron supplement Antibiotics via IV Your cardiac and other medications will be reviewed daily and adjusted as necessary	Aspirin Vitamins and iron supplement Antibiotics are stopped
Treatments	You will be shaved (neck to ankle) Shower Antiseptic skin prep Enema is given	You will arrive in the SICU asleep with an endotracheal (breathing) tube in your mouth, cardiac monitoring lines, and a urinary catheter in place	Chest tubes are removed You will receive supplemental oxygen Perform breathing and coughing exercises Dressings will be changed	Supplemental oxygen will be given Your cardiac rhythm will be monitored You will be weighed daily (weight gain is expected during surgery from fluid retention	Urinary catheter will be removed
Diet	No food or drink after midnight (NPO)	Intravenous fluids given (NPO)	Intravenous fluids given Begin drinking fluids	Begin cardiac diet with fluid restriction	Advance to cardiac diet
Activities	Physical therapy assessment and instruction Surgical and anesthesia evaluations		With assistance you will be repositioned in bed	With assistance get out of bed and walk in room or to bathroom	With supervision get out of bed and walk in hallway
Communication	Leave phone number and location of family spokesperson to be contacted after surgery	Your family and cardiologist will be called when the operation is finished	Your family may come to visit you at designated times Family spokesperson may call SICU at any time	Social service or nurse will evaluate discharge needs Receive family brochure	Discharge information will be introduced

EXHIBIT 4 Patient Education Pathway

	Post-op Day 3	*Post-op Day 4*	*Post-op Day 5 Discharge Day*	*Post Discharge*
Patient Goals	Attend diet class Learn about medications and purpose Review all discharge material	Attend discharge class Name medications, purposes, and any expected side effects	You should know about: • signs and symptoms to report to physician • wound care • medications • activities/exercises • diet • follow-up appointment Tests	
Tests		EKG, chest X-ray, blood tests		
Meds	Aspirin, vitamins, and iron supplement Your cardiac and other medications will be reviewed daily and adjusted as necessary	Aspirin, vitamins, and iron supplement	Aspirin, vitamins, and iron supplement	
Treatments	Temporary pacing wires will be removed	Shower with assistance		Take discharge medications as instructed
Diet	Fluid restriction will be eliminated Review discharge diet			
Activities	Walk at least 250 ft. in hall four times a day with supervision if needed	Walk independently 500 ft. four times per day; up/down stairs; shower	Review post-discharge plan Independent in all personal care activities	Follow home exercise programs as instructed Check incisions each day Elevate legs
Communication	Ongoing review of discharge information Attend diet class	Attend discharge class	Discharge note sent to referring physician	A nurse will call you on first and third day home Call MD office to schedule follow-up appointment

was medically necessary. For decades, fee-for-service had been the dominant payment method; however, over the last decade (as pressures to reduce health care costs increased) this method had largely been phased out.

Diagnosis-Related Groupings (DRG). This system was created by the federal government in 1983 as a way to pay for Medicare patients. A DRG was a three digit number that described a particular medical diagnosis. For example, DRGs 106, 107, and 546 were all variants of CABG surgery. A hospital received the same fee from the government for all patients diagnosed as a DRG 106 regardless of how sick the patient was, how costly the patient was to treat, or how long the patient stayed in the hospital, giving hospitals an incentive to reduce treatment costs and length of stay. Under this system, while the hospital was paid a standard fee for each DRG, the doctor was still able to bill the government on a fee-for-service basis. The DRG system had been adopted by many private insurance companies and approximately 80% of MGH's CABG patients were on this type of payment plan.

Global Fee. The global fee method was similar to DRG; however, doctors were not allowed to bill on a fee-for-service basis. Rather, the hospital and doctor together were paid a standard fee for the DRG and they were left to negotiate how this fee would be split. The advantage to the payer was that the total cost per patient was known. However, this method could create problems at the hospital over the split, particularly when multiple doctors were treating the same patient. In late 1994, this method was not used as extensively as the basic DRG method.

Capitation. Under this system, the provider received a fixed payment each month to cover a group of patients—regardless of the number of patients actually treated or the amount of treatment required. Payers formed HMOs by grouping patients together to gain power over providers and create incentives for providers to reduce costs. HMOs chose the doctors and hospitals its members could use based in part on low costs. Thus, in order for a hospital to attract a group of patients, it had to have costs lower than its competitors. This created competition between hospitals, forcing contin-

ual cost reductions to ensure access to the growing number of HMO patients.

The amount MGH charged a patient for a CABG depended on the severity of the patient's condition and on the patient's length of stay. However, by 1994 the amount MGH was reimbursed was independent of what it charged. Further, although 80% of MGH CABG patients were on DRG type payment plans, the actual amount received by MGH through these plans varied, because each insurer negotiated separately the amount it would pay for each DRG. In only a small percentage of cases was the MGH reimbursement based on costs or charges.

HOSPITALS REDUCE COSTS

To reduce costs in the 1990s, hospitals had begun to examine where they were incurred. Among other issues, many hospitals found that a number of patients were staying longer in the hospital and often receiving more tests and expensive medications than were medically necessary. They also found that nurses and other highly trained, highly paid technicians were performing functions that could be done by less expensive personnel. To address these issues, hospitals developed procedures where, for example, patients would not be admitted the day before surgery, but rather on the morning of the surgery. In other cases, procedures that had required an overnight stay were now done on an outpatient basis. Further, some hospitals reduced the number of nurses and increased the number of medical assistants so that nurses were only used where their higher skills were needed.

Health care was particularly costly in the Boston area. Massachusetts was a leading center for treating the most seriously ill patients using the most advanced, high-tech medical equipment. Besides MGH, there were nine other major teaching hospitals in Boston alone. With the pressure to reduce costs and lengths of stay, it was generally believed that there were more hospital beds, and perhaps more hospitals, than the market could continue to support.

Merger with Brigham & Women's

In response to these pressures, MGH announced in December 1993 that it would merge with Brigham & Women's hospital. Long fierce competitors, MGH and Brigham & Women's were the top two hospitals in Boston and were nearly equal in terms of size, services offered, severity of illnesses treated, and prestige. As of late 1994, little change had occurred in the two institutions since the merger; however, it was expected that in the years to come, bed counts would be reduced, services would be consolidated, and fewer employees would be needed.

MGH'S EFFORTS TO CHANGE

In the early 1990s, MGH administrators formed a number of groups to examine ways to improve practices and reduce costs throughout the hospital. One such group, the Clinical Data Management Unit, attempted to review historical data to get ideas for medical practice improvements. Bohmer explained some of the difficulties in trying to use the data:

> U.S. hospitals in general have not had good cost accounting systems. For example, for a given group of patients, we do not know how many received a particular blood test or how many blood tests were performed on each patient. Nor do we know what kind of cement was used in a particular knee replacement. We could get some of this information by going back through individual patient records one at a time, but that is not practical.

> The information that is readily available is much more general. We know, for example, the primary and secondary diagnoses of the patients (why they came to the hospital), when they came to the hospital, who treated them, and demographic data about the patient. As far as designing improvement programs, however, this information is not so useful.

Bohmer further explained that hospitals tended to look at outcomes on a case by case basis. If, for example, a patient had a complication after surgery, the staff would review how that patient was treated and what might have been done differently. What hospitals had not been doing well was examining how the last 500 patients were treated and which treatment methods had produced better outcomes on average.

A second group at MGH, the Clinical Improvement Steering Committee, was examining whether Total Quality Management techniques (developed by industry practitioners) could be ap-plied in a health care setting. The group concluded that TQM methods would have to be adapted to be acceptable to the hospital community. Bohmer continued:

> One thing that has hindered TQM's acceptance in the health care industry is the management jargon and the quasi-religious enthusiasm that surrounds it. The hype is viewed with a bit of distaste in the medical community—physicians don't want to hear their patients referred to as "customers." I teach a three day training program at MGH called clinical quality improvement (CQI) where we talk about the tools and techniques of TQM as applied to a hospital.

A third group, the Clinical Practice Council, comprised 40 multi-disciplinary doctors, nurses, and administrators. It was charged with identifying specific areas within the hospital for improvement and then starting the improvement programs.

Knee Replacement Care Path

In the early 1990s, an orthopedic surgeon who practiced medicine at MGH (but independent of the above groups) had worked to develop a care path for total knee replacement surgery. This surgeon, after unsuccessfully trying to interest the orthopedic surgeons group at MGH in creating the care path, decided to assemble one himself. Once completed, the surgeon put his new patients on the path and the results were dramatic: costs and length of stay were reduced by over 30% with no apparent reduction in quality of outcome. Other orthopedic surgeons who performed operations at MGH, upon seeing this success, gradually began putting their patients on the care path as well.

Care Paths Selected as the Method of Improvement

Although MGH had taken a number of steps to identify areas for improvement and had initiated a number of improvement projects, efforts to-date had been somewhat piece-meal. Bohmer believed that a broader, more comprehensive approach was needed to initiate significant change. Care paths, one such comprehensive approach, were viewed as a way to reform the whole system of care. Bohmer noted, "You can't make changes in a process until you have identified and defined the process you're trying to change." Creating a care path was analogous to getting the process under control before trying to make incremental improvements. Bohmer continued:

> There is a lot of room for improvement in health care. Currently, there is no uniformity of process, no standardization—partly because standardization has been equated with being insensitive to patient requirements. It is only recently that we have begun to realize that we can pay attention to individual patient needs within the context of having a relatively stable process of care. As a result, wherever anyone has looked for variation, they have found it. So the mileage to be gained from standardizing a process is significant—we're talking about 20%–30% drops in length of stay.
>
> Because of those numbers, many people in health care view critical pathways as an end. I believe, however, that pathways are only the beginning. Once you have a stable system, you can begin to make improvements and see whether they are related to improvements in outcomes that you care about. Thus a more significant use of critical pathways is still a number of years away—both at MGH and at other hospitals around the country. In the meanwhile, creating a critical pathway is a good first step both for initial gains and for building a framework for continuous improvements in the future.

CABG IDENTIFIED AS THE FIRST CARE PATH PROJECT

Once care paths had been selected as a primary technique for improvement programs throughout the hospital, the Executive Committee of the Clinical Practice Council had to identify which area of the hospital would be the first to implement the new model. The success of the first care path project was considered critical.

The committee started with a list of the top 10 resource utilizers at MGH in terms of total charges (what patients were charged) and total bed days (see Exhibit 5).[2] Upon examination of the list, the cardiac care area—with three out of the top four DRG clusters—quickly became the focus of attention. As Torchiana stated, "People rob a bank because that's where the money is. It made sense to examine cardiac care as the possible first pathway project."

Next, the committee examined how MGH's CABGs compared with those of other U.S. teaching

DRG Group	Sum of Charges	Sum of Bed Days
CABG (106, 107, 546)	$20,187,874	7,245
Valve replacement (104, 105, 454)	15,979,149	5,742
Joint replacement (hip & knee) (209, 471, 558)	14,416,327	6,856
Angioplasty (112, 550)	12,878,856	6,682
Craniotomy (001, 002, 530)	12,442,024	5,066
Bowel procedures (148, 149, 585)	10,898,968	6,339
Upper G. I. (154, 155, 585)	7,860,626	4,197
Strokes/TIAs (014, 015, 532, 533)	7,543,366	5,445
Respiratory infections (079, 080, 089, 090, 474, 540)	7,472,705	4,488
Lobectomy (075, 538)	7,384,719	3,306

EXHIBIT 5 High Resource Utilization DRG (Diagnosis Related Grouping) Clusters: The Top 10 Resource Utilizers (Charges)

hospitals. Analysis revealed that, in general, MGH had longer lengths of stay (see Exhibit 6). MGH also had longer lengths of stay when compared to three other Boston hospitals (see Exhibit 7). This indicated to the committee that reducing the length of stay—and thus costs—should be possible.

Several other factors were considered in determining which area would implement the first care path. The committee agreed they would need a leader who could bring together the diverse medical specialties necessary to develop a pathway that people would be willing to follow. Moreover, the leader should be a spokesperson for the value of using pathways throughout the hospital. Torchiana, although a relatively junior member of the cardiac surgical staff, was identified as a potential team leader because he already had been involved with several process improvement committees at MGH. Additionally, his knowledge of the hospital and his ability to work for consensus was well respected. He also was interested in the improvements that care paths could produce and was willing to take on the time-consuming task of leading the team. This latter attribute was especially important given that team members would not be

---

[2] MGH used total charges to target where to cut costs because, like many hospitals, it had scant information on the actual costs of performing a given procedure.

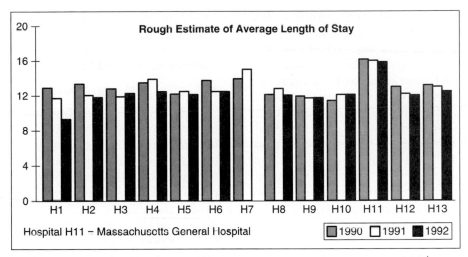

EXHIBIT 6 Average Length of Stay[a] at 13 Consortium Hospitals for DRGs 106 and 107[b]
[a]Average length of stay includes days spent in the hospital before, during, and after surgery.
[b]DRGs 106 and 107 are both CABG procedures.

EXHIBIT 7 Inter-Hospital Comparison of Length of Stay (LOS) for DRG 107[a]

Hospital[b]	Number of Stays	Median LOS	Mean LOS	Charlson Index[c]
Beth Israel	235	9	9.63	.60
Brigham & Women's	326	8	9.57	.93
Mass General Hospital	347	10	11.38	.73
New England Deaconess	378	9	10.00	.52
Total	1,286	9	10.20	.70

[a]Sum of FY 1992 and first quarter of FY 1993.

[b]Beth Israel, Brigham & Women's, MGH, and New England Deaconess were all Harvard University affiliated teaching hospitals.

[c]The Charlson Index roughly measured the severity of illness of the average patient served. Higher index numbers indicate sicker patients.

Source: Trimmed Harvard Hospitals data.

compensated for the extra time spent on the care path's creation.

A final factor in selecting the CABG area for the project was the relatively identical recovery path for most patients.[3] Although CABGs were complex medical procedures that involved several major areas within the hospital, post-surgery treatment was routine enough that a standardized care path could be created.

Putting Together the Care Path Team

In January 1994, Bohmer and Torchiana assembled a care path team including a cardiologist (the general heart doctor), a surgeon, a anesthesiologist, various residents, and personnel from the operating room, the SICU, Ellison 8 (the hospital floor where CABG patients stayed until ready for discharge), and physical therapy, as well as dieticians, social workers, and other non-medical

---

[3] In contrast, the pre-surgery care path was affected by a variety of forces. The patient group was quite diverse, for example, and patients came to the hospital for a variety of reasons (e.g., angina or a recent heart attack). Moreover, they already had undergone a range of treatments—from no previous treatment to the use of drugs, balloon angioplasty, or even a previous CABG. Some patients had been scheduled weeks in advance while others came from the emergency room or a floor bed; still others had been transferred from another hospital. Further, some patients were otherwise healthy 55 year olds while others were obese, diabetic, and 80.

staff—some 25 people in all, each representing a different area or department. Torchiana selected some members, while others were asked to participate by their area managers. Meetings were held once per week and were open to both team and non-team members. Various personnel thus attended meetings when items of particular interest to them were up for discussion.

While the team pulled representation from every corner of the CABG service, naturally, some had more to contribute than others. Torchiana at times questioned whether too many people were involved, thus making the process less efficient. He believed, however, that it was better to include everyone than risk alienating a group. Team members were charged with going back to their departments to discuss the issues under consideration and to get agreement on what the team member

would present to the care path team. Because the cooperation of all departments ultimately would be necessary to successfully follow a care path, Bohmer considered this role critical.

Developing the Care Path

The first few meetings were spent educating the team members about care paths and the need to make improvements in the CABG area. The team then set out to produce a flow diagram of the current process (see Exhibit 8). A primary purpose of the flow diagram was to structure and organize the team's discussions. Each step in the flow diagram was examined to generate a problems list, which was divided by the three areas of service: the operating room, the SICU, and Ellison 8 (see Exhibit 9). The problems identified centered on communication, coordination, and

EXHIBIT 8 Abridged CABG Process Flow Diagram for MGH

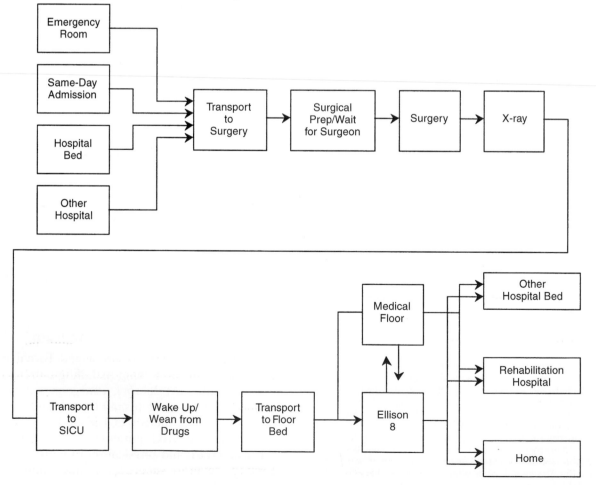

Day of Surgery
- Variable start times for first cases, operating room (OR) schedules
- Delay from first case finish to start of second case
- Transport delays to both the OR and the surgical intensive care unit (SICU)
- Information to families, what communications and by whom, telephone in OR
- Lack of SICU staffing

SICU
- Communication of schedule, SICU not called from OR
- Timing of ventilator wean,[a] extubation[a] at night
- X-ray and pharmacy delays
- Control of hypertension
- No beds on Ellison 8
- Report to SICU staff—individuals must know patient; need Q&A period; who is giving/getting report?; are they informed? Communication of information regarding patients, current medications, and conceptual information.

Ellison 8
- Bed availability
- No currently designated floor for patient overflow
- Limited transfer time, usually no later than 6:00 PM
- Use of oxygen
- Diet/nausea

Delays in Discharge
- Medical complications—atrial fibrillation, anemia, anticoagulation issues[b]
- Determination of rehabilitation needs, availability of rehab bed, lack of weekend admissions to rehab facilities
- Information on discharge planning is scattered
- Communication between hospital and referring physician
- Patient/family expectations different than physicians
- Social situations at home

[a]Patients coming out of surgery were dependent on a ventilator for breathing and also had a feeding tube. The patient was "weaned" or gradually removed from the ventilator while in the SICU. Extubation was the removal of the feeding tube. Both were significant early steps towards recovery and had to occur before the patient could leave the SICU.

[b]Atrial fibrillation (an irregular heart beat), anemia (a blood disorder characterized by a below normal number of red blood cells), and anticoagulation issues (related to proper blood clotting) were three potential complications faced by CABG patients during recovery.

EXHIBIT 9 Abridged Problem List

patient flow; the care path would attempt to address these problems.

To help understand some of the areas of opportunity for improvement, the team employed a software product widely used by insurance companies to deny payments for people who did not need to be in the hospital. Some physical therapy, for example, could be performed on an outpatient basis. The software helped identify patients receiving only treatments that did not require hospitalization who could be sent home or to a lower cost rehabilitation hospital. The care path team used this software to examine past CABG patients and found numerous instances where patients were in the hospital longer than medically necessary.

After the initial education of the team and the analysis of the existing CABG method, the team formed several subgroups. These subgroups—

including the operating room personnel, physical therapists, and social workers—met off-line and discussed their progress at the weekly team meetings. Bohmer felt that two key functions were served by the subgroups. First, they moved much of the technically detailed work out of the large team meetings. Equally important, they allowed broader participation in the creation of the pathway. Bohmer hoped this would foster greater buy-in by the staff when the care path was eventually implemented.

The Physical Therapy Group. The experience of the physical therapy group highlighted some of the issues encountered and addressed during the creation of the care path. The primary roles of physical therapy were to instruct and assist the patient in performing various breathing and coughing exercises, which helped prevent postoperative lung complications, and to improve the patient's functional mobility after the surgery. Under the current system, patients received a preoperative educational visit from a physical therapist for the purpose of practicing the breathing and coughing techniques that would be used after surgery. Patients also received a preoperative functional evaluation by the physical therapist. All patients were then treated by a physical therapist on a daily basis after their surgery.

However, patients admitted on Sunday for a Monday morning surgery did not always receive the educational visit because fewer physical therapy personnel were on duty. This raised the question of whether the education was truly necessary. Additionally, physicians did not feel that every patient required treatment (although some patients—especially those with preexisting respiratory problems—had a clear medical need for physical therapy). Moreover, some of the work being done was routine nursing care, and did not require a physical therapist to perform. Thus the care path team asked the physical therapy subgroup to look at its practice patterns in CABG surgery and come back with a plan to reduce costs without impacting patient outcomes.

Brian Roy, physical therapy supervisor and a member of the care path team, agreed that some patients received more treatment than necessary because, historically, physical therapy had been ordered for all cardiac surgical patients, and it was difficult to change an accepted standard without

everyone's buy in. However, his subgroup believed that if physical therapy were ordered only when a physician determined a patient's need, there was a potential for delay in early intervention and discharge planning. Such delays, Roy noted, had been a problem for other physical therapy departments in the U.S. that had worked on care paths in their hospitals. The physical therapists believed they should be the ones to determine physical therapy need.

Roy saw the care path as a way to develop a set of criteria or triggers that would indicate the level of treatment each patient required. This would allow therapists to spend their time more efficiently by concentrating on those patients who most needed their services. Under this plan, physical therapists would evaluate all patients at several key points in their hospital stay to determine whether treatment was necessary. (An evaluation took less than five minutes while a treatment lasted about 30 minutes.) Further, prior to surgery, all patients would receive an educational visit—even those admitted on a weekend. Roy and his group provided evidence that pre-operative education reduced post-operative length of stay. Roy believed that the use of the physical therapists' plan would reduce the overall amount of physical therapy needed by CABG patients.

Bohmer reviewed the physical therapy situation:

> Ultimately, we have to give a lot of credit to the physical therapy group. They had the most to lose in this process, but they ended up having a positive influence on the team. They put together a detailed report that outlined criteria under which they believed physical therapy was medically necessary. We expect the use of these criteria to reduce substantially the need for therapy, and their report set a high standard for other groups to follow when examining their own areas.

Torchiana felt it important to keep in mind the difficulty of making service reductions without adversely affecting the quality of the CABG outcome while still reducing costs and ensuring that those charged with providing professional care accepted the results. He stated:

> There are a number of indicators you can look at when evaluating the use of a treatment such as physical therapy. A big indicator in heart surgery is mortality rate, and I doubt what we have done with

the physical therapists will affect that. Another indicator we carefully track is readmission to the SICU from the floor. Our rate now is very low, about one percent, but if it should rise as a result of increased respiratory problems, we would have to reexamine the use of physical therapy. An extra day in the SICU costs far more than any possible reduction in the use of physical therapists.

The physical therapy issue raised several questions about the creation and use of care paths. Bohmer wondered if the best treatment method had been selected. Should he rely on the individual medical areas to decide what treatment methods should be used on the path, or should the team make such decisions? If such decisions were taken away from the specific medical area, how would this affect the implementation of the care path?

While key compromises had been made among the physical therapists, in part because of the direction given by the full team, at times Torchiana and Bohmer left less critical issues alone during the creation of the pathway. They felt that creating a care path that everyone accepted was more important than creating the most efficient or least costly pathway. Once implemented, changes could be made in the future to perfect the path.

Patient Education.   A major consideration behind everything that went into the care path was how it affected the patient. While the path was not expected to reduce medical quality in general, the team was careful not to reduce the patient's perception of quality. Patient Educator Mimi O'Donnell felt that a large part of a patient's quality of care rating depended on how well he or she understood what was going on and what to expect. The care path would formalize and guide the existing patient education program.

O'Donnell met with every patient before the surgery to explain what to expect on each day in the hospital, focusing particularly on post-surgery recovery. Patients were given a simplified version of the care path and O'Donnell would review it with them. She also met with every patient every morning after the surgery to reinforce what would happen on that day. O'Donnell explained that patient education went a long way toward increasing the trust the patient felt for the hospital staff:

> What often happens after the surgery is that, from our perspective, the patient is doing great—or at least exactly how we expected them to do. The

mistrust arises because they feel so bad they believe we're not telling them something. But if they remember we told them they'd feel like a truck ran over them on Day 3, they'll be less worried when that happens.

Patient education was also expected to be a useful tool in keeping patients on the care path. O'Donnell continued:

> People often hear that CABG surgery patients are in the hospital for about 10 days following the surgery. We've started to tell our patients five to seven days, and when we start the care path, it will be five days. Telling people five days keeps both the patient and the staff focused on the expected discharge date and meeting the goals along the way. We no longer ask a patient "Are you ready to go home or do you think you want to stay another day?" Rather, we tell them "You are ready to go home." This doesn't mean we discharge people who are not ready to go home. But lengths of stays are dropping now and expectations are an important factor in this.

Lowering Costs and Average Length of Stay

Costs and length of stays typically were somewhat unevenly related. Although patients remained in the hospital for five or more days after CABG surgery, Torchiana believed that half of the total costs generated were incurred on the first day in the operating room and the SICU: operating room costs approached $2,000 per hour in surgery and SICU costs per day were three or four times those of a regular patient floor. A substantial portion of the time spent in the operating room was determined by the amount of surgery performed by the resident. Torchiana believed that operating room time could be cut in half if residents did not perform operations. Cutting costs in this area, however, would adversely affect the quality of resident training. Thus the care path needed to consider broader goals, not just those of the procedure.

Other operating room costs had been examined as well. One potential change was to decrease the number of units of blood prepared prior to surgery. Standard practice was to prepare four units of blood matched for each patient at a cost of $150 per unit. Upon review by the care path team, it was discovered that this blood was rarely used during surgery; if it was needed, there was sufficient time to obtain it from the blood bank. Despite its findings, the team was not willing to recommend eliminating the setting up of blood in advance, but recommended that the amount be reduced from four units to two. Additional operating room costs were similarly reduced as the team examined each drug and procedure used during the surgery.

During 1993 and 1994, the average length of stay for the MGH CABG area dropped by several days (see Exhibit 10). Three factors played a role in this decrease: knowledge that other hospitals had shorter lengths of stay; general pressure to reduce costs throughout the health care industry; and expectations in 1994 that the efforts of the care path team would reduce the average length of stay. Little if any of this reduction was attributable to new or improved technologies. Overall costs were expected to be lower under the care path both because of shorter lengths of stay and because of using fewer and less expensive tests and medicines.

Implementing the Care Path

In December 1994, the care path developed by the team was ready for implementation, although it still was considered a work in progress and revisions were expected. For example, the path

elicited extensive information on each patient that was entered into a computer database. Ultimately, it was hoped the data would help answer such questions as why certain groups of patients fell off the path; the path might then be modified to better care for these patients, or different paths might be outlined for different patient groups.

Moreover, some issues remained unresolved. A fundamental change under discussion involved charting by exception, which would significantly reduce the amount of time nurses spent on long-hand record keeping. Under the current plan, nurses would maintain a care path check sheet in addition to normal, and extensive, records for each patient's permanent medical record. Brigham and Women's Hospital, however, included its care path sheet as part of the medical record and charted by exception. Written notes were required only when a complication arose with a patient, and normal progress required only a mark on the check sheet.

Bohmer and Torchiana realized there were many potential strategies for executing the care

EXHIBIT 10 Average Length of Stay[a] at MGH for DRG 107, by Fiscal Quarter, 1993–1994

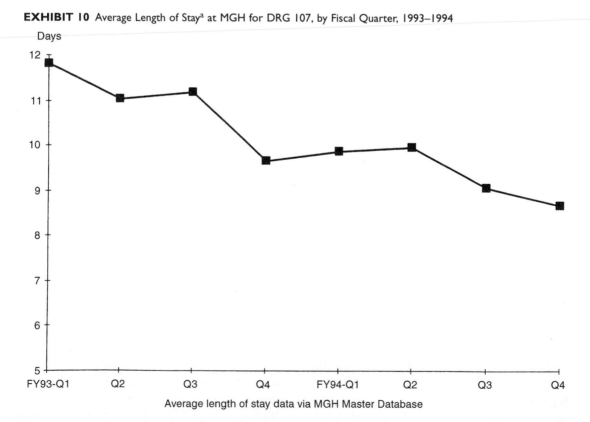

Average length of stay data via MGH Master Database

[a]Does not include days spent in the hospital before surgery.

path; whichever route they chose, they hoped the team's efforts would be rewarded by a smooth implementation. Bohmer was particularly concerned with the path's roll-out because he knew he would be involved in other care path projects in the future.

One option for CABG was the slow approach used by the orthopedic surgeon's group on total knee replacement. If Torchiana were the first (and only) surgeon to utilize the path, for example, he could demonstrate over six months that patients had shorter length of stays. Furthermore, these patients could be tracked after surgery to verify that the rate of complications had not increased, and the results could be used to convince other surgeons to employ the path. An additional benefit to this option was that modifications to the path would not necessitate retraining for the entire group.

A second option was to simply pick a start date in January and begin implementation by all surgeons simultaneously. A small pilot program had been run successfully, and speedy implementation might more quickly convince other MGH departments of the value of the care path method.

Other options existed, but regardless of how they proceeded, Bohmer and Torchiana had to consider potential effects on the staff. The creation of the path had been a very political process with many employees striving to justify their importance and their jobs. Bohmer also had to keep in mind that the physicians and the hospital maintained a cooperative environment. The hospital would not order physicians in any department to use a care path. The physicians and staff had to believe that care paths were a better way to treat patients and improve quality. Poorly implemented, the use of care paths could be fiercely opposed in some areas of the hospital. Yet in the increasingly cost conscious and competitive health care industry, failure to control costs in some manner was not a viable option.

Solagen: Process Improvement in the Manufacture of Gelatin at Kodak

William Bolten, gelatin plant superintendent, was in his Kodak Park office in June 1982 preparing for a meeting to be held the next day. Dr. Brian Woolsley (director of the chemistry division), Dr. George Searle (director of the manufacturing services organization), and Bolten would have to decide whether Kodak should begin construction of a production plant for Solagen, a new gelatin manufacturing process. The estimated cost for the plant was about $41 million, in addition to the more than $3 million already spent on Solagen R&D costs and pilot plant expenses.

Gelatin was a key ingredient in the manufacture of high quality photographic film and paper, core Kodak products. The new Solagen process promised a number of benefits. The most obvious was reducing the length of a key step in the production process from the present range of 30–80 days to a mere 48 hours. The Solagen process could also potentially increase the yield of the process from its present level of 40% to at least 80%. Substantial inventory benefits were associated with the reduced processing time and increased yield. Additionally, R&D promised improvements in photograph quality (clearer, crisper pictures) and film manufacturability (e.g., by reducing variability and simplifying the coating of gelatin onto the film base).

Thus, in some ways, Bolten felt it was absolutely critical that Kodak make the investment in order to keep pace with the cost and quality levels dictated by competition. However, he also felt there were reasons to question seriously if now were the right time to move ahead, because the Solagen process was made up of new technologies,

parts of which were largely unproven. While statistics from testing had been encouraging, they were not conclusive. Moreover, Solagen was expensive: it necessitated new equipment and a new plant, whereas the old plant was fully depreciated. Finally, any changes to the gelatin-making process could have wide-ranging, long-term effects on Kodak's films and photographic papers.

For some time, Bolten had thought it desirable to move the "art" of gelatin making closer to a "science." As a general manager at Kodak Park had noted in the early 1970s:

> There is a large quotient of witchcraft in successful gelatin making. You have to forget much of everything else you have learned about modern principles of manufacturing. There is no better or worse; a batch either works or doesn't work with a given film or paper, and there are no reliable techniques for telling in advance which is which.

Bolten pondered, "Have we learned enough about the gelatin-making process to help make the giant leap from 'witchcraft' to the precision required for Solagen's success?" (See Exhibit 1 for the Solagen project time line.)

COMPANY HISTORY

In 1878 when, at age 24, George Eastman decided to vacation in Santo Domingo, an engineer suggested he make a photographic record of the trip. Eastman was thus introduced to photography. Seven years afterwards, in 1885, Eastman started his own business in the field, registering the trademark "Kodak," a name he made up, three years later.

In 1982, Eastman Kodak logged sales of $10.8 billion. Film, photographic paper, and more than 900 chemicals used in their processing were produced at the company's largest manufacturing plant, the Kodak Park Division in Rochester, New

This case was prepared by Brian DeLacey under the direction of Dorothy Leonard-Barton. Copyright © 1986 by the President and Fellows of Harvard College. Harvard Business School case 687-020.

July 1977	Carson becomes head of R&D's Chemical Processing and Engineering Lab.
August 1977	Carson proposes gelatin R&D project to manufacturing plant. Wolanski hired; Morrow joins project.
December 1977	Basic elements of new Solagen process discovered.
September 1978	Bench scale tests supported by other research groups, which characterize and begin testing the gelatin and emulsions derived from the Solagen process.
June 1980	Larger bench scale facility designed and operated; favorable results stimulate the request for a pilot facility project involving the gelatin plant and R&D.
August 1980	Meeting with Blanchard (CEO); project approved to build pilot plant with intent to begin construction of full-scale plant in September 1983.
	Favorable results from bench scale tests in fall 1980 and spring 1981 accelerate the schedule for design and construction of the pilot facility.
July 1981	Pilot facility begins first runs.
January 1982	Pilot plant produces enough gelatin to allow film and paper making operations to begin testing.
June 1982	Solagen Steering Committee calls for a recommendation on going forward to full-scale production or terminating the project.

EXHIBIT 1 Key Events for the Solagen Project

York. More than 30,000 people worked at this site, which stretched over three miles and included nearly 200 major buildings.

THE EXISTING PROCESS OF MAKING GELATIN

Gelatin was essential to photographic film and paper manufacturing throughout Kodak (see Exhibit 2). It was a critical component in 400 different emulsions for 980 different types of film and 270 kinds of photographic paper (see the Appendix for a glossary of terms). Because of the clarity demanded in photography, gelatin used as a coating in film making had to be purer, and more transparent, than the gelatin that went into familiar food products (such as Jell-O). The basic process for making gelatin was more than 150 years old and had been largely uninfluenced by new technologies during that time.

In the simplest terms, gelatin making consists of three steps: (1) extraction of collagen from animal bones; (2) purification; and (3) partial hydrolysis, where the purified collagen reacts with hot water. Kodak's gelatin-making process (see Exhibit 3) was complex, time consuming, and highly variable; furthermore, a critical step, liming, was subject to elements beyond the control of people in the gelatin plant. Temperature and humidity influenced the rate at which the liming reaction took place in the open wooden and stainless steel vats. The composition of the lime varied by source, as

did the quality of the animal bone that came from sources in the U.S. and India. An experienced gelatin maker commented, "You don't know where the cow has been, what it has eaten, what environment it's been exposed to, so it's difficult to know what quality bone you are getting. It's not like something synthetic where you know the exact composition."

Randall Sudbury, a foreman in one of Kodak's gelatin plants, exemplified the kinds of skills required in the liming process. For 13 of his 22 years at Kodak, he decided when the liming step was complete and instructed the three shifts working in the liming area what corrective actions to take if the liming step was proceeding too quickly or too slowly. Sudbury tested the limed ossein by sight, feel, and smell.

First, he could tell whether enough lime had been added simply by looking at the color of the ossein in the pit. Second, he would penetrate the surface of a fistful of ossein with his fingernail, always applying the same pressure. The way the ossein peeled back off his fingernail indicated whether the liming step was complete. This "finger test" was confirmed by the "squeeze test." Sudbury took a fistful of limed ossein, rolled it in his hand, and squeezed it, applying the usual amount of pressure, to assess texture and firmness. Finally, Sudbury smelled a fistful of limed ossein. Based upon the amount of chlorine he could detect, he confirmed or invalidated the conclusions from his previous tests. He could usually tell after taking

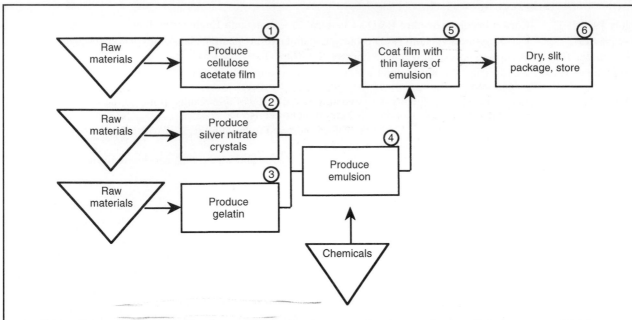

1. Cotton linters and pure wood pulp are dissolved and processed to form a plastic cellulose acetate, which becomes the film base.
2. Silver, the essential light-sensitive material, is dissolved in nitric acid. The resulting silver nitrate is crystallized, dried, stored in barrels and shipped to Kodak's emulsion-making operations.
3. Gelatin is produced from animal bones.
4. The silver nitrate crystals are combined with inorganic halide salts (potassium bromide) in the presence of gelatin and other chemicals to produce a photographic emulsion.[a]
5. Layers of this emulsion are then coated onto the film base.
6. The film base with dried emulsion coating is slit to proper widths and packaged as rolls, reels, or cartridges. Film is stored, under proper protective conditions, then shipped to dealers.

EXHIBIT 2 Major Steps in the Manufacture of Photographic Film

[a]In producing the emulsion, a chemical process occurs in addition to the physical distribution of the silver chemicals throughout the gelatin-based emulsion. Ultrafine crystals of silver halide are produced. The size, spatial density, and distribution through the emulsion layers of these microcrystals combined with additional chemicals determine the characteristics of the film or paper product. For example, very high resolution film requires very fine and very uniformly distributed crystals. The film speed and its use (e.g., medical x-rays or simple family photos) will determine which of the 400 emulsions are used to create the film.

two samples whether or not the lot would be good. According to Sudbury, a lot rarely turned out bad, and if it did, usually someone had erred (by forgetting to add enough lime, for instance).

Sudbury had learned his job from his predecessors, who in turn had learned what differentiated good from bad limed ossein from those who performed the tests before them. "At the time I started," Sudbury recalled, "anyone who wanted the job could have had it. All you had to do was stick your hand in the liming pit. If you had sensitive skin you were in real trouble, because the lime irritates it. In fact, I've had good luck; I still have my skin."

After liming came washing and cooking, and the output of the cooking step was dried and stored in containers sorted according to the characteristics of each batch. Gelatin from the various batches was then blended as needed to meet the specifications of different internal customers. For instance, the top 15%–20% in quality was reserved for making very sensitive film, because this gelatin was the purest and would serve as an inert carrier of the light-sensitive chemicals without side effects. For photographic paper (the largest consumer of gelatin), color characteristics (as measured by yellow density) were more important than chemical properties.

EHS

EXHIBIT 3 Kodak's Existing Gelatin Manufacturing Process

Processing Time (days)

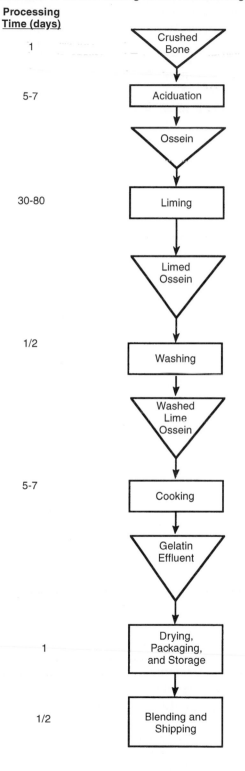

Crushed animal bone was received in trainloads from various suppliers in the United States and India.

Crushed bone was mixed in large wooden or stainless steel vats and mixed with a dilute hydrochloric acid solution; several hundred vats were active at any given time, processing thousands of pounds of bones. Grease and unwanted minerals were removed from the bone. The output was the impure organic collagen (ossein), minus the inorganic mineral (e.g., the calcium compounds) of bones.

The ossein was fed, via ducts, directly into liming pits—either holes in the ground or stainless steel vats. Two people monitored the pits/vats to ensure that the ossein reacted with the lime at the right rate. If the reaction moved too quickly or slowly, the pits/vats were drained, the lime washed off, and a new amount of lime added. Duration of this step depended upon the composition of the ossein and lime, humidity, and temperature.

Limed ossein was ready in 30 to 80 days (50 to 60 being the norm), as determined by the squeeze and finger tests (described in the case). The limed ossein had to be used in the five- to six-day period after passing the squeeze test or it would spoil.

After liming, the limed ossein was washed and fed via ducts to the cooking facility.

The washed limed ossein was placed in vats where water was added and brought to a boil.

Six to seven cooks (cycles) took place; after each cook, the vats were drained of the effluent, steam cleaned, refilled with water, and reheated. During the cook, the purified collagen reacted with water (hydrolyzed) and was converted to gelatin, which remained suspended in the aqueous solution. After the final cook, the remaining unusable solids were disposed of, all the useful collagen having been extracted in the previous cooks.

The suspension was filtered, concentrated (via evaporation), and the solution further purified (via deionization) to provide the final gelatin mass.

The final step involved drying gelatin on a 200-foot conveyor before packaging in four-foot-tall barrels used for storage prior to being shipped to film/paper manufacturing.

When an order for gelatin was received from a film or paper manufacturing plant, a blend of gelatin batches, which varied in properties, was prepared from the barrels of dried gelatin in inventory to meet the requirements of the film/paper to be produced.

THE SOLAGEN PROPOSAL FOR A NEW GELATIN-MAKING PROCESS

The new approach for gelatin making was a result of creative thinking and experimentation in Frederick Carson's research group. Carson joined the Polymer Development Laboratory in 1968. In 1977, he became head of the Chemical Processing and Engineering Laboratory, a department within the Research and Development area, and reported to Dr. Brian Woolsley. In planning for his new position, Carson identified a number of key areas he wanted to work on. At the top of his list was gelatin; he felt no other process or ingredient was so critical and less understood at Kodak. A lack of technology as well as methods to measure gelatin characteristics on a fundamental level had contributed to the lack of process-related research efforts in the past. Carson decided it was important to look for ways to improve the existing gelatin manufacturing process. He recalled:

> We had never interacted with the plant people; we had never even met them. We were seen as the ivory tower. I asked them to let us take at least a one-year crack at seeking improvements in the gelatin-making process. If results were positive after a year, then we could continue. I sent a proposal outlining this to Wayne LaFrance, gelatin plant superintendent at that time. In it I pointed out that making gelatin was so poorly understood that we needed to improve our understanding of gelatin and the way in which it was manufactured.

Although the proposal met with no active opposition, the plant showed little interest. Many in the plant viewed Carson's project as a joke. The lack of enthusiasm was not a significant hurdle, however, since Carson had funding from the Research Division. He started researching gelatin, bringing in full-time help. "We hired Peter Wolanski in 1977, from Princeton, with a Ph.D. in chemical engineering," Carson said. "He started working on the basic understanding of the gelatin process since so little was known about it. Peter's research was topnotch and greatly helped in understanding the critical steps in the process—acid decomposition of bone (or aciduation—see Exhibit 3) and liming." Carson also assigned Keith Morrow to work on the process: "Keith has a master's in chemical engineering and is an excellent go-getter with the talent to look at a process and pull together all the loose ends."

Over the next several months, Wolanski and Morrow developed a prototype of a rapid gelatin-making process. By adding several chemicals to the raw materials in a reactor instead of a liming pit and accelerating the reaction through the application of chemistry, their bench-scale prototype process completed one of the ossein chemical conversion steps in 48 hours (in contrast to two to three months). The temperature and other reaction conditions could be controlled and the chemicals served as a catalyst to accelerate the necessary reaction. This new process came to be known as Solagen, short for *sol*ubilized coll*agen*. (See Exhibit 4 for a comparison of the process flows for the liming and gelatin extraction steps associated with the new and old processes, and Exhibit 5 for a cost/benefit analysis.)

By late spring 1980, Wolanski and Morrow had proven that the new process was technically feasible; the key remaining questions needed to be resolved as part of larger scale testing by the gelatin plant staff working in conjunction with the Chemical Processing and Engineering Lab. Wolanski moved on to other projects while Morrow continued to work full time on Solagen.

PLANNING THE PROJECT

The CEO of Kodak, Alex Blanchard, had heard about the Solagen project early on from an assistant who had visited the R&D labs and was very enthusiastic about its potential. From time to time, the R&D group visited Blanchard's office and made presentations. An August 1980 meeting, which included representatives from the gelatin plant, resulted in a proposed schedule for pilot and full-scale plants (see Exhibit 6).

William Bolten, Gelatin Plant Superintendent

In 1980, William Bolten was sent to the Gelatin Division as an assistant superintendent to oversee development of the Solagen project. In 1981 he was promoted to superintendent to fill the spot vacated by Wayne LaFrance, who was retiring after working in the Gelatin Division for 33 years, 17 of them as superintendent (see Exhibit 7 for an organization chart). Bolten had five years' experience as assistant superintendent in the Synthetic Chemicals manufacturing plant, a bachelor's degree in chemical engineering, and an MBA from Rochester Institute of Technology. Several project

EXHIBIT 4 Steps in Current and Proposed Gelatin-Making Process (simplified)

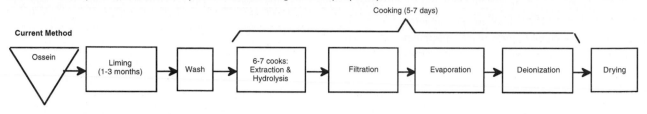

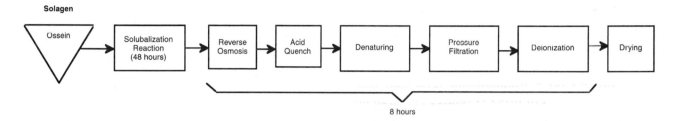

EXHIBIT 5 Annual Potential Operating Effects on Gelatin Division (dollars in millions)

Operating Savings	
Raw materials[a]	$10.9
Utilities	2.1
Waste water treatment	1.5
Inventory carrying cost[b]	3.8
Additional Costs	
New chemicals required	$8.5

[a]At 80% yield. The chart below indicates the calculated relationship between raw material savings and gelatin yield:

[b]Based on projected $15 million reduction in gelatin inventory.

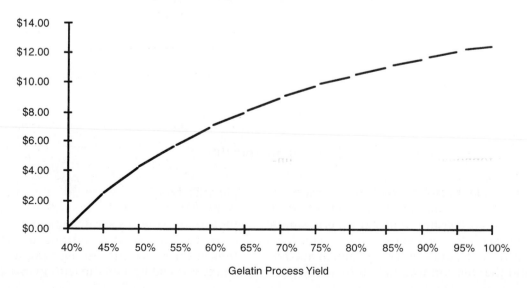

Gelatin Process Yield

Quarter	R&D Activities for Solagen	Testing for Solagen
4th, 1980	Gather data (R&D and gelatin production staffs)	
1st, 1981	Specify pilot plant equipment	
3rd, 1981	Install pilot plant equipment	
1st, 1982	Begin pilot operations	Trials with full-width photographic film; specific product trials
1st, 1983	Design prototype plant	Begin twelve-month product storage tests
2nd, 1983	Gain special expenditures funding for installation and operation of new gelatin making plant	Special expenditures request approval
3rd, 1983	Begin construction of new plant	
4th, 1984	Complete installation of new plant	Further testing of other products
1st, 1985	Begin operation of new plant	Convert one film and one paper product to new gelatin formulation

EXHIBIT 6 Proposed Project Schedule (from the 13 August 1980 meeting with Blanchard)

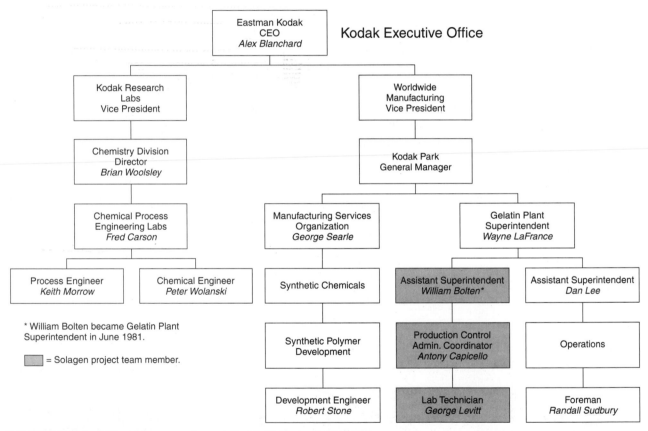

EXHIBIT 7 Organizational Structure, Eastman Kodak Company, August 1980

members considered Bolten to be on the fast track at Kodak; he was young and highly regarded for what he had accomplished in his previous position.

In his first few days on the job, Bolten discovered that the plant itself was old and in need of repair, and the division was staffed by many peo-ple who had been there 20 or more years: they were effective in what they did, he thought, but their skills were deep rather than broad and they were not very good at introducing changes into their environment. It also was not clear what the change should be. Gelatin, although a key element in making high quality film and paper, was a commodity-type product—it was simply the carrier for the valuable silver compounds. The existing process produced a widely varying gelatin product that had been sorted and blended for decades; all the current film and paper manufacturing plants had learned to design their processes around the resulting blends. The expense was in film and paper making, not gelatin manufacturing.

Bolten quickly realized that, for him at least, the Solagen project was a no-win situation. Management, from the CEO down, was already convinced that the new process was a success; thus, if he managed the implementation successfully, his efforts would be perceived as no great accomplishment. On the other hand, Dan Lee, the other assistant superintendent, told Bolten when he arrived that Solagen just wouldn't work. Lee had worked in the gelatin plant for 28 years, had earned the respect of every technician and staff member there, and was openly opposed to the Solagen project. And he was not alone. Most long-term employees in the gelatin plant felt that 10 years or more with the gelatin-making process were needed to really understand it. Carson's group, though technically qualified, clearly had little experience actually making gelatin.

The Gelatin Plant's Response to the Prototype Process

Antony Capicello was one of the few people in the plant who had, in 1977, favored looking into the process Carson proposed. Capicello's job was primarily process optimization, but he also had responsibility for scheduling gelatin production and the small in-plant development lab, and he was the designated interface between R&D and the gelatin plant. He suspected the existing manufacturing process could be improved upon, and having worked on a successful project with Carson several years earlier in another division, he wanted to give Carson's proposal a chance.

Capicello was aware that his position was not popular. A similar process, attempted by a well-known European supplier of gelatin, had failed, and the company had been nearly ruined financially. Attempts by R&D to learn more about the details of that recent disaster had proven unsuccessful. Moreover, argued most plant personnel, Kodak's current gelatin-making process was much more flexible. In the traditional process, gelatin

makers had a production window of up to five days during which the limed ossein could be used. The continuous process used in the Solagen method meant that every step was tightly linked, which required precise timing. Referring to the necessity to follow the reverse osmosis step immediately with acid quenching (see Exhibit 4), one veteran gelatin maker observed: "If you don't hit that baby just right, you're in real trouble."

One senior manufacturing manager with extensive gelatin-making experience commented:

> It takes people close to a job to really know what a quality job is. For the longest time the assistant superintendents would make all the decisions regarding when the limed ossein was ready. Later this decision was put in the hands of the foreman, who was closer to the liming process. You need to have people close to the job making decisions about what they are doing; this keeps them committed to doing a quality job. I'd like to see every person out there an artisan, a person interested in what they are doing. Sometimes introducing a new technology will put technology between the person and the craft, and people can become less committed to quality as a result.

THE PILOT PLANT

In summer 1980, once gelatin strength, viscosity, and color had all been tested in liter quantities, R&D started using larger scale lab equipment. This was followed by a joint development effort between R&D and the Kodak Park gelatin plant. Morrow, Carson, Capicello, Bolten, George Levitt (a lab technician with six years of experience with gelatin making), and another experienced technician made up the project team for the new Kodak Park pilot plant in the early stages. The $300,000 spent on building the pilot plant brought total expenditures on Solagen to over $2 million as of July 1981.

One Technician's Point of View

"I would say that I have the most experience of anyone who has worked on Solagen," said Levitt, assigned to run the Solagen pilot plant. He elaborated:

> I've averaged probably 12 hours per day on just Solagen for about a year and a half. My son was real small at the time, and I can remember many a night when I was holding his bottle in one hand and Solagen data in the other (see Exhibit 8 for representative Solagen test data). Gelatin making is

extremely complex. It isn't like adding A and B and coming out with C. It's very, very temperamental. It's not easy to work with. Unless you know the ins and outs, it's a bear.

I'm the only one in the building who really knows what's going on with Solagen. The only other person I know who has worked these kinds of hours also works on Solagen. In fact, he and I sometimes have a contest to see who can stay awake the longest—I hold the record at 37 hours.

Levitt carried out testing under the direction of his boss, Capicello, along with a development engineer from the Manufacturing Services Organization.

EXHIBIT 8 Selected Test Data for Batches from the Solagen Process

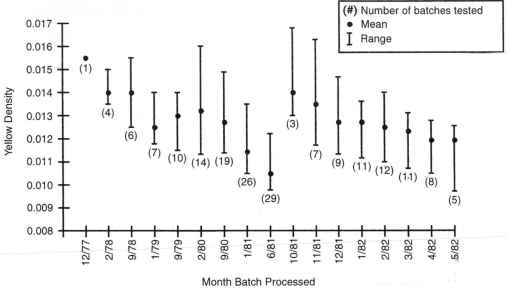

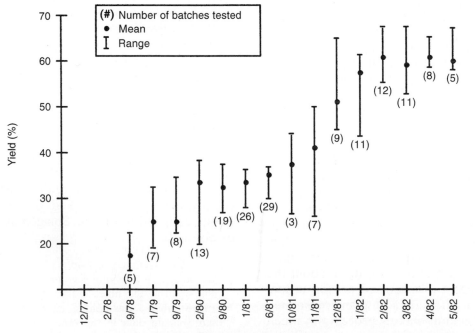

The pilot plant studies defined the steps for the Solagen process, and refinements of the parameters for each step yielded improvements to the process. Enough gelatin was produced to test the emulsion-making processes and several of the film and paper manufacturing processes. Toward the end of the pilot plant phase, Levitt felt that the output could reach the process's goal of 0.010 to 0.011 yellow density level only if another step were added to the process. His supporting evidence, however, was drawn from a limited amount of testing, and the benefit of the additional step was more of a hypothesis than a conclusion. Because the raw materials going into the process were, by their nature, highly variable, his suggested change would have to be tested across a large number of batches before anyone could be certain the results were not due to the characteristics of a few particular batches of raw stock. Furthermore, the gelatin output from the current Solagen process had already been extensively tested by the film and paper divisions. Because adding one more step would require an enormous amount of retesting and could introduce additional variability to the process, the Solagen Steering Committee decided against pursuing the idea further.

Phototesting the New Gelatin

According to Tom Fritsch, representative for the Film Division (a major consumer of the output from the gelatin plant):

My job is to take the emulsions made from the gelatin produced by R&D and the pilot plant and run tests on various films and photographic paper to look for significant differences from the existing gelatin. This type of testing is standard procedure for new products or for any process changes being introduced. Making better photos is the result of hundreds of complex interactions. Gelatin plays such a unique role in the behavior of photographic material that if you use a new gelatin, you have to go back and reformulate the film from the ground up. Because of the impact this would have on film manufacturing, some of the plant managers aren't particularly enthusiastic about the Solagen project.

It has become clear that the new gelatin has some unique physical properties different from the existing gelatin. We have determined, however, that there are no exceptionally good or bad properties and the Solagen process gelatin has acceptable qualities for use in film manufacturing.

Morrow's Comments

Keith Morrow commented on the project's development to date.

We had process objectives we were trying to meet, we had a specification on the product to meet, and we had a facility we wanted to build. All three require different kinds of information. The process people want to tinker to see what the process can do; the product people want you to demonstrate that the product is stable and very reproducible, so they don't want you to tinker around with the process; the process design people are looking to do major things, like try out a completely new piece of equipment in the plant.

All these areas are pulling on each other to get information. Of course, the design person doesn't want to be the one who built the multimillion dollar plant that didn't work; the product person wants 100% certainty that you can consistently make the product per specification; the process person, me, wants the maximum amount of latitude in tinkering with the process in order to reach its optimal levels. All this is compounded by a compressed time frame.

SOLAGEN AT A CROSSROADS

In June 1982, when Woolsley called to schedule the next day's meeting, Bolten was reviewing reports on the Solagen program and his notes from Thursday's weekly meeting of the Solagen Steering Committee. The stated goals of the Solagen process were to develop a single, continuous process for producing gelatin with a yellow density in the range of 0.010 to 0.011 and a yield of at least 80%. Since most of the output of the present gelatin plant production process ranged from 0.013 to 0.014 (see Exhibit 9), Solagen promised significant improvement. Marketing anticipated that the increased quality of prints made with the new gelatin would be noticeable to customers, and would result in a competitive advantage for Kodak's photographic products.

One report Bolten had was a checklist of tests the Solagen Steering Committee had laid out five months earlier as a set of objectives to be accomplished over the next six months. If the objectives had been met, then Bolten could easily support a request for funds to build a new gelatin manufacturing facility. Unfortunately, quality (e.g., yellow density) and process yields of the new gelatin still had not provided statistically significant results as originally promised by R&D. R&D argued,

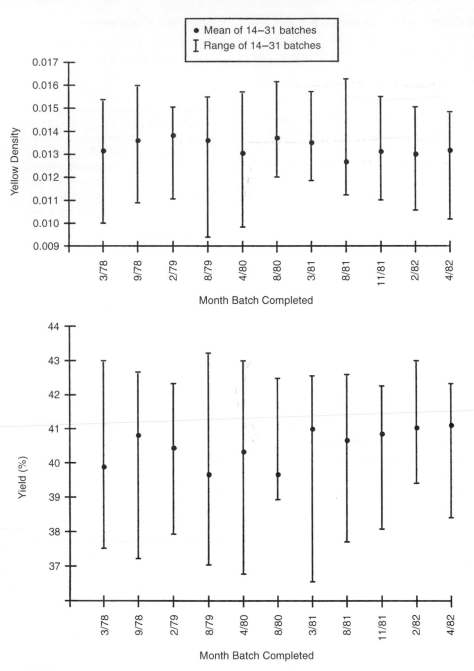

EXHIBIT 9 Selected QC Department Data from Kodak Park Gelatin Plant Production Runs

however, that significant progress had been made and more would follow.

The last report from the pilot facility highlighted several significant technical questions that could only be adequately addressed with further expensive testing on production-size equipment. This eleventh-hour crisis was a serious oversight because the problem of measurement and testing had been identified at the initiation of the Solagen project (see Exhibit 10).

One final point had been bothering Bolten for some time. The original proposal from R&D argued that the quality improvements would be significant, and testing to date showed some promise, but quality improvements were hard to quantify and didn't fit neatly into any of the

EXHIBIT 10

To: Wayne LaFrance, Gelatin Plant Superintendent
From: Fred Carson, Chemical Processing and Engineering Lab
Re: Gelatin Tests and Measures
Date: 19 September 1977

I hope you have had time to study my proposal for research to improve your manufacturing process. As an element of our research project, I would like to propose that we establish new quantitative tests that allow us not just to sort and batch the gelatin for each of the film or paper plants, but to achieve a science-based methodology for understanding and eventually controlling our gelatin process to tighter specifications. We have few quantitative standards other than yellow density by which to statistically evaluate current or future gelatin products. Our subjective measures and tests combine the effects of many phenomena and are therefore not very helpful in managing your operations.

I would propose the development of new or improved quantitative tests for: (1) process yield; (2) yellow density; (3) gelatin aging; (4) emulsion characteristics; (5) emulsion layer formation characteristics; and (6) predicting deleterious side effects. We have a pretty good handle on the first two:

- *Process Yield*—measurement of the mass of gelatin produced relative to the theoretical amount if all of the bone collagen were converted first to ossein and then to gelatin. These data need to account for losses in specific batches resulting from separation, filtration, and handling inefficiencies as well as from flaws in the chemical processes.
- *Yellow Density*—determines, quantitatively, the optical transparency of the gelatin product. Batch-to-batch variation in the physical and chemical nature of gelatin at the molecular level can cause it to absorb more light and appear yellowish. The lower the yellow density number, the more transparent (water clear) the gelatin. Yellow gelatin may become a quality defect on photographic paper giving photos a yellow tinge.

The remaining four tests all require substantial involvement with the film and paper operating units because the manufacturing practices may overshadow other effects:

- *Gelatin Aging*—heat, humidity, oxygen, and trace impurities all have the potential of changing the properties of gelatin during storage or transport. No detectable change in key properties must occur for a period of many months in sealed barrels at manufacturing locations around the globe. We need tests to predict aging properties rather than QC procedures to catch degraded gelatin.
- *Emulsion Formation*—although most of the emulsions contain similar constituents, the most significant being the light sensitive silver salts which record the photographic image, the detailed properties of emulsion formations are specific to the hundreds of different Kodak film and paper products as well as the different processes used to apply the emulsion layer.

There are numerous traditional tests for measuring gelatin-based emulsion formation characteristics. Our current practice requires that formulations containing constituents from new suppliers, plants, or processes be verified on actual production equipment which require substantial costs. We need to improve our tests and the correlation of these tests to what occurs in gelatin and emulsion production.

- *Emulsion Layer Formation*—the major purpose of the gelatin is to provide a matrix for the light-sensitive silver compounds which need to be dispersed evenly as microcrystals over the area of the film or paper as well as through the thickness of the emulsion layer. The uniformity of the thickness during forming and drying and a priori control according to specified targets is critical. It must also be strong and tough; it can't peel off the acetate or paper substrate. Can these characteristics be predicted without carrying out production runs?
- *Side Effects*—pure gelatin is inert (does not react chemically) to film, paper, or silver compounds. However, small amounts of impurities or residues from incomplete reactions from the gelatin-making process may cause negative side effects. Can we develop tools to test for these before going into production runs?

established corporate methods for capital project evaluation. He had received more than one reminder from the financial office that hundreds of research projects were competing for scarce resources. It had been increasingly difficult to justify spending money on a project that was failing to meet the specifications clearly set out for the process. "Projects take on a life of their own," one manager observed. "Sometimes you just have to bite the bullet and shut a failing one down."

Bolten felt the company had already benefited from the Solagen project in that a great deal had been learned about gelatin over the last four years, which would certainly leave Kodak better prepared for the future.

In the meantime, several recent and related developments had begun to influence the decision on approving the $41 million allocation for a new plant:

1. A report from marketing showed that demand for gelatin would be less than had been predicated two years ago. Thus the potential cost savings to be realized through the new process were no longer as great an incentive. Original projections had put utilization of current gelatin capacity at 115% to 120% by 1983, whereas actual data showed present utilization at about 85%. There was no need to build a new plant to meet increased capacity requirements; however, a new plant would still be needed to house the Solagen process because it was so different from the existing gelatin-manufacturing process. Given the new capacity projections, it was likely that a new plant would be used to continue the experimentation on the Solagen process, in anticipation of renewed demand, rather than to produce gelatin immediately for the current volume of film and paper products, as originally projected. Thus, any anticipated savings would be delayed several years.

2. Several technical questions remained. There existed too few standard specifications for comparing the "new" to the "old" gelatin, so it was difficult to judge how much better or worse the new gelatin was. The yellow density of the new process was slightly better than that of the old process, but whether the pilot scale process would be representative of the full-scale plant process was uncertain. Additionally, the yield figures were closer to 60% than the 80% originally targeted (although still better than the 40% yield of the old process). However, since portions of the testing were done on expensive equipment in different labs throughout Kodak Park, it was unclear whether the lower yield was a result of limitations in the new process or simply a result of test samples being trucked around Kodak Park. Another question often asked was "Can you assume the yield from each separate unit test will give a meaningful overall yield in a continuous process when everything is tied together?" Such questions could be answered only by building the new plant.

3. Finally, the market environment was changing. Heightened competition from Japanese film manufacturers was challenging Kodak in the areas of quality and cost. Attempts to understand their gelatin-making process had proved unsuccessful; not surprisingly, they were very secretive.

Kodak prided itself on its position among the elite of R&D spenders, making it possible to undertake projects such as Solagen. But the strong and steadily increasing sales of the past (Exhibit 11) were less certain in the future, making it more difficult than ever before to justify R&D dollars.

EXHIBIT 11 Excerpts from 1981 Kodak Annual Report (dollar amounts & shares in millions)

	1981	*1980*	*1979*
Sales	$10,337	$9,734	$8,028
Earnings from operations	2,060	1,896	1,649
Earnings before income taxes	2,183	1,963	1,707
Net earnings	1,239	1,154	1,001
Supplemental Information			
Sales:			
• Photographic Division	$8,258	$7,904	$6,458
• Chemicals Division	2,349	2,070	1,777
Research and development expenditures	615	520	459
Employees at close of year:			
• In the United States	91,900	84,400	80,800

Having spent considerable time weighing the evidence and considering the issues, Bolten recognized that he must now pull together his own recommendations. He also recognized that, whatever the final decision, execution would ultimately determine Kodak's success. Should he push forward for the construction of the full-scale plant, continue with the project less aggressively, or cancel the project entirely? Which plan would most benefit Kodak?

APPENDIX

Glossary of Terms

Acid Quench   the addition of excess acid to quickly terminate the basic or caustic reaction.

Aciduation   the separation of collagen from the mineral constituents of bones by the reaction of ground bone with hydrochloric acid.

Cellulose Acetate   a clear resin used to make photographic film that is derived from cellulose, the main constituent in all plant tissues and fibers.

Collagen   the fibrous protein substance found in animal bone, cartilage, and connective tissue.

Cotton Linters   inexpensive cotton fibers; the short fibers that cling to cotton seeds after the first gleaning.

Deionization   the removal of ions from a solution (such as calcium and chlorine) in the water used to make gelatin from bones; if the water is simply evaporated, the ions that are left behind may contaminate the gelatin.

Denature   neutralize the solution (suspension) which was acid quenched.

Emulsion   a suspension of fine droplets or particles of one or more substances in a viscous fluid; common examples include mayonnaise and paint. The light-sensitive ultrafine particles of silver compounds used to produce photographs are dispersed in a viscous dispersion of gelatin and water, an emulsion, so that they can be uniformly coated onto photographic films and papers.

Gelatin   obtained through the partial hydrolysis of collagen, which, in turn, is derived from the principal protein tissue of animal bones and hides. The physical and chemical properties of gelatin, such as color, solubility, stability, and emulsion forming characteristics, are functions of the source of the collagen raw material, the method of manufacture, conditions of thermal history, the acid-base conditions, and the chemical nature of impurities or additives. In a common food form known as Jell-O®, the "polymeric molecules" of gelatin readily dissolve and are suspended in hot water but rigidize (gel) when cooled and thereby lock up the water in the gelled matrix. Gelatin is a common material used in food, photography, and medicine.

Liming Reaction   the second step in the process of extracting collagen from animal bones using a derivative of calcium carbonate (a plentiful, natural mineral) to create a caustic chemical reaction.

Ossein   the name for collagen in the intermediate state of purification following its removal from bone.

Pressure Filtration   use of pressure to force more rapid flow of a water solution through filter paper or fabric for the purpose of separating unreacted bone byproducts from the fluid.

Reverse Osmosis   a form of molecular filtration through a semipermeable membrane (when applicable it is more discriminating than simple filtration).

Solubilized   to make substances (such as fats or proteins which are not appreciably soluble under normal conditions) soluble through the action of additives.

Yellow Density   a quantitative measure of the optical transparency of the dried gelatin product. The lower the value, the more transparent the gelatin—i.e., the more it is like pure water or glass. Differences in the chemical nature of the gelatin will cause it to absorb light and appear yellow.

McDonald's Corporation

Whether in Moscow or Massachusetts, the same experience would greet a customer in any of the 12,611 McDonald's quick-service restaurants worldwide. McDonald's had distinguished itself in the quick-service industry through its remarkable consistency across all units. To competitors and customers alike, the Golden Arches—the corporate emblem that adorned every restaurant—symbolized pleasant, fast service and tasty, inexpensive food.

In the United States alone, McDonald's served over 20 million customers every day.[1] Although such a number testified to the restaurant chain's success, it also suggested a troubling question for management. With McDonald's already serving so many customers, how could it possibly attract more business? External pressures reinforced the dilemma. Demographic trends were reshaping American eating habits while competitors were attacking the quick-service giant from all sides. From chains specializing in speed and service, to those offering wider variety and those that featured deeply discounted menus, McDonald's faced competitors poised to challenge the industry leader on all fronts. McDonald's had built its success on a legendary operating system that amazed competitors and the financial community by generating an average annual return on equity of 25.2% from 1965 through 1991, and an average an-

nual earnings growth of 24.1%. However, sales per unit had slowed between 1990 and 1991, causing management to wonder whether the company's operating system, so vital in guaranteeing uniform quality and service at every McDonald's outlet, was suited to the new circumstances the company faced.

Consumers were changing: in addition to an increasing, yet variable, concern for "healthy" food, there was a growing concern for the environment among consumers. A study of Americans in the summer of 1989 had found that 53% of those questioned had declined to buy a product in the previous year because they were worried about the effects the product or its packaging might have on the environment.[2] Aware of the growing importance of environmental stewardship, McDonald's had recently undertaken a bold collaboration with the Environmental Defense Fund, which seemed to offer some concrete methods by which operations could adapt to the benefit of the environment.

Top managers considered three vexing challenges:

- To what extent should McDonald's change its operations strategy to accommodate the growing need for flexibility and variety in products. Was it merely tweaking—or a dramatic change—which would support the company's volume growth objectives?

- To what extent would environmental concerns compromise McDonald's traditional strengths and complicate an already challenging competitive situation?

- Finally, could the lessons learned in the recent collaboration with the EDF help McDonald's as it sought solutions to the continuing competitive challenge?

---

[1]With 250 million people living in the United States, McDonald's was serving roughly 8% of the U.S. population daily.

This case was prepared by David M. Upton and Joshua Margolis. Copyright © 1992 by the President and Fellows of Harvard College. Harvard Business School case 693-028. The information presented in this case does not necessarily represent the opinion of McDonald's Corporation. Thanks are due to Terri Capatosto and Shelby Yastrow of McDonald's along with Jackie Prince and Fred Krupp of the EDF. The following provided background material for this case: John F. Love, *McDonald's: Behind the Arches* (New York: Bantam Books, 1986) and Lois Therrien, "McRisky," *Business Week*, October 21, 1991.

---

[2]Frances Cairncross, "*Costing the Earth,*" pp. 190–191. Harvard Business School Press, 1992.

THE SPEEDEE SERVICE SYSTEM

Dick and Mac McDonald opened their first drive-in restaurant in 1941, relying on carhops—waiters who went from car to car—to take orders from patrons parked in the restaurant's large lot. In 1948, the brothers abandoned their popular format and introduced self-service windows, 15-cent hamburgers, french fries, and milk shakes. They standardized their preparation methods (in what they termed the "Speedee Service System") with exact product specifications and customized equipment. Every hamburger, for example, was prepared with ketchup, mustard, onions, and two pickles; the ketchup was applied through a pump dispenser that required just one squirt for the required amount. Ray Kroc, who held the national marketing rights to the multimixers used in the restaurants to make milk shakes, met the McDonald brothers in 1954. He was so impressed by their restaurant and its potential that he became a national franchise agent for the brothers, and founded the McDonald's chain. Like the McDonald brothers' first restaurant in San Bernardino, California, the McDonald's chain featured a limited menu, low prices, and fast service. From the moment in 1955 when he opened his first McDonald's, in Des Plaines, Illinois, Kroc made the operating system his passion and his company's anchor. Whereas many competitors could prepare products that were similar to McDonald's, most focused on recruiting franchisees, whom they promptly ignored, and on identifying the lowest-cost suppliers.

Kroc, on the other hand, sought (i) to make sure McDonald's products were of consistently high quality, (ii) to establish a unique operating system, and (iii) to build a special set of relationships between the McDonald's corporation, its suppliers, and its franchisees (see Exhibit 1).

GETTING IT RIGHT— AGAIN AND AGAIN

McDonald's designed its operating system to ensure consistency and uniformity across all outlets. Operating procedures guaranteed customers the same quality of food and service visit after visit, store after store. Every hamburger, for example, was dressed in exactly the same way: mustard first, then ketchup, onions, and two pickles. One competitor, who operated 250 Kentucky Fried Chicken restaurants, marveled at McDonald's record of consistency:

> I've been to McDonald's in Tokyo, Vienna, and Australia, and I get a great sense of having the same product from each one of their locations. Most people haven't been able to bring the discipline needed in fast food to get that type of consistency.

McDonald's operating system concentrated on four areas: improving the product; developing outstanding supplier relationships; improving equipment; and training and monitoring franchisees. In its quest for improvement, McDonald's revolutionized the entire supply chain, introducing innovations in the way farmers grew potatoes and

EXHIBIT 1 McDonald's Original Menu

HAMBURGER	15c	ROOT BEER	10c
CHEESEBURGER	19c	ORANGEADE	10c
FRENCH FRIES	10c	COCA COLA	10c
MILK	10c	COFFEE	10c
MILK SHAKE Chocolate Strawberry Vanilla			20c

ranchers raised beef, altering processing methods for both potatoes and meat, and inventing efficient cooking equipment tailored to the restaurant's needs. Most revolutionary, perhaps, was McDonald's attention to detail. Never before had a restaurant cared about its suppliers' product beyond the price, let alone the suppliers' methods of operation.

McDonald's was able to spend as much time and effort as it did in perfecting its operating system because it restricted its menu to ten items. Most restaurants in the 1960s and 70s offered a variety of menu items, which made specialization and uniform standards rare and nearly impossible. Fred Turner, one of Kroc's original managers and later Senior Chairman of McDonald's, stressed the critical importance of menu size in attributing success of the company's operating system:

> It wasn't because we were smarter. The fact that we were selling just ten items, had a facility that was small, and used a limited number of suppliers created an ideal environment for really digging in on everything.

Turner developed the first operations manual in 1957, which, by 1991, reached 750 detailed pages. It described how operators should make milk shakes, grill hamburgers, and fry potatoes. It delineated exact cooking times, proper temperature settings, and precise portions for all food items—even prescribing the quarter ounce of onions to be placed on every hamburger and the 32 slices to be obtained from every pound of cheese. French fries were to be 9/32 of an inch, and to ensure quality and taste, no products were to be held more than ten minutes in the transfer bin.

McDonald's patrolled suppliers and franchisees scrupulously. The meat in McDonald's hamburgers, for example, had particular specifications: 83% lean chuck (shoulder) from grass-fed cattle and 17% choice plates (lower rib cage) from grain-fed cattle. Fillers were unacceptable. Whereas other restaurants merely accepted what suppliers provided and complained only when meat was visually inferior, McDonald's routinely analyzed its meat in laboratories.

In 1991, McDonald's spent $26.9 million on its field service operation to evaluate and assist each of its restaurants. Each of the company's 332 field service consultants visited over 20 restaurants in the US several times every year, reviewing the restaurants' performance on more than 500 items ranging from rest room cleanliness to food quality and customer service. Turner was the first corporate employee to visit and evaluate each restaurant, and, as early as 1957, he summarized his evaluations by assigning a letter grade to a restaurant's performance in three categories: quality, service, and cleanliness (QSC). For more than thirty years, therefore, McDonald's had prided itself on QSC and a fourth letter—V for value.[3]

McDonald's meticulous attention to detail and careful analysis of quality and procedures did not come from an unbending need for regimentation. Instead, McDonald's sought to study every component of its operation to learn what worked and what failed, to determine how best to offer consistently good service and food. Whereas other chains ignored both franchisees and suppliers, McDonald's sought to elicit commitment from them—commitment that required not only adherence but experimentation. Turner explained:

> We were continuously looking for a better way to do things, and then a revised better way to do things, and then a revised, revised better way.

SUPPLIERS

A simple handshake secured every arrangement between McDonald's and a supplier, and it symbolized the way McDonald's revolutionized the entire relationship. Jim Williams, head of Golden State Foods, which supplied McDonald's with meat, contrasted the traditional supplier-restaurant relationship with the changes McDonald's introduced:

> Deals and kickbacks were a way of life. How long you let a guy stretch out his payments was more the determining factor of whether you got the business than the quality of the product you were selling. Kroc brought a supplier loyalty that the restaurant business had never seen. If you adhered to McDonald's specifications, and were basically competitive on price, you could depend on their order.

When McDonald's first approached the established food processing giants, such as Kraft,

---

[3]Franchisees could not be graded on value because it violated antitrust regulations, which prohibited rigid pricing and required that independent business owners be given the latitude to set prices on their own.

Heinz, and Swift, the restaurant chain received a cold response. The established suppliers refused to accept McDonald's concepts and specifications and continued to concentrate solely on the retail market. Only small, fledgling suppliers were willing to gamble on McDonald's, and in turn, McDonald's created a whole new set of major institutional vendors. Each McDonald's restaurant ordered 1,800 pounds of hamburger meat per week and 3,000 pounds of potatoes. By meeting McDonald's strict standards and price requests, suppliers were guaranteed future volumes from a burgeoning restaurant chain. Kenneth Smargon, whose Interstate Foods supplied McDonald's with shortening, described the novel relationship that developed:

> Other chains would walk away from you for half a cent. McDonald's was more concerned with getting quality. They didn't chisel on price and were always concerned with suppliers making a fair profit. A lot of people look on a supplier as someone to walk on. But McDonald's always treated me with respect even when they became much bigger and didn't have to. That's the big difference, because if McDonald's said "Jump," an awful lot of people would be asking "How high?"

Suppliers grew alongside McDonald's and were thus carefully attuned to the company's needs. As one supplier commented, "You've got to be deaf, dumb, and ignorant to lose McDonald's business once you have it."

FRANCHISEES

McDonald's referred to its 3,500 U.S. franchisees as its partners for good reason. By 1992, McDonald's generated 39% of its revenues from franchise restaurants. When Ray Kroc first sold franchises, he made sure that his "partners" would make money before the company did, and he insisted that corporate revenue come not from initial franchise fees but from success of the restaurants themselves. That philosophy continued to be at the center of McDonald's franchise and operating practices.

Franchise owners did indeed see themselves as partners, developing such products as the Filet-O-Fish sandwich and the Egg McMuffin in the 1960s and the McDLT in the 1980s. Franchisees also formed powerful regional cooperatives for both advertising and purchasing. Their regional advertising budgets enabled them to "customize" local promotions while also supporting national programs, and the buying cooperatives gave franchisees a channel for challenging suppliers to be innovative, even when those suppliers were meeting corporate requirements.

Together with corporate management and suppliers, franchisees infused McDonald's with an entrepreneurial spirit. All three partners balanced one another, just as the entrepreneurial inventiveness within each balanced their collective emphasis on disciplined standards of quality.

COOKING UP PRODUCTS

Nothing exemplified the success of McDonald's operating system like the development of its food. From french fries to Chicken McNuggets, McDonald's had distinguished its menu offerings by drawing both on the rigorous operating system, with its focus on uniformity, and on the orchestra formed by corporate management, suppliers, and franchisees.

In Pursuit of the Perfect Fries

When McDonald's first began operating, french fried potatoes accounted for approximately 5% of the entire US potato crop. By 1985, french fries accounted for more than 25% of the U.S. market. McDonald's had made french fries standard fare for an American meal, but more important for McDonald's, french fries became the restaurant chain's most distinctive item. Ray Kroc was well aware of the importance of the chain's fries:

> A competitor could buy the same kind of hamburger we did, and we wouldn't have anything extra to show. But the french fries gave us an identity and exclusiveness because you couldn't buy french fries anywhere to compete with ours. You could tell the results of tender loving care.

McDonald's did indeed apply tender loving care in preparing its french fries. At first the company simply monitored the way french fries were cooked in its restaurants, trying to determine the exact temperature and settings that yielded the best french fries. They discovered, however, that temperature settings on the fryers had little connection to the temperature of the oil in the vat once cold potatoes were dropped in. By putting temperature sensors in the vat and on potato slices, McDonald's charted temperature readings during the cooking process. When a batch of cold, wet potatoes was thrown into a vat of melted shortening, the shortening's temperature dropped radically. Each batch of fries fell to a different temperature, but, McDonald's researchers discovered, the fries were always perfectly cooked when the oil temperature rose three degrees above the low temperature point. This discovery enabled the company to design a fryer that produced perfect french fried potatoes every order.

The initial research team eventually learned that potatoes also need to be cured for three weeks to produce perfect french fries: in that period of time the sugars within potatoes convert into starches. To prevent excessive browning and permit uniform crispness through the fry, McDonald's only accepted potatoes with a 21% starch content. Members of the company's field operations staff visited produce suppliers with hydrometers, a floating instrument that measured the starch content of potatoes when immersed in a bucket of water.

As the number of McDonald's outlets grew to over four hundred in the early 1960s, the company's potato consumption surpassed six million pounds a year. That gave McDonald's and its suppliers sufficient purchasing power to influence growers of Idaho Russet potatoes to adhere to planting practices that yielded potatoes with high starch content. McDonald's also began looking for potato processors willing to invest in storage facilities with sophisticated temperature controls.

In the early 1960s, Jack Simplot, a major potato grower who supplied 20% of McDonald's potatoes, approached McDonald's with an idea for improving the chain's french fries. He agreed to spend $400,000 to put Idaho Russets in cold storage during the summer, when they typically were not available. During the summer months, McDonald's relied on California white potatoes, less suited to production of crisp french fries. Although his gamble failed, and all of the stored potatoes rotted, Simplot returned with another, bolder suggestion in 1965. He recommended that McDonald's consider converting from fresh to frozen potatoes. Reluctant though the company was to tamper with its renowned french fries, Ray Kroc recognized the distribution problems involved in supplying fresh potatoes to his growing chain. Sim-

plot pitched his idea to Kroc on the basis not of price but of quality, as he later explained:

> They were having a hell of a time maintaining potato quality in their stores. The sugar content of the potatoes was constantly going up and down, and they would get fries with every color of the rainbow. I told him that frozen fries would allow him to better control the quality and consistency of McDonald's potato supply.

McDonald's studied the freezing process carefully, learning that the traditional process robbed structure and flavor from french fries. Ice crystals would form in the potato during freezing, rupturing the starch granules. McDonald's developed a process to dry french fries with air, run them through a quick frying cycle, then freeze them. This reduced the moisture in the frozen fry while preserving its crispness. Simplot volunteered to build the initial production line that implemented this process, and by 1992, his company supplied McDonald's with 1.8 billion pounds of french fries—close to 50% of the chain's domestic potato business. Only a small, local supplier when he first approached McDonald's, Simplot's organization grew to a $650 million frozen potato processing giant.

McDonald's even improved the way restaurant crews filled orders for french fries. Operators had complained that employee productivity suffered because the metal tongs traditionally used to fill french-fry bags proved clumsy. In response, a McDonald's engineer, Ralph Weimer, designed a V-shaped aluminum scoop with a funnel at the end that enabled operators to fill a french-fry bag in one motion and, in addition, align the fries in the same vertical direction within the bag.

Fast Break from Competitors: Breakfast and the McMuffin

In June 1976, McDonald's franchisees introduced the chain's most significant new product: not just a new menu item but a new meal, breakfast. Most operators were sufficiently busy keeping their restaurants open between 11:00 A.M. and midnight, but a Pittsburgh franchisee looked at these hours as a limitation that offered an opportunity:

> We were paying rent, utilities, and insurance twenty-four hours a day, but we were only open for business for half that time. We had all those morning hours before 11:00 A.M. to do some business.

This franchisee began opening his restaurant at 7:00 A.M., serving coffee, doughnuts, sweet rolls, pancakes, and sausage. Without detracting from McDonald's existing menu, he generated entirely new business.

Other franchisees would agree to extend morning hours only if they happened upon a breakfast item that promised enormous sales growth. Herb Peterson, a franchise operator in Santa Barbara, California, believed that to launch a new meal, McDonald's required a unique product that could be eaten like all other McDonald's foods—with the fingers. He turned to a classic egg dish—Eggs Benedict—for inspiration.

In 1971, he developed a sandwich and a special utensil that could, in classic McDonald's style, guarantee foolproof production of the sandwich. A cluster of six Teflon-coated rings could be used on a grill to give eggs the rounded shape of an English muffin while giving them the look and taste of poached eggs. When a slice of cheese and bacon were added, McDonald's had developed the cornerstone product of its breakfast menu: the Egg McMuffin.

McDonald's rolled out a complete breakfast menu in 1976, featuring the Egg McMuffin, hotcakes, scrambled eggs, sausage and Canadian style bacon. McDonald's had again distinguished itself from competitors, none of whom responded until the mid-1980s, by which time McDonald's held a virtual monopoly on breakfast, which accounted for 15% of average restaurant sales.

McDonald's once again turned to suppliers for support in developing the Egg McMuffin; some were responsive while others lost a revolutionary opportunity. Pork processors, for example, worked with McDonald's to build equipment that could cut round slices of bacon instead of strips.

Chicken Comes to the Golden Arches

In the late 1970s, McDonald's official chef, Rene Arend, tried to develop an onion product—deep-fried chunks of onion—but the variation in onion supplies made it difficult to control quality. Instead, CEO Fred Turner suggested that Arend substitute bite-sized chunks of deep-fried chicken.

McDonald's immediately turned to two suppliers to help develop the product in record time. Gorton, the original supplier of fish for McDonald's Filet-O-Fish sandwich, was selected to solve the breading and battering challenge as it had done previously with fish. McDonald's handed the most difficult challenge to Keystone, one of McDonald's meat suppliers: find an efficient way to cut chicken into bite-sized, boneless chunks. Arend, meanwhile, developed four sauces to accompany the nuggets. The collaborative effort between McDonald's and its suppliers produced breakthroughs that made the new product, Chicken McNuggets, not only possible but unique: a modified hamburger-patty machine that cut boneless chicken into nuggets, for example, and a special batter that gave the nuggets the taste and appearance of being freshly-battered.

By March 1980, just five months after beginning work on McNuggets, McDonald's was testing them in a Knoxville restaurant. Within three years of introducing Chicken McNuggets throughout its chain, McDonald's was deriving 7.5% of domestic sales from its newest product. The giant of the hamburger business had suddenly become the second-largest chicken retailer in the food-service industry, positioned behind Kentucky Fried Chicken. Keystone's efforts on behalf of McDonald's again provided proof of the success bred by loyalty: by 1992, Keystone had 65% of McDonald's chicken business, transforming the meat supplier into a major chicken producer as well.

Competitors and Growth

McDonald's had built the most successful quick-service franchise in the world, maintaining phenomenal growth for over 35 years. Distinguishing itself from other chains by adhering tenaciously to an operating system focused on uniformity, it worked with its franchisees and suppliers as partners to improve the operating system and introduce new products. But as management reviewed McDonald's performance in recent years, many wondered if the company's traditional strategy still suited the dramatic changes it now seemed to face.

McDonald's share of the U.S. quick-service market had dropped from 18.7% in 1985 to 16.6% in 1991, even though the company gained sales from a bigger quick-service "pie." Despite this, between 1988 and 1990, sales per U.S. outlet dropped an average of 3.7% in real dollars. After years of double-digit income growth, McDonald's 1991 net U.S. income grew just 7.2% to $860 million. It was estimated that by 1995, profit from overseas outlets would surpass profit from U.S. outlets.

Overseas business, in fact, showed the greatest growth in recent years, with operating income rising from $290 million in 1987 to $678 million in 1991. Although international expansion clearly offered McDonald's its most fertile frontier, McDonald's had to concentrate on U.S. operations. There were 2,500 franchisees in the United States, over 8,814 restaurants (1,416 company-operated), and 25% of company revenues came from franchise fees based on a percentage of sales. U.S. business accounted for 60% of profits, and it simply had to be bolstered.

Moreover, McDonald's had to consider demographic trends. Hamburger consumption had dropped from 19% of all restaurant orders in 1982 to 17% of all orders in 1990. (Hamburger consumption at *McDonald's* had nevertheless increased over the same time period.) Increasingly, though, consumers were becoming more conscious of nutrition and dietary *options* without compromising taste. The change in dietary preference was, however, certainly not universal, and there was a strong constituency of customers who continued to enjoy McDonald's traditional fare.

The quick-service industry had grown at an average annual rate of 8.7% in the 1980s but was projected only to keep pace with inflation during the 1990s. Perhaps most confusing in its implications, the number of meals eaten off the premises of quick-service restaurants had increased from 23% in 1982 to 62% in 1990. McDonald's responded with double drive-thru windows to keep pace with changing consumer preference, as well as new venues for its restaurants, such as schools, sporting arenas, museums, airports and hospitals. It also developed new smaller restaurants, less expensive than its traditional designs, which could service customers profitably in "seam" areas between existing McDonald's restaurants.

New Competition

The once-simple quick-service market had been complicated by the entry of specialist competitors who had emulated McDonald's strategy to capture their own segment of the market. Michael Quinlan, Chairman of McDonald's, acknowledged just how fierce the competition had become. "Our competition is much tougher, no question about it. And not just in numbers but in quality." McDonald's most menacing competition no longer came from Burger King, Wendy's, or Kentucky Fried Chicken—the traditional rivals.

Chili's and Olive Garden catered to customers searching for full-service and greater variety. Both were family-style restaurants where patrons sat down to be served. Menus offered a wide variety of foods, yet prices remained competitive with those at McDonald's. (See Exhibit 2 for McDonald's menu.) Casual dining restaurants were likely to grow in the 1990s as their most frequent patrons—people between the ages of 40 and 60—increased in number by about 20 million.

Two hamburger chains, Sonic and Rally's, offered drive-through service only and specialized in delivering burgers fast. For four years Sonic sales per restaurant grew an average of 11.3% per annum, and in 1991 alone, sales per unit increased 13%. There were 1,150 Sonic units and 327 Rally's.[4] Taco Bell featured Mexican food and a menu with 26 items under one dollar. Along with Kentucky Fried Chicken and Pizza Hut, Taco Bell was owned by PepsiCo and had seen the greatest increase in sales of any quick-service chain in the late 1980s. By learning from McDonald's, Taco Bell shifted food preparation to outside suppliers, reduced kitchen space in its outlets, and used a cost-based strategy to compete—prices were always kept low. Between 1988 and 1991, Taco Bell served 60% more customers and sales rocketed 63%.

Early Responses from McDonald's

McDonald's drew on its traditional strengths to respond to competitors' challenges and customers' new habits. Careful product development, closely gauged to customer tastes, again formed the focus of attention as McDonald's turned to suppliers and franchisees for assistance. To address concerns about nutrition, McDonald's had introduced salads, chicken, and muffins. In conjunction with Keystone and Auburn University, it developed the first-ever 91% fat-free burger, McLean Deluxe. Keystone also convinced McDonald's to experiment with chicken fajitas, which proved an instant success in initial tests. The chicken arrived precooked and seasoned, so it only required heating and did not slow operations. The fajitas sold

---

[4]Therrien, "The upstarts teaching McDonald's a thing or two," *Business Week,* October 21, 1991, p. 122.

APPROVED NATIONAL MENU ITEMS—Listed on Menu Board—(Effective 6/1/92)

Regular Menu Items

1. Hamburger
2. Cheeseburger
3. Quarter Pounder with Cheese
4. Big Mac
5. McLean Deluxe (and cheese option) (8, 12, 16 oz.)
6. McChicken Sandwich
7. McNuggets—6 piece
8. McNuggets—9 piece
9. McNuggets—20 piece
10. Happy Meal—Hamburger
11. Happy Meal—Cheeseburger
12. Happy Meal—4 pc. McNuggets
13. Filet
14. Chunky Chicken Salad
15. Chef Salad
16. Garden Salad
17. Side Salad
18. Small Fries
19. Medium Fries
20. Large Fries
21. Lowfat Milk Shakes
22. 1% Milk
23. Drink—Child Size (12 oz.)
24. Drink—Small (16 oz.)

25. Drink—Medium (21.9 oz.)
26. Drink—Large (32 oz.)
27. Orange Juice
28. Coffee (8, 12, 16 oz.)
29. Decaffeinated Coffee Fresh Brewed
30. Hot Tea
31. Iced Tea (12, 16, 21.9, 32 oz.)
32. Apple Pie
33. Chocolate Chip Cookie
34. McDonaldland Cookies
35. Sundaes
36. Cones

Breakfast Menu Items

1. Egg McMuffin
2. Sausage McMuffin w/Egg
3. Big Breakfast
4. Hotcakes and Sausage
5. Sausage Biscuit
6. Sausage/Egg Biscuit
7. Bacon/Egg/Cheese Biscuit
8. Breakfast Burrito
9. Hash Browns
10. Apple Bran Muffin (fat free)
11. Cereal (Wheatics & Cheerios)

APPROVED NATIONAL "VALUE MENU COMBOS"—Listed on Menu Board— (Effective 6/1/92)

Regular Menu

1. Big Mac, Lg. Fry, Med. Drink
2. 2 Cheeseburgers, Lg. Fry, Med. Drink
3. Quarter Pounder w/Cheese, Lg. Fry, Med. Drink
ᵃ4. McChicken, Lg. Fry, Med. Drink

Breakfast Menu

1. Egg McMuffin, any size drink
2. Bacon Egg & Cheese Biscuit, any size drink
3. Sausage McMuffin w/Egg, any size drink
ᵃ4. Sausage Biscuit w/Egg, any size drink

ᵃThe #4 position can be used as a flexible option with provided options being McLean DeLuxe, 2 Chicken Fajitas, Filet-O-Fish, or Hotcakes during Breakfast.

EXHIBIT 2 McDonald's Menu: 1992

well in market tests and were soon scheduled for national introduction.

Just as McDonald's had spent five years perfecting its breakfast menu for national roll-out, the company spent seven years developing a pizza suitable for its restaurants. Meticulous product development included design of advanced technology, as it had when McDonald's engineers introduced a special french-fry scoop and a grill that prepared hamburgers in half the time by cooking them on both sides simultaneously. Now McDonald's engineers had invented a pizza oven that could cook McDonald's Pizza in under five minutes. In addition, McDonald's was developing new staging equipment—high-tech temperature and moisture controlled cabinets—that would allow parts of a product to be prepared ahead of time without detracting from food quality. Toasted buns, for example, could be stored in these containers without becoming dried out.

In early 1991, McDonald's returned to a value menu, cutting prices an average 20%. Cheeseburgers sold for only 69 cents and McDonald's Happy Meals™—complete children's meals (sandwich, fries, drink, and toy in a colorful box)—for just $1.99. As a result, sales of hamburgers increased by 30% and customer counts rose. Revenues and profits, however, increased less dramatically.

These initial moves suggested a fundamental tension between McDonald's expanded efforts to provide greater value, on the one hand, and enhanced variety, on the other. As Fred Turner noted, "We're a penny-profit business," and with a value menu, volume was critical. That made the chain's hallmark of speed more vital than ever, yet a wider variety of menu offerings posed the risk of slowing each unit's service. Variety and value had to be carefully balanced. Management's challenge was to sustain McDonald's painstaking attention to products and service in achieving that balance.

FLEXIBILITY AND GROWTH

McDonald's had achieved success by focusing on a simple formula: limited menu, low prices, and fast service. The Golden Arches symbolized a uniform product—primarily burgers, fries, and shakes—delivered in a consistent manner. Whereas uniformity and consistency had formed McDonald's focal point for thirty-five years, the company's new advertising slogan seemed to suggest a subtle yet significant shift: *What You Want Is What You Get at McDonald's Today."* Catering to customers had always been the company's focal point, but to meet changing and divergent customer needs, McDonald's was exploring many different options, and management thought a basic question had to be answered. Would the chain's new concern with flexibility in meeting customers' changing needs require a fundamental change in McDonald's bedrock strategy? Or was this just a new, albeit incredibly complicated, situation once again adaptable to the company's traditional approach?

Early responses to new customer desires and intensifying competition represented just a piece of the company's maelstrom of creative activity. Further efforts were in progress as well. For example, McDonald's had developed a number of new building prototypes, from drive-through-only models to compete with Rally's and Sonic, to small cafes suitable for small towns. Menu diversification offered the greatest area of experimentation. A wide range of items were being tested, including lasagna, carrot sticks, corn on the cob, fruit cups, and oven-baked chicken. McDonald's was also looking for new ways to address nutritional concerns revolving around calcium deficiency and sodium and fat reduction.

McDonald's changes to date had not threatened its traditional operating system, but increased variation throughout the chain—whether in menu offerings, building plans, or eating experience—would pose formidable challenges to McDonald's in maintaining its remarkable quality control and speed of service. The operating system had been constructed to ensure uniformity, quality, and speed at all McDonald's restaurants. If the chain intended to offer a wider variety of foods, such as spaghetti and meatballs or baked chicken, it could disrupt an operating system built around a limited menu.

McDonald's traditional rival, Burger King, afforded an example of the dangers contained in variety. Burger King flame-broiled its hamburgers, which some perceived would be tastier than McDonald's grilled burgers—*if* the flame-broiled Burger King burgers were cooked correctly. But flame-broiled hamburgers were inconsistent in quality and Burger King was not able to implement an operating system that could sustain consistency across all units.

Increasing variety posed another potential dilemma for McDonald's. As the chain responded to pricing challenges from competitors like Taco Bell, higher volume became imperative. To generate higher volume at each restaurant, speed became even more important, and speed could not be risked on a cornucopia of new products. Although the new menu items McDonald's had thus far tested, such as chicken fajitas, had not clogged operations and were well-received by franchisees, McDonald's had to guarantee similar smoothness with some of the more exotic products under consideration, whether chicken, spaghetti, or corn on the cob.

The sheer number of additional products could also detract from the speed of service. McDonald's perfected its operating procedures and equipment in part to accommodate its work-force, whose annual turnover rate was greater than 100% (this was, nevertheless, the lowest in the industry). While McDonald's commitment to training continued to set the industry standard, no McDonald's outlet could afford to engage in complicated preparation processes for new products that might work at cross-purposes with speed of service.

If those challenges did not prove sufficiently daunting to the quick-service giant, it also had to consider restaurant image if it hoped to expand its business through enhanced variety. McDonald's had built its image as the place for hamburgers and quick-service—not for other food and not for casual dining. If people sought Mexican food, they would go to Taco Bell. If people wanted pizza, they would go to Pizza Hut. If they wanted to sit down to a leisurely, reasonably priced meal, Olive Garden, Chili's, Perkin's, TGI Friday's, and Friendly's all came to mind before McDonald's. Not only did McDonald's have to extend its own image, it also had to confront the established reputations of competitors.

These challenges appeared especially troubling because dinner presented perhaps the final frontier of potential growth. Only 20% of McDonald's sales came from dinner, and to entice customers to visit the Golden Arches for dinner required a new menu—as it had for breakfast—and even a different ambience. To defend against competitors, McDonald's could not introduce dinner items one by one. Competitors could tout their specialties and thus respond easily. McDonald's, therefore, had to present an entire dinner menu at once, and the earliest possible date for such a roll-out appeared to be the spring of 1993.

Dinner differed in other ways too. Lunch and breakfast customers were most concerned with speed and convenience, but dinner was more of an event, and customers expected full meals and more complete service. Table cloths and table service, for example, did not seem out of the question. With 62% of 1990 quick-service sales coming from off-premises eating, compared to just 23% in 1982, the trends for lunch and breakfast seemed to be headed in the opposite direction.

While these competitive pressures mounted, a new challenge had been growing: protecting the environment. While many companies had seen the outbreak of environmentalism in the late 1980's as a threat—McDonald's saw an opportunity: the chance of knitting a responsible environmental policy into its evolving operations strategy.

Management considered all of these challenges and knew McDonald's would like to maintain the same core menu, operating systems, and decor. The chain would nonetheless have to allow greater latitude across units and provide a broader variety of products and experiences for the customer. But would there still be such a thing as a standard McDonald's?

STEPPING INTO THE FUTURE: MCDONALD'S AND THE ENVIRONMENT

"We're not wild-eyed zealots who are going to give away the store, but we'll always ask, 'Are we doing the right thing?' And remember, we live where we work, and we care about where we live."—Keith Magnuson, Director of Operations Development.

One recent development proved that there still could be a standard McDonald's, despite the most basic changes in operating procedures. On October 10, 1989, Ed Rensi, president of McDonald's U.S.A., met with Fred Krupp, the Environmental Defense Fund's executive director, at EDF's request. EDF recognized McDonald's substantial existing initiatives in recycling, and its critical role as an industry leader. McDonald's recognized EDF's expertise in solid waste management and the importance of seeking expert opinions.

When McDonald's accepted EDF's suggestion to help assess the company's solid waste stream and explore ways to reduce it, McDonald's was making a bold move. It was engaging a new partner to help address environmental concerns, one aspect of the increasingly complex situation in which the company now found itself. For a private corporation of McDonald's stature to collaborate with an environmental organization entailed significant risk and required a willingness, by both parties, to consider new ways of thinking about operating practices. The partnership, however, turned out to be a noteworthy success, generating advances in areas beyond waste reduction. "We went about finding environmental solutions," commented Bob Langert, "and we discovered efficiencies we never saw before."

THE NEWEST PARTNER: ENVIRONMENTAL DEFENSE FUND

The Environmental Defense Fund (EDF) was founded in 1967 on Long Island, New York, to stop the spraying of DDT, a pesticide which threatened birds by causing their eggshells to thin. By 1990 EDF had become one of the nation's most respected and effective public-interest organizations working to protect the environment. It had over 200,000 members and recorded more than $18.5 million in 1991 revenues. Although most widely known initially for its legal work, especially its suits against private companies and the government, EDF now had twice as many economists and scientists as attorneys on staff. In the 1970s and 1980s EDF produced studies linking sulfur emissions to acid rain, lobbied successfully for legislation reducing the lead additives in gasoline, and designed several water conservation projects. EDF had helped fashion the Clean Air Act of 1990, taking a controversial stand by working with the government to create policy and by recommending market-based incentives to reduce pollution. The organization's sound economic and scientific studies and its practical approach garnered respect from all sides of environmental issues. However, actually collaborating with a private company—especially McDonald's, often referred to as the symbol of today's disposable society by many organizations in the environmental community—entailed tremendous risk and EDF, after all, would take no money from McDonald's. Jackie Prince of the EDF outlined EDF's views:

> Despite all the risks, we felt it was worth it— we *have* to explore a variety of different strategic alternatives and look for approaches which will find solutions and produce results for the environment.

Waste Reduction Task Force

In August 1990, four senior managers from McDonald's joined two staff scientists and an economist from the Environmental Defense Fund to form the Waste Reduction Task Force. In April 1991, the task force released its comprehensive report, which not only covered every aspect of McDonald's solid waste stream but also offered testimony to a successful relationship.

Bob Langert was one of the members of the task force and acknowledged the stereotypic suspicions both sides had at first. Quickly, however, McDonald's and EDF came together and began thoroughly examining solid waste at McDonald's. "We didn't decide to get married on first sight," recalled Langert. "At some point we came together. It was a mating game." To build rapport and gain a true understanding of McDonald's business, EDF participants were given access to all corporate information and even worked in a McDonald's for a day. For its part, McDonald's felt that a separate department dedicated to environmental issues would only belittle the company's efforts, so all environmental initiatives were to be directed through operations development.

The task force designed an action plan that met three criteria. First, the plan was comprehensive, covering all materials and all aspects of McDonald's operations. Second, it offered incremental solutions. "There is no single answer, no grand-slam home run," Langert mused. "While we were looking for this grand solution, though, we grasped the scope of the problem." The task force therefore identified an array of solutions, each complementing the others. Third, the plan made environmental action an ongoing activity at McDonald's: the report outlined areas where McDonald's developed new environmental criteria to be considered on a par with other business considerations. The joint task force delineated 42 distinct initiatives revolving around the environmental hierarchy of reduction first, reuse second, and recycling third. A set of management mechanisms accompanied each initiative to incorporate it into McDonald's standard operating procedures and ensure accountability.

The 42-step waste reduction plan included initiatives such as the introduction of reusable shipping containers and other materials, substantial packaging changes, use of unbleached paper products, new and expanded recycling efforts, composting trials, and employee retraining. Together, these initiatives would cut the waste stream at the chain's 8,500 U.S. restaurants by more than 80 percent.

Through careful study, the task force calculated that each McDonald's generated an average of 238 pounds of on-premise solid waste per day, or .12 pounds per customer. That did not even include the solid-waste generated by take-out customers, who represented 40% to 60% of store business. (See Exhibit 3 for characterization of McDonald's solid waste). Although McDonald's was perceived by some as an environmental demon because its products were all served in disposable containers, the task force determined that 80% of the chain's solid waste was in fact produced behind the counter. Its challenge, as a result, loomed even larger than expected: McDonald's could not simply tinker with the packaging of its products. Whatever course McDonald's pursued, its efforts to reduce solid waste could not disrupt any unit's service, had to involve numerous suppliers, and required sufficient flexibility to accommodate franchisees operating in different regions.

McDonald's sought to set ambitious goals for its franchisees while permitting sufficient latitude

EXHIBIT 3 Summary of McDonald's On-Premises Waste Characterization Study[1]

Over the Counter (OTC)		*Behind the Counter (BTC)*	
	% of Grand Total		*% of Grand Total*
Uncoated Paper	4%	Corrugated	34%
Coated Paper	7%	Putrescibles	34%
Polystyrene	4%	LDPE	2%
Non-McDonald's Waste	4%	HDPE	1%
Miscellaneous	2%	Liquids	2%
		Miscellaneous	6%
TOTALS	21%		79%

Grand Total
238 lbs/day/restaurant
0.12 lbs per customer served

Definitions and Examples

Over the Counter	Waste in the customer sit-down area and from outside waste receptacles
Behind the Counter	Waste behind the register counter, including kitchen and storage rooms
Polystyrene	Hot cups and lids, cutlery, salad containers
Miscellaneous OTC	Condiment packaging
Corrugated	Shipping Boxes
Putrescibles	Food waste from customers, egg shells, coffee grounds, other food scraps
LDPE	Low-density polyethylene film wraps and plastic sleeves used as inner packaging in shipping containers
HDPE	High density polyethylene plastic mostly used for jugs, e.g., syrup jugs
Liquids	Excess, non-absorbed liquids measured during waste audit
Misc, BTC	Durables, equipment, office paper, secondary packaging other than corrugated boxes

[1]Based on a two-restaurant, one-week-long waste audit performed 11/12–11/18/90 in Denver, CO, and Sycamore, IL. Figures have been adjusted to reflect conversion from sandwich foam to paper wraps. Adapted from Page 31 of the Task Force Report.

for each unit to achieve those goals. "We can allow for local autonomy," commented Langert, "as long as we're being as aggressive as possible." It would be left to each franchisee to determine the most viable means for achieving goals. In densely populated states, such as Massachusetts, California, and New York, franchisees might address solid waste issues by relying heavily on recycling. McDonald's units in Texas, on the other hand, might find lower landfill fees and less reason to explore recycling as vigorously, and instead focus primarily on composting.[5] Here too Langert offered a realistic outlook.

> Some percentage of the 42 initiatives will fail. We might not get it right the first time, but we'll test again. Composting may be difficult at first, so we'll learn to develop new packaging that can in fact be composted better.

The task force evaluated possible actions according to their effect on four parties, each considered of equal importance: customers, suppliers, franchisees, and the environment. Shipping pallets provided an example of a transparent change McDonald's made (with minimal impact on operations) and was now encouraging suppliers to make. Standard pallets had been used an average of 1.8 times, creating an expense on two ends: constant replacement and landfill fees. McDonald's adopted a durable pallet that could be used between 30 and 40 times, reducing waste, decreasing costs, and having no effect on operations.

Although the task force sought foremost to reduce the materials McDonald's used and the solid waste generated, it stressed the importance of examining the full lifecycle of all materials. The task force identified ways to reduce environmental impacts arising during initial stages—raw materials acquisition, manufacturing, and distribution—as well as during actual use and handling after use, whether discarded, reused, or recycled. To make sure that recommended actions had a net positive effect on the environment, the task force scrutinized each solid waste reduction option from the perspective of lifecycle assessment (see Exhibit 4).

Brown Bags

The changes inspired by environmental analysis came after deliberation over all the alternatives, deliberation that demanded more than scientific calculation. For example, one supplier presented McDonald's with a bag that was 17% lighter and thus used less material and generated less waste. Another supplier, however, offered a bag containing 65% recycled newsprint, which subsequently led to a bag constructed from 100% unbleached, recycled material—50% post-consumer waste and 50% post-industrial waste. After careful evaluation, the task force recommended the 100% recycled bag, which contained the least amount of virgin material. Because the new bags used unbleached material, they were brown instead of white. Initial customer reaction was tepid, yet the task force discovered in restaurant testing that once consumers understood why the bag looked different, they felt good about it. McDonald's did in fact adopt the 100% recycled bag, suddenly recognizable in its advertising campaign and thoroughly explained in brochures available at each restaurant.[6]

Corrugated Boxes

Corrugated boxes made up one of the two largest components of McDonald's on-premise waste, accounting for 34% of solid waste by weight. Every McDonald's restaurant went through 300 to 400 corrugated boxes per week. As it had done so often in other areas of its operations, McDonald's again turned to suppliers. Boxes contained an average 21% recycled content, but McDonald's commissioned an outside consultant to survey the paperboard industry's capacity to increase that level. Suppliers worried that additional recycled content would weaken the boxes and make them more expensive and heavier. One small supplier, though, approached McDonald's with a new box containing 21% old newsprint. With the consultant's findings and a sample box in hand, McDonald's fixed an ambitious objective of 35% recycled content for its corrugated boxes. In September 1990, McDonald's mandated a 35% level for all suppliers and established a system to monitor and track adherence to this goal. Envi-

---

[5]Composting is a natural biological process. In open-air piles or vessels, microbes break down organic materials into a soil or humus. Organic materials include items such as coffee grinds, eggshells, food scraps, and soiled paper packing.

[6]McDonald's Corporation/Environmental Defense Fund Waste Reduction Task Force, *Final Report,* April 1991, p. 94.

SYSTEM BOUNDARY

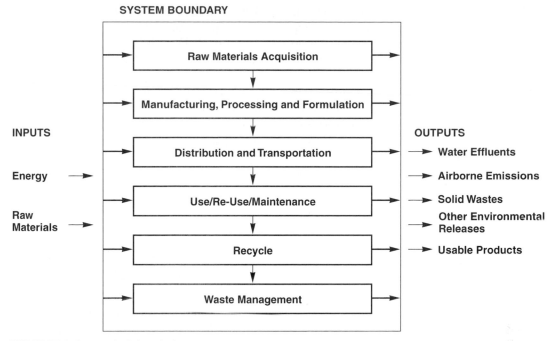

EXHIBIT 4 Scope of a Lifecycle Assessment
Each of the phases of the lifecycle are examined with respect to inputs and outputs, environmental impacts arising from them, and potential improvements that could reduce such impacts.
Source: Society for Environmental Toxicology and Chemistry, "A Technical Framework for Lifecycle Assessment," Washington, DC. January, 1991.

ronmental criteria were now as important as all other criteria in McDonald's review of supplier performance.

By making such challenging demands, McDonald's did more than extend its dedication to quality into the environmental realm. McDonald's created a market for the recycled materials its stores would be generating. And the few McDonald's outlets that had already begun recycling corrugated boxes already realized reductions of $250 to $600 per month on garbage collection.

McRecycle USA

Prior to McDonald's collaboration with EDF, McDonald's had announced its McRecycle USA. program. This program called for McDonald's to spend $100 million annually on using recycled products when constructing, renovating, and equipping McDonald's outlets in the United States. Almost 350 new McDonald's were built every year in the United States, and close to 1,000 were remodeled. Just as McDonald's was doing in mandating 35% recycled content in corrugated boxes, the company was strengthening a market for recycled materials. Over 500 suppliers and manufacturers had already registered to participate in McRecycle USA.

Sandwich Packaging

McDonald's generated tremendous controversy when it decided to abandon the polystyrene clamshell it had been using to package its sandwiches since 1975. But the decision represented the most careful analysis the task force completed on any one issue and perhaps the most environmentally conscientious move McDonald's had ever made. By shifting to quilted wraps, McDonald's reduced the volume of waste from sandwich packaging by 90% and the volume of shipping packaging by over 80%.

McDonald's selected its packaging on the basis of three criteria: availability, functionality, and cost. To be suitably functional, sandwich packaging had to perform highly in four areas. First, it had to provide proper insulation to keep the food warm for a specified time in the holding bin. Second, the packaging had to keep the food tasty and moist without allowing it become either soggy or dry. This was called "breathability." Third, food-packaging was evaluated for its handling ability. Did the packaging sustain product integrity—did it, for example, allow employees and customers to handle the sandwich in a sanitary manner? Fourth, packaging had to meet standards of appearance. It had to permit printing and graphics that would enable crews and customers to recognize the sandwiches quickly.

To evaluate the quality of sandwich packaging, McDonald's conducted a battery of tests. The company measured internal food temperatures as well as temperatures at different time intervals. The company used blind taste-tests and moisture analysis. McDonald's also judged grease resistance, product appearance, locking mechanisms, and folding characteristics. Every form of food packaging came with a set of procedures for wrapping the food and with training materials that connected preparation of the menu item with the appropriate method of packaging.

To these rigid standards the Waste Reduction Task Force added a new set of specifications. Every form of packaging would be evaluated according to the reduction it represented in materials and in production impacts (such as energy use and emissions). Packaging was also judged for its use of reusable material and recyclable material, as well as for its recycled content and use of materials that could be composted.

To improve performance of its packaging, McDonald's had, in 1975, switched from paperboard sandwich packages to polystyrene (foam) clamshells. Contrary to the confusion surrounding McDonald's switch from polystyrene packaging in November 1990, McDonald's did not return to paperboard packages. It introduced a thinner, paper-based wrap, once again making a switch based on performance criteria, which now included environmental standards.

The new sandwich packaging consisted of a three-layered wrap: an inside layer of tissue, a sheet of polyethylene in the middle, and an outer sheet of paper. Unlike paperboard containers, the layered wrap performed as well as the foam clamshells on the traditional packaging criteria and met higher environmental standards: it promised a large reduction in solid waste.

Just prior to the switch, McDonald's had announced an ambitious program to test plastic recycling in conjunction with plastic manufacturers.

The switch from clamshells, therefore, elicited sharp reactions in the media. Immediate response accused McDonald's of pandering to public misconceptions about the environment. McDonald's was accused of exploiting the clamshell's notoriety as an icon of the throwaway society, eschewing the less popular and more difficult solution. "Had we only been out to score with the public," Langert retorted, "we would have returned to paperboard, which is actually worse for the environment but is perceived by the public as preferable to plastic." The analysis of alternative packaging did include an assessment of existing and potential recycling of foam clamshells. (See Exhibit 5 for comparison of sandwich packaging.)

Nonetheless, McDonald's had serious qualms about the switch. Moving away from foam clamshells affected five suppliers, and two in particular felt a significant impact. The company hated to abandon a supplier and wondered how the move might affect its relationships with other suppliers. McDonald's considered those relationships sacrosanct, but relationships with suppliers all revolved around providing the best available product. In fact, it was an existing supplier that approached McDonald's with the layered wrap in the spring of 1990 after two years of preliminary testing.

From the spring of 1990 until the wrap's introduction in November, both the supplier and McDonald's tested and developed the packaging further. When it met standards for heat retention, appearance, moisture control, and waste reduction, the wrap was tested in several McDonald's restaurants on the Quarter Pounder with Cheese.

Meanwhile, McDonald's asked EDF to compare the environmental merits of the new packaging to foam clamshells. The layered wrap promised three areas of reduced waste when contrasted with the clamshell. First, the volume of the boxes in which the layered wrap was shipped paled in comparison to clamshells. Second, production of the wrap entailed less industrial pollution than that associated with the manufacture and handling of polystyrene. Third, the layered wrap was itself of lower volume, so it promised to reduce the impact of waste disposal.

Plans to recycle polystyrene could hope to capture only the foam from products eaten on the premises of a McDonald's, so even if each restaurant could recover every clamshell used on site, that would constitute just a 40% to 50% reduction

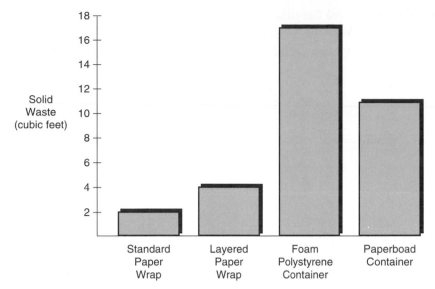

EXHIBIT 5 Total Solid Waste for Sandwich Packaging per 10,000 units

Source: Adapted from "Resource and Environmental Analysis of Sandwich Wraps" by Franklin Associates, Ltd. for Perseco, 1991.

in disposed waste. In contrast, the layered wraps themselves represented a 90% reduction in volume over clamshells. When compared on energy use, air emissions, waterborne wastes, and solid waste generation, the layered sandwich wrap appeared far preferable to polystyrene foam: the wrap required 85% less energy, generated 40% less air emission, produced 80% less discharge into water and 60% less solid waste. (See Exhibit 6 for overall environmental comparison of packaging alternatives.) Despite the clear choice implied by both performance tests and environmental studies, the task-force report carefully described McDonald's switch to layered wraps:

> It is critical to note that McDonald's decision to phase out polystyrene packaging and substitute paper-based wraps cannot be evaluated as a generic "paper vs. plastic" issue . . . Not all plastics or paper materials are created equal. Therefore, the specific nature of the materials involved—their mode of production, their current rate of recycling, and so on—dramatically affects their relative environmental consequences and must be carefully taken into account in any comparison.

PLANNING FOR THE FUTURE

As McDonald's managers reviewed the work of the task force, they wondered what lessons they might draw from the experience with the task force. Had it all been worth it?—or was this just a distraction from the competitive pressures challenging McDonald's as it strived to maintain its growth targets? Was this just a transient issue, like the energy crisis of the seventies, or should it become a primary goal of McDonald's future operations? Throughout the effort, one member of McDonald's top management recalled, McDonald's never forgot its business. "We're in the business of making hamburgers—of serving quality food at a low price. We're not in the packaging business." That business was growing more complex even without the environmental initiative. McDonald's was faced with unprecedented challenges for variety and flexibility in its service. The choices were clear. First, the company could rely on its traditional recipe based on consistency and quality through standardization, one which had made it the paragon of success in the quick-service business. Alternatively, McDonald's could make some changes in its basic strategy—by allowing even more franchisee autonomy and continuing to provide a growing variety of offerings and service in its restaurants. But how far was too far?

On October 1st, 1992, Burger King announced a dinner menu, and that it would begin table service between 5 p.m. and 8 p.m. in its company-owned restaurants.

EXHIBIT 6 Environmental Comparison of Packaging Alternatives

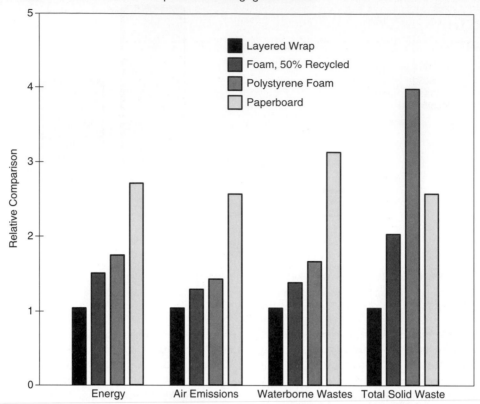

Note: The presentation of data in this chart for 50% recycling of polystyrene foam is hypothetical. Such a rate is far from being achieved anywhere in the US, and therefore represents a highly optimistic assumption — one that is far higher than even the goal of the polystyrene industry itself to be recycling 25% by 1995.

For ease of presentation, impacts are shown relative to the layered wrap, which was assigned a value of 1.0.

Source: Adapted from Waste Reduction Task Force, Final Report, Page 41.

What Really Makes Factories Flexible?

David M. Upton

Manufacturing managers in a broad array of industries agree that achieving low cost and high quality is no longer enough to guarantee success. In the face of fierce, low-cost competition and an army of high quality suppliers, companies are increasingly concentrating on flexibility as a way to achieve new forms of competitive advantage. The flexible factory, they hope, will enable them to respond to customer orders quickly, provide a broad product range, or introduce new products to the range effortlessly. The push to make factories more flexible has been spreading throughout manufacturing and currently is even permeating industries such as chemicals and paper, in which the assumption for decades has been that the plants with the longest production runs are typically the most competitive.

Having acknowledged the importance of flexibility, managers in industry after industry are finding it frustratingly difficult to improve. Some have organized cross-functional teams in the hope that new ways of working will generate greater agility. Many have collectively invested tens of billions of dollars in hardware and software in the hope that computer-integrated manufacturing (CIM) will transform their factories into highly flexible operations. Time and time again, managers have been disappointed and frustrated because they have not understood exactly why enhanced flexibility has eluded them. Was it the degree to which they automated their operations? Was it the software, whose complexity and cost they had underestimated? Or was it the inability of employees to take advantage of the new technologies?

In a quest to help manufacturing managers understand why the improvement of flexibility has been so elusive, I embarked on a study of 61 factories in North America that manufacture fine

Reprinted by permission of *Harvard Business Review*. Article from issue July–August 1995.

paper. At first glance, the paper industry may seem like an unusual starting point for the study of flexibility. It is rarely characterized as flexible and has not, until recently, given high priority to improving flexibility. However, there are some less obvious characteristics that make the paper industry an ideal place to begin.

Unlike most industries in which different plants make different products—and, indeed, in which the same plant may make different products—the paper industry's products are comparable across plants and are always manufactured by the same fundamental process. There are only a small number of ways in which one type of paper differs from another type—the most fundamental being the basis weight, or area density, of the paper. These characteristics, or grades (each particular pulp and weight combination is a grade), are straightforward to measure. Those facts enabled me to develop concrete measures of both the range of products that a given plant could produce and the time it took a plant to switch from making one product to making another product.

My findings turn much of the conventional wisdom on its head. In the plants I studied, there was little direct correlation between the degree of computer integration and the degree of operational flexibility. I found that large plants were not inherently less flexible than small plants. Contrary to what many believe, newer, bigger processes were typically better able to perform quick changeovers than older, smaller machines. And although experienced workers provided powerful advantages in some situations, they impeded a plant's ability to be flexible in others.

The primary revelation of my research concerns the role of people—both managers and operators. The flexibility of the plants depended much more on people than on any technical factor. Although high levels of computer integration can provide critically needed advantages in quality and cost competitiveness, all the data in my study point to one conclusion: Operational flexibility is determined primarily by a plant's operators and the extent to which managers cultivate, measure, and communicate with them. Equipment and computer integration are secondary.

At many of the plants in my study, however, managers embraced computer integration as the solution to the growing need to forge new capabilities. In reality, computer systems were often a quick fix that helped managers avoid the tremendously difficult task of defining precisely what kind of flexibility they required from a plant and then setting goals, revamping measurement and compensation systems, building training programs, and overhauling work practices in order to achieve that flexibility.

To state it simply, most managers put too much faith in machines and technology, and too little faith in the day-to-day management of people.

WHAT IS FLEXIBILITY?

Ten or 15 years ago, quality was much like flexibility is today: vague and difficult to improve yet critical to competitiveness. Since then, managers and academics have studied and experimented with ways to improve quality; as a result, there is currently an enormous variety of quality-improvement techniques and a plethora of textbooks and gurus from which to choose.

Flexibility is only beginning to be explored. If managers aim to improve a plant's flexibility, where should they start? The first problem is one of definition. Flexibility means different things to different people. At the plant level, flexibility is about the ability to adapt or change. But there are many ways to characterize such an ability. One manager might be talking about the cost of changing from one product to the next. Another might be talking about the ability to ramp production volumes up and down to fit the demand of the market. Yet another might be talking about the ability to increase the range of available products. All these abilities might be called flexibility, but they require very different courses of action to develop.

The type of flexibility a given company should emphasize should be determined by its competitive environment. Whether one is referring to products, production volumes, or manufacturing processes, flexibility is about increasing range, increasing mobility, or achieving uniform performance across a specified range.

Product range can mean different things. For example, a plant can have the ability to make a small number of products that are very different from one another, or it can have the ability to produce concurrently a large number of stock-keeping units that are only slightly different from one another.

Mobility means a plant's ability to change nimbly from making one product to making another. It is this kind of flexibility that is associated with quick response times—mobility minimizes the need for long runs and allows production to follow demand without excessive inventory.

Finally, there is uniformity of performance. Plants always have one product that they would much rather make than others because that product maximizes productivity, quality, or some other measure. When a plant moves away from its favored set of parameters, performance falls off. If it falls off steeply, many managers will label the plant inflexible. According to that definition, a flexible plant is one that can perform comparably well when making any product within a specified range. It is this capability that is most important to a full-range manufacturer; the uniformity of performance across the range, more than the size of the range, will protect a plant from cherry-picking predators. Uniformity of performance also applies to production volumes: Some plants are able to work productively over a broad range of output volumes, while others are unable to increase or decrease volumes without incurring considerable penalties.

Once managers have defined the kinds of flexibility they want to develop, they face another set of issues. First, because flexibility is not easy to measure, improvement in flexibility is also difficult to measure. For example, is a plant that can produce 200 different colors of paint 100 times more flexible than a plant that can make 2 products (say, a car and a truck) on the same line? Clearly, simply counting products won't suffice in defining flexibility because it doesn't account for the "differentness" of the products concerned.

Second, the products that a plant actually makes do not necessarily reflect its flexibility. Those products that a plant could make matter, too. For example, a factory can have the flexibility to machine titanium without a chip of titanium ever being cut. Unlike most other sources of manufacturing advantage, such as low cost or high quality, flexibility is sometimes about a potential ability rather than a demonstrated one.

Third, it is often unclear which general features of a plant must be changed in order to make its operations flexible. For instance, many management experts preach that cross-functional empowered teams and computer integration help make plants more flexible. But do they always translate into operational, competitive capabilities that the company can sell? The answer is often no. Similarly, one type of equipment may be capable of making a large range of products, while another may possess quick-changeover capabilities, and both may be called flexible. Yet the latter will be of little value if the market demands great variety. The same holds true for training programs, information systems, incentive schemes, and measurement methods. They, too, must be aligned to provide precisely the form of flexibility that is needed from the overall system. Few factories have actually aligned those elements.

SURPRISING DISCOVERIES

Managers at many of the plants I studied deemed an astounding 40% of flexibility-improvement efforts to be unsuccessful or disappointing. In the vast majority of those cases, the cause could be traced to a failure to identify precisely what kind of manufacturing flexibility was needed, how to measure it, or which factors most affected it.

A paper mill usually consists of a pulp plant, which provides pulp for a group of two to ten converting plants that turn the pulp into paper.

The paper-making process is essentially a water-removal procedure. Water is removed from a pulp slurry by use of gravity, squeezing, and heating. The pulp slurry is laid onto a moving fabric belt from which water drains off. The pulp web is squeezed and heated by a series of rollers until it is strong enough to support its own weight. Further heating then takes place until the paper's moisture content is just below that of the ambient atmosphere. The paper is then collected on a reel and sliced into roll sizes that are convenient for customers and sheeting machines.

By collecting production data and interviewing managers, supervisors, and operators, I was able to measure the breadth of paper grades that each plant was capable of producing and the changeover time that each plant required to switch between grades. In addition, I measured the experience of the workforce by length of service, the vintage of the technology, the level of computer integration, the scale of the plant, and the degree of emphasis that management placed at each plant on various types of flexibility. In order to assess the latter, I asked the shop-floor people responsible for running the plant how much emphasis they thought that managers were placing on a whole range of factors, from safety to quality to the various types of flexibility. (See Exhibit 1, "Plant Flexibility: Factors and Findings.")

I found large differences in the flexibility of the plants. Changeover times varied from one minute to four hours, even for similar types of change on comparable equipment. I found that the potential range of product variation in the plants

EXHIBIT 1 Plant Flexibility: Factors and Findings

Description	Units	Mean	Minimum	Maximum
Changeover times	minutes	15.40	1	240
Range of plant	pounds	64.6	1	161.0
Change frequency	changes per month	29.02	0	500
Date of last major rebuild	year	1973	1919	1991
Width of paper web	inches	159.8	76.0	348.0
Speed	feet per minute	1,466	250	3,200
Net output	tons per day	236.8	18	1,200
Average crew service	years	17.6	1	25
Degree of computer integration (general)	scale of 0.0 to 8.0	5.16	1.83	8.0
Break frequency	breaks per week	16.0	1	60

Note: The data are drawn from a study of 61 fine-paper plants in North America.

differed by a factor of 20. This discrepancy is not surprising given the wide variety in the capacity and vintages of the plants in my study. What is surprising, however, is that very few of my assumptions about the reasons for such disparities—the same assumptions, incidentally, that prevail within the industry at large—turned out to be correct.

First, I found that the degree of computer integration in a plant was not in itself associated with either increased range or improved changeover times. (See Exhibit 2, "Computer Integration Reduces Flexibility.") Indeed, even computer hardware and software designed specifically for the purpose of improving the changeover process, such as automatic grade-change systems, did not decrease the time required to make grade changes in the plants and actually inhibited the ability of plants to produce a broad range of grades. This discovery is especially important because managers often have difficulty justifying computer-integration projects on the basis of cost savings or quality improvements and therefore justify them on the basis of the improved flexibility they will provide.

Second, I discovered that there were no de facto relationships among the various forms of flexibility. In other words, just because a factory is flexible in one way does not mean it will naturally be flexible in others. To explore whether there are generally flexible and generally inflexible plants, I looked at the relationship between two forms of flexibility in each paper plant: its mobility (measured by changeover times) and its range (the breadth of product characteristics it could produce). I found no relationship between the two types of flexibility. (See Exhibit 3, "There Is Little Relationship Between Two Types of Flexibility.")

Third, while there was a clear relationship between the scale of an operation and the breadth of products it could produce (larger plants made a smaller range of product characteristics), I found no clear link between the scale of an operation and its ability to change swiftly between products. Although it is true that the cost of downtime resulting from changeovers is higher in bigger plants (because the lost output and investment involved are much larger), it is also true that the advantages of quick changeovers, which provide the ability to undertake just-in-time production, could be accrued at a proportionately larger scale.

Fourth, workforce experience, an important factor in building flexibility, affected different types of flexibility in different ways. In general, the more experience a workforce had (as measured by length of service), the greater the range of products the plant could make. Surprisingly, however, changeover times, or mobility, were worse in plants with more experienced workforces.

Finally, much of the variance in plant flexibility (both range and mobility) could be explained by managerial action—the extent to which managers emphasized the importance of a particular kind of flexibility to operators—rather than by the structural characteristics of the plant. Plants whose managers had not made flexibility a clearly understood goal were much less flexible than those whose managers had.

EXHIBIT 2 Computer Integration Reduces Flexibility

Plants with more CIM have less range...   **and longer changeover times**

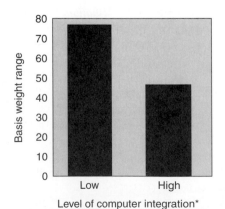

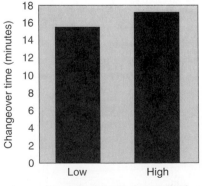

*The data have been corrected for factors other than CIM, such as scale and workforce experience.

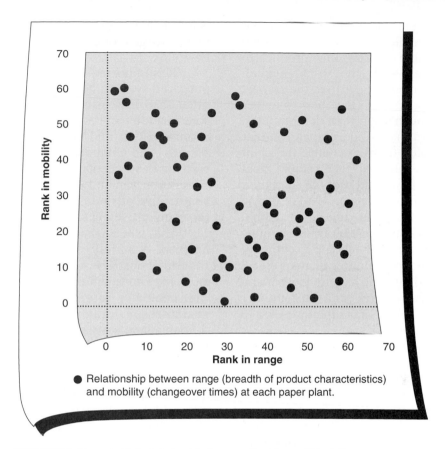

● Relationship between range (breadth of product characteristics) and mobility (changeover times) at each paper plant.

EXHIBIT 3 There Is Little Relationship Between Two Types of Flexibility

THE UNFULFILLED PROMISE OF CIM

Why is it that huge investments in computer-integration systems have failed to increase flexibility? Let's think about how computer integration affects the range of work that a plant can do. Imagine a plant designed to manufacture a range of products. When the process is computerized, any competent engineer will ask, Over what range of conditions should this system work? After the possible operating range has been identified, the engineer will come up with a dollar figure for the computer systems needed to coordinate the process. When the company's manager is taken aback by the price, the engineer will point out that the extremes of the range are pushing up the price. The manager will then decide to sacrifice the extremes on the grounds that they are seldom needed.

But look at what has been given up. Although handling the extremes was difficult when the plant was being operated manually, an experienced and skilled crew could coax a plant to make those products. With the processes computer integrated, the plant runs into the "there isn't a button for that" problem. At such plants, the range of products often fell by 20% to 30% after the mill made a major investment in CIM. What's more, the operator skills required to perform such acrobatics typically atrophied from lack of use.

Some of these problems were recognized 30 years ago when "hard" automation reigned supreme. The hope was that software-based CIM would solve such problems. Although it is true that computer integration may be changed to accommodate new requirements, many companies have been misled by the soft in software. Soft implies easily changeable or malleable. Experience shows that manufacturing-integration software is often anything but. As one manager pointed out, "I'd be better off with a flame cutter and a hacksaw than I would with a team of software engineers. At least I'd be able to see what was taking so long to change."

One of my more surprising findings was that computer integration did not decrease the time needed to switch from making one product to making another one. While the worst manual-change system took much longer than the slowest computer-integrated system, the best manual-change teams were much faster than the computer. Many teams of operators had developed routines and tricks that enabled them to change the plant over efficiently, and the best teams took great pride in the fact that they could beat the computer. "The computer is really slow; it gets kind of boring sitting and watching the plant run, so we figured out a better way to change manually," one young operator in the Midwest said, echoing a sentiment expressed by many people in other plants. "We all practiced and worked out who should do what and when, and now we can always beat the computer and do changeovers more quickly than we used to do them with the computer."

The operators' ability to outperform computers can be explained as follows: One of the primary risks in making any change is that of catastrophic failure, such as a paper break, which is akin to a tool breakage in machining. When the paper running in the machine breaks, it must be rethreaded, which is always time-consuming and expensive. To avoid downtime, the methods for changing between products under computer coordination are conservative. People, however, may be a little more daring. They have access to sensors that are unavailable to computerized systems, such as the sound of the process or the feel of the pulp. Some managers might fear that such practices will result in higher breakage rates and more downtime. My data show that, to the contrary, the computer-integrated systems not only were slower than the manual systems but also resulted in a higher breakage rate in the average plant.

Why would managers invest in such equipment if it is not particularly effective in boosting flexibility? The answer is that they often do not know how effective—or ineffective—it is. In most traditional industries, managers do not routinely benchmark flexibility. While flexibility can provide a powerful means for increasing revenues, most managers still focus on comparing cost figures—if they make any comparisons at all. Even those paper-plant managers who did routinely benchmark flexibility were unable to collect data from a sufficiently large sample of plants; as a result, they were unable to see that computer integration was failing to generate a clear advantage in process flexibility.

It is important to point out that many computerized systems have been installed for reasons other than increasing plant flexibility. Those reasons include facilitating the tracking and delivery of information and improving the quality of the process. And computerized systems used to those ends have succeeded. Judicious use of computer integration can provide valuable new sources of competitive advantage when closely aligned with the competitive needs of the business.

Still, when I have shown my study to managers in a variety of industries, particularly in process industries such as glass, chemicals, and steel, they have sighed. They, too, have discovered that computer integration does not necessarily guarantee greater flexibility. In many cases, the additional complexity resulting from computer integration has been a competitive millstone around their companies' necks, demanding new and expensive skills that have not translated into clear advantages in the market. More data is not the same as more information. Systems often sidetrack manufacturing organizations from the tasks they should be doing well. Many continue to hail computer-integrated manufacturing as a panacea. But unless it is treated as a tool rather than as an end in itself, CIM may exclude most people in an organization from the process of shaping and improving the way the operation runs.

The approach of "investing one's way to flexibility" through computer integration can be damaging in two ways. Not only is computer integration not the panacea for flexibility problems but it also comforts managers with the thought that they are doing something, when all along they should have been doing something else. The implication for managers, as Robert S. Kaplan pointed out in "Must CIM Be Justified by Faith Alone?" (*HBR*, March-April 1986), is that the blanket acceptance of computer-integration projects on the grounds that they will improve flexibility must be replaced with a healthy skepticism.

BUILDING THE RIGHT WORKFORCE

It is not a revelation that people can often become less flexible in their work patterns as they become more accustomed to a particular way of doing their jobs. But my research raises a more complex question. Setting aside work practices, how does experience affect those capabilities that can more directly contribute to a company's success? How does experience affect operational flexibility? While my research shows that a workforce's experience is an important factor in determining the flexibility of an operation, it also shows that experience affects different types of flexibility in different ways: Long service had a positive effect on the range of manufacturable products and a negative effect on the ease with which the plant could switch between those products. This finding makes sense. In order to work on unusual jobs at the extremes of a plant's range, people need experience to know how to get the job done. Experienced people know how to run the plant without breaks when making very thin paper or how to get the paper dry without burning it when making very thick paper.

A few theories could explain why plants with more experienced workforces were less mobile. First, many of the more experienced crews held the view that each individual plant was made to do one thing well and that changeovers that went beyond those established parameters were making improper demands on the plants. Less experienced crews, however, had learned papermaking at a time when flexibility had started to become critical. Many of these crews had developed their own novel ways of making changeovers and saw them as a welcome switch from the tedium of machine tending. In particular, they often viewed change as a defining part of their jobs. I don't think that it is a coincidence that one outstandingly mobile plant had the following rule when selecting its operators (although not its supervisors): You must never have worked in this industry before.

PURSUING FLEXIBILITY

How, then, should managers approach the challenge of making their manufacturing operation more flexible? The first step is to ask, What form of flexibility does the company need from its plants? For example, a manufacturer that wanted to excel at customizing products would need to develop the ability to carry out a large range of jobs in the plant, while one that wanted to use quick response as its primary competitive weapon would need to focus on building quick changeovers into the manufacturing process.

Once they have identified those capabilities, managers must determine the type of workforce or equipment they need to enhance flexibility. For example, the manufacturer emphasizing customized products would require an experienced workforce that could make even the most difficult products. The company hoping to be flexible through quick response would be better off with a workforce less steeped in the traditional ways of operating, a workforce that is ready to adapt to an environment of continuous change.

Next, managers should find ways to measure the type of flexibility sought and should emphasize the importance of those measures to the workforce, letting them make industry comparisons and providing them with incentives to underscore the point. Most managers at the plants I studied were still clinging to measures that had no connection to flexibility. For example, plant managers and their superiors tended to focus on measures that made sense when their plants were big enough to be able to compete on cost: capacity utilization and tons of output per hour. To expect a plant both to be flexible and to continue to focus solely on the utilization of its equipment and the cost of production makes no sense. The plants that were flexible in terms of range and mobility tended to have clear, nonfinancial measures of the flexibility they were trying to develop—changeover times, lead times, or process range.

Training is an important mechanism for building operational flexibility. On the surface, training simply provides the skills people need to carry out new tasks. Its ancillary roles, however, are much more critical. First, training plays an important part in moving people beyond a "this is the way we've always done it" mentality. In industries in which people are trained primarily by serving as understudies to those with more experience, the new mind-set is particularly critical. Second, training builds confidence: Many people in manufacturing are reluctant to try new approaches or techniques because they are afraid of exposing their ignorance. Third, it builds an esprit de corps and helps emphasize the growing competitive need for the right kind of flexible operation—providing a sense of common purpose from a common experience.

Increasing flexibility may be costly in the short run, but it gets easier over time. Plants become more flexible because their managers emphasize the importance of flexibility and because they practice being flexible. A self-reinforcing process then begins. Because such plants are flexible, they are assigned varied and quick-response work, which in turn makes them still more flexible. And just as a plant with mediocre quality can be stretched by challenging it to produce higher-quality goods, previously inflexible plants can be made more flexible by changing the work assigned to them.

Once manufacturing managers have determined the type of flexibility they need, they have to give careful thought to how they will develop that capability. Designing the right mix of machines, computer systems, and people, and figuring out the most effective way to orchestrate them are hard work. But turning only to machines, hardware, and software as the solution will not suffice. People count more than machines.

COMBINING COMPUTERS AND PEOPLE TO BUILD FLEXIBILITY*

Managers and engineers have long preached that computer systems should complement, rather than replace, the skills of operators. In the end, however, most have embarked on a path to computer integration that caused them to place machine over man and resulted in less flexible rather than more flexible factories.

What accounts for the disparity between idea and execution? The problem rests with how—or whether—managers define the type of flexibility to pursue and then choose the appropriate computer systems, work practices, training programs, incentives, and measures. To create a highly flexible computer-and-people-integrated manufacturing system, managers of each individual factory have to come up with their own unique formula. The managers of Mead Corporation's Escanaba Mill, in Escanaba, Michigan, which makes coated fine paper and employs 1,300 people, did just that.

---

*Photos: Jeffery Davis/Black Star.

In the early 1990s, the Escanaba complex, like the paper industry in general, was struggling: The market was in a deep slump, there was a glut of capacity, and price cutting was rampant. To make matters worse, the mill was facing intensifying competition from a growing number of competing mills with bigger and newer machines. Finally, a spurt of imports from Europe raised concerns that foreign producers, which had never posed a threat, might be planning a major assault on the North American market.

Like most of their peers in the paper industry, Escanaba's managers had long believed that the key to competitiveness was to achieve the lowest possible costs through long production runs and few product changeovers. But suddenly many in the industry were forced to rethink those assumptions and look for new ways to distinguish themselves from competitors.

The answer for Escanaba, its managers decided, was to be more responsive to customers than their competitors were. They would accomplish that goal by being highly mobile—able to change production schedules quickly so that they could fill orders much faster than competitors could. At that point, the industry's customers might have to wait as long as two weeks to receive an order, even in slack times. Escanaba's managers set out to slash that time to one or two days.

The new strategy of emphasizing responsiveness demanded a new way of working in the mill: It required faster product changeovers and nimble decision making. When managers analyzed how the mill had been operating, they came to a sober conclusion: The plant was slow in switching from one product to another and in changing schedules to accommodate new customers' requirements. It took too long to execute a production-schedule change, and grade changes often generated product-quality problems or mistakes. They also realized that the plant was not inherently incapable of quick changeovers; changeovers hadn't improved, because improving them had not been a high priority. Managers had been judged primarily on their success in maximizing the mill's capacity utilization and product quality, and they simply focused on long production runs to achieve their performance targets. The long runs meant that operators did not have to learn how to improve changeovers. They also produced a culture that placed very little value on responsiveness to customers. "We make it; you [the sales force] sell it—that's the way the manufacturing people used to see things in this  mill," recalled Henry Swanson, the mill's manager of process control and information.

The mill's managers also realized that computerization in itself was no panacea. Some of the machines in the mill were relatively highly computer integrated. "Even though we had a lot of computers on the plant, sometimes we'd make a couple of hours' worth of production before someone realized that something was wrong," Swanson said. "It was just too easy to trust that the computers had got it right." In addition, the opaque computerized system prevented workers from learning how they might improve operations. So one of the first steps that managers took to transform Escanaba was to rip out the old millwide computer systems. They replaced them with a new system called QUPID (for Quality and Information for Decisions). Unlike the turnkey systems that previously coordinated manufacturing processes, QUPID was custom designed to support operators in each operation; the operators controlled the manufacturing process and would be free to make changes, depending on what they saw happening on the production line. In other words, the system was designed from the outset to help workers make better decisions rather than to cut them out of the decision-making process.

To that end, the mill's managers insisted that operators be intimately involved in the system's design and development. "If the previous system taught us anything, it taught us that we didn't want black-box computer integration that only the vendor really understood," said Glendon Brown, the mill's vice president of production technology. "We needed an architecture that we were part of and that was much more open and easy to change."

Rather than depending on a single supplier, the mill bought the system's building blocks from several different sources. There were two fundamental criteria for choosing those sources: Each had to be a leader in its area of expertise and be willing to customize the system for Escanaba.

Significantly, Escanaba designed the system's interfaces in-house. Each function designed its own interface to ensure that its people got the information they felt they needed to do their jobs and in the format that was easiest for them to understand. "If we were going to succeed in the longer term, we needed the ability to make changes 24 hours a day, seven days a week—times when most managers aren't around," Brown said. "We needed to provide useful information to our operators at the lowest level in the organization, so that they could make decisions."

The mill also overhauled its training programs. But it took several attempts before managers hit on the right approach. First, Mead made a common mistake: It used technical people to explain to the operators how the new computer systems worked. "It was a disaster," Swanson said. "The technical guys knew too much about the systems and told people more than they needed to know about technical issues and not enough about the business issues and why we needed to work differently."

The mill's managers dropped that program. In its place, they created one designed to help workers understand what they had to do to satisfy customers. The program explained why quick changeovers were critical to the mill's long-term success. And it emphasized that the systems were only a tool to help them perform their jobs better. Operators who had long assumed that keeping the machines running was all that mattered began to look at their work differently.

That program has since evolved. Originally, a professional trainer conducted classes in a seminar-like setting. However,  managers came to believe that learning and training should be part of all their employees' jobs. With that goal in mind, managers trained a team of the mill's supervisors and operators to teach others on the floor and in classrooms.

The result of the training program is a plant that now excels at learning. Armed with an intimate knowledge of different jobs and their challenges, the new trainers have played an instrumental role in helping operators become increasingly adept at carrying out quick changeovers and responding to the demands of new customers. Operators are no longer mere machine tenders.

Managers also wisely realized that the mill's measurement and incentive systems had to bolster its new strategy. Accordingly, measures and incentives aimed at maximizing capacity utilization and output and minimizing costs have given way to measures and incentives aimed at maximizing responsiveness and customer satisfaction.

Each year, the mill surveys customers to identify what it is doing well and how it needs to improve. Using the survey, a

team drawn from managers and employees throughout the mill then generates specific operating goals. For example, the team might challenge Escanaba to reduce changeover losses by 25% within six months. (This kind of focused goal is much more effective than simply declaring, like managers at all too many factories still do, "We should strive to improve flexibility.") The compensation of managers and superintendents is based on the mill's success in achieving those goals.

The results have been astonishing. The mill's responsiveness and customer satisfaction have increased dramatically. In 1993, it sold the most paper in its history. Escanaba is now the most productive mill in Mead's fine-paper group and has dramatically increased its market share. By emphasizing

what workers need to do and providing them with the information they need to do it, Mead has proved that a factory can increase flexibility and, at the same time, boost productivity and lower costs. It's just a question of figuring out precisely what kind of flexibility one wants to achieve and giving people the support they need to achieve it.

BUILDING FLEXIBILITY YOU CAN'T SELL

When factory managers don't carefully assess their strategies before embarking on a flexibility program, the results can be competitively destructive. One U.S. mill, which I'll call Kildare, had just such an experience. A complex equipped with medium-size paper machines, Kildare made relatively high-volume fine papers and employed about 1,500 people.

In the early 1990s, Kildare's markets were in the grip of a severe slump, and mills with giant, lower-cost machines had come to dominate the business. With Kildare losing market share and struggling to stay in the black, its managers soberly concluded that they could not stand still and wait for the market to rebound. Several competitors had launched reengineering programs aimed at improving their responsiveness, that is, their ability to fill customers' orders quickly. Deeply worried, Kildare's managers decided that they had better follow suit and began to reengineer the order-to-delivery process to make the mill even more responsive than the competition.

To that end, the mill created a training program to teach operators the skills that would enable them to make the swift product changeovers required by the new strategy. In addition, the computerized recipes and other procedures used to produce each grade of paper were carefully documented and routinized. The only aspect that management overlooked was the measurement and reward system, which continued to focus on the plant's capacity-utilization rate. Delivered in the form of praise and criticism as well as pay, the message to supervisors was to keep utilization high. With its emphasis on fewer and longer production runs, that message flew in the face of management's contention that responsiveness was now what mattered most.

Nevertheless, by mid-1993, after an intense, year-long effort, Kildare had cut its lead times in half and had achieved its target of becoming world class in responsiveness. But managers then made a painful discovery. The mill's vastly improved responsiveness had enabled it to hold on to existing customers, who were delighted by Kildare's ability to fill their orders more quickly. But for two reasons the mill had not been able to increase its market share or sales significantly. First, competing mills had made similar strides, and many of them had the advantage of bigger machines. Second, there was simply not enough business in Kildare's particular market.

Kildare's managers realized that they would have been better off had they focused on expanding the range of products that the mill made. A series of opportunities to make a challenging array of relatively high-volume products that were outside the mill's traditional product range sparked the epiphany. The main opportunity was a chance to supply papers to be used to make lottery tickets sold in Central America. The papers had to be difficult for would-be counterfeiters to forge, yet cheap and sturdy.

Kildare's experienced crews were able to manufacture these difficult products. But they found that the systems and procedures installed to improve responsiveness, which assumed a core set of standard, unchanging papers, were a hindrance. For example, the emphasis on perfecting a routine and documenting the procedures and computerized programs for making each paper grade was counterproductive when no two orders were exactly alike and when success depended on excelling at figuring out how to make a particular order during trial runs rather than on delivering that order quickly. In other words, the systems and procedures designed to make the plant more responsive discouraged the development of the skills required to excel at experimentation. Conversely, the trial runs, whose duration was impossible to predict, produced the kind of constant scheduling headaches that one tries to minimize or eliminate if responsiveness is the top priority.

About six months after managers had targeted the new markets, they finally recognized the problem and dismantled many of the changes they had instituted to increase the mill's responsiveness. For example, operators no longer have to enter the programs for making every paper grade into the computer that controls production. Other practices introduced to improve responsiveness—for example, a streamlined order-processing system—did not have to be dismantled.

In addition, the mill changed its measurement and reward system to relax pressure on operators to keep the machines running and make fast changeovers. As a result, although responsiveness is no longer the top priority, Kildare has been able to hang on to its traditional customers and win new ones. The mill's sales and profits are soaring. Admittedly, the end of the industry's recession is one reason for its success. But, more important, the mill now excels at a type of flexibility that it can sell.

Stermon Mills Incorporated

As he sat at his desk, waiting for the improvement team to arrive, Stan Kiefner, President and CEO of Stermon Mills, stared blankly at the letter in front of him. The letter was from Pete Cushing of the Renfield Consulting Group:

10/1/92

Dear Stan

I have given a lot of thought to our conversation of last Friday. Having looked at the latest price figures and the projections for the next five years, I would say that I have to agree with you: Stermon is unlikely to be competitive on the basis of cost without an investment in a new, state-of-the-art paper machine. Given the over-capacity projected for the industry, and the $500m cost—I'd say you have to find an alternative! Stermon just can't keep chiselling on price. In my opinion, the only way to maintain and grow your customer base is to offer something the bigger companies can't—you have to become more flexible than the competition.

. . . .

The letter confirmed what Kiefner already knew. It was no longer possible for Stermon to match the price being offered by the large mills for commodity grade paper (see Exhibit 1). With the huge economic rewards available to large scale technology in paper-making, Stermon's small machines simply cost too much to run for the output they produced. Since he left Boise Cascade in 1990, Kiefner had known Stermon was headed for trouble without some dramatic changes. But it was only recently, as the real price of Xerox grade paper hit a twenty year low, that the urgency of the situation had become clear.

If it was to continue to be viable, in both the short-term and the long-term, Stermon had to be-

come more flexible. Kiefner had put together a team of his best managers to look at the problem. He had asked the head of the team, Bill Saugoe, to put together a two-year flexibility improvement plan, which would specifically address the competitive problems facing Stermon, and detail the steps which needed to be taken in order to make Stermon flexible.

EXHIBIT 1 Monthly Statement of Income for Machine 4: September 1992

Item	$ per Ton
Gross Sales—Paper	**769**
Freight & Other	(79)
Net Sales—Paper	**690**
Variable Costs	
Wood	58
Purchased Pulp	125
Chemicals and Additives	94
Electricity	28
Fuel	54
Other Materials	29
Total Variable Cost	**390**
Variable Contribution	300
Fixed Costs	
Mill Operating Labor	99
Mill Maintenance Labor	36
Contractor Maintenance	22
Maintenance Materials	27
Operating Supplies	19
Mill Supervision	17
Mill G & A—Salaries	6
Mill G & A—Other	16
Depreciation/Amortization	78
Insurance and Taxes	12
Total Fixed Cost	**332**
Total cost of goods sold	722
Income—Paper operations	(32)
Non operating income (expense)	(2)
Net Income	**(34)**

This case was prepared by David M. Upton. Copyright © 1992 by the President and Fellows of Harvard College. Harvard Business School case 693-053.

Kiefner was unsure about the whole business. It was a lot easier to work on costs, he thought. You could count dollars after all. But flexibility was a different matter. How could they improve something if they weren't really clear what it was? How could they measure their competitors' performance? How would they even know if they had improved? This was not going to be easy.

Kiefner sat back, and waited for Saugoe's knock at the door.

THE STERMON STORY

Stermon Mills Incorporated was a small, independent fine-paper producer. It was founded by Tom Brasker, a second-generation Scot, in 1910. Located in the town of Fond du Lac, in Northern Minnesota, Stermon's (single) paper mill was a collection of some twenty buildings, housing one pulping plant and four paper machines of varying vintages (See Exhibit 2). The oldest (#1) was the original machine installed when the company was founded. Though a giant in its time, it was now the smallest machine in the plant and was affectionately known as "Little Jack."

Stermon had added two additional machines in the 1950s—#2 and #3 machines were also the giants of their day. The #4 machine had been added in 1976 and was the largest machine on site: 186" wide, it ran at a speed of 1700 feet per minute (about 20 miles per hour). Total output from the site was 570 tons of paper a day, with 280 tons of that being produced on machine #4 (see Exhibit 3).

The company's major products had always been uncoated wood-free papers (see Exhibit 4). This market was dominated by the demand for Xerographic paper, although many other papers were produced in the general category of uncoated fine paper. For example, Stermon also made book paper and paper for writing tablets. Coated papers required extensive additional coating equipment, while mechanical papers could not be produced in Stermon's pulping plant. For this reason, Stermon restricted itself to the production of uncoated fine papers.

Uncoated fine paper was differentiated from other types of papers by both its end uses and its manufacturing process. The primary end uses were printing and writing, and included, for example, the paper on which this case was printed. The end uses

EXHIBIT 2 The Stermon Plant in Fond du Lac

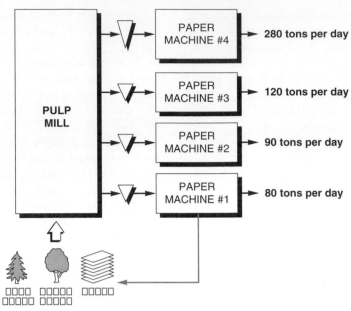

EXHIBIT 3 Schematic of Fond du Lac Plant

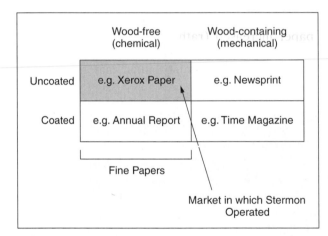

EXHIBIT 4 Types of Paper and Pulping Processes

could be categorized into four segments: publishing (books), commercial printing, office/business (computer printers and copiers), and writing. Such papers varied from each other in a number of ways. First, and most important, was the basis weight of the paper. Paper could vary in area density from 15 lbs per unit area to 100 lbs per unit area in Stermon's plant. Xerox paper weighed 20 lb per unit area. Second, paper could include different proportions of chemicals in the pulp that was used. This was called the furnish. Third, paper

could be dyed in order to produce different colors of paper. Colored paper was made only on the smaller machines. The machines required a lengthy wash down after each run of paper and few companies could afford to keep their larger machines idle for this task—Stermon was no exception.

MAKING PAPER

The first step in making paper and paperboard, after the wood was cut, involved "pulping." This process refined the wood so that only the cellulose, the substance required in paper, remained. Wood consisted of approximately 50% fiber, 30% lignin, a tough, resinous adhesive that gave structural support to the tree, and 20% extractable oils and carbohydrates. During pulping, the cellulose fiber was separated from the other components so it could be processed further; pulping could be done either mechanically, by grinding the wood, or chemically, by boiling the wood with chemicals. Although newsprint manufacturers relied on mechanical pulping, the grinding process broke the cellulose into shorter fibers when tearing them apart and left some lignin in the resulting pulp. This created a weaker paper that turned yellow more quickly. Only products with less rigid quality requirements—newspapers and telephone books, for example—used mechanical pulp. Unlike mechanical pulping, which used 90–95% of the wood harvested, chemical pulping used 45–50%. Chemical pulp yielded 1.25 tons of paper per ton of pulp because inert "fillers" were added in the process.

When transformed into fine paper—the bright white type used in business and printing—chemical pulp went through an intermediate step: bleaching. Bleached pulp allowed producers to make a strong, bright paper that did not discolor during storage or when exposed to sunlight. It thereby satisfied the needs of paper products with high demands for purity, brightness, and permanence. Once the pulp was bleached, it was processed into "stock": a suspension of fibers and additives in water. Individual fibers of pulp were suspended in water and then "beaten" and refined to produce fibers with the proper characteristics of length, flexibility, surface area, and density. Chemicals could then be added to the stock: rosin, aluminum sulphate, or synthetics to reduce absorbency for writing papers; starch to add strength; dyes for colored paper. At the end of this process, stock could be made into a sheet of paper.

To produce a finished sheet of paper, a paper machine had to remove water from the stock—between 100 and 500 tons of water for every ton of pulp. Water was removed by three methods in sequence: first by gravity, second by squeezing, and finally by heating. In the "wet" end of the paper machine, the stock was deposited on a "wire"—a continuous belt of mesh material—with inclined blades of metal or plastic ("foils") underneath it, the wire drained the water from the stock. From the end of the wire, what was now a fragile paper web moved into the presses. Protected from above and below by continuous belts of felt, the paper moved through rollers, which pressed the sheet and drained water into catch basins (so the water could be used again). The paper web then travelled to the "dry" end of the paper machine. There the paper crossed double rows of steam-heated, cast-iron cylinders, again held by felt belts.

In the calender section, the paper was pressed further, as a set of hardened cast-iron rollers improved the surface-finish of the paper. From there the paper was wound onto a steel spool. In the final step of making paper, broadly called "finishing," large reels of paper were rewound into smaller reels, some were made into stacks of sheets (reams), and the paper was in-spected. Fine paper, once inspected and packaged, was sold to merchants, who supplied end-users, or directly to the users themselves.

THE NORTH AMERICAN FINE PAPER INDUSTRY

Land of the Giants

The North American market was the world's largest consumer and producer of uncoated fine paper. In 1989, the North American market accounted for an estimated 45% of the world's uncoated fine paper capacity, and 44% of the world's consumption. Almost all of the demand for uncoated fine paper in North America was met by domestic (US and Canada) production. Exports and imports were not significant (around 5%) but had been growing spasmodically in recent years in top-end (high quality coated) and bottom-end (commodity uncoated) fine papers.

Despite industry fears to the contrary in the late 1970s, growth in demand for uncoated fine paper increased (rather than abated) because of information processing in the office/business segment. Since 1982, U.S. uncoated fine paper shipments had increased at 4.7% per year compared to 3.8% per year for the other three paper classifications. However, the strong growth in demand for uncoated fine paper during the 1980s had contributed to the industry's reduced profitability in the early 1990s. Significant capacity expansions to meet projected long-term demand, combined with the softening of demand during the 1989–92 recession, had led to excess capacity and depressed prices. It was generally agreed that real prices for fine paper were currently the worst the industry had seen for many years.

International Paper was the world's largest paper company with sales totalling $12.96 billion in 1990. Uncoated fine paper accounted for about 18% of International Paper's total sales. The company was a full line producer of uncoated fine paper, possessing well known brands such as Hammermill and Springhill reprographic, printing, envelope and tablet papers. A survey among users of laser paper showed that Hammermill had a 30% brand preference compared to 12% for the next leading competitive brand. Georgia-Pacific was the world's second largest paper company after its acquisition of Great Northern Nekoosa (GNN) for $3.7 billion in March, 1990. In 1990, Georgia-Pacific had sales totalling $12.67 billion. The GNN acquisition not only strengthened Georgia-Pacific's full line of uncoated fine papers, but also added paper distribution and envelope converting businesses. With the mid-1991 start up of a new 290,000 metric tons per year machine at Ashdown, Arkansas, Georgia-Pacific matched International Paper's uncoated fine paper capacity of 1,905,000 metric tons per year.

For the other top ten producers of uncoated fine paper [Exhibit 5], the production and distribution of printing and writing papers (including uncoated fine paper) accounted for a significant percentage of their total sales. For example, the proportions for Champion International and Boise Cascade in 1990 were 40% and 53% respectively. The other producers competed primarily on the basis of having focused product lines, providing product and service flexibility, and/or owning channels of distribution. For example, Domtar, Canada's leading producer of fine papers, had its own distribution company and was developing a

niche in the recycling and brokerage of waste paper. Paper companies that had a distribution company often needed to complement their limited product lines by carrying products made by other paper manufacturers.

Recycling

The most important change in the market for fine papers had been the growing emphasis on recycling. The very visible problem of the disposal of solid waste, of which, in the United States, 41% is paper and paperboard, had spurred businesses and governments to demand fine papers that contained significant amounts of recycled fiber. Unfortunately, the demand for recycled fine papers was not being adequately met because of a limited supply of suitable waste paper. The traditional sources of suitable, or high grade de-inking waste paper, such as printing and converting waste, were already being heavily exploited. The current North American recovery rate for these pre-consumer waste sources was about 85%. The largest untapped source of high grade de-inking waste paper was office/business waste. However, this source

EXHIBIT 5 The Top Ten North American Producers of Uncoated Fine Paper

Company	Annual Capacity (000 Metric Tons)	Market Share (%)
1. International Paper (U.S.)	1,905	14.6
2. Georgia-Pacific (U.S.)[a]	1,905	14.5
3. Champion International (U.S.)[b]	1,112	8.5
4. Boise Cascade (U.S.)	1,093	8.3
5. Union Camp (U.S.)[c]	816	6.2
6. Weyerhaeuser (U.S.)[d]	694	5.3
7. James River (U.S.)[e]	662	5.0
8. Domtar (Canada)	590	4.5
9. Mead (U.S.)	472	3.6
10. Willamette (U.S.)	435	3.3

[a]New 290,300 metric ton per year machine at Ashdown, AR, started up mid-1991
[b]Year-end 1990 capacity
[c]New 226,800 metric ton per year machine started up at Eastover, SC, mid-1991
[d]Include Prince Albert Saskatchewan.
[e]Includes carbonless base stock

Market share of top five companies:	62.3%
Market share of top ten companies:	77.0%
Total 1991 North American capacity[f]	13,149 million metric tons

[f]Includes all other companies

was limited due to logistical and technical difficulties. The logistical challenge involved the setting up of efficient and low cost collection programs for offices and businesses. The technical challenge was twofold. The first was controlling the variety of contaminants in the office waste. The second difficulty was the inability of current de-inking technology to remove key contaminants such as xerox and laser print.

These challenges had major implications for both consumers and paper companies. Consumers would assume a critical role in shaping not only the demand, but also the supply for recycled fine papers, since they would be generating and sorting the raw material to be used in the manufacture of the product. For paper companies, it was clear that the distribution of fine papers to businesses might become increasingly tied to the collection of high grade de-inking waste from those businesses.

STERMON'S INTEGRATED MILL

Plants in the industry were either "integrated" or "paper only." Integrated mills, like the one in Fond du Lac, had a pulp plant on site, while "paper only" mills had to ship in dried pulp from outside. Because of the cost of drying and transporting pulp, modern mills tended to be integrated, and only a few specialty mills now ran without pulping capacity on site. Larger pulp facilities were very much more efficient than smaller ones and the output of even a modest modern pulping plant exceeded the requirements of the world's largest machines [Exhibit 6]. Because of the disparity in minimum efficient scale between pulp plants and paper machines, integrated mills usually included a central pulp plant feeding three to six paper machines on the same site (see Exhibit 3). Plants were almost always located near a plentiful supply of both water and trees. Two types of tree were used to make fine paper. Pine trees supplied long-fiber pulp for strength, while deciduous trees supplied short fiber pulp for smoothness and consistency. For this reason, there were paper plants in both the North and South of the USA. Plants in the North shipped in short fiber pulp, while southern plants shipped in the faster growing long-fiber. The ideal recipe for paper was around 50% of each type of pulp.

Plants within Plants

The four paper machines at Fond du Lac were like factories within factories. Each was housed in its own building, and was supplied with pulp through pipelines from the pulping plant. The huge buildings were old and splattered with dried pulp, particularly those housing the older machines.

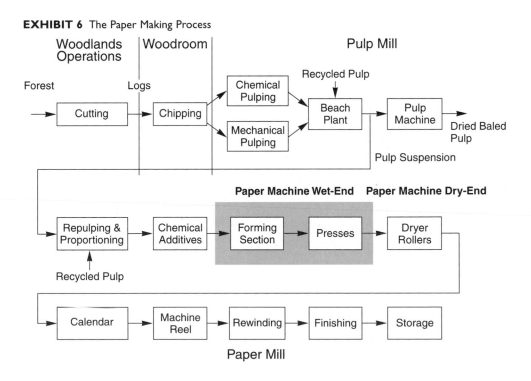

EXHIBIT 6 The Paper Making Process

Each machine operated three shifts a day, seven days a week, with a two-week shutdown in the summer for maintenance. About 30% of the hourly workers in the plant worked in maintenance. The remaining direct operators worked in the pulping, paper-making, reeling/winding and shipping areas.

Each machine required between four and six operators to run. Operators' tasks were ranked: from machine tender (the highest rank) to spare hand (the lowest). Movement through the ranks was strictly by seniority, and a bright young addition to the shop floor staff at Stermon could look forward to being a machine tender after about fifteen years of service. The average length of service of the machine tenders in the plant was 24 years. While there were often disagreements within a shift on any machine, a shift formed a tight cluster of people who knew each other well, and had to solve problems arising on their machine, day and night. In keeping with the tradition of the paper industry, the key measure by which operators were judged was the utilization of the machines. Lew Frowe was a back-tender on #4 machine:

> There has been a big push recently on improving safety in the plant. A few weeks ago, a guy got caught in a storage tank when it filled with pulp: he died. We have far too many accidents. We've also had management pushing us on quality. Seems like whatever we do it isn't good enough. When all's said and done though, there's only one thing that really counts: "Tons is King" is what everyone knows in the paper industry. You try to get lots of other things right, but if you don't make your tons, your neck is on the block.

Stermon's hourly workers belonged to the United Papermakers Union (UPU). Disputes were frequent (274 recorded in 1991 alone), and in two-thirds of cases centered around overtime allocation. Senior union members were supposed to take precedence for being allocated overtime, though management would often try to circumvent this rule. However, the most troubling disagreement for the plant's management concerned the demarcation of functions. Dave Yarrow, the pulp plant manager, commented:

> Let's take unloading as an example. Pumping chemicals off a tanker coming into the rail yard is a pretty straightforward job. Here, it needs two people. You need a pipefitter to connect up the coupling, but you need a materials handler to actually turn the valve! It sounds ridiculous and it is, but it's true! The

two of them have to sit there like twenty buck an hour hatstands while they watch the tanker empty.

Employee turnover was low in the plant—Stermon was by far the highest paying employer in the area, and the union protected its employees well. There was a long waiting list for jobs at the plant. "You've got to wait till someone dies!" commented Frowe.

Machine operations had been dramatically altered in the 1980's when digital control was added. Rather than running around the plant altering the speed of drives manually, the operator of the machine used computer control, operated from a central cab mid-way down its length. A graphical display showed the condition of almost any motor or valve on the equipment. Stermon had found that computer control greatly improved utilization as the computer was able to adapt quickly to slight changes in input materials without production problems. While the computer system on machines 3 and 4 allowed grade changes to be carried out automatically, operators on machine 3 claimed that the computer was far too slow, and changed grades manually by altering valves and drive speeds. The most common type of grade change was a simple change in basis weight—the most important way in which one type of fine paper differed from another.

> The computer never quite does it right—but it never messes up too bad either. We just let it take the reins in the middle of a run. For grade changes though, we prefer to do it on our own. (Back-tender, machine 3)

The smaller machines carried out four or five grade changes within a day, but machine 4 averaged one grade change a day, because of the high cost of having it not producing paper. Each machine ran on a two week cycle, and progressed up and then down the basis weight range for the machine, changing furnishes as it went. The order was important, since gradual grade changes kept the paper-making process more stable than large shifts. The machines stayed on each grade for a varying length of time depending on the orders for that particular grade.

SELLING THE SHEET

Sylvia Tannar had worked in the sales department at Stermon for almost fifteen years. "We've seen slumps before," said Tannar, "but never one as bad as this. We've got guys in this plant who say their fathers don't even remember it being this tough. Paper prices are through the floor. 20 lb Xerox paper has been selling as low as 650 bucks a ton. We can't even get close to that!"

In 1991, three new uncoated fine paper machines came on line in the United States. Georgia Pacific, Union Camp and Boise Cascade all introduced state-of-the-art machines running at 4000 fpm, producing 850 tons per machine each day. All three were focused on 20 lb Xerox paper, with occasional runs of 18 lb or 24 lb. These gargantuan new machines took advantage of the tremendous economies of scale in the technology. Paper machines had consistently grown in size and speed since the early twenties. With each new machine introduced into the industry, its owner hoped to grab greater economies than competitors, and win out on price or margins. Each of the 1991 machines cost $500m. Historically, the big companies had often invested in new capacity at about the same time, each seeing the same window of opportunity. This magnified the already cyclical nature of the paper industry and 1991 saw the biggest capacity glut the world had ever seen. Fine paper prices fell from $950 per ton in 1988 to $650 per ton for comparable grades of paper in October, 1992.

While such prices were hurting Georgia Pacific, Boise Cascade, and Union Camp, they were devastating to a small company like Stermon, which lacked the scale economies of the bigger machines. "We've had to find new ways to win orders," noted Tannar. One way Stermon had kept machine 4 busy was to begin making grades which were lighter and heavier than were usually made on the machine. "We might not be able to run flat out on one grade," said Tannar, "but we can try to keep busy by selling some cats and dogs at the ends of the range. People can come to us for stuff they can't buy elsewhere."

Forty-two percent of Stermon's paper went to paper merchants, who sold their paper to converters. Converters turned the paper into envelopes and forms. In the last two years, merchants and other customers alike had shown an increasing reluctance to carry inventory, pushing the inventory back into the struggling paper plants. "They want it Just-In-Time or not at all," complained Tannar. "I never thought I'd see the day when this JIT business would hit a process industry, but it's here.

If we don't deliver in bits and pieces, we lose the business. It either ends up with us carrying the inventory, or pushing really short runs onto the machines. The manufacturing guys hate it—but what can we do?"

ARE WE A CESSNA OR A 747?

Together with the other five members of his crew, Charley Jonn was responsible for keeping #4 machine running. Jonn had worked the night shift tending machine 4 for 21 years.

> There's been a lot of pressure around here lately. I usually get in around 10ish, and deal with whatever problems the late shift has left me with. I set the machine back in trim: Hank on the last shift never does set it on its sweet-spot. Then, I start to take a look at any changes coming up in the schedule.

The paper machine operator's job was essentially one of monitoring the machine, keeping an eye open for equipment problems and making changes in paper grade from the control booth at the center of the machine. Operators generally liked to keep a machine stable, running on one grade. This gave the process stability and avoided a common but catastrophic source of failure—a paper break. As the name suggested, a paper break occurred when an instability in the process or some impurity in the web caused the paper running in the machine to tear. Paper tangled everywhere and the machine would shut down while the web was re-threaded. This meant having the whole crew clamber over the machine, tearing out paper. One intrepid member would throw the leading edge of a new web into the machine while precariously balanced between two rollers. It took anything from 10 minutes to 8 hours to repair a break, during which time production was at a standstill. Breaks were much more likely with thin papers and unfamiliar grades. Curiously, they seemed to occur much more often at the beginning of a shift than any other time.

Jonn threw his hands up in despair at the increasing frequency of grade changes the crew was being asked to make.

> A big paper machine is like an airliner. It takes time to get up in the air and time to come down. If you want to do small hops, you go in a Cessna not in a 747. This paper machine was made to stay in one spot. We lose 30 minutes of production time every

time we change grades. That might be OK on machines 1,2 and 3 but this is a high output machine and we lose a lot of output in 30 minutes. I know that times are hard, but if you're always changing over, you never have time to make paper.

> We're all measured on output. The bottom line is and always has been tons per day. You don't make your tons—you've got problems, so we're really careful when we change grade. We're careful and we try to get it right.

Even so, time lost due to grade changes had almost doubled from 6% in the early 1970s to 10% in 1992. On average, #4 machine was making twice as many changes as it had in 1990, and productivity was suffering. "It's bad enough as it is, without losing all this time and making all this broke[1] changing grades."

Quality

"We've always prided ourselves on making a real quality product," noted Lars Robikoff, superintendent of machine 4, "but some of the problems we've been having recently have really taken us by surprise." A large piece of holed paper pinned to the wall was testament to this. "This hole cost us $5,981.28" said the felt-penned inscription.

> It's only in the newer grades—we're so used to making 20 lb, that we make a mistake here and there on the heavy stuff and the light stuff. Customers are coming back screaming at us—you can't blame a printer for crying out when he's got a web with holes the size of lumberjack's thumbs breaking in his press.

Stermon relied heavily on sampling inspection to insure the quality of the product shipped. Inspectors would check for moisture content, ash content, color and a host of other features. Any discrepancies would be reported back to machine operators, who would take the appropriate action. Product quality was also monitored continuously by computer on machine 4—even so, the occasional problem slipped through the net.

Robikoff attributed the quality problems to the instability in the paper making process, due to the higher frequency of changes and the "odd" pa-

pers which were becoming more common. He was nevertheless optimistic.

"All of these changes have to end soon. Once business picks up again we'll be back making one or two grades I'm sure—It'll be the same as it was before."

NO PAPER TIGER

"I don't think it's ever going to be the same as it was before," said Kiefner. "No matter what happens, we can't compete with the likes of Boise Cascade and Union Camp. We just can't hit those kind of costs in this plant. We'll always be marginal. But you know we're small—and we can do one thing those guys can't—we can be flexible." It was the only way to continue to compete. "Even if things pick up," he said "we'll still need something we can be really good at—we need to become excellent at being flexible."

Kiefner had charged Saugoe with the job of developing an improvement program to set Stermon on a path which would make it, once again, a world-class plant. But now it would be world-class in terms of its flexibility rather than its cost. The improvement scheme would begin on November 10th, 1992, and was to set clear goals and milestones. The initial focus of the plan would be machine #4, the largest machine in the plant, and the one considered the most important and the least flexible.

Saugoe had been included in a number of improvement schemes in the past. In August, 1977, he had set up a real-time cost analysis system in the plant. In March 1983, he had led the Total Quality Initiative (TQI), with the specific aim of reducing defects in the paper. Saugoe had looked at a number of Quality Improvement Programs in the process industry before the team finally agreed on a scheme developed by Manzax Chemical in the UK, based on Philip Crosby's methods. Both schemes had been a considered a success by management. But flexibility seemed different. What did it mean to "get flexible"? Saugoe didn't know, so pulled together a team to find out.

Flexibility in Manufacturing

On September 12th, Saugoe's team of manufacturing specialists discussed the flexibility improvement scheme. A handful of worried people

---

[1]Broke was the term used for off-standard paper. Between runs, the off specification paper made was re-pulped and cycled back through the plant.

crowded into his office. He had asked each of them to come up with ideas on how to improve flexibility.

Davie Pemthrall was superintendent on machine 3.

We should figure out how to push this machine a little more. If we improved some of the process control systems, and put in higher powered dryers on machine 4, we'd really be flexible. We'd be able to dry real heavy papers, but still be able to control the process well enough to make light papers. We'd be able to make almost anything if we did that, then we'd really be flexible.

Peter Lohresich (Machine 2 superintendent) differed:

I don't know, Pem, I saw it a little differently. I think we need to improve the changeover times so we can switch between the grades a little more easily. Grade change time and paper breaks are really starting to eat into the efficiency on machine #4. Some of the guys on 3 have got together a fire-brigade. They figured out a way to beat the computer every time on grade changes. They run around like crazy when it comes to changing the machine. The computer does it in ten minutes. These guys are incredible! They do it in two or three.

Yes Pete, but number 3 is a little machine, you can play around with that kind of thing there. Machine 4 is making almost 300 tons a day. You need to be safe when you change grades.

I still think we should work on speeding up grade changes on 4. I don't see any reason why it can't start getting really flexible, just like number 3.

Lars Robikoff (Superintendent, Machine 4) disagreed:

No, I don't think either of these things really makes us flexible. It's all very well saying we should work on getting machine 4 to make a large range of weights or to changeover quickly, but you'll never be really flexible until you fix the fundamental problem: the machine was built for 20 lb Xerox paper. It likes to run there—that's where it's most efficient. You should forget about getting it to do real heavy, light and all those other weird papers. Let's get it to be efficient across the range of papers we make now—on 15 lb, 18 lb and 24 lb—get the yields up there. Then we won't care which we produce—we'll really start to be flexible.

Pemthrall agreed:

We have really patchy quality across the grades we make now on 4. Customers shouldn't have to put up with holes in the web just because we're making stuff our machine doesn't like. As well as that, there are folks out there who've got machines that are set up specifically for 15 lb or 24 lb. We better learn to be as good as them, or they'll win every time.

Flexibility in Sales

"It means doing what the customer wants," said Elly Ryesham in the sales department. "Flexibility means being all things to all people—of course, you can never do it; but you do your best. It means giving the customer exactly what they want, when they want it, I suppose."

Saugoe wasn't sure that helped. What kinds of things did the customers want, and what exactly did they mean by flexibility? Saugoe set Ryesham a task. "Go back to your salespeople, and see if you can put together a list of things we need to do, to be what our customers call "being flexible." Break them into categories, and see which kind of request comes up the most."

Two days later, Ryesham returned.

Well, it wasn't real clear, but I guess we came up with three things. The first need is for customized paper—one-offs and specials—that kind of thing. Some of our customers would really like us to be able to make paper tailored to their specific needs, even real lights and heavies. Second, customers want us to deliver just-in-time frequently rather than pushing a whole run onto them. Finally, I guess they like the fact they can do one stop shopping here; we've got a lot of product lines. I have my own opinions about which of these is most important, but I also asked the salespeople.

Ryesham had taken a straw poll of the sales force, asking which of these were most important. "They all are!" replied one saleswoman. Eventually the committee ended up with a list, grading each type of flexibility from A (important) to E (unimportant) (see Exhibit 7) Unfortunately, some salespeople had added more "flexibility" items to the list.

"There are all types of flexibility," said Saugoe, "but now we have a better idea of what's really important to the customer. Saugoe still wasn't sure how this translated into a flexibility plan for the plant. One complicating problem was that

EXHIBIT 7 Survey of Sales Force

Requirement	Andy Newland	Liz Foxell	Jimmy Mellor	Tracy Shaw	Nick Walker
Customization	A-	A-	B-	D	B-
Responsiveness in delivery/JIT	A	A+	A+	B+	A
Having a broad product line	B	A	B	B	B-
Having flexible, helpful salespeople	B	A	C	C	B
Bring in new products frequently	D	E	B	E	C

there was already a flexibility improvement program in operation. For the past two years, HRM people had been negotiating a flexibility scheme with the union. Union officials had agreed to begin to relax the traditional constraints on workers taking each others' jobs. Aidan Waine, UPU representative in the pulp plant, commented on the rumors he had heard:

> We've been negotiating this deal for three years and now they're saying we've got to be even more flexible! Sounds to me like another way of getting something for nothing.

FLEXING THE FACTORY

Saugoe sat in his office putting together his presentation on overhead foils for Kiefner. He felt that Kiefner had been losing some patience with the team recently. It took them two weeks just to work out what a flexibility improvement program meant! Kiefner was a man with cold, steely heart for warm, fuzzy ideas. Two weeks ago, the team had come up with some comparatively vague suggestions for an improvement program. Kiefner had insisted that nothing would ever happen if the results could not be measured. Besides, he was concerned that Saugoe had no idea how to rank the various schemes in terms of their importance. Saugoe had remade a list of the flexibility improvement options, and was now working on which of these should be carried out.

First, Stermon could upgrade machine 4 with computer control, extra dryer capacity, and better training, so that it could make a much broader range of basic weights. With better control, the number of "recipes" the machine could make would also be increased. This would clearly improve the flexibility of the machine. If the machine were able to make heavier weights as well as slightly lighter weights than it could now, Stermon could make money by tailoring paper to customers' specific requirements both within the existing range of the machine, and outside it. Marketing estimated that a 7% premium (before freight) could be charged for such a service on these grades, though the machine would only produce such specialty jobs for 30% of the time. The capital cost of improving the flexibility of the machine in this way was $3.1 million.

The second option relied much more on the people in the plant being able to adopt new ways of working. It would mean completely breaking with paper industry tradition. Machine 4 could be taken to a one week cycle, and run through the existing grades every week instead of every two weeks. This would certainly save on inventory costs—but even if inventory stayed the same, marketing estimated that Stermon could charge a 5% pre-freight premium for the ability to make weekly "JIT" production runs. This was not at all straightforward though. If changeover times remained the same, it would mean a lot more time lost due to grade changes on machine 4. Ten percent of available machine time was currently lost due to changeovers. Would the machine operators be able to learn to change over faster? Perhaps some of the machine tenders from machine #3 could help the crew on #4 to become more flexible among the grades.

The third option was to improve the yield on machine 4 on the less frequently produced grades. In general, paper produced on the machine split into four categories, as shown in Exhibit 8. Machine 4 was strongly focused on 20 lb Xerox paper. Over the past year, however, demand had been very soft for this paper because of the new capacity in the industry. For 28% of the past year's two-week machine cycles, there had been no demand

EXHIBIT 8 Yields and Proportions of Output on Machine 4

Grade	≤15 lb	18 lb	20 lb	24 lb
Yield[a]	78%	86%	95%	89%
Usual proportion of production	14%	16%	62%	8%
Proportion when no 20 lb demand	37%	42%	-	21%

[a] Yield figures are net of grade changes. These are the yields once the machine is running the grade.

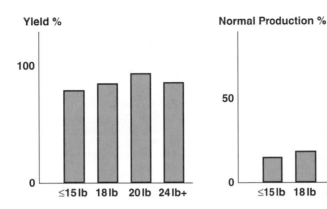

for 20 lb paper, and the capacity of the machine was shared among the other grades in their "normal" proportions to each other. This situation was expected to continue for at least two more years. These abnormal weeks were very unpopular on the floor, since it meant spending two weeks without running the machine on its sweet spot. The machine was not sufficiently flexible to produce all grades well. To improve this flexibility among the grades, a new expert system for process control could be installed. This system promised to raise the yields for 15 lb to 24 lb paper made on the machine so that they would be comparable to that for 20 lb, providing the machine with much more flexibility across its grade range. The machine would then be much more tolerant of a lack of demand for its "favorite" grade. In addition, quality would become more consistent across the grade range. The cost of this system and the associated actuator network was $5.05 million.

Finally, Saugoe could recommend accelerating the flexibility program which was being worked out with the union. There had been other fires to fight in recent months, and a lot of the original impetus in the program had drained away. This program had the advantage that it was already underway, and was important in improving the effectiveness of the labor in the plant. Seeing people sitting around waiting for the "right" job to show up was getting to be really demoralizing for everyone in the plant.

While Stermon could go ahead with all four plans, Saugoe knew from his experiences with other improvement schemes that it would be much better to focus attention on one or two. In addition, he was concerned that some combinations of the flexibility improvement plans would conflict. He sketched out some notes to himself on how the plans might interact (see Exhibit 9). Saugoe wondered if there might be another way out. "Maybe we should work on having enough flexibility to get out of this business altogether!" thought Saugoe, half-cynically, half-seriously, as he put together the slides for his presentation to Kiefner [Exhibit 10].

As he checked his recommendation in indelible pen on the slide. Saugoe thought, "No changing my mind now, I guess." With no flexibility left, he knocked on Kiefner's door.

EXHIBIT 9 Combinations of Improvement Plans

	Increase Range	*One week cycle*	*Uniform Yields*
One week cycle	Might be difficult just to make new grades *without* trying to change between them quickly. Combination of unfamiliar grades and process instability might cause paper breaks and/or quality problems		
Uniform Yields	Would be too difficult to improve yields at the same time as stretching the machine. With the new grades being anticipated, would not expect any yield improvement on existing grades.	In order to improve yields, would probably need to stay on grades for at least as long as current run lengths. Unlikely to get process stable enough to improve yields if more changes. Could do it—but results would be to raise non-20 lb yields only about 3%	
Labor Multi Skilling	Could use existing skill base and use this as an opportunity to cut across functional lines. People generally enthusiastic about "difficult" papers. Would need to relax "output" pressure.	Might cause a lot of discontent if people were being asked to change over faster/more often, as well as performing multiple functions. Not likely to work well.	This would already be seen as a way of improving output rather than improving flexibility. Hard to combine with a push on multi-tasking.

EXHIBIT 10 Marketing Projections—Best/Worst/Expected for 20 lb Xerox

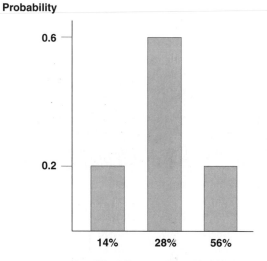

Fraction of two-week cycles in the next two years in which there will be no 20 lb paper produced

MODULE 2

Operations Systems and Information Technology

OVERVIEW

Information Technology (IT) is no longer an ancillary subject in Operations Management. Companies have traditionally left this facet of their operations to the Information Systems department to manage. Today, however, IT has become an integral part of managing and improving operations. By 1996, for example, 87% of operations managers cited at least a joint responsibility for IT decision-making.[1] There are a number of reasons for this. First is the need for quick-response operations, the explosion of variety, and the increasing brevity of product life-cycles.[2] In such circumstances, there is both more information to manage and greater advantages to managing that information well. Information technologies, therefore, become a crucial part of the operation. Second, new distributed computing architectures have increasingly placed information technology in the hands of users rather than with central data processing departments. These new tools, including powerful desktop machines, client-server architectures, and open standards for information sharing, allow operations functions an unprecedented amount of control over their own information systems. Finally, and most important, many companies are using information technology to create powerful new operations-based competitive weapons, as we will see in a number of cases in this module.

The promised advantages of effective IT management in operations have been well documented. The National Research Council found, for example, that the computer-integrated operations in their sample reduced overall lead time by between 30% and 60%, increased operations productivity by 40–70%, and increased product quality by a factor of between 2 and 5.[3] Such new capabilities provide manufacturing and service operations not only with the opportunity to reduce a range of costs, but—probably more important—to generate new revenue by either growing existing markets or entering new ones. Some research studies in the late 1980s suggested that gains to investment in information technology were, at best, insignificant, leading to what has been termed the "Productivity Paradox." More recent and more detailed data, however, show that paradox to be partly an artifact of the samples used in previous work. Brynjolfsson's work shows investments in information technology to be at least as productive—dollar for dollar—as more traditional investments.[4] More telling, however, is that Brynjolfsson's study found gains to be disproportionately high in the manufacturing sector in his sample of 367 firms. Kelley also found significant efficiency advantages to information technology in manufacturing operations.[5]

Despite these promised riches, operations managers repeatedly cite information technology

---

[1]Fulcher J. (1996). Ahead of the Pack. *Manufacturing Systems*. 14: 5–18. May 1996.

[2]Wheelwright, S. C. and K. B. Clark (1992). *Revolutionized Product Development*. New York, Free Press: 3–4.

[3]*Toward a New Era in U.S. Manufacturing: The Need for National Vision.* Washington, D.C., National Research Council. Washington D.C., 1986.

[4]Brynjolfsson, E. and L. Hitt (1996). "Paradox Lost? Firm-level evidence on the Returns to Information Systems Spending." *Management Science* 42(4): 541–558.

[5]Kelly, M. R. (1994). "Productivity and Information Technology: The Elusive Connection." *Management Science* 40(11): 1406–1425. November 1994.

as one of their biggest headaches. IT projects are notorious for cost and delivery overruns[6] as well as for their labyrinthine complexity. In addition, some highly touted technologies such as Robotics and Flexible Manufacturing Systems have yielded many expensive catastrophes on the shop floor. Finally, information technology can often cement an operation to a particular set of technologies, systems, or ways of doing business. In doing so, it can severely constrain the operation's strategic flexibility.

With these facts in hand, the operations manager can no longer sit on the sidelines and be quizzed by IT people in the hope that they will ultimately come up with a "system" that will do what they want. Operations managers need to understand the technology in a way that allows them to make decisions that are right for their operations, and take much greater control of it than they have in the past. This is both a blessing and a curse. A blessing, in that it allows technology to be forged into the operation in a way that builds strengthened competitive advantage, by combining it with a deep understanding of how the operation works and what it needs to deliver. A curse, in that it demands knowledge that is distant from that imparted to traditionally-trained operations managers.

Part of the solution, at least, is for operations managers to learn more technical detail about information technology. While technical understanding is rarely a hindrance, understanding the technology is not enough. There are fundamental and peculiar *managerial* issues concerning the integration of Information Technology and Operations that neither field addresses wholly on its own. These issues are relevant to the design, management and improvement of IT-enabled operations systems.

A Path-based Model for Information Technology Development in Operations

There are (at least) two models for how operations design and develop their IT base. The first is progressive waves of large "systems," which are put out to tender or programmed by an IT depart-

ment, and which periodically become obsolete as time goes on. IT projects are large, long, and complex. They deliver value when they are complete.

Users are involved before the project is started (to determine requirements), and after the technical work is done (to help people feel that they "own" the system). At the time of their development, these projects promise to solve the IT problem "once and for all." The major challenges with this approach are to specify precisely in advance all the requirements of the system, manage the vendor or the IT group to avoid cost and delivery overruns, and to find ways to insure against premature obsolescence and the possibility that circumstances may have changed by the time the system is complete. Much effort is expended trying to predict the future, on a periodic basis, and going through painful "transitions." The IT and operations environment has changed so radically over the past few years that the world in which the first model might have been appropriate—the mainframe world—is rapidly disappearing.

This module introduces a new perspective—a second model for how operations can design and develop their IT base. It views IT development in an operation as a "path" in which multiple technological phases (such as networking, software and processing devices) overlap, evolve, and are mutually dependent (see Table 1). In these circumstances, the computer resource is continually being renewed at different levels, and the prime concern is the ability to integrate and provide compatibility with existing modules. Projects are small and fast and intended to start paying off quickly, allowing local experimentation and delivering value along the way. Users are involved as part of this process. This requires less long-range planning and large-project management, but more ongoing direction-setting and technical expertise in the operation to understand fully the implications of a given piece of new technology and to learn about what might come next.

The path-based approach to the application of information technology appears to promise many of the advantages that are associated with the principles of "continuous improvement" in operations processes. There is an important difference, however. Information systems require an architecture. An architecture defines how the components of a system will function and fit together

---

[6]Xenakis, J. J. (1996) "Taming SAP." *CFO:* 23–30. March 1996.

TABLE I Two Models for IT Development in Operations

	Periodic-New-System-based	Path-based
Role of IT	Supportive/Peripheral to Operation	Integral part of Operation
Project size and number	Large, few, infrequent	Small, many, frequent
Development Approach	Build then install	Prototype and evolve
Delivery of Value	When project is complete	On-going
Source of technology/software	Custom-built, heavy use of custom code, proprietary standards	Off the shelf, little custom code, standards in common use
Primary functional concerns	Control, efficiency, accommodating all requirements at once	Integration, interconnection, flexibility, progressive delivery of requirements
Locus of Technical Control	Vendor/IT group	Operation itself
Experimentation	Limited	Frequent opportunities
Primary Managerial Effort	Installation, Project and Vendor Management	Ongoing management of interconnection standards

as a coherent whole.[7] Since operations systems increasingly emphasize the connections between components rather than the components themselves, the architecture of the system is increasingly important. Traditional information systems management satisfies architectural needs by monolithic design: the system is designed at a point in time so that all of its components fit together well and function together. Rather like the design of a house, this can be achieved by pre-specifying how the house should look and function as a whole, and how all of the bricks, mortar, and other materials will fit together to achieve that goal. When the house no longer fits its function or is outdated, it is demolished, though a clever architect might find a way to adapt the legacy building to fit into a new environment.

A path-based approach to information systems does not demand that all components be specified (or even anticipated) in advance. It sees the existence of legacy systems as a fact of life, and accepts at the outset that new modules and new technologies will be added, and the system will evolve progressively as time goes on. One might suspect that a path-based approach to information systems development might result in haphazard

systems, which have no coherent architecture. However, this simply requires a different definition of the word "architecture"—in dynamic rather than static terms. To maintain architectural coherence in a system whose components are added, removed and changed over time, the architecture needs to be defined in terms of principles rather than substantives. Rather than specifying, in advance, precisely which components will form part of the whole, a dynamic architecture specifies the *principles* by which they are added or changed. As such, the architectural metaphor is closer to that of a town or city. The architecture of a city is defined in terms of the principles by which new components are added (zoning restrictions, planning rules, etc.), rather than by substantive, one-off prescriptions of the components that will constitute it.[8]

A dynamic architecture means more than being modular. A modular architecture would simply define, in advance, all the interfaces that exist, and ensure that components adhered to those interface standards. However, interfaces are also subject to change and technical advance. Therefore, the principles themselves should evolve over time (just as planning commissions change their criteria for additions to cities) so that the architecture itself can adapt to changing circumstances as

[7]Henderson, R. M. and K. B. Clark (1990). "Architectural Innovation: The Reconfiguration of Existing Product Technologies and the Failure of Established Firms." *Administrative Science Quarterly* 35: 9–30. March 1990.

[8]With some notable exceptions such as designed cities like Brasilia and Canberra.

time goes on. For most cities, as for most IT systems in operations, this is where efforts for long-term planning are best placed.[9]

With this model for information systems management, there are three important roles in managing the IT path of an operation. First is in *designing* and orienting the path: providing direction so that the progressive addition of modules delivers the form of competitive advantage the operation is seeking. Because IT tends to deliver different kinds of value to operations than more traditional investments, it needs to be evaluated differently. It more often provides greater benefits in responsiveness, reliable delivery, and ability to customize than in lower costs and higher quality (as might a more traditional investment in capital equipment). In doing so, it opens up a range of opportunities for the operation to compete in new ways, as well as support existing ones, but it also demands a broader perspective on the assessment of prospective investments.

Second is in *managing* the path: building design principles that ensure the progressive addition of modules results in a harmonious whole, in which modules are easy to network to each other and provide flexibility to change as requirements and objectives change. The danger of frequent design-build-test cycles of many, small projects is that elements of information technology that are collected together begin to diverge, resulting in an unintegrated polyglot collection of modules. The solution to this architectural problem lies in the management of standards and, increasingly, in applying the concept of *open systems,* which is discussed in detail later in this section. While this issue would seem to be merely technical, no other factor is more significant in determining the long-term flexibility of IT-based operations systems. Careful stewardship of standards allows an operation to change its information technology with its competitive environment, to expand easily and quickly, and to adopt innovations in technology in a modular way, without having to redesign all other modules in the operation to accommodate the change. Decisions about which standards should be used require operations managers' full involvement and understanding, since the right decisions depend on

how the operation will function and what kinds of change can be expected in the future.

Third is building an Information Technology path that provides a foundation for ongoing operations *improvement*. Much of the emphasis in the past, particularly in manufacturing, has been on the role of information technology in automating operations, and dispensing with the people who used to perform the associated functions. However, if designed well, IT can streamline routine and repetitive functions and free operators to improve rather than simply execute processes. It can reinforce new, more effective ways of coordinating work and provide a structure to prevent a reversion to old ways of doing things. Finally, it increasingly offers the possibility of broad and open connectivity, allowing whole networks of disparate operations to improve the way they work together.

MODULE STRUCTURE

The module comprises ten cases, each of which concerns issues related to the design, management and improvement of IT-enabled operations. The first four cases address issues at the shop floor level and technologies that affect *physical processes*. The next three cases look at information management at the plant level and IT systems for *coordinative processes,* such as Manufacturing Resource Planning and Enterprise Integration. The last three sessions look at *linkage processes:* operations and information technology to connect outside the operating unit and how the development of new operations-based capabilities in information technology can be exploited outside the operation for which they were originally developed.

In building upwards in this way, the module first introduces the building blocks of systems, then looks at how these elements are aggregated at the next level, where a different set of issues often exists. The discussion in later cases relies on the earlier cases to provide an understanding of the lower level technologies. This reflects the hierarchy developed by the National Institute of Science and Technology (NIST).[10] McLean and Jones[11] suggest

---

[9]In traditional architecture, the idea of principles rather than prescription to guide changing, hierarchical architectures (city—suburb—street—house) is explored in Alexander, C., Ishikawa, S. et al. (1977). *A Pattern Language.* New York, Oxford University Press.

[10]*Information Technology for Manufacturing: A Research Agenda.* Washington, D.C., National Research Council: 138–139. 1995.

[11]McLean, C. and Jones, A (1986). "A Proposed Hierarchical Control Model for Manufacturing Systems." *Journal of Manufacturing Systems* 5 (1): 15–25. January 1986.

that the key issue in building a conceptual model for computer integration is an understanding of the levels at which a particular piece of technology is operating, and the module reinforces this by examining issues at progressively higher levels in the systems hierarchy. The technologies introduced (see Figure 1) are by no means an exhaustive list of those employed in modern operations systems. They are representative, however, of the technologies used at each level, and capture the kinds of managerial issues faced. For example, many of the issues concerning operators' freedom to program CNC machines locally (in John Crane) would also apply to industrial robots or automated assembly machines; Kanebo's concerns about the ongoing availability of the proprietary method they use to network stores to their plant by modem would also apply to many wide-area-network-based systems.

It is very difficult to have a useful discussion about the role of information technology in operations without an understanding of what the technology is and what it does. Each class in the module therefore has two objectives. It explores what the particular technology *is,* then addresses the broader managerial issues that arise from the case.

One of the most important of these managerial issues is whether the information technology path being followed in the case is *changing* or *reinforcing* the operations' competitive focus. Information technologies that change the competitive focus of an operation are more likely to demand other significant changes in the company's operations strategy, since the whole operations "ma-

chine" will often need to be re-designed to adapt to the changed mode of competition.[12] The NIST hierarchy does not shed any light on this issue, so another conceptual dimension is needed in organizing the cases in the module. As Figure 2 shows, the cases are almost evenly split between those that "change the game"[13] and those that aim to strengthen performance in the existing one. In two cases (FASTech and AeroTech) this distinction is not clear, since the technologies can be used for both purposes. This two-dimensional framework stresses that IT in operations is not *always* about transforming the organization.

MAJOR THEMES

1. Designing the Path: Shaping IT-based Operations Systems to the Competitive Role of the Operation

An important danger that awaits the operations manager looking to invest in IT is that of installing a "world-class" system, using the very latest technology, in the hope that this will deliver world-class performance. As the Cybertech case shows, this is a perilous assumption. First, it is not at all clear that "world-class" technology guarantees exceptional

---

[12]As described in Hayes, R. H., Pisano, G. P., et al., Eds. (1996) *Strategic Operations: Competing through Capabilities.* New York, Free Press.

[13]Nalebuff, B. J. and A. Brandenburger (1996). *Co-opetition.* Doubleday, New York.

FIGURE 1 Module Structure

Class	*Technologies Introduced*
1. John Crane	Computer-aided design; computer-aided manufacturing; computer numerical control
2. The Cybertech Project	Monolithic architectures; sensor technology
3. Motorola, Inc. The Bandit Pager Project	Modular architectures; robotics
4. FASTech	Manufacturing execution systems
5. EG&G Rotron	Pull-based shop floor control
6. DEC Endpoint	Manufacturing resource planning systems
7. Vandelay	Enterprise information systems/SAP
8. Kanebo	Electronic data interchange; flexible manufacturing
9. John Deere	Group technology; open systems
10. AeroTech	Internet/Intranet technologies; open systems; wide-area networking

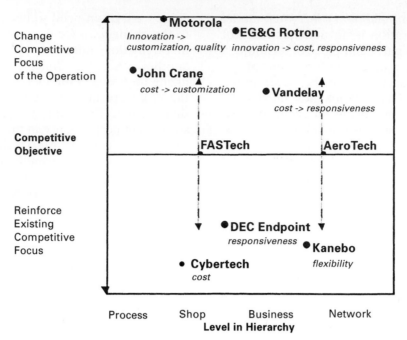

FIGURE 2 Competitive Objectives and Level of Projects in Module

performance. Second, as underlined by Hayes and Pisano,[14] a more important question than whether or not to be "world-class" is what one should be world-class *at*. The ability to mold information technology in a way that delivers performance consistent with the competitive strategy of the firm is critical to success.

The CIM zealots who led the Cybertech project may have made the mistake described by Grant, et al.:

> [This] enthusiastic endorsement of advanced manufacturing technologies is dangerously simplistic. First, it accepts as axiomatic the benefits of automation and computer-integrated manufacturing without heeding the substantial costs and risks.[. . .] Second, current wisdom suggests that companies must choose between continuing with their mechanized, specialized production systems and leaping into the future with the adoption of fully automated CIM. In fact, new manufacturing processes comprise a broad menu of technologies, including *engineering* techniques such as computer-aided design and engineering; *manufacturing* techniques such as robotics, computer-aided manufacturing [. . .] flexible manufacturing sys-

tem (FMS), automated storage and retrieval, and cellular manufacturing; and *management* techniques such as MRPII, Just-in-Time (JIT), Total Quality Management and autonomous work groups. Although some of the new technologies are complementary, others are alternatives, and when selecting particular technologies companies must make important choices about the degree of automation, the extent of integration and the dimensions and scope of flexibility.[15]

To ensure a match between technology and the external competitive objective, the task is to identify the primary *functional* objectives of information technology projects and match these with the competitive/improvement goals of the operation. Table 2 provides some example information technology functions in operations and marries them with the competitive objectives that would be consistent with that function. While information technology will perform a number of operations functions, a new project or module will often have a primary underlying functional objective. If this functional objective is inconsistent with the projected competitive role of the operation, then the

[14]Hayes, R. H. and Pisano, G. P. (1994). "Beyond World-Class: The New Manufacturing Strategy." *Harvard Business Review:* 77–86, January–February, 1994.

[15]Grant, R. M., Krishnan, R., et al. (1991) "Appropriate Manufacturing Technology: A Strategic Approach." *Sloan Management Review:* 43–54. Fall 1991.

TABLE 2 Matching Information Technology Function to Competitive Role

Information Technology Function	*Consistent Competitive Need*
Reduce material waste Eliminate labor Reduce cost of a business process.	Decreased Cost
Improve consistency of processes Trap errors/mistakes Track process parameters Provide better process information to operators	Improved Conformance Quality and Product Reliability
Provide broad availability of order information Ensure information accuracy Track physical flow of material	Enhanced delivery reliability
Management and distribution of programs for programmable machines Facilitate rapid design changes/modification Deliver production process information to shop-floor operators	Enhance ability to customize product, deliver broad product range
Connect customers/suppliers to operations electronically Speed information flow through the operations system Allow reduction in work-in-progress through greater control	Improved responsiveness
Provide virtual test-beds Facilitate design work Generate automatic recipes/part-programs	Rapid Innovation

effort and investment would be better put else-where.

Information technology that allows the operation to compete in new ways often demands a broadening of traditional investment appraisal methods, especially in manufacturing. Many Computer Integration enthusiasts dismiss traditional capital investment appraisal as merely a "barrier to implementation." Information technology, however, should not be outside economic rationality and, indeed, should certainly not be justified, in Kaplan's words, by faith alone.[16] There are, however, some key advantages that IT-based solutions tend to offer that are unusual for more traditional operations. For example, manufacturers focused on cost reduction too often have appraisal systems that are not capable of recognizing the revenue-generating potential of operations and in particular, of information technology as an amplifier of that capability. This lack of recognition also applies in the IT-world: for example, only 4% of IT directors say they had been appointed to exploit the possibility of the computer to capture market share.[17]

John Crane, Kanebo, Motorola, and Cybertech each provide opportunities to discuss these issues. Crane and Kanebo are both moving down an IT path that builds capabilities to generate revenue rather than simply reduce costs, and have based their initiatives on the competitive strategies of the respective firms. Crane is focused on reducing order-to-delivery lead times, and to do so has streamlined both its physical flows (primarily through manufacturing cells) and its information flows (through the CAD-CAM link). Kanebo is concentrating on using IT as a signaler (about what is selling well) and as an input to the production control systems in its plant to ensure that the product is available. Motorola is using advanced manufacturing technology to improve quality and flexibility—each of which has been identified as a critical market requirement through benchmarking. Conversely, it is not yet clear that the solution developed by the Cybertech engineers

[16]Kaplan, R (1986). "Must CIM be Justified by Faith Alone?" *Harvard Business Review:* 87–95. March-April 1986.

[17]Grindley, K. (1995). "Why Appoint an IT Director?" *Managing I.T. at Board Level.* London, Pitman: 51.

addresses the prevailing competitive needs of the meat industry.

In class, a fundamental question is, "What competitive need does this system address and how does it do it?" This is comparatively easy to answer in the case, say, of Kanebo. It is much more difficult in the Vandelay case.

2. Managing the Path: The Growing Importance of Open Systems

"The nice thing about standards is that there are so many of them to choose from."
—ANDREW S. TANENBAUM

In the past, the primary technology in information systems was the central processor. Whether a mainframe, a mini-computer, a Programmable Logic Controller, or a stand-alone PC, the emphasis was on the processing device itself. The evolution of increasingly distributed architectures (in which processing power is spread across many devices) and the growth and commoditization of computing power mean that processors are no longer the central issue in computing. Connectivity is. Few managerial problems now arise because "The MRP run didn't complete on time" (because of lack of processor power). We are nowadays much more likely to hear problems like:

- "System A doesn't talk to System B and so we have to enter the data manually."

- "Our competitor is connected to his suppliers through Electronic Data Interchange, but we have to use fax machines, because of the cost of interfacing our production control system to the EDI boxes."

- "We need to re-program our circular knitting machines all the time. The problem is, we only have one person who knows how to do it. Those machines use a completely different programming language from the others in our plant."

- "We have three different networks around the plant. Originally, that was fine, because the pulping operation didn't need to be connected to the papermaking operations. But now, we want to connect the two so we trigger production of pulp when the paper machines need it. It's going to be very expensive."

Part of the answer to such problems is the judicious selection of the standards by which computers communicate with each other and with humans in an operation. Increasingly, significant and strategic operations problems can result from not being able to network effectively. Of course, it is always *possible* to connect one system to another. The question is—at what cost? Fortunately, a broader understanding of the importance of standards, open protocols, and internetworking technologies means that managers can avoid such strategic cul-de-sacs. It is from here that the ability to forge dynamic, flexible architectures springs, and where the operations manager's technical understanding of IT is most valuable.

This knowledge is becoming increasingly important. First, as computing power has become more and more distributed, connections between devices have become increasingly important. Second, the pervasiveness and variety of computers in operations mean that it is unlikely that one manufacturer will be able to supply all the computing devices involved. With one manufacturer, it is fairly straightforward to decide how machines will communicate. The vendor will often use their own, proprietary standards. When multiple suppliers are involved, broadly available standard methods for communication with both humans and other machines are critical. Third, it is increasingly the case that new information technology is progressively added to a system *over time*. This means ongoing vigilance to ensure that the system functions as a coherent whole. Finally, as the environment becomes more changeable and operations more fluid and adaptable, there is a greater need to move equipment around in the system, re-program it, and add new subsystems. Each of these factors means that there are significant advantages to being able to construct operations systems that continue to fit together in a modular way. Just as Lego™ brick models (in which the bricks have a pre-defined "interface" to each other) can be reconfigured and reshaped, so standard computer interfaces greatly enhance the long-term flexibility of the operation. Open standards play an increasingly important role in delivering this capability.

What is an Open Standard?

In the early nineteenth century, every British factory that needed to bolt one thing to another invented its own threading system to do so. Slowly, manufacturers of fastening systems emerged, and nuts and bolts were made by a variety of specialized manufacturers. While many vendors sold nuts and bolts, it was only rarely that a nut from one manufacturer would fit on the bolt of another. Vendors who sold particular systems of nuts and bolts were not altogether upset by this—after all, a sale of their fastener system to a particular customer meant that they would have a "lock" on them for many years to come. In 1841, Joseph Whitworth made a recommendation to the equivalent of the U. S. Department of Defense (Woolwich Arsenal) for the standardization of coarse-thread bolts. The adoption of this standard for nuts and bolts meant that products from different fastener manufacturers could be substituted, with the knowledge that nuts and wrenches would still fit. The Whitworth thread standard was widely published, and since no one company owned the standard, no one could be precluded on proprietary grounds from making nuts and bolts to the standard. It thus became an *open* standard. An open standard is an agreed-upon interface between modules, that is not subject to proprietary control.

Multi-vendor open standards, then, are not a new phenomenon and one might suspect that all that is needed to offer similar advantages in computer systems would be to provide a standard method for one computer to communicate with another. Unfortunately, this is not so easy. The reason is that computers, like human beings, communicate at many different levels. Consider the English and Indonesian languages. While both use the Roman alphabet (an open standard), knowledge of that standard is not enough to allow one person to understand another. Esperanto (another open standard) was an attempt to solve the standard problem at this "higher" level. Computer devices also communicate at many levels, and there are closed (proprietary) and open standards dotted throughout these levels. For the task of delivering a message from one computer to another, the OSI (Open Systems Interconnect Group) has agreed upon a standard model for what those levels are. The lowest levels are concerned with the physical connection of the devices; the middle levels define how the message is addressed to where it is going and how it ensures it arrives in one piece; at the higher levels, the standards prescribe how the information is encoded and compressed and how it is delivered to the program listening at the other end. At each of the seven levels in the model, there are many available protocols. This layering of protocols is further complicated when humans are involved. Communications with humans and physical devices demand even higher levels (such as programming languages) to carry *meaning*. Standards also exist at these levels. For example, "KILL" might mean "STOP" to one robot, but mean something quite different to another!

An open system is one that relies on open standards at the various levels. Probably the most prominent example of an "open" system is the Internet, which relies on the Internet Transport Protocol (TCP/IP) to get data transmitted to the right place in the right order. In spite of the availability of alternative technology, TCP/IP[18] has become a dominant, non-proprietary method for achieving this task. Another example of a standard that we would like to be "open" (but isn't as far along) is SQL (Structured Query Language), for which there is an ongoing effort by ISO-ANSI to create an open standard.[19] SQL enables users to query relational databases in a standard way. Although IBM originally invented SQL (delivering its first commercial product in 1981), there quickly arose a whole plethora of competing SQL "dialects" from competitors, each purporting to deliver some advantage over its peers. This meant that—if one should decide to change database vendors—one would have to change all the code that queried the existing databases. At this point ISO and ANSI stepped in to begin the process of standardizing SQL. While it is not easy to chase a moving, innovating target, such efforts are critical in enabling systems to talk to one another, be interchangeable, and help users avoid being "locked-in" to one supplier *purely by the standards*. However, an individual IT provider may claim that its proprietary product is so superior to the prevailing open standard that it is worth the strategic risk. So, for example, Oracle has produced PL/SQL—its own language for constructing SQL queries. Fortunately, many of the standards used in operations have progressively become *open* standards. DEC's Ethernet, for example, a low-level networking protocol, has progressively become an open standard. Some proprietary standards are now so prevalent that they provide as many of the advantages to modularity as open standards do. "Openness,"

[18]Comer, D. E. (1995). *Internetworking with TCP/IP: Principles, Protocols and Architectures*. Englewood Cliffs, NJ, Prentice Hall.
[19]Bowman, J. S., Emerson, S. L., et al. (1993). *The Practical SQL Handbook*. Reading, MA, Addison-Wesley.

then, is on a continuum, determined by the extent to which one firm has and exerts control over the standard, either to change it for its own purposes or to limit its use.

Given that decision making in this complex situation is increasingly a critical determinant of an operation's long-term flexibility, how should operations managers make decisions concerning the standards used in their operations? Few operations have the luxury of a "clean-sheet" for IT, and many of the standards used will be inherited from legacy systems. Some choices, therefore, will already have been made. However, there is much an operations manager can do to ensure future flexibility when adding new pieces of information technology to an existing operations system. There are three primary decisions to be made when considering the addition of new IT-based technology to an operation as part of an overall path.

First, the manager needs to decide which standards are relevant. If the equipment or system is self-contained and the programming and communications interfaces to it operate according to a standard that is acceptable in the operation, then it does not matter what methods the system uses internally. As a contained system, with understood methods of interfacing outside itself, it is defined as a *module*[20] and the only relevant standards are those that the module uses externally. However, it is important to consider the possibility that the module will be broken up, to be changed or adapted to future needs. In this case, the internal methods and languages used will *become* relevant. In the 1980s, many FMS systems were sold as "turnkey" systems, which connected machine tools and materials handling systems to a supervisory computer using peculiar and proprietary protocols. When times changed, and the machine tools needed to be reconfigured, it was extraordinarily difficult and expensive to program and reconnect the system in the new configuration. Many expensive, proprietary systems became white elephants, and were abandoned. Will the "module" remain a module? If so, what standards are relevant in communicating with it? Would we be able to communicate with the internal elements of the module if we should ever need to break it up?

Second, the manager must decide if those standards will *function* with the existing and projected modules in the rest of the operation with which it might need to communicate. Does the module communicate with standards that are used elsewhere in the operation? How widespread and stable are those standards? Will they continue to be so in the future? How difficult will it be to connect the module with new systems? Are there peculiarities of the particular dialect that the module uses?

Third, having decided how well the set of standards associated with the module fits with the operation, the manager then needs to look at the *aggregate* effect of any new standards and languages on the operation as a whole. Figure 3 shows where various combinations of closed and open standards are appropriate. In general, an operation's systems grow more expensive to maintain and support as the number of different standards used increases. It will also be more difficult to staff with the breadth of expertise required. For this reason, the manager must consider whether the addition of a new standard (rather than the use of extant standards in the operation) is justified. The likelihood of encountering difficulties in interfacing and programming systems also increases with the degree to which standards in the operation are *closed*. However, it is important to remember that a closed standard will often be technically superior, locally, to the open equivalent (assuming one exists) in the short term. This is because the vendor will shape its standard to be closely tailored to the equipment with which it is associated. In the long term, however, the proprietary nature of the standard can constrain flexibility and limit the ability to interconnect with unanticipated modules. Suppliers will often favor closed standards, for fairly obvious reasons, though customer pressure and increasing need for integration between "alien" modules have meant a growing availability of open-standards-based modules.

Most operations are in the upper-right hand quadrant of Figure 3, even though the variety of tasks and technical performance of the closed standards does not justify their being there. Why is this? Operations tend to add equipment and computer systems progressively, and vendors often have a zealous bias towards their own, proprietary standards. For capital equipment in particular, physical requirements will often overwhelm IT concerns. With too little thought given to the effect

---

[20]Parnas, D. L. (1972). "On the Criteria to be Used in Decomposing Systems into modules." *Comm. ACM* 5: 1053–1058. December 12, 1972.

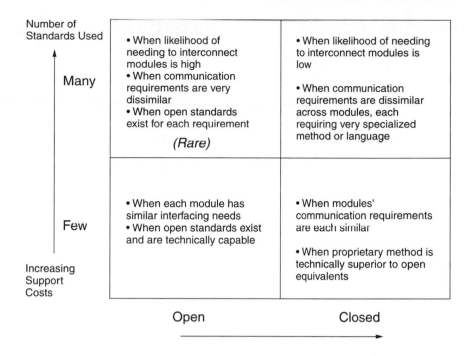

Number of Standards Used

Many

	Open	Closed
Many	• When likelihood of needing to interconnect modules is high • When communication requirements are very dissimilar • When open standards exist for each requirement *(Rare)*	• When likelihood of needing to interconnect modules is low • When communication requirements are dissimilar across modules, each requiring very specialized method or language
Few	• When each module has similar interfacing needs • When open standards exist and are technically capable	• When modules' communication requirements are each similar • When proprietary method is technically superior to open equivalents

Few

Increasing Support Costs

Open   Closed

• Increasing likelihood of subsequent interconnection problems (Vandelay)
• Increasing difficulty in adapting to local needs (Crane)
• Increased danger of proprietary lock-in (Kanebo)

FIGURE 3 Appropriate Combinations of Standards of IT in Operations

of the growing pool of proprietary standards, there eventually emerges a zoo of systems, which can be connected with one another only at great cost, with custom-written interfaces. Because the equipment and systems used are often highly specific to the "mechanics" of operations, IT managers are not in a good position to trade off the advantages of a parsimonious, open architecture with operational functionality. The answer is for the operations manager to take greater control of the computer architecture on which she increasingly depends. In the long term, this is an issue of stewardship, since there are many short-term advantages to accepting the introduction of new standards to a system. Without such attention, IT-based operations will suffer overwhelming complexity and paralyzing inflexibility.

Standards issues appear in a number of the cases in this module, as shown in Table 3. Kanebo and Vandelay must each wrestle with the dilemma of short-term functionality versus long-term flexibility. John Crane must manage the consequences of

rejecting the "closed" IBM CAD-CAM system and developing its own internal system, while AeroTech is looking for ways to exploit open standards to grow its network-based manufacturing community.

3. Building a Foundation for Improvement

3a. Operations Improvement-driven IT versus IT-driven Operations Improvement

Conventional wisdom holds that companies should first decide what their business processes must be, then employ and specify information technology to facilitate those processes. To do otherwise would be to put the cart before the horse. Philosophically, this seems to be the right approach, and—in general—it probably is. There is a balancing view, however, which manifests itself often enough not to be dismissed as mere technologists' folly: that view is that information technology will often spur improvement in unanticipated ways. In what circumstances would one tend to use a particular set of information technologies to

TABLE 3 Open Standards Issues in Cases

Class	Standard Used	Open Equivalent	Operations Issue
John Crane (CAD format)	CADAM (closed)	No Open Standard for CAD representation	Production Engineers unable to interface proprietary CAD-CAM module to CNC machines. Built a new Crane-specific method.
John Deere	Proprietary Group Technology Classification System	OPITZ, MICLASS*	Does the proprietary part/process representation have value outside Deere or is it so peculiar to Deere's manufacturing processes that it is not broadly useful?
Vandelay Industries	SAP: Proprietary Enterprise-wide system	No Open Standard	Can SAP interface with other systems, or will it simply require the purchase of additional modules (from SAP)? To what extent is the firm locked into SAP's technology?
Kanebo Ltd.	NTT/Captain	No Open Standard	What will happen if NTT discontinues the system after Kanebo has convinced stores to adopt it and build their operations around it?
AeroTech	TCP/IP, HTTP	(Open)	Use of open networking standards to create multi-partner manufacturing system.

*Source: Hyer, N. L. and Wemmerlov, U. (1985). "Group Technology Oriented Coding Systems: Structures, Applications, and Implementation." *Production and Inventory Management* 26(2): 55–78. Second quarter, 1985.

drive an improvement initiative? There are three general situations:

(i) As a source of structure to foster and reinforce new ways of working

In the 1980s, many firms had struggled for years to remove excessive work-in-progress from their batch-manufacturing shop floors, and considered the possibility of buying Flexible Manufacturing Systems (FMS) to invest their way out of the problem. In a survey of FMS installations in the 1980s, Ingersoll Engineers found that 40% of the benefits of FMS were realized before a single piece of equipment had been installed.[21] The specter of new information technology, and the formalization of processes, at last provoked plants to re-think what work was carried out, how it was planned, and how material and information moved around the plant. The discipline that the technology demanded caused long-standing vagaries and rules-of-thumb to be challenged and examined to an extent that might have been difficult without it. The DEC case looks at the tensions and practical problems that can arise when leading improvement using Information Technology to provide discipline and structure.

(ii) To build new IT-based capabilities

With the Bandit Pager project, Motorola was able to use IT not only to tackle a prevailing competitive problem, but also to develop new IT-based operating capabilities within the organization, ready to be exploited in unanticipated, innovative ways. Similarly, many firms are now installing Intranets (in-house versions of the Internet) in spite of the fact that their current usefulness is far from compelling. They are leading projects aimed at using this particular technology primarily to develop new capabilities and knowledge. These capabilities can then be used to pounce on new opportunities for exploiting the technology.

(iii) To take advantage of new and superior off-the-shelf information technology

While every operation would like to use systems that are perfectly tailored to it in every way, there are often considerable advantages to using off-the-shelf technology where it is a close approximation to what is actually needed.[22] This is particularly true in the case of "better mousetrap" technologies (which the SAP R/3 system is advertised to be). In

[21]*The FMS Report.* Kempston, UK, Ingersoll Engineers: 179. 1982.

[22]*Information Technology for Manufacturing: A Research Agenda.* Washington, D.C., National Research Council: 138–139. 1995.

these circumstances, there may be severe competitive disadvantages in *not* using the new technology, in which case that particular software or hardware would drive the improvement project. The difficulties that can arise in these circumstances are explored in the Vandelay case.

3b. Facilitation vs. Substitution

"Give us the tools, and we'll finish the job"
—WINSTON CHURCHILL

The "Factory of the Future" envisioned in the 1980s[23] is markedly different from the future being forecast today.[24] In the 1980s, many were predicting that Flexible Manufacturing Systems and associated technologies would ultimately displace people in many industries, resulting in the creation of "lights-out" factories. While the exclusion of people from operations *has* taken place in many processes (microchip manufacture, for example), we have not seen the widespread substitution of shop-floor based people, even in industries like metalworking, which FMS aimed to revolutionize. Why is this? One reason is that people have a powerful advantage over current machine technologies: the ability to learn and deal with unforeseen circumstances.[25] In spite of important advances in artificial intelligence,[26] machines are still miserably pedestrian in their ability to create new knowledge from experience, in a way that informs future action and allows them to adapt to changing circumstances. In an environment where product and market requirements change rapidly and technology becomes broadly available very quickly, the ability to learn is a valuable commodity and, currently, a uniquely human one. As new products and services are developed, the need to learn about a process or technology often requires the provision of mechanisms to involve people in the system, using IT to facilitate their work, rather than using IT to substitute for them. Zuboff[27] identifies this

dual role of information technology as the capacity to both automate and *informate*. She suggests that managers often over-emphasize the former role, because of a perceived need to exert control through the technology. This is precisely what is observed in the Cybertech case.

There are, however, some processes and systems in which the opportunities to learn and improve are either meager or competitively unimportant or where new technology can provide a vastly superior solution. We can (though oversimplifying a little) divide operators' roles into three hierarchical functions. Execution (the performance of the process), Control (determining the output of a process, correcting for changing conditions), and Learning (the improvement of the process and the development of new skills). If we exclude, for now, the possibility of information systems learning,[28] then the question is, when should information technology substitute for the role of operators in execution and control of a task, and when should it be used merely to facilitate that task?[29]

While this is a complex issue, there are clearly some circumstances that would favor one approach over the other at both levels (see Figure 4). If execution is repetitive or hazardous, the degree of variety is within the range of programmability, requirements are comparatively stable over time, and/or there are compelling productivity/quality advantages to be gained, then a substitution based approach is more likely to be beneficial. Conversely, if output is highly customized, if the process is at a low stage of knowledge, or if the task is undergoing constant change, then IT will be more useful as a facilitator rather than a substitute. At the control level, if the rules for control are well understood and concrete, decision making is frequent, and the range of circumstances over which control is required is limited, then IT may well play an important role in substituting for routine operator control, provided the system is sufficiently transparent that the operator understands what it is doing and why. If, however, there are a large number of contingencies, which are abstract and infrequent in nature or when there remain untapped opportunities to learn and experi-

[23]Jaikumar, R. (1986). "Postindustrial Manufacturing." *Harvard Business Review:* 69–76. November-December, 1986.

[24]Morton, O. (1994). "A Survey of Manufacturing Technology." *The Economist.* March 5, 1994.

[25]Gerwin, D. and Kolodny, H. (1992). AMT at the Level of the Individual. *Management of Advanced Manufacturing Technology,* John Wiley and Sons: 186–228.

[26]Kusiak, A., Ed. (1988). *Artificial Intelligence: Implications for CIM,* IFS (Publications) Ltd./Springer Verlag.

[27]Zuboff, S. (1988). *In the Age of the Smart Machine.* New York, Basic Books.

[28]While automatic learning systems do exist, they are sufficiently limited in their application to be excluded for most practical purposes.

[29]Walton examines this issue in detail in Walton, R. E. (1989). *Up and Running: Integrating Information Technology and the Organization.* Boston, MA., Harvard Business School Press.

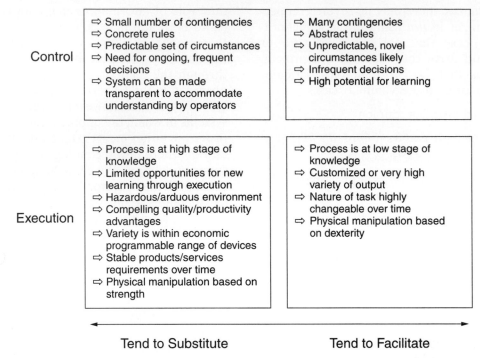

Control	⇨ Small number of contingencies ⇨ Concrete rules ⇨ Predictable set of circumstances ⇨ Need for ongoing, frequent decisions ⇨ System can be made transparent to accommodate understanding by operators	⇨ Many contingencies ⇨ Abstract rules ⇨ Unpredictable, novel circumstances likely ⇨ Infrequent decisions ⇨ High potential for learning
Execution	⇨ Process is at high stage of knowledge ⇨ Limited opportunities for new learning through execution ⇨ Hazardous/arduous environment ⇨ Compelling quality/productivity advantages ⇨ Variety is within economic programmable range of devices ⇨ Stable products/services requirements over time ⇨ Physical manipulation based on strength	⇨ Process is at low stage of knowledge ⇨ Customized or very high variety of output ⇨ Nature of task highly changeable over time ⇨ Physical manipulation based on dexterity
	Tend to Substitute	Tend to Facilitate

FIGURE 4 Circumstances Under Which One Would Use IT Either to Substitute or Facilitate

ment with the process, then IT's role should emphasize facilitation of control over substitution.

The issue of visibility in control is an important one, since operators will often be excluded from a process, and less likely to be able to improve it if they have no idea why a computer-based controller is doing what it does. The managers of Mead's paper plant in Escanaba, Michigan, for example, realized they had made a mistake on their automation initiative and reacted by tearing out their comparatively new fully-automatic "opaque" information system, substituting a system designed to deliver more information to people supervising the systems on the shop floor. In doing so, they provided a way for operators to remain engaged in the process, and were able to improve its performance over time.[30]

This decision of when to substitute and when to facilitate fuels the John Crane case, and is a fundamental issue in the Cybertech case. Both cases look at the issue of replacing vs. supporting people with an automated, IT-based system. Vandelay looks at the multi-plant version of this problem: is SAP's R/3 a hard automated system for running an operation that substitutes for and homogenizes plants' ad hoc production control systems? Or is it the basis of a facilitating toolbox to provide a base for continued improvement, which can be tailored and changed by each plant to fit its changing competitive requirements?

DESCRIPTION OF CASES

The first case, **John Crane (UK) Limited,** introduces a number of themes that will be seen in the rest of the module. Crane has spent ten years slowly improving its plant by reorganizing shop layouts, changing loading policies, and—most importantly—by increasing the skill and responsibility levels of its operators. In doing so, the operators have grown more able to control the WIP levels in the shop and have also learned to program their own Computer-Numerically-Controlled (CNC) machine tools on the shop floor. Performance increased dramatically as a result of these changes, and operators became much more engaged in the competitiveness of the company. However, in 1990, it became clear that there was a great opportunity for Crane to connect its Computer-Aided-Design system directly to the shop floor machines: essen-

[30]Upton, D. M. (1995). "What Really Makes Factories Flexible?" *Harvard Business Review:* 74–84. July–August, 1995.

tially cutting the operators out of the loop and obviating the need to have them program their machines. Crane's operators had been convinced to embrace a new information-based manufacturing technology, only to find another one waiting in the wings to take their place. Crane's dilemma then, was whether to build the new CAD-CAM link. On the one hand, managers had built an organization whose performance (particularly around *physical* flows) relied on the continued involvement of people on the floor. At the same time, there were compelling advantages of building the CAD-CAM link to streamline the *information* flows in the business.

Crane introduces some important issues in operations improvement and looks at how new technology interacts with that improvement. It also shows how important it is to give advance thought to how fundamental computer-automated process elements will fit into the system as a whole, even though the entire system might be, as yet, incomplete.

The Cybertech Project also looks at the issue of process and shop-floor integration—using a very different method. The Australian meat industry had traditionally been composed of slaughterhouses relying on arduous, labor-intensive processes. The meat industry's research association developed a system (Cybertech) aimed at creating an automated slaughterhouse. Cybertech engineers developed both new process technology and a way of integrating processes together using information technology. Here, however, we see a radically different approach to the gradual one used by Crane. Cybertech is an example of a demonstration project (as is Motorola—the following case). The development of new process technology and information technology in this case takes place away from the existing operations, in a cloistered environment sponsored by the meat industry's research association. The fundamental challenge with any demonstration project is how to spread the learning and the technology to existing operations once the system has been developed.

Motorola Inc.: The Bandit Pager Project also describes a demonstration project for developing new shop-floor integration technology. Faced with ominous benchmarking data from Japan, which showed clear problems concerning quality, Motorola decided it needed a radically different approach for manufacturing its pager products. Like Cybertech, the new approach was developed as part of a separate demonstration project to insulate it from existing practices.

By this stage in the module, three very different approaches to developing advanced operations systems have been explored. **FASTech Integration** looks at a firm making software tools that allow the rapid development of such systems. FASTech introduces a number of important concepts, in that it specifically addresses the issue of software development for operations. It first looks at why developing software for a physical environment is so different from developing, say, a payroll package. Software engineering is a much bigger problem in the development of advanced operations systems than one might think. Even without the added complexity of a physical environment, software projects always seem to take longer than a company anticipates. As the old saying goes, *the first 90% of the work takes 90% of the time: the last 10% takes the other 90%.* The question is why. Part of the reason is that engineers will often re-invent the software wheel when developing systems. FASTech provides re-usable software modules that permit engineers to use existing, tested elements to build and run their system—either from Unix machines or PCs. FASTech's software communicates with all of the processes in a system and coordinates the flow of materials and information between them in a customizable way. It is thus an example of how an MES (Manufacturing Execution System) can be built.

However, because of the way FASTech prices its software (by the number of computers it runs on), some users have started to cram too much functionality onto too few PCs, and the performance of the software has begun to degrade, making FASTech's customers' systems (the primary showcase for new customers) appear faulty. Second, some customers have developed "souped-up" devices (somewhere between a PC and a Unix machine) so that they can get the performance of a Unix machine from the software with the price for a PC.

Finally, there is a large degree of "deal-cutting" in which FASTech's salespeople try to figure out what advantage can be gained from the software and then try to price it accordingly. In contrast to FASTech, **EG&G Rotron** involves very little recognizable information technology, but still looks at the development of a system. It marks the transition of the module from process-based physical-coordination tasks to the higher level tasks of production control. Rotron is using a new technology for production control: pull-based production. Its delivery performance, however, has begun to suffer. As Rotron made its move from defense-based businesses to commercial OEM-based work, its managers decided to move towards carrying much less inventory and to producing to demand more than to forecast. After a few missed deliveries, debate at Rotron started to heat up: should they or should they not continue with the JIT project? Zealots sat in each camp as the company became more and more polarized over the issue.

Digital Equipment Corporation explores a similar set of issues, against the backdrop of a computer-based implementation of a production control system (MRP II). Digital's Auburn operation was a feeder plant designed to produce components for other plants building computer systems. The case describes the implementation of an MRP II system, aimed at improving the plant's responsiveness to its downstream cousins. During implementation, however, the plant receives an "emergency" request, which demands that the new system be overridden. Digital's Auburn plant was originally in chaos, and the MRP II system has begun to impose some discipline and control in the plant. That control, however, has come at a price. The regimentation of the MRP system means that "emergency" requests can no longer be satisfied without sacrificing the integrity of the system. However, in the longer term, as it improves, there is no doubt that the new system will enable the plant as a whole to be much more responsive.

Vandelay Industries moves further up the hierarchy and introduces Enterprise Information Systems (EIS). The German firm SAP has, with its product R/3, come to dominate the market for Enterprise-wide Information Systems. Indeed, this software package has itself spawned a whole industry of implementers that have ridden the dual waves of reengineering and enterprise integration. The Vandelay case looks at a particular installation of R/3 at Vandelay Industries. Vandelay, a company that has grown by acquisition, has in the process acquired a large number of disparate information systems. Over time, the market in which they operate has come to value responsiveness very highly. The combination of unintegrated computer systems and this changing competitive need has begun to damage operations effectiveness. To address the problem, Vandelay decided to install SAP R/3 with the help of Deloitte & Touche Consulting Group/ICS.

Kanebo Limited looks at information technology to connect the operation outside the factory walls, as well as the development of a new Flexible Manufacturing System. Kanebo, the second-largest cosmetics manufacturer in Japan, is faced with increasingly volatile demand and a need to provide much higher product availability in the thousands of stores that sell its products. To do this, Kanebo is looking at a point-of-sale based system (BellCap) that would allow it to observe a representative sample of stores and adjust the production of its various lines to fit the emerging demand. **Deere & Company: Computer-Aided Manufacturing Services Division** looks at the development and exploitation of operations technology-based capabilities. As a result of company-wide efforts to build new capabilities in information technology and operations, Deere & Co. has built new expertise in both systems integration and a computer-based form of Group Technology. Deere is considering exploiting this new capability by selling it to other manufacturing companies.

AeroTech Services Inc. describes a revolutionary project that uses the Internet to create communities of factories, which can then begin to share much richer information than the previous technologies have allowed. With McDonnell Douglas (MDA) as a focus, AeroTech provides a channel by which MDA can access its suppliers' computers and vice versa. It does so by using open-standards and building gateways to any proprietary standards that might exist. In doing so, it has changed the way MDA's network functions. Drawings now take minutes rather than days to transfer; new members can join the electronic manufacturing community without excessive hardware or training costs, and MDA has access to a much broader range of suppliers (who can bid on subcontracted work electronically). The AeroTech case explores some important Internet-working technologies, and looks at how these might change the way in which plants and networks of plants work.

The AeroTech case underscores the value of open standards, but also looks at how an understanding of information technology combined with an understanding of operations management can create new opportunities that allow firms to manage their operations in completely different ways than they might have done in the past.

John Crane UK Limited: The CAD-CAM Link

It was a crisp July morning in 1990. As usual at this time of day, the M25 London Orbital Motorway was a parking lot. Bob Gibbon, Operations Director for John Crane UK Limited, sat in his car, and thought about the previous day's meeting with John Carr, Engineering Systems Manager, and Alex Luboff, Engineering Systems Engineer. The CAD-CAM issue was getting to be a problem at John Crane's Slough[1] plant. Carr's team had demonstrated the feasibility of generating programs for computer-controlled production machines directly from the company's design database. At the same time, Crane's shop-floor operators had made astounding progress in learning to program the machines themselves from engineering drawings. They had become progressively more skilled over the past few years, chiefly as a result of their involvement in the manufacturing cells project, one of a handful of projects which had brought Crane manufacturing from mediocrity to world-class excellence. The operators were keen to continue to use their newly-acquired expertise.

Carr had put it plainly the day before: "We need to think about who should be writing these programs, now that we have a choice: should they be written automatically in Production Engineering, or should the shop-floor operators be writing them?"

THE CRANE STORY

On March 9th, 1917, Crane Packing Company was founded in Chicago, Illinois, by Frank Payne. The company's first product was invented by John Crane. He devised a system for sealing rotating shafts by packing material tightly around the shaft, thus preventing the fluid surrounding the shaft from leaking out. Payne set up a British subsidiary of Crane in Slough in 1923. By 1989, John Crane UK Limited was the main European arm of John Crane International (JCI), whose 1989 profit before interest was £32m on turnover of £239m (£1.00 = $1.85 at the time of the case). JCI was owned by the TI Group, a British company with diversified engineering interests, and had defined its corporate strategy to be congruent with that of the TI Group as a whole:

> *"TI's basic strategic thrust is to be an international engineering group, concentrating on specialized engineering businesses, operating in selected niches on a global basis, and commanding sustainable technological and market share leadership."*
>
> —CHRISTOPHER LEWINTON,
> CHAIRMAN AND CHIEF EXECUTIVE,
> TI GROUP, 1989

John Crane UK Limited managed the EMA (Europe, Middle East and Africa) region of John Crane International. This region generated 30% of JCI's revenues. John Crane EMA had subsidiaries in Austria, France, Belgium, Germany, Holland, Italy, Sweden, Spain, Switzerland and a joint venture in China. It had numerous agencies in other countries as sales and distribution points for its products and services. In 1989, over 70% of its business came from outside the UK.

THE PRODUCT: MECHANICAL SEALS

Mechanical seals had become complex engineering products with a wide variety of applications. For example, they were used around the propeller shafts of submarines to prevent sea-water from leaking past the shaft and filling the vessel; they

---

[1] Pronounced like *plough*

This case was prepared as the basis for class discussion rather than to illustrate either effective or ineffective handling of an administrative situation. Some information has been disguised.

This case was prepared by David M. Upton. Copyright © 1990 by the President and Fellows of Harvard College. Harvard Business School case 691-021.

were used on the shaft of chemical pumps to contain the fluids being pumped. The most common use was in the water-pump of an automobile, to contain the coolant around the pump drive shaft. Despite the variety of applications, all seals performed a similar function. They provided a barrier between two regions through which a common shaft rotated (see Exhibit 1). Exhibit 2 shows some examples from Crane's product range. Crane supplied seals for most applications. Customers came with a particular sealing problem, and Crane provided a solution in the form of either a standard or a custom seal, along with a housing design if necessary. Sixty percent of seal sales were replacements for seals which had reached the end of their useful life. John Crane UK manufactured 64% of the EMA region's seals by sales volume. The principal seal families are shown in Figure 1.

While there were many standard products, others were very specialized and complex, requiring superlative engineering design. For example, gas seals were special seals in a high-growth product category, on the "leading edge" of seal technology. These highly complex seals could cost tens of thousands of pounds, and demanded a high degree of production expertise.

THE MARKET

Revenues from sales of seals manufactured in the UK in 1989 were £46m. Customers for mechanical seals generally belonged to one of the following three categories:

(i) Projects

Project sales came from customers who were involved in building a large scale plant, such as an oil rig or chemical plant. Competition for these orders was intense since projects tended to be large and relatively few in number. Success in this market resulted in future sales of spare parts for the whole plant since the life of the pump being sealed was often five times longer than the life of the seal. Each seal would probably be replaced four or five times during the life of the pump.

(ii) Original Equipment Manufacturers (OEMs)

OEMs (for example, pump manufacturers) bought seals to install in their equipment before they sold to their customers. Their products were manufactured to a firm schedule, which meant that reliable delivery by Crane was essential. Again, competition was fierce, as the volumes tended to be larger and more stable, often forcing higher levels of

EXHIBIT 1 Mechanical Sealing

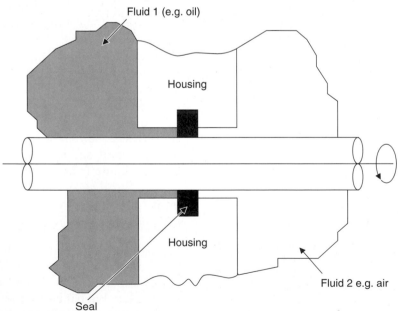

EXHIBIT 2 Examples of Products

| | | *1990 UK Production* | |
Product	*Application*	*Sales (%)*	*Typical Price (£)*
automotive and appliance	e.g. automotive coolant pump	7	1
standard rubber bellows	water-based industries	21	15
standard wedge ring	petrochemical industries	31	30
special seals	various specialist applications	41	80

FIGURE 1 Product Families

price discounting. OEMs and Project sales shared similar levels of replacement business.

(iii) End user

The majority of sales of seals and replacement parts were made to end users. Two extremes of this market were large multi-national companies which specified Crane seals in all their plants worldwide and owners of swimming pools which required seals for their filtration pumps. Larger users required reliable, though not always immediate, delivery. Small users required reliable seals with prompt replacement service.

In general, the market was conservative, and not eager to try out new products. This meant that there were some very long product life cycles: the 1A seal, one of the best selling seals, had been in the market for 40 years. At the same time, customers continued to push for improved responsiveness for applications design.

Competitors fell into four categories. First, and most important, were those similar to John Crane who offered a wide range of sealing solutions. Second, were low variety, high volume producers. They concentrated on a very small range of seals, and often lost customers as soon as they had requirements out of the range of their expertise. Third, competitors in local markets often emerged from companies expanding from seal servicing. Finally, and increasingly more worrisome, were "pirate" competitors who put Crane's name on a sub-standard seal and passed it off as genuine. Crane held approximately 30% of the European market across the range of segments it currently served, and was widely considered to be the leader in seal technology.

Crane's market had evolved markedly over the previous ten years. There had been a steady shift away from standardized products to specially designed products, which had grown from 7% of revenues in 1981 to 41% of revenues in 1989.

MANUFACTURING AT JOHN CRANE UK

Most UK employees were based in the towns of Slough and Reading[2] (20 miles apart) in the south-east of England. There were 170 production employees in Slough and 70 in Reading. The main steps in manufacturing a mechanical seal were component production and assembly. Metal-machining was the dominant method by which Crane produced seal components, although it produced some by machining PTFE[3] (10% of value) and by pressing sheet steel (20% of value).

The two main processes for machining metal components were turning and milling. In a turning process, the component was rotated and cut by a stationary tool, while in milling, the component was held still and was cut by a rotating tool. Turning resulted in round, rotationally symmetrical features, while milled features were generally asymmetrical or prismatic. Because seal features were usually round (to fit around shafts), most of the productive effort was spent turning components on lathes or turning centers (which were sophisticated lathes). All machined components were turned as part of the production process, while only some components had milled features. A typical process for a metal-machined component was:

1. Make blanks from metal stock;
2. Perform first set of primary turning operations on turning center (called Op. 1);
3. Turn component around in the work holder, and perform the second set of primary turning operations (Op. 2);
4. Mill and drill features which cannot be turned;

---

[2] Pronounced like *heading*

[3] PTFE (polytetrafluoroethylene) was a low-friction polymer. PTFE machining was carried out in a separate facility as was sheet steel work. Automotive seals were also produced in a separate local facility in Slough.

5.   Finish turn components to final tolerance; and

6.   Store for later assembly (see Exhibit 3)

Component machining work was split into two categories: Make to Order (MTO) and Make for Stock (MFS). MTO comprised 35% of machined component production value and was produced in the Slough factory. MFS made up the remaining 65% and was produced in Reading. MTO was further split into "specials" (32% of MTO unit volume), which were components specially designed for a particular order, and "stan-dard," which had already been engineered (68% of MTO unit volume). In 1989, the Slough factory machined 34,000 components while Reading produced 400,000.

Assembly was relatively straightforward and in general, Crane assembled to order. A mechanical seal comprised about 8 components assembled into a finished unit. There were nearly 100,000 finished assembly types even though there were only 6,000 standard components. While complex metal components were usually machined in-house, many components were produced by vendors

EXHIBIT 3 Manufacturing Process for Metal Machined Components

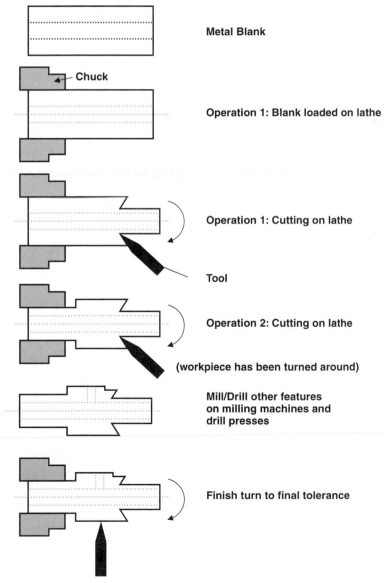

(bought-outs). Bought-outs were often non-metallic and relatively simple: carbon faces or grubscrews for example. Though Crane manufactured a large variety of seals, only a few products were made in large volumes. This meant that much of Crane's manufacturing task was that of a job-shop: making a large variety of components effectively. Sixty-five percent of Crane's components had an annual demand of less than 10 per annum. This included all MTO components and half of MFS.

> When we talk about economies, they are economies of variety, not scale. We are not trying to increase production to spread our costs over any particular product. We are trying to minimize the impact which product variety has on us. If we can aggregate our products cleverly, we gain a great advantage.

THE READING FACTORY: 1981–1983

In 1980, most of the machines (in both Reading and Slough) were 20 to 30 years old. Capital investment had slowed to a trickle of about £50,000 per annum over the previous five years. There were many different machines to cope with the enormous variety of material sizes, batch quantities, and types of product. Machines in both Reading and Slough were arranged functionally: all the lathes were together in one area, all milling machines in another and so on (Exhibit 4 shows such a functional layout). Having machines of the same type grouped together in departments meant that components had to visit multiple departments, making the flow of components through the shop very complicated. Work would slowly wend its way

EXHIBIT 4 Old Shop Layout in Slough

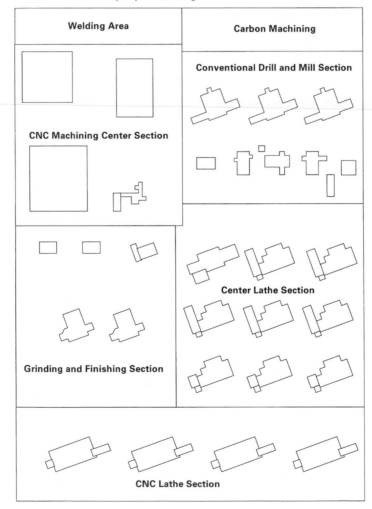

through the shop, spending most of the time sitting and waiting on the floor. A component could travel literally miles between the time the raw material went onto the floor and the time the component went into finished components stores. There was very little grouping of components in manufacturing. If anything, it was based on the volume of parts produced. Small volume components tended to be produced in Slough, and higher demand components in Reading, but there were many exceptions. A third factory in Havant handled medium volume components. Production costs were divided roughly evenly between these three factories.

In all factories, the objective was to keep machines busy. Shop loading was aimed at maintaining machine utilization. Unfortunately, the large number of components in process meant that there were very long lead times. Gibbon commented on the Reading factory.

> In Reading, we could have 8, 10 or 12 weeks worth of work sitting at a given machine. We often had to interrupt a batch to put on a rush job, and the work-in-process reflected our lead times of about 3 months in make-to-stock (90% of value) and 6 months in make-to-order (10% of value). The mix gave rise to a complex logistical problem.

The Reading factory ran two shifts, five days a week, and made about 300,000 components a year. Components were being produced in a very wide variety of batch sizes; some of the larger batches were 2000–3000 components. Occasionally these long jobs were punctuated with rush orders, which usually meant re-setting some machines and losing considerable productive time.

In the middle of 1982, the Havant factory was burnt down by an arsonist. While this was a short-term disaster, it gave Crane a golden opportunity to resite and reorganize production. Havant production was brought to Reading. Gibbon, in his mid-twenties at the time, was made Production Superintendent and put in charge of the move. Reading was divided into a stock shop (for make-for-stock components) and a non-stock shop (for make-to-order components), to increase the visibility of make-to-order work by manufacturing it separately. This was the first attempt at grouping components within a factory. (The non-stock shop was moved to Slough in 1984). This separation greatly improved the visibility of non-stock work

in the shop, and reduced the lead time for non-stock components from 26 weeks to 12 weeks. Within each of these shops, a number of changes were made:

> We wanted to use the opportunity to make production more flexible. We tried to make machines more similar to each other and we trained people to operate a number of machines.

The replacement labor was new. In the old factory, people on the shop-floor were either setters (who performed machine set-ups) or operators. The change in labor force meant that this tradition could be changed, and workers were employed as setter–operators rather than one or the other. While this was a small step, it meant a great increase in flexibility in the shop. Improvements were limited, since the machines were fire-damaged and the labor was new. Even with this hindrance, make-for-stock lead times were reduced to 6 weeks. Despite weathering the fire, and making improvements along the way, the way the Reading factory was being run was still a headache.

> As things were, we threw work at the shop because that's what the order point system demanded. In 1981, I had made a computer model of the factory using CAN-Q[4] (see Exhibit 5), so that we could understand our plant better and demonstrate the advantages of any changes in the system. We validated the model and found it accurate to within 2 or 3%. We explored the relationship between the amount of work-in-process on the shop floor and the output we got from the plant (see Exhibit 6). This made it even clearer to me that the way we were loading work onto the shop was a big problem. I just couldn't win on this point!—people genuinely believed it was the production's fault that lead times were so long, rather than the policies we were using. Countering the traditional beliefs about shop loading was very difficult.

Gibbon was convinced that the policy of keeping the shops loaded down with work was hurting effectiveness and was causing long lead times. The results he had gleaned from the computer model further steeled his conviction that changes were needed. Frustratingly, he was unable

---

[4] CAN-Q was a computer program which used queueing theory to mathematically model the flow of work around a factory. It gave information such as expected queue lengths and throughput times.

Term	Definition
2D-Drafting	The use of design systems which rely on two-dimensional representations of three-dimensional objects.
CAD	Computer Aided Design.
CADAM™	IBM proprietary CAD system.
CAM	Computer Aided Manufacture.
CANQ	Computer Analysis of Networks of Queues: A simple, generalized mathematical model of a manufacturing system developed by James Solberg at Purdue University.
CAPP	Computer Aided Process Planning: The use of computers to generate methods for producing a product, either through interaction with the user (interactive) or automatically (generative).
CIM	Computer Integrated Manufacturing: The philosophy or tools associated with ensuring use of common computer information in products, processes and business systems.
CNC	Computer Numerical Control: A system for operating the axes and motors of machine tools using computers and electromechanical drives, rather than human motion. Sequences of motions are stored in a part-program and run on a CNC machine controller.
Discrete Event Simulation	The modelling of a system, usually on a computer, by describing the changes that occur to it at discrete points in time. Examples of computer software packages to do this are XCELL and SLAM™.
Machine tool	A device for shaping or cutting a product which incorporates driven spindles, along with two or more axes of motion for either the tool, the workpiece, or both. Examples of machine tools are lathes, milling machines, and grinding machines.
Offline programming	The production of part programs without stopping the machine on which they are to run.
NC	Numerical Control: The precursor to CNC, which used paper tapes and electromechanical systems rather than computers.
Part program	The computer program which a CNC machine tool uses to direct its motors and axes, containing detailed instructions on how to produce a component.
Post processor	A computer program which adapts a generalized computer-based process plan to produce a part program for a particular machine tool.
Turning	A method of machining which involves rotating the workpiece and cutting it with a stationary tool. This is carried out on a lathe or a turning center.
Turning Center	A sophisticated lathe, which provides additional machine capabilities, such as driven tools.

EXHIBIT 5 A Glossary of Terms

to convince people that there could be a better way of doing things.

CNC and Cells in Reading, 1984–1986

Having had such difficulties changing shop-loading practices within the status quo, Gibbon changed tack and turned to new production technology and the problem of flow. The age of the machines in the Reading shop often made it difficult to hold tolerances and efficiently produce a high-quality product. Gibbon and his team set about justifying an investment of £350,000 in new, Computer Numerically Controlled (CNC) machine tools. As the name implies, a CNC machine has a dedicated computer controller which tells the machine all it needs to know to make a part, such as the spindle-speed, the position of the tools, the tooling to be used and so on. On traditional machines, the operators performed these functions using levers and dials. Computer-control was much faster and more reliable. The controller had a computer program (a part-program) for each part which the machine would make. This could be read into the controller's memory from punched tape, magnetic media, or another computer by a communications link.

Some non-CNC machines did a similar job using mechanical automation, but the set-up time for each batch was long, so these machines were relatively inflexible. CNC machines required only a change of program and the appropriate tooling to switch jobs. The new machines would thus be more flexible since the penalty of changing from one job to the next would be reduced. The machines also tended to be more versatile because they could make many more types of components

CAN-Q Results—Reading Shop—1981

Mean WIP (components)	Mean Lead Time (working days)	Mean Output Rate (components/day)
4970	15.1	329
7456	16.1	464
9941	17.1	581
12426	18.2	683
14912	19.3	771
17397	20.5	847
19882	21.8	912
22368	23.1	967
24853	24.5	1014
27338	25.9	1054
29824	27.4	1086
32309	29.0	1113
34794	30.7	1134
37280	32.4	1151
39765	34.2	1163
42250	36.0	1173
44736	37.9	1179
47221	39.9	1182

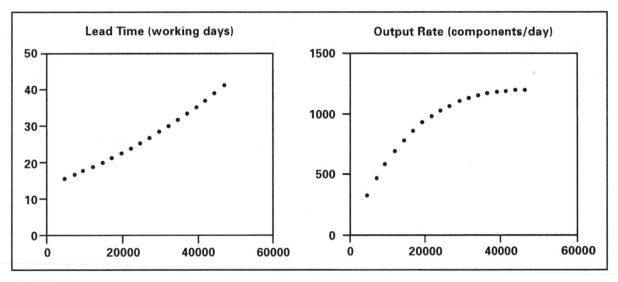

EXHIBIT 6 CAN-Q Results

than the old machines. This was a large investment for Crane and came at a time when capital was short. To be sure that the project was accepted, the justification carried out was unusually rigorous, thorough, and extensive.

The proposed investment in the new machines gave Crane the chance to look very carefully at the way it ran its production operation, and issues such as material flow were closely examined. During the project, in 1983, Crane looked at the prospect of a Flexible Manufacturing System (FMS): a complex system with an automated materials-handling system connecting unattended machines together, the whole shop being scheduled by a central computer. The team decided that the technology was too new, and too inflexible to adapt to Crane's needs. However, the process of carrying out the analysis for the FMS crystallized Crane's production-system needs. A great deal of use was made of discrete-event simulation,[5] which now became an important instrument of persuasion. After considering all the alternatives, Crane decided to rely on the following to improve their manufacturing system:

- Manufacturing cells
- Advanced production technology (in the form of CNC machines)
- Better-trained people

---

[5] See Exhibit 5

Manufacturing cells were formed on the principle that machines in a shop should be located based on the parts they were producing rather than the type of machine they were. In effect, minifactories were created within an existing plant. Gibbon set up 3 different types of cells in Reading, as shown in Exhibit 7. Components were grouped to be produced by particular cells. In Reading the groupings were made by distinguishing between those components which required only turning (turned rings) and those which required turning and subsequent milling (drilled rings). Rather than making a long, weary journey from department to department, batches of components passed quickly around a close-knit U-shaped "cell" of machines, visiting 2 or 3 of them. Each cell contained all the machines necessary to complete its type of job along with a small group of operators who ran the cell.

Union rules in the shop had always been that one machine should be tended by one person.

EXHIBIT 7 New Shop Layout in Slough

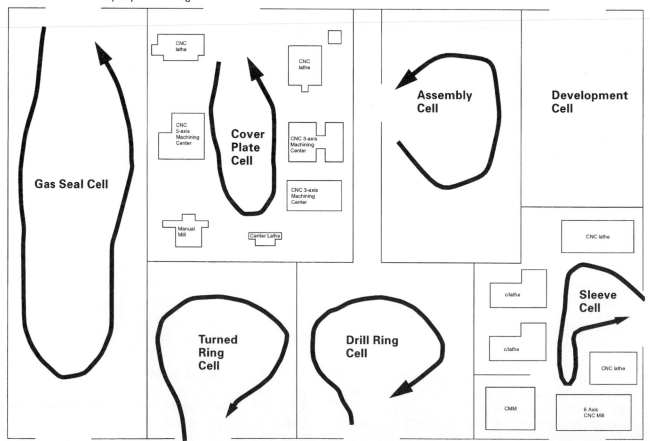

However, the change in machine technology made this policy clearly unreasonable. Operators could often tend multiple machines if computers tended low-level operations. Operators assigned to work on the cells were thoroughly trained in the new technology. When the new machines were commissioned, performance targets based on learning curves were set for the operators, many of whom took these targets as a personal challenge. They became very committed to the project as they learned more about the technology and the new production system. The move towards cells meant a very different style of work for them. Instead of having the next operation for a batch on the other side of the shop and possibly several weeks away, the subsequent operation was performed a few meters away and possibly only minutes after the original operation. This link fostered cooperation between people on the shop-floor. Rather than sitting in isolation, plodding through an endless pile of work waiting for the same operation, people became aware of the total production process. Gerry Cusack, a Production Engineer at the time, pointed out:

> A big part of the success of this project came from the bottom. A lot of work was put in by everyone, but the people on the machines could have made it work or killed it off. They made it work.

By mid-1986, the project was clearly a success:

> To be fair, it would have been difficult to fail using such new equipment. Even so, output per operator increased by 13%, and lead times fell by 65%. Both of these are key measures for Crane. People liked the project and the technology gained acceptability. We were on a roll!

The experiment had paid off. Not only had the introduction of cells and CNC improved performance, but it had, at last, clearly demonstrated the advantages of not overloading the shop with work. During 1986, batch quantities were reduced dramatically as manufacturing and stock management became more aware of these advantages. This new way of working was not without its problems, however:

> Operators were used to having a mountain of work in front of them: there was always something to do. Now, they had to get used to the idea that they only got work when it was needed. This was uncomfortable for some people.

To limit work in the shop, Crane painted 1.5 meter squares on the floor for finished work. That square also held the input buffer for the next operation. Operators were given a "make list" each week, but were also told that they could only put their finished work in the square while there was room: if it got full, they were to stop and find out why it wasn't being emptied. Four years later, the painted squares were long worn away, but the work-in-process continued to be as low as when they were fresh on the floor. The control system in Reading started to shift from a re-order point system (fixed quantity, variable time) to a time-phased system (fixed time, variable quantity). This meant that similar components could be grouped together more easily. These changes in production control decreased lead times by a further 50%.

Not everyone was happy with the new methods. About 5% of the operators just didn't like it: they preferred the old way of working. In general, however, the project resulted in an enormous improvement in morale. Operators helped to make video recordings of each other setting up machines so that they could improve their work-methods. They wrote, produced and edited a video tape of the cells, demonstrating how much better the manufacturing system was, now that the cells were in place. The title music they chose was Bachman Turner Overdrive: "You Ain't Seen Nothin' Yet."

Cells in Slough

In 1988, the lease ran out on Crane's London Road plant in Slough. Rather than renew the lease, the whole factory was moved to a new building in Slough in October 1988. The experience of installing cells in Reading and the factory move meant that the time was ripe for moving to the cell system in Slough for production of non-stock components. The Slough operation demanded much more flexibility of its manufacturing system because of the sheer variety and novelty of components that were produced. Along with the move, several new CNC machines were bought, primarily turning centers. By July 1990, six cells were working in Slough on two shifts. These are shown in Exhibit 7. As in Reading, these cells produced components according to their geometry, although the gas ring and assembly cells were separate. The move to cells was a similar success in Slough. Operators were paid 25p per hour more for each new skill learned. Thus, a turner who could also mill could make £2.00 per day more by learning the skill. Mark Glennerster, Production Controller at Slough, commented:

> In the old plant, it was easy for work to be obscured by the general mess. With the cells though, everyone can see the work sitting in a particular cell waiting to be worked on—problems can't be hidden. It really is management by sight.

In the old plant, WIP could be dismissed as being on its way from one machining area to another. With the cell system, it was obvious that WIP was the responsibility of the people in that cell which made the whole manufacturing system much easier to keep under control for both managers and operators.

Since 1981, Crane's continual manufacturing development had helped to greatly improve the EMA region's operating performance, as evidenced in Figure 2.

CIM AT CRANE

While the cells were being developed on the shop floor, changes were made in manufacturing philosophy at the top of the organization. By 1985, Computer Integrated Manufacturing (CIM) became an important issue.

> By 1985, FMS was dead. Everyone read "The Goal." OPT and JIT were the fashionable things. The emphasis moved very much to the "Whole Business" issue and Computer Integrated Manufacturing was a natural progression.

Technologies such as Computer Aided Design (CAD) and Computer Aided Manufacturing (CAM) had been developed at Crane but management knew that such technology could also be bought by competitors. In its simplest terms, computer integration meant ensuring that computer information generated by one part of the company could be used directly in all others. For example, subsidiary companies needed to be able to access data from the central design database and the ordering system needed to be integrated with production planning. CIM was both a set of technologies and a philosophy. In 1985, it was common for people to carry boxes of computer-printout from one part of the Slough headquarters to another. This was the antithesis of the CIM philosophy. Management at Crane were convinced

	1981	1990	Change
Turnover (£m)	28	70	+150%
Inventory/Sales			–45%
Return on Assets			+120%
Sales/Employee (£000)			+130%
Lead time (days):			
MTO	180	7	–96%
MFS	90	9	–90%
Components produced (Reading)	300,000	400,000	+33%
Components produced (Slough)	10,000	34,000	+340%

FIGURE 2 Performance Improvement, 1981 to 1990

that instilling CIM "thinking" in the firm was the key. Gibbon pointed out:

> CIM meant the integration of the whole manufacturing business. We had simplified a lot of our processes, and automated them: the key was integration. CIM, for us, was CIM. Because it involved so many departments and personal interests, it really needed commitment and perseverance right at the top of the organization to carry it through. It's good to have as much technical understanding as you can at the top level—even when there is a lot of trust—top people need to know the technology so they can play devil's advocate. They also need enough technical knowledge to deal with all of the changes which take place, and not be overwhelmed by technology.

The push towards CIM was intense. A team with representatives from Finance, Engineering Design, Logistics, Production Engineering and Data Processing was assembled to look at business integration.

> Although the brief was business integration, CIM was our fashionable flag. We went away for a week to discuss it, and slowly we developed a CIM strategy. We assessed what we thought were the current and future needs of the business in terms of financial performance and satisfying customer demands. To improve, we used information and product flows along with lead times and development times and how we might reduce them. We then asked the Board to commit to a feasibility study.

The team recognized that a CIM "philosophy" was something too intangible to impart to the organization. It needed to be made clear by projects which would be pilots for the company's direction, and which would use CIM technology to achieve their ends. This process generated eight CIM foundation projects, as shown in Exhibit 8.

> CIM gave us a shared vision. The technology forced people to talk to one another, and made information transfer come naturally. The process of developing the projects was probably as important as the projects themselves. It gave people a more holistic view of the business.

One CIM project was the development of an expert system: The process of providing a customer with a seal suited to the particular application demanded considerable judgment and expertise on the part of the sales engineer. The

knowledge required for seal-selection had become progressively more expansive and complex. Experienced sales engineers were not easy to find and there was considerable disparity amongst them. In general, older salespeople recommended standard "conservative" solutions, while younger, newer employees tended to suggest novel solutions using the latest seal technology. Sales engineers often disagreed about the best solution for an application. To resolve some of these problems, Crane developed an expert system for seal selection. This was a program which could run on a laptop computer, and could ultimately be carried by sales engineers to their customers. The program used

EXHIBIT 8 CIM Report

Computer Integrated Manufacturing, (CIM), is a never-ending road to continual business improvement. It requires us to be constantly aware of present and future developments in technology and to plan the future with these advances in mind.

However, to ensure that we make best use of these developments as they arise, it is very important that we get and keep our company in the right shape. To achieve this we have established 8 major projects which will form the foundation of our CIM strategy.

Because any company, including our competitors, can buy computers, CNC, CAD, etc., we must ensure that the benefit John Crane gains from such investments is greater than that achieved by our competitors.

The key to this success is YOU.

The adaptability, flexibility and ingenuity of every employee to make best use of these technologies and systems is the key to us maintaining our number 1 position in the world.

To date, the building blocks of CIM already in use (CAD, CNC, JIT, Mainframe, mini and microcomputer systems, etc.) and the subsequent corporate focus since we first committed ourselves to CIM in 1985 have made significant contributions to our corporate objectives.

Continuing to stay on top had to be our aim so the 8 CIM foundation projects are practical actions for further improvements to Crane's competitiveness now, and in the future.

We have set ambitious, but realistic targets and John Crane's board and senior management are committed to achieving them.

To realise these ambitions *everybody* has to play their part.

KEY CIM PROJECTS AND TARGETS

Projects	*Targets (December 1988)*
1. CAD Development	Install CADAM in major subsidiaries
2. Expert Systems	Install Seal Selection System to Subsidiaries/Sales Offices
3. Made-in Non-Stocks	Lead time reduction • Sales order to supply order—2 weeks • Standards—2 weeks • Specials—4 weeks
4. Made-in Stocks	Service Level—95% Lead time reduction—1 week
5. Order Processing System	Update
6. Just-in-time (JIT) Purchasing	Lead time reduction • Stock items—2 weeks • Non-stocks—4 weeks
7. JIT Purchasing (by John Crane)	Lead time reduction • Stock items—2 weeks • Non-stock items—4 weeks
8. New Factory	Improved Communication Reduced Indirect Costs

Artificial Intelligence (AI) techniques to embody the expertise of the sales engineers as a whole, as well as the engineering department, and asked the user a response-dependent sequence of questions. After gathering the responses, the program would provide a seal suitable for the application, according to a standardized selection procedure. This and the seven other foundation projects steered Crane firmly on a course towards computer integration.

CIM became the central theme in the development of manufacturing at Crane. The link between CAD and CAM was one of the prominent motifs.

COMPUTER AIDED DESIGN

In the late 1970s, Crane had a very traditional design office in which people sat at boards with pencils and erasers and produced the engineering drawings which conveyed their designs. By the early 1980s, it was clear that things had to change. The tremendous expertise which had been built up over the years needed to be used more effectively: customers required more responsiveness from Crane and their competition, and the time it took designers to produce drawings caused a bottleneck. CADAM™[6], a 2-dimensional drafting package which ran on a mainframe, was introduced in 1983. To produce a drawing using CADAM™, a designer sat at a workstation with a light pen and a button box, and produced the engineering drawing which expressed the details of the seal design. Many short-cut features in the software meant that designers no longer had to worry about time-consuming geometric constructions. The computer did these for them and freed them to concentrate on the design process itself. Much more importantly, CADAM™ allowed the designers to edit existing designs to produce a new one. For John Crane's business, this was a great boon. Very few of the "specials" were truly completely new designs; they were almost always adaptations of an existing design using perhaps a different material or a different dimension here and there.

By early 1985, the average time to produce an engineering design had been halved to one week, and by 1989, the CADAM™ mainframe system operating within the UK was used to generate all

special and standard drawings for manufacture and assembly. The system soon allowed subsidiaries to access the design and gave them much faster and more accurate interaction with the design office.

COMPUTER AIDED MANUFACTURING

Traditionally, skilled operators had been able make items directly from an engineering drawing (see Exhibit 9A and Exhibit 10) on manually-controlled machines. However, when the first CNC machines were bought and installed, programs were written by the Production Engineering Department. Production Engineers worked from computer-generated paper drawings and devised the tool paths required to produce the geometry in metal (see Exhibit 9B). Stand-alone microcomputers translated that plan and tailored it for a particular machine. Punched tapes were then produced and taken to the machine tool. Each manufacturer's machine tools required that slightly different dialects be produced to allow for particular physical designs and controllers. Programs which translated the code into the right dialect were called post-processors. Fortunately, Crane was using CNC machine tools from only a handful of manufacturers at the time, and post-processor software was available for all these machines

Production Engineers became the link between the CAD system and the computer-controlled machine tools on the floor. The operators' jobs were made much more straightforward because they became responsible simply for running and tending the machines. Even so, they frequently re-checked the Production Engineers' work after the tape was read into the machine.

Despite the advantages of this manufacturing method, a number of Production Engineers were still dissatisfied with it. Alex Luboff commented:

> It was ludicrous. We were drawing a component on CAD, printing this off onto paper and typing the dimensions back into another computer to produce a part-program. It was time to buy a system that could automatically combine CAD and CAM. The CAD system did have the ability to allow machine-tool programmers to interact with the system and produce process plans and part-programs automatically, but at the beginning of 1987, CADAM™'s CNC software was very basic, and was seen by the

---

[6] CADAM is a trademark of IBM Corporation

EXHIBIT 9 Stages of Design–Manufacturing Links at John Crane UK Limited

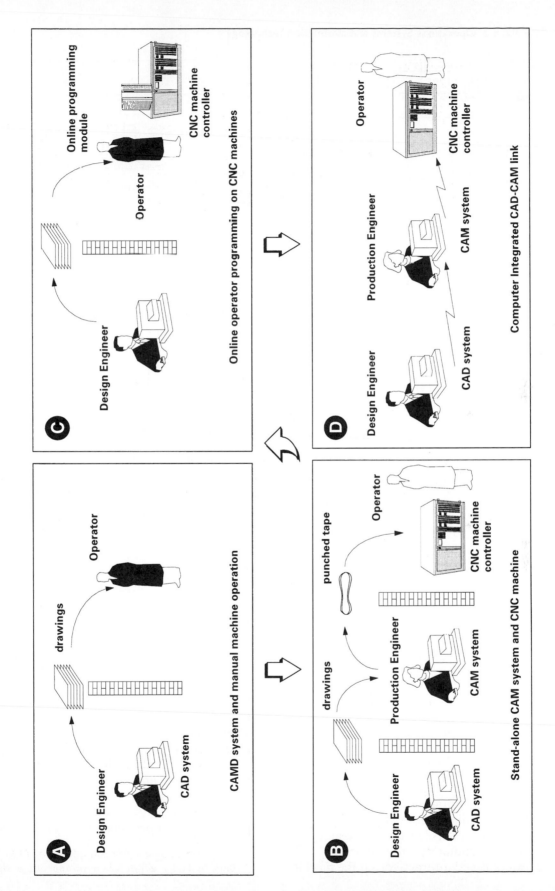

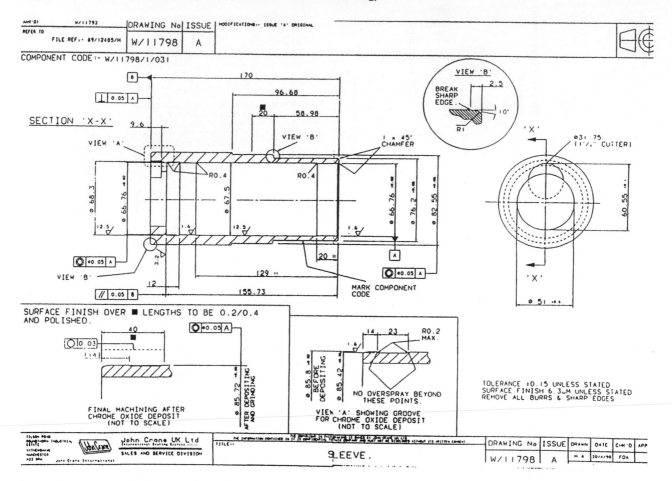

EXHIBIT 10 Drawing of a Seal Component

Production Engineers as worthless for Crane's purposes—it just didn't produce usable programs. By the middle of the year IBM's CADAM™ group had announced vast improvements to their software and we agreed that this was the way to go. In 1988, a new mainframe computer was installed in Slough together with 16 workstations and the CADAM™ upgrade (including a package from IBM from which it was possible to create a post processor for any machine tool simply by filling in a questionnaire). We set ourselves a target of one year to set up the CAD-CAM system for all the machine tools in Slough. At the same time, six new turning centers were purchased, all with advanced on-machine programming facilities.

The new machine tools understood a different dialect of programming language and there was no software available to post-process the Production Engineers' plans on the stand-alone microcomputers. Fortunately, the machine tools could be programmed interactively at the machine

console using a friendly, graphical language. Their controllers dealt with the post-processing internally. As there was no other way to produce programs for the machines, the operators were trained in this "online" programming (see Exhibit 9C). Meanwhile, engineers eagerly awaited the new CADAM™ CNC package. Disappointingly, it was much inferior to expectations. The engineering team was frustrated: many years of discussion with the supplier still had not produced a usable system. There were numerous software errors, and the engineers complained of "tediously slow" processing. It was also very difficult to create post-processors for the system, and engineers found that it lacked many features necessary for the type of work Crane did. Gerry Cusack pointed out that the process plans it produced were also a problem:

Take a sleeve for example—CADAM™ made cuts of equal depth when boring out a sleeve. A skilled operator makes very fine cuts towards the end of the job because a sleeve is a long, vibrating thin object. There's still some art in programming a CNC machine, and a computer can't capture it that easily.

The Engineering Systems group spent the rest of the year trying to trick and cajole CADAM™ into producing usable programs for the new machines. At the end of the year, they still faced the problem that they couldn't get "into" the software to alter it. It just could not produce programs as good as those the operators were producing.

By mid-1989, the project was put on hold in anticipation of an early 1990 re-release of CADAM™. The new version promised to provide licensees direct access to CAD data so they could write their own software, and offered an ideal chance for Crane to build its own CAD-CAM software to exact specifications. Bob Gibbon and the Engineering Systems team carried out a feasibility study of the new "Crane written" system when the new CADAM™ release arrived. By the beginning of February 1990, the development of the Crane CAM software was well underway and trials were resoundingly successful; by July, the software was nearing completion of the initial stage (turning for one type of CNC turning center). (See Exhibit 9D.)

Tests of the new software produced impressive results—at last, a Production Engineer could sit at a terminal in the drawing office, pull up a component's CAD drawing, generate a part-program and post-process it without errors. The engineers were elated: the CAD-CAM link had been forged.

THE SITUATION IN JULY 1990

Online Programming

The purchase of six new turning centers combined with the inadequacies of the CAD-CAM system had made further operator training a necessity. Operators became highly skilled in producing part-programs on the machines from paper drawings produced by the CAD system. The fact that only one department was involved in producing a part-program meant that lead time was much shorter. Programming and proving times improved because operators were familiar with both the part-program they had written and the machine it was being written for. Many of the operators pointed out that

they found their jobs more satisfying when they were able to do the programming themselves. The new turning centers were distributed amongst the cells, and performed both Operations 1 and 2 on each job they produced. Operators estimated their programming time to be 30 minutes for Operation 1 and 15 minutes for Operation 2. Operator time was not a significant constraint, since CNC machines ran without interaction once the component was loaded.

The problem with online programming was that machines were not productive while the operator was programming on them. The combination of machine and operator cost approximately £100 per hour. While it was technically possible to program on the machines while they were cutting another job, the fact that jobs could be produced in very short runs made this impractical and difficult. A sample of operator time sheets showed an average of 1.96 jobs (batches) for each of the six turning centers per shift. Although a job may have been done before (in exactly the same way in some cases), operators often "re-programmed" the machine. This could be solved by storing and pooling tapes, but would operators trust each others' part programs as much as their own?

Machine controllers were idiosyncratic. When all the CNC part-programs were being written by Production Engineering, the operators only had to know how to run a machine. If they had to program machines as well, their flexibility in moving from machine to machine in the cell was reduced. While they were, in general, enthusiastic, a handful of operators disliked programming, and some were much better at it than others. Online part-programming also meant that design-for-manufacture problems often were not spotted until they held up an operator on the floor.

Offline Programming

The advantage of programming machines offline was that the machine could be running while the part-program was being prepared. Programming was carried out on a separate computer, allowing the machine tool's control computer to be used exclusively for production.

The stand-alone microcomputer-based offline programming was still used by Production Engineers for the older CNC machines. The new in-house software would enable them to produce offline programs for the new machines using data direct from the CAD system. The cost of employing a Production Engineer as a part-programmer was around £16,000 per annum. If the offline programming could be done from CADAM™ using the new software, then there would be no manual translation of dimensions from the drawing. This would improve quality by eliminating transcription errors, and the time it took the engineer to produce a part program would be halved in comparison to operators using the online method. It would also allow a more straightforward path for future computer integration: the component design, part-program and measurement program would all be derived from the same data file, integrating both the design and measuring processes with fabrication. Eventually, the costing system (for example) could be integrated using this link. The annualized cost of a CADAM™ workstation was estimated at £3000.

THE CIM CELL DILEMMA

Should part-programming be carried out offline, by Production Engineering on CADAM™ workstations in the Production Engineering office, or by the operators using the machine's local control computers on the shop-floor? Paul Sefton was an engineer on the CIM team:

> Computer Integration is a sound philosophy for manufacturing, but to integrate, you have to do some standardization. Take the expert system project for example—we can't get people to agree on a standard seal-selection procedure despite the fact that

we need one badly.[7] Look at CAD-CAM: the operators have really put their weight behind improving things on the shop-floor, but they all do programming differently and its getting to be very inefficient. Perhaps they'll just have to stand aside now and let the Production Engineers write standard programs again. CIM will give Crane advantages that it just cannot let slip away.

Crane's CIM project was the cornerstone of its manufacturing strategy. Eventually Crane would be able to integrate all its manufacturing departments, allowing them to achieve "sustainable technological leadership" in manufacturing. The push towards CIM from the top of the company was clear and strong.

At the same time, the cells had been built by helping operators to become autonomous and responsible. Crane saw their commitment and energy as the central element of its improved manufacturing performance. In the main, they had taken to the task of programming their machines with great enthusiasm and were doing an excellent job of transferring the skills they had developed from years of manual work to computer-based machine tools. Now, there was an alternative to the online programming skills which the operators had learned: true integration with the CAD system. Gibbon sat back amidst the juggernauts on the motorway and considered the dilemma.

---

[7] By 1990, the seal-selection expert system was still having difficulty gaining acceptance in the UK. Whereas sales engineers sometimes provided different solutions to each other, they could usually be relied upon to disagree with the expert system.

CASE 10

The Cybertech Project (A)

Jack Crawford, Chief Executive of Cybertech Pty looked out over the green Queensland pasture at Wollagong Meatworks as his mobile phone rang for the third time in as many minutes. There were some things to be proud of today. The production trials had been a great success. Even so, it was still not clear what the future held for the Cybertech project.

Cybertech was the world's most advanced meat processing facility, and was poised to provide a beacon to the world in introducing automation to the largely manual meat processing industry. Developed by a meat industry research organization, it provided a complete, computer-integrated system of linked processing stations to replace age-old methods and work-practices.

Yet, despite its technical excellence, the way in which the Cybertech project technology might be exploited was unclear. While many meat processing managers had praised the system as a shining example of a first-class technical demonstration project, some were skeptical about its benefits. Still others were intrigued by the potential of some of the processing stations developed for the system and were keen to adopt them as modules in their plants, but were reluctant to invest in the whole system. It would mean a radical departure, after all, for the way the whole industry was run, let alone for the brave plants who undertook the challenges of being the site for the next generation of the Cybertech experiment.

Crawford was steadfast in his belief that the greatest promise of the Cybertech system lay in the wholesale computer-integration of each of its elements, and that piecemeal adoption would result in benefits falling far short of its potential. This was an astonishing technological leap, mused Crawford. Could it be that this incredible achievement would really be chopped up, adopted in bits and pieces, here and there, and that the 15 year dream of a fully-integrated, computer-controlled meat processing system would never find a place in what was, after all, one of the backbones of the Australian economy?

Crawford mulled over three questions:

- How should he convince the meat industry that Cybertech was the best path to improve its long-term performance?

- What strategy should he employ to ensure the dissemination of the Cybertech production technology, as a computer-integrated whole rather than as isolated islands of automation?

- What steps should he take to ensure that the second commercial project—Cybertech 2—would be less expensive than the over-engineered Cybertech 1, and how much cheaper did it need to be?

MEAT PRODUCTION

Meat production had long been regarded as an arduous and particularly physical industry in which to work. Meat production legislation in the U.S.A. underwent radical changes concerning both safety and hygiene after the publication of Upton Sinclair's novel "The Jungle" (see Exhibit 1), which described life in meat processing plants in Chicago at the turn of the century. It was said that Theodore Roosevelt, reading the serialized novel during his breakfast of steak and eggs, went to his window in the White House and vomited, giving rise to a renewed personal vigor on his part to pursue not only much stricter control over the processing of meat, but also new labor laws which began to protect people from the prevailing horrors of the meat-packing plants.

The workers in each of [the processes] had their own peculiar diseases. And the wandering visitor might be sceptical about all the swindles, but he could not be sceptical about these, for the worker bore the evidence of them about on his own person—generally he had only to hold out his hand.

There were the men in the pickle rooms, for instance where old Antanas had gotten his death; scarce a one of these that had not some spot of horror on his person. Should a man so much as scrape his finger pushing a truck in the pickle rooms, and he might have a sore that would put him out of the world; all the joints in his fingers might be eaten by the acid, one by one. Of the butchers and floorsmen, the beef-boners and trimmers, and all those who used knives, you could scarcely find a person who had the use of his thumb; time and time again the base of it had been slashed, till it was a mere lump of flesh against which the man pressed the knife to hold it. The hands of these men would be criss-crossed with cuts, until you could no longer pretend to count them or to trace them. They would have no nails—they had worn them off pulling hides; their knuckles were swollen so that their fingers spread out like a fan. There were men who worked in the cooking rooms, in the midst of steam and sickening odours, by artificial light; in these rooms the germs of tuberculosis might live for two years, but the supply was renewed every hour. There were the beef-luggers, who carried two-hundred-pound quarters into the refrigerator cars—a fearful kind of work, that began at four o'clock in the morning, and that wore out the most powerful men in a few years. There were those who worked in the chilling rooms, and whose special disease was rheumatism; the time limit that a man could work in the chilling rooms

was said to be five years. There were the wool-pluckers, whose hands went to pieces even sooner than the hands of the pickle men, for the pelts of the sheep had to be painted with acid to loosen the wool, and then the pluckers had to pull out this wool with their bare hands till the acid had eaten their fingers off. There were those who made the tins for the canned meat; and their hands, too, were a maze of cuts, and each cut represented a chance for blood poisoning. Some worked at the stamping machines, and it was seldom that one could work long there at the pace that was set, and not give out and forget himself, and have a part of his hand chopped off. There were the "hoisters," as they were called, whose task it was to press the lever which lifted the dead cattle off the floor.

They ran along upon a rafter, peering down through the damp and the steam; and as old Durham's architects had not built the killing room for the convenience of the hoisters, at every few feet they would have to stoop under a beam, say four feet above the one they ran on; which got them into the habit of stooping, so that in a few years they would be walking like chimpanzees. Worst of any, however, were the fertilizer-men, and those who served in the cooking rooms. These people could not be shown to the visitor, for the odour of a fertilizer-man would scare any ordinary visitor at a hundred yards; and as for the other men, who worked in tank rooms full of steam, and in some of which there were open vats near the level of the floor, their peculiar trouble was that they fell into the vats; and when they were fished out, there was never enough of them left to be worth exhibiting—sometimes they would be overlooked for days, till all but the bones of them had gone out to the world as Durham's Pure Leaf Lard!

EXHIBIT 1 Excerpt from *The Jungle*

Even though meat processing had come a long way since the days of Sinclair's novel, it remained an unglamorous industry, which failed to attract many graduates. Despite wide consumption of meat and its importance to the economy, meatworks were often used by parents in Australia as an example of where *not* to work. It was, however, a critical export industry. As the nation's Eurocentric roots began to wither, an increasingly vigorous trading network was growing with the Pacific Rim countries. While a trend towards "healthy" lifestyles in the US had begun to stem growth in certain red-meat categories, demand in Asia was growing at 7% a year—twice that of the OECD countries. In 1964, 58% of Australian export meat was destined for the United States, but by 1993, 40% of the business was done with Korea and Japan, versus 37% with the U.S.

THE PHOENIX PLANT

The Glenfillon Meat Works in Phoenix, Queensland, was one of the best examples of a modern (but traditional) meat-production process in the industry. Phoenix was a plant with 550 people on-site running a two shift operation, processing 850 beasts per day. The process of producing meat was broken into four steps: slaughtering, boning, slicing and packaging.

Slaughtering

Cattle were killed by first rendering them insensible and then killing them by passing a heart-stopping current through the torso. The carcass was then "disassembled"—taken apart in a series of discrete steps by a group of 40 slaughterers, knife-hands and general laborers. In the Phoenix plant, carcasses were carried on overhead powered conveyors. After killing, the carcass was bled in a process called "sticking" (a rod being pushed through the animal's thorax) and trimmed of extremities such as horns, tail and hooves. Operators were strictly graded (A, B and C slaughterer according to the skill required for their operation). For example, the process of cutting out orifices in the carcass which might be sources of infection was considered a highly skilled job, as was the process of removing the hide from the beast. In each case, mistakes could cause costly product safety or quality problems.

The exact sequence of the remaining core processing steps was highly regulated, and the USDA required certification of all processes which produced for the US market. After being trimmed, carcasses were eviscerated, and the viscera sac separated off and fed through the floor of the plant to the by-product plant. After head-removal, the carcass continued through a number of stations where people progressively trimmed the carcass up, eventually sawing it lengthwise to leave the slaughter floor as two "sides" of beef. The carcass moved around a U-shaped free (rather than powered) overhead conveyor, being pulled from station to station by the operators themselves.

The slaughter floor of any meatworks was not an immediately attractive sight. People worked hard to keep up with the line, and many had spent their working lives in conditions which most people (despite a continued taste for the final product) found immensely distasteful.

In addition to the standard process, there were a growing number of "custom" processes even in slaughtering, which continued to expand in variety as new markets evolved. The parts of an animal considered directly edible was strongly culturally derived, and because of the growing number of cultures that provided markets, more and more "delicacies" were emerging. For cattle slaughtered for these markets this meant shuffling and adding to what had been a standard set of operations until a few years ago. For this reason, many of the people who had traditionally been considered knife-hands or general labor were beginning to require even more skill [Exhibit 2].

At the end of the slaughtering process, carcass halves were labeled, and stored in refrigerators to be chilled overnight. Such chilling had traditionally been necessary to arrest any microbi-

A certified slaughterer should be able to carry out the following actions safely. (This skill list corresponds closely to the process flow in slaughtering):

- Feed cattle from race into knocking box (holds head of animal)
- Safely load and use the knocking gun
- Safely shackle the right hind leg, and hoist onto the rail (shackling)
- Correctly bleed the beast
- Rod and tie weasand
- Correctly remove horns (mechanical cutters) and mark front hocks
- Clear and drop rectum, skin first leg, remove first leg and change first leg
- Skin and remove second leg
- Carry out flanking, skinning of brisket and foreshank
- Completely remove head, place on rail and skin head [check dentition]
- Fit and remove hide stripping chains
- Safely and correctly operate hide stripper to remove hide
- Remove fore feet, skin sinews, mark and saw brisket
- Carry out gutting procedure on the beast
- Safely saw down the carcass with a splitting saw
- Correctly trim the sides to comply with standard carcass trim

EXHIBIT 2 Skill List for Beef Slaughtering, 1994*
*Department of Employment, Vocational Training and Industrial Relations. TAFE•TEQ. Syllabus CN938: Certificate in Meat Industry Processing. Module MIA005. 20/4/1994.

ological action (infection) which may have resulted from the slaughtering process, as well as to stabilize the carcass for deboning. Chiller capacity had to be carefully managed since warm carcasses could not, legally, be mixed with cold.

Deboning

After about a day of chilling (the core temperature of the carcass had to reach 20°C in 20 hours by regulation), the carcass passed through to deboning, where the major bones were removed and the primary meat sections were removed from the animal. Deboning required great skill and strength as well as some degree of ambidexterity. Operators needed to pull a joint with one hand and cut with the other, in precisely the right places. Boners needed around six-months practice to build dexterity and muscle before they could carry out the job effectively. New boners were added to the team as learners alongside skilled boners until they were able to "cut tally"—to reach a minimum

so-called "buddy-cuts"—the accidental injury of one operator by another. The biological hazards of the plants were also of great concern to both operators and managers. Three diseases transmitted from the animals: brucellosis, Q-fever and leptospirosis had traditionally plagued the industry, though advances in rearing techniques had dramatically reduced the incidence of these.

The Football Player Syndrome

Finally were long-term effects of exerting similar forces, over and over again. Slaughterers had been likened to professional footballers—this was a young person's job and few people lasted longer than 10 years of the constant wear and tear on the joints. For all these reasons, meat-processing remained a form of processing that had been stubbornly defiant of attempts to automate, yet was a hazardous job, fraught with control difficulties and operating inefficiencies [Exhibit 5].

AUSTRALIA'S OPERATIONS STRATEGY FOR MEAT PRODUCTION

By 1993, there were fewer than 220 meatworks in Australia, down from 550 in 1972. Despite this, overall production had risen from 450 kilotonnes to over 2700 kt. The number of employees fell from 50,000 in 1977–78 to around 25,000 in 1994, due primarily to slaughterhouse closings and improve-

ments in productivity. The average slaughterhouse in Australia produced 7.5 kt of meat in 1990 compared to 4.4 kt in 1972. Facilities were therefore becoming more concentrated, though some had suggested that this change in concentration of facilities was slowing (see Exhibit 6). Most slaughterers bought animals from the 75,000 Australian farms producing livestock. In 1992, there were around 25 million cattle in Australia, with 42% of these in Queensland. Many processors bought animals under either explicit or implicit contracts, though the way in which animals were acquired varied considerably from state to state. In Victoria, for example, the average lot size might be two or three cattle, while in Northern Australia a forward contract might be written for 500 or 1000 head.

Over the previous two decades, the industry had suffered from year-to-year variation in demand (see Exhibit 7). In addition, there was a strong seasonal factor in the production of meat, the extent by which the maximum production month in the year exceeded the minimum was 22%, 64% and 52% for beef, veal and mutton respectively. The greatest variation occurred in the tropical north of the country, where slaughterhouses usually closed for several months during the rainy season. Some slaughterhouse operators tried to maintain capacity utilization by slaughtering a broader range of species, as well as obtaining livestock from elsewhere in the country.

EXHIBIT 5 State of the Art Manual System

EXHIBIT 6   Concentration of Meat Production in Australia, 1991–1992 (ASIC 2115)*

1987–1988	%	Sites #	Sites %	Employment #	Employment %	Wages/Salaries A$m	Wages/Salaries %	Turnover A$m	Turnover %
Largest 4 firms	1.2	22	5.6	7,274	23.7	165.9	24.2	1,358.8	26.3
8 firms	2.4	35	8.9	9,775	31.9	227.9	33.3	1,981.7	38.4
12 firms	3.6	43	11.0	11,591	37.8	281.0	41.1	2,397.2	46.4
16 firms	4.8	50	12.8	13,628	44.4	325.6	47.6	2,732.6	52.9
20 firms	6.0	54	13.8	14,713	48.0	351.2	51.3	2,987.6	57.9
Total 336 firms	100.0	392	100.0	30,671	100.0	684.3	100.0	5,164.0	100.0
1991–1992									
Largest 4 firms	1.3	27	7.7	8,193	29.9	240.7	32.0	1,785.7	33.3
8 firms	2.6	32	9.1	9,909	36.2	282.4	37.5	2,366.1	44.1
12 firms	4.0	38	10.8	10,921	39.9	313.3	41.6	2,780.7	51.9
16 firms	5.3	42	11.9	12,529	45.8	357.0	47.4	3,137.6	58.5
20 firms	6.6	46	13.1	13,863	50.7	394.7	52.4	3,419.7	63.8
Total 302 firms	100.0	352	100.0	27,364	100.0	752.8	100.0	5,360.0	100.0

*Source: ABS 1992e, Cat.No. 8221.0

EXHIBIT 7   Australian Beef and Veal Production, 1970–1991

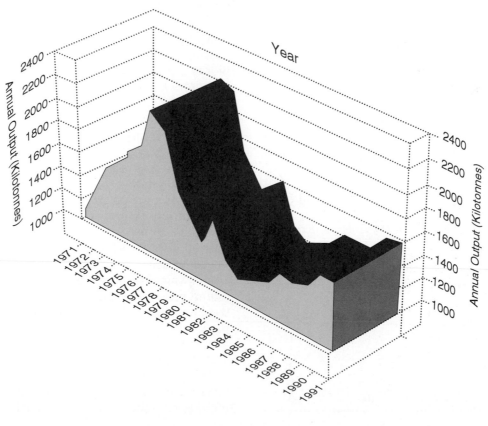

The industry remained labor-intensive with comparatively little investment in technology in most operations. A typical breakdown of the cost in the processing and marketing channel for beef is shown in Table 1.

Quality standards were very strictly laid down by both domestic and international regulation. The Australian Quarantine and Inspection Service (AQIS) carried out inspection of meat in all export-certified establishments. Thus, external inspectors were a common sight in most operations. Complaints about the burden this bureaucracy imposed on the industry were common. Quality Assurance schemes (QA), which aimed to build quality into the product through the *process* rather than through inspection were very much in their infancy in 1994, and inspection was still the primary method of guaranteeing quality in this potentially lethal product.

The Australian Department of Commerce had, in 1989, noted the critical importance of workforce skill and motivation for international competitiveness in meat processing yet characterized the industry as one in which unskilled workers dominated. Indeed, no other sector of the food processing industry had fewer skilled and semi-skilled workers than the red meat industry. 63% of workers did not finish high school. 23% of meat workers had some post-school qualification versus 49% for manufacturing in general. The Australian Bureau of Statistics calculated that the number of days lost to industrial action in the industry was very high—with 2.28 days lost per employee due to industrial action compared with 0.29 in the manufacturing industry as a whole. In addition, the ADC noted that *"in the slaughter industry, work is dirty, the degree to which workers participate in the decision-making process is minimal and career paths are almost non-existent."* Even by 1994, the industry's safety record was lagging other industries by a factor of ten to one. Workers' compensation levies for the meat industry in Queensland were 14% of the total payroll (compared with 1.4% for industry as a whole).

Tallying and Seniority

Twenty percent of the workforce worked on a tally (piece-rate) system, but this 20% generally worked in slaughtering and boning, and determined the output rate of follow-on operations. On average, forty-percent of skilled operators in a meat plant worked on the killing floor. A slaughterer's pay structure was complex. It comprised three elements. A guaranteed minimum wage based on a "minimum tally" of a set number of animals; bonus payments at a rate of 25% per animal more than the minimum tally rate—up to the "maximum tally" (25% above minimum headcount), and additional payments of 37.5% over the minimum per head rate for output in excess of the maximum tally. The way in which the tally system was applied to workgroups was one of the primary causes of industrial disputes. In addition, the tradition of "seniority" (first-in a department, last-out) meant that operators keen to avoid losing their job when the industry cycled down also avoided moving around the meatworks to acquire new skills. The tally system and seniority made this undesirable.

The systems of tallying and seniority were enshrined in Australia's "industrial award" system, which had characterized industrial relations since federation. Section 51(XXXV) of the Australian Constitution empowered the Commonwealth to legislate on the prevention and settlement of industrial disputes which extend beyond the limit of one state. This power resulted in an elaborate system in which the bureaucracy determined the minimum wage for each industry, occupation and sometimes an individual site, part of a state, company or groups of companies. In the meat industry alone there were, in November 1994, 45 federal and 39 state awards. Part III of the Federal Meat Industry Award covered the piece work and tally systems, with 16 general divisions of labor, and numerous classifications within each division. Pay

TABLE I Typical Cost Breakdown for Beef Processing

Cost Component	Domestic (%)	Export (Japan) (%)
Livestock Cost (Purchase and Procurement)	72	65
Processing Costs		
• Labor	10	12
• Materials and Services	11	10
• Fixed Costs (inc. Depreciation and Management)	2	1
Total Processing	23	23
Delivery Costs	5	12
Total	100	100

rates depended on both the classification and the location of the plant.

Production planning was difficult in such a seasonal industry. In general, plants worked on a demand-based (rather than forecast-based) system, drawing off an inventory of live animals on the farms and ranches of the country. Meat was sold by marketing and sales people, then buyers searched for cattle to fulfill the order. While plants tried hard to keep production quantities level, capricious weather or soft world-prices for meat often caused lengthy slack times. As one production manager pointed out—"you can lay people off, but you can only put them on the gate for so long. Pretty soon—they'll have to find something else."

BENCHMARKING AUSTRALIA

There was growing evidence to suggest that performance of Australian slaughter facilities had been falling behind that in other countries. In 1993, Booz-Allen and Hamilton conducted a study which compared the cost of best-in-class processing facilities in Australia, the US, Argentina, Ireland and New Zealand. The results of the study are shown in Table 2.

Many pointed out that the processing cost differences reflected the fact that Australian cattle were grass-fed (and thus tended to be smaller than grain-fed stock), as well as government mandated charges such as inspection costs and industry levies. Indeed, as one subsequent report pointed out, conclusions about capital and labor productivity might be misleading because of the different costs of each in various countries, and that the

benchmarking study should not be considered alarming.

Still others heard a loud call to arms.

THE CYBERTECH PROJECT

The Cybertech concept was born of an ambitious plan to leapfrog world competition through the application of advanced manufacturing and information technologies to the meat industry. Seventeen years previously, in 1977, the AIRC (Australian Industrial Research Council) embarked on primary research to explore the feasibility of an automated system for meat processing.

Ned Pilcher of the AIRC was a Ph.D. biologist who began the "Alternative Slaughtering Technology" project:

In 1976, I remember seeing photographs of meat-processing in Chicago in the late 1800's—really the first appearance of a production line for meat-processing. They had rails that slid the carcass from man to man, with each person specializing in a particular part of the butchering process. It occurred to me, that despite all the technological advances in other industries, the meat industry was virtually untouched by technology.

The AIRC's job was to do basic research on this kind of problem. It was our job to ensure that there was a technology available to the industry, so in 1977, I put together a team of people to take a look at it: one engineer, two technicians and a draughtsman. I didn't think it was wise to hire engineers who were steeped in the existing methods of the meat industry, so I appointed engineers who had never worked in the business before. That worked out really well. We found lots of solutions that would have not been thought of otherwise.

TABLE 2   Cost Profiles of Delivering Ready-for-Market Meat to the United States (Aust.cents/kg)

	Australia	U.S.A.	Argentina	Ireland	NZ (traditional)	NZ* (hot-boning)
Animal Cost	340.5	465.8	269.9	736.9	291.0	329.9
By-Product Revenue	56.2	82.0	41.5	94.2	58.9	65.7
Animal Cost Net of BPR	284.3	383.8	228.2	642.7	232.1	264.2
Processing	112.7	41.2	105.1	85.7	71.7	60.6
Transportation	37.1	9.7	50.9	15.1	28.4	29.3
Total Costs	434.1	434.7	384.2	743.5	332.2	354.1

*The New Zealand comparison was also carried out by comparing against a comparatively new technique called hot-boning, in which a highly regulated and sterile slaughtering process permitted safe boning without chilling the carcass.

It quickly became clear that the slaughtering process was much more difficult to automate than originally anticipated. The dual problems of a compliant, flexible carcass and inevitable biological variation between beasts brought challenges that caused the seasoned automation engineers to throw up their arms in despair.

Much of the processors' tasks relied on craftspersonlike skills—the process was much closer to an art form than a specifiable, replicable process. Conventional operations wisdom was that, in such circumstances, the process might succumb to automation through a scientific understanding of the process and progressive reduction in sources of random variation. Unfortunately, much of the random variation in meat processing was inevitable—each carcass was (rather stubbornly and inconveniently) different from the next. AIRC's solution to this general problem was to develop automated processes that reduced variation whenever possible, and used sophisticated adaptive-control techniques where variation in the input was unavoidable.

Initial Research on a Few Processes

The team decided to attack the beginning of the process first—where the animal was led up a race and encouraged to put its head in a fixture which held it stationary (capture). A wooden mock-up was built at the local slaughterhouse to find out how cattle behaved within the race. A prototype was built in which the animal walked up a ramp from which an inverted V-shape progressively got higher between its legs, presenting a rising profile in the floor, until the point where it could support the animal painlessly. At this point, the hoof-ramps were dropped from underneath its legs. The V-shape separated the legs and stopped the animal crossing them as it walked. The race would thus suspend the beast by its belly, with its head immobilized. With its legs dropped away, it was given a heart-stop current and a simultaneous head-stun, to kill it painlessly, and without frightening the animals behind it (important both for humane reasons and for meat tenderness). This device worked well, so the team began work on other modules such as Automatic Hock Removal and Carcass Tipping (where the carcass was inverted to supine position for underbelly work).

By 1984, we had modules for lead-up, capture, stunning/killing, automatic hock removal, carcass tipping and brisket cutting. All of these had been developed so they were under automatic process control and working really well. It had been difficult but it worked, and we felt we had done a good job on the primary research. Now it was time to move it on to the development stage. We decided to look for some manufacturing industry input. We put a bid out to tender for people interested in developing the technology commercially.

No one came forward who had the resources to do it well. We therefore decided to do sort of a semi-commercial partnership with a slaughterhouse called Cray Brothers, who said we could install it module by module—creeping down the line as we built and proved each processing station—as long as it kept working! They would then have the option of buying it or getting rid of it at our expense.

Industrialists were fascinated by the project, and the AIRC let everyone in to see the original technology, running in a paddock at the AIRC laboratories in Brisbane. The tremendous interest, particularly in the front-end processes, spurred the engineers to be even more aggressive in their goals, and the team was enthusiastic about working with Cray Brothers and developing the process module by module.

"Build a Whole Prototype Rather Than a Station by Station Project"

Then, in 1984, the government undertook a review of research funding bodies, and the AIRC's team were faced with a change in funding partner—a new body, the AMC (Australian Meat Development Corporation) would now oversee commercialization. The AMC were equally enthralled by the project, but not about the strategy for commercialization.

Andy Wilson at the AMC had been a meatworks manager during the time that another a new technology, downward hide-pulling, was introduced. The story was a sad one for the New South Wales meat industry, at least as they see it. The industry went to the Industrial Relations commission, saying "Look—we have this new technology which will help the men on the line in terms of stress and strain, and which is also quicker than the manual method, so we'd like you to change the award for an increased tally on this part of the operation.

The tally ended up being **decreased** by 2½! So the industry had introduced new technology and had all the productivity advantages given away—and more! Andy was more than unhappy about this.

Andy said "There's *no way* we are going to let AIRC introduce this technology module-by-module, because the unions will pick us off piece by piece and we'll have a compounding deficit along the whole line."

The plan, therefore, developed into one of building a monolithic demonstration system that would be built as a functional whole, rather than module by module. This was a very unpopular decision with the team, who believed that the best technical solution lay in building modules. Technically, the project had gained some revolutionary advantages, and despite concerns about the all-or-nothing approach, its proponents were keen to put the technology—and its associated renewed investment—to work as soon as possible.

The Prototype

Ned Pilcher described the progression from the primary research to the full laboratory prototype.

> It all went secret, and, as I said, using the philosophy of a complete system introduction rather than "module by module." We had only got a few processes done. Since then, though, things like hide-pulling technology have been developed, along with evisceration, carcass splitting, head-removal, H-bone splitting—all this was done later with a brand new team, though I must admit, I haven't seen it—it would have been too upsetting. After all, it was handed over to a completely new team! I would have felt like an interfering grandfather.

By 1988, a full-scale computer-integrated prototype was built and running at the AIRC's labs. The prototype, and its successor, relied on a combination of automation of key processes and computer integration working alongside manual operators who performed those tasks too difficult to automate.

In July 1985, the Corporation for Research on Meat and Allied Industries (CRMAI) had been formed as the result of an industry supported Government initiative with the charter of managing research and development for the meat and livestock industry in Australia as an independently funded corporation.[1] The newly-formed corporation was funded through levies on livestock producers and meat processors which were matched by contributions from the Commonwealth Government.[2] The CRMAI had become the project's shepherd—and it was renamed—Cybertech.

CYBERTECH MARK I

Having learned critical lessons from the prototype laboratory system, a team from EJD Engineering was contracted to carry out the feasibility study for a commercial system. The commercial system would be differentiated from the prototype in that it would aim for higher reliability, and more thorough "production quality" equipment, rather like the transition manufacturing systems make to hard-tooling in the automotive industry.

From August of 1991, EJD pored over the technical and commercial details of the prototype system. In December, they concluded that the technology was ready for commercial implementation, provided key amendments were made. There remained a critical problem however: which company would volunteer to install commercially untested technology in an industry notoriously sensitive in industrial relations, and highly dependent on continual, uninterrupted operations? Many plants expressed keen interest in becoming Cybertech's *second* commercial site.

Cybertech found a commercial home at the Wollagong Meatworks, 120 miles north west of Brisbane. Wollagong was one of the industry's leading plants with an existing capacity of 300 head of cattle and 800 small stock per day. The plant employed 250 people, concentrating on high quality products for the domestic and export markets. Many people pointed to Wollagong's technological foster-parentage as an example of courage and foresight for the industry as a whole. Wollagong chairman, Brian Starling, commented on the decision to install Cybertech.

> You can look at it in many ways. It could be courage, or it could be we're too scared not to install it. If it's successful and we didn't have it, we'd be in a mess.

By the end of 1993, Cybertech Mark I was up and running at Wollagong. [Exhibit 8 and 9]

[1]Annual Report, 1992–1993.

[2]By June 1993 the CRMAI was funding over 200 red meat research projects including genetic engineering, new meat products, vaccines, chemical residue reduction, meat marketing and automated tenderness control.

EXHIBIT 8 Partial View of the Cybertech Mark I System

THE SYSTEM

Cybertech Mark I was a semi-automated system to perform operations from the cattle-race to the delivery of carcass sides to the chillers. The capacity of the Mark I plant was 600 cattle per eight-hour shift, with the ability to process beasts between 300–800 kg live weight. The Cybertech building was a two story concrete structure with a steel frame. By-products were processed on the ground floor, where the hide chiller and offal freezers were also located. The system was about one and a half times the size of conventional slaughterfloors (1050 m^2) and operated at about the same speed as a conventional plant, with a process time of around 40 minutes from animal entry to sides entering the chillers. Here, however, the similarity to conventional slaughterhouses ended.

CONTROL AND SENSING

At the center of the system was a computer-control booth, reminiscent of chemical plant control rooms (see Exhibit 10). The control room featured three computers which allowed managers to monitor the operations in the plant, along with sophisticated trouble-shooting software that pinpointed problems. An alarm screen showed failure points by flashing and automatically called up a maintenance screen which showed schematics of the relevant pieces of equipment. The screens also showed whether each module was operating in automatic or manual mode, and where any delays had occurred. Additionally, 16 closed circuit video cameras allowed the control room operator to see key work areas, via four small screens, in the console. The floor of the Cybertech building was

EXHIBIT 9   Cybertech System: Evisceration Conveyor

color-coded—red in danger zones where sensors picking up movement could close down the plant, yellow in hazard areas, grey in working areas and beige in viewing zones.

The system bristled with sensors. Over 3000 input/output ports were incorporated. The automated plant used state-of-the-art feedback and feedforward control to manage carcass variability, many of the techniques learned from FMS (Flexible Manufacturing Systems) control methodologies, as well as technologies from Artificial Intelligence, such as fuzzy logic.

COMPUTER INTEGRATION AND AUTOMATION OF THE SYSTEM

The Cybertech plant automated many of the conventional slaughterfloor functions though each au-

tomatic station had manual back-up. Details of the system's process are in Exhibit 11. A particular process (horn-cutting) is shown in Exhibit 12.

Jack Crawford described the importance of maintaining the integrity of the system:

This system is an incredible engineering achievement. I would say that 70% of the advantage of the system comes from the fact that computer integration is used to measure and adapt to the carcass at each stage. Each sub-system feeds forward what it has measured and the precise work it has carried out to the following stations, so we don't end up having to make the same measurements twice. In addition, computer integration of all the modules gives us the ability to tweak the system, as a whole, so we don't have variation in one part of the process messing up something we had just fixed in a another part. If it were split into modules, all of these advantages would be lost.

EXHIBIT 10 Cybertech Control Room

In addition, it is designed to be monolithic because that's the only way of radically changing the nature of work practices in the industry.

NEWS CONFERENCE

In November, 1993, a media tour was conducted around the Cybertech plant. One industry observer at the tour described it as "A magnificent engineering accomplishment." Another observer, staring aghast at the clinical whir of robot motors, and the huge processing stations, described it as "a monstrosity."

THE PHOENIX EXPERIMENT

"It's been hijacked by the engineers!"

Bill Moore's unequivocal view of Cybertech echoed the concerns of a small but vocal group of people in the industry. Moore ran the Glenfillon Meat Works in Phoenix, Queensland. Phoenix had undertaken a radically different approach to improvement.

Training and Development

Rather than wait for the Cybertech project to prove itself to be a sound alternative to more manual methods, Phoenix had built an innovative training program (run in a separate facility) that was unusual in the industry. The training began with basic literacy skills, and built on this with courses in classification and boning. Workbooks were developed to go with each component of the training, so that people could be seen to progress through it.

Charlie Aitken described the steps taken to build Phoenix' training program:

Our first task was to start building people's self-esteem and begin to build a career path for them. We began by giving people training in beef specification. They needed to understand why they were doing things. Doing a tenderloin the "easy way," for example, can cost $60,000 over a year. It was critical that people understand things like this. On average, everyone now spends at least half an hour a week on training, and goes through 3–4 courses a year.

EXHIBIT 11 Description of Cybertech Process

The automated functions include lead up, capture, stun, sticking, bleeding, horn removal and inversion of the carcass. The carcass was then prepared manually for the further automated processes of hide removal, aitch-bone split, head removal, head transfer to the head chain, head wash, brisket cut, evisceration, tail cut and carcass split. Manual trimming and inspection of the carcass then followed.

Animals were sorted in the yards to present batches of six similar-sized cattle to a ride-on conveyor. Once a beast entered Cybertech, a pusher moved down behind it to prevent it retreating. The animal then stood on the moving floor, legs spread either side of an inverted-V, and was conveyed forward to the knocking box. At the knocking box, sensors on the head restraint confirm that the animal's head was through, then activated head clamps. The floor dropped away and the automatic stunner operated. After killing, a trolley gripped the animal's neck, the gates opened and the beast was automatically pulled forward to the automatic sticking station. Here, the horn cutter swung down with sensors that located the horns, which were then cut off. After sticking, the animal was lowered onto the bleeding rail (with head support) and bled for 90 seconds. The blood drain was located beneath the conveyor for direct collection and a scraper on the conveyor made it self cleaning. It was this module, from the ride-on conveyor to bleeding, that had attracted most interest from industry to date. At the end of the module, a two-stage lifter turned the animal off the bleeding conveyor onto the dressing conveyor—a wide moving floor which presented three bed dressing cradles at once. At each cradle, operators manually opened and laid back the hide, tied the weasand and did some preparation for evisceration. Three or four teams of two were able to work on this inversion conveyor. It took several minutes from the animal being deposited on the conveyor to its removal at the hide pulling module. Hocks, udders and other trim dropped from this inversion conveyor onto a trim conveyor at the end. The last task on the inversion conveyor was placing hooks in each tendon. The carcass was then lifted up in four-leg suspension onto the chain and slung between two rails (i.e. legs up). Two manual stations allowed operators to do the head work-up, dropping muzzles and trim into a chute.

The hide puller involved four pieces of equipment—called GA, G1, G2 and G3. State-of-the-art sensors on each machine pre-set the following machine to the carcass parameters. GA was a pre-set station which measured the angle and height of the suspended carcass. G1 was a mighty machine, unlikely to be damaged by a dinosaur carcass falling on it! It clamped the hide on each side of the carcass and pulled it down, leaving a narrow strip attached to the carcass, G2 used a special clearing tool to slice this narrow strip of hide from the carcass, and strip the hide off the tail. G3 pulled the hide over the head, rolled it up and dropped it down a chute. The carcass then continued along the chain, tilted and moved around a corner to the manual bunging station and the automatic aitch-bone cutter, which was again set by sensors. The carcass then tilted and turned another corner and was presented for automatic head removal. The Cybertech team described the head removal module as "second-generation equipment," providing a glimpse of the sleeker equipment Mark II might hold.

Sensors located the back of the head, the head was clamped and then blades cut it off. Another machine transferred the head automatically to the head chain, where it went through an initial wash. After a full wash the head was inspected, and brains, tongue and cheeks removed manually. The head then fell down a chute. The brisket cutter was also automatic and directed by sensors. It took three cuts on a large carcass, two on a small one. At the automatic eviscerator, the carcass was tilted head up at 45 degrees. A sensor then determined the height of the brisket, the eviscerator swept the cavity and the viscera fell into the viscera pan conveyor beneath. The large square pans contained compartments for paunch, edible offals and tail. The pans were tilted up if anything was condemned, emptying contents down a condemned chute. The carcass then moved through the automatic tail removal module. A laser sensed the tip of the tail, the tail was cut off and dropped into the viscera pan. The carcass tilted again (30 degrees head down) at the last automatic module, the carcass splitter. Sensors found the backbone and guided the splitting saw. The sides were finally released from their slung position and passed manual trim stations before heading for automatic wash, high voltage electrical stimulation and chilling.

I was never happy with any of the training that was developed elsewhere—it was always too basic and just not well-put together. We are now the only plant in Australia with our own structured training scheme. AUS-MEAT is now sending its trainers here to learn how to train. We've built training modules for each of the functions in the plant. For meat-processing skills, they do it half on their time, and half on ours. If they want to do anything else, from Computer Science to Japanese, they can just come to us and we will organize and pay for the course, though they do it in their own time.

We have also included a compulsory course in basic literacy skills, in a communications module, as we call it. Everyone has to go through this as well as the courses for their particular function. It's amazing what people can do once they have an understanding of what the cuts really should be, and what the costs of making mistakes are.

I don't know much about this Cybertech system—but give me $20m for training and I'll build a system designed by meat workers for meat workers: productivity would rocket.

Mechanically Assisted Boning

Phoenix had also begun experimenting with a new method for boning beef. The system provided a set of powered hooks above the production line. The hooks were attached to the carcass by the operator while working. The hook would then augment and assist the pulling action of the operator as he or she made incisions in the joint.

A group of 7 boners, 7 slicers and 7 packers were selected to form a cell using the new system. The team were pulled "off the street": none of them had any experience in the industry, and the line was physically separated, in a different room, from the rest of the plant. The cell provided 20% of overall boning capacity. A local agreement with the Union allowed everyone in the cell to be multi-skilled, and within three months, all of them were on one rate of pay.

While there was suspicion and some sneering about the cell from the rest of the plant (much machismo was expended in deriding the "wimps" in the new area), the new operators performed well in their tasks and a recent climate survey had shown them to be the people in the plant most satisfied with their jobs.

"People should be able to work till they're sixty," said one operator. "This will let us do it."

A HUNDRED MILES AWAY

A hundred miles away, back at Wollagong, Crawford was working on error-recovery routines with one of the software engineers on the Cybertech system. The engineer had heard a rumor that an American company was working on a similar system. His source estimated that their team were about two years behind the Cybertech project.

Crawford thought about the future. First, was the difficulty of disseminating the technology now it was basically working. The Mark II system would have to be considerably cheaper—but there was considerable scope to do this, since the Mark I had been so over-engineered. The engineers would be much further down the learning curve on the Mark II.

A Cheaper System

The problem was, that no one was quite sure how far and how fast the cost would come down. No one had ever built this kind of system before, and much of the cost came from debugging and re-designing the equipment after it had been installed. Even though some estimated the project costs, so far, to be $38m, building another Mark I system, with the same design, would cost A$13m. Crawford estimated that the system would have be brought down in cost to A$5m to be viable. While he was sure it could be done, how would he convince another meat plant to invest in the Mark II system? Wollagong managers had raised some questions about the fact that the plant ran at only 80% uptime versus the 99.5% as specified in the original contract with BHP [see Exhibit 13].

Disintegration

Second, Crawford was under considerable pressure to break the system up, and sell affordable, individual modules to meatworks. He was very reluctant to do this, since so much of the advantage of the system came from computer integration of the modules which allowed constant monitoring of the whole system, as well as more control. In addition, he felt that further development of the computer integration systems would be critical if the industry was to learn more about such computer integration methods. *"The integration and the software **is** the technology now,"* remarked Crawford.

EXHIBIT 12 Horn Cutting Robot

	Phoenix (2 shift, 250 days/year)		Cybertech Mark II Estimates (3 shift, 250 days/year)	
Capacity (Cattle/Day)		850		1800
1994 output (Cattle)		146,000		—
1994 output (tonnes of finished meat)		24,000		—
Capital Cost (Slaughter only) (A$)		2.5m		13m
Annual Costs				
Direct Labor (A$/year)	80@25k	2.0m	90@25k	2.25m
Indirect Labor (A$/year)	12@35k	0.48m	24@60k	1.2m
Materials and Services (A$/year)		2.5m		4.5m

EXHIBIT 13 Cost Comparison of Cybertech and Phoenix Slaughter Floors

The Phoenix Plant

Finally, there were rumblings from a few renegade plant managers that the system was not the right path for the industry at all. The Phoenix experiments had achieved well-publicized success. Phoenix' experience pointed to a different model for building improved performance, yet Crawford believed Phoenix' success was strongly dependent on the trust that existed at that particular plant, as well as the skill of the managers involved.

There are 72 registered export plants in Australia. If we develop this system further, the whole kill could be processed by 15 Cybertechs. If we are to do the right things for the industry, how should we capitalize on what we have learned from the project so far? We have to find a way to get this computer-integrated technology out there. Australia's meat industry could be on the line—and the Americans are right behind us. But what should we do now?

References

1 *Industry Commission Report on Meat Processing. Report Number 38.* Australian Government Publishing Service, Melbourne. 20 April, 1994.

2 *The Australian Meat Processing Industry, International Development Opportunities for Processed Red Meat Products for Human Consumption.* AGPS, Canberra, August 1989.

3 *The Jungle,* Upton Sinclair, 1906.

4 *Meat Research Corporation. Annual Report,* 1992–1993.

5 Acknowledgments for photographs and other material are due to the publisher of *AUS-MEAT Feedback,* November/December 1993. AUS MEAT is a division of the Australian Meat and Livestock Corporation.

Motorola, Inc.: Bandit Pager Project (Abridged)

The Bandit project demonstrated several important points. First, we proved that building an automated factory was worthwhile, financially. Second, with adequate resources and clear goals, ambitious targets can be achieved. Finally, you can't overplan the project. On Bandit, there were clear milestones defined for each prototype cycle, and each station on the production line had someone in charge who knew what had to be done. Managers did not have to get involved in those details. (Laura Saucier, staff industrial engineer.)

From June 1986 to December 1987, the Bandit project had developed and implemented a fully automated line for manufacturing Motorola's Bravo pagers. Now, in October 1989, the Bandit line was near its goal of producing almost half of all the Bravo series pagers, the remainder being made in the company's Puerto Rico and Singapore plants. Further, not only did the Bandit line pagers hold the highest quality record in Motorola's history, the project's $8 million–$10 million investment had already been paid back in cost—and quality—savings.

Buoyed by these results, the Paging Products Division was embarking on a new project, dubbed Son-of-Bandit, which would emphasize product, not just process, technology. The division's vice president and general manager, Merle Gilmore, was aware that Son-of-Bandit posed significant challenges:

> The Bandit program was a tremendous success, showing once and for all that American manufacturing can compete with offshore production. The challenge now is to take what we have learned on Bandit and apply these lessons to the next generation of pagers and throughout the rest of the company.

This case was prepared as the basis for class discussion rather than to illustrate either effective or ineffective handling of an administrative situation.

This case was prepared by Steven C. Wheelwright. Copyright © 1991 by the President and Fellows of Harvard College. Harvard Business School case 692-069.

MOTOROLA COMPANY BACKGROUND

Motorola, one of the world's largest electronics companies, with 1988 annual sales of $8.25 billion, was founded in 1928. Initially, the company produced car radios, moving into military electronics during World War II and then semiconductors in 1952. The company also entered the consumer electronics field, becoming the number-three producer of color TV sets in 1965 and introducing the first U.S.-made all-transistorized TV set in 1967 (the Quasar line). In 1974, Motorola exited consumer electronics completely because of foreign competitive pressures, selling its color TV business to Matsushita of Japan.

Foreign competition continued unabated through the 1970s, and by the early 1980s, Motorola was leading the charge for protection against Japanese semiconductor manufacturers. Robert Galvin, Motorola's chairman, felt that the Japanese were employing unfair trade practices by dumping chips to gain market share.

During the mid-1980s, Motorola management familiarized themselves with Japanese manufacturing quality and defect-level standards. Although the Japanese unfair trade practices remained a focal point, management reexamined their firm's own quality, defect-level standards, and manufacturing processes. A formal "benchmarking project" ended in 1986 with a report made to Motorola president and CEO, Bill Weisz. Bruce Piltch, director of manufacturing operations for the Paging Products Division, recalled:

> The report compared Motorola performance to worldwide state of the art, function by function. It was a cold slap in the face. We had been lulled into complacency, reading newspaper accounts about how good we were. It was a real education. Not only did we discover that we weren't so hot, but we also came to realize that things were getting worse instead of better.

According to Piltch, what motivated Project Bandit was foreign competition: "We needed to make sure that we would have the skills we'd need to participate in the business in the future." It was clear that Motorola's manufacturing capabilities had to be improved, and emphasizing manufacturing excellence became a corporate strategy, a major thrust of which was a companywide drive to obtain six-sigma-quality levels in all its manufacturing operations (see Exhibit 1).

The Paging Products Division

During the 1980s, Motorola was structured in six major business segments and a New Enterprises organization. The Paging Products Division was part of the Communications Sector, the largest of the six, averaging $3.2 billion in sales annually.

Other products in the Communication Sector included portable and mobile FM two-way radio communication systems, microwave communication systems, and portable data terminals.

Motorola sold its pager to carriers (like Metro Media and Bell South) that owned an infrastructure system. These carriers in turn leased or sold the pagers to end users. In addition to the cost of the pager, the end user paid a monthly service charge to be connected to the system. Motorola's pagers varied in size, type of paging (numeric, alpha-numeric, voice, tone-only), and range.

The Paging Products Division, like the rest of Motorola, was under extreme pressure from Japanese competitors. Moreover, from 1979 to 1989, all other U.S. manufacturers of pagers (including RCA, GE, Bell & Howell, Harris, and

---

EXHIBIT I Six-Sigma Concept

WHY 6-SIGMA?

Consider a product—its performance is determined by the margin between the actual characteristic values of design requirements and its parts. These characteristics are produced by factory processes and at the suppliers.

Every process attempts to reproduce its characteristic values identically from unit to unit, but variations occur. Processes that use real-time feedback have a small variation but other processes may have a large variation.

Variation of the process is measured in standard deviations (sigma) from the mean. Normal process variation is considered to be ±3-sigma.

Under normal conditions, about 2,700 parts per million will be outside the normal variation. This, by itself, does not appear disconcerting. But a product containing 1,500 parts will have 4.05 defects per unit. This would result in fewer than two units out of every hundred going through the entire manufacturing process without a defect.

Thus, we can see that for a product to be built virtually defect-free, it must be designed to accept characteristics that are significantly more than ±3-sigma from the mean.

It can be shown that a design that can accept twice the normal variation of the process; ±6-sigma, can be expected to have no more than 3.4 ppm defective for each characteristic, even if the process mean were to shift by as much as ±1.5-sigma.

In the same case, for a product containing 1,500 parts, we would now expect only 0.0051 defect per unit. This would mean that 995 units out of 1,000 would go through the entire manufacturing process without a defect.

The goal is to design a product that will accept maximum variation and processes that produce minimum variation, ultimately reaching zero defects. Motorola's 1992 step toward this objective is to achieve ±6-sigma capability.

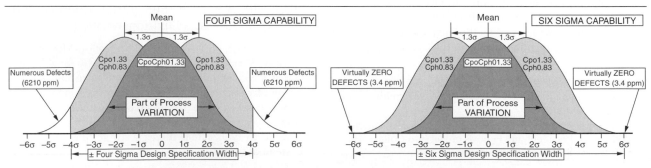

Source: J. Wolak (May 1987). "Motorola Revisited." *Quality, 5,* pp. 18–23. Reprinted with permission.

Stromberg Carlson) dropped out of the market. Edward Holland, a staff engineer in the Advanced Manufacturing Technology/Robotics Group, recalled that period:

> Motorola was always a product-oriented company. We made sales by having the best product with the most features before anyone else. During the early 1980s, we began to discover that having the best product was not enough—people could copy us very quickly. One obvious answer was to increase our quality level by improving the manufacturing process, using robotics and automation. The Robotics Group, started with half a dozen people, was a strategic move in that direction. We began by automating small parts of the process with robots—developing small islands of automation. At that point it was more learning than anything. It was reasonably successful, and we gained some credibility.

Upper management, as a result of their tours of Japanese facilities during this period, were also convinced that Motorola would have to automate in order to compete. Likewise, the Paging Products Division decided that automation and design for manufacturability were necessary for it to remain competitive.

In February 1986, top technical people from the Paging Products Division met off site with some people from the Advanced Manufacturing Technologies/Robotics Group to develop an approach for designing a totally automated line. Said Holland: "It was really a bunch of smart people locked up in a hotel room for a week to hash out a project plan." They developed an approach based on the Bravo product (see Exhibit 2), which was in pilot production under the code name Jstar at the time.

The Jstar pager was selected because it was mechanically more conducive to automation than other designs. Also, because Bravo was to be a high-volume product in the middle of Motorola's pager line, its automation could take full advantage of any economies of scale. Finally, the Jstar Bravo was being started up in conventional plants in Puerto Rico and Singapore, which provided a safety net if the automated factory failed or was late.

From the beginning, it was clear that this project had strategic significance. Chris Galvin, then general manager of the Paging Products Division (and son of Robert Galvin), felt that Motorola needed to develop new skills to survive in the competitive paging market, and Operation Bandit, as the Bravo automation project came to be known, was a way to learn them. The project also was consistent with Motorola's new strategic emphasis on manufacturing; it would raise the level of expectations for U.S. manufacturing and prove that it was not necessary to go offshore to obtain low cost, as the Jstar version had done.

George Fisher, then the assistant general manager of the Communications Sector (and later CEO), personally made the funding request presentation to the Motorola board of directors to get approval for Operation Bandit.

OPERATION BANDIT

Philosophy

The original plan for Bandit called for the development and implementation of a fully automated pager line for the Bravo pager within 18 months. The schedule for the project was tied to a December 1987 target date for shipping product from the line; all the other dates were determined by that end date. Bruce Piltch, director of manufacturing operations for the Paging Products Division, assumed the role of project manager. Although Motorola had a history of schedule slippage on some past projects, Piltch was determined to hold this one to its schedule.

Piltch was a highly driven and persuasive leader, whom team members described as a "crusader," a "renegade," and a "workaholic." His philosophy of project management fit his personality. As he described it:

> America is best at crisis management—our culture is oriented toward crisis management, tactics, emotional involvement, instant gratification. That's how we put a man on the moon. We take advantage of that in managing our teams—if you don't have a crisis, create a few.

> Project Bandit had this same kind of feeling. We were in a crisis most of the time anyway, but we had to foment a few crises as well. And you would not believe the output you can get out of a team of U.S. engineers—phenomenal increases in productivity—100% or more.[1]

---

[1]From "This Bandit Is Not a Thief: A Case Study of Advanced Manufacturing at the Paging Products Division of Motorola, Inc.," by Thomas W. Schlie, Associate Professor of Business Administration, Illinois Institute of Technology, 1989, p. 21.

EXHIBIT 2 Bravo Pager Product Description

On the Go? Stay in touch with the BRAVO Numeric Display Pager!

When your lifestyle demands that you be on the move, the BRAVO Numeric Display Pager will help you keep important lines of communication open. It actually displays phone numbers or coded information so that you can make more efficient use of your time!

Compact, easy to use

Motorola knows that convenience is essential when it comes to pagers. That's why we designed the BRAVO Numeric Display Pager!

The BRAVO pager is equipped with a sturdy belt clip so that you can affix it to your pocket, belt or purse. It's easy to remove the clip so you can also slip the pager into your pocket or briefcase. We even have an optional lanyard that can be used with or without the clip.

Return calls at your convenience

Don't panic if you can't answer your messages immediately upon receiving them! At times like these you'll appreciate the BRAVO pager's memory. It can hold up to five messages in memory so that you can return calls when it's best for you. The most recent messages stay in memory, pushing the oldest ones out. Each message can include not only the phone number but other important information such as extension, caller identification number or degree of urgency. When you read your messages, you can freeze the numbers on the display so that you can write them down. Duplicate messages won't take up valuable memory space. The pager scans each message so that duplicates will not be entered into memory more than once.

Should you choose, you can save up to three important numbers for future reference by protecting them. These numbers cannot be overwritten by other messages and will stay in memory until you remove their protection or turn your pager off.

This pager offers you a variety of alerts

During standard operations, the pager will bleep for several seconds (or until reset) when a page is received. However, you can set the pager to emit only a single discreet beep if you prefer. If you need privacy, or don't want to disturb others, two options are available: You can choose to have the discreet beep removed leaving only the flashing message light; or you can choose our VIBRA-PAGE option which alerts you by means of a gentle vibration. The latter is great for places where silence is important such as conferences, hospitals, quiet zones, as well as in high noise environments, such as construction sites, manufacturing plants, and airports, where a beep tone might not be heard. Whether you choose the beep tone or silent alert, a red light will also flash to indicate that you have a message.

The display tells it all

The 12-digit liquid crystal display tells you more than just your messages. At a glance you can see whether your pager is on, what type of alert it is set to, how many new messages you have to read, and if your battery is starting to run low. There is even a built-in light for use when viewing the display in low-light environments. All of this information helps to make the BRAVO Numeric Display pager a valuable communication and business tool.

BRAVO Pagers manufactured by:

 MOTOROLA

1301 East Algonquin Road
Schaumburg, Illinois 60196
(312) 397-1000
Specification subject to change without notice. Ⓜ, Motorola, BRAVO, and VIBRA-PAGE are trademarks of Motorola, Inc.

Best of all—Motorola reliability

At Motorola, providing quality products is a commitment we make to all of our customers. Part of the process of building reliable pagers is the extensive testing that's done during the design and production phases. Our accelerated life test (ALT) program is one such example. For the BRAVO Numeric Display Pager, this testing simulates five years of field stress in a few weeks, enabling us to design out potential problems. The result is pagers that stand up to the most demanding situations, when used under normal conditions.

Try one today! We think you'll agree that using a Motorola pager is the best choice you can make.

Shown actual size.

Piltch did not agree with the standard Motorola methods for managing and evaluating a project; he felt that project performance was measured only subjectively, by how one interpreted the fine print. He therefore introduced a "contract book" containing agreements between the development team and management. The book set out clear financial and technical benchmarks against which the project was to be evaluated. It also laid out the method by which those goals were to be achieved.

While the content of the contract book mostly resembled Motorola's existing standard operating procedures, its implementation differed. With the standard operating procedures, each group set its own goals more or less independently. Because these goals often conflicted, when the project fell short in some area, responsibility for the shortcoming was difficult to ascribe. With the contract book, all the relevant groups agreed to a single document; responsibility was clearly stated and shared.

To meet their timetable, Piltch felt they should develop as few new technologies as possible. Indeed, the project was named Operation Bandit to emphasize the importance of eliminating the "Not Invented Here" (NIH) syndrome. Outside the entrance to the project area a sign read: Please don't leave the area without leaving us a good idea. George Keller, the engineering manager for Bandit, recalled the philosophy of the project:

> NIH would have killed us, given the chance. In the past we rewarded the designer who came up with the newest, the greatest, the latest thing. We should have been looking for the designer who took something that basically worked and optimized it.[2]

Piltch elaborated:

> Our biggest problem has been cultural—thinking that only Motorola had or could develop the best technology. The Japanese are much less myopic in this regard. They view the problem as a clean-sheet opportunity and are willing to take ideas and technology from anywhere. That was part of our mission in doing the benchmarking—to raise expectations at Motorola of what could be done, and foster a clean-sheet mentality that would welcome ideas and technology from all sources.[3]

---

[2]From "How They Brought Home the Prize: A Visit to Motorola's Bandit Plant," *Manufacturing Systems,* April 1989, p. 27.

[3]From "This Bandit is Not a Thief," p. 21.

Staffing

The project was staffed using Motorola's Internal Opportunity System, where job openings were posted so that anyone who was interested could apply. Despite the project's ambitious goals, its visibility enabled Piltch to attract large numbers of applicants. Because of the multidisciplinary nature of the project, it turned out to be somewhat difficult to free up people who had the necessary qualifications, however.

The team comprised about 25 engineers from different engineering disciplines: robotics, industrial engineering, manufacturing, mechanical, electrical, tooling, and test systems (see Exhibit 3). Eventually, an accountant was assigned to the team, because Piltch recognized that with a totally automated production line, most of the standard accounting measures would have to be altered. Since the product was a redesign of the Jstar pager with no change that affected the customer, marketing was not involved day to day on the team.

All team members were moved to an office area adjacent to the Bandit production line and the division's main assembly area. The walls enclosing the Bandit area had large glass windows, which had been installed partly so that the factory workers did not feel that management was trying to hide its automation efforts, and partly so that the Bandit team would feel that it could not hide its mistakes.

The Bandit team worked fairly autonomously. As one team member put it: "We were all a team in one room with no red tape. . . ." The testing department provided some specialized support, performing Accelerated Life Tests (ALT) on the prototypes for the team. Part of the Computer Integrated Manufacturing (CIM) system was also developed outside the team. The higher-level CIM system was the responsibility of a member of the Material Control Systems (MCS) Department. Bandit also entered into a joint development contract with Hewlett-Packard to help develop a software backplane to link all the cell controllers. Although other major computer firms also bid on the job, HP was selected because it was willing to work as a partner with Motorola.

Suppliers

The Bandit team started to screen suppliers very early on to make sure only those who could meet the six-sigma-quality goal were selected.

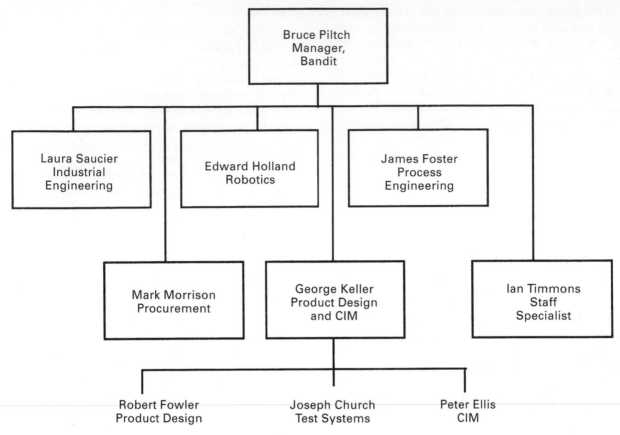

EXHIBIT 3 Bandit Project Team Organization (Late 1986)

They started with a list of 300 eligible suppliers and reduced that to 60 based on Motorola's prior experience with them. Bandit team members visited these 60, examining their manufacturing processes, and the 22 best were ultimately selected. Mark Morrison, procurement manager for component and product quality, commented on supplier relationships:

> In searching for ways to make dramatic improvements in our operations, we discovered we needed to develop better working relationships with our suppliers. This was evidenced by the fact that outgoing quality was maintained by screening out at least one order of magnitude defective materials in the production process.
>
> We found that this was not necessarily due to problems with our suppliers, but rather outdated and cumbersome Motorola systems. Our specifications were outdated and poorly written, our ordering system was confusing, and we put too much emphasis on price rather than value. We also found

that we had too many suppliers—several hundred too many.

> I concentrated my efforts on electrical components like transducers first . . . but I should have looked first at the mechanical parts, like the plastic housing for the pagers. It took longer to get the mechanical parts suppliers up to our requirements—to get their tooling improved—than it did the electrical, and we ran into a time crunch with them on Bandit.[4]

Keller elaborated on what happened when he and others went to talk to suppliers about improving the quality of their product:

> We went out to talk to them, but they also talked to us, and the poor quality of our component specs was their biggest gripe. They showed us stacks of paper for a single part, and we couldn't even understand everything. So we entered into a major effort with our Bandit suppliers to rewrite all the specs—make them short, simple, easy to understand.

---

[4]Ibid., pp. 48–50.

Piltch (as quoted in *Manufacturing Engineering,* April 1989) also recalled this aspect of the problem:

> We would ask to see the blueprints we had sent them, and the blueprints were antiquated or contradictory—they were a real mess . . . We had to scrap the entire process we had been using to describe to our suppliers what we wanted. . . . That procedure took us close to four months and a great deal of very precious engineering resources. Once components were defined and goals were established, suppliers were sought.

Design/Redesign

Several internal components and subassemblies of the Bravo pager had to be redesigned for assembly by the automated line. This redesign involved mainly small changes to the geometry of components to provide flat surfaces that the robots could grab when placing the component. For the customer, division management decided that the pager itself had to be functionally equivalent and visually identical to the Jstar Bravo pager. Because the new design had to take into account both manufacturability and quality issues, the team tried to be conservative in their choices.

The design of the printed circuit board that carried and integrated all the electrical components (e.g., chips, resistors, and capacitors) was a good example of the kind of trade-offs that were made. Originally, to make the assembly of the printed circuit board easier, the board was designed so that all the components could be placed from one side. But because only one side would be used, the components had to be tightly packed and the traces (wires) that connected them could be only two mils wide.

Keller realized that getting six-sigma quality out of this state-of-the-art board design would be impossible and insisted that it be redesigned to have components on both sides; this change would make the spacing less critical and allow standard chips to be used. He explained:

> I found myself becoming a process designer also. Prior to this experience, we used to go through endless negotiations with the process engineers, kind of formally with memos and position papers. With Bandit, there were 30 minutes of screaming and yelling at each other, and then we would reach a compromise.

It worked the other way too, the process engineers becoming involved in the product. The process engineers kept pushing for one single-sided printed circuit board, but we finally convinced them that the board density would be too great. So we had the choice of two boards or one board on both sides, and we chose the latter approach. That choice meant 90 extra feet of conveyor and $200,000 more for equipment—two more robots, another oven, and so forth.

Redesigning Bravo to meet Motorola's six-sigma-quality goal was also an exacting process, explained one engineer:

> So with electrical components, we would take capacitors, for example, and measure them, calculate the means, and design them so that tuning adjustments on the Bandit Bravo could meet six-sigma requirements. On the mechanical side, we measured hundreds of the plastic housing units, developed tolerance requirements, and worked with our vendor so he could hold dimensional tolerances within .002" and also meet six-sigma standards.[5]

The production line was built up from automated cells like those used in conventional production lines. These were modified slightly to fit into the fully automated Bandit line. The engineers started with the beginning of the line and added cells one by one until the line was completed. By January 1987, the date of the first prototype build, the line was completed, although not debugged.

Subsequently, the project revolved around four major prototype cycles and a pilot production run, whose dates remained tied to the December 1987 goal. Prior to each cycle, the design was temporarily frozen. The line, as it existed at that point, was used to produce all prototype units (see Exhibit 4). This approach to prototyping cycles, referred to as *periodic prototyping,* differed dramatically from that used traditionally by Motorola and others. Under the traditional approach, early prototypes tested engineering feasibility, functionality, and design, and later cycles tested manufacturing processes. Furthermore, a given prototype cycle occurred after a set of tasks was completed (which, if late, delayed prototyping), not at scheduled intervals.

With periodic prototyping, the entire set of cross-functional efforts was evaluated in each cycle according to a preset schedule. Thus, each

---

[5]Ibid., p. 24.

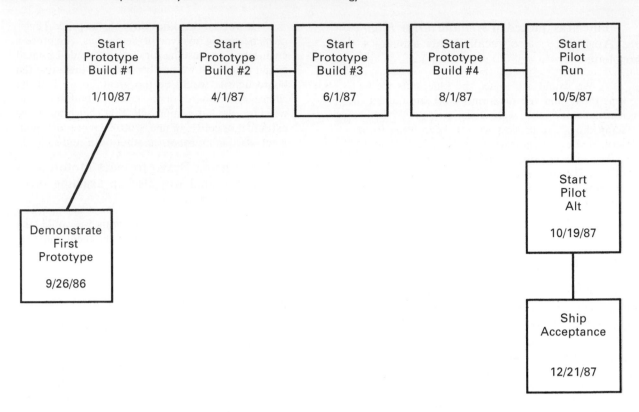

	Demo	Prototype #1	Prototype #2	Prototype #3	Prototype #4
Location of Build	Lab	Pager Factory Front End Manual Bandit Back End	Partial Bandit Front End Manual Bandit Back End	Complete Bandit Build with Manual Assistance	Full Bandit Line
Status of Bandit Line	Not Started	Initial Design	Front End Largely Complete AutoTest in Back End (with Manual Assembly)	Hardware Complete CIM Control Started	Bandit Line Completed

EXHIBIT 4 Bandit Prototype Schedule

cycle was a test of how all functions and elements of the system were progressing, not just a subpart. Because the dates were preset for every few months, they provided a recurring focal point for assessing the status of each part of the project and helped direct efforts needed to get back on track by the next prototyping date. Also, because each cycle produced 50 to 100 units, every group had a number of units they could test and work with between prototyping cycles.

Although Bandit was the first project at Motorola to use periodic prototyping, all the prototype dates were met within one or two days. While not all of the planned technical progress had been made prior to each cycle, any shortcomings were generally made up within a few days and *always* by the next prototyping cycle. When the computer system was down, the engineers built the prototypes by hand. In the first two prototyping cycles, the full line was not completed, so the prototype units were only partially built on the line. By the third cycle, however, complete units were assembled on the line. In addition to the prototype cycles, project milestones were also reviewed quarterly with Chris Galvin. For most of these reviews George Fisher was also present. On the whole, these reviews were regarded positively because of the increased visibility they gave the project.

Robert Fowler, product design manager, contrasted the Bandit development process to its predecessor:

> In the old system, the design engineers would do two or three prototype runs; then it would be transferred to manufacturing, and they would try to get all the problems out in one pilot run (which would often turn into two or three pilot runs). On Bandit, we scheduled periodic prototype cycles, and manufacturing was involved in every one of them.

> This approach to prototyping had several advantages. Since everyone had to be ready for the prototype build, no excuses were accepted for delay. It also greatly facilitated communication among all the groups. Furthermore, by running the prototypes down the Bandit line, we were able to build many more units at each cycle, which enabled widespread distribution of the prototype units for testing. In most projects, the model shop would build only a few prototype units because it was too expensive to build very many. Because of the availability of Bandit prototype units and because of the high priority of the Bandit project, we were able to do an Accelerated Life Test (ALT) at each prototype cycle.

> By doing the ALT, we discovered several problems that were caused by interaction of the process and product design. For example, we found that over time the pagers' frequency drifted from the set point. On investigating, we determined that it occurred because of the short cycle time on the Bandit line; the pagers were still warm from the soldering oven when they were tuned. As they cooled down, the frequency tended to drift. To fix this problem, we had to change the material in the PCB and change the design of the oscillator. If the prototypes had not been built on the line and then put through an ALT, we would not have found this problem until much later, and the schedule would have been severely affected.

By December 1987, the line was up and running and had passed the required benchmark—five-sigma quality performance on a batch of 1,000 units. While the final goal was six-sigma quality, sign-off was tied to reaching demonstrated five-sigma quality.

The Bandit Line

The result of Operation Bandit was a fully automated factory that was driven by individual customer orders. The order, placed by a salesperson (or even directly by the customer) into the pager order system on the corporate IBM mainframe, could contain any number of pagers in any one of 21 million possible feature combinations. Order data were then passed to the Communications Sector's Material Control System (MCS), which generated a bill of materials and a shop order. These data were then transferred to a Stratus computer that prioritized, scheduled, and assigned serial numbers to the order. The Stratus also performed plantwide CIM tasks such as production line summary reporting. The order was then sent to the Bandit line controller, which instructed the line to build the required pagers. (See Exhibits 5 and 6.)

The Bandit production line was a true lot-size-of-one, flexible production facility. All the production line functions were completely automated with the exception of component material handling, which was purposely not automated because to do so was far more costly than the benefits justified.

The U-shaped Bandit line was about 450 feet long, with 34 workstations connected by conveyors. Each workstation had a status light. If the light was green, all was normal; if yellow, the workstation had detected an anomaly but was still functioning; if red, the workstation was down (nonfunctional). The line was staffed each shift by approximately 12 workers who corrected the problems that caused the red and yellow lights, kept the machines supplied with materials, and performed maintenance tasks on the machines. They were supported by a shift supervisor and two engineers.

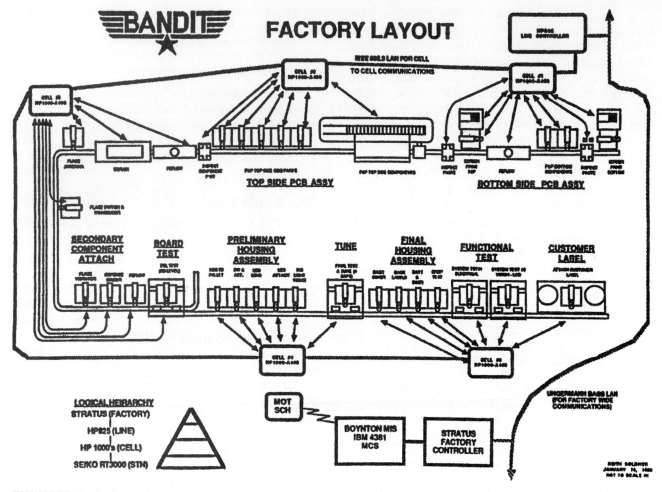

EXHIBIT 5 Bandit Factory Layout

Early Bandit Production (December 1987 to October 1989)

During the year and a half of production that followed the project's official completion, conflicts arose between meeting production goals and experimenting to enhance the operation of the line. For example, to pick up components, some of the robots used "grippers" that required adjustments every few days. To eliminate this problem, the engineers wanted to switch to a different kind of gripper, but doing so would have cost several hours of production, and so the change was postponed.

Recalled Richard Spira, Bandit production manager (as of March 1989):

> One thing we learned after the project was officially completed was that we had to get the engineering people off the production line. They were

constantly trying to optimize the system. When I took over, my charge was to concentrate on producing pagers. Once the engineers were off the line, the biggest problem I had was that we could never get statistically significant trends because of robot downtime. Achieving five-sigma quality day in and day out is a world apart from briefly demonstrating five-sigma quality. We learned that one key was the preventative maintenance (PM) schedule. We started with the standard PM schedule used on robots elsewhere in the plant but still had problems. It turned out that we had to rewrite the PM schedule just for Bandit because the Bandit robots are used very differently. In the rest of the factory, robots may move in a 10- or 20-degree arc, but on the Bandit line, they move a full 180 degrees.

> We also had problems with slow morning start-ups, after being shut down at night. The first step in solving this problem turned out to be easy—I just put

EXHIBIT 6 Close-up of a Bandit Line Robot Cell
Automated soldering robot performs its operations on the Bravo circuit board with a high degree of
consistency . . . another step toward six-sigma quality.

in a third shift. My motto has become "The Factory Never Stops." Having solved these problems, we are now concentrating on throughput, some minor equipment capability modifications, and continuously improving the line's performance.

Other problems cropped up as well. Despite early vendor involvement, obtaining a continuous supply of high-quality components was difficult. When production started to ramp up, not all the vendors consistently met the production and quality demands. The Bandit team had to help them solve their problems.

The CIM system also had several start-up difficulties. Increasing production volume generated much heavier processing loads, and an additional cell controller computer had to be added to the line. A great deal of work also was done on the CIM system to integrate it more fully with the corporate MIS systems for order entry and material requisitions. Noted Bruce Keller:

> Probably the most impressive technology to come out of Bandit was the CIM system. We don't know of anyone else in the United States that has developed a factory running on lot sizes of one based on actual customer orders in a totally automated environment. We also are able to do real-time statistical process control that gives the workers immediate feedback on how everything is going. These real time data will be extremely important as we push toward six-sigma quality, because to obtain six-sigma we not only have to identify problems quickly, but also must track trends in order to anticipate problems and avoid them. We can never get to six-sigma quality without anticipating problems in this manner.

Peter Ellis, CIM engineer on Bandit, added:

> The software connection of all the different elements of the CIM system was the most challenging part of the Bandit project, and the newest to the company. A major problem was communication between the different groups. Although the CIM group was brought in early, we spent most of the early period worrying about the overall architecture of the system, not working on the detailed level of how to communicate with the robots. As a result, when we tried to integrate with the robotics, we did not know what to expect, and CIM was often the bottleneck.

Piltch and other managers felt, however, that the absence of difficulties would have signaled that they had not attempted enough. Although the Bandit project met its required five-sigma performance during a production run in December 1987, it did not reach that level of performance on a day-to-day basis for another 18 months. However, by August 1989, the Bandit line had stabilized at five-sigma quality, was producing substantial volume, and was considered a great success throughout Motorola. Albert Cameron, strategic marketing manager, explained:

> The Bandit production line has finally given us the ability to ramp up quickly to meet demand. The pager business is very seasonal, and even though it is growing about 20% per year, there is a big spurt in demand in the second quarter followed by a sharp *decline* after the summer. Every year, we have problems getting enough pagers out in the second quarter, and so we risk losing market share. In 1989, the Bandit line provided the flexibility to enable us to meet demand much more effectively—reducing our second-quarter delivery problems dramatically.

> While I know the product line marketing manager would have liked to have had more input on Bandit, the team had to concentrate on getting the job done.

One marketing manager voiced a different opinion, however:

> The Bandit people thought that because they were not changing any of the customer features, they did not have to involve marketing. However, they ended up making some decisions to simplify their tasks that caused me considerable grief. For example, they decided to use a five-spot crystal, which limited the type of pagers they could produce to only high-band pagers. When they made that decision, the bulk of the market was high-band. Since then, however, the market has shifted to 900-Mhz pagers, and I've had to tell half of my customers that they can't get a Bandit Bravo—they can get only a Jstar Bravo. The customers get real upset when they hear this—in part because the Bandit people sent out brochures explaining how good the Bandit line is and how high the quality is. I didn't even see one of these brochures until a customer showed it to me!

Nevertheless, the Bandit line received considerable attention from the business press, and some industry analysts felt Bandit's success was influential in the decision to award Motorola the first Malcolm Baldrige National Quality Award in 1988. Furthermore, senior corporate management saw periodic projects such as Bandit—involving significant jumps in product and/or process performance every two to four years—as a primary source of improvement in competitive advantage. By late 1989, several Motorola divisions, with top management's encouragement, were pursuing major "home run" projects using an approach very similar to that used by the Pager Division on Bandit.

BEYOND BANDIT

By October 1989, most of the start-up problems had been ironed out, and Merle Gilmore, vice president and general manager of the Paging Products Division, was concerned with optimizing the payback on the Bandit investment. Both direct and indirect returns from Bandit were important. Line utilization on Bandit had to be as high as possible to maximize the direct return; yet everyone felt that the line could be made more efficient with experimentation and further process development. Furthermore, the Bandit line's flexibility made it very attractive for prototyping and even initial production of other products. All but the final assembly of pilot production on Motorola's new wristwatch pager was done on the Bandit line, for example. Such "external" demands for the line were often in direct conflict with obtaining the optimum line utilization.

In addition, having two internal designs for the Bravo pager itself had intrinsic difficulties because two separate product lines had to be maintained. Any change in one had to be made in the other. For example, one of Motorola's customers had trouble with water leakage, and the Jstar pager had to be redesigned slightly. The customer also insisted that the Bandit version be redesigned, even though it was not clear that the Bandit pager had the leakage problem. Such problems required substantially more support effort.

Nonetheless, from the beginning, Chris Galvin had told Piltch that the success of the Bandit line was only half the job. The other half was to transfer the knowledge gained in the Bandit operation throughout the division and the company. It was clear that, given the rate of change in most of Motorola's businesses, top management saw the bulk of the company's performance improvement coming from significant projects such as Bandit, with tuning and refining taking place between such projects. Thus, one obvious successor to the legacy of Bandit was the next-generation Bravo pager, appropriately nicknamed "Son-of-Bandit," a project directed at improving the product while supporting some further gains in the productivity of the process.

Son-of-Bandit Issues

Pagers were differentiated by a variety of features, for example, size, battery life, number of messages stored in memory, message display (e.g., type, readability), and ability to lock and delete messages. Motorola's product development strategy had been to compete aggressively on such features. By continually changing the customers' view of what the standard pager should consist of, Motorola dominated the pager business. Over time, marketing developed a series of guidelines for new product specifications: (1) smaller is better; (2) pagers should be more attractive physically; (3) features customers accept remain unchanged

(so the end user need not learn how to use a pager with each generation); and (4) being alert for "gotchas." A marketing manager explained the last-named guideline:

> A gotcha is when a competitor designs in a feature that customers feel is superior, and you don't have it in your pager. For example, NEC developed a display that would automatically light when the surrounding lighting is low. On our display, you have to push a button to light the display. Many customers feel NEC's display is superior because of that feature, and we have lost some sales because of it. Of course, gotchas work both ways, and we try to design in our own.

Historically, marketing obtained most of their feedback by discussing with big carriers what they would like in the next-generation pager. Marketing then developed specifications for the new product and passed them on to product development. If product development had problems with the specifications, they would meet with marketing and hammer out a compromise.

Because of the pager market's rapid growth, however, pagers were becoming more of a consumer business. To adapt, marketing initiated a drive to identify the end users and which market segments had high or low penetration, so Motorola could focus its marketing (and some product development) effort on certain segments with high growth potential. The results of this effort were not expected until the end of 1990, when the Son-of-Bandit development would be well under way.

For his part, while he hoped that Son-of-Bandit would learn from the Bandit project, Gilmore felt that it was important not to copy the Bandit process blindly. There were significant differences in the goals of the two projects: Bandit had been a big push in *process* technology, and Son-of-Bandit had to concentrate on pushing *product* technology. There was also the question of whether Son-of-Bandit should have only a single, fully automated production process or retain the combined automated/conventional approach used for Bravo.

Gilmore felt that many of the reasons for the success of Operation Bandit had been understood, but he wanted to make sure these lessons were disseminated and applied effectively throughout the division and company.

CASE 12

FASTech Integration Inc.

In January 1994, Jim Pelusi, CEO and cofounder of FASTech, was debating how his company's manufacturing automation software, CELLworks, should be priced. The CELLworks suite, which allowed customers to build computer-integrated manufacturing systems quickly, ran on personal computers and workstations; its English-like language permitted "alien" machines from different manufacturers to communicate with each other simply, and its graphical interface was easy for operators to use. Despite this, the purchasing manager at Silcor, FASTech's largest customer, had just called to inform Pelusi that Silcor was planning to cut back significantly on its purchases of CELLworks, which would endanger FASTech's 1994 revenue growth target and any hope for 1994 profitability. Silcor had discovered that by switching its hardware configuration from a cutting-edge distributed computing system onto one centralized workstation, it could save 80% of its control software expenses.

Pelusi and his young management team believed that while their pricing policy had been a major contributor to FASTech's growth and profitability, both the level and the basis for pricing could be improved. Moreover, if the company was to reach its potential, pricing issues would have to be resolved quickly. In 1992, FASTech had grown by 62% to $7.6 million in revenue; 1993 growth, however, was only 14%. Moreover, losses in 1993 and 1992 totaled nearly $2.3 million (although 1993 losses were only $800,000, and forecasts for 1994 had indicated a return to profitability along with higher growth).

This case was prepared as the basis for class discussion rather than to illustrate either effective or ineffective handling of an administrative situation. Professors Benson Shapiro and David Upton revised the marketing information in the case. Data have been disguised.

This case was prepared by Paal Gisholt and Robert Jones under the direction of David M. Upton. Copyright © 1994 by the President and Fellows of Harvard College. Harvard Business School case 694-028.

That FASTech's price structure had caused its largest customer to retreat from its commitment to distributed computing simply to save on software costs deeply troubled Pelusi. How many other customers would be forced to make similar technological compromises? And how much revenue and profit might FASTech be losing due to unintentional incentives built into its present price structure? The situation could not have surfaced at a more critical time. The market for software to integrate manufacturing equipment and factory information systems had grown tremendously, driven by manufacturers' need to improve manufacturing productivity and reduce time-to-market in an increasingly competitive marketplace. This growth had attracted numerous competitors. An intense battle was underway to see which vendor's software would emerge as the industry standard.

Although Pelusi had long recognized the potential to improve FASTech's price model, he had been reluctant to deviate from standard industry pricing practice. A unique approach to pricing would prevent direct price comparisons between FASTech and other vendors, giving competitors the opportunity to mislead customers into believing that FASTech's product was more expensive. Pelusi promised Silcor that he and his management team would analyze alternative approaches to pricing. The goal would be to solve Silcor's problem by developing an improved overall price model that better captured the value that FASTech's products provided to its customers.

FASTECH'S ORIGINS

Jim Pelusi and Hans Bukow started FASTech Integration in December 1986. At the time, they were working for GMF Robotics, a vendor of robots and automated manufacturing systems.[1] Al-

[1]GMF Robotics was a joint venture between General Motors and Fanuc, a Japanese robot producer. In 1992, Fanuc acquired full ownership and changed the name to Fanuc Robotics.

though GMF considered itself a hardware vendor, customers increasingly required that GMF help develop the software that integrated its robotics with its customers' factory information system.

This integration software usually had to be written using a low-level computer language called C (see Exhibit 1).[2] Because most manufacturing engineers did not know how to write programs in C, software engineers did the programming. And integration software was notoriously difficult to write. One problem was the communication between "alien" devices: different elements of a man-

ufacturing system (such as a machine tool or a robot) often were made by different vendors and used entirely different languages and protocols for communication. Moreover, integration software had to deal with a physical and unforgiving world, which added tremendous complexity. In a program used to calculate a payroll, for instance, the program could run in its own time overnight and a bug might cause, say, an addition error without immediate physical consequences. In contrast, if integration software called up the wrong part-program or caused a communications error, a robot might crash into a machine. Finally, manufacturing software had to run in "real time"—the software had to run synchronously with the devices on the shop floor.

---

[2]A computer language is described as "low-level" if it is closer to the computer's native language (machine code) than human language.

EXHIBIT I   Sample C Program to Compare Two Words

```
register char *s1, *s2;
{
/* case INSENSITIVE: Compare strings: s1>s2: >0 s1==s2: 0 s1<s2: <0
*/
register char c1,c2;

for(;;) {
c1 = *s1++; if (c1 <= 'Z') if (c1 >= 'A') c1 += 040;
c2 = *s2++; if (c2 <= 'Z') if (c2 >= 'A') c2 += 040;
if (c1 != c2) break;
if (c1 == '\0') return(0);
}
return(c1–c2);
}

#ifdef AMIGA
#ifndef isascii
#define isascii(c) ((unsigned)(c)<=127)
#endif
#endif

#define DOWNCASE(x) (isascii(x) && isalpha(x) && isupper(x) ? (tolower(x)): (x)
)
int ULstrncmp(s1,s2,n)
char *s1, *s2;
int n;
{
/* case INSENSITIVE: Compare strings, up to n chars:
s1>s2: >0 s1==s2: 0 s1<s2: <0
*/

register int i;
register int result = 0;

for(i = 0;(s1[i] | | s2[i]) && i<n && !result;++i){
result = DOWNCASE(s2[i])—DOWNCASE(s1[i]);
}
return(result);
}
```

In addition to these problems, writing good integration programs was a challenge because software engineers rarely understood the manufacturing engineers' description of the process. And it was extraordinarily difficult to modify the programs once the system had been installed.

After seeing many examples of time-consuming miscommunication between software engineers and manufacturing engineers, Pelusi and Bukow decided that the only efficient way to integrate a work cell was to let manufacturing engineers do it themselves. They set out to find a set of software tools that would enable manufacturing engineers—most of whom had only rudimentary programming skills—to perform the integration. Despite interviewing dozens of outside manufacturers, they failed to unearth any such software packages.

Recognizing this important and unmet market need, Pelusi and Bukow resigned from their jobs at GMF, formed FASTech Integration, and began to design the new product. Based on their prior experience, they knew the software must meet three criteria to be successful:

- It should be easy to use, delivering clear and quick improvements in development productivity and time-to-market that would be easily recognized by conservative manufacturers;
- It should perform well on distributed computing systems, which were rapidly gaining acceptance at leading-edge manufacturers;
- It should offer the customer unparalleled flexibility by using object-oriented technology to make the computer code written by engineers easily reusable and reconfigurable.[3] Exhibit 2 shows the type of language used in the FASTech product.

Despite their background and connections in the auto industry, the founders decided to focus on the semiconductor and electronics businesses. They reasoned that semiconductor and electronics manufacturers, who typically needed to shave precious months off time-to-market, would be willing to pay a premium price for a tool that offered faster development of integration software applications and thus would provide dramatically increased manufacturing flexibility. Making its first commercial sale in 1988, FASTech had grown steadily. By 1994, the company had sold over 1,500 systems, broadening its commercial focus beyond the semiconductor and electronics industries to include process industries and automotive assembly.

TECHNOLOGY FOR TRANSLATION

The CELLworks Family of Products

FASTech developed and marketed a family of manufacturing integration software tools under the name "CELLworks." These products helped different pieces of factory equipment in a work cell communicate and work together effectively. For example, in a plant producing calculators, one work cell—that included robots, chip insertion machines, and perhaps a bar-code reader—would be devoted to "stuffing" electronic components into the circuit board. Machines in this type of automated work cell required synchronized instructions telling them what tasks to perform and when. Machines also had to be able to pass data back and forth regarding their status. The CELLworks family of products made the production of software to coordinate, communicate with, and control the cell easier than it had ever been.

The CELLworks product family comprised five modules of software. The licensing of each module was controlled through a software device called an enabler. While real-time control software could be developed using CELLworks, the user would not be able to execute the code unless each computer running the execution software also had an enabler. The five modules were:

1. The Application Development and Execution Environment—This module comprised a graphical fourth generation programming language (4GL) and an execution environment. The 4GL made it possible for process engineers to write a set of prose-like instructions, called an application, to control the operations of factory equipment. This application would be used by the execution environment in real time to control the work cell. Since applications developed with CELLworks needed an enabler to run, enablers had to be loaded on every computer used to control the work cell. FASTech sold two versions of CELLworks: a development license, which contained the 4GL tools

---

[3]Object oriented software was composed of a number of highly discrete, interchangeable modules. These modules, called "objects," could be easily reused or "plugged in" to other programs.

EXHIBIT 2 Example of a CELLworks Application to Control a Station

CELLworks
Everything CELL CONTROL Should Be
Powerful Graphic Cell Programming & DeBugging Tools

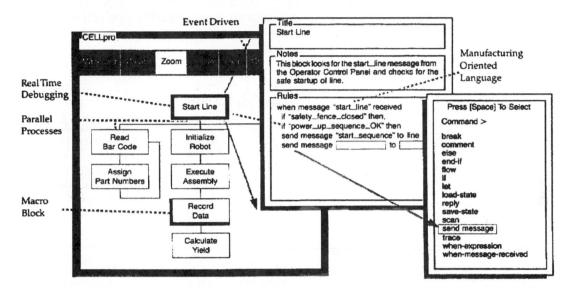

Largest Library of Interface and Application Modules

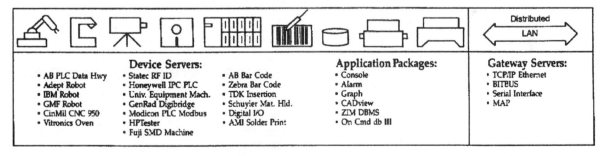

Device Servers:

- AB PLC Data Hwy
- Adept Robot
- IBM Robot
- GMF Robot
- CinMil CNC 950
- Vitronics Oven

- Statec RF ID
- Honeywell IPC PLC
- Univ. Equipment Mach.
- GenRad Digibridge
- Modicon PLC Modbus
- HPTester
- Fuji SMD Machine

- AB Bar Code
- Zebra Bar Code
- TDK Insertion
- Schuyier Mat. Hld.
- Digital I/O
- AMI Solder Print

Application Packages:

- Console
- Alarm
- Graph
- CADview
- ZIM DBMS
- On Cmd db III

Gateway Servers:

- TCP/IP Ethernet
- BITBUS
- Serial Interface
- MAP

Complete, Integrated Development Environment and Run Time System

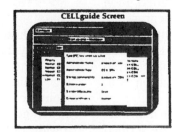

- Menu driven CELLguide
- CELLview, CELLtrace, & CELLtalk Debug Tools
- Transparent Networked Messaging
- Virtual Cell Control Architecture

- Real Time, Multi-tasking without complexity
- Available for IBM 286/386 class computer
- Integrated Database Management System
- Device Interface Development System

necessary to write an application; and a runtime or execution license, which contained the enabler that made it possible to run the application on the factory floor.

2. MBX: A Messaging Bus—The MBX was a message-based communications mechanism that allowed the various CELLworks modules to work together and communicate with each other.

3. Human Interface Servers—FASTech's human interface servers comprised configurable sets of forms, graphs, alarms, and animation objects, which allowed a straightforward interface to be designed for the machine operators who would run the system on a day-to-day basis.

4. Equipment Servers: The Rosetta Stone in Software—Equipment servers were special software bridges that enabled a piece of equipment, with its own unique specifications and communication protocols, to be easily integrated into a work cell. Equipment servers were the computer equivalent of a language phrase book for the integration computer. Each equipment server would know how, for example, to translate "stop" in the language of the equipment for which it was designed.

5. Other Types of Servers—In addition to communicating with each other, factory machines often needed access to systems that were not "physical" manufacturing devices. For example, it might be necessary to communicate with a company database to collect information on the details of a given product, or inform higher level computers when a particular batch had been completed. These other servers enabled CELLworks to communicate easily with a wide variety of commonly used packages.

A Typical Application

Most of FASTech's products were sold to customers installing new manufacturing lines. Customers generally would begin the process by specifying the production machines needed, then the computer hardware necessary to integrate the line. CELLworks was used to develop and execute applications to control the activities of this group of devices—for example, those in a station used to manufacture cellular phones. Such a station is illustrated in Exhibit 3.

The coordination and control of the many activities taking place in a work cell was prescribed by a software application, a program written in a prose-like language by the manufacturing engineers developing the cell. The prose-like nature of these commands made it much easier for the manufacturing engineers to write and debug the application. It was also relatively easy for those other than the original author to modify this type of code.

Using the cellular phone example, a work cell might be organized in 10 stations (see Exhibit 3). In order to control such work cell hardware, the customer would require software from FASTech as follows:

Module	Description
Application Enabler	The execution or "runtime" version of the CELLworks software that could execute the application
Messaging Bus	Permits the equipment, computers, and operators in a work cell to communicate with each other
Human Interface Package	To build and execute displays for the operator
Servers: • Programmable Logic Controllers • Bar Code Readers • Assembly Robots • Test Equipment	Each equipment required its own server to enable it to communicate with the rest of the manufacturing control system, although a single server could be used for multiple units of identical equipment

THE CELLWORKS ACCOUNT BASE

The manufacturing cell control software market for 1993 was estimated to be about $73 million, with five year growth estimated at about 10% per year. Actual customer acquisition of cell control software was about twice the $73 million, but about half the market was taken by software developed internally by user companies.

FASTech concentrated on the semiconductor manufacturing and electronic assembly markets. Semiconductors were manufactured in highly automated "fabs" costing several billion dollars each. The industry was very capital-intensive and growing rapidly. Electronics assembly involved the manufacture of computers, telecommunications, switch gear, telephones, consumer electronics, and a wide range of other products. Typical processes including stuffing printed circuit boards with com-

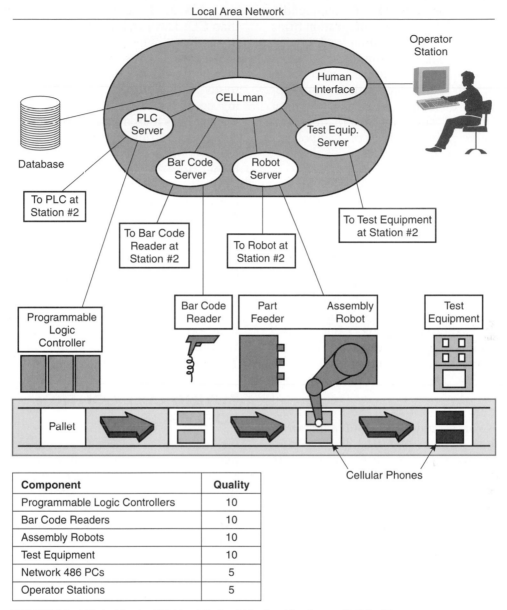

Component	Quality
Programmable Logic Controllers	10
Bar Code Readers	10
Assembly Robots	10
Test Equipment	10
Network 486 PCs	5
Operator Stations	5

EXHIBIT 3 A Typical Station Within a Workcell Used to Manufacture Cellular Phones
The software required to run this system is outlined in Exhibit 4.

ponents and loading the boards into frames. FASTech's revenues by industry were:

Semiconductors	55%
Electronic Assembly	20%
Auto and Metal Working	15%
Other	10%

Its customers included many large companies such as AT&T, Digital Equipment Corporation, Hewlett-Packard, Hitachi, Motorola, Philips, Sam-

sung, and Silcor. FASTech management estimated that 20% of the total $73 million cell control software market was in semiconductor manufacture, and 12% in electronic assembly.

System integrators, ranging from large multinational, cross-industry firms such as Andersen Consulting and EDS, to small highly focused manufacturing automation firms, provided much of the installation and support in many projects. In others, the customer's own employees provided the installation and support expertise. Recommendations and references from system integration firms were important aids in the selling and buying processes. FASTech was working hard to build partnerships with system integrators who could provide clients with requirements definition, project management, development and installation support, and even full "turn key" installations. The impact of any change in FASTech pricing policies and levels on these firms was unclear.

Competition

FASTech had several direct competitors in the manufacturing automation software market. Two other classes of products coexisted in this market: a lower-end product that functioned primarily as a systems monitoring tool and a high-end product that provided more application power than CELLworks. The latter, high-end product did not require as much post-purchase programming (it was ready to run "out of the box"), but this also limited its flexibility. For the most part, FASTech's primary competitors were considerably larger in revenues, and were also older, more-established companies.

The primary competitors in the low-end segment were Sysworks and Century Software, which offered products similar to CELLworks; Pelusi thought, however, that his firm's tools were quicker, more powerful, and more robust. He also felt that these characteristics justified a higher price level for CELLworks than for comparable products by Sysworks and Century. These products performed best when used for simple systems monitoring but often "ran out of steam" when used for controlling elements of the manufacturing process in real time. Initially, these products were PC-based and priced on a CPU-based scheme. As the software evolved to Unix-based systems, CPU-based pricing was still used, but Unix nodes were priced at a higher level by both competitors. Century's sales had grown to $18 million (projected) in 1993. Overall, Century's sales had grown by approximately 11.6% over the past five years. Profits were expected to be much healthier in 1993, at over 8% of sales after several years of 1% (of sales) profitability. Sysworks 1993 sales were projected to be over $10 million, with profits of nearly $2 million. In each of the past two years, Sysworks had nearly doubled its sales and more than doubled its profits.

A second class of products was priced higher than CELLworks, and offered the type of applications that engineers would have to *build* with CELLworks. In some cases, when their needs matched available products, companies were able to save the additional programming and engineering costs that would be necessary with CELLworks. FASTech mainly competed against two companies in this segment, Prologix, and BYCIM. These companies' products were VAX-based and higher priced than CELLworks. Each used a classification system that allocated prices according to power of the VAX being used. BYCIM used only five classification categories; Prologix used eight different classes. Prologix had been in business for more than 17 years, and had experienced its most rapid growth during the mid to late 1980s. Prologix's 1993 sales topped $14 million but experienced a bottom line loss of over $2 million. BYCIM sales were lower than Prologix's at $8 million projected for year-end 1993. However, BYCIM also projected profits, albeit modest at 2.5% of sales, for the fifth consecutive year.

BUYING CELL CONTROL SOFTWARE

Cell control software was a complex and involved purchase for major customers. The manufacturing organization focused on such issues as efficiency in the plant, reliability, and durability—manufacturing managers wanted to know if the software would work. The software engineering organization, on the other hand, focused on ease of use and efficiency in program development and software engineering, and often was the "easiest sell." The information technology organization was most interested in connectivity to their corporate information systems, industry standards, cost, and vendor technical support. The procurement function focused on price and discount (in fact, some procurement departments were evaluated on the size of the discounts they negotiated, regardless of actual price).

Companies with in-house, captive supplier operations, of course, presented much different purchase situations than those in which FASTech competed only with other outside vendors. Captive suppliers tended to be viewed as "fixed costs" applied to a wide range of products. Human resource issues sometimes limited the way customers viewed employees such as software programmers. Additionally, some potential clients viewed their manufacturing automation software capability as a core competence and distinct competitive advantage.

FASTech management had seen a preponderance of "large deals" in its revenue base, with large sites accounting for 30% of transactions yet 80% of revenue. Revenue per year at one large, multi-site client had risen from $300,000 in 1990 to $1.6 million in 1993, with sales in several of the corporation's operating units.

In a typical outsourced manufacturing automation project, cost components were:

1. In-house and/or systems integrator support   38%
2. Down time because of product reliability   15%
3. Material handling hardware   15%
4. Automation hardware   14%
5. Supplier support   10%
6. Supplier software   8%
   100%

FASTech supplied both software (70% of revenue) and support (30% of revenue, including consulting, customization, maintenance, and training).

In many companies, top management was skeptical at worst and unenthusiastic at best regarding investments in manufacturing software. The CEO at a large metal goods manufacturer publicly stated, "We have spent a fortune on manufacturing automation software, but I can't find any related productivity or efficiency improvements. We will be damned careful in the future with such capital projects." Other top managers were hesitant to walk away from the promised improvements in manufacturing efficiency and competitive effectiveness. The potential rewards in an intensely competitive manufacturing environment seemed too good to pass up.

FASTECH'S SALES AND PRICING APPROACH

FASTech sold through a nine-person direct sales force in the United States and through distributors outside the United States. Reporting to Jeff Cassis, vice president of sales and marketing, were two U.S. regional sales managers as well as an European manager, an Asian manager, and various headquarters marketing people (e.g., product marketing, marketing communication). The U.S. sales-

people were paid a base salary averaging $40,000, plus a commission based on sales revenue and a quarterly bonus for attainment of specific account and product related sales goals. Commissions and bonuses accounted for an average of 50% of total compensation.

FASTech maintained a standard set of list prices, although salespeople were allowed to offer discounts of up to 10% at their own discretion. Larger discounts had to work their way up the sales organization chain, with significant discounts going all the way to Pelusi. The largest discount, involving a site license, was about 25%.

Software pricing involved a unique set of challenges that rarely arose when pricing manufactured goods. Cost of goods sold (COGS)—in this case, diskettes, and manuals—typically amounted to less than 5% of product cost. By far the largest proportion of a software vendor's costs were fixed and up front. Development costs varied little with sales volume. Because marginal costs were not particularly useful in establishing software prices, most software was priced based upon some estimation of value to the end user. And this was extraordinarily difficult to determine (particularly with innovative software that could be used as flexibly as CELLworks).

CPU-Based Pricing

Many comparable software vendors used CPU-based pricing, which required that the customer pay a separate software license fee for each computer, or central processing unit (CPU), on which the software was installed. CPU-based pricing could be found in both the mass market segment of the software market (for products such as Lotus 1-2-3) and in the larger system arena (software for mainframes and minicomputers). Larger, more powerful CPUs were capable of supporting multiple users running the same program, so the license fee charged for faster, more powerful CPUs was generally some multiple of that charged for a desktop computer.

CPU-based pricing worked well in the mass market segment because it was easy to administer—one simply counted PCs. For software applications that ran across a variety of hardware platforms (including distributed PCs, RISC workstations, minicomputers, and mainframes), however, CPU-based pricing often failed to correspond to customer value received. If, for example, an individual was using a program loaded on a powerful minicomputer, that single user would be significantly overcharged, because the software price would have been based on the power of the machine and the possibility of multi-user execution. Given the weak relationship between price and value, a number of software vendors—particularly the large relational database companies—had been experimenting with alternative approaches to pricing, including

- charging per user,
- charging per concurrent user (two people using the software at the same time)
- charging by computer terminal, and even
- charging per transaction (e.g., in an equity trading application, per trade).

FASTech's Price Structure in 1993

FASTech used a straight CPU-based pricing structure to charge for its products: the price charged for each software module was multiplied by the number of computers running that module. Returning to the cellular phone example, Exhibit 4 outlines the price FASTech would charge for its software tools to run the work cell components shown in Exhibit 3.

While this particular work cell was driven by PCs, more powerful computers like RISC workstations could control roughly two to four times the number of factory devices as a PC before performance would deteriorate.[4] Because configurations using workstations typically could operate

---

[4]RISC, or reduced instruction set computing, was a type of processor design that allowed much faster execution of programs.

with half as many CPUs, FASTech charged roughly twice as much per workstation as per PC in order to generate comparable revenues.

A SHORT-TERM CRISIS: THE SILCOR PROBLEM

Silcor, one of the largest electronics companies in the United States, had been a strong supporter of FASTech since that firm's inception. It had purchased numerous systems each year and served as a valuable reference account, allowing customers to see FASTech's products in action. The relationship had deepened in recent months, and Silcor had funded FASTech's efforts to develop a new software product. All had gone well until Grover Freeman, Silcor's director of manufacturing technology, called to let Jim Pelusi know about Silcor's recent decision to reduce the amount paid to FASTech for an upcoming manufacturing line by reconfiguring its factory control hardware. Silcor, which itself manufactured and sold computer hardware, had developed a new workstation that combined four microprocessors into one computer. This "souped up" workstation, termed a multi-processing server workstation, was capable of driving roughly 10–20 times the amount of equipment driven by a PC, and five times that driven by a traditional workstation, at only twice the price.

Because CELLworks was designed for a distributed computing environment, FASTech originally priced it without concern for the capabilities of more powerful computers. FASTech's price list had only two CPU classes: PC and workstation. With the advent of the multi-processing server

EXHIBIT 4 Execution Mode Pricing

Module	Price per CPU	Number of CPUs	Total
Application Enabler	$4,000	5	$20,000
Messaging Bus	$2,000	5	$10,000
Programmable Logic Server	$1,000	4	$4,000
Bar Code Reader Server	$1,000	4	$4,000
Assembly Robot Server	$1,000	2	$2,000
Test Equipment Server	$1,000	2	$2,000
Human Interface Package	$1,500	5	$7,500
Total:			$49,500

The software modules shown above would be required to run the system shown in Exhibit 3.

workstation, however, Silcor planned to replace its usual network of 5 PCs with a single workstation server, a move which would cut FASTech's revenues from $49,500 to $21,500—a whopping 57% decrease. And this was just the tip of the iceberg. Pelusi knew that Silcor planned to buy 20 additional systems in 1994. Thus, the current pricing structure could cost FASTech nearly $600,000 in revenue in the following year.

Pelusi was worried about Silcor's plans for several reasons. First, he had just committed to his board of directors that he would achieve an aggressive set of monthly financial projections. The loss of $600,000 in volume, most of which represented contribution to profit, was a serious setback. Second, and more important, if other customers followed Silcor's lead and implemented similar systems to reduce their software costs, he knew FASTech's long-term viability would be jeopardized. FASTech's direct sales approach depended upon average revenue per transaction of $50,000 plus. A $20,000 average revenue per transaction simply would not provide enough to support direct sales while maintaining sufficient profitability. Pelusi knew he had to take action.

The easiest action would be to add another, higher performance CPU class to the price list to reflect the development of the multi-processing server workstation. Pelusi worried, however, that by doing so, Silcor might perceive FASTech to be singling out its most important customer for selective pricing. The addition of a CPU-class was further complicated by the fact that Silcor itself was the manufacturer of the server in question.

As he considered the risks of simply patching this problem with a potentially contentious additional CPU class, Pelusi sensed an opportunity to overcome what he viewed to be FASTech's real pricing problem—its reliance on CPU-based pricing.

Broader Problems with FASTech's Pricing Scheme

Pelusi believed FASTech's pricing problems extended far beyond the Silcor situation. In preparation for his meeting with Grover Freeman, he held a brainstorming meeting with his senior managers. They generated the following list of problems:

CPU Overload. Some customers had slowed the performance of FASTech software by integrating too many pieces of equipment with each PC or workstation. This posed a dual problem for FASTech: the company generated less revenue from these customers because they bought fewer software licenses, and the customers were often disgruntled as well as expensive to support, because they frequently called for technical support when their system failed to perform as expected.

Overpricing Highly Distributed Systems. The sales force believed FASTech was dramatically overpricing systems to customers with highly distributed configurations—for example, those in which a cheap 386 model PC was dedicated to every piece of equipment. Many of these customers, believing FASTech's prices to be unreasonable, stayed with in-house custom C programming. Some of these orders had been saved by FASTech salespeople's convincing senior managers to override the price list's maximum 10% discount.

Excessive Deal-Cutting. Senior managers were devoting an increasing proportion of their time to cutting special deals to overcome failures of the pricing structure. In addition to this being a distraction from other responsibilities, the team worried that with every special deal the credibility of FASTech's price list diminished.

Failure to Adapt Prices to New Technology. As evidenced by the Silcor situation, FASTech's price list had failed to keep up with changing technology. Senior managers wondered if they needed to increase the number of different hardware classes for prices to correspond more closely to hardware power. With computer hardware technology changing so fast, would this need to be readdressed every six months?

CPU as Poor Proxy for Value. Was the CPU-based pricing structure a stable and appropriate measure of value for FASTech's software? Or was some other measure really more appropriate?

ASSESSING THE VALUE OF TOOLS FOR COMPUTER INTEGRATION

The common theme underlying all these problems was poor correspondence between price charged and value received. Because FASTech wanted to ensure that its prices corresponded to customer value, the team sought information from customers as well as the sales force to refine their understanding of the value that the product delivered. This was more difficult than they thought. They found that the drivers of value depended on whether the software was employed in development mode (to write applications) or in execution mode (to run applications on the factory floor).

Development Mode

In purchasing application development tools, customers valued programmer productivity and the flexibility to adapt to changes in the way the manufacturing system worked. A system that was easy to learn and use would require minimal training and start-up investment. Well-designed tools also enabled the manufacturing engineer to program more quickly and effectively. Faster programming provided two distinct benefits. First, fewer engineers had to be hired to integrate a work cell. The "fully loaded" cost of a customer software engineer was $100,000 to $120,000. Second, good tools could cut application development time by several months, greatly accelerating production ramp-up. In industries with short product life cycles, such as semiconductors, this lead time could have an enormous impact on competitiveness.

Structured development tools enabled engineers to organize applications into well-defined modules and assemble subsequent applications by combining modules from their existing library. This accelerated the company's adaptation to changes in production processes over time, while capturing the learning from previous experiences.

Runtime Mode

In runtime or execution mode, requirements were quite different. Customers valued "connectivity" and execution speed. They also valued being able to connect a large number of robots, machines, and factory information systems, and control them as a group with one application. Connectivity also implied the ability to connect many different makes and models of factory equipment without having to undertake the time-consuming process of developing custom-made servers (language and protocol translators) in C. Customers also valued execution speed. Work cell execution software had to process information and execute commands quickly.

Setting Objectives

After investigating both the source of FASTech's pricing problems and the way customers valued its product, the team felt they had a far more robust understanding of the problem. To prevent themselves from being too reactive, however, the team established an explicit set of criteria against which any pricing scheme should be judged:

1. maximize revenues by pricing the product in a manner which corresponded to customer value;
2. maximize profitability;
3. help CELLworks become an industry standard;
4. remove the price structure as a major influence in the customer's hardware platform configuration decisions;
5. make prices easy for the customers to understand and justify internally;
6. make pricing easy for the sales force to explain, justify, and apply; and
7. adapt readily to changing technology without the appearance of constantly changing prices.

PRICING OPTIONS

The team quickly reached consensus regarding how development licenses should be priced. They would employ user-based pricing, charging customers separately for each manufacturing engineer developing applications on the system. The team believed this method of pricing development licenses corresponded closely to value received by the customer. There was far less agreement surrounding runtime pricing, however, which was far more important because execution systems accounted for roughly 70% of revenues.

The team came up with four runtime pricing options, each of which had unique strengths and weaknesses.

Connection Based Pricing. The most radical alternative identified by the team was to price runtime licenses based solely upon the number of pieces of equipment being connected. They saw significant benefits to being able to price the entire system (including CELLworks, the MBX messaging bus, human interface packages, and servers of all types) by giving the customer a "per connection" price (i.e., $2,500 per equipment connect). This option appealed to the group for several reasons. Most important, connectivity—the performance attribute that most closely corresponded to customer value—was solely responsible for the price level. With this method, customers could make a direct connection between the $2,500 paid for Cellworks and the $200,000 piece of equipment it integrated. In addition, it would allow customers to use whatever type of hardware they wished, without any effect on software cost. This pricing concept was also easy to explain and justify to customers.

Status Quo.   This option, termed the "do nothing" option by the team, avoided the risk involved with deviating from standard industry practices. Those advocating this option pointed out that every vendor in the industry experienced these very same problems. As long as FASTech's problems weren't significantly worse than those experienced by competitors using CPU-based pricing, they argued, the impact on FASTech's competitive position should be negligible. Advocates of this option pointed to FASTech's success to date, and argued that the risks of changing the pricing system outweighed the benefits.

A Modified Status Quo.   The modified status quo option retained a CPU-based pricing structure, but increased the number of CPU classes from two to five. This option would require that every make and model of hardware be classified in one of the five categories, and that the list be updated monthly to include newly introduced machines. The major improvement over the status quo option was that by creating additional hardware grades, there would be a better match between a runtime license price and its capacity to integrate factory equipment. This change would resolve the Silcor problem directly, and would make it more difficult for customers to exploit underpriced hardware configurations.

A Hybrid Approach.   The final approach to pricing identified by the team involved a compromise between the connection-based pricing scheme and traditional CPU-based pricing. This pricing structure required that FASTech's prod-

ucts be divided into two groups: discrete products and system products. Discrete products corresponded to a specific part of the hardware configuration, such as a piece of equipment or an operator station. These included Equipment Servers and Human Interfaces and would be priced per equipment connection or per operator station, independent of the number of CPUs involved. System products consisted of software that gave the work cell a general capability, such as enabling applications to be run or facilitating communications. Systems products included CELLworks runtimes and the MBX messaging bus, and would be priced based upon the number and type of CPUs employed. Overall, the hybrid price structure was approximately as sensitive to the number of connections as it was to the number and type of CPUs chosen.

Each customer would view any changes primarily from the perspective of how it affected its costs. Furthermore, competition in the work cell integration market was intense, and practical implementation considerations would weigh heavily in this decision. Pelusi tried to take the customer's perspective. Which of the proposed structures would be easiest for customers to understand and appreciate? If FASTech went with one of the more radical alternatives, how should it communicate this change to existing and new customers? Such a major change in pricing would result in some customers' benefiting, while others would likely be hurt. Should FASTech do something to protect those harmed by the change, such as grandfathering the price list?[5] If so, which customers would be grandfathered, and for how long? Pelusi was equally concerned with the competitive dimension. Did FASTech, a relatively small vendor, really want to lead the industry in such a fundamental pricing change? Was the advantage to be gained worth taking the risks? And finally, what was the revenue impact anticipated from a pricing change, both in the short term and long term?

---

[5]Grandfathering meant allowing customers for whom the new prices were less favorable to continue to buy products under the old pricing scheme for a specified period of time.

Must CIM Be Justified by Faith Alone?

Robert S. Kaplan

When the Yamazaki Machinery Company in Japan installed an $18 million flexible manufacturing system, the results were truly startling: a reduction in machines from 68 to 18, in employees from 215 to 12, in the floor space needed for production from 103,000 square feet to 30,000, and in average processing time from 35 days to 1.5. [1] After two years, however, total savings came to only $6.9 million, $3.9 million of which had flowed from a one-time cut in inventory. Even if the system continued to produce annual labor savings of $1.5 million for 20 years, the project's return would be less than 10% per year. Since many U.S. companies use hurdle rates of 15% or higher and payback periods of five years or less, they would find it hard to justify this investment in new technology—despite its enormous savings in number of employees, floor space, inventory, and throughput times.

The apparent inability of traditional modes of financial analysis like discounted cash flow to justify investments in computer-integrated manufacturing (CIM) has led a growing number of managers and observers to propose abandoning such criteria for CIM-related investments. "Let's be more practical," runs one such opinion. "DCF is not the only gospel. Many managers have become too absorbed with DCF to the extent that practical strategic directional considerations have been overlooked."[2]

Faced with outdated and inappropriate procedures of investment analysis, all that responsible executives can do is cast them aside in a bold leap of strategic faith. "Beyond all else," they have come to believe, "capital investment represents an act of faith, a belief that the future will be as promising as the present, together with a commitment to making the future happen."[3]

But must there be a fundamental conflict between the financial and the strategic justifications for CIM? It is unlikely that the theory of discounting future cash flow is either faulty or unimportant: receiving $1 in the future is worth less than receiving $1 today. If a company, even for good strategic reasons, consistently invests in projects whose financial returns are below its cost of capital, it will be on the road to insolvency. Whatever the special values of CIM technology, they cannot reverse the logic of the time value of money.

Surely, therefore, the trouble must not lie in some unbreachable gulf between the logic of DCF and the nature of CIM but in the poor application of DCF to these investment proposals. Managers need not—and should not—abandon the effort to justify CIM on financial grounds. Instead, they need ways to apply the DCF approach more appropriately and to be more sensitive to the realities and special attributes of CIM.

---

[1] This example has appeared in several articles on strategic justification for flexible automation projects. Clifford Young of Arthur D. Little has traced the example to *American Market/Metal-working News,* October 26, 1981. Other examples of the labor, machinery, and throughput savings from flexible manufacturing system installations are presented in Anderson Ashburn and Joseph Jablonowski, "Japan's Builders Embrace FMS," *American Machinist,* February 1985, p. 83.

Author's note: Especially helpful comments on the preliminary draft were made by Robin Cooper and Robert Hayes (Harvard Business School), Alan Kantrow (*Harvard Business Review*), George Kuper (Manufacturing Studies Board), and Scott Richard and Jeff Williams (Carnegie-Mellon). Mr. Kaplan is Arthur Lowes Dickinson Professor of Accounting at the Harvard Business School and a professor of industrial administration at Carnegie-Mellon University, where for six years he was dean of the business school. His first article for *HBR,* "Yesterday's Accounting Undermines Production" (July–August 1984), was a McKinsey Award winner.

[2] John P. Van Blois, "Economic Models: The Future of Robotic-Justification," Thirteenth ISIR/Robots 7 Conference, April 17–21, 1983 (available from Society of Manufacturing Engineers, Dearborn, Michigan).

[3] Robert H. Hayes and David A. Garvin, "Managing as if Tomorrow Mattered," *HBR* May–June 1982, p. 70.

TECHNICAL ISSUES

The DCF approach most often goes wrong when companies set arbitrarily high hurdle rates for evaluating new investment projects. Perhaps they believe that high-return projects can be created by setting high rates rather than by making innovations in product and process technology or by cleverly building and exploiting a competitive advantage in the marketplace. In fact, the discounting function serves only to make cash flows received in the future equivalent to cash flows received now. For this narrow purpose—the only purpose, really, of discounting future cash flows—companies should use a discount rate based on the project's opportunity cost of capital (that is, the return available in the capital markets for investments of the same risk).

It may surprise managers to know that their real cost of capital can be in the neighborhood of 8%. (See Part I of the *Appendix* at the end of the article.) Double-digit hurdle rates that, in part, reflect assumptions of much higher capital costs are considerably wide of the mark. Their discouraging effect on CIM-type investments is not only unfortunate but also unfounded.

Companies also commonly underinvest in CIM and other new process technologies because they fail to evaluate properly all the relevant alternatives. Most of the capital expenditure requests I have seen measure new investments against a status quo alternative of making no new investments—an alternative that usually assumes a continuation of current market share, selling price, and costs. Experience shows, however, that the status quo rarely lasts. Business as usual does not continue undisturbed.

In fact, the correct alternative to new CIM investment should assume a situation of declining cash flows, market share, and profit margins. Once a valuable new process technology becomes available, even if one company decides not to invest in it, the likelihood is that some of its competitors will. As Henry Ford claimed, "If you need a new machine and don't buy it, you pay for it without getting it."[4] (For a more realistic approach to the

evaluation of alternatives, see Part II of the *Appendix* at the end of the article.)

A related problem with current practice is its bias toward incremental rather than revolutionary projects. In many companies, the capital approval process specifies different levels of authorization depending on the size of the request. Small investments (under $100,000, say) may need only the approval of the plant manager; expenditures in excess of several million dollars may require the board of directors' approval. This apparently sensible procedure, however, creates an incentive for managers to propose small projects that fall just below the cut-off point where higher level approval would be needed. Over time, a host of little investments, each of which delivers savings in labor, material, or overhead cost, can add up to a less-than-optimal pattern of material flow and to obsolete process technology. (Part III of the *Appendix* shows the consequences of this incremental bias in more detail.)

Introducing CIM process technology is not, of course, without its costs. Out-of-pocket equipment expense is only the beginning. Less obvious are the associated software costs that are necessary for CIM equipment to operate effectively. Managers should not be misled by the expensing of these costs for tax and financial reporting purposes into thinking them operating expenses rather than investments. For internal management purposes, software development is as much a part of the investment in CIM equipment as the physical hardware itself. Indeed, in some installations, the programming, debugging, and prototype development may cost more than the hardware.

There are still other initial costs: site preparation, conveyors, transfer devices, feeders, parts orientation, and spare parts for the CIM equipment. Operating and maintenance personnel must be retrained and new operating procedures developed. Like software development, these tax-deductible training and education costs are part of the investment in CIM, not an expense of the periods in which they happen to be incurred.

Further, as some current research has shown, noteworthy declines in productivity often accompany the introduction of new process technology.[5] These productivity declines can last up to a year, even longer when a radical new technology like CIM is installed. Apparently, the new equipment

[4]Quoted in John Shewchuk, "Justifying Flexible Automation," *American Machinist,* October 1984, p. 93.

introduces severe and unanticipated process disruptions, which lead to equipment breakdowns that are higher than expected; to operating, repair, and maintenance problems; to scheduling and coordination difficulties; to revised materials standards; and to old-fashioned confusion on the factory floor.

We do not yet know how much of the disruption is caused by inadequate planning. After investing considerable effort and anguish in the equipment acquisition decision, some companies no doubt revert to business as usual while waiting for the new equipment to arrive.

Whatever the cause, the productivity decline is particularly ill timed since it occurs just when a company is likely to conduct a postaudit on whether it is realizing the anticipated savings from the new equipment. Far from achieving anticipated savings, the postaudit will undoubtedly reveal lower output and higher costs than predicted.

TANGIBLE BENEFITS

The usual difficulties in carrying out DCF analysis—choosing an appropriate discount rate and evaluating correctly all relevant investment alternatives—apply with special force to the consideration of investments in CIM process technology. The greater flexibility of CIM technology, which allows it to be used for successive generations of products, gives it a longer useful life than traditional process investments. Because its benefits are likely to persist longer, overestimating the relevant discount rate will penalize CIM investments disproportionately more than shorter lived investments. The compounding effect of excessively high annual interest rates causes future cash flows to be discounted much too severely. Further, if executives arbitrarily specify short pay-back periods for new investments, the effect will be to curtail more CIM investments than traditional bottleneck-relief projects.

But beyond a longer useful life, CIM technology provides many additional benefits—better quality, greater flexibility, reduced inventory and floor space, lower throughput times, experience with new technology—that a typical capital justification process does not quantify. Financial analyses that focus too narrowly on easily quantified savings in labor, materials, or energy will miss important benefits from CIM technology.

Inventory Savings

Some of these omissions can be easily remedied. The process flexibility, more orderly product flow, higher quality, and better scheduling that are typical of properly used CIM equipment will drastically cut both work-in-process (WIP) and finished goods inventory levels. This reduction in average inventory levels represents a large cash inflow at the time the new process equipment becomes operational. This, of course, is a cash savings that DCF analysis can easily capture.

Consider a product line for which the anticipated monthly cost of sales is $500,000. Using existing equipment and technology, the producing division carries about three months of sales in inventory. After investing in flexible automation, the division heads find that reduced waste, scrap, and rework, greater predictability, and faster throughput permit a two-thirds reduction in average inventory levels.(This is not an unrealistic assumption: Murata Machinery Ltd. has reported that its FMS installation permitted a two-thirds reduction in workers, a 450% increase in output, and a 75% cut in inventory levels.[6])

Pruning inventory from three months to one month of sales produces a cash in low of $1 million in the first year the system becomes operational. If sales increase 10% per year, the company will enjoy increased cash flows from the inventory reductions in all future years too—that is, if the cost of sales rises to $550,000 in the next year, a two-month reduction in inventory saves an additional $100,000 that year, $110,000 the year after, and $121,000 the year after that.

[5]See Robert H. Hayes and Kim B. Clark, "Exploring the Sources of Productivity Differences at the Factory Level," in *The Uneasy Alliance: Managing the Productivity-Technology Dilemma,* ed. Kim B. Clark, Robert H. Hayes, and Christopher Lorenz (Boston: Harvard Business School Press, 1985), and Bruce Chew, "Productivity and Change: Understanding Productivity at the Factory Level," Harvard Business School Working Paper (1985).

[6]"Japan's Builders Embrace FMS," *American Machinist,* February 1985, p. 83.

Example of an FMS justification analysis

With the following analysis, one U. S. manufacturer of air-handling equipment justified its investment in an FMS installation for producing a key component:

1

Internal manufacture of the component is essential for the division's long-term strategy to maintain its capability to design and manufacture a proprietary product.

2

The component has been manufactured on mostly conventional equipment—some numerically controlled—with an average age of 23 years. To manufacture a product in conformance with current quality specification, the company must replace this equipment with new conventional equipment or advanced technology.

3

The alternatives are:
Conventional or numerically controlled stand-alone.
Transfer line.
Matching cells.
FMS.

4

FMS compares with conventional technology as Table A shows.

5

Intangible benefits include virtually unlimited flexibility for FMS to modify mix of component models to the exact requirements of the assembly department.

6

The financial analysis for a project life of ten years compares the FMS with conventional technology (static sales assumptions, constant, or base-year, dollars) as Table B shows.

7

With dynamic sales assumptions showing expected increases in production volume, the annual operating savings will double in future years and the financial yield (still using constant, base-year dollars) will increase to more than 17% per year.

On the basis of this analysis and recognizing the value of the intangible item (5), which had not been incorporated formally, the company selected the FMS option.

Table A

	Conventional equipment	FMS
Utilization	30%–40%	80%–90%
Number of employees needed (including indirect workers, such as those who do materials handling, inspection and rework)*	52	14
Reduced scrap and rework	—	$60,000 annually
Inventory	$2,000,000	$1,100,000†
Incremental investment	—	$9,200,000

* Each employee costs $36,000 a year in wages and fringe benefits
† Inventory reductions because of shorter lead times and flexibility.

Table B

Year	Investment	Operating savings	Tax savings ITC and ACRS depreciation	After-tax cash flow 50%
0	$9,200	$ 900‡	$ 920	$–7,380
1		1,428§	1,311	1,370¶
2		1,428	1,923	1,675
3		1,428	1,835	1,632
4		1,428	1,835	1,632
5		1,428	1,835	1,632
6		1,428		714
7		1,428		714
8		1,428		714
9		1,428		714
10		1,428		714

After-tax yield: 11.1%

Payback period: during year 5.

‡$ 900 = Inventory reduction at start of project.
§$1,428 = 38 fewer employees at $36,000/year + $60,000 scrap and rework savings.
¶$1,370 = (1,428)(1 − 50) + (1,311)(0.50).

Less Floor Space

CIM also cuts floor-space requirements. It takes fewer computer-controlled machines to do the same job as a larger number of conventional machines. Also, the factory floor will no longer be used to store inventory. Recall the example of the Japanese plant that installed a flexible manufacturing system and reduced space requirements from 103,000 to 30,000 square feet. These space savings are real, but conventional financial accounting systems do not measure their value well—especially if the building is almost fully depreciated or was purchased years before when price levels were lower. Do not, therefore, look to financial accounting systems for a good estimate of the cost or value of space. Instead, compute the estimate in terms of the opportunity cost of new space: either its square-foot rental value or the annualized cost of new construction.

Many companies that have installed CIM technology have discovered a new factory inside their old one. This new "factory within a factory" occupies the space where excessive WIP inventory and infrequently used special-purpose machines used to sit. Eliminating WIP inventory and rationalizing machine layout can easily lead to savings of more than 50% in floor space. In practice, these savings have enabled some companies to curtail plant and office expansion programs and, on occasion, to fold the operations of a second factory (which could then be sold off at current market prices) into the reorganized original factory.

Higher Quality

Greatly improved quality, defined here as conformance to specifications, is a third tangible benefit from investment in CIM technology. Automated process equipment leads directly to more uniform production and, frequently, to an order-of-magnitude decline in defects. These benefits are easy to quantify and should be part of any cash flow analysis. Some managers have seen five- to tenfold reductions in waste, scrap, and rework when they replaced manual operations with automated equipment.

Further, as production uniformity increases, fewer inspection stations and fewer inspectors are required. If automatic gauging is included in the CIM installation, virtually all manual inspection of parts can be eliminated. Also, with 100% continuous automated inspection, out-of-tolerance parts are detected immediately. With manual systems, the entire lot of parts to be produced before a problem is detected would need to be reworked or scrapped.

These capabilities lead, in turn, to significant reductions in warranty expense. When General Electric automated its dishwasher operation, for example, its service call rate fell 50%. Designing manufacturability into products, making the production process more reliable and uniform, and improving automated inspection can all contribute to major cash flow savings. Although it may be hard to estimate these savings out to four or five significant digits, it would be grossly wrong to assume that the benefits are zero. We must overcome the preference of accountants for precision over accuracy, which causes them to ignore benefits they cannot quantify beyond one or two digits of accuracy.

We can estimate still other tangible benefits from CIM. John Shewchuk of General Electric claims that accounts receivable can be reduced by eliminating the incidence of customers who defer payment until quality problems are resolved.[7] Consider too that because improved materials flow can reduce the need for forklift trucks and operators, factories will enjoy a large cash flow saving from not having to acquire, maintain, repair, and operate so many trucks. All these calculations belong in a company's capital justification process.

INTANGIBLE BENEFITS

Other benefits of CIM include increased flexibility, faster response to market shifts, and greatly reduced throughput and lead times. These benefits are as important as those just discussed but much harder to quantify. We may not be sure how many zeros should be in our benefits estimate (are they to be measured in thousands or millions of dollars?) much less which digit should be first. The difficulty arises in large part because these benefits represent revenue enhancements rather than cost savings. It is fairly easy to get a ballpark estimate for percentage reductions in costs already being incurred. It is much harder to quantify the magnitude of revenue enhancement expected from features that are not already in place.

---

[7]John Shewchuk, "Justifying Flexible Automation."

Greater Flexibility

The flexibility that CIM technology offers takes several forms. The benefits of economies of scope—that is, the potential for low-cost production of high-variety, low-volume goods—are just beginning to flow from FMS environments as early adopters of the technology start to service after-market sales for discontinued models on the same equipment used to produce current high-volume models. We are also beginning to see some customized production on the same lines used for standard products.

Beyond these economy-of-scope applications, CIM's reprogramming capabilities make it possible for machines to serve as backups for each other. Even if a machine is dedicated to a narrow product line, it can still replace lost production during a second or a third shift when a similar piece of equipment, producing quite a different product, breaks down. Further, by easily accommodating engineering change orders and product redesigns, CIM technology allows for product changes over time. And, if the mix of products demanded by the market changes, a CIM-based process can respond with no increase in costs. The body shop of one automobile assembly plant, for example, quickly adjusted its flexible, programmed spot-welding robots to a shift in consumer preference from the two-door to the four-door version of a certain car model. Had the line been equipped with nonprogrammable welding equipment, the adjustment would have been far more costly.

CIM's flexibility also gives it usefulness beyond the life cycle of the product for which it was purchased. True, in the short run, CIM may perform the same functions as less expensive, inflexible equipment. Many benefits of its flexibility will show up only over time. Therefore, it is difficult to estimate how much this flexibility will be worth. Nonetheless, as we shall see, even an order-of-magnitude estimate may be sufficient.

Shorter Throughput & Lead Time

Another seemingly intangible benefit of CIM is the great reductions it makes possible in throughput and lead time. At the Yamazaki factory described at the beginning of this article, average processing time to per work piece fell from 35 to 1.5 days. Other installations, including Yamazaki's Mazak plant in Florence, Kentucky, have reported similar savings, ranging from a low of 50% reduction in processing time to a maximum of nearly 95%. To be sure, some of the benefits from greatly reduced throughput times have already been incorporated in our estimate of savings from inventory reductions. But there is also a notable marketing advantage in being able to meet customer demands with shorter lead times and to respond quickly to changes in market demand.

Increased Learning

Some investments in new process technology have important learning characteristics. Thus, even if calculations of the net present value of their cash flows turn up negative, the investments can still be quite valuable by permitting managers to gain experience with the technology, test the market for new products, and keep a close watch on major process advances.

These learning effects have characteristics similar to buying options in financial markets. Buying options may not at first seem like a favorable investment, but quite small initial outlays may yield huge benefits down the line. Similarly, were a company to invest in a risky CIM-related project, it could reap big gains should the technology provide unexpected competitive advantages in the future. Moreover, given the rapid pace of technological change and the advantages of being an early market participant, companies that defer process investments until the new technology is well established will find themselves far behind the market leaders. In this context, the decision to defer investment is often a decision not to be a principal player in the next round of product or process innovation.

The companies that in the mid-1970s invested in automatic and electronically controlled machine tools were well positioned to exploit the microprocessor-based revolution in capabilities—much higher performance at much lower cost—that hit during the early 1980s. Because operators, maintenance personnel, and process engineers were already comfortable with electronic technology, it was relatively simple to retrofit existing machines with powerful microelectronics. Companies that had earlier deferred investment in electronically controlled machine tools fell behind: they had acquired no option on these new process technologies.

THE BOTTOM LINE

Although intangible benefits may be difficult to quantify, there is no reason to value them at zero in a capital expenditure analysis. Zero is, after all, no less arbitrary than any other number. Conservative accountants who assign zero values to many intangible benefits prefer being precisely wrong to being vaguely right. Managers need not follow their example.

One way to combine difficult-to-measure benefits with those more easily quantified is, first, to estimate the annual cash flows about which there is the greatest confidence: the cost of the new process equipment and the benefits expected from labor, inventory, floor space, and cost-of-quality savings. If at this point a discounted cash flow analysis—done with a sensible discount rate and a consideration of all relevant alternatives—shows a CIM investment to have a positive net present value, well and good. Even without accounting for the value of intangible benefits, the analysis will have gotten the project over its financial hurdle. If the DCF is negative, however, then it becomes necessary to estimate how much the annual cash flows must increase before the investment does have a positive net present value.

Suppose, for example, that an extra $100,000 per year over the life of the investment is sufficient to give the project the desired return. Then management can decide whether it expects heightened flexibility, reduced throughput and lead times, and faster market response to be worth at least $100,000 per year. Should the company be willing to pay $100,000 annually to enjoy these benefits? If so, it can accept the project with confidence. If, however, the additional cash flows needed to justify the investment turn out to be quite large—say $3 million per year—and management decides the intangible benefits of CIM are not worth that sum, then it is perfectly sensible to turn the investment down.

Rather than attempt to put a dollar tag on benefits that by their nature are difficult to quantify, managers should reverse the process and estimate first how great these benefits must be in order to justify the proposed investment. Senior executives can be expected to judge that improved flexibility, rapid customer service, market adaptability, and options on new process technology may be worth $300,000 to $500,000 per year but not, say, $1 million. This may not be exact mathematics, but it does help put a meaningful price on CIM's intangible benefits.

As manufacturers make critical decisions about whether to acquire CIM equipment, they must avoid claims that such investments have to be made on faith alone because financial analysis is too limiting. Successful process investments must yield returns in excess of the cost of capital invested. That is only common sense. Thus the challenge for managers is to improve their ability to estimate the costs and benefits of CIM, not to take the easy way out and discard the necessary discipline of financial analysis.

APPENDIX:

Getting the Numbers Right

PART I: THE COST OF CAPITAL

A company always has the option of repurchasing its common shares or retiring its debt. Therefore, managers can estimate the cost of capital for a project by taking a weighted average of the current cost of equity and debt at the mix of capital financing typical in the industry. Extensive studies of the returns to investors in equity and fixed-income markets during the past 60 years show that from 1926 to 1984 the average total return (dividends plus price appreciation) from holding a diversified portfolio of common stocks was 11.7% per year. This return already includes the effects of rising price levels. Removing the effects of inflation puts the real (after-inflation) return from investments in common stocks at about 8.5% per year (see Table A).*

---

*Roger G. Ibbotson and Rex A. Sinquefield, *Stocks, Bonds, Bills and Inflation: The Past and the Future* (Charlottesville, Va.: Financial Analysts Research Foundation, 1982). The author has updated this study for returns earned during 1982–1984. This estimate should be adjusted up or down, depending on whether the project's risk is above or below the risk of the average project in the market. A detailed discussion of appropriate risk adjustments is beyond the scope of this article. Good treatments can be found in David W. Mullins, Jr., "Does the Capital Asset Pricing Model Work?" *HBR* January–February 1982, p. 105, and in chap. 7–9 in Richard Brealey and Stewart Myers, *Principles of Corporate Finance,* 2d ed. (New York: McGraw-Hill, 1984).

TABLE A Annual Return Series (1926–1984)

Mean annual returns

Series	1926–1984	1950–1984	1975–1984
Common stocks	11.7%	12.8%	14.7%
Long-term corporate bonds	4.7	4.5	8.4
U. S. Treasury bills	3.4	5.1	9.0
Inflation (CPI)	3.2	4.4	7.4

Real annual returns net of inflation

Series	1926–1984	1950–1984	1975–1984
Common stocks	8.5%	8.4%	7.3%
Long-term corporate bonds	1.5	0.1	1.0
U. S. Treasury bills	0.2	0.6	1.6

These historical estimates of 8.5% real (or about 12% nominal) are, however, overestimates of the total cost of capital. From 1926 to 1984, fixed-income securities averaged nominal before-tax returns of less than 5% per year. Taking out inflation reduces the real return (or cost) of high-grade corporate debt securities to about 1.5% per year. Even with recent increases in the real interest rate, a mixture of debt and equity financing produces a total real cost of capital of less than 8%.

Many corporate executives will, no doubt, be highly skeptical that their real cost of capital could be 8% or less. Their disbelief probably comes from making one of two conceptual errors, perhaps both. First, executives often attempt to estimate their current cost of capital by looking at their accounting return on investment—that is, the net income divided by the net invested capital—of their divisions or corporations. For many companies this figure can be in the 15% to 25% range.

There are several reasons, however, why an accounting ROI is a poor estimate of a company's real cost of capital. The accounting ROI figure is distorted by financial accounting conventions such as depreciation method and a variety of capitalization and expense decisions. The ROI figure is also distorted by management's failure to adjust both the net income and the invested capital figures for the effects of inflation, an omission that biases the accounting ROI well above the company's actual real return on investment.

The second conceptual error that makes an 8% real cost of capital sound too low is implicitly to compare it with today's market interest rates and returns on common stocks. These rates incorporate expectations of current and future inflation, but the 8.5% historical return on common stocks and the less than 2% return on fixed-income securities are real returns, after the effects of inflation have been netted out.

Now it is possible, of course, to do a DCF analysis by using nominal market returns as a way of estimating a company's cost of capital. In fact, this may even be desirable when you are doing an after-tax cash flow analysis since one of the important cash flows being discounted is the nominal tax depreciation shield from new investments. I have, however, seen many a company go seriously wrong by using a nominal discount rate (say in excess of 15%) while it was assuming level cash flows over the life of their investments.

Consider, for example, the data in Table B, which is excerpted from an actual capital authorization request. Notice that all the cash flows during the ten years of the project's expected life are expressed in 1977 dollars, even though the company used a 20% discount rate on the cash flows of the several investment alternatives. This assumption of a 20% cost of capital most likely arose from a prior assumption of a real cost of capital of about 10% and an expected inflation rate of 10% per year. But if it believed that inflation would average

TABLE B Example of a Capital Authorization Request*

	Alternative 1	Rebuild Present Machines					
Year	1977	1978	1979	1980	1981	...	1986
Sales	$6,404	$6,404	$6,404	$6,404	$6,404	...	$6,404
Cost of sales:							
Labor	168	168	168	168	168	...	168
Material	312	312	312	312	312	...	312
Overhead	1,557	1,557	1,557	1,557	1,557	...	1,557

	Alternative 5	Purchase All New Machines					
Year	1977	1978	1979	1980	1981	...	1986
Sales	$6,404	$6,724	$7,060	$7,413	$7,784	...	$7,784
Cost of sales:							
Labor	167	154	148	152	152	...	152
Material	312	328	344	361	380	...	380
Overhead	1,557	1,440	1,390	1,423	1,423	...	1,423

*Adapted from Robert S. Kaplan and Glen Bingham, *Wilmington Tap and Die,* Case 185–124 (Boston: Harvard Business School, 1985).

10% annually over the life of the project, the company should also have raised the assumed selling price and the unit costs of labor, material, and overhead by their expected price increases over the life of the project.

It is inconsistent to assume a high rate of inflation for the interest rate used in a DCF calculation but a zero rate of price change when you are estimating future net cash flows from an investment. Naturally, this inconsistency—using double-digit discount rates but level cash flows—biases the analysis toward the rejection of new investments, especially those yielding benefits five to ten years into the future. Compounding excessively high interest rates will place a low value on cash flows in these later years: a 20% interest rate, for example, discounts $1.00 to $.40 in five years and to $.16 in ten years. If companies use discount rates derived from current market rates of return, then they must also estimate rates of price and cost changes for all future cash flows.

PART II: MEASURING ALTERNATIVES

Look again at the capital authorization request in Table B. The cash flows from alternative 1 assume a constant level of sales during the next ten years; the cash flows from alternative 5 show a somewhat higher level of sales based on a small increase in market share. The difference in sales revenue as currently projected, however, is not all that great. Only if managers anticipate a steady decrease in market share and sales revenue for alternative 1, a decrease occasioned by domestic or international competitors adopting the new production technology, would alternative 5 show a major improvement over the status quo.

Obviously, not all investments in new process technology are investments that should be made. Even if competitors adopt new technology and profits erode over time, a company may still find that the benefits from investing would not compensate for its costs. But either way, the company should rest its decision on a correct reading of what is likely to happen to cash flows when it rejects a new technology investment.

PART III: PIECEMEAL INVESTMENT

Each year, a company or a division may undertake a series of small improvements in its production process—to alleviate bottlenecks, to add capacity where needed, or to introduce islands of automation based on immediate and easily quantified labor savings. Each of these projects, taken by itself, may have a positive net present value. By investing on a piecemeal basis, however, the company or division will never get the full benefit of completely redesigning and rebuilding its plant. Yet the pressures to go forward on a piecemeal basis are nearly irresistible. At any point in time, there are many annual, incremental projects scattered about from which the investment has yet to be recovered. Thus, were management to scrap the plant, its past incremental investments would be shown to be incorrect.

One alternative to this piecemeal approach is to forecast the remaining technological life of the plant and then to enforce a policy of accepting no process improvements that will not be repaid within this period. Managers can treat the money that otherwise would have been invested as if it accrued interest at the company's cost of capital. At the end of the specified period, they could abandon the old facility and build a new one with the latest relevant technology.

Although none of the usual incremental process investments may have been incorrect, the collection of incremental decisions could have a lower net present value than the alternative of deferring most investment during a terminal period, earning interest on the unexpended funds, and then replacing the plant. Again, the failure to evaluate such global investment is not a limitation of DCF analysis. It is a failure of not applying DCF analysis to all the feasible alternatives to annual, incremental investment proposals.

EG&G Rotron Division

The Sunday evening rain drummed rhythmically against the windows of Scott Miller's office in the EG&G Rotron plant at Woodstock, New York, amplifying the distant rumble of the Woodstock anniversary rock festival. "*It'll be turning muddy over at the festival,*" said Miller, Plant Four manager, "*but I'm stuck in a lot worse here. When those motor casings came in on Friday I thought just-in-time was really starting to work for us. Then I find half the housings are unusable and the other half will need a lot of work to machine them down to the right size.*"

The housings were components for a shipment of motors to Airdex, an important new customer in Rotron's Hi-Rel (high reliability) transportation products business. The anxious new customer expected delivery on Tuesday, which meant shipping on Monday. The housings had been delivered on the last possible day for completion of the order, in accordance with Rotron's new just-in-time production system, but when they were inspected, half of the covers had blow-holes in the cast-metal while the other half were salvageable (with some time-consuming extra work)—but were not manufactured according to the specification, even though the supplier had always performed well in the past. Miller was not looking forward to the prospect of calling a hard-won customer to tell him that his entire first order of air-conditioner motors would be late.

Miller rubbed his eyes with his oil-soaked knuckles as he walked back out onto the floor. The weekly planning meeting in the morning would mean even more excitement. Everyone in the plant now knew about the problem with the Airdex order, and it was sure to reopen the debate

on the role of just-in-time (JIT) manufacturing at Rotron. As Jeff Solomon—Miller's manager—had remarked on Friday, "*If it wasn't for JIT, we'd have one less dissatisfied customer.*" Solomon had never been a fan of JIT, insisting that making motors was altogether different than making cars or washing machines. The debate over how far to push JIT at Rotron had ebbed and flowed over the past three years, but seemed to have been settling down recently. Miller himself had become a convert, and even the old-time operators had warmed to it as the plant began to see the kind of improvements in lead times and quality that Tom Peters had promised them in the evangelical videotape they had all watched. This latest problem was going to make the sparks fly again. There would be plenty of "I told you so"s to give the meeting a productive edge, thought Miller. He would have to figure out what he would say if he got stuck in the middle of an argument, and more importantly what he would say to Airdex. He walked back into his office, sat in his chair and reluctantly listened to the lollapaloozal beat against the window.

EG&G ROTRON IN 1976: MOTORS AND FANS

EG&G Rotron was founded in the late-1940s by Konstant Von Rijn, a Dutch electrical engineer, who had identified a need for high-frequency switching devices in a range of electrical systems. In 1976 it had been acquired for $5.5m by EG&G,[1] a large manufacturing company based in Wellesley, near Boston, whose customers were primarily the US Department of Energy (USDoE) and prime contractors to the US Department of Defense (USDoD). At the time of the acquisition by EG&G, Rotron had total annual sales of $15m, mainly made up of AC motors and air moving equipment (fans and blowers) sold to USDoD and its prime contractors. The company had also been

[1] *Electronics News,* March 1, 1976

operating a commercial business which sold low-cost fans for computer equipment with annual sales of $18m. This business was sold in 1986, when the computer industry looked ready to nose dive.

In 1984, Bill Roppenecker took over as company General Manager, having joined the company in 1973. Roppenecker became President in 1987. Roppenecker advocated "managing by walking around," talking to managers and staff, and making sure to acknowledge good work. In his view, "people will listen to words, but they'll follow actions."

Generating New Opportunities

When he became General Manager, Roppenecker targeted growth as his primary objective. His first step was to introduce a standard framework for analyzing new projects, using objective measures of Net Present Value (NPV) to prioritize projects. There had previously been substantial disagreement within the company over which projects to pick, and projects were often selected by a loudest voice system. The NPV framework made the decision-making process transparent, and allowed people to understand the decisions being made even if they were hard to agree with. It was two years before the new system was accepted completely.

Roppenecker pursued growth by diversifying aggressively into new markets. Prior to 1985, Rotron had only sought "sole source" business—for which the customer relied entirely on Rotron for its supply. In 1985, the company dropped the policy, and began to chase business as second-source suppliers. In Roppenecker's words, "*we became both the highest priced and lowest price competitor.*" The goal was to deny safe pockets of business to competitors, and to exploit any scale advantages to Rotron of the additional business.

Design engineering prowess became the competitive lever that Rotron used to prise open the doors to new markets. In 1985, Roppenecker established a separate electronics department to develop a low power (10–20 watt) Direct Current (DC) motor. In 1986, the company developed a high-power DC blower for chemical warfare protection. For these applications, Rotron produced a brushless DC motor (with the trademark *ECDC*—Electronically Commutated Direct Current). *ECDC* technology employed electronic systems to convert Direct Current into Alternating Current (see Exhibit 1), rather than carbon brushes and commutator rings. The main advantage of this design was its long lifetime and very low maintenance costs compared to brush-commutated DC motors.

EXHIBIT 1 Motor Commutation

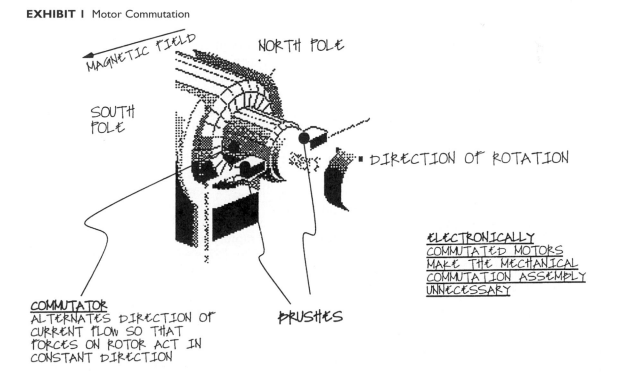

MAGNETIC FIELD

NORTH POLE

SOUTH POLE

DIRECTION OF ROTATION

ELECTRONICALLY COMMUTATED MOTORS MAKE THE MECHANICAL COMMUTATION ASSEMBLY UNNECESSARY

COMMUTATOR ALTERNATES DIRECTION OF CURRENT FLOW SO THAT FORCES ON ROTOR ACT IN CONSTANT DIRECTION

BRUSHES

Also in 1986, Roppenecker instituted a new program for long-range business planning. The assembled managers at the first meeting all agreed that the large military budgets of the 1980s were unsustainable, and identified three markets as the most fertile for new business: transportation, commercial aerospace, and military motors (for applications other than air-moving). In-house development teams were created to explore the potential of the new markets, using a matrix-like organization to involve staff managers in the decision-making process and broaden their knowledge. Kevin Hagen, for example, who had worked almost exclusively in marketing for the military side of the business, became a key member of transportation market development team. Ongoing long-range planning was further systematized into quarterly meetings during 1987, using EG&G's corporate planning procedure as a template.

Finding New Opportunities: Mixed Results

The teams' efforts produced mixed results. Rotron's efforts to find other military applications for its motors met some formidable barriers. The major obstacle was the large installed base of motors. These motors were generally upgraded with incremental design improvements by their original manufacturers after they had won initial acceptance. Success in this market would therefore require radical (and proprietary) innovation with clear benefits to the customer to make a dent in the incumbents' positions. Loyalties to existing suppliers were strong, purchase volumes low, and there was little commonality of design with Rotron's current products (most motors had different speed/torque requirements than those for air blowers). By 1994, Rotron had built sales of about $500,000 annually, but eventually transferred the business back into the existing Mil-Aero division.

The commercial aerospace team adapted the previously developed chemical-warfare air blower and generated a 40% share of the commercial aerospace market for brushless motors. Sales peaked at $1.5m in 1991, then declined to $1m in 1993 as the commercial aviation market collapsed. In the winter of 1995, this business was still in a "holding pattern." Bad luck, it seemed, had stymied this promising new commercial opportunity.

In the transportation business, there were substantial barriers to overcome as Rotron came to grips with the underestimated multitude of dif-

ferences between commercial and military customers. Cost, however, was by far the most dominant obstacle. Rotron's target prices were 3 to 5 times those of competitors (Rotron's product was much more reliable), but to reach even these levels, cost reductions of 50–70% from extant 'military' costs were required. Nevertheless, with an unremitting attack on costs through design and production changes, Rotron overcame these problems, and by 1995, sales in the transportation (Hi-Rel) market reached 35% of Rotron's total sales—the Hi-Rel seedling planted in 1986 had blossomed.

EG&G[2]

EG&G was founded in 1947 by Harold Edgerton, Kenneth Germeshausen and Herbert Grier, three nuclear engineers from MIT. During the second world war they had been active in the US effort to construct an atomic bomb, and were asked to continue the management of nuclear weapons programs by the US government after the war. Shortly after founding their company, the three hired Bernard O'Keefe, a former employee of Dr. Grier during the war. O'Keefe, a self-professed "card-carrying member of the military industrial complex," was said to have wired the controls of the bomb that destroyed the Japanese city of Nagasaki, and, in the early 1950s, had climbed a 300 foot test tower to disarm a live hydrogen bomb that had failed to explode.

The company concentrated on government contracts until 1960, when it started to consider expansion into environmental work. At the same time, the three founders retired from management of the company, leaving O'Keefe in charge. Although the specific environmental proposals did not reach fruition, they heralded a period of expansion and diversification via acquisition: EG&G bought thirteen companies between 1964 and 1967. Interest in the environment was rekindled at the end of this period, as environmental awareness grew rapidly in the US.

The 1970s were a difficult period for EG&G. While prospects for nuclear power soared in late 1973 during the oil embargo, they vanished just as rapidly with the end of the embargo, in part a victim of the growing US environmental movement. Meanwhile, other company developments, such as

---

[2]EG&G Company data book

a flash tube for photocopiers (an off-shoot of the stroboscopes used in nuclear weapons testing), were beaten to market by rival firms. Finally, the end of the Vietnam war and the beginning of detente placed a strain on military funding, the mainstay of EG&G's business.

Like many Defense contractors, EG&G prospered during the years of the Carter-Reagan military build-up. The company also won business from NASA, testing Shuttle electrical components and managing Cape Canaveral. A further boost was the contract to manage the Rocky Flats nuclear components plant in Colorado, won from Rockwell Corporation in 1989. Just previous to this period O'Keefe had retired from EG&G, and was ultimately replaced by John Kucharski.

EG&G's Exit from Government Contracting

As military spending wound down in the late 1980s and into the 1990s, EG&G began to look even more to commercial ventures over government contracts. The focus on the commercial arena sharpened tremendously in the summer of 1994: EG&G announced that it was withdrawing from almost all of its government contract work.

MARKETS

By 1995, Rotron comprised three divisions, each focussed on a different market:

- Mil-Aero: the military market for air blowers, traditionally Rotron's core business
- Hi-Rel (High reliability): Rotron's new commercial market for motors in transportation applications, such as bus air conditioners or engine pump motors.
- HFS (High Frequency Switching): A comparatively new off-shoot of the Hi-Rel business making High-Voltage transit car power supplies.

Total sales for 1994 were $22m: 60% from Mil-Aero, 35% Hi-Rel and 5% HFS.

It had quickly become clear that the three markets had very different competitive requirements.

Mil-Aero

The main feature of the Mil-Aero business was the need for products to conform precisely to detailed military specifications. Military applications had to meet extremely high performance requirements, reflecting the critical conditions under which they were likely to be used. Typically, the lowest priced bid that met specifications would win a contract. Products were made to order once a firm had successfully bid on a contract.

Rotron sold to three types of customer in this business. Some products were sold directly to the USDoD, while others were purchased by military OEMs, who would assemble Rotron air moving products into more complex pieces of equipment (for example in electronics cooling, or in the air conditioning systems of tanks). Finally, Rotron also sold some products to foreign military agencies.

Orders arriving for military applications were quoted long lead times, averaging around 18 weeks. Delivery dates were known with a high degree of precision, as Roppenecker pointed out: "the military know when they'll need the product." Moreover, since the products were built to meet military specifications, the normal practice was to pay companies for work done even if, as a result of a change in specifications after the contract was placed, the product changed and the work was wasted.

Products were priced on a "cost plus" basis. This meant that prices were set by costs plus added profits. In Roppenecker's words, "*cost plus profit equalled price.*" There had been little competition between firms in the military air-moving industry until 1985, when Rotron initiated its new policy of chasing second-source contracts.

In 1995, the main change in this market was the change in procurement taking place in the US. There were increasing signs of a move away from tightly specified contracts and cost-plus pricing towards a method of purchasing based on commercially available products. In spite of such speculation, there was still considerable uncertainty over how, and how fast, Mil-Aero customers would change their purchasing practices.

Hi-Rel

Rotron found the beginnings of its success in the transportation motors market in 1987, by adapting products from its military business. The new markets' requirements were, however, very different in this new, commercial world.

Rotron supplied motors for a range of applications to a broad variety of customers. Customers included public transportation utilities as well as commercial firms. Products were shipped to OEMs, to end-use customers, and to provide spare parts. As a result of the disparity in customers, orders were characterized by widely differing lead times. A sample of 48 orders in 1995 showed that 75% had a lead time of less than 8 weeks, while 10% had lead times of less than a week. Short lead times were typical of spare parts orders. The company made four basic Hi-Rel products, with 25–30 variants or SKUs (in total) reflecting different voltages, mounting plates, duty requirements and so on.

One of the most significant differences to the military business was the lack of pre-defined customer specifications. According to Norm Smith, manager of the custom business segment, the customer usually just asked "does this work in my application?" Prices were determined externally, by the market, rather than internally, by cost. "*Profit equals price less costs,*" observed Roppenecker.

Product requirements in the Hi-Rel market were determined by performance rather than by design specifications. Engineers at Rotron viewed commercial markets as having more demanding requirements than military markets in some respects: "*the commercial environment is harsher than the military one. Our equipment is often running for 16–18 hours a day, versus sitting in a warehouse for military products.*"

Competing in this market presented a number of difficult new challenges for Rotron. The company entered the Hi-Rel business with an "over-confident attitude," assuming that any product meeting the arduous demands of military service during a global thermonuclear conflict would also meet commercial standards. It had apparently not considered the possibility that its products would come to be used in the New York Subway system.

Rotron suffered a number of early product failures. For example, bus air-conditioning motors were sent to several cities' public transport utilities for test and evaluation. Units were returned, destroyed, in about 6 weeks. In Cleveland, the motor units suffered from excessive salt corrosion; in the south, the citric acid (a by-product of fruit processing) used to clean the buses also corroded the motors. In New York, a number of motors were destroyed when 'maintenance' staff drove screws through the threaded holes in the motor casing, destroying the motor inside its housing. Rotron had to perform extensive re-designs of its prod-

ucts, to lower the cost, avoid corrosion and to prevent failure from similarly creative maintenance techniques.

Rotron prices were some 3–5 times those of its competitors in the transportation business, since its products were sold on a life-cycle cost basis. Rotron motors, being brushless, would last perhaps 10 years versus the one year people could expect from a brush-commutated motor. Reaching profitability, even at these prices, had not been easy. Cost reductions of 50–70% from military cost levels had been necessary.

The key feature of the design, the brushless-commutation of the motor, was central to Rotron's success. Public transport utilities were a major buyer of Rotron products, and according to one Rotron customer, "*maintenance in utilities is worse than in any other industry.*" Absence of brushes in the design removed one of the major sources of motor failure, giving customers greater reliability. Reliability was considered the most important attribute in many of Rotron's commercial products, from bus air conditioners ("buyers are concerned about not being embarrassed by product failures. Their customers are often the people who voted them into their job") to locomotive fuel pumps ("if a fuel pump fails in a locomotive crossing North Dakota in the winter, the fuel will freeze and the engine will stop. That's both very dangerous, and expensive to recover.")

HFS

The HFS business combined some of the characteristics of the two other main lines of business. Products were made to order and frequently had well-developed specifications (although seldom with as much detail and precision as military specifications). At the same time, profit was determined by Rotron's ability to fill orders at an acceptable cost. Customers were typically public transportation utilities such as the San Francisco area BART. Customers typically had an approximate delivery schedule, but could not be depended on to stick precisely to agreed delivery deadlines.

Competitors

Competitors varied by business segment. In the Mil-Aero business, Rotron's main competitor had been IMC Magnetics, a subsidiary of NMB

(USA) based in Hauppauge, Long Island, New York. In 1985, when Rotron adopted its second-source policy, IMC sales were estimated by Rotron at $4m versus the $15m that remained in Rotron after the divestiture of the commercial business. By 1994, IMC was losing money and was in the process of exiting the business.[3]

Within the Hi-Rel business, there were a variety of competitors in different markets. In bus air conditioners, Rotron had built a $1.5M business by 1995. This volume of business was felt to be sufficient to attract large, powerful engineering firms such as Reliance Electric and GE.

ROTRON ORGANIZATION

The Woodstock site was built around a foundry for casting motor formers and housings, and two assembly plants (called plants One and Four for historical reasons) in which housings were finished, motors wound, and products assembled. Other key departments included order processing, design and engineering, purchasing, and marketing. In 1994, the organization was undergoing changes initiated by the decision in 1991 to use just-in-time (JIT) manufacturing techniques to reach shorter lead times and lower costs (the JIT initiative is discussed in detail below).

Purchasing

Purchasing was headed by Larry Bruck, who also worked in quality assurance (the two functions were combined at Rotron). In 1994, he managed relationships with over 500 suppliers. 180 of these provided 93% of the total dollar value of Rotron purchases. Bruck had set a target of 120 suppliers overall, based on a need for 70 key components.

In the military business, suppliers had traditionally been selected based on lowest bids. Rotron was now moving to establish longer-term relationships with suppliers, focusing primarily on quality of supplies. Bruck explained, "*If we are getting in parts that are below our quality requirements, being lowest cost or even on time is immaterial.*" However, in the JIT regime, timeliness was also crucial. He added, "*we want it right and on time.*"

Bruck had worked with suppliers to help them understand the importance to Rotron, and

Rotron's customers, of quality and timeliness. Some suppliers' operations and quality people had been invited to visit Rotron and participate in games designed to underline the importance of timeliness, and Bruck and others from Rotron had visited suppliers to advise them how they could shorten their lead times on orders. On occasion, Bruck had worked with suppliers even after their poor delivery performance had cost them their Rotron accounts.

Bruck had also begun working with people from other companies within EG&G, both to find internal sources for parts and to gain purchasing economies. In this way, he was able to arrange supply of Rotron's electronic circuit boards from an EG&G unit at lower cost, and with shorter lead times, than from the previous supplier.

Order Processing

Order processing and order entry were carried out in the customer service department, with a staff of six. Orders were taken from customers, then would be passed directly to scheduling if they were for standard products, or would be directed to the design and engineering department if the work required custom design. Once the order had been scheduled, the customer would be contacted (usually in 1–4 days) and informed of the expected completion date.

Orders were entered into a Material Requirements Planning system (MRP I), which exploded the bill of materials for the customer order and provided lead time information on the component parts. In 1994, the system lacked the capability to incorporate shop capacity and hence to provide order fulfillment dates. This task had to be done off-line by the plant management staff. Internal development efforts were under way to improve the MRP system to incorporate capacity planning and scheduling.

Design and Engineering

The design and engineering department was most involved in processing custom orders. Orders were first passed to one of Rotron's three applications engineers, whose job was to provide a bridge between customers and the Rotron design engineering group. The applications engineers would make a decision on whether or not to accept a

---

[3]*Long Island Newsday,* 30 September 1994

particular order. Typically, orders would likely be declined if they required significant retooling. Most of the custom orders that were accepted involved small changes to existing products, and were termed Special Product Requests (SPR). While such special requests took considerably more time and effort than standard orders, they were often the seedlings from which new standard products were grown: 40% of 1993 sales were a result of new products introduced over the previous five years.

Once an SPR had been accepted, the order was passed to the design engineering team, who were responsible for building a prototype. Prototype construction was normally accomplished in about two weeks, with the team working from "red-line" prints (hand-amended blueprints). Considerable judgement was needed, however, to balance the need for speed against the possibility that the design might change, resulting in the need to construct an additional prototype.

The design team was supported by a PC-based CAD system called CadKey, in place since the beginning of 1994 when they had switched from a minicomputer-based system, Unicad. While the CadKey system was functionally similar to Autocad, Rotron was finding it difficult to recruit people with knowledge of CadKey and so had begun hiring and retraining people with Autocad expertise.

The design engineers were supported in their work by technician designers. Technicians were responsible for the actual fabrication of prototypes, and also made a lot of the detailed design decisions. For instance, the technician was expected to keep track of the cost of a particular design, and was also partly responsible for ensuring design-for-manufacturability (DFM) (e.g., determining the number of fasteners on a motor housing).

In their DFM role, the technicians spent a lot of their time talking to people in manufacturing. The idea, according to Norm Smith, was to "*let the design technician talk to the operator, rather than getting the engineer in.*"

In late 1994, the engineering team was focused on reducing engineering lead times. The key obstacle was the need to package information for various groups within Rotron (for example, financial data for the accounting/control department, or set-up data for the plants). Engineers estimated they spent perhaps a third of their time working on

drawings and two thirds packaging information for other users. In Norm Smith's view, the need to package information was "*one of the biggest obstacles to engineering cycle time reduction. Even simple changes seem to take for ever.*"

Manufacturing

The two fabrication areas were focused plants; Plant Four dealt with large motors intended primarily for the Hi-Rel business, while Plant One fabricated small motors for the Hi-Rel business and all the military motors. Plant One also contained the HFS unit, in a self-contained space in the basement of the plant. The core components of a motor were the former (around which the electrical windings were made) and the housing—the metal case of the motor. Formers and housings for Rotron's products were either bought in from outside suppliers, or were cast on-site in the foundry.

The Foundry

The foundry cast many of the smaller mountings and casings used in the plant. Parts were also bought in from outside vendors when specialized work or extra capacity was needed. The casting equipment dated from the 1960s and was characterized by long set-up times. Consequently, it was used to produce long runs of parts, which were held in stock for use when required in the fabrication shops. The driving reason for an on-site foundry was the strong interaction between design and the manufacturing process. Rotron had developed its designs based on an ability to cast steel laminations very precisely into aluminum rotor housings—providing much superior electromagnetic characteristics, and hence outstanding motor performance.

While the foundry was inflexible in the sense that changing between products took between a few hours (same metal) and a day (different metal), the cast parts were produced only semi-finished and could be machined to fit a variety of product specifications. One cast part could normally be used in several different motor designs, giving greater flexibility to the foundry than was at first apparent. Between 100 and 500 parts were produced in a run, taking two or three hours, so like many small-batch operations, most of the foundry's time was absorbed in switching between one product and the next.

Plant One

Plant One was headed by Peter Stewart, whose job had grown to cover plant management as well as sales and marketing by the end of 1993. The plant contained several distinct areas. On the lower level, the HFS business was sited in a small floor. Here the seven-person HFS team assembled and tested products. A range of products were produced at any one time. Assemblers were highly skilled and capable of all assembly tasks. Dedicated HFS engineering staff were co-located.

On the upper level, the Mil-Aero products were fabricated by 70 direct people and 50 staff and indirects. In the electronics area circuit boards were tested, while the machine shop finished aluminum parts for specific products, using two Computer Numerically Controlled (CNC) machines. Coil winding and assembly were performed in 30 individual production cells. Once parts had been assembled they were taken directly to testing prior to being shipped.

The people within these areas had not, so far, been trained to move outside their particular cell, although within a cell, most of the workforce were cross-trained. Production controllers sat in a doorless, glass-walled office in the centre of the shop, though they were usually found out on the shop floor. Overall, the main floor of Plant One felt quite cramped, despite the absence of significant work-in-progress or supplies.

Through the summer of 1994, Stewart's objective was to extend the cellular organization further into the plant, with the next area of attention to be the electronics area.

1991: THE VCI INITIATIVE AND JIT

The reorganization of the fabrication plants into cells was intended in part to support the push towards JIT manufacturing at Rotron. The JIT policy was in turn driven by an EG&G corporate initiative, the VCI (value-cost-improvement) initiative. Despite the feeling amongst some Rotron managers that VCI was just one more TLA (three letter acronym), "*it's just another example of the MBA (management by acronym) approach to management,*" as one person put it, the initiative took hold.

JIT and Plant One

Cells were first introduced into Plant One in the coil-winding area. There were parallel work flows through the plant, for AC and DC products. The implementation of cells described here is for the AC products; however, the implementation for DC products followed the same pattern at the same time.

Initially, there were three cells for AC products, with each cell performing the same sets of operations. After about six months, cells had been introduced into the assembly area, again, initially, with all cells performing the same operations. Over time, the workflow through the cells changed, with one cell in winding and assembly focusing on low-volume special products and the other two on the main product lines. The change came from the people working in the cells. According to Stewart, "*you have to listen to the people. They know what works and what doesn't.*" Nevertheless, it took time before the workforce adapted to the new working environment and began to suggest changes to the workflow. Stewart estimated it had taken a year of patience and encouragement before the ideas had begun to flow.

As an example of how the JIT system worked, Stewart described the AC assembly area. Operators were given *kanban* cards permitting from 60–120 components at any one time in the cell. Working desk space was restricted to minimize the possibility of accumulating inventory, and WIP cradles (trays and other equipment for carrying WIP from one station to another) were built with low capacity (for example, a typical cradle to carry AC wound cores held only six cores).

The introduction of cells had a dramatic impact on the operation of Plant One. WIP levels plummeted in current dollar value, between 1991 and 1994, from about $1.1m to about $0.4m, freeing large amounts of space on the plant floor. Further space was freed up by eliminating the winding shop in favor of the winding cells. The additional space allowed consolidation of all fabrication activities onto the same floor of the plant, including work previously performed five miles away in Bearsville. "*Before, communication was terrible. Now, everyone knows what's hot,*" commented Stewart.

There were other improvements. The distance travelled by a typical product during fabrication within the Woodstock site fell from 5.2 miles to 0.3 miles. Lead times fell, defect levels declined substantially, and workforce productivity improved. The overall impact on cost from implementing Just-in-Time was estimated by Norm Smith as a reduction of around 20% by the summer of 1994. Finally, on-time delivery performance had improved substantially.

Cells posted daily and weekly performance charts at the entrance to each cell. The charts recorded productivity, rework and customer returns. In some cases, charts were built by the supervisors. In cases where a cell was working well and had been fully-trained, the people in the cell were responsible for monitoring and recording their own daily performance.

Plant Four

The fifty people in Plant Four built transportation products for the Hi-Rel business. In 1994, the shop floor was being reorganized into cells following the example of Plant One. The approach was similar and the impact as significant, although as the Hi-Rel products were physically much larger than the Plant One range, there was occasionally a substantial volume of inventory and WIP visible in the plant.

THE JUST-IN-TIME DEBATE

There had been fiery discussion within Rotron about how to implement JIT. The key questions were how far, and how fast, to push the philosophy. Concerns raised included cost and quality, as well as responsiveness to customers.

One of Rotron's main challenges was in ensuring timely deliveries of orders to customers in the Hi-Rel business. For these customers, timeliness and fast response were often critical, and a late response could easily mean a lost order. Moreover, future orders could be jeopardized if, say, the company could not turn around a spare parts order quickly enough.

While the issue was clear, the response was the subject of heated debate. Advocates of JIT made a number of arguments in favor of pursuing JIT more aggressively. Excessive inventory costs were fuel to the fire of their argument. Rotron estimated that direct warehousing costs were about 12% of the value of parts per year stored, while the associated system costs were typically 4% of parts value per year. Finally, inventories incurred oppor-

tunity costs on the capital tied up, currently estimated at 9% per annum.

The advocates also pointed to the cost reductions that had been achieved with the introduction of JIT to date as evidence of future potential benefits, as well as the harder to quantify advantages in terms of improved quality and responsiveness. One advocate's view of where the company should be heading was provided by Kevin Hagen, the Mil-Aero marketing manager:

> I tell our people to think of L. L. Bean. When I place an order, I get a choice of product, price information, and dispatch and delivery dates. Things have improved a great deal round here, but we still aren't there yet. And all our customer demands are tightening up.

A number of people in the plant began to voice concerns, however, about "JIT-mania." These people preferred to adopt a more cautious approach to JIT, in spite of its promised benefits. They argued that there were substantial costs incurred in pushing JIT too fast, given that filling customer orders depended in many instances on Rotron's suppliers delivering on time. While it was more difficult to quantify the costs of not filling orders on time, it was clear qualitatively what the consequences could be: lost business now, and lost customers in the future. This alternative view was summed up by Norm Smith:

> We currently hold buffers of WIP and finished goods inventory. The Just-in-Time people are completely opposed, but our suppliers aren't reliable enough, they aren't flexible enough given the range of products we have to hold. In the end, we need to do a cost benefit analysis of inventory costs versus lost order costs. It's kind of strange really—we've tempered our JIT plans **because** our customers want their orders just-in-time.

The JIT debate was one that had touched all of the managers at Rotron. Bill Roppenecker was concerned to balance the need to improve the organization with the need to preserve relationships with Rotron's customers:

> A lot of people have theories about how the world should be, but if you have to deal with reality you have to make modifications. Our problem is that we can't train the customer, and in our new markets the worst thing you can do is fail to meet your commitments. So, in a sense, inventory is a marketing expense.

At the same time, we can't afford to alienate our zealots too much. The zealots are the agents of change in the company, we have to let them try things out, let them win some of the time. If we are going to build capabilities that let us compete successfully, we have to allow people to experiment.

THE AIRDEX ORDER

Miller had been convinced he could run Plant Four with little or no inventory. Indeed, he had been inspired by the experience in Plant One, where on-time delivery performance had improved to over 90% and cells were now being extended into the electronics area. While there was still a stocking policy for some items, Miller was sure that even these items—at least the ones with steady demand—could be produced just in time. The motor for the Airdex order was one of the first group that had been selected to be made on a Just-In-Time basis—since it had a steady demand, and was a well-understood product in the plant. The pressure to build up inventory again after this Airdex fiasco would be strong—and if the JIT zealots couldn't hold the line with this motor, they would find it difficult to justify JIT for the rest.

Miller knew from past experience what arguments to expect at the following day's planning meeting. The zealots were sure to argue that this was merely a "glitch" and point to the need for squeezing more time out of the system, creating closer links with suppliers and working with them more closely. For them, this latest problem was above all another opportunity to work on improving Rotron's manufacturing processes. On the other hand, those anxious to slow the pace of JIT would point to the damage to a new customer relationship. As Peter Stewart said, "*I don't want to see my customer suffer for the sake of someone's theoretical beliefs.*"

Miller ran through the problem in his mind. First, there was the financial issue—how much stock—if any—did it make sense to hold for this line of motors? This was a profitable and fairly high-volume product (see Exhibit 2 and Exhibit 3 for data on prices and costs for various order sizes) with orders coming typically either for spares in ones and twos, or in quite large volumes. He'd gathered together the data on the pattern of orders in this line of motors for the past year or so, and the business managers had provided estimates of the probability of losing orders through stockouts at different levels of finished goods inventory (see Exhibit 4). The business managers thought that eight weeks of inventory would remove *any* chance of losing orders through supplier unreliability and other unexpected events, such as machine breakdowns.

On the other hand, there was the cost of holding the stock (currently 25% per year) and the longer-term benefits of JIT to think about. Even if there did appear to be a financial advantage in holding inventory in this line, did it make sense to do so? Perhaps the head of steam for manufacturing improvement that had been growing would just fizzle without the pressure of producing without inventory. As the rain drummed ever heavier against the window pane, Miller turned back to the

EXHIBIT 2 Income, Price and Cost Data by Size of Order

Income by order size for standard motor product*

Order Size	1–5	5–10	10–20	20–40	40+
Income/Order ($)	$120	$225	$450	$750	$1,200

Price and cost data by order size for standard motor product

Order Size	1–5	5–10	10–20	20–40	40+
Parts cost ($)	$22	$22	$22	$22	$22
Manufactured cost ($)	$83	$80	$75	$72	$68
Selling price ($)	$123	$110	$105	$97	$88
Income/Motor ($)	$40	$30	$30	$25	$20

**Note:* The average large order was 60 units

Monthly orders by order size for standard motor product

Order Size	Orders/Month	Units/Month
1–5	23	69
5–10	2	15
10–20	5	75
20–40	7	210
40+	1	60
Total	38	429

EXHIBIT 3 Breakdown of Orders by Order Size

	Order size			
Number of Weeks of Inventory	*1–5*	*5–10*	*10–20*	*20–40*
0	10%	15%	20%	20%
2	5%	10%	10%	10%
4	5%	5%	10%	10%
6	0%	0%	5%	5%
8	0%	0%	0%	0%

EXHIBIT 4 Estimated Probabilities of Losing an Order by Order Size at Various Inventory Levels

blank notepad on his desk. The painful experience with this order had started to sway his view about JIT. How should he decide whether re-instituting inventory in this line was the right thing to do for the business?

In the blank absence of a clear, logical basis for a decision, the plant's future policy looked set to be decided by the age-old "loudest-voice" system at the meeting tomorrow. Perhaps, he mused, he could persuade one of the caterwaulers at the festival to come and shout for his side of the argument.

If only he knew what it was.

Getting Control of Just-in-Time

Uday Karmarkar

Like all good revolutions, just-in-time manufacturing is producing revolutionaries who don't know when to stop. It is also producing over-reactions from people determined to make them stop. Consider the curiously vexed debate about how to get materials to, and work in process through, the shop floor.

Pick up virtually any manufacturing magazine these days and there will be some articles and pages of advertisements by consultants extolling the virtues of JIT over such computer-driven control systems as materials requirements planning (MRP) or materials resource planning (MRP II)—as if JIT principles were opposed to MRP and to the use of computers. One recent ad put the choice this starkly: "JIT vs. MRP II—JIT is the key to your survival!"

MRP, proponents of JIT explain, is merely a "push" technique. An MRP II program promises manufacturing managers more precision than it can deliver, requires unnecessary information, and demands more formal discipline than the shop floor needs. In contrast, JIT people seem especially drawn to such computerless, "pull" techniques as *kanban,* the system used extensively in Japan's auto and electronics industries. For JIT, presumably, human pull is good, computer push is bad.

What must be particularly confusing to manufacturing managers who get wind of this debate is that kanban systems are used most successfully by the same Japanese and American corporations that are famous for spearheading the use of advanced computer automation—Toyota or Hewlett-Packard, for example. In crucial respects, MRP II aims to be a JIT system, while kanban cannot.

Note: Uday Karmarkar is the Xerox Professor of Operations Management and Director of the Center for Manufacturing and Operations Management at the William E. Simon Graduate School of Business Administration of the University of Rochester.
Reprinted by permission of *Harvard Business Review.* Article from issue September–October 1989.

Worst of all, doesn't kanban look suspiciously like the old order point, order quantity (OP, OQ) system that MRP once discredited and replaced?

This debate needs clarity, and then it needs to end. The idealized conception of the shop floor one gets from some extreme JIT advocates—a line, inherently flexible, inventoryless, even computerless, replenished by infinitely responsive suppliers—may actually prevent manufacturing managers from using the tools they need to run their operations. JIT principles should certainly not preempt the use of MRP II. Indeed, most advanced manufacturing companies find that they require a hybrid system of shop floor control systems—tailored systems, including innovative pull systems like kanban, as well as time-tested, computer-driven push systems like MRP II.

At the same time, shop floor managers should know just when MRP II is an unnecessary burden and when kanban can't work—when push comes to shove and pull comes to tug. All managers can learn interesting strategic lessons from their choices. The question of how to manage inventory cuts quickly to the basics of manufacturing in an age of intense global competition: How much automation is enough? How should the factory respond to customers? How much can you load on workers? How do you deal with orders? What is waste? The shop floor is still a microcosm of the whole business.

PULLING AND PUSHING AT JIT

The basic difference between pull and push is that a pull system initiates production as a reaction to present demand, while push initiates production in anticipation of future demand. Thus a fast food restaurant like McDonald's runs on a pull system, while a catering service operates a push system.

At McDonald's, the customer orders a hamburger, the server gets one from the rack, the hamburger maker keeps an eye on the rack and makes new burgers when the number gets too low. The manager orders more ground beef when the maker's inventory gets too low. In effect, the customer's purchase triggers the pull of materials through the system; the customer initiates a chain of demand.

In a push system, the caterer estimates how many steaks or lobsters are likely to be ordered in any given week. He reckons roughly how long it takes to broil a steak or serve a party of four; he figures out how many meals he can accommodate and commits to buying what he needs in advance. He can account for the special event that he knows is scheduled to take place in midweek. In other words, the caterer gets a picture of production in his mind and pushes materials to where he expects them to be needed.

What Is JIT Anyway?

When you drop everything to take care of a walk-in client, you are reacting, implicitly, to a pull system. When you plan for a meeting, you are in the push mode. What does either method have to do with JIT?

Nothing directly. Think of JIT as a statement of objectives. It underscores the importance of lead-time management in all aspects of manufacturing. It asserts that incremental reductions in lead times are crucial indices of manufacturing improvement. JIT presumes that to achieve such reductions the system should deliver to every operator, in any conversion process, whatever he or she needs just when it is needed. It saves the money tied up in downstream inventories, protecting against long lead times. Shorter lead times mean improved responsiveness and flexibility.

JIT promises to preempt the delays and confusion associated with the stack-up of materials. Correspondingly, it saves the money that would otherwise go into indirect labor for storing and moving work-in-process (WIP) inventory and storing and handling buffer stock.

An analogy to commuter traffic may be useful. Say a thousand cars have to get through the Lincoln Tunnel every ten minutes. Wouldn't it be ideal for the economy (and sanity) of New Yorkers if each driver left home at precisely the right time to fall into the line at the entrance, so each car entered, one after another, like cars in a train? Would New Yorkers need six-lane divided highways leading to the tunnel if they could enforce this JIT ideal?

To be sure, there are a number of established materials control techniques—pull techniques—associated with JIT, particularly as Japanese companies have realized it. There are synchronized deliveries from proximate suppliers, who can also deliver more or less as production needs fluctuate. There are floor layouts and kanban systems in which materials are constrained to flow consecutively along predictable paths and at a pace determined, in effect, by the last operator in the chain.

These pull techniques, excellent as they are, should not, however, be confused with JIT's governing principles. JIT aims to manage lead times and eliminate waste. There is nothing inherent in push systems that makes them incompatible with JIT. On the contrary. The goal is to get drivers to leave home at just the right time to take their places at the tunnel entrance. JIT advocates shouldn't care whether the signal to leave comes as a computerized call or as a wave from the next-door neighbor.

The Limits of Pull

There is no denying that pull systems are very effective in disciplining production to meet demand just-in-time and, in certain environments, are more effective than push systems. But are pull systems inherently JIT? No pull system, in fact, can constrain workers consciously to produce just-in-time for some future event—because pull systems do not recognize future events. The inventory level triggers production; the pull system aims to fill up depleted inventory—whether it's Big Macs or machined parts.

Pull systems are fine if your McDonald's franchise is downtown with a steady daily stream of customers. But if you're next to a football stadium, how can a pull system alone prepare you for the day of a game? Similarly, it's easy to see how implausible a pull system would be in solving the Lincoln Tunnel's JIT problem. Wouldn't it be more sensible to stagger the cars according to some kind of push system—say, "blue cars leave at 7:45"— than to expect all commuters acting individually to leave for work in perfect synchrony?

There is a paradox here. JIT advocates admire pull systems and look askance at computer-governed push systems like MRP. Yet the latter inherently aims to be a JIT system, while pull systems do not really recognize the future events you are supposed to be just-in-time for. This confusion has a history.

Forty years ago, the most common control system was OP, OQ, a pull system that seeks to exploit the presumed efficiencies of batch manufacturing. It was not known for its quick responsiveness to customers. Inventory managers determined the point below which materials and parts should not fall, and clerks ordered stock whenever it fell below that point. You put a line in a pail of bolts; when you exposed the line, you ordered more bolts. The order was based on average demand, and the fixed trigger point for releasing an order was based on typical behavior.

These techniques were more or less suitable for managing retail operations, though even in those settings there were problems like the McDonald's franchise on the day of a game. If you ran a garage, for example, it would be tough to restock snow tires quickly after a big blizzard because every tire store would hit its order point and there would be a flood of reorders. The OP, OQ system would not react and place an early order when a blizzard was forecast.

If OP, OQ could be annoying to retailers, it could be disastrous to manufacturers. For want of a part, whole lines were shut down. And job lot orders, when they finally did come in, often forced manufacturers to tie up cash in more stock than they needed. Nor did OP, OQ integrate all information that was available when initiating production: How long does it take to build a product? What is likely external demand? In fact, parts and components are often built for in-house demand rather than for outside customers, and their requirements are well-known.

Managers often took obviously inappropriate action because of the old OP, OQ method. Demand surges invariably caused shortages; small shortages triggered production of parts even when people knew there would be no near-term demand for the part. Against this flawed system, MRP—the first generation of what is now MRP II—had obvious merit and won wide acceptance very quickly.[1]

---

[1]Early *HBR* coverage included Jeffrey G. Miller and Linda G. Sprague, "Behind the Growth in Materials Requirements Planning," September–October 1975, p. 83.

MRP to the Rescue

The concept behind MRP was straightforward, and MRP II is no real departure. In the same way that the caterer plans and conceives the whole week's production, the MRP system explodes the entire manufacturing operation into discrete parts making up the whole. It then projects demand, the time it would take to meet it, and the materials needed.

The key to MRP is that you have to tell it the lead time to manufacture a part, component, or assembled product. If parts production is intended to support, say, final assembly of a telephone, MRP orders only the parts that are actually going into the phones you expect to sell—not some preset job lot determined by "efficient scale."

So instead of building according to a fixed inventory position of various parts, MRP mandates building to the scheduled delivery of the final product. That, at least, is the theory. The best feature of MRP is its demonstrated capacity to work through the bills-of-materials relationships by which parts and subassemblies become the final product. MRP calculations start at the end items to be shipped and proceed stage by stage through bills of materials, releasing orders for the various parts or assemblies, according to a predetermined quantity and timing. The process then automatically repeats for the next level of parts going into each planned component or assembly.

Penetration of MRP methods into manufacturing has been substantial, especially in industries characterized by complex bills of materials, large numbers of open orders, and many needs for materials coordination among plants, vendors, and customers. Indeed, MRP has become so much the standard for materials management that it has led to the professionalization of the task, as exemplified by the American Production and Inventory Control Society. At the same time, owing to the heavy computer demands of MRP, systems managers and MIS departments have taken over a good deal of manufacturing management.

PUSH COMES TO SHOVE

MRP II—more exact than MRP before it—initiates production of various components, releases orders, and offsets inventory reductions. MRP II grasps the final product by its parts, orders their delivery to operators, keeps track of inventory positions in all stages of production, and determines what is needed to add to existing inventories. What more could JIT ask?

A major barrier to MRP, though, is the cost of hardware and software for a complex computerized system—no minor barrier especially to smaller producers. And even more important are the costs of training and implementation. You have to teach your workers a lot that they don't know about computers. And in order to enter the right data and the right relationships, you have to spend a great deal of time finding out things about your system that you don't presently know: How should parts be timed to be put together just the way you want them? How long will it take for delivery of all the critical parts?

MRP does not conflict with JIT, but MRP must assume a fixed production environment with fixed lead times. Even with the best intentions, people who set up MRP systems base them on established and often flawed methods of conceiving conversion processes—methods that could be full of inefficiencies and that could be easily improved if workers were not constrained by MRP expectations.

In this context, the professionalization of materials control is a handicap, not a benefit. MRP standards have become a kind of orthodoxy, so people resist the introduction of new methods to the shop floor. New methods can threaten the positions of MIS managers, materials managers, MRP vendors, consultants, and educators who have become attached to the standards.

Of the many standard assumptions made by MRP, the fixed lead times are the most troublesome. Why is MRP so susceptible to getting lead times wrong? The best answer is that production lead times vary depending on the degree of congestion or loading within the shop. The fallacy in MRP is that its releases produce the very conditions that determine lead times, but these lead times have already been taken as known and fixed in making the releases. Consider again the cars traveling to the tunnel. The time it takes for any one car depends on traffic conditions and starting times. Change the pattern of departures, and you change the load on the system and the time it takes.

There is another way of looking at this. A single lead-time number must suffice in MRP for all situations faced on the floor. Consequently, the number has to be set high enough to cover all variations up to the worst case. If an order is ever late, people have an incentive to increase the planned lead time in the system so that the delay does not occur again. A commuter who might encounter an accident or traffic jam will leave early to protect against such contingencies. Similarly, orders will usually be released too early and will often complete early, thereby increasing inventories in the system.

Incentives for Improvement

Perhaps the most pernicious aspect of MRP is the removal of any responsibility for lead-time reduction from the shop floor. How can there be incentives to reduce lead times if there are no rewards for completing work faster than MRP's fixed standards say?

Another big problem with MRP is its unnecessarily complex and centralized nature. MRP II systems plan and coordinate materials flow and produce order releases to the shop floor. But in many situations, the shop floor can be more flexible than MRP II.

For example, an assembly group might want to change its build schedule because parts aren't available for some current schedule. Yet change is stymied because the appropriate paperwork is unavailable and won't be available until the next run of the MRP system—say, next week. It often makes no practical sense to run an MRP plan every day. It takes time to collect and distribute all the data involved. Also, a good-size MRP system can tie up the central computer for hours. The same computer might be used for everything from word processing to payroll and general ledger accounting. Yet some shops would be better off working in just such short cycles.

Some MRP enhancements have addressed these problems. MRP vendors have created "shop floor control" modules—actually monitors, not controllers, which track progress on the shop floor. The resource management tools in MRP II analyze capacity and resource loading. Perhaps the best known of these systems is "rough-cut capacity planning." This method analyzes the load that MRP order releases create on the shop floor. If this load exceeds the capacity of a work center, the implication is that the work in the shop will not get done within the time allowed. The human planner must now find some way to cure the problem diagnosed. Sophisticated techniques for evaluating the lead-time consequences of MRP releases are also available now, including order release methods (X-FLO, for example), scheduling techniques (OPT, CLASS, MIMI), and simulations (FACTOR).

While helpful, these methods increase MRP costs and can be subject to the same criticisms as the system they are meant to restore: they remove responsibility and incentives from the shop floor and they are only as good as the information put into them.

DOES PULL EVER COME TO TUG?

If MRP superseded OP, OQ, the kanban method is often prescribed as a JIT technique that overcomes the deficiencies of MRP. Presumably, if you set up a production system that works like a bucket brigade, you can forget about providing incentives for continual improvement or gathering what may prove to be incorrect information. The team will discipline itself according to the next customer's needs.

To the extent that kanban works like a bucket brigade, it is indeed a JIT system. Everyone in the chain takes about the same amount of time to pass a bucket, and the system can work without any inventories of buckets between people. If the output end slows down, the whole chain will react and slow down; if it speeds up, the chain will react and speed up as much as possible, until limited by the slowest bucket passer.

Nor is kanban just warmed-over OP, OQ. With kanban systems, workers can see clearly the value of lead-time reduction. Unlike other pull systems, kanban combines production control with inventory control. The interaction between lead times and inventory levels becomes obvious to everybody on the line.

Moreover, the production supervisor owns the inventories that are produced; they are not pushed into other hands. He or she is thus forced to recognize that increasing the lead time of manufacturing increases WIP as well as finished inventory. This is completely unlike conventional pull systems like OP, OQ in which the inventory management function is separated from production or replenishment.

Indeed, the kanban method of posting circulating work orders makes the current work commitment of the manufacturing cell immediately obvious to everybody in the cell. Planning setups in advance, therefore, or opportunistically consolidating batches to save setups can become routine. The mix changes and demand surges that call for personnel reassignments become more transparent.

Kanban has another virtue that JIT people like. The fixed pool of cards in a kanban cell reduces the extent to which demand fluctuations are passed on by the cell to other upstream cells. The cards provide an upper bound that filters out extreme variations. At the same time, the system disciplines the downstream customer by punishing wide fluctuations or demand surges. A sudden surge will not be satisfied until the limited number of cards circulate many times. This encourages uniform demand and level schedules on the downstream side.

Kanban Is Reactive

Kanban is not without difficulties, though, which show up especially when it is forced to operate in complex operations where variations are too great or too intractable to be disciplined easily. Toyota's kanbans discipline suppliers, but a supplier's kanban cannot discipline Toyota.

The kanban method works best where there is a uniform flow—a level-loaded, synchronous, or balanced system. It does *not* plan well. JIT enthusiasts should realize that when a kanban system is implemented in an environment full of variations in supply and demand, it is even less likely than MRP to operate in a stockless manner—that is, without a burdensome amount of WIP. Variability causes the same extreme problems that it does in other pull systems. Extra cards or containers—buffers, for example—have to be introduced to cover variability and avoid back orders. Nothing in a kanban system magically reduces inventory levels due to some internal rule or formula.

Since the system is reactive, changes in demand level percolate slowly from stage to stage. Even if it is perfectly obvious that demand is rising, there is no standard way to prepare for the situation. Some U.S. assemblers that work with Japanese suppliers using pull systems have commented that if there is a steep change in demand levels, the suppliers take from three to six months

EXHIBIT I Tailored Production Controls

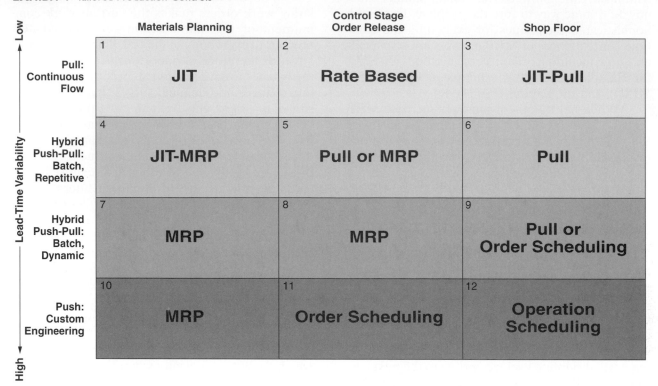

	Materials Planning	Control Stage Order Release	Shop Floor
Pull: **Continuous** **Flow** *(Low)*	1 **JIT**	2 **Rate Based**	3 **JIT-Pull**
Hybrid **Push-Pull:** **Batch,** **Repetitive**	4 **JIT-MRP**	5 **Pull or MRP**	6 **Pull**
Hybrid **Push-Pull:** **Batch,** **Dynamic**	7 **MRP**	8 **MRP**	9 **Pull or** **Order Scheduling**
Push: **Custom** **Engineering** *(High)*	10 **MRP**	11 **Order Scheduling**	12 **Operation** **Scheduling**

Lead-Time Variability (vertical axis, Low at top to High at bottom)

Continuous Flow: The production process is dedicated to one or a few similar products. Production is continuous and level so that the lead time for production is uniform and predictable. Some examples are assembly lines, transfer lines, and dedicated-flow lines.

1. Since production rates are uniform and predictable, material can be delivered to the process in a JIT manner.

2. Work orders are not required since production is level. A blanket order specifying a "going rate" is adequate. Occasionally, if the production mix is changed, the rates may be changed, but these changes are infrequent.

3. The predictability of the process and the production rate make it possible to design for smooth JIT materials flow on the shop floor. If there are points at which small inventories are accumulated for quality control or accounting purposes, they can be replenished in a pull manner.

The author is grateful to Indur Shivdasani for his contribution to this exhibit.

to adjust to it and encounter plenty of problems until the system reaches smooth operation again.

TAILORED CONTROLS, HYBRID SYSTEMS

Where does all this leave us? Which system should the manufacturing manager choose? The simple fact is that there is no need to choose between push or pull. These methods are not mutually exclusive, and each has its pros and cons. The best so-lution is often a hybrid that uses the strengths of both approaches.

Pull methods tend to be cheaper because they do not require computerization—hardware or software. They leave control and responsibility at a local level and offer attractive incentives for lead-time management. MRP systems are good at materials planning and coordination and provide a natural hub for inter-functional communication and data management. When it comes to work release, they are good at computing quantities even

Batch, Repetitive: Parts of the process may resemble a continuous-flow system while others involve multiple products produced in batches. Lead times are fairly constant and predictable. The product mix is relatively constant but may have variations from month to month. Typical is production of parts and components for a high-volume end product—such as cars or electronics.

4. Some parts and materials that are used uniformly can be delivered in a JIT manner. In other cases, with long lead time items, MRP is required to plan purchasing, delivery, and coordination between plants.

5. Since lead times are predictable, MRP works well, but so do pull methods—and they are cheaper. MRP may be required for master scheduling when work orders are generated; inventory must be managed; and work centers must coordinate.

6. Work on the shop floor flows relatively smoothly, and pull systems can be used to move work on the shop floor. If MRP systems are used, the trick is to coordinate pull on the floor with MRP work orders. One simplifying device is to combine several levels of the bill of materials into fewer levels so that the points of coordination with MRP are minimized. Tandem hybrid systems work well

Batch, Dynamic: Production is in batches, and the output mix and volume can vary; many customers come in with their orders on a weekly and monthly basis. The load on the facility changes; bottlenecks can shift, with backlogs appearing here and there; lead times become variable. Examples are parts and product manufacturers supplying several customers, factories supplying retail outlets with multiple parts, and medium- and low-volume plants.

7. As production mix and volumes change, many different materials and parts are required; departments must coordinate production. MRP becomes essential to match purchasing with production and coordinate parts fabrication and assembly. Production volumes can be smaller than lots likely to be purchased. Inventories build up and must be tracked.

8. Output varies too much for pull systems to work well. Look ahead, and build what will be needed. Even if MRP's timing isn't perfect, it does all the bookkeeping on quantities, inventory availability, and requirements, net of inventories.

9. At the shop floor level, work orders must be tracked. In some early common operations such as metal pressing, blanking, or molding, volumes may be high enough and level enough to use a pull system. Work orders, generating a master schedule, tie together purchasing, parts, subassemblies, assemblies, and customer orders. All are "pegged" and tracked with the MRP system.

Custom Engineering: With low-volume, complex engineered products or with custom manufacturing, there is no regularity in production patterns. The load on the facility can vary widely; what took two weeks when ordered in January might take four months in June. Queues and congestion are a major concern, and load-time management requires a high level of analysis and detail. Examples of such facilities are machine tool manufacturers, custom-equipment builders, and products with a high option and custom content.

10. There is no regularity in materials usage; some materials may be ordered only after a customer order is received. MRP is invaluable as an information management tool. It books orders, maintains bills, whether custom or standard, and coordinates customer orders, ship orders, and purchasing orders.

11. The factory runs on work orders generated by MRP. But MRP's poor understanding of lead times and capacity limits means that the order releases are of little use for good time and delivery performance. MRP still plays a role, however, in maintaining information about materials and inventory availability and coordination between departments

12. Scheduling systems (OPT, CLASS, MIMI) that can handle the complexity of detailed operational scheduling are only just appearing. They are too complex and costly for smaller shops.

if they are weak on timing. A successful hybrid system can use each approach to its best advantage.

The key to tailoring production control lies in understanding how the nature of the production process drives the choice of control method. The accompanying exhibit summarizes various manufacturing control methods and process characteristics. For a continuous-flow process, ongoing materials planning is not essential and JIT supply techniques work well. Order releases do not change from week to week, so a rate-based approach can be used. At the shop floor level, JIT

materials-flow discipline combined with pull release—kanban, for example—is effective.

In a repetitive manufacturing environment with fairly stable but varying schedules, materials planning can be a combination of MRP II and JIT methods. Order release may require MRP calculations if changes are frequent or if it is necessary to coordinate with long lead times or complex materials supply and acquisition. Pull methods work well on the shop floor.

As we move to more dynamic, variable contexts—like job shop manufacturing—MRP becomes invaluable for planning and release. Pull techniques cannot cope with increasing demand and lead-time variability. Shop floor control requires higher levels of tracking and scheduling sophistication. Materials flow is too complex for strict JIT.

Finally, in very complex environments, even job release requires sophisticated push methods. Where these are too expensive, the only option is to live with poor time performance, large inventories, and plenty of tracking and expediting.

The Best of Both

The dividing line between push and pull is obviously not sharp. In many situations, the two can coexist and are complementary. Most important, it is perfectly possible to take elements of one system and add them to the other. If pull systems have natural lead-time reduction incentives and push systems do not, for example, there is nothing to prevent managers from instituting a program of incentives in the context of a push system. Given the importance of lead-time reduction, in fact, it is crucial for managers to measure lead-time performance and provide feedback on response and turnaround times to each work center and shop. Though MRP systems do little to encourage good lead-time performance directly, managers can introduce measurement and incentive schemes based on MRP's data collection capabilities.

There is nothing to stop managers from compensating for the deficiencies of pull systems either. Pull systems, for instance, have no means of lot tracking—pegging lots to specific customers. But customers may want to keep track of their orders, and there may be special regulatory or quality control reasons for maintaining a lot's identity. So why not add lot tracking and data collection systems to a kanban line, leaving the release function as a pull system? (One simple and effective approach is to accumulate the information physically, with the lot itself as it moves through various process stages, and then record it electronically at inventory points in the process.)

Theoretically, there is no limit on the variety of control methods that can be developed. Most are hybrids. Attempts to implement pure push systems are usually accompanied by the growth of some informal, reactive pull procedures. The most common, alas, is the "hot list," by which assembly tells manufacturing what parts it wants most on a given day.

In a way, such informal procedures are only piggy-backing on the official MRP system, using short-term release information that MRP has not yet processed. The trouble with any informal procedure, however, is that it is very unsystematic; it may be based on assembly's guess of what it can get from parts and does not take into account the actual position of open orders in parts. Moreover, it undermines the credibility of the official system. Since there can be no coordination between the two, disbelief in the official system becomes self-fulfilling. Instead of such informal overrides of MRP II, consider one of the following hybrids.

JIT-MRP

There are now several modifications of existing MRP II systems, which add pull elements and remove some of the problems connected with the system's lack of responsiveness. Some such modifications are "synchro-MRP," "rate-based MRP II," and "JIT-MRP." These systems are appropriate for continuous-flow or level-repetitive processes, where production is at a level rate and lead times are constant. In these situations, the order release and inventory management functions are of little value. The facility can be designed to operate in a JIT manner so that any material that enters the facility flows along predictable paths and leaves at predictable intervals. Work is released by a pull mechanism, so there is no WIP buildup on the floor.

Such a JIT-MRP line produces to meet a daily or weekly build rate rather than build to specific individual work orders. This means that inventory position isn't necessary for release calculations. Inventory levels can be adequately calculated after the fact on a so-called "back-flush" or "post-deduct" basis by subtracting to allow for production that has already taken place. In short, MRP serves mainly for materials coordination, materials planning, and purchasing and not for releasing orders. The shop floor is operated as a JIT flow system.

Tandem Push-Pull

In a repetitive batch environment where lead times are fairly stable, either an MRP or a pull approach can achieve order release. MRP would be best for purchase planning of items with long lead times. Actual build routines closely correspond with the MRP II schedule, yet the timing of subassembly and assembly releases can be eliminated to allow the shop floor to change rapidly in response to short-term demand pull. Subassembly and assembly are flexible, short-cycle processes that can easily be run on a pull basis.

In this common situation, push and pull systems can simply be juxtaposed—MRP II to ensure parts availability based on end-item schedules and kanban for actual subassembly and assembly releases. MRP can be run only as frequently as necessary for parts purchasing and planning. Since the floor schedules can change quickly, the MRP database will always be playing catch-up with actual part withdrawals. This approach has been particularly successful in subassembly and assembly environments in which manufacturing cycle times are much shorter than parts purchasing and fabrication lead times.

Requirement-driven Kanban

Consider another situation where individual cells within the manufacturing chain can be run with kanban control, although MRP II runs much of the rest of the process. This can occur where final assembly schedules are unstable with respect to volume and mix, yet certain portions of the production process see fairly steady demand. A plastics injection molding cell that makes the same bottle for different shampoos is a good example. The MRP system can predict requirements for plastic parts quite well; kanban could run the injection molding cell.

One approach for such a case is to use MRP II to plan the number of cards in the cell on the basis of the gross requirements for all the parts produced by the cell. The MRP system doesn't have to monitor the inventory level in the cell or match demand with available inventories since the system doesn't make order releases. The gross requirements are an aggregate forecast of demand from the cell. Of course, as the gross requirements increase, additional cards are introduced into the cell in advance of the demand increase. They are withdrawn as the requirement level drops. MRP thus plays the role of planning adviser to the cell, setting the budget level in terms of the number of cards but not specifying the "expenditure" or release of the cards.

Many component manufacturing shops supplying subassembly and assembly operations, where the mix may change substantially but the total volume does not vary much, can use this approach. Other users are builders of common components or subassemblies like motors, similar

components like PCBs, and metal-forming operations like blanking, shearing, and pressing.

Dynamic Kanban

Pull methods like OP, OQ typically do have some push component, such as seasonal expectations. Forecasts of demand patterns can be used to set new values for the order quantity and for the order point. In this manner, the otherwise passive pull system is able to anticipate predictable changes.

Similarly, the card quantity in a kanban system can be altered in response to regular changes in demand forecasts—not only seasonal variations but obvious trends or planned promotions. In these cases, the forecast can be used to calculate the number of cards necessary to support the changed level of demand. The cards become a planning parameter driven by forecasts of activity.

Looking Ahead to CIM

There are no panaceas for manufacturing management problems. A single approach will not suffice for all situations. Managers have to design and refine solutions. Kanban itself, like so many JIT techniques, evolved over many years.

I believe that future advances in pull systems will most likely accommodate even more computerized and automated factory environments. The challenge will be to create incentives for process improvements in the automated factory. Expert systems will have important roles in troubleshooting and diagnosing problems, sometimes even substituting for shop floor supervisors.

The fastest growing area for push methods is "factory management systems"—new methods oriented toward shop floor management rather than materials planning. These new systems monitor manufacturing and collect production data and merge with technologies like smart cards and bar coding. Even newer techniques of scheduling and cell management are leading to a bottom-up style of factory management. Indeed, as information technology evolves further, push techniques, like the pull approaches, will tend to decentralize control to the local, cell level.

In today's manufacturing settings, we are witnessing a drift toward the ultimate JIT factory, in which the needs of a JIT cell are perfectly coordinated with the output of all others and matched to customers' varying demands. Expressed in those terms, that's the ultimate CIM factory too.

Digital Equipment Corporation: The EndPoint Model (A)

In October 1986, Paul Stevens, the Distributed Systems Manufacturing (DSM) Group manufacturing manager at Digital Equipment Corporation, reflected on the activities of the past 18 months: "It's difficult to manage change in a successful company. Doing things differently is not natural behavior. Old habits die hard. And most employees want to see results indicating that change is "the right thing to do" before offering their full commitment."

In April 1985, Stevens had been assigned responsibility for the DSM group, including support engineering, value engineering, purchasing, and all manufacturing activities across three plants. Within months, his staff had developed a new manufacturing strategy—called the EndPoint model—and had launched a wave of new programs to implement the strategy. Now that the programs were well under way, Stevens wanted to review the group's progress and identify the challenges that remained.

THE COMPANY: ITS HISTORY AND PRODUCT STRATEGY

In 1986, Digital Equipment Corporation (DEC) was the world's second-largest manufacturer of computer systems, with revenues of $7.6 billion and 94,700 employees. Founded in 1957 by Kenneth Olsen, an MIT engineer, DEC had changed the way that people computed by introducing the first inexpensive minicomputer, the PDP-8. Before DEC, all computers were mainframes, housed in special centers and used to process large batches of

data. DEC's small, rugged machines allowed scientists and engineers to computerize a variety of routine tasks such as machining, typesetting, and medical scanning. The widespread use of minicomputing helped lay the groundwork for the personal computer revolution.

In 1979, Digital's chief engineers won approval to develop a new generation of superminicomputers, based on a single computer architecture called VAX. Ranging from small desk-top machines to computer clusters that could compete with mainframes, the proposed VAX-based machines would be fully compatible, use uniform operating system software, and communicate across shared networks. This product strategy differed from the then standard industry practice of developing different computer architectures and software systems for different sizes and classes of computers. According to DEC's engineers, the new VAX-based computers would enable customers to build computer networks of almost any size and scope, from a few desktop systems linked by a single cable within the same room, to ones involving hundreds of large, powerful computers spread throughout a global organization. "The concept was very simple," said Olsen, "but there were billions of dollars involved in doing it."[1]

Networks soon became a cornerstone of Digital's corporate mission. According to Olsen:

> Our goal is to connect all parts of an organization—the office, the factory floor, the laboratory, the engineering department—from the desktop to the data center. We can connect everything within a building; we can connect a group of buildings on the same site or at remote sites; we can connect an entire organization around the world. We propose to connect a company from top to bottom with a single network that includes the shipping clerk, the secretary, the manager, the vice president, even the president.[2]

This case was prepared as the basis for class discussion rather than to illustrate either effective or ineffective handling of an administrative situation. All names and some data have been disguised.

This case was prepared by Janet L. Simpson under the direction of David A. Garvin. Copyright © 1988 by the President and Fellows of Harvard College. Harvard Business School case 688-059.

---

[1]P. Fuhrman, "Brickbats into Roses," *Forbes,* September 22, 1986, p. 160.

[2]Digital Equipment Corporation, 1986 Annual Report, p. 3.

In Digital's pursuit of this vision, the Distributed Systems Manufacturing group, which made DEC's network products, was a key player.

THE MANUFACTURING ORGANIZATION

In 1986, Digital's manufacturing function employed 28,800 people in 108 sites worldwide. DEC's products were manufactured by one of six groups: Computer Systems Manufacturing (CSM) produced midrange and large VAX-based systems; Small Systems Manufacturing (SSM) made microVAX systems, workstations, and personal computers; Storage Systems Manufacturing (STORAGE), produced tapes, disks, and disk-drives; Low End Systems and Technologies (LEST) made printed circuit boards, terminals, and printers; and GIA and EUROPE produced a combination of systems and options for European and other markets.

Distributed Systems Manufacturing (DSM)

DSM, part of the Computer Systems Manufacturing Group, manufactured 500 line items including local area network[3] and communications products, modems, expander cabs, and power controllers. DSM employed 1,100 people in four design centers, one central business organization, and three manufacturing plants located in Maine, Ireland, and Puerto Rico.

Historically, DSM was not a significant part of Digital's revenue stream; its traditional products were shipped to six DEC plants in an arrangement that one manager likened to "supplying transmissions for cars." But by 1986, DSM's network products were also being sold directly to original equipment manufacturers (OEMs), end users, and distributors. The growth of internal and independent demand for DSM's products boosted 1986 revenues by 32%, to several hundred million dollars. DSM's revenues were projected to grow 60% more in 1987 and double again by 1989.

[3]A local area network (LAN) is a data communications link over an inexpensive carrier (generally coaxial cable or twisted pair wire) that acts as an intra- or inter-premises electronic highway to transport information among communication devices such as office automation equipment, microcomputers, and peripherals. Digital's LAN is called DECnet Ethernet.

DSM'S MANUFACTURING STRATEGY

In April 1985, Stevens and Jeff Lockwood, the business planning manager, met to discuss DSM's five-year business plan. At the time, DSM's charter was to become the high-quality, low-cost supplier of network and communications products worldwide. DSM had also been given ambitious business goals: to double ROA and improve margins by 10 percentage points over the next five years. "Such goals," said Stevens, "could not be achieved through incremental changes." He continued:

> We were not currently under competitive pressure to make changes in our manufacturing strategy. But we recognized that we had a leadership position in networks and a two- to three-year window of opportunity before IBM and others entered the market. We wanted to capitalize on that advantage.

To develop their manufacturing strategy, DSM managers assessed future customer requirements, the activities of competitors, and advances in manufacturing process technology and business systems.

Customer Requirements

Over the next five years, DSM's customers were expected to become more demanding in the areas of quality and product performance. Equally important, they were expected to require DSM to respond quickly and predictably to changing product needs. Stevens explained:

> A *minimum* requirement for future success was the ability to supply high quality products that met customers' performance requirements. Customers were also likely to demand responsiveness from suppliers in the form of just-in-time purchasing. "Ease of doing business" was expected to become increasingly important in vendor selection.

DSM managers realized that future customer demands could not be met without reducing their manufacturing cycle time—the time from vendor shipment of parts and materials to customer delivery of finished products. In 1985, DSM's cycle time averaged 40 weeks.

Competitive Analysis

DSM staff reviewed what other manufacturers were doing to reduce cycle time through co-location of vendors or more sophisticated process technologies. They identified three approaches:

a) the "GM model": large centralized production facilities with vendors required to locate nearby;

b) the "generic industry" model: decentralized production facilities co-located near suppliers; and

c) the "IBM model": a centralized, highly automated, vertically integrated facility in which computer-aided manufacturing methods were employed.

According to Stevens:

> To remain competitive, we knew that DSM had to link closely all elements of supply, manufacturing, and sales without centralizing operations. But none of the models we identified were a good fit with our three geographically dispersed plants and 2,000 suppliers. So, we came up with the idea of "virtual integration," in which our plants, vendors, engineering staff, and customers would remain geographically dispersed, but would be "virtually integrated" through networked systems.

This "virtually integrated" model—a multi-plant computer-integrated manufacturing system connected by networks to vendors and customers—represented DSM's vision of its future. Within the DSM plants, networked systems would gather, track, and route information among members of the purchasing, marketing, finance, design, and manufacturing departments. New or updated product designs would be transferred automatically from engineering to production planning, while flexible manufacturing systems[4] on the factory floor would automate manufacturing processes and material handling. Externally, customers and vendors would be connected on-line with the plants, exchanging order information and, in some instances, production schedules and plans. DSM managers called this "virtually integrated" system the End-Point model (Exhibit 1).

THE ENDPOINT MODEL

Instituting and operationalizing the EndPoint model became the goal of DSM's five-year business plan. The planning staff also reviewed DSM's manufacturing process to establish a cycle time target for the EndPoint model.

The Manufacturing Process

In 1985, DSM's manufacturing cycle had four major stages: component test and burn-in (6 to 8

---

[4]Flexible manufacturing systems (FMS) are often considered to be the building blocks of total factory automation. An FMS may include robotics, numerically controlled machines, tool-changing systems, and material handling systems.

EXHIBIT I DSM EndPoint Model: Virtual Integrated Manufacturing

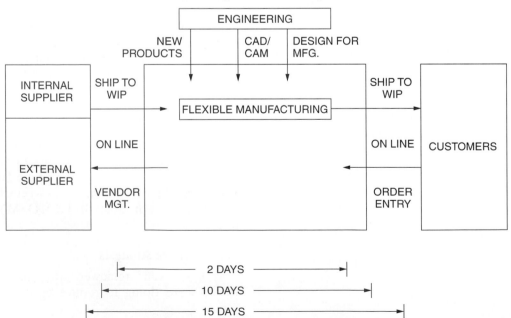

weeks), module assembly (20 weeks), systems integration (6 to 8 weeks), and distribution (6 weeks).

Component Test and Burn-In. Components from vendors were not shipped directly to DSM's plants. Instead, they were first delivered to a centralized testing facility for 100% inspection. A stress test, called burn-in, was used to screen out key components that would fail in the field. Inventory and test time totaled 6 to 8 weeks.

Module Assembly. After passing the test and burn-in process, components were shipped to one of three DSM plants for printed circuit board assembly. Inventory and in-process assembly at the plants accounted for 20 weeks of cycle time.

Systems Integration. The printed circuit boards not incorporated into stand-alone units were shipped to one of two facilities for systems test with a CPU system. Systems integration added 6 to 8 weeks to cycle time.

Distribution. Customer orders were consolidated at one of three distribution warehouses. In 1985, these warehouses contained 6 weeks of inventory.

Cycle Time Target

Through inventory reductions, automation, and computer integration of functional tasks, DSM planners estimated that cycle time could be reduced to 15 days by 1990 (Exhibit 2). The 15-day

EXHIBIT 2   Cycle Time Reduction Model

	Test and Burn-In	Board Assembly	Systems Integration	Distribution Warehouses	Total Cycle Time
Original Manufacturing Cycle Time	6–8 weeks	20 weeks	6–8 weeks	6 weeks	40 weeks
Step 1.					
• Move warehouse inventory from all distribution points and field offices to manufacturing location				(5 weeks)	35 weeks
Step 2.					
• Develop Ethernet set of products which do not require systems integration					
• Develop quality certification at board level to eliminate need to test at systems level			(6–8 weeks)		
• Eliminate inventory holdings as hedges for delivery performance	(5 weeks)				23 weeks
Step 3.					
• Eliminate component test of incoming materials	(8 days)				
• Eliminate kitting; pull to WIP					
• Achive Class A, MRPII; reduce safety stock, WIP, FGI; eliminate receiving inspection		(10 weeks)		(2 days)	11 weeks
Step 4.					
• Eliminate safety stock					
• Reduce cycle time through automation		(5 weeks)			
Step 5.					
• Eliminate finished goods inventory; build to order		(3 weeks)			3 weeks
Endpoint	2 days	10 days	0 days	3 days	15 days

Note: A step does not have to be fully completed before the following step is begun.

Source: Company records.

total included 2 days for receipt of raw materials; 10 days to build the product in-plant (of which only 2 days were work-in-process); and 3 days for systems integration and shipment to customers.

DSM's managers believed that the key to achieving the 15-day target was improving information accuracy and velocity—the care and speed with which information was exchanged. One manager explained:

> An internal study found that 75% of the transactions done in manufacturing were information transactions, such as compiling numbers from different reports; the remaining 25% were material transactions. It was clear that in the long run, information velocity, not material velocity, would determine how close we could get vendors and customers to lie within the same "box" in the EndPoint model.

In this area, senior managers felt that DSM had a strong competitive advantage. One of them explained:

> There are two pieces to the integration of a manufacturing system. The first piece is the hardware—the computer equipment and networks. Unlike many of our competitors, DSM is already very

integrated from a hardware perspective. Because of this, we can focus on the second piece of systems integration: integrating the data and information that flows over the network.

THE ENDPOINT PLAN

The DSM planning group developed a five-year timeline of programs and activities to achieve the EndPoint model and reduce cycle time to 15 days (Exhibit 3). The plan focused on integrating four elements:

a) *systems information and management tools,* including software and computer-aided design;

b) *control,* measured by progress toward achieving build-to-order capabilities;

c) *physical manufacturing processes,* such as automated material handling systems and local area networks, which impacted both the material and information flow on the factory floor; and

d) *programs and philosophies,* such as customer/vendor partnerships and work force reskilling.

The EndPoint plan sequenced the programs required, at both the plant and group levels, to

EXHIBIT 3 The EndPoint Plan

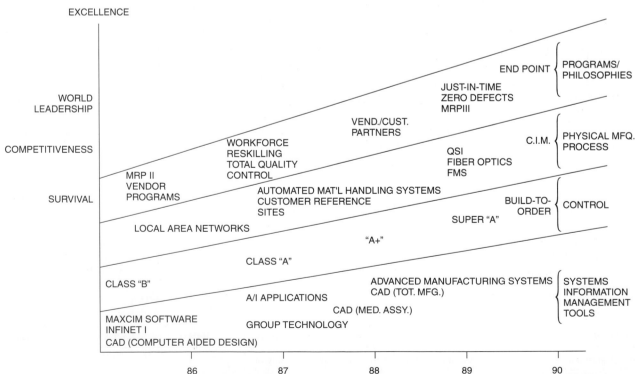

systematically reduce cycle time. Vendor partnerships, managed at the group level, would address raw material procurement time and cost. Programs at the plant level, such as Manufacturing Resource Planning (MRPII), Just-in-Time (JIT), and Total Quality Control (TQC), would reduce product-in-process time. And pilot studies regarding information velocity would be conducted by the group staff, supported by corporate manufacturing development funds.

Many of these programs were not new to DSM's plants. In fact, the plants had been working on a variety of projects to reduce manufacturing cycle time. But, according to Stevens:

> We had islands of automation in the factories—tactical solutions, not strategic solutions. We didn't understand how facilities, process technology, and people could work together synergistically. The EndPoint plan pulled these efforts together.

MANUFACTURING RESOURCE PLANNING (MRPII)

Several programs in the EndPoint plan were launched or under way in 1985; the first milestone was for DSM to become certified as a Class A, MRPII manufacturer.[5] MRPII, a computer-supported planning and scheduling system that links a firm's business, operating, and financial systems, was thought to be a necessary first step because of the tight integration it imposed. MRPII requires that all departments use the same set of numbers; it therefore provides management with a tool for monitoring performance throughout the manufacturing process. Users of MRPII systems are rated from "Class A" to "Class D." Class A firms use MRPII as a companywide game plan for sales, finance, manufacturing, purchasing, and engineering; Class D companies have the system working only at the data processing level.

To achieve Class A status, discipline in decision making is required. MRPII integrates a firm's financial and sales plans with the constraints imposed by delivery or design lead times and plant capacity. An effective MRPII system therefore requires accountability in demand forecasts by product line, accurate inventory records, and careful planning and schedule maintenance. At DSM, MRPII was considered essential for just these reasons. Stevens explained:

> DEC's dramatic growth has historically depended on and rewarded those behaviors tied to informal systems such as expediting. MRPII forces functional executives to come together monthly to develop the production plan. It's a tough discussion. But management discipline is essential if the EndPoint model is to be achieved.

In June 1985, seven plant managers in the Computer Systems Manufacturing (CSM) Group signed a statement in which they agreed to achieve a Class A rating by June 1986. DSM's plant in Augusta, Maine, was one of the seven plants. Carl Porter, Augusta's plant manager, recalled, "If there was one goal that we were determined to reach in 1986, it was Class A status."

MRPII: THE AUGUSTA PLANT

By June 1985, the Augusta plant had been working on manufacturing systems and software integration for two years. The plant had a variety of computer-supported systems in place, including a shop floor control system, called Infinet, used to schedule and track orders released to the production floor, and a materials requirement planning system, called MC-10, used to schedule and order materials. Each of these systems was a discrete entity, using software tailored to the needs of a single functional area. The result, according to one materials manager, was a disjointed information flow:

> We had sophisticated systems that never talked to one another. As a result, most of the time, the functional organizations were trying to second-guess what others were doing. For example, suppose there was a need to build 1,000 units. Production control (PC) might decide to order 1,100 units, because they didn't always get what they wanted from material control. Material control might think, "PC never get their forecasts straight; I know they'll ask for more." So, they might add 20% to the PC request. Purchasing would then receive a request to order material for 1,300 units, 300 more than required. Such "just-in-case" scenarios were common because the original need was never visible at the back-end of the system.

Systems differences were as significant among the CSM plants. One manager noted, for example, that although all CSM materials

---

[5]For a more complete explanation of MRPII, see *A Note on Manufacturing Resource Planning (MRPII),* HBS Case Services, No. 687–097.

organizations used the MC-10 software, "each system had been customized to the point that no two looked alike." Thus an MRPII system, based on uniform software, would not only allow all functional areas within a plant to work with a common set of numbers, but would also, if required, allow all seven plants to share information.

MRPII IMPLEMENTATION

Porter selected an experienced materials manager, Jerry Sabel, to spearhead the MRPII implementation. At Porter's request, Sabel became a regular participant in Augusta's senior management staff meetings. Sabel's MRPII project team included representatives from finance, engineering services, personnel, MIS, manufacturing, and materials.

Performance Metrics

Sabel and the six MRPII program managers (one from each plant) established 13 performance metrics to measure progress toward meeting Class A requirements (Exhibit 4). Each metric was a measure of business, scheduling, planning, or record accuracy. For example, the sales plan was evaluated by measuring the accuracy of forecasts by product line; the master schedule, by comparing scheduled units to units completed; and purchasing, by the on-time delivery record of vendors. An average total score of 90% for two consecutive months was required to become certified as a Class A manufacturer.

Software Selection

The software selected for the MRPII system was called MAXCIM, a closed-loop manufacturing system that had production planning and master scheduling capabilities as well as the elements required to generate financial figures, marketing forecasts, and engineering plans. MAXCIM also provided management with tools to monitor schedules and plans.

At Augusta, the conversion to MAXCIM was targeted for January 1986. During the summer of 1985, 22 individuals were trained on the MAXCIM system. These employees, in turn, conducted MAXCIM training sessions in each functional area. By 1986, the 600 Augusta plant employees had received 68,000 hours of training. But one manager recalled: "Some people didn't take the training to heart. It was difficult getting them to see that this was more than a materials system—that they, and their jobs, were part of a plantwide system rather than an isolated entity."

In January 1986, the MAXCIM system was installed. The plant had prepared for the conversion by stockpiling two weeks of finished goods inventory and creating manual back-up systems for each functional area's computer-supported activities. One team member explained the scope of the task: "To change an operating system means that you essentially rip out the guts of the plant and replace it. All of the knowledge accumulated over the years ceases to exist. Despite our best efforts, we underestimated the magnitude of the task."

EXHIBIT 4   MRPII: DSM's 13 Performance Metrics

Measurement of:	*MRPII Component*	*Performance Metric*
Top Management Planning	1. Business Planning	Return on Assets
	2. Sales Plan	Sales Plan Accuracy
	3. Production Plan	Validity of Production Plan
Plant Performance	4. Master Schedule	Master Schedule Planning
	5. Material Plan	Reschedule Reliability
	6. Capacity Plan	Plan Capacity Properly
Data Base Accuracy	7. Bills of Material	Accurate Bills of Material
	8. Inventory Control	Inventory Record Accuracy
	9. Routings	Routings Accuracy
Plant Execution	10. Material Acquisition	Schedule Performance
	11. Shop Floor Control	Schedule Performance
	12. Schedule Performance	Customer Satisfaction
	13. Order Execution	Executable Orders

Source: Company records.

One crisis arose over unfilled purchase orders. MAXCIM required a purchase order format that was not compatible with Augusta's old system. Thus, all outstanding purchase orders had to be reentered into the MAXCIM system. Buyers were moved to the receiving floor to help manage receiving. Temporary clerical help was hired to input the new data. "We almost buckled under the strain of the data input alone," one team member recalled. When plant performance was evaluated at the end of January, the Augusta plant's metrics averaged 80%, up from 65% the prior year. To further focus attention on achieving Class A requirements, a 4' × 8' board was installed in the Augusta cafeteria, listing the name of the plant staff member responsible for each of the 13 performance metrics, and an updated weekly score. Porter's name appeared next to the business performance metric.

MRPII: DSM GROUP MATERIALS MANAGEMENT

In addition to the activities at the Augusta plant, DSM's group materials staff focused on developing accurate sales projections for each of DSM's product lines. David Chandler, the group materials manager, explained:

> We could not attain a Class A rating or performance without accurate product forecasts. It is these forecasts that drive manufacturing to allocate resources, order material, and have labor available to produce and ship to plan.

> Because DEC is a systems company, sales were projected by computer systems, not units of network products. To obtain the level of detail required for MRPII, we had to broaden our role in manufacturing and develop a detailed sales plan for DSM's network products.

In 1985, most of DSM's products were sold internally to six DEC systems plants. Because network products were a small portion of the total cost of computer systems, these plants maintained high inventory levels of DSM's products and often ordered more than needed to meet systems production requirements. In 1985, DSM took back all of its products inventoried at the systems plants. Chandler recalled: "The plants were assured that they would get products when they ordered them. They were only too happy to give up their inventory—in some cases, they had as much as several years' supply. Stevens and Porter took the hit in their numbers."

According to DSM managers, this action gave DSM more control over internal demands for its products. But it also put additional pressure on the group materials department to improve product forecast accuracy. As one manager explained, "You can't hold up the sale of a computer system because you've run out of a relatively inexpensive network component."

Chandler's staff thus turned to the more difficult problem of translating corporate sales projections in dollars to units of network products by product line. Unpredictable sales growth and new product introductions made the task challenging. To clarify sales demand, the group materials staff held frequent meetings with customers and attended a weekly forum with product management, marketing, and manufacturing. Chandler commented:

> We had to do a lot of education within DEC to overcome the perception that we were the "poor cousin," the Class "C" component supplier. In the past, that attitude had created situations where Porter and the plant frequently had to respond to last-minute requests for network products. With MRPII, the sales plan had to be frozen 13 weeks prior to the beginning of each quarter.

From these meetings, the group materials staff developed a sales plan by product family type. This unit sales plan was then converted to a production plan for the three DSM plants. The group materials staff met formally with the plants on a monthly basis and reviewed the numbers weekly. Changes were made as needed, usually once per week.

According to Chandler, MRPII changed the focus of DSM's group materials management: "Historically, we focused on obsolescence and inventory. Now we're concerned with sales, marketing, product planning, and pipeline planning." But the formality of the MRPII system changed Chandler's normal operating style. He observed:

> In the past, if sales exceeded plan, I could call Porter and ask him to expedite 20,000 more units. With MRPII, I lose two to three weeks of time working through the formal system. Initially, MRPII looked as if it was there to get in the way. But the informal system didn't show the trauma that people at

the plant went through. And from a business perspective, my request actually might have hurt the company, causing us to lose a sale from another customer. With MRPII, you make the trade-offs explicitly.

Chandler also noted that MRPII added accountability to the sales-planning process: "MRPII took informality and finger-pointing and formalized it. If the manufacturing facility builds to plan and the plan is not accurate, it's not the plant manager's fault. With MRPII, you understand the boundaries. Still, no one liked the discipline."

In May 1986, the Augusta metrics averaged 90% for the first time. In June, the plant achieved its Class A rating. Porter observed: "Implementing MRPII is like trying to run a four-minute mile. You start at 5.5 minutes, then 5.4, 5.3, and so on. Each step gets harder and harder to achieve. We consider Class A to be our first step. There are many more beyond it."

OTHER DSM PROGRAMS

By the fall of 1986, several additional programs had been launched to move DSM toward the End-Point model.

Information Velocity

In 1986, the DSM group staff received corporate manufacturing development funds to conduct pilot studies for improving information velocity. While some of these studies focused on the mechanics of data integration, such as developing a data highway, others were concerned with improving information flow. One project, for example, aimed to reduce inefficiencies in DSM's production planning process. Two industrial engineers were assigned to evaluate the process from product forecast through order generation to identify inefficient methods, meetings, or procedures, and make recommendations for corrective action. The staff intended to apply the methodology and lessons learned from this pilot project to all information-intensive processes at DSM.

The Partnership Program

The DSM group staff also launched a partnership program with several key vendors/customers. Ellen Phillips, DSM's external ventures business manager, explained the purpose of the partnership program: "Our goal is to work together to implement programs that achieve excellence in manufacturing performance—thereby reducing cycle times and improving the quality of our business." By the fall of 1986, DSM staff had approached five firms with the intention of creating a partnership arrangement. These firms had been selected from DSM's vendors and customer base after an exhaustive screening process. All potential candidates were rated using two lists of selection criteria: descriptive criteria, including geographic location, relationship with DSM (vendor, OEM, or customer), and use of diverse computer equipment; and evaluative criteria, which were weighted more heavily, including Class A MRPII status, advanced product manufacturing (i.e., a producer of high-tech products), and excellence in human resource management. Information came from DEC's customer account managers, purchasing managers, and published sources such as annual reports and the trade press.

After narrowing the list to five candidates, DSM staff worked with DEC's account managers to customize programs for each firm. During initial meetings with the firms, the staff shared DSM's EndPoint plan and the objectives of the partnership program. Phillips explained: "We knew that vendors almost could not say "No" to DEC, because of our leverage with them. However, our intent was to work on issues that would be mutually beneficial. In the past, we gave vendors a performance report; now we wanted them to give us one."

To lend credibility to the program, DSM agreed to give the vendors product forecasts on a monthly basis so that they could plan their production runs accordingly. DSM further agreed to finance a review of its specifications, at a cost of $250,000. In return, vendors were expected over the long term to improve delivery time while working with DSM to reduce total cost.

The partnership program was not without risk. Phillips explained:

> These firms are also five of DSM's top ten customers, so our credibility is at risk if we don't follow through. Short term, we are also asking our people to expose themselves while implementing changes in our manufacturing practices; the partners will see us making mistakes. But the risks are worthwhile. Without a strong partnership program, we will not meet the goals of the EndPoint model. In the short run, the

issue is survival. In the long run, it is world-class performance.

Toward the Endpoint

Once MRPII was in place, DSM launched three complementary programs to reduce manufacturing cycle times: CIM (Computer-Integrated Manufacturing), which focused on information collection and control; TQC (Total Quality Control), which had as its goal zero defects in both product and information quality; and JIT (Just-In-Time), which focused on eliminating waste and reducing inventories to zero.

CIM

In the spring of 1986, while group staff members studied data integration among DSM's plants, a CIM project team was assembled in Augusta to focus on data and information integration within the plant. The MAXCIM software gave each functional area a common tool for planning and scheduling, but it was not able to collect data, such as direct labor hours or machine output, on a real-time basis. That capability would be required to support a just-in-time manufacturing process. The CIM team's goal was to develop a communication vehicle consisting of networks, standards, and a common database, that would allow managers to collect data in real-time and would provide all functional areas with access to the data in the format required.

TQC

In the fall of 1986, a Total Quality Control (TQC) program, which focused on improving both product and data quality, was also on the launching pad. Historically, DSM's product quality was

monitored by macromeasures such as AQLs (acceptable quality levels), and reliability (mean time between failures). Vendor quality was assessed by incoming inspection. The TQC program's objectives were to attain zero defects in products and information, and establish a "ship to WIP" relationship with vendors.

JIT

Reducing lot sizes, shortening lead times, and eliminating safety stock were essential if DSM was going to meet its 15-day cycle-time target. In the fall of 1986, the Augusta plant staff was involved in a fact-finding and educational process aimed at understanding the JIT concept. At DSM, MRPII was envisioned as the vehicle for moving toward a just-in-time production process. Stevens explained:

> MRPII provides the complete information needed to run a quality manufacturing operation. But the system does not question manufacturing lead times, lot sizes, queues, or safety stocks. By tightening the requirements for MRPII performance metrics while making physical changes in our manufacturing processes, we can set goals for continuous improvement. For example, today we consider a vendor delivery to be on time if it is shipped within three days of schedule. In 1987, on-time delivery will mean within one day of due date. In 1988, Class A vendor delivery will mean within one day of the due date, with zero defects. Through such a process, MRPII can be used to focus attention on those areas that contribute most significantly to cycle time.

The Results

By October 1986, the impact of these programs was evident in DSM's financial and performance statistics (Exhibit 5). Cycle time had already

EXHIBIT 5   DSM's Performance

			EndPoint Model		
	FY84	*FY85*	*FY86 (YTD)*	*FY87*	*FY88 (Forecast)*
Revenue growth (%/yr.)	NA	26%	32%	54%	70%
Revenue/person growth (%/yr.)	NA	28%	19%	26%	68%
Revenue/square foot growth (%/yr.)	NA	26%	31%	56%	59%
Inventory/revenue dollar	$0.28	$0.33	$0.15	$0.15	$0.07
New products shipped	6	6	3	11	25

NA = not applicable.

Source: Company records.

dropped 10%; an ambitious schedule of programs was expected to reduce it another 50% by 1988. DSM managers were encouraged by their success. However, one manager questioned the pace of change:

> How quickly can people assimilate these programs? MRPII was a backbreaker. It required dra-

matic changes in behavior . . . a lot of stress. JIT and TQC are much more difficult. MRPII just works on basic manufacturing discipline; JIT and TQC actually change the way you manufacture products.

> Today, the plants also have to deal with a changing product mix and 30% to 40% projected growth. Is it wise to divert management's attention away from growth to implement these programs?

A Note on Manufacturing Resource Planning (MRPII)

Manufacturing Resource Planning (MRPII) is a computer-based planning and scheduling system designed to improve management's control of manufacturing and its support functions. MRPII translates a firm's business, sales and production plans into specific day-to-day tasks through such well-defined techniques as master scheduling, materials planning, capacity planning, shop floor control and vendor scheduling. The system enables management to set priorities, anticipate crises, and measure performance to schedules and plans.

MRPII evolved from Material Requirements Planning (MRP), a computerized tool for scheduling and ordering materials. MRP is a technique for exploding bills of material to calculate net materials requirements and plan future production. Early MRP systems used four pieces of information to determine what materials should be ordered and when: the master production schedule, which describes when each product is scheduled to be manufactured; bills of material, which list exactly the parts or materials required to make each product; production cycle times and materials needs at each stage of the production cycle; and supplier lead times. The master schedule and bills of material indicate what materials should be ordered; the master schedule, production cycle times and supplier lead times then jointly determine when orders should be placed. Over time, such features as capacity planning, vendor scheduling, and work-in-process tracking were added to MRP systems, so that management could also monitor operating performance.

MRP is only one element of a complete MRPII system. Technically, MRPII marries an MRP operating system to the firm's financial system, allowing all departments to work from a single, visible set of numbers. Equally important,

MRPII provides a management process for integrating financial planning, marketing, engineering, and purchasing with manufacturing. As one user has observed: "To work well, MRPII has to cut across business disciplines. These disciplines are driven by differing motivations; normally no one is rewarded for integrating them."[1]

COMPONENTS OF MRPII

An MRPII system has three components: Top Management Planning, Operations Management Planning, and Operations Management Execution (Exhibit 1).

Top Management Planning

In a fully integrated MRPII system, a firm's business, sales and production plans are fed into the MRPII execution model and updated monthly.

Business Planning sets specific goals for margins, return on assets (ROA), and other business objectives. These goals are drawn from the firm's strategic plan for markets, products and profits.

Sales Planning provides product projections—rather than dollar forecasts—based on anticipated market demand.

Production Planning balances the sales plan with available capacity and constraints derived from engineering (time to release new designs), vendors (lead times), and manufacturing (facilities, equipment and people). Resource allocation decisions based on capacity, inventory levels, and the desired level of customer service are then incorporated into the production plan.

Operations Management Planning

The master scheduler converts the production plan into a **Master Production Schedule,** a specific statement of what products are to be built, in what quantities, and when. The master production

This note was prepared by Janet L. Simpson under the direction of David A. Garvin. Copyright © 1987 by the President and Fellows of Harvard College. Harvard Business School case 687-097.

[1]John Teresko, "MRPII: A Strategic Tool for Survival," *Industry Week* 9/30/85, p. 42.

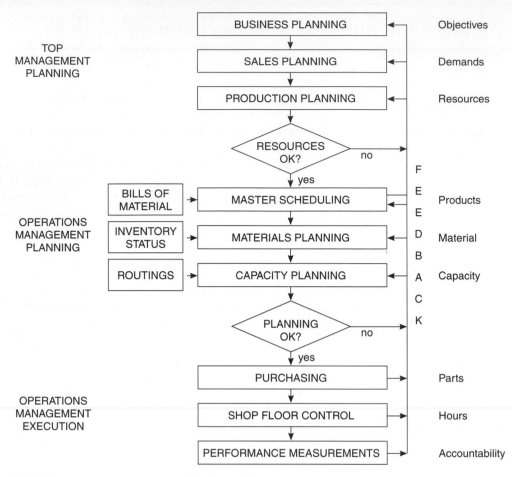

EXHIBIT I Manufacturing Resource Planning (MRPII)
Source: David W. Buker, Inc., Chicago, Illinois. Reprinted with permission.

schedule then drives the ordering and scheduling of all material (**Materials Planning**) and provides direction for optimal use of labor and machine capacity (**Capacity Planning**). These plans are evaluated weekly; proper execution requires accurate bills of material, inventory records and routings.

Operations Management Execution

Operations management plans are communicated, in the form of daily schedules, to engineering, tooling shops, purchasing, and the production floor. The material plan provides **Purchasing** with schedules for material acquisition that specify parts, quantities, and dates. The capacity plan and master schedule generate daily work center schedules to assist shop supervisors in setting priorities and assigning work to people or machines. **Shop Floor Control** encompasses all of these daily lists, plus work-in-process tracking, shop order delivery,

and scheduling and rescheduling controls. On-time vendor delivery and shop floor performance are essential if master schedule targets are to be met.

CLASSIFICATION OF USERS

A checklist and an ABCD rating scheme are widely used to measure how well a firm is operating its MRP or MRPII system. Using the checklist, independent consultants evaluate technical considerations (such as the mechanics of capacity planning), data integrity, ongoing employee education, and performance to plans and schedules. Firms are then rated from "Class A" to "Class D," based on the following generally accepted industry criteria:[2]

---

[2]The description of rating criteria was adapted from O. Wight, *The Executive's Guide to Successful MRPII* (NH: O. Wight Publications, 1984), pp. 107–108.

Class A

A Class A MRP company has material requirements planning, capacity planning, shop floor dispatching, and vendor scheduling systems in place and being used. Management participates in production planning and constantly monitors the accuracy of inventory records, bills of material, and routings, as well as the attainment of master schedules, and capacity plans.

A Class A MRPII user has tied its financial system to its MRP system. Simulation capabilities have been developed so that "what if" questions can be answered. Management uses MRPII to run the business and monitor performance. In a Class A firm, the system provides a companywide game plan for sales, finance, manufacturing, purchasing, and engineering. Each of these functions uses the formal system; there is no attempt to override schedules through expediting or shortage lists.

Class B

A Class B firm uses components of an MRP or MRPII system for production and inventory control. The Class B company typically has materials requirements planning, capacity planning and shop floor control systems in place, but has done little with purchasing. Top management does not use the system to run the business directly and shortage lists tend to override shop schedules.

Class C

A Class C company uses MRP/MRPII primarily as an inventory ordering technique rather than a scheduling tool. Shop scheduling is still done from a shortage list, and the master schedule is typically inaccurate.

Class D

A Class D company has MRP/MRPII working only in its data processing department. Typically, inventory records are poor. If the company has a defined master schedule, it is usually grossly mismanaged. In 1985, a survey of 1,123 American MRP/MRPII users found that fewer than 200 plants met Class A criteria.[3] Those that did reported a 28% improvement in customer service, a 25% reduction in inventory levels, a 16% increase in productivity, and an 11% reduction in purchase

costs. These improvements produced significant costs savings. For example, 40% of the Class A users reported annual savings exceeding $1 million, while only 2% reported savings of less than $100 thousand annually. Other classes of users also reported improvements in customer service, productivity, and inventory reduction, but their cost savings were markedly lower (Exhibit 3).

MRPII IMPLEMENTATION

In practice, MRPII users employ a series of performance metrics to monitor progress toward achieving a Class A rating. These metrics typically address the accuracy of each key component in the MRPII model. For example, the sales plan may be evaluated by measuring the accuracy of forecasts by product line; the master schedule, by comparing scheduled units to units completed; and purchasing, by on-time vendor delivery. Systems are said to be operating at a Class A level when the average accuracy of these metrics reaches 90%. A sample list of metrics appears in Exhibit 2.

While the proper use of these metrics can highlight problem areas during implementation of

EXHIBIT 2 MRPII: Representative Performance Metrics

MRPII Component	Performance Metric
Top Management Planning	
Business Planning	Return on Assets
Sales Planning	Product Forecast Accuracy
Production Planning	Production Planning Accuracy
Plant Performance	
Master Scheduling	Scheduling Accuracy
Materials Planning	Accurate Material Priority Planning
Capacity Planning	Accurate Work Center Scheduling
Database Accuracy	
Bills of Material	Accurate Bills of Material
Inventory Control	Accurate Inventory Records
Routings	Routings Accuracy
Plant Execution	
Purchasing	On-Time Vendor Delivery
Shop Floor Control	On-Time Shop Order Completion

[3]The Oliver Wight Companies 1985 Newsletter: *Control of the Business,* (1985: Newbury, NH).

MRPII, they may also be used to improve performance once the Class A rating is achieved. For example, vendor delivery may initially be considered "on-time" if deliveries arrive within one week of the due date. Once that target is achieved, on-time delivery may be redefined to mean deliveries arriving within one day of the due date. Through such practices, a firm can use MRPII to gain continuous improvement in its manufacturing performance. According to the 1985 survey cited above, companies spent an average of $907,000 to implement MRP/MRPII systems. Class A users spent $1,181,000. Surprisingly, Class D users spent nearly the same amount,

EXHIBIT 3 1985 O. Wight Survey of MRP/MRPII Users

1. What is the approximate dollar volume (in millions) of your plant or division?

	All MRP Companies	Class A Companies
Under $10 million	10%	4%
$10–24 million	20	12
$25–49 million	22	31
$50–99 million	18	19
Over $100 million	30	34

2. What were your approximate costs (in thousands) in implementing MRP/MRPII?

	All MRP Companies	Class A Companies
Computer Hardware	$257	$394
Computer Software	176	175
Inventory Record Accuracy	52	108
Bill of Material Accuracy	43	52
Routing Accuracy	29	39
Education	66	97
Consulting	45	48
Other Costs	239	268
Total	$907	$1,181

3. What would you estimate to be your yearly benefits from MRP/MRPII?

	All MRP Companies	Class A Companies
Under $100 thousand	25%	2%
$100–249 thousand	19	11
$250–499 thousand	16	26
$500–749 thousand	12	14
$750–999 thousand	5	7
$1.0–1.4 million	10	14
$1.5–1.9 million	3	9
$2.0–2.9 million	5	6
$3.0–3.9 million	1	—
$4.0–4.9 million	1	1
$5.0–5.9 million	—	1
Over $6 million	3	9

(continued)

$1,002,000. However, sharp differences between the groups were reported in two areas: top management commitment, and education. Only 20% of Class A users felt they had not received enough top management support; by contrast, 78% of the Class D users reported a lack of management commitment. In addition, while more than half the companies surveyed reported they should have done a better job educating their employees, Class A companies had been far more active. For example, 82% of the A users had educated their top management at outside classes against only 50% of the D users. A summary of these survey results appears in Exhibit 3.

EXHIBIT 3   *(Continued)*

4. In implementing MRP/MRPII, which of the following did your plant or division do?

	All MRP Companies	Class A Companies	Class D Companies
Top Management Education	64%	82%	50%
Formal Cost/Benefit	46	66	36
Full-Time Project Leader	68	83	49
Proven Implementation Plan	43	60	24
MRP Consultant	51	73	44
Key Mgrs. Educated Outside Classes	69	86	58
Video-Assisted Education	62	70	55
Ongoing Education—Classes	47	73	32
Ongoing Education—Video	32	49	24

5. What would you have done differently in implementing MRP/MRPII?

	All MRP Companies	Class A Companies
More Education	55%	35%
Better Software	28	23
Top Management Commitment	48	20
Other, Not Listed	21	18
Would Do Nothing Differently	11	39

Source: The Oliver Wight Companies 1985 Newsletter: *Control of the Business* (1985: Newbury, NH). Reprinted with permission.

Vandelay Industries, Inc.

On a Monday morning in January, 1996, Elaine Kramer was in her Philadelphia office catching up on e-mail. She had been in Minneapolis the previous week for a series of meetings between her firm, Deloitte & Touche Consulting Group/ICS, and the executives and plant managers of Vandelay Industries Inc., a major producer of industrial process equipment. The week had ended with the two companies signing a contract to work together on a large information systems implementation project.

Her phone rang.

"This is Elaine Kramer."

"Hi, Elaine, this is George Hall. I manage Vandelay's Dunbarton plant; we met at the project kickoff meetings last week."

"Oh, yes—how are you, George? I really enjoyed the presentation on your pull-based manufacturing project. You guys have generated some really impressive results. What can I do for you?"

"I was just wondering if I could start getting my people signed up for training on the R/3 system. I know it's early, but we're really eager to dig in here. Your presentation got a lot of people excited about getting rid of our plant's old mainframe. We want to get an R/3 team together so we're ready to work on the system as soon as it's installed at Dunbarton."

"Well, we haven't started putting training schedules together yet . . . "

"Well, keep us in mind when you do. Like I said in the presentation, we're a bunch of tinkerers,

and that's what has helped us improve so much over the past few years. We think R/3 can really help us past some of our current roadblocks, so we're eager to start experimenting with it."

"OK, let me get back to you once we're further along with training plans."

After Kramer hung up the phone she mentally replayed the conversation; it raised an issue that had been in the back of her mind since the meetings. How much should the plants in the network be encouraged to modify their local set-up of the new computer system once it had been installed?

PROJECT BACKGROUND

Vandelay had decided in 1995 to implement a single Enterprise Resource Planning (ERP) information system throughout the corporation. The firm had chosen the R/3 system from SAP AG, a German company that was the market lead in ERP products. Vandelay hoped that the R/3 implementation would end the existing fragmentation of its systems, allow process standardization across the corporation, and give it a competitive advantage over its rivals.

Vandelay managers realized that putting R/3 in place would be an enormous effort, of which installation of hardware and software was only a small part. For help with all aspects of the project, from the technical details of an ERP system to widespread business practice changes, Vandelay had engaged the Deloitte & Touche Consulting Group/ICS. ICS assisted clients in managing fundamental changes of the kind entailed by an ERP system, and had significant expertise with SAP's R/3 product.

Kramer, who had been with the firm for over 5 years, had been chosen to lead the project. At the meetings in Minneapolis she had been impressed with Vandelay's enthusiasm for the project. The plant managers seemed especially excited; many of them had said that they considered their existing information systems an impediment, rather than an aid, to efficient production.

George Hall certainly seemed pleased at the thought of R/3 in his plant, but Kramer was not entirely calmed by their conversation. Hall had evidently assumed that Dunbarton would be free to modify the system at will; Kramer knew that this would not be the case. She wondered how to respond to his request for training, and how to let him and the other plant managers know that all decisions about R/3 were not under their control.

VANDELAY INDUSTRIES

Company Background

Vandelay Industries, Inc. was an $8B corporation that manufactured and distributed industrial process equipment used in the production of rubber and latex. The company was founded in Minnesota during World War II; its initial products proved important on the home front, enabling the much greater productivity required by the war effort. From the beginning, Vandelay's offerings were known for their design quality and innovative engineering; company lore held that this was because wartime rubber shortages necessitated precise, wasteless production.

Markets for Vandelay products were extremely healthy throughout the following decades, and the firm steadily expanded, partly by building new sites and partly by acquiring smaller firms.[1] The company also steadily expanded its product lines, eventually supplying a range of process industries. Vandelay plants were treated as revenue centers and typically were allowed a high degree of independence, provided that they maintained acceptable profit margins. At its peak, the company employed 30,000 people and manufactured on four continents. Employees tended to remain with Vandelay for a long time, taking advantage of generous pay and benefits and a stimulating work environment.

The company began to experience difficult times beginning in the mid 1980s as a result of market shifts and severe competitive pressures. Three strong foreign competitors emerged, offering less expensive alternatives in many of Vandelay's product lines. These machines typically did not include all of the features of the comparable Vandelay product, but were substantially (20–30%) cheaper. As a result, the American company's traditional emphasis on features and customizability became a liability. Its manufacturing operations were never intended to be low cost, but its products could no longer command a large price premium once suitable substitutes were available. The firm's traditionally long lead times also became a problem; the new entrants could fill customer orders much more quickly.

Vandelay fought hard over the next ten years to learn new technologies and new ways of doing business. It adopted lean production methods, rationalized its product lines, and introduced new, simpler and cheaper machines. It also closed three plants, leaving eight in operation[2] and had the first layoffs in its history, reducing its total headcount to 20,000 people. Many of these efforts paid off, and the company returned to profitability in the mid 1990s.

During this decade of realignment Vandelay's executives realized that they would have to accord much higher priority to manufacturing and order fulfillment in order to further drive down costs. They also needed to become quicker; the company's new machines were popular, but still had longer lead times than competitors. Internal investigations had shown that actual manufacturing and material movement times accounted for less than 5% of total lead times experienced. Large parts of the remaining time, Vandelay found, were devoted to information processing and information transfer steps. This was partly because the computer systems in use across the firm to guide order fulfillment and production activities were poorly integrated, and in some cases completely incompatible.

Information Systems

Each plant had selected its own system for manufacturing resource planning (MRP), the software that translated customer demands into purchasing and production requirements. In addition, many sites had also installed specialized software to help with forecasting, capacity planning, or

---

[1]Half of all new Vandelay sites from 1945 to 1985 were bought rather than built.

[2]4 in North America, 2 in Europe, and 2 in Asia.

scheduling. Information systems for human resources management had also been selected individually. There was a single corporate financial information system, to which each site had built an interface for automatic electronic updates, but this was the only example of corporation-wide systems integration.

As Vandelay reviewed its operations, it uncovered several examples of how this patchwork of information systems added time and expense to the production cycle. Examples included:

- *Scheduling:* The plants' dissimilar manufacturing software often made integration across sites difficult. For example, one of Vandelay's American plants made a variety of machined and stamped metal parts which were used by the other North American assembly sites. This plant used an outdated MRP system which required all data to be entered manually. Requirements from all downstream users were keyed in at the beginning of each week, a task that required almost a full day. No other inputs were allowed during the week, and the plant was deluged with complaints about its responsiveness.

- *Forecasting:* Vandelay's European planning group used a forecasting program which grouped all demand for an item into one monthly "bucket." Plants were then free to decide when to build the product within that month. Customer orders, however, usually requested delivery within a specific week. If these requests did not line up with the month's production plan by chance, late shipments resulted.

- *Order management:* Customer orders were taken manually by an inside sales organization in each region (North America, Europe, and Asia), then routed via fax to the appropriate plant where they were keyed in to that site's order entry system. Faxes, and therefore orders, were sometimes lost.

- *Human resources:* When a Vandelay employee transferred from one location to another, her complete employee record had to be copied. Because of incompatible human resources software, this data often had to be manually re-entered. In addition to being redundant and time-consuming, this meant that the confidentiality of the information was difficult to guarantee.

- *Financials and Accounting:* The manufacturing software used within most Vandelay plants was not integrated with the site's financial package, so information such as labor hours charged to a job, materials purchased, and orders shipped had

to be entered into both systems. This introduced potential for error, and necessitated periodic reconciliations.

Business Practices

Vandelay sites' operations practices were as varied as their information systems. There was no uniformly recognized 'best' way to invoice customers, close the accounts at month end, reserve warehouse inventory for a customer's order, or carry out any of the hundreds of other activities in the production process that required computer usage or input. At the kick-off meetings, Kramer had heard 'horror stories' about flawed processes uncovered by plant managers. Some of them were quite vivid:

> I walked down to my receiving dock a few days ago and just watched what happened each time a supplier's truck unloaded. First, our receiving guys would verify the quantities. Then they'd leave the boxes on the dock and take the packing lists over to a terminal for our quality system. If it said that the part needed incoming inspection, they'd move the boxes over to quality control. If there was no inspection, they'd take the list over to another terminal and enter the received quantities into the purchasing system, then they'd move the boxes and the list over to stores. Meanwhile, the stores guy is working through a backlog of these boxes, entering the stockroom bin numbers of all the items he's shelved. And if there's a discrepancy in the packing list or a high-priority item hits the dock, things get real complicated.
>
> —TERI BUHL,
> FORT WAYNE (IN) PLANT MANAGER

> When I started at the plant last year, I couldn't believe how work got scheduled on the floor. They'd started a system of putting a green tag on high priority work orders to flag that they should be at the head of the queue. That worked for a while, but then someone decided that really high priority jobs should get a red tag. You can guess how it went from there. By the time I got there, no job had a prayer unless it had some kind of tag on it and there were at least a half-dozen color combinations in play. Our starting queues looked like Christmas trees.
>
> —ALAIN BARSOUX,
> MARSEILLES PLANT MANAGER

To alleviate these problems with systems and practices, Vandelay decided to purchase and install a single ERP system, which would incorporate the functions of all the previously fragmented software. The company would also use this effort as an opportunity to standardize practices across sites.

Vandelay saw one other major benefit from an ERP system: gaining visibility, in a common format, over data from anywhere in the company. The company anticipated that once the software was in place, authorized users would be able to instantly see relevant information, no matter where it originated. This would provide the ability to co-ordinate and manage Vandelay sites more tightly than ever before; plants could see what their internal customers and suppliers were doing, and network-level managers could directly compare performance across locations.

After a review of leading ERP vendors and implementation support consultants, Vandelay decided to purchase SAP's R/3 software and put it in place with the help of Deloitte & Touche Consulting Group/ICS.

THE SOFTWARE VENDOR: SAP

Company Background

SAP AG was founded in 1972 in Walldorf, Germany, with the goal of producing integrated application software for corporations. These applications were to include all of the activities of a corporation, from purchasing and manufacturing to order fulfillment and accounting. SAP's first major product was the R/2 system, which ran on mainframe computers. R/2 and its competitors came to be called Enterprise Information Systems (EISs). Within manufacturing firms they were also known as Enterprise Resource Planning (ERP) systems to reflect that they incorporated and expanded on the functions of previous MRP systems.

SAP was one of the first ERP vendors to realize that powerful and flexible client-server computing technologies developed in the 1980s were likely to replace the established mainframe architectures of many large firms. The company began work on a client-server product in 1987 and released the R/3 system in 1992. R/3 capitalized on many of the advantages of client-server computing, including:

- *Ease of use.* Client-server applications often used personal computer-like graphical user interfaces. They also ran on the familiar desktop machines used for spreadsheets and word processing.

- *Ease of integration.* The flexible client-server hardware and operating systems could be more easily linked internally (to process control equipment, for example) and externally, to wide-area networks and the Internet.

- *Scalability, or the ability to add computing power incrementally.* Companies could easily expand client-server networks by adding relatively small and cheap machines. With mainframes, computing capacity had to be purchased in large 'chunks.'

- *More open standards.* The operating systems most used for client-server computing were non-proprietary, so hardware from different manufacturers could be combined. In contrast, most mainframe technologies were proprietary, so a mainframe purchase from IBM or Digital locked in the customer to that vendor.

As Figure 1 shows, R/3 was extremely successful and fueled rapid growth at SAP. By 1995, the firm was the 3rd largest software company in the world (see Exhibit 1). Expansion was especially rapid in North America, where SAP went from a very small presence in 1992 to $710M in sales in 1995. This success was due to several factors, including:

- *Client-server technology.* As large firms moved from mainframe to client-server architectures in the early 1990s, the R/3 system was available to them. Meanwhile, many suppliers of existing 'legacy systems' did not have client-server applications ready for market.

- *Modularity, functionality, and integration.* R/3 functionality included financials, order management, manufacturing, logistics, and human resources, as detailed in Exhibit 2. Prior to the arrival of ERP, these functions would be scattered among several systems. R/3 integrated all of these tasks by allowing its modules to share and transfer information freely, and by centralizing all information in a single database which all modules accessed.

- *Marketing Strategy.* SAP partnered with most large consulting firms. Together, they sold R/3 to executives as part of a broader business strategy, rather than selling it to Information Systems managers as a piece of software.

R/3 Usage: Transaction Screens and Processes

On a user's machine, R/3 looked and felt like any other modern personal computer application; it had a graphical user interface and used a mouse for pointing and clicking. Users navigated through

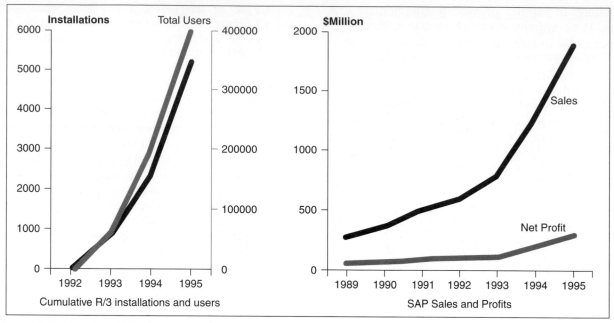

FIGURE I Growth of SAP and the R/3 System (Source: SAP)

Vertical and Cross-Industry Applications Worldwide Software Revenue, Top 10 Vendors Worldwide, 1993–1995 ($M)

Company	1993	1994	1995	1995 % Share	1994 % Share	Growth 1994–95 (%)
Microsoft	1,246	1,688	2,484	6.2	4.8	47.1
IBM	1,647	1,607	1,711	4.3	4.6	6.5
SAP AG	414	843	1,322	3.3	2.4	56.9
IBM/Lotus	281	401	540	1.4	1.1	34.6
Computer Associates*	431	425	478	1.2	1.2	12.5
Autodesk	351	392	455	1.1	1.1	16.1
Novell	603	477	443	1.1	1.4	–7.1
Adobe Systems	324	387	438	1.1	1.1	13.3
Cadence Design	336	391	435	1.1	1.1	11.2
Siemens Nixdorf	350	365	361	0.9	1.0	–1.1
All other vendors	24,238	27,895	31,240	78.1	79.9	12.0
Worldwide solutions revenue	30,273	34,930	39,989			14.5

EXHIBIT I World's Largest Software Companies

*Includes revenues of Legent Corp. for entire year
Source: International Data Corporation, 1996

R/3 by moving from screen to screen; each screen carried out a different transaction. Transactions included everything from checking the in-stock status of a component to changing an assembly's estimated cost; Exhibit 3 gives an example of a transaction screen.

A full SAP implementation, including all standard functions, incorporated hundreds of possible transactions. Most common business processes included multiple transactions and cut across more than one functional area or software module. Figure 2 outlines the process of taking a

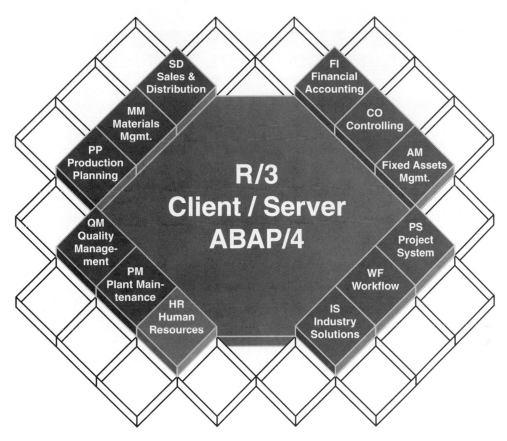

EXHIBIT 2 Functions Included in SAP's R/3 System
Diagram trademark of SAP

customer order, and shows the SAP modules involved at each step. It shows that without ERP this process could involve three separate information systems—Sales and Distribution, MRP, and Accounting and Financials. With R/3, each step would require a different transaction screen, but they would all be part of the same system. They would thus be sharing and updating the same information. This elimination of redundant entry and "hand-offs" between applications was one of the chief advantages of ERP systems.

R/3 Usage: System Configuration

Configuration Tables. Although R/3 was intended as a "standard" application that did not require significant modification for each customer, it was still necessary to configure the system to meet a company's specific requirements. Configuration was accomplished by changing settings in R/3 configuration tables.

R/3's approximately 8000 tables defined every aspect of how the system functioned and how users interacted with it; in other words, they defined how all transaction screens would look and work. To configure their system, installers typically built models of how a process should work, then turned these into 'scripts,' and finally translated scripts into table settings. For example, after writing a script that defined how a new customer order would be entered, Vandelay would know whether the order taker should have the ability to override the product's "price" field on the order entry screen.

During an implementation, this configuration activity had to be replicated for all relevant processes and required a great deal of time and expertise. People who were adept at this work, and who understood the impact of each table change, were a feature of every R/3 implementation. Kramer would be relying on several of them at ICS to work closely with the Vandelay project team.

EXHIBIT 3 Sample SAP Screen

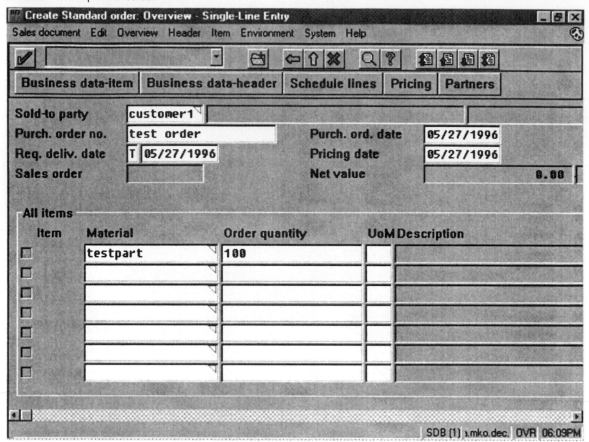

© 1996 SAP America, Inc.

FIGURE 2 SAP Modules Involved in a Single Business Process

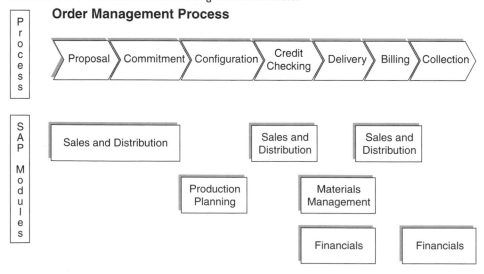

Added Functionality. Although the R/3 system was generally recognized to contain more functionality than its competition, it typically could only satisfy 80–95% of a large company's specific business requirements through standard configuration table setting work.[3] The remaining functionality could be obtained in four ways:

- Interfacing R/3 to existing legacy systems

- Interfacing R/3 to other packaged software serving as "point solutions" for specific tasks

- Developing custom software that extended R/3's functionality, and was accessed through standard application program interfaces

- Modifying the R/3 source code directly (This approach was strongly discouraged by SAP and could lead to a loss of support for the software.)

THE CONSULTANTS: DELOITTE & TOUCHE CONSULTING GROUP/ICS

Company Background

Deloitte & Touche Consulting Group (the Consulting Group) was the consulting division of Deloitte & Touche, one of the 'Big 6' audit and tax firms and the product of the 1989 merger of Deloitte, Haskins & Sells and Touche Ross. Consulting had been an important activity for the predecessor firms since the 1950s, and accounted for over 15% of total Deloitte & Touche revenues by the mid-1990s.[4] In 1995, the Consulting Group generated slightly over $1 billion in revenues and employed 8,000 professionals in more than 100 countries.

Deloitte & Touche Consulting Group/ICS was the subsidiary of the Consulting Group which specialized in SAP implementations, offering complementary software products, education and training, and consulting in business process reengineering and change management. ICS was one of the largest worldwide providers of SAP implementation services and one of the most rapidly growing sections of the Consulting Group, employing over 1300 professionals on four continents in 1995.

ICS had developed a considerable knowledge base in SAP systems; over 50% of its consultants had more than two years experience with the products. ICS had won SAP's Award of Excellence, which was based on customer satisfaction surveys administered by the software maker, every year since its inception. SAP had also named ICS as an 'R/3 Global Logo Partner.' According to SAP,[5]

> The aim of these partnerships is to establish, extend and enhance R/3 expertise. In order to keep these logo partners up to date with the latest developments, SAP maintains very close contact with them, providing an intensive flow of information and offering the following services:
>
> - an R/3 System for internal training;
> - regular R/3 logo partner forums, workshops and training sessions;
> - access to SAP InfoLine, SAP's internal information system;
> - second level support from SAP Consulting, including the consultant hotline.

ICS professionals ranged from general management consultants to SAP specialists. The specialists focused on a functional or technical area of SAP and worked as, for example, experts on the Materials Management functions or programmers in the systems' native ABAP/4 language. Management consultants, meanwhile, had experience with process re-design, systems implementation, change management, or project management. More senior personnel often combined both types of skills.

Technology-Enabled Change

ICS consultants had adopted a common set of principles for leading large-scale change in a firm. According to Kramer:

> Change occurs at several levels in an organization: strategy, process, people, and technology. Depending on the particular client situation, there are two approaches which can be taken. The first is 'clean sheet,' where all four dimensions of organizational change are explored without constraints. The second is 'technology-enabled change.' In this situation, the primary technology is selected early in the process and more strongly influences the other three dimensions of strategy, people, and processes, but still en-

[3] According to an SAP estimate
[4] "Professional Service Trends: Deloitte & Touche" Dataquest ® report, February 25, 1994

[5] From SAP Web site. http://www.sap.com. Downloaded 3/1/96

ables significant overall business change. The introduction of powerful, flexible, enterprise-wide solutions such as SAP is driving this approach as clients are looking to concurrently replace mainframe legacy systems *and* achieve significant operating improvement.

The 'right' approach to change is determined based on client's situation. In Vandelay's case, the latter approach is more appropriate since they have already made the decision to go with SAP. To guide a client through all phases of implementation, ICS uses a structured approach tailored to the client's situation. This methodology captures the collective learning of the practitioners and creates a roadmap for the SAP implementation.

Figure 3 illustrates how ICS viewed the difference between the 'technology-enabled' and 'clean sheet' approaches to process redesign.

THE VANDELAY PROJECT

Vandelay management projected that the implementation would take 18 months and require the full-time efforts of 50 people, including consultants

(both process redesigners and SAP specialists) and employees, as well as part-time involvement from many employees at each site. The total budget for the project was $20 million, including hardware, software, consulting fees, and the salaries and expenses of involved employees. Based on her prior experiences, Kramer felt that the timeline and budget were very aggressive for the scope of the implementation; she wondered whether all of the elements were in place to achieve the desired change.

R/3 software was to be implemented at Vandelay's eight manufacturing sites and four order entry locations,[6] and at the corporate headquarters in Minnesota. The plant installations would take the longest; each one would require a lengthy preparation period to align its operations with the new business practices. Kramer estimated that two thirds of all Vandelay employees would need training on how to use the new system, with the amount

---

[6] Order entry locations: 2 in North America, 1 in Europe, and 1 in Asia.

FIGURE 3 ICS's View of Two Models for Business Process Re-design

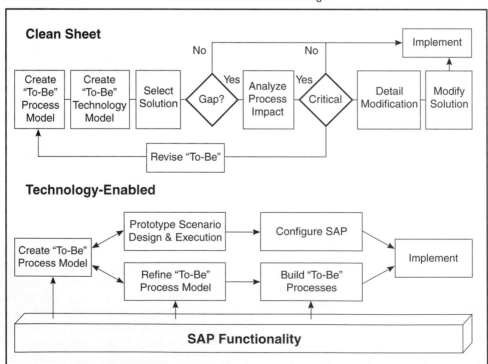

of training required ranging from one day for casual users to two weeks for those who would use R/3 heavily in their jobs.

Initially, the project team would focus about 80% of its effort on designing the "to be" process model of the organization, and 20% on issues relating to the system implementation. This reflected the fact that the project would begin by establishing the need for business change and setting performance targets, rather than installing software. In the later phases of the implementation the required mix of consulting skills would shift to deeper SAP expertise. During the activities of system configuration, testing, and delivery, the emphasis would be reversed; 80% concentration on SAP implementation, 20% on process design.

Team Structure

As Kramer put it:

> A project like this one requires a variety of skills. I think the most important are project management ability, SAP expertise, business and industry understanding, systems implementation experience, and change leadership talent. We'll need to field a joint client/consultant team with the right mix of skills at the right time.

Vandelay and ICS had decided to use two teams for managing the project. While senior management on the steering committee would decide strategic issues relating to the implementation, Table 1 shows that the project team would be responsible for the bulk of the decisions made, and for the ones which determined how the system would actually work. For this reason, Kramer was eager to structure this team correctly.

Kramer's experience had shown her that there were two basic ways to select participants for the project team. She could simply present a list of the required skills and characteristics for team members to senior-level management and ask them to nominate and approach the people who they felt would be best for the job. Alternatively, she could mandate that the team contain at least one representative from each of Vandelay's implementation sites around the world. While this approach might sacrifice some quality and depth on the team, it could also help to ensure that each site would have a project champion from the outset.

Managing Change

Selecting the best development team was only one of Kramer's considerations as she prepared to dig in on the Vandelay engagement. She had led ERP implementations before and was aware of the challenges involved in assisting a large organization as it attempted to change and standardize its practices. She placed these challenges into a few categories:

Centralization vs. Autonomy. There was no way to involve all users in the decisions that would affect them and their jobs. This could create a strong temptation for people to second guess these choices, and to alter the system that was delivered to them. This was especially true at Vandelay, which had a strong tradition of encouraging innovation and autonomy among its employees, as George Hall had demonstrated. Should this tinkering be encouraged, or should systems and processes be 'locked-down' as much as possible? Could Kramer and her teams be confident that

	Team Composition and		% of Total Issues
Team Name	Time Commitment	Issues Addressed by Team	Addressed by Team
Steering Committee	Division VPs 8 people, meeting monthly	*Business Strategy,* e.g. sequence of site installations, planned changes in mfg. strategy.	5%
Project Team	Operations employees, e.g. planner/buyers, financial accountants: 20 people, full-time.*	*Implementation specifics:,* e.g. rules for reserving inventory for a customer order, horizons for planning and scheduling.	95%

TABLE 1 Vandelay Project Team Structure

*Includes only client business operations team members; does not include consultants, IT resources, or other staff for project activities such as testing, training, and documentation.

their decisions were the right ones throughout Vandelay? If so, should processes be tightly centralized and controlled, and tinkering (and therefore possible innovation) strongly discouraged? If not, what was the point of the long and thorough development and implementation cycle? Kramer had a strong bias toward "input by many, design by few," but how could she put this rule into practice?

She knew that this issue was particularly important for global companies like Vandelay. Just as cultures and currencies varied across countries, so did standard business practices, outlooks, and relationships between customers and suppliers. The implementation team would have to be sure that any universal processes did not run afoul of local ones.

A closely related question concerned standardization on externally defined 'best practices.' Much of the consultants' expertise came from their previous engagements; they knew what had worked and what hadn't for other clients. In addition, SAP's standard capabilities were the result of the firm's accumulated knowledge about the requirements for ERP software. There was thus a set of outside practices involving systems, operations, and processes that could be used at Vandelay. Kramer wondered how they should be incorporated into the project—were they a starting point or the final word?

Kramer could already see one area where plants would have to give up some of their autonomy. R/3 required that each item have a single, unique part number, and Vandelay executives wanted common part numbers across all sites so they could see accurate consolidated information about production, orders, and sales. Each plant, however, had developed its own internal part numbering system over time. Replacing these schemes would be a major effort, involving everything from stockroom storage bins to engineering drawings to part stamping equipment. In addition, plant personnel would have to forget the previous numbers, which they often knew by heart. Kramer saw that part number standardization would be part of the Vandelay R/3 implementation, that the plants would probably resist it, and that they would have no choice in the matter.

Change Agents and Organizational Inertia. Kramer also knew from experience that large implementations went best when a critical mass of early leaders—people who were enthusiastic about the work of change and who were respected within the firm—had been built. She also knew, however, that even with committed change agents in place, most people did not completely accept a new system until they really believed that it was inevitable. She found this paradoxical; companies committed substantial resources up front and stated clearly that the new system was a given, but most employees remained skeptical for a long time. Why was this, and what could she and her early movers do about it?

Software. Although R/3 had broad capability, there would be situations where it would not exactly fit the desired Vandelay process design. Kramer had observed three primary alternatives to addressing this situation:

1. Change the business process to match the capabilities of the software
2. Interface R/3 to another package or custom solution
3. Extend the R/3 system to precisely match the business requirements.

What guidelines should she follow in selecting among these options?

Kramer knew that she would have to get back to George Hall soon about training for his site, but she was unsure what to tell him. If his people weren't allowed to experiment with the system as much as they wanted, would his enthusiasm for the project turn into hostility?

CASE 16

Kanebo Ltd.

INTRODUCTION

In early 1988, senior managers of the Cosmetics Division of Kanebo Ltd. were preparing to implement a strategy for improving their responsiveness to consumer demand. The strategy consisted of two parts. First, they proposed to introduce a new POS (point of sale) information system that they hoped would both stimulate demand for Kanebo products and eventually make it possible to obtain accurate, up-to-date sales information from the division's 30,000 retail outlets around Japan. This would enable them to identify products that were selling much better or worse than expected, so they could make changes in both their production schedules and their marketing approaches.

But the equipment and workforce policies in use at their Odawara factory prevented it from being able to respond as quickly as the new market information required. Therefore, the second part of the new strategy was to invest as much as ¥2 billion[1] at Odawara in new "FMS" flexible manufacturing lines. These lines not only would require fewer workers and be able to change from one product to another much faster than could the existing lines, but they could also be run with a skeleton crew at nights and on weekends, when the factory normally was shut down. The ultimate goal of this combination of POS and FMS was to be able to respond promptly—and, in fact, automatically—to unexpected changes in the demand for any of Kanebo's products.

---

[1] ¥127 = U.S.$1.00, approximately, at the time of this case. At this rate of exchange, a simple way to estimate the dollar equivalent of a Yen amount is by dividing it by 1000 and then multiplying the result by 8.

This case was prepared as the basis for class discussion rather than to illustrate either effective or ineffective handling of an administrative situation. Certain information has been disguised.

This case was prepared by Robert H. Hayes and Hirokaza Kono. Copyright © 1991 by the President and Fellows of Harvard College. Harvard Business School case 691-105.

Recently, however, a number of people had begun to express concerns about both projects. One group was uneasy about basing the new POS system on NTT's (Nippon Telephone and Telegraph's) new nationwide video-text system. The NTT system allowed users to gain instantaneous access to a large central information bank through a simple video terminal. Kanebo had modified and expanded this system so that the stores could also gain access to information about specific Kanebo products and advice about how to deal with typical skin or beauty problems. Even more important, the Kanebo system was equipped with a bar code detector that made it possible for store managers to record automatically information about customer purchases onto a memory card. At the end of each day, the contents of this memory card could be transmitted back to Cosmetics Division headquarters for analysis. This would make it possible both to institute corrective action, if necessary, and to compare the performance of different stores.

Unfortunately, NTT had recently run a test of its new system in one small region in Japan and had experienced disappointing results. Not enough people had signed up to use the system, even at a heavily discounted leasing price, and many of those who did had experienced difficulties with it. Few had renewed their subscriptions to the system after the trial period. Rather than attach Kanebo's POS system to an NTT system that had lost much of its credibility, some Cosmetics Division managers argued for a whole new approach. They recommended that Kanebo develop a system based on low-cost personal computers, which could transmit data periodically to headquarters through standard telephone lines.

Concerns were also being expressed about the factory automation project. While the pilot model of the new FMS packaging line required many fewer workers than existing lines, and less time to make changeovers between products, some managers felt that the degree of improvement still was not sufficient to justify its cost. "The goal was to reduce the number of workers to at most one or two, and to make a changeover in less than 10 minutes," explained one. "But at present it looks as though at least three people will be required, and the changeover time is closer to an hour than 10 minutes. Moreover, small bottles still can not be produced efficiently on the FMS. Perhaps we should wait until the system is operating closer to its goals before putting it into our factory."

These concerns and suggestions for alternative approaches were reported to Mr. Kazutomo Ishizawa, Kanebo's president and one of the early advocates of such a system. Although he still felt that the Cosmetics Division needed to become more responsive to market changes, it no longer was clear to him that the approach being proposed was the best one for Kanebo. On the other hand, he felt it was important for the organization to improve its flexibility, and was concerned that waiting for the development of a whole new approach might cause an unacceptable delay in making this improvement.

COMPANY BACKGROUND

Kanebo celebrated its 100th birthday in 1987, making it one of Japan's oldest companies. At one point in the 1930s it was also the largest, in terms of sales, privately-owned company in Japan. Its corporate symbol—a ringing bell (the Japanese word "kane" means "bell")—was well known throughout the country because of the company's age and size, as well as its penetration into a number of consumer markets. In 1987 its nearly 9,000 employees generated sales of over ¥380 billion, and a profit after tax of ¥2.3 billion. Additional financial information is contained in Exhibit 1.

Kanebo limited its activities to the textile and related industries for most of its first 75 years, but in 1961 it began a broad program of diversification. Beginning with toiletries and cosmetics, it gradually added specialty foods, pharmaceuticals, housing and environmental products, industrial materials, electronics (including the production of integrated circuits), and information systems. In 1981 it announced that in the future it would place top priority on its fashion, cosmetics, and pharmaceutical businesses, while deemphasizing standard textile products.

By 1988, textiles and fashion products still represented almost 50% of total sales, while cosmetics and toiletries accounted for about 30%. Most of these sales occurred within Japan, but international sales—particularly of cosmetics—were becoming more important. Some of Kanebo's production of textiles was carried out by affiliated

EXHIBIT I   Financial Summary (in ¥ billion)[a]

	1987	1986	1985	1984
Net sales[b]	381.8[(29.0)]	352.5[(33.8)]	330.8[(35.3)]	326.5[(34.8)]
Cost of goods sold	266.9	249.7	236.3	236.0
Sales and administrative costs	90.5	83.7	74.4	70.9
Operating Earnings	24.4	19.1	20.1	19.6
Nonoperating expenses (including net interest)	17.2	13.0	12.0	12.3
	—	—	—	—
Ordinary earnings	7.2	6.1	8.1	7.3
Earnings before taxes (after extraordinary earnings and expenses)	5.2	5.2	5.0	5.7
Net earnings	2.3	2.8	2.8	2.4
Assets:				
Current	299.9	268.0	235.3	236.5
Fixed	171.5	159.2	107.1	111.8
Total assets (including deferred assets)	478.5	434.5	349.1	354.4
Liabilities:				
Current	355.4	314.0	241.9	250.7
Long-term	73.9	72.0	62.5	60.3
Stockholders' Equity	49.2	48.5	44.7	43.3

[a]Fiscal years ending March 31 in 1988, and April 30 in other years
[b]Cosmetic sales, as percent of total, are contained in parentheses

companies in other countries. Aside from a small cosmetics factory in Taiwan and a small independent joint venture in Europe, however, the production of all other products took place in Japan. The increasing value of the Yen relative to most other currencies therefore was making it more and more difficult for Kanebo to compete in foreign markets.

Although corporate headquarters was in Osaka, Kanebo's fashion, cosmetics, pharmaceuticals, and foodstuffs divisions all had their headquarters in Tokyo. Each division was given considerable autonomy, and conducted its own R&D. The company also had a central R&D Laboratory that focused on three fields having broad application across the different divisions: biotechnology, electronics/information systems, and new materials/polymer chemistry. Its goal was to identify technological synergies among the various divisions, and ensure that technological developments in one part of the company could be exploited by others.

THE COSMETICS DIVISION: MARKETING

After growing rapidly in the 1960s and early 1970s, Japan's cosmetics industry appeared to have matured by the mid-1980s. The industry growth rate fell below 10% in 1977 and to less than 1% in 1987. As the growth rate fell, competition intensified among the many companies competing for a share of this market. Shiseido, the largest of these companies, held about 28% of the market while Kanebo, the second largest, held about 13%. Other companies, such as Clinique and Estee Lauder, tended to specialize in particular market niches. Giant Kao, sometimes called the "Procter & Gamble of Japan," focused primarily on low-cost, high-volume cosmetics and toiletries. It held only about 3% of the market for major cosmetic products.

In the face of this stiffening competition, which both reduced its gross margins and caused its growth to stagnate, Kanebo put increasing emphasis on innovation and customer service. Introducing new products at a rapid rate, its product line grew from about 1,100 to almost 2,500 items between 1980 and 1988; this included over 200 shades of lipstick alone. (Exhibit 2 depicts a representative sample of these products.) Many of these new products were seasonal, in that their colors

and scents were tailored to a specific time of the year.

Periodic conferences, which included sales managers, store managers, beauty consultants, and Cosmetics Division personnel, were held to choose the products that were to be made the focus of new promotional campaigns. These campaigns generally lasted two to three months, and featured catchy songs, pretty "campaign girls," and heavy advertising. In 1988, products promoted in this way accounted for about 20% of Kanebo's units sold, and 40% of its total sales revenue.

As a result, cosmetics products increasingly displayed the characteristics of fashion items, making it difficult to predict the likely demand for individual items. The demand for the most popular shade of lipstick, for example, was often more than 100 times that of the least popular. By the time Kanebo became aware that one of its newer products was selling much better than expected, it was often too late to increase production before that item's selling season was over. The Cosmetics Division estimated it had lost over ¥1 billion in sales because of stockouts during 1987 alone.

Different competitors chose different approaches to distributing their products. Shiseido and Kanebo, among others, used the "Seido-hin" system, in which wholly owned sales companies were responsible for all sales within specific geographic regions. Each sales company purchased products from its parent company and distributed them through a large number of independent retail outlets in its territory. Kanebo, for example, owned 72 sales companies, which served 30,000 retail outlets throughout Japan with a sales force of about 1,100 salesmen (called Area Managers). Almost 80% of these outlets were chain stores, while supermarkets, department and convenience stores accounted for the rest.

Most of these retail shops were quite small in size; only about 13% of them sold more than ¥1.5 million worth of Kanebo products a month, while almost half sold less than ¥450,000. Their average monthly sales was about ¥600,000. Slightly more than half of them handled Kanebo products exclusively, and they accounted for about 45% of total Kanebo sales. The others offered competing products as well, which made them somewhat difficult to control. Much of a salesman's time, therefore, was devoted to cultivating relationships with store owners and motivating them to sell his products rather than those of other companies.

EXHIBIT 2 Kanebo Cosmetics Products

[1] Alga Milky Lotion (Skin Moisturizer: 80 ml., ¥2500)
[2] Alga Lotion (Skin Conditioner: 150 ml., ¥2500)
[3] Faircrea Whitening Lotion (Skin care for sun exposure: 150 ml., ¥3800)
[4] Alga Soap (Scrubbing Facial Soap: 120 gr., ¥2500)
[5] Chyria Milky Water (Skin Moisturizer: 170 ml., ¥4000)
[6] DaDa Essence (Medicated Skin Conditioner: 30 ml., ¥10,000)
[7] Blanchir Whitening Spots (Sun Shield and Conditioner: 2 @ 15 ml., ¥10,000)
[8] Affinique Summer Foundation (Cream Foundation with special applicator: 35 gr., 15 ml., ¥10,000)
[9] RS-102 Lipstick (¥3500)
[10] Raphaie RS-75 Lipstick (¥4500)

Moreover, these small stores usually were managed in a very informal way, and decisions were made in an ad hoc manner. They seldom carried enough inventory of all products, and therefore expected delivery of items ordered from the sales company within a day or two.

Salesmen were hired by Kanebo itself, and underwent one year of training at one of the sales companies. A typical salesman was responsible for about 26 stores, and visited 8 to 10 per day. During their periodic visits to stores they confirmed the delivery of previously-ordered items, checked the stock of Kanebo products (which was the only way to get an accurate estimate of actual sales), took orders for additional items, informed store personnel about new products, and answered whatever consumer questions had arisen.

The store, in turn, could ask the salesman to return unsold stock to the sales company for credit. One of a salesman's most important tasks, therefore, was to limit the amount of returned merchandise by maintaining good communication with store managers. Salesmen prided themselves on their knowledge of local market conditions and trends, as well as the situation at each of their retail stores. They were paid a monthly salary, plus incentives based on actual sales. Other companies, particularly those specializing in very high priced items, had adopted a much different system in which the sales companies that distributed their products were independently owned. Moreover, the sales forces of these sales companies sold their products directly to customers through personal visits to their homes or offices. Finally, Kao and other companies that emphasized lower priced items used still another approach—the so-called "Ippan-hin" system—in which they distributed their products through huge independent wholesalers. These wholesalers serviced the whole range of retail outlets, from small specialty and grocery stores to large department stores. Kanebo itself increasingly was using an Ippan-hin system for distributing its line of toiletries.

In 1988, companies using the Seido-hin system accounted for just under 40% of cosmetics sales in Japan, whereas those using the Ippan-hin system accounted for just under 30%. There was evidence, however, that the latter companies were slowly gaining market share from those that used other systems. It was suspected that this was largely due to the growing acceptance of lower priced items, particularly among young people.

Despite the recent slowdown in the growth of cosmetics sales in Japan, some industry observers predicted renewed growth during the 1990s. This resurgence would be based, they felt, on both Japan's growing affluence and its changing demographics and behavior patterns. Not only were younger women increasingly using cosmetics, but so were women over 40—and the number of people in this latter category was increasing rapidly as Japan's population aged. These trends were expected not only to encourage growth in the cosmetics market, but to cause it to fragment as well. As Japanese women broadened the range of activities they engaged in, to include travel, sports, and cultural pursuits, they demanded a broader range of colors and styles.

They also wanted more and better information to guide them when buying cosmetics. Kanebo's marketing department estimated that only about 30% of its products were "self-selling," in that customers did not request any advice or other assistance from a sales person when making the purchase decision. Partly because of this, small retail stores (which had limited product lines and expertise) were expected to lose their attractiveness, relative to the larger department and retail stores, to this new breed of consumers.

COSMETICS DIVISION: MANUFACTURING

Just over 50% of the bottling and packaging of Kanebo's cosmetics took place at its factory in Odawara, Japan, about 40 miles southwest of Tokyo. Lower cost, less fashionable items tended to be sourced from subcontractors in Japan, who primarily packaged formulations that were produced in bulk at Odawara. Shipping costs and legal restrictions combined to make it impractical to supply Kanebo's Japanese customers with products packaged at its factory in Taiwan.

The Odawara complex consisted of the factory itself, an administration building, two technology centers (one specializing in biotech research), a raw material warehouse, and separate dormitories for unmarried men and women. It employed about 350 people, of whom over two-thirds were women and 15% worked part-time. The factory usually operated one 7.5 hour shift each weekday, and one every other Saturday. Under Japanese law, women were not allowed to work after 10 o'clock at night. Because of the tight labor market in Japan, it was becoming increasingly difficult to recruit people to do factory work—much less at night or on weekends.

A typical factory worker at Odawara earned about ¥1.6 million per year in salary and another ¥750,000 in bonuses. In addition, Kanebo paid roughly ¥150,000 for social benefits. Workers received a 20% premium for working beyond the usual quitting time; such overtime, however, was limited for women workers to three hours a day, six hours per week, and 150 hours per year. Workers also received a 50% premium for working after midnight or on holidays.

The factory produced three major types of products; skin care (largely creams and lotions), makeup (lipsticks and face powder), and fragrances (perfumes and toilet water). Most used the same batch production process, which involved four separate stages. First, ingredients were measured into a stainless steel vat, following the directions of a recipe stored in the factory's computer. Liquid ingredients were introduced directly, under computer control, while operators measured dry ingredients on an electronic scale following directions displayed on a computer video terminal. The capacity of these vats ranged from 2,400 to 5,000 kilograms. The batch sizes of emulsified products could be as low as 200 kg. or as high as 5,000, and averaged about 1,300.

Next, these materials were heated and mixed. In the latter stages of this emulsifying process, a semi-vacuum was introduced into the vat to facilitate the removal of air in the mixture as it was gradually cooled back to room temperature. The mixing/degassing/cooling stage required about two hours, most of which time was consumed by the cooling process. After cooling, the mixture was inspected and held in storage vats for several hours (or several weeks, in the case of perfumes) so that it could stabilize.

After this stabilization period the mixture was transferred through glass tubes to one of the plant's 23 bottling/packaging lines. Four of these lines were dedicated to lipsticks and three to foundation powders. A typical bottling/packaging line was staffed by nearly 20 workers, and operated at a rate of between 1,500 and 7,500 units per hour (averaging about 5,000 per hour for bottled products and 1,500 per hour for lipsticks). A nonstandard item requiring special packaging might need as many as 25 workers, however. After packaging, the finished item was again inspected and shipped immediately to the Division's nearby central warehouse. From there it was sent to one of nine distribution centers around the country. It took three days, on average, for a product to proceed from unmeasured raw material to finished goods. Once packaged, it could be delivered to a retail store within 5 days.

The containers used for skin care products, which consumed the bulk of the bottling activity at Odawara, consisted of three basic types: bottles, tubes, and jars. Each of these, in turn, came in three basic sizes: small, medium, and large. Additional complications were introduced by the fact that some bottles were of the "pour" type, while others were of the "pump" type. Because of the difficulty of changing over a bottling line from one of these type-size combinations to another, each line was

dedicated to one such combination. As a result, on any given day some of Odawara's lines would be operating at capacity while others would be idle—but the lines falling into each category were constantly changing.

This made it difficult to calculate the factory's capacity, particularly for skin care products. Because it involved fewer lines and container shapes, the packaging capacity for lipsticks was somewhat easier to determine. It was estimated to be about 1.2 million units per month, somewhat greater than the average lipstick demand of about 935,000 units per month. Demand had risen to almost 2.5 million units a month during peak selling periods, however.

The cost structure for cosmetics varied by item and price level, but the usual practice of companies using the Seido-hin system was for a sales company to sell products to its retail stores for about 20% more than the price it paid its parent company. The retail store, in turn, priced the product so as to receive a margin of somewhat over 50%. The factory's total manufacturing cost was usually about 30% of its selling price to the sales company, and raw materials (including packaging materials) accounted for about 75% of this. Direct and indirect labor, depreciation, and light and power costs accounted for the other 25%.

The factory had been continually examining and improving its performance, concentrating in recent years on reducing costs and improving its ability to produce small lots economically. For example, cleaning out the glass transfer tubes between batches had been reduced from 90 to 30 minutes in 1984, when a steam cleaning process had been introduced. Changing over a packaging line to a new container shape or size used to take two skilled workers about half a shift. Recently, however, the changeover time had been reduced to about 1.5 hours on average (and, in some cases, to less than one hour), and could be carried out by one unskilled worker. Similarly, the factory's production lead time—from ordering materials to final shipment—had been reduced from 75 to 45 days, largely through improvements in its raw material ordering process and production scheduling system. It was now limited primarily by the time required to obtain packaging materials.

Despite such improvements, increasing the number of different products produced at the factory had dramatically reduced its effective capacity. In an effort to reduce the time lost through changeovers, Kanebo had worked to rationalize its product line. For example, it had redesigned its lipstick products so that three basic holders (which could be embellished in a variety of ways) replaced the 30 holders offered previously.

Scheduling production for the factory took place through a hierarchical process. First, the 72 sales companies estimated the demand a year ahead for each of Kanebo's products. These estimates were combined and used as input to a computerized demand forecasting system that incorporated each item's demand history (if such historical data were available). From the resulting forecast an aggregate production schedule was prepared for the next three months and used as the basis for ordering raw materials from suppliers. A detailed production schedule, divided up into three 10-day periods, was prepared a month in advance and "rolled forward" every 10 days. This schedule indicated when a given product could be delivered to retail stores. Factory management had some freedom to revise daily production schedules to reflect the availability of specific equipment and raw materials. Preparing and implementing new production schedules was not an easy task, both because the number of workers assigned to a given packaging line could vary according to the product and line specifications, and because the difficulty of hiring new factory workers required that the existing labor force be fully utilized.

Because the total capacity of the factory's skin care packaging lines exceeded the average demand rate, each line was in operation only about half the time. When operating, a line typically produced two different products during each shift; the average run length was roughly one month's estimated sales. About two weeks' worth of raw materials were held at Odawara, which facilitated changes in the production schedule if they became necessary. The factory's ability to change production volumes was limited, however, by the fact that it usually took over a month to obtain packaging materials from suppliers.

In addition, nearly two months' worth of packaged products, on average, were held in Kanebo's distribution system. Because of the extremely seasonal nature of demand, production of most items had to begin well in advance of the target selling period. Kanebo was willing to hold as much as three months' supply of an item if it was

sure it could be sold. Nevertheless, sales companies quickly ran out of products that sold much better than forecasted, while they had to take back products whose sales were well below forecast. The value of such returned products had been somewhat over ¥2 billion in 1987, and most of them were thrown away.

IMPROVING THE FLOW OF INFORMATION FROM RETAIL STORES

Relying on salesmen to transmit information, recorded by hand, about estimated sales at the stores they visited made it difficult for Cosmetics Division managers to get accurate, timely data about retail sales trends. The variation in total demand from month to month made it even more difficult to predict the demand for individual items accurately enough to ensure adequate supplies from the factory. Therefore, the Cosmetics Division had been working for several years to develop better methods for obtaining data about product sales from its retail stores.

Its first attempt was the so-called "Sellable Store" system, which was introduced in 1983. This system combined a POS terminal with a personal computer, and was designed for large retail stores. Such stores not only wanted to keep accurate records of the sales and inventories of different items, but also needed to maintain background information and purchase histories for individual "Member Customers." These were repeat buyers whose business was cultivated through individualized attention, including telephone calls and frequent mailings providing information about new products, skin problems, or beauty tips. The Sellable Stores system maintained these customer files, and also could generate product reorders and promotional letters automatically.

The number of stores that were potential users of this system was limited, however, by the system's monthly leasing cost of ¥30,000 to ¥50,000 and the burden of maintaining up-to-date information about customers' changing needs and preferences. The 500 or so stores that kept records for over 1,000 Member Customers each were potential users; they accounted for over 700,000 Kanebo customers. A sample of this size was expected to provide a useful indication of the purchasing behavior of the other six million or so regular buyers of Kanebo cosmetics. By early 1988 about 150 stores had adopted the system.

By 1985, with the Sellable Store system launched, Kanebo's attention turned to the development of a simpler, lower cost system that would be more appropriate for servicing its smaller retail stores. In 1987 it began experimenting with an "Electronic Diary," a hand-held computer with a removable IC Memory card that salesmen used to record the stocks of various Kanebo products in the stores they called on. Periodically the information on this memory card was transmitted to Division headquarters, and used in estimating sales rates. The capability of this simple device was limited, however, by the frequency with which the salesman could call upon a store and count its stocks.

Dissatisfaction with this approach led Kanebo to begin designing a simpler version of the Sellable Stores system. This new system would not be required to maintain individual customer files, so would not have to accept information from a keyboard, but would provide information about the daily sales of each product. This would both facilitate the reordering process and provide more accurate information about demand patterns for diagnostic purposes. It was known that both Shiseido and Kao were developing such systems.

There was debate among Kanebo managers about the relative merits of a system based on a low-cost personal computer, which could both provide promotional information at the store level and collect sales data for periodic transmission to headquarters, or one based on a large telecommunications network. The second type of system could provide a wider range of more sophisticated information through a powerful central computer. The systems being designed by Shiseido and Kao were of the first type, but Kanebo was leaning toward adopting the second. Personal computers with sufficient capabilities cost around 800,000 yen without a printer. Although they could transmit 80 to 100 characters per second, transmission of graphic material took much longer, and retail stores were required to input information through a typewriter keyboard. Kanebo proposed to build a system around NTT's newly developed CAPTAIN (Character And Pattern Telephone Access Information Network) system, which was expected to have about 80,000 subscribers by the end of 1988 and 110,000 by the end of 1990. If it went ahead with this approach, Kanebo would be the first company

in Japan to base a nationwide retail store information system on the CAPTAIN system.

The proposed "BellCap" (a combination of Kanebo's familiar symbol and CAPTAIN) system was composed of a POS register, equipped with a wand capable of reading bar-coded information that could then be stored on a removable IC memory card, and a low-cost color terminal attached to a telephone outlet. Kanebo was in the process of designing the POS register with Mitsubishi Electric, which would then manufacture them, while NTT would provide the terminal. Kanebo was modifying this terminal so that it could accept information from the removable memory card and transmit its contents periodically to division headquarters. It also proposed to design a low-cost printer to attach to the terminal; this would enable the store to obtain a hard copy of information displayed on the terminal. The terminal did not contain a keyboard, but the operator could request assistance and certain kinds of information by using the wand to select from among a number of bar-coded instructions. The system was designed to be simple enough that an eight-year-old child could operate it.

Data could be transmitted to the store's video terminal very rapidly, enabling "snapshot" images to be displayed (transmission took around 1 minute per single shot, about 4 times faster than if a personal computer were used). Sequences of such images could be used to promote selected products or assist in beauty consultation. The store could also use the system to keep track of inventories and transmit replenishment orders to its sales company, thereby speeding up the delivery of high selling items. Moreover, store managers and customers would have access to all the data in the CAPTAIN data bank. This enabled them to order tickets to various events, make hotel reservations, and obtain information about what nearby stores were having sales, where child care facilities were located, the weather forecast for different parts of Japan, etc. Finally, store managers could use the system to assist them in evaluating their store's performance and in guiding changes. For example, they could ask the system to provide graphs comparing their sales with those of the average store in Japan or their local area.

The great advantage of this system over a PC-based system was its very low telecommunication cost. The usual telephone charge for a local call in Japan was only ¥10 for three minutes, but this rate rose rapidly as the distance increased. For example, the same amount would pay for only 10 seconds of a call at night between Tokyo and Osaka, a distance of 300 miles. The cost of communicating anywhere in Japan over the CAPTAIN system, however, was ¥10 per minute during the day and ¥6 per minute at night. Large blocks of information could be transmitted very quickly to a BellCap terminal, which could then store this information in its memory for repeated play. As a result, it was anticipated that the store would only have to be connected to the system ten to twenty minutes each day.

The participation of Mitsubishi Electric, NTT, and NTS (the company providing the videotext network) in developing the BellCap system reduced Kanebo's development cost to about ¥35 million. Mitsubishi was not a market leader in the POS register business, and regarded the BellCap project as a way to acquire advanced technology and experience. Kanebo proposed to lease the BellCap system to stores at ¥12,000 per month, ¥5,000 less than its actual cost. Alternatively, stores could purchase the system for about ¥1 million, about 30% of which was for the CAPTAIN terminal. In either case the stores would pay their own transmission cost.

Through this system Kanebo hoped to achieve four goals. First, by establishing closer linkages with its stores and enabling them to provide better service to their customers, it hoped to build stronger loyalty to Kanebo products among store managers. This was particularly critical in the case of stores selling competitors' products as well as Kanebo's. Second, it hoped that store customers would be so pleased by the additional information the system made available to them that they would buy more Kanebo products. Third, Kanebo expected that the daily information provided by the system would help it in identifying emerging consumer trends. This would be useful in crafting promotional campaigns and guiding new product development.

Finally, access to daily information would help Kanebo improve the efficiency of both its marketing and manufacturing operations. Analysis of each store's sales would enable marketing to identify those stores that were selling certain products at more than the average rate (so that the approaches they were using could be studied and applied to other stores) or less (in which case they

might benefit from a salesman's assistance). Just as important, information about daily sales would improve production scheduling, and enable the factory to make better use of its limited capacity. Such information was particularly valuable early in a selling season, as Kanebo's marketing people believed the ultimate success of a newly-introduced product was largely determined during the first couple of weeks after its introduction.

Kanebo proposed to introduce the BellCap system, on an experimental basis, to 30 of its larger stores in late-1988. If it worked satisfactorily, another 400 stores would be added to the network. Assuming that enough stores volunteered to adopt BellCap, Kanebo hoped that 3,000 stores would be involved by 1993, and 7,000 by 1995. Moreover, direct transmission of orders would allow Kanebo to reduce from 250 to 100 the number of people currently occupied with receiving and summarizing the daily barrage of orders received by telephone and fax.

THE INTERNAL DEBATE

The critics of the proposed BellCap system were uneasy both about basing it on the CAPTAIN system and whether it would be accepted by the retail stores. Some argued against BellCap on technological grounds. "Already over two million people in Japan are using PC's," one person stated, "but only a few thousand have ever used the CAPTAIN system. Moreover, given the way computer technology is evolving it is reasonable to expect that soon we could install a very powerful PC, having much broader uses, in a store for less than the leasing cost of the BellCap system." Another pointed out that, while stores could receive information very quickly through the BellCap system, they could only transmit at a rate of 8 characters per second. "Transmitting sales information back to Division headquarters could turn out to be very expensive for them," he observed.

Others based their criticism on the effect the proposed system would have on store managers and Kanebo salesmen. "The stores will not adopt this system, even if we reduced its cost to nothing, unless they feel it will improve their sales and simplify their jobs," stated one person. "Instead, it appears to complicate their jobs, and it is not clear that it will improve their sales. Moreover, they will resist being monitored so closely."

Another talked about the reaction of Kanebo's salesmen. "The BellCap system will have to be sold to our retail stores and their managers trained to use it effectively. This will simply add to the burden on our salesmen, who already work very hard. And what will be their reward for this added work? If the computer becomes the source of all important information, and the main communication link with the company, what is there left for the salesman to do?" he asked. "And what pride can he take in his job?"

Still others observed that stores selling other companies' cosmetics (as well as Kanebo's) would probably be reluctant to use the BellCap system to record the sale of competitors' products, as this would transmit competitive information to Kanebo. This implied that they would have to use different methods for recording sales, depending on whose product was being purchased. Worse, when Shiseido came out with a competing system, the store might have to lease both systems—in addition to the electronic cash registers that many of them were already leasing.

Others pointed to the problems the BellCap system would create for manufacturing. "It will provide more data than the factory can use," argued one. "Our purchasing/manufacturing system is basically not very flexible, and continual changes in the production schedule will simply cause confusion and inefficiency." Another was concerned that faster feedback from the retail stores would simply relieve the sales organization of the pressure to develop good forecasts. "This just gives them an excuse to dump their mistakes on the factory more frequently, and expect it to solve their problems for them. Besides, getting more accurate forecasts requires that several thousand stores adopt BellCap, and even under the most optimistic projections we won't have that many stores on the system for at least five years."

Improving the factory's flexibility, of course, was the goal of the proposed FMS bottling line. Developing a prototype of this line had taken Kanebo engineers several years. It had been improved to the point where it could now change from one shaped bottle to another, under computer control, in less than one hour. At least three people were needed to operate the line, which bottled at the same rate as Kanebo's standard lines. The high cost of the FMS, combined with uncertainty about whether and when it would achieve its goals of single-digit (less than 10 minutes) changeover times and a single operator had delayed its introduction. Also, it was still not possible to handle very small (50 milliliter or less) bottles, which Kanebo used for its most expensive skin lotions. Finally, it was not known how much of the potential capacity of the FMS lines could be utilized. It was becoming so difficult to persuade workers to work outside of normal hours, many people felt it was unlikely the lines could be operated more than two shifts (90 hours) a week.

Converting an existing skin care bottling line to one that was both automated and could fill different sized bottles was estimated to cost about ¥270 million, while converting a lipstick line would cost over ¥120 million. These estimates were for hardware costs alone; the cost of the software that had been created by Kanebo personnel was not included. These costs were somewhat over twice the cost of one of the semi-automated bottling lines that Kanebo had purchased in the early 1980s.

"Clearly, it is difficult to justify such an expenditure on the basis of labor savings alone," commented Mr. Ishizawa. "But can we justify it on the basis of the additional flexibility it will give us? And how many new lines will we have to install in order to make a significant improvement in the ability of the factory to respond to large changes in sales forecasts?"

Deere & Company (A) The Computer-Aided Manufacturing Services Division (Abridged)

"A Window to the World"

Striding briskly across the glass-encased bridge leading to the main building of the Deere & Co. Administrative Center, Bill Rankin betrayed, in a broad smile, elation at having just received conditional approval to proceed with a plan to market some of the software and systems his division had developed over the past five years. Tom Hein and Dave Scott, managers in the Computer-Aided Manufacturing Service Division, were returning with Rankin from the meeting with some of the firm's senior executives. They had presented a business plan, developed with input from their engineers, that projected financial returns too good to be rejected. Nevertheless, their presentation had not been without some anxiety, for becoming a manufacturing systems software vendor represented a major departure from the John Deere tradition of being one of the world's foremost manufacturers of heavy duty agricultural and industrial equipment.

Rankin's presentation had stressed the potential benefits of the proposal beyond the revenues it could be expected to generate. He had argued that the venture would be "a window to the world" that, if properly exploited, would assure Deere of remaining a dominant manufacturing force internationally. Their conviction notwithstanding, Rankin and his managers were aware that final approval had been influenced as much by a prolonged depression in the firm's principal markets as by the strength of their arguments. The firm's earnings per share had fallen to a record low in the past year, and business conditions were not expected to improve in the short term.

A booming farm economy had encouraged farmers to invest in massive amounts of farm equipment during the 1970s. But as federal programs changed in the 1980s, consumer preferences in farm machinery shifted away from large "fully loaded" products toward equipment that performed basic tasks more productively and cost effectively. A similar trend toward smaller, more productive equipment also was evident in the industrial equipment market in which Deere competed, and was accompanied by vigorous price competition.

After a prolonged period of striving to adjust to the deepest farm recession in decades by reducing costs in its core business, Deere began to explore some additional sources of revenue, such as new product lines and services. Of particular interest were ventures that would provide some protection against the cyclical nature of its traditional businesses. A joint venture to manufacture diesel engines with General Motors was under investigation, along with plans to make the firm an even more dominant force in the lawn care products industry. Approval of the CAM services plan was in keeping with this willingness to entertain new ideas.

Rankin was aware that a number of problems remained unresolved. The conditional nature of the approval created a need to generate early sales, which was particularly worrisome because a ban on recruiting from outside the firm would force him to draw the salesforce from the existing group of engineers, none of whom had any sales experience. This would undoubtedly put some strain on the engineering resources available to the group, and Rankin was concerned that progress on new projects might be impaired. He also had to consider how to exploit the large potential market for his organization's services so as to maximize the benefits to Deere.

This abridged case was prepared as the basis for class discussion rather than to illustrate either effective or ineffective handling of an administrative situation.

This case was prepared by Robert H. Hayes. Copyright © 1992 by the President and Fellows of Harvard College. Harvard Business School case 693-051.

THE GROWTH OF A GIANT

In 1836, a young blacksmith, discouraged by the depressed business conditions in Vermont and the fires that twice had destroyed his shop, decided to seek his fortune in the West. Captivated by the beauty and fertility of the Rock River Valley, John Deere and some fellow Vermonters decided to settle in the small commune of Grand Detour, Illinois, where Deere established a new blacksmith shop. He soon learned that the plows brought west by the pioneers would not scour in the rich black soil of the prairies. Every few steps the iron moldboards, designed for sandy eastern soil, had to be scraped of the heavy soil that stuck to them. Many farmers were quitting the area in despair.

After experimenting with different shapes and materials for plow bottoms, in 1837, Deere developed the first successful self-polishing steel plow. In its first trial, the black earth fell smoothly away from the highly polished surface and curved shape of the moldboard and share. This new plow helped open the West to agricultural development.

As demand for his new ploughs increased, in 1847 Deere moved to Moline, Illinois, to take advantage of the transportation and water power provided by the Mississippi river. By 1850 production had reached 1,600 plows per year using special steel rolled to Deere's specifications by mills in Pittsburgh. Subsequently, Deere introduced the reaper and thresher as alternatives to more primitive harvesting methods. Over the next hundred years Deere and Company evolved into the largest producer of farm equipment in the world and a leading manufacturer of industrial equipment. In the decade of the 1970s alone, Deere's sales grew from $1.5 billion to $5.4 billion and its market share in farm equipment increased an estimated 35%. Its construction and industrial products businesses grew too, though less dramatically.

As Deere's volumes increased and new products were introduced, its factories tended to become larger and more complex. (See Exhibit 1.) Rankin observed:

> We're a very traditional company, and as we've grown slowly and deliberately, so also we've grown outward. With every increment of growth you don't have time to go back and erase the blackboard and redesign the facility. As product volumes change over time, and new products get introduced, things tend to get added on the periphery, resulting in a great deal of process complexity. If you take a top

view of a traditional manufacturing facility, like many of ours at the time, you'll see a complex material flow with material moving from building to building without any apparent rational pattern.

When the problem became pronounced in the early 1970s, Deere initiated a major modernization and reorganization program. At its largest manufacturing facility in Waterloo, Iowa, two new plants were constructed to simplify and "focus" manufacturing operations for a line of diesel engines and tractor assembly, while at the same time freeing space for other manufacturing activities.

THE GROUP TECHNOLOGY APPROACH

To aid in rationalizing the organization of the remainder of the factory, the Administrative Services Division proposed that "Group Technology" be utilized. This was a software-driven system for analyzing and classifying parts into groups, which facilitated the identification of parts whose function could be performed by other parts, the design of new parts that could replace several existing ones, and the creation of production processes that were customized to the needs of a part group.

Subsequently, a reorganization of machine tools in one part of the factory was undertaken using manufacturing cells as the fundamental building blocks. This involved moving away from large process-based departments to individual operating units that were designed to transform raw stock into finished parts as efficiently as possible. To minimize cross flow, manufacturing cells were designed to incorporate all, or nearly all, of the operations in their assigned part families. Encouraged by the success of these two projects, a Group Technology System department was established to advance the technique and make it more accessible to other divisions.

Tom Hein explained the objective of the group at the time.

> Group Technology was initially introduced simply because we had a reorganization problem in the plant and GT looked like the way to solve that problem. As we looked at other, related problems, however, the shortcomings of [our initial] system quickly became evident and, in 1978, we began developing our own proprietary GT system. As a starting point, we interviewed approximately 400 engineers throughout the company to determine

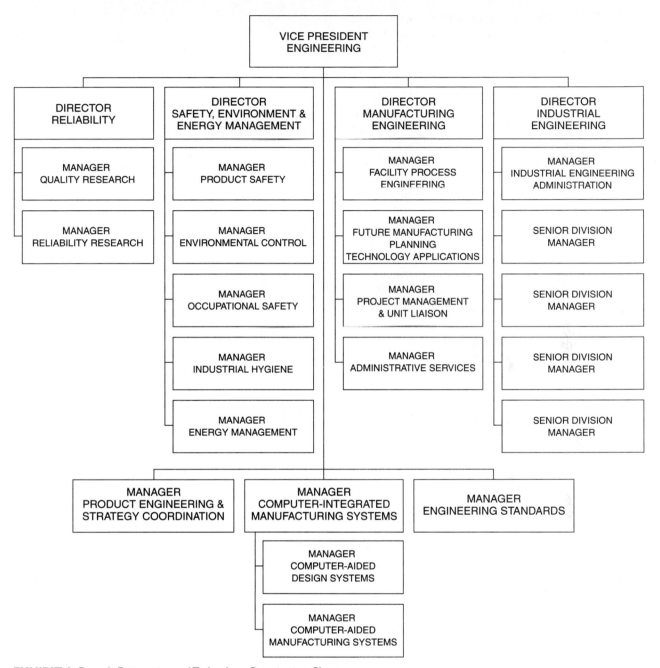

EXHIBIT 1 Deere's Engineering and Technology Organization Chart

what types of information about parts they required to do their jobs. The results of this exercise reinforced the idea that a new set of software tools had to be developed.

Fueled by internal demand for help in forming manufacturing cells, the department grew steadily and attracted some of Deere's best engineers. GT team members were also selected from among the region's top-of-the-class engineering students, who were attracted by the firm's stature as a leading edge manufacturer and major employer in the Midwest. Many of these students had advanced engineering degrees and some had obtained MBAs through evening programs, under an educational assistance program sponsored by Deere.

By 1982, the small, strained organization was evidencing a need for additional skills to assist in product development. Rankin was selected to head up the newly reorganized department in the fall of that year. A successful young manager with extensive experience in applying simulation techniques both in the Army and in John Deere's materials management system, Rankin brought an open and participative style of management to the job. He provided the carefully selected members of the department with ample freedom to work on projects they were personally interested in and, whenever possible, made decisions by committee. Following the reorganization (see Exhibit 2), and with the intent of establishing the firm as a leader in computer-integrated manufacturing, the newly renamed Computer-Aided Manufacturing Services division moved quickly to develop a range of tools built around the enhanced GT software.

THE JOHN DEERE GROUP TECHNOLOGY SYSTEM

The nature of the set of products that constituted the Deere Group Technology system was elaborated by Tom Hein, manager of software development.

> The heart of our package is a classification and coding system designed to capture key geometric characteristics of a part. Working from engineering drawings at a computer terminal, part coders at any one of our factories can input data on new and revised parts through an interactive menu-driven program. The system generates a 35-digit code that acts as a reference to a part's features. In addition to creating the code, our system, unlike other commercially available GT packages, retains complete, detailed, geometric data about the part that can be used routinely for selection and analysis. The system is also designed to access, from other corporate and factory data bases, additional production data, including standard costs, weights, routings, future requirements, etc. for parts.
>
> To analyze this augmented GT data base, we have developed a variety of flexible retrieval and analysis programs that are available to all Deere engineers. The software comprises thirty major programs organized in six modules (see Exhibit 3) that variously provide the capability to put data into the system, modify data already in it, isolate groups of parts based on any combination of geometric features and/or production data, and perform statistical,

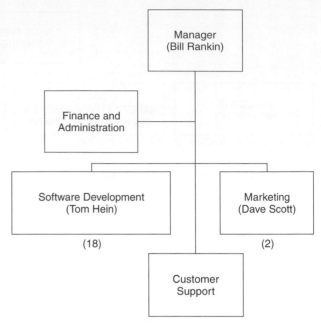

EXHIBIT 2 CAM Services Organization Chart

> graphical and sensitivity analyses. The system also incorporates a number of sophisticated file management routines...and "help" screens containing comprehensive on-line instructions and definitions.
>
> Currently, the system is accessed daily by nearly all of Deere's factories in the United States and Europe, providing reference data for process planning, facilities and capacity planning studies, procurement of machine tools, and to control parts proliferation and assess new manufacturing technologies.

A more specific accounting of the benefits of the GT system was provided by the group's new marketing manager, Dave Scott. "The GT system," Scott said,

> has been the key to the firm's movement toward cellular manufacturing and the adoption of just-in-time production concepts. It has been a major contributing factor in the increased productivity of our engineers, allowing analyses to be performed that couldn't even be conceived before its existence. Our tools have been credited with providing major savings to the corporation.
>
> For example, because our code is based on manufacturing features, such as holes, threads, splines, and slots, a designer can go to a terminal and get a listing, in the terminology that he or she normally thinks in, of all the parts that fit the description

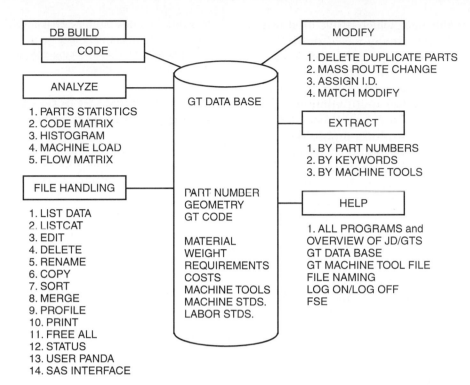

EXHIBIT 3   The John Deere/Group Technology System (JD/GTS) Software Package

of a new part that's being designed. Several things can happen when this occurs. First, an existing part might be found that will do the job. When this happens, besides eliminating the need to create a new design and the associated downstream paperwork for tooling, processing, etc., it allows us to exploit economies-of-scale by increasing the production requirements for the existing part, or to go to a more efficient process.

I have heard industry estimates, by the way, that the manhour cost of launching a new part design through tooling, process engineering, and manufacturing is about $11,000. So an up-front savings of this amount comes every time we avoid a new design. Similar, though I imagine lower, savings are realized when, by modifying an existing design to meet the new part function, we can fit the part into a family and still get the economies of scale. Eventually we might find that a part designed for a product manufactured at one plant is being made at another because it fits into an existing family at that plant.

Perhaps most importantly, though, the GT system has provided a foundation for computer-integrated manufacturing (CIM) at Deere. GT's feature-based representation of parts provides a common neutral "language" to bridge computer-aided

design (CAD) and computer-aided manufacturing (CAM), a fundamental requirement for CIM. With our system, the design data base becomes the same base used for manufacturing. What this means is that eventually, instead of trying to create families of parts by design similarities, we can think in terms of families that lend themselves to similar processing.

COMPUTER-AIDED PROCESS PLANNING

With GT as an experience base, the group began to develop computerized process planning tools. Process planning was the link between design and manufacturing. It entailed the conversion of design data into manufacturing plans and costs; as Hein had put it, "It's where CAD meets CAM."

A process plan, the specification of the manufacturing operations to be performed in the production of a given part, was developed by a planner who used a blueprint supplied by the designer to decide how each feature should be produced, which machine to use, and what machine settings to apply. Typically in excess of 50% of a company's manufacturing engineering manpower was consumed by this task, which drove all downstream functions. It was usually based on the experience of a few critical people, and yielded inconsistent results.

The logic required to develop an "optimal" process plan was frequently quite complex. The philosophy behind the John Deere Process Planning System (JD/PPS) was to decompose the task into smaller problems, each comprising a module. Thus, a process plan for a part that required turning, milling, and drilling would be developed using three logic modules, one for each of the different tasks. This approach had a number of advantages. One was that the logic of any single module was less complex than that of the whole plan. Another was that efficiency increased when a plan's development could be distributed among several engineers. Finally, developing logic modules for generic classes of operations, and providing a flexible method of integrating the modules, made the system usable in any manufacturing environment.

Logic modules for drilling and turning had already been developed. Hein explained:

> Let's say a process engineer wants to drill a hole in 4140 stainless steel. The hole is to be ½" diameter and a coolant will be used in the process. The engineer also specifies the machine on which the job is to be done. Having been provided with this information, the JD/PPS system calculates, based on stored information about the capabilities of the particular machine, the most appropriate speed and feed rates for drilling the hole in the specified material. This information allows the engineer to determine what capabilities new equipment should have, and is useful in process design.

> We began with these two modules because quite a bit of research had already been done on the processes, providing us with a scientific base of knowledge. Much of production, though, is more art than science, and for these operations the JD/PPS was designed to capture rules used by an "expert." It was here that the modular decomposition feature paid the greatest dividends, since a system engineer could work on a particular process with experts, possibly drawn from different Deere facilities, to develop and maintain logic modules. In addition, the modular structure of the system allowed us to develop and add new modules for new technologies as they became available.

> The problem with all of this is the magnitude of the task involved. I estimate it will take another five years before we have a system we're fully satisfied with, and this assumes we'll have the system engineers to work continuously on it. Nevertheless, we feel this is key to Deere being able to fully optimize its manufacturing operations.

COMPUTER-INTEGRATED MANUFACTURING (CIM)

Group technology and computer-aided process planning provided valuable data and tools for improving communications among the design, planning, and manufacturing functions. "The problem," Hein said,

> is that the language of CAD is geometry based. Data input by the designer is stored by the computer in the form of points and equations that allow lines, arcs, and circles to be combined and displayed to represent a finished part. Interpreting these line diagrams presents a great deal of difficulty for manufacturing, as there the language is based on manufacturable "features."

To provide a communication link between CAD and CAM, the group had begun to develop a feature-oriented part description data base that was a logical extension of the GT data base.

To help resolve its hardware interfacing problems, Deere was the first company to implement a Manufacturing Automated Protocol (MAP) local area network. Scott remarked: "When fully implemented, the MAP network will allow us to simply plug in the computers and hardware for both CAD and CAM systems and be off and running." Following the first MAP installation at the Harvester Works, Deere's CAM systems engineers undertook a number of installations in other facilities.

FLEXIBLE MANUFACTURING SYSTEMS (FMS)

The members of the CAM systems group were aware that many of the successes of CIM to date had been achieved by focusing on very narrow families of parts. "Flexible manufacturing systems are effective through similar focusing," Hein had said.

Deere had been one of the first users of FMS technology. Its first system was installed in the Waterloo facility in 1981, when many local firms were just learning of the existence of the technology. In addition, the firm had a number of flexible manufacturing cells in operation at other locations. Its Waterloo installation was perhaps the most publicized American system in the trade journals, and Deere was widely consulted by other firms interested in installing FMSs. As it had been involved in the development and implementation of some of these projects, the CAM systems group had significant experience with the technology.

A TYPICAL CONSULTING PROJECT

The group's reputation spread rapidly by word of mouth. As news of the results achieved in the reorganizing of the Waterloo manufacturing facility was publicized throughout the decentralized organization, requests for the group's assistance in analyzing and developing reorganization plans for other operating facilities began to come in. The case of the hydraulic cylinder cell was typical.

Hydraulic cylinders were integral components on a wide range of the heavy industrial and agricultural equipment that Deere manufactured. They converted fluid power into directed motion to move backhoe arms, and to lift and tilt front end loader and bulldozer blades. (See Exhibit 4.) Consistent with its tradition of customer service, the company retained on its active parts list almost every cylinder used in any of its products for the last 50 years.

Traditionally, hydraulic cylinders were manufactured by an unwieldy batch process carried out in a 340 thousand square foot, three-floor factory. The functionally laid out plant suffered from all the shortcomings of batch processes. Lead time for production was long, work in process inventory was enormous, and a large indirect labor pool was employed in machine set-up and teardown, material movement, tool crib attendance, inspection, and maintenance. The need for expediting remained high despite having introduced a sophisticated MRP program. Jobs were often very late or even lost.

After coding all the cylinders and performing a preliminary analysis, the CAM engineers decided to develop a cell for manufacturing the heavy duty agricultural cylinders. These products constituted a significant portion of the regular production workload and shared common physical and manufacturing characteristics. A few days later, they learned that another CAM engineer was in the middle of a related project to control the proliferation of cylinders by forming design families. While the set of cylinder designs being "standardized" by the group was used primarily in medium-duty industrial equipment, there nevertheless was a considerable overlap in design specifications for the two groups of cylinders.

The industrial and agricultural products that used these cylinders were produced in geographically and organizationally separate facilities. Product designers in one division typically had been unwilling to "compromise" their designs to incorporate components designed for another, even if manufacturing efficiencies would result. This had begun to change as the firm's business environment increased pressure for improved efficiency.

Out of these efforts emerged a new cylinder class—the 120 series—which doubled as a medium duty mobile construction equipment cylinder and a heavy duty agricultural equipment cylinder. Designed for ease of manufacture, these cylinders reflected a greater awareness of the constraints and capabilities of the manufacturing system. A new cylinder design could be developed quickly by selecting the appropriate components from each family, or by modifying a "standard" design if an appropriate component did not already exist. In either case, the task would be easier than designing a component or cylinder from scratch. Since all such cylinders would conform, within limits, to a standard design, manufacturing efficiencies would also be achieved.

A manufacturing cell was then developed to produce this new family. Of the 62 machine tools that comprised the cell, 37 were existing machines that had been relocated and 25 were newly acquired. Results of the change are shown in Exhibit 5. The part count fell from 405 to 75, and nonstandard parts were eliminated. Manufacturing was rationalized by minimizing the number of product routings. Routing simplification is illustrated in Exhibit 6, which compares the barrel routings in the batch process with that in the 120 series cell. The ratio of direct to indirect workers went from 123:50 to 57:1, and all material handling, set-up, and tool changing was done by the direct work force. Two process planners scheduled work through the cell, compared to seven to schedule an equivalent workload through the batch process. Making the work force responsible for inspecting the quality of its own work eliminated the need for roving inspectors. By allowing defects to be identified

EXHIBIT 4 The Hydraulic Cylinder

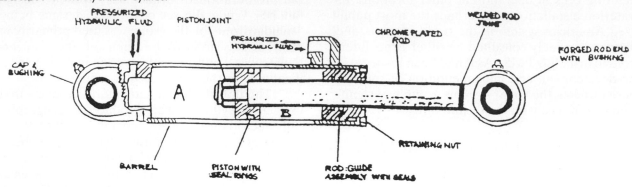

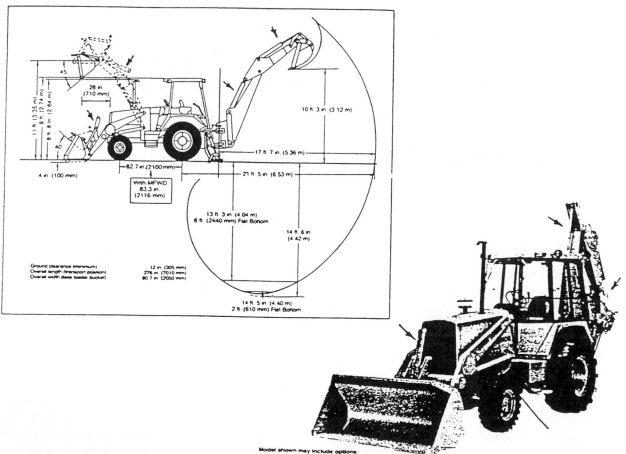

immediately, this approach facilitated a just-in-time system, in which work pieces moved almost immediately to adjacent workstations.

The manufacturing cell was managed by four supervisors (two on the day shift, one on each of the other shifts), and staffed by two programmers and two engineers. Engineering projects had previously been performed by engineers from a centralized pool who serviced the entire Plow and Planter facility. This limited continuity of interest

GT Cell Cost Reductions

	Before	*After*
Inventory	21 days	10 days
Material handling	26%	14.5%
Scrap	51%	14% (last 3 months, less than 10%)
Maintenance	36%	22%
Inspection	17%	3%
Crib attendants	17.4%	0%

EXHIBIT 5 Summary Statistics for Modular Manufacturing Implementation
All costs are stated as a percent of the total direct labor charges/week incurred in the cell.

in a particular project, and substantial delays between identifying needs and implementing projects were common. Under the new approach, as soon as a project was identified one of the engineers immediately became involved. Over time the two engineers developed an intimate knowledge of the system and developed close working relationships with the supervisors. By combining their more scientific perspective with the extensive process experience of the supervisors, who viewed manufacturing as essentially an art, they quickly became "experts" in the specific processes within the cell.

Based on this success, the Plow and Planter Works, in association with the Hydraulic Design division, decided to develop a second cell for manufacturing heavier duty cylinders. Only 38% of the design engineering resources and 8% of the manufacturing engineering resources consumed in the first cell's development were required to develop the second.

EXPLOITING THE POTENTIAL

Marketing the group's services within the firm had not been a problem, given its string of successes, and now Rankin, Hein, and Scott contemplated how to exploit Deere's external market. The potential market seemed huge. All three were convinced of the value of their systems and tools and, with the revamping of the U.S. and European industrial bases in response to the competitive threat from the Far East, demand for such services could be enormous. A number of small companies had begun to offer engineering systems software for

specific niche markets but, except for some quite sophisticated CAD tools, most of the software was primitive compared to Deere's. The flurry of activity in the area had also attracted a large number of independent consultants into the market.

Deere's excellent position derived from its long involvement and record of success. All Deere systems and software tools were tested internally, and customers could see them in action in Deere facilities. None of the firm's competitors was positioned to offer this kind of "live" demonstration. Consequently, Deere considered all segments of the market open to exploitation. Though estimates of market potential varied widely in the various segments, all were very high and anticipated rapid growth.

Opinions varied on the marketing issue. Scott favored pricing the integrated GT software package at the high end to reflect the inherent quality of the product, and providing training and consulting at cost. Some of the engineers, however, recommended pricing the software low enough to generate quick sales and charging substantially higher rates, commensurate with management consulting fees, for after sales service. Hein also was concerned by what he perceived to be an accelerating shift away from developing new systems toward modifying existing tools for applications outside the metal fabrication industry. He was under pressure from Scott, for example, to allocate some resources to the development of a new code structure for the GT system that would make it applicable to the electronics industry. Rankin, however, felt that marketing, at least initially, should be concentrated in the metal fabrication industry to allow engineering resources to be focused on projects directly relevant to the firm's own operation. This, he believed, would make it easier to leverage Deere's huge experience and parts base.

Earlier in the year, Brian Rugh, one of Rankin's engineers, had demonstrated some of the newer GT tools at a Deere operation in France. When Rugh keyed in from a product blueprint the dimensions of a part used by the French plant, the system generated a list of 15 parts used at the Dubuque facility that fit the criteria. Keying in another feature of the part reduced the number to three. Rugh had then called up the tools, routing, production plan, and standard hours involved in the manufacture of one of the parts and from these calculated its cost. This experience had convinced

EXHIBIT 6 Example of Routing Simplification/Standardization

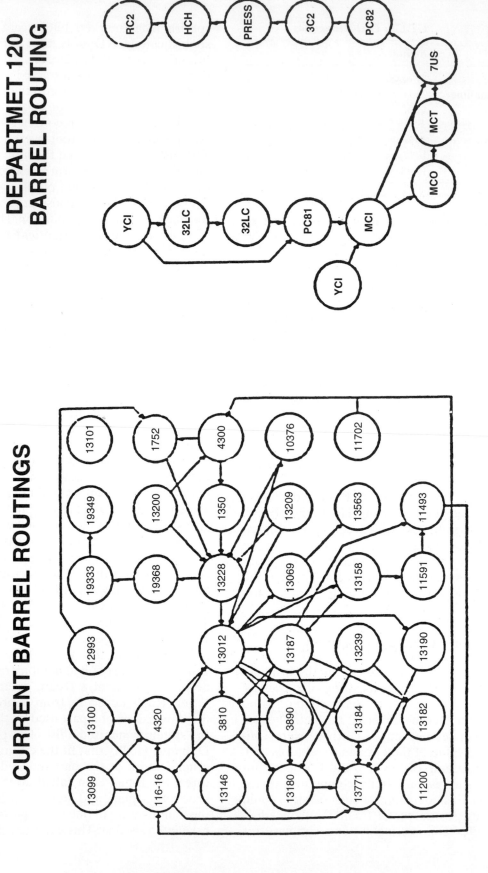

CURRENT BARREL ROUTINGS

DEPARTMET 120
BARREL ROUTING

both Rugh and Rankin that the 200,000 part number database already coded and residing in the company's computer was a potentially marketable resource that could easily be augmented with data on customer products. A number of uses could be made of this database. A client interested in analyzing cell arrangements for the production of a family of parts, for example, could use the database to extract illustrative costs and production times for a similar set of parts, thereby significantly reducing the data collection required.

About another possibility, Rankin was less sure. The depressed state of the firm's core business coupled with the success of its "reorganizing" and "refocusing" projects had left many of Deere's manufacturing facilities (including the Cylinder plant at the Plow and Planter Works) with excess capacity. With the high overheads they had to carry, some of the division managers had begun manufacturing related products for outside consumption. Rankin suspected that the knowledge of firms'

needs obtained through his group's sales and consulting activities could be exploited by matching those needs with the capabilities of Deere facilities. The CAM Systems group, inasmuch as it controlled the common database for the entire firm, might serve as a broker for this service.

However, the most important contribution his group could make, he believed, was in improving Deere's ability to keep abreast of the latest advances in production technology. New processes and techniques were appearing with greater frequency. In order to exploit them for competitive advantage it would be necessary to learn about them as soon as they appeared, and to capture this knowledge in a form that would make it more widely available within Deere. As its engineers provided consulting services to other firms, they would be able to identify new technologies and gain access to the knowledge of the experts in these new processses. Rankin wondered what long-term impact this might have on Deere.

AeroTech Service Group, Inc.

In early July of 1995, in a small building not far from the St. Louis Airport, AeroTech Service Group president George Brill was crimping connectors onto Ethernet cabling. Some new computers had just arrived, and Brill wanted to wire them into AeroTech's network immediately. The routine of the work allowed his mind to wander, and he mulled over a business proposition. AeroTech had recently been asked to submit a bid on a project by Tyrell Corporation, a large aerospace and defense contractor that was similar in many ways to AeroTech's current customer, McDonnell Douglas Aerospace (MDA). For the previous two years, AeroTech had been working with MDA to facilitate electronic information sharing among the company and its suppliers, customers, and other partners. The system they had built, called CITIS, was useful, robust, and widely praised by its users. It was also growing quickly.

This success had begun to attract attention, and AeroTech had been contacted by several potential customers. He found the Request for Quote, or RFQ, from Tyrell particularly interesting because it asked for services very much like the ones provided to MDA. It could allow AeroTech to charge differently for them, however, and perhaps to realize greater revenues. At the same time, though, the volume and variety of inquiries indicated to Brill that there was strong demand for the expertise that AeroTech had developed. He thought that his company could easily sell consulting services to clients interested in expanding the variety and scope of their electronic collaborations. Consulting appeared to be a lucrative busi-

ness, and Brill was confident that AeroTech could be successful at it.

Earlier in the day, he had received another offer. Brill's main contact at MDA had called to propose an additional systems integration project to AeroTech. This one was smaller and more straightforward than implementing CITIS; it involved building an interface between the Internet and an aging mainframe computer. MDA was offering an attractive sum of money for completing the task, and Brill was fairly confident that his firm could do it effectively.

Brill felt that AeroTech had to choose between responding to Tyrell's RFQ and establishing itself as a consultancy; the company did not have the resources to commit to both efforts. He had just begun to evaluate the financial implications of the two choices. He also felt that AeroTech could respond immediately to MDA's proposal no matter which of the two other options it chose, but he wondered whether it would sidetrack the company at a time when focus seemed so important.

AEROTECH

The AeroTech Service Group was founded by Brill in 1991 with personal funds and a loan from his family. It was originally an engineering consulting firm. Brill intended to take advantage of the aerospace industry's trend toward increased subcontracting by bidding for individual projects that MDA wanted to outsource. In 1993, he developed a plan for copying and shipping paper MDA spare parts drawings to companies who wanted to supply the U.S. Government.

The project brought him into contact with the group at MDA responsible for electronic commerce. This team had developed a prototype of a new information system called the Contractor Integrated Technical Information Service, or CITIS. CITIS was a response to a directive from the Department of Defense known as Military

This case was prepared as the basis for class discussion rather than to illustrate either effective or ineffective handling of an administrative situation.

This case was prepared by Andrew McAfee under the direction of David M. Upton. Copyright © 1996 by the President and Fellows of Harvard College. Harvard Business School case 696-094.

Standard 974, which was intended to reduce paperwork and spur the development of new technologies for collaboration. It required prime contractors on defense projects to make electronically available to their customer (the Federal Government) contractually required information such as maintenance manuals, safety test results, and lists of subcontractors.

For aerospace projects, this information could be voluminous. It was commonly estimated, for example, that the paper required in support of a Boeing 747 would not fit inside the airplane. For the military airplanes that MDA built, there would be an even higher level of mandatory documentation. MDA saw CITIS as a way to speed construction of the required digital database. If the system were used by all involved groups to share information, it would not be necessary to recreate electronic documents from a mountain of paper at the end of a project.

AeroTech and the MDA team quickly realized that CITIS would be an ideal vehicle for transferring drawings of spare parts. On a pilot project, Brill demonstrated his ability to connect an outside supplier to CITIS, and soon received purchase orders for six more installations. At the same time, MDA was looking for an outside firm to take over management and administration of the service. Mike Burnett, a software engineer who had worked on early prototypes of CITIS, had formed a solid working relationship with Brill. Brill had also met another talented engineer, Bruce Draper, who began working as a consultant to build more functionality into the service.

Because the three men had spent so much time with the system, AeroTech was the logical choice to receive the CITIS contract from MDA. The AeroTech Service Group, by this time a partnership among Brill, Burnett, and Draper, became a McDonnell Douglas "Strategic Alliance Company" in May, 1994.

THE CITIS SYSTEM

Purpose

The CITIS software appeared like any other program on a user's computer. Its function was to serve as a gateway to other information resources. These resources fell into two categories: information pools and applications. An information pool was a collection of data stored on a remote computer, for example a purchased parts database, a directory of computer-aided design (CAD) drawings, or a list of suppliers qualified to manufacture a certain category of parts. An application, meanwhile, was a computer program such as software for manufacturing requirements planning (MRP) or a three-dimensional CAD package.

CITIS's primary function was to make available information pools and applications that were not resident on a user's machine. In other words, CITIS freed its users from the requirement that they be sitting in front of the computer that contained the data or program of interest. The importance of geographic distance and organizational boundaries was thus diminished for CITIS users; they could access the information and applications on any computer they were authorized to use, even if that computer were located in another time zone, country, or firm. Table 1 shows some of the most common activities carried out using CITIS; Exhibit 1 gives a simplified graphical view of how CITIS and AeroTech facilitate these tasks.

CITIS Technology

To enable remote access to information and applications, CITIS used protocols developed for the Internet, a large public network that connected millions of dissimilar computers around the world. Machines on this network adhered to a common set of rules for passing data, which were collectively called the Internet Protocols; if a group of machines abided by these rules, they could reliably share information with each other. These protocols were well-developed by the early 1990s, and could be implemented on virtually any computer hardware. The CITIS team recognized them as ideal building blocks for their system, and so tried to mimic the Internet instead of re-inventing it.

Four protocols in particular guaranteed that CITIS could provide extremely high functionality; Table 2 lists them in increasing order of sophistication, and provides an example of how MDA and its partners used them.

Internet protocols were not the only possible choices for enabling the tasks described in Tables 1 and 2. As "open" standards, however, they were particularly attractive. They were not owned by

TABLE 1 Principal Uses of CITIS

Capability: Example	Usage Volume	Comments
Directory access and file transfer: MDA moved CAD files (electronic versions of part drawings) to a private directory allocated to one of the firm's suppliers. The supplier then accessed the directory and downloaded the information to a local computer.	In June 1995, CITIS users transferred approximately 25,000 files to each other, not including bid requests. The mean file size was 2 Megabytes (Mb).	File transfer was the most common use of the CITIS system. It eliminated a great deal of lost time and expense.
Electronic distribution of bid requests: MDA creates an electronic "buy-to" package and moves the data to the directories of all potential suppliers. Suppliers access the data, review it on-line, and interactively submit their bids.	The average user downloaded one of these a month. The average electronic bid request package was 3 Mb in size.	MDA estimated that savings from this use alone paid for AeroTech's services.
Information referencing: MDA maintained a list of suppliers qualified for specific production processes. Other subcontractors could consult this list to find partners.	The average user downloaded 20 of these reference documents each month. Mean file size for these references was 0.5 Mb.	AeroTech used World Wide Web technologies as a means to convey this type of information.
Terminal emulation: A military customer anywhere in the U.S. could log onto an MDA mainframe in St. Louis and check the final delivery schedule for a system.	In June 1995, CITIS handled approximately 3000 of these sessions, which lasted an average of 12 minutes.	Terminal emulation was widely used for database queries, production and inventory updates, and other text-based tasks.
Remote use of applications: An outside designer, without leaving her firm, could use MDA's CAD system to view a solid model of a part and check its fit within a larger assembly.	In June 1995, CITIS handled approximately 1000 of these sessions, which lasted an average of 25 minutes.	This type of graphics-based task required higher bandwidth, and so was not available to all CITIS participants.

any one entity or company, the details of their operation were widely available, and they could be incorporated into any software or system without incurring licensing fees or other such costs.

Two consequences of these standards' openness were important for the CITIS team. First, it was easy to find and install software based on Internet protocols for virtually any computer. Because CITIS participants were using many different hardware platforms and operating systems, this universality was important. Second, Internet protocol bundles were not expensive; many were distributed without charge, or with a minimal "shareware" fee. This meant that CITIS installation was not expensive.

Protocols developed for the Internet provided the building blocks for extensive electronic collaboration among CITIS participants. AeroTech's effort in constructing the system, however, entailed far more than simply distributing software to users and then troubleshooting during installation. To satisfy MDA and all of its partners, including the U.S. government, two significant challenges remained: insuring the security of the system, and building the fastest possible internetwork.

Security

The Internet protocols described above were designed for circumstances in which all connected computers would share information freely. This was emphatically not the case for an aerospace and defense firm like MDA, whose computers contained large amounts of sensitive Department of Defense data. There appeared, then, to be a fundamental incompatibility between the technology underpinning CITIS and the project's security requirements. MDA would not allow its computers to be accessed by outsiders unless it could be assured that security would not be compromised in any way.

AeroTech addressed this concern in two ways. First, it did not replace or alter existing protection on any member computer with CITIS. Login procedures, User ID names, passwords, and all other safeguards remained unchanged on all

EXHIBIT 1 Examples of CITIS in Operation

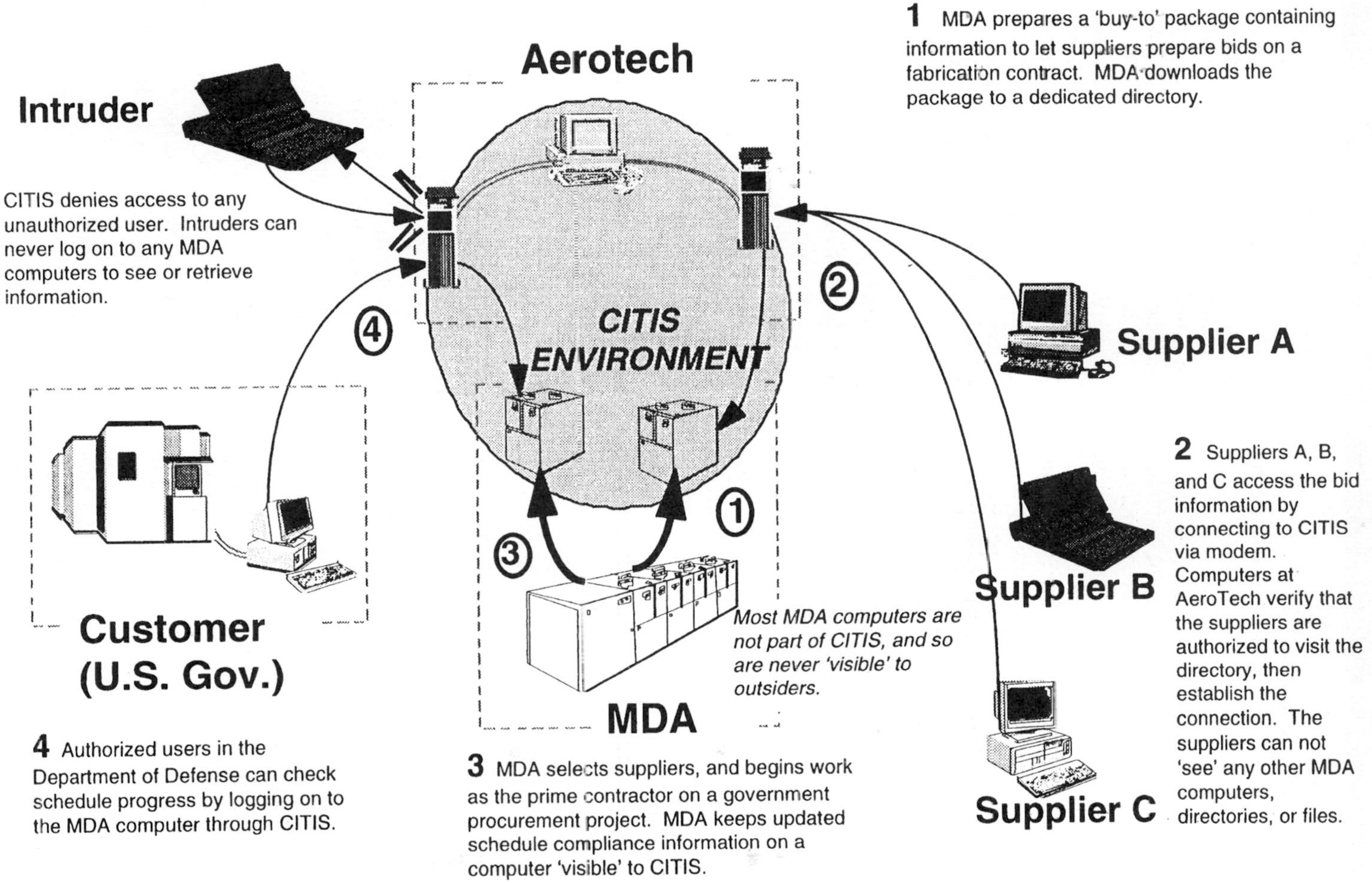

Aerotech

CITIS ENVIRONMENT

Most MDA computers are not part of CITIS, and so are never 'visible' to outsiders.

MDA

Supplier A

Supplier B

Supplier C

Customer (U.S. Gov.)

Intruder

1 MDA prepares a 'buy-to' package containing information to let suppliers prepare bids on a fabrication contract. MDA-downloads the package to a dedicated directory.

2 Suppliers A, B, and C access the bid information by connecting to CITIS via modem. Computers at AeroTech verify that the suppliers are authorized to visit the directory, then establish the connection. The suppliers can not 'see' any other MDA computers, directories, or files.

3 MDA selects suppliers, and begins work as the prime contractor on a government procurement project. MDA keeps updated schedule compliance information on a computer 'visible' to CITIS.

4 Authorized users in the Department of Defense can check schedule progress by logging on to the MDA computer through CITIS.

CITIS denies access to any unauthorized user. Intruders can never log on to any MDA computers to see or retrieve information.

313

TABLE 2 Internet Protocols Used to Provide CITIS Functionality

Protocol	Purpose	CITIS Example
mail protocols (smtp, pop, imap)	Allowed users to exchange messages	MDA engineer in St. Louis notified a machine shop manager in Los Angeles that a new version of a Computer Aided Design (CAD) drawing was available
file transfer protocol (ftp)	Allowed users to access files on a remote machine and transfer them to a local hard drive	Machine shop manager accessed CITIS, which established a link to a St. Louis mainframe, then downloaded an archived CAD file to her PC.
telnet	Allowed users to access/log on to a remote machine and use the applications resident on it.	Department of Defense employee in Washington DC logged onto St. Louis mainframe via CITIS to access program schedule information.
X-Window	Allowed users to display "windows" of text, graphics, or applications that reside on a remote machine.	Machine shop manager used CITIS to access Phoenix computer and view drawings created with a UNIX-based viewer.

machines. CITIS simply delivered users to the "front door" of a computer; they still needed the appropriate keys to enter it.

Second, AeroTech kept track of which "front doors" each user could visit. It would be disastrous if a hacker used CITIS to crash an MDA system or copy a classified file, but it would also be unacceptable if a user could see sensitive directories and filenames, even if they could not be copied. CITIS included a database which maintained a list of all users and the exact files, directories, and computers for which they had authorization. Before allowing any user to access a remote machine or pool of information, CITIS first verified that the user was authorized for that activity and then validated the user. Authorizations were granted by a group within MDA and maintained by AeroTech. As discussed above, this security was layered on top of other authorization checks; after CITIS granted access to a remote computer a user still had to pass through that machine's native security system.

Bandwidth

A final important concern for AeroTech in designing the CITIS system was how to make the system as "fast" as possible for its users. The speed and responsiveness of any internetwork, or collection of physically separate computer networks, is largely a matter of bandwidth, or the information carrying capacity of the links between them. A system which used only modems and normal telephone lines, for example, would be cheap but slow.

An internetwork which used high speed, dedicated telecommunications links would be much faster, but more costly to implement and maintain.

AeroTech realized that not all CITIS users would have the same bandwidth requirements. A machine shop which connected to CITIS only to download electronic drawings would probably be satisfied with modem speeds. A large aerospace firm that was collaborating with MDA and wanted to conduct design reviews via videoconferencing, however, would need much more bandwidth.

AeroTech used its telecommunications expertise to build a variety of communications links and create a bandwidth "patchwork" among users. Those with minimal or sporadic needs accessed the system with modems, while more permanent participants (e.g. distant MDA sites, customers within the government, other large aerospace firms) used more dedicated, higher bandwidth links.

Economics

The contract for CITIS management and administration provided for variable weekly expenditures against a yearly budget. AeroTech typically charged a flat weekly fee and billed MDA for unexpected support requests. AeroTech did not charge based on the number of users added or the amount of traffic on the system, because such increases did not increase the cost of running the system. The firm did charge for special projects, such as connecting a large partner with high bandwidth requirements, that required significant amounts of time.

MDA estimated that by mid-1995 the CITIS system was paying for itself, taking into account only the cycle-time related savings realized from distributing bid request packages to suppliers electronically rather than manually.

Summary

CITIS, then, was essentially a security and authorization database that presided over an internetwork of computers running Internet protocols, using appropriate bandwidth. The only dedicated physical manifestations of the system were two small networks of computers, one at AeroTech, the other at MDA, and the communications links between MDA's corporate network in St. Louis and other large partner sites. Beyond this, CITIS was purely a method, developed and implemented by AeroTech and MDA, of exploiting the information resources of a number of geographically dispersed partners.

When Brill added the first external supplier in mid-1993, there were fewer than 50 people, all of them within MDA, authorized to use the system. By the fall of 1994, after AeroTech had taken the CITIS contract, there were 400 internal and external users. A year later, there were 1300. Figure 1 graphs this increase, and includes AeroTech's estimates for continued growth as of June of 1995.

In response to this growth, AeroTech had hired two additional engineers in late 1994 and two more in the first quarter of 1995. This team was responsible for CITIS maintenance and administration, and for responding to customer troubleshooting requests. While Burnett and Draper were still involved in CITIS, especially for difficult problems and complicated projects, the system no longer required their full-time attention.

By mid-1995, CITIS had already begun to reduce information transmission costs for MDA and its partners. It had also eliminated needless travel and time lost searching and waiting for information. With increasingly heavy use, the discovery of new applications, and the addition of more users, both AeroTech and MDA anticipated that CITIS would continue to grow in both size and importance.

NEXT STEPS FOR AEROTECH

Brill realized that AeroTech's experience in building CITIS had given the firm a significant lead in constructing "virtual factories" in which industrial users could collaborate and share information. The company's demonstrated expertise in the use of Internet protocols, network security, databases and user tracking, telecommunications, and the many other technologies that made up CITIS was both rare and valuable. As the Internet continued to grow explosively and more firms decided to explore its possibilities, Brill felt that demand for AeroTech's services could only grow.

AeroTech as Consultants

Because half of all CITIS users were outside MDA, AeroTech had worked with many companies over the previous two years. Throughout that time, Brill had received phone calls from them asking if AeroTech would be available for other projects, or to help develop a strategy and implementation plan for greater connectivity or electronic commerce. Brill had turned these requests down, but was now wondering if he could build a business around them. He, Burnett, and Draper had gained a great deal of experience leading projects at companies, and felt that they understood managers' concerns in this area well and knew how to address them effectively.

Brill realized, however, that he had no experience managing a consulting company and didn't even know what his chief concerns should be. He thought that demand for AeroTech's services would not be a problem, but what about supply?

FIGURE 1 Growth of the CITIS System
Number of Registered Citis Users

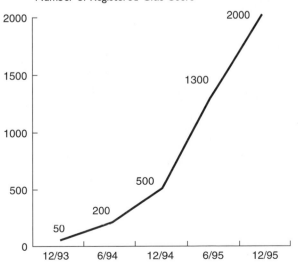

Could he find people who were both knowledgeable enough to address the range of problems that clients would have, and who had the personal skills required to be effective consultants? Brill had met many outstanding engineers and technicians who lacked these skills, and he knew that sending such people to clients would be disastrous. However, he felt that the four engineers he had hired to maintain CITIS would all have made good consultants, and this gave him hope that he could find and recruit others like them. Brill assumed that, as a consulting company specializing in industrial internetworks, AeroTech could hire and train five people every six months over the next two years. He also anticipated promoting one person from consultant to manager each six months, while maintaining Burnett and Draper as consulting partners. He feared that faster growth than this might compromise the quality of the services that they could offer.

To help understand billing rates and salaries, and to estimate revenues and expenses, Brill used a report published in early 1995 by an association of management consulting firms. It summarized a survey of the group's members, and Brill found it informative, even though AeroTech would not be positioned as general management consultants. He felt that his company could charge comparable rates to these firms. Exhibit 2 contains excerpts from the report, and Exhibit 3 shows the "percentage income statement" that it included. Brill was planning to use this information to make an esti-

EXHIBIT 2 Excerpts on Billing from 1994 Survey of Management Consulting Firms

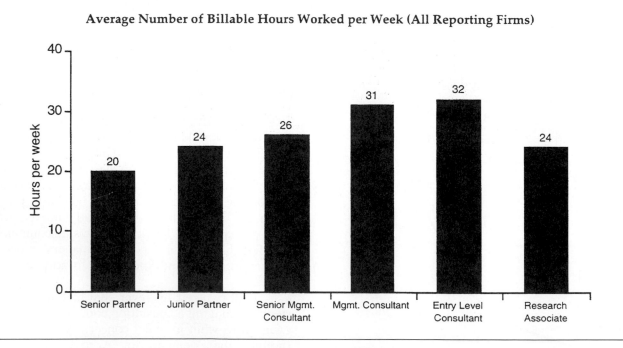

Establishing billing rates is, to some extent, as much an art as a science. Essentially, the goal is to charge clients at a rate that is consistent with the value of services provided while at the same time allowing the maximum possible revenue and hopefully allowing an adequate profit for the firm after expenses. This suggests, therefore, that if billing rates are too high, staff utilization (i.e., hours billed to and collected from clients) may be low, thus resulting in less than desired revenues. Likewise, if billing rates are too low, utilization may be high but revenues may still be less than desired. The key, therefore, is to set billing rates at a level that, when combined with staff utilization, results in the maximum possible revenues.

The typical hourly billing rate charged for employees earning $125,000, $75,000, $60,000, and $35,000 per year during 1993 was $210, $160, $128, $78, respectively. These were somewhat lower than that of the prior year.

Average Number of Billable Hours Worked per Week (All Reporting Firms)

Source: 1994 Survey of United States Key Management Information, ACME—World Association of Management Consulting Firms. Copyright © 1994, ACME.

	Typical	*Middle Range*
Total Consulting Fee Revenues	100.0	100.0–100.0
Revenues from Billed Expenses	12.9	5.2–19.2
Total Revenues from Consulting Operations	112.9	105.2–119.2
Salary Expense (without Bonuses/Profit Sharing)	51.4	40.8–56.3
Fringe Benefit Expense	9.0	6.3–10.8
Total Outside Labor Cost	8.0	1.0–10.3
Business Development Expense (excluding time)	4.3	1.9–5.1
Staff Recruiting, Selection, and Relocation Expense (excluding time)	0.6	0.0–0.8
Professional Development Expense (excluding time)	1.6	0.4–2.0
All Other Operating Expenses	20.4	14.6–36.6
Total Operating Expenses	95.3	89.9–105.2
Net Operating Profit Before Taxes, Bonuses, or Profit Sharing	17.6	7.0–26.6
Other Related Information		
Unbilled Work in Process as a % of Consulting Fees	6.3	2.7–9.0
Average Level of Backlog (i.e. projects sold but not yet started) as a % of Consulting Fees	9.5	4.1–21.4
Average Number of Work in Process Days that are Unbilled at any Given Time	22	9–32
Bad Debt Expense as a % of Consulting Fees	0.1	0.0–0.5

EXHIBIT 3   "Percentage Income Statement" from 1994 Survey of Management Consulting Firms 1993 Percentage Income Statement (All Reporting Firms) (All numbers expressed as a % of consulting fee revenues)
Source: 1994 Survey of United States Key Management Information, ACME—World Association of Management Consulting Firms. Copyright © 1994, ACME.

mate of revenues and costs for an AeroTech consultancy over its first two years.

Brill's primary concern with establishing AeroTech as a consulting firm was not around demand or even its ability to supply these services; instead, he was concerned about sustaining expertise. The skills that he and his colleagues had developed came largely from the CITIS project and the learning that it had provided. If AeroTech turned its focus away from doing this type of work, Brill was not sure how it would accumulate new expertise. In an industry as turbulent as AeroTech's it was important to have up-to-date skills, but if most AeroTech employees were full-time consultants their skills might stagnate. Brill was concerned that they would be doing more teaching than learning.

The Tyrell Proposal

Tyrell was a large aerospace contractor based in Wisconsin. It had grown rapidly throughout the 1990s, mainly by acquiring other firms as the defense industry consolidated. Its most visible product was a radar system that had a high-profile role during the Gulf War. It was also involved in many other ongoing procurement projects, both on its own and in partnership with other contractors.

The RFQ document from Tyrell was intriguing; it seemed to offer an opportunity tailor-made for AeroTech. Tyrell was asking for proposals to construct an information sharing system that would fill much the same role as CITIS, and that would be used in the same industry. Brill was not surprised that Tyrell was asking for such a familiar system; AeroTech had brought one large group at Tyrell into the CITIS environment because Tyrell was working with MDA on a procurement project. People within this group became heavy users of the system, and had made inquiries to AeroTech in the past about replicating it.

The RFQ represented the formalization of those inquiries. It asked for proposals to build a system that would provide a subset of the functionality of CITIS, and that would have comparable security features. Tyrell wanted its system to provide the first three of the capabilities listed in Table 1. The company only wanted to transmit files and access stored information; it did not specify a system that would allow terminal emulation or remote use of applications. Because most Tyrell employees already had access to the Internet the RFQ stated that bidders would not have to provide this service, and so it would not be necessary for AeroTech to purchase large numbers of modems, gateway computers, and other similar equipment.

The winning bidder would receive a two year contract for the system, provided that the contractor maintained adequate service levels. The first users to be connected were 40 engineers divided among three teams in Wisconsin, Texas, and California. According to the RFQ, later users would be added based on the requests of specific departments, teams, or projects. Brill expected that, over the length of its contract, Tyrell's system would grow much like CITIS had.

Pricing While there was a fixed yearly budget with MDA for CITIS, Tyrell's RFQ specified three different pricing methods. Bidders could submit proposals based on any of these, and could submit proposals that included more than one pricing scheme. The three methods were:

Monthly usage fee: Bidders were to specify a per-user fee for monthly use of the system. At the end of each month, Tyrell would pay an amount equal to this fee multiplied by the number of users registered to use the system.

By user: Bidders were to specify a flat per-user fee for use of the system over the life of the contract. At the end of each month, Tyrell would pay an amount equal to this fee multiplied by the number of *new users* registered to use the system during the course of the month.

By volume of information transferred: Bidders were to specify a fee for each megabyte of information downloaded through the system. At the end of each month, Tyrell would pay an amount equal to this fee multiplied by the number of megabytes transferred during that month.

Brill was sure that other companies had received the RFQ, but he felt that AeroTech had a good chance at winning the contract. His company

had made a good impression on the Tyrell employees that it had worked with. AeroTech could also build the required system most cheaply, in Brill's opinion. The Tyrell project would be largely a replication of CITIS, so much of the software written to track usage, manage authorization, and insure security would be transferable. Other bidders would have to create much of this from scratch.

Tyrell's current computing environment was different from MDA's so the contract, if AeroTech won it, would not be as simple as installing the software written for CITIS. Brill estimated that required code modifications, implementation, and "baby-sitting" of a Tyrell system would take up most of Burnett and Draper's time for about six months. It would also require two additional employees, a computer workstation, and a telecommunications line; Exhibit 4 gives Brill's estimate of the costs of each of these.

Brill had asked his contacts at MDA if the company would object to AeroTech submitting a proposal in response to the Tyrell RFQ. MDA encouraged AeroTech to bid; a CITIS equivalent at Tyrell would make it easier for the two large companies to share information.

As he began to prepare a proposal in response to the RFQ, Brill faced two concerns. First,

EXHIBIT 4 Estimates of Expenditures Required in Support of Tyrell RFQ

Brill's initial estimates for hardware and telecommunications costs and the salary expense involved with the Tyrell system.

Hardware	*Estimated Cost*
Workstation to act as server for Tyrell system	$50,000
Two CSU/DSU devices, or high speed modems to connect server at AeroTech with Tyrell computer over a T1 telecom. line (see below)	$6,000
Telecommunications	
One high speed T1 telecommunications line between AeroTech and Tyrell	$3,000/mo.
Salary Expense	
Two engineers, full time	$16,000/mo., fully burdened
Draper and Burnett, for first 6 months of project	$20,000/mo., fully burdened

he was unsure which pricing method or methods to use, and how to set fees. MDA paid for its system with a simple yearly budget, but the Tyrell system would be financed very differently. Brill thought that experience gained from CITIS left his firm in a good position to anticipate how the Tyrell system would grow and be used, but he still had to translate that experience into at least one concrete pricing plan.

His second concern echoed his hesitation about repositioning AeroTech as a consultancy. Winning the Tyrell contract would commit his company to building another "virtual factory" much like the one it had already constructed. Was this the business that AeroTech should be in? Would it have the opportunity to explore alternatives, if it won this contract? Before committing to this effort, Brill wanted to be sure that it would place his company on a desirable course.

The DSTAR Project

A final consideration for Brill was whether to accept a relatively short-term project that MDA had offered to AeroTech. MDA was the prime contractor and final assembler for the DSTAR program, about which Brill knew little because his security clearance was not high enough. DSTAR had begun in the 1970s, and most of its production and process information came from software that MDA had written specifically for the project. This software was written in COBOL, a language that was no longer commonly used, and ran on a 20 year old mainframe.

Despite its archaic computer systems, the Department of Defense customer for DSTAR had decided to use it as the pilot project to develop new methods of information sharing. MDA was to periodically extract data, such as production schedules and test results, from the DSTAR information system, encode these data so that they could not be read by unauthorized people, and transmit them over the Internet to customers at the Pentagon and elsewhere in the military. This process was to be largely automated. MDA thought it possible that information routing of this type could become a requirement much like Military Standard 974, but did not anticipate that this would happen within the next 2–3 years.

Because of the abilities it had demonstrated with CITIS, MDA had offered this project, named DSTARNet, to AeroTech for the flat fee of $250,000. Brill knew that CITIS itself could not be used to build DSTARNet, but thought that there might be some commonality between the two efforts; both, for example, involved using Internet protocols to securely send MDA information. He also knew that it would take significant effort to automate the extraction of the required information from DSTAR's outdated information systems. Burnett knew COBOL, but had not programmed with it for many years.

Brill estimated that the project would require three months from both Burnett and Draper. He knew that this estimate was little better than a guess, though, and that no one would know how much work DSTARNet would require until the project began. It could be almost trivial to build a system to extract and exchange the information, but Brill doubted that this would prove to be the case. MDA appeared to be inflexible on the fee for the project, and indicated that other contractors were available who would accept that work at that rate.

As Brill inserted the last Ethernet connector, he knew that decisions needed to be made back in his office. Should AeroTech undertake the DSTARNet project? Whether or not it did, should he prepare a bid in response to the Tyrell RFQ, or should he and his partners move AeroTech into consulting?

The Real Virtual Factory

David M. Upton and Andrew McAfee

By now, the monolithic factory was supposed to have given way to the virtual factory: a community of dozens, if not hundreds, of factories, each focused on what it does best, all linked by an electronic network that would enable them to operate as one—flexibly and inexpensively—regardless of their locations. This network would make it easy for companies with dissimilar computer systems to exchange information about inventory levels and delivery schedules. It would allow companies with different CAD systems to collaborate electronically on designs. It would permit potential suppliers to gain entry to the system in order to bid on jobs with minimal hassle and little or no investment. And finally, it would allow a small manufacturer to have the same access to information as a large partner.

For most companies, however, true electronic collaboration remains elusive. Networks for producing autos, textiles, and many other products do exist. But when one looks at how they share information, one is reminded of what Dr. Samuel Johnson said: "It is not done well; but you are surprised to find it done at all." Even highly sophisticated companies have found—and continue to find—the task of creating seamless electronic networks of lean, computer-integrated manufacturing operations to be frustrating and difficult. Managers at most of these companies are still struggling to make their information systems more flexible. They are perplexed about why so much paper is still being shuffled around. They are desperate to figure out how to extend the network to more of their partners without causing costs and overhead to balloon. And they do not understand why their heavy investments in IT have not radically changed the way their companies work.

Clearly, the three main technologies that companies have employed to create the virtual factory—electronic data interchange (EDI), proprietary groupware (such as Lotus Notes), and dedicated wide-area networks—are not complete solutions. Although that conclusion is hardly a revelation, many managers do not understand exactly why these technologies are not delivering. The reasons become clearer if one thinks about the different demands a network must meet for a large-scale virtual factory to succeed.

Working with companies in industries such as electronics, white goods, paper, and aerospace, we discerned three basic demands on such a network:

- It must be able to accommodate network members whose IT sophistication varies enormously—from the small machine shop with a single PC in the corner to the large site that boasts an array of engineering workstations and mainframes.

- While maintaining a high level of security, it must be able to cope with a constantly churning pool of suppliers and customers whose relationships vary enormously in intimacy and scope.

- It must give its members a great deal of functionality, including the capacity to transfer files between computers, the power to access common pools of information, and the capability to access and utilize all the programs on a computer located at a distant site.

EDI, groupware, and wide-area networks can each deal with some of these demands, but none can deal with all of them, nor can combinations of the three technologies. Does this sad fact mean that the virtual factory remains a mirage—a wonderful destination that can't ever be reached? The answer is no. Real virtual factories are now being built. For example, AeroTech, a small, relatively young information-services company, has built one for McDonnell Douglas Aerospace that represents a radical departure from the approaches that others have taken. (See the section titled "The Real Virtual Factory That AeroTech Built.") AeroTech has created a networked manufacturing community that is open and friendly to even the most unsophisticated users, provides a very high degree of functionality, and works even though the community's membership is constantly changing.

Two critical elements make this type of networked manufacturing community possible: a function we call an information broker and open standards based on the protocols established for the Internet. As anyone who has used the Internet's World Wide Web knows, open standards make it relatively easy for members of a community to share information regardless of differences in their individual IT systems. In addition, they make it possible for members to use one another's computing power. Finally, the Internet's open standards permit each member of an internetwork to pick the communication channels—from a normal phone line to a high-speed connection—that are best suited for it to carry out its role in the virtual factory. In a real virtual factory, the network is the factory.

The information broker, which is an outside vendor in McDonnell Douglas's virtual factory, performs a variety of functions. It signs up new partners. It keeps track of the network's members and the number and level of relationships that each has with others in the network. It oversees security, constantly ensuring that each partner has the proper security clearance and access codes. Although AeroTech does not yet do so, an information broker could also serve as a converter, employing powerful conversion software to permit partners who have different formats or proprietary software to exchange information.

THE DEMANDS OF A VIRTUAL FACTORY

Before laying out the mechanics of an information-brokered manufacturing internetwork—a real virtual factory—it might help if we first explored why existing forms of EDI, groupware, and wide-area networks are inadequate. To that end, let's examine how each can or cannot satisfy the three main demands on a virtual factory: (1) that it be able to incorporate partners at any stage of a relationship, (2) that it be able to incorporate partners with all levels of IT sophistication, and (3) that it be able to provide all required functionality.

Different Stages.   Like people in a romantic relationship, manufacturing partners typically move through progressively closer stages—from dating through engagement to marriage. During the exploratory stage, companies learn about each other and establish norms of interaction and bases for further involvement. For companies, exploratory activities include requesting, sending, and obtaining information about products and services; distributing requests for bids and receiving quotes; and establishing contracts and purchase orders. Collaboration entails more sharing and planning. Companies at this stage have agreed, for example, to work together as customer and supplier and therefore want to exchange and review more detailed data, such as CAD/CAM files and manufacturing-process documentation. Integrated manufacturing partners expect a continuing relationship—for example, in a joint venture. Their activities include sharing data about production, inventory, and schedules and accessing the information and applications resident on each other's machines.

At any one moment, it is common for a company to be at different stages with its various partners. It may have several joint-venture partners and at the same time may be constantly shuffling customers and making changes in its relationships with suppliers. To support many relationships at all stages, information systems must be easy to enter and leave: a network that is expensive or difficult to join will discourage exploration. In addition, networks must be secure: potential participants will not join a system that will expose their internal networks or their transmissions to spies and hackers.

Different Levels of IT Sophistication.   Regardless of the stage of their relationship, participants in a virtual factory will vary greatly in their level of sophistication about information technology. That level is a combination of several factors, including the type and power of installed hardware and software; the average and highest level of computer expertise among site personnel; and the degree to which people on the site are already connected to one another by an internal network.

Within the typical large manufacturing company, different groups are themselves at different levels. A design group might have a cluster of linked workstations running advanced drawing and modeling software. The production control function might access mainframe manufacturing-resource-planning (MRP) software from dumb terminals. A sales manager might have a lone PC. And it would not be unusual if none of the three could interact with the others electronically, even if they were all on the same site.

There is also tremendous variation across smaller companies. For example, a subcontractor specializing in finite element analysis or other modeling techniques is likely to have an advanced computing environment, whereas a supplier of packaging materials may have only rudimentary systems. The wide range means that any technology underpinning a real virtual factory must be easy to implement, even on low-end hardware.

High Functionality.   Manufacturing groups have both heavy and complex information-sharing requirements. By heavy, we mean the great volume of information involved in any manufacturing process. For example, consider the body of documentation needed to specify how to build even a relatively simple part, the different information formats typically used, and the information required to move the item through the production process. As the part moves among partners' sites, this ever mounting pile of information must go with it. For complex parts, the amount of information required can be staggering. The paper required to fully describe the production of a Boeing 747 undoubtedly would not fit inside the airplane itself.

Information-sharing requirements within manufacturing are also complex. The IT process required to send a purchase order, for example, is very different from the process required to send an assembly. The former is a simple transmission of text, whereas the latter is an interactive manipulation of graphical data. Both, however, are common activities that a real virtual factory should support.

Sharing and manipulating all information on a network involve three distinct types of functionality. In ascending order of complexity, they are: simple data transmission, data access, and access to applications, or what we call telepresence.

Transmission is the most straightforward; it is simply sending a packet of information from one place to another. Partners in a virtual factory need to exchange all kinds of information, from E-mail to purchase orders to numerical control programs. Transmissions such as videoconferences need to occur in real time, but most do not.

Data access capabilities permit members of the community to share common pools of information in more sophisticated ways than simply by passing messages to one another. For example, by creating virtual bulletin boards and file cabinets that authorized users can open, companies can make sure that all participants in a product development project are abiding by the same schedule, that updated CAD files are always available to suppliers, or that regulators can monitor emissions levels. A real virtual factory must be able to permit some users to add or change information in databases in addition to viewing it.

The highest level of required functionality is telepresence, a capability that allows all authorized people to see and use the programs resident on a given computer, whether the users are company insiders or outsiders and whether they are on-site or far away. This attribute is one of the key advantages of the Internet, which lets cybernauts jump from machine to machine around the world, making use of the information and applications on each.

Telepresence is extraordinarily useful within a virtual factory. For example, it allows small companies to use the number-crunching power of a large partner for computationally intensive simulations, and it permits a customer to check the status of an order by logging on to a supplier's order-management system. That kind of activity can even be performed by means of a home page on the World Wide Web. (See the section titled "Virtual Factories, the World Wide Web, and Java.")

A real virtual factory, then, provides all this functionality to its partners, regardless of the stage of their relationships or their level of IT sophistication. The diagram "Three Factors Determine the Ease of Information Sharing" provides a framework that can help managers analyze whether their current solutions are adequate for their needs. The figure shows, for example, that it is much easier for companies at the integrated stage to agree on and build an information sharing structure than it is for companies that are only at the cooperative stage. Similarly, it shows that it is much harder to connect naïve IT users than sophisticated ones or to provide access to applications—real telepresence.

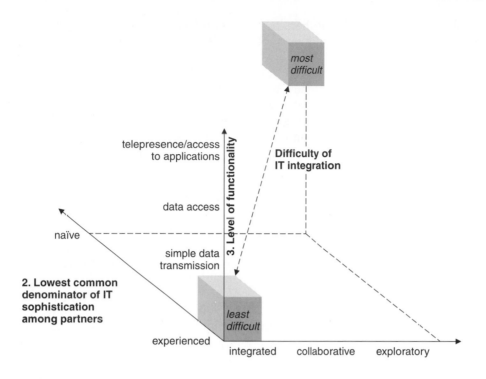

Three Factors Determine the Ease of Information Sharing

CURRENT APPROACHES

To compare different approaches to electronic collaboration, note how much of the cube each fills. A system that fills a lot of the space, especially one that reaches close to the back corner (where unsophisticated companies at the exploratory stage can transparently use others' machines), makes real virtual factories possible. Let's take a look at the three different categories of technology currently in use and see how they stack up.

Electronic Data Interchange. EDI is the oldest form of electronic collaboration among manufacturers; it grew out of a need to simplify the paperwork for administering the Berlin airlift. Today's EDI uses a collection of common formats for communicating data between companies. It is used most frequently to exchange data such as purchase orders, to execute transfers of electronic funds, or to provide delivery information to customers. EDI standards specify how each of these information transfers should be structured so that any party using those formats can accept transmission from any other party using them.

However, conventional forms of EDI cannot satisfy all the demands of a virtual factory. Despite the existence of some common standards, many systems are still inflexible and proprietary. As a consequence, it is expensive and time consuming both to add new members to such a network and to expand the types of information exchanged on it. Depending on the particular network, it can cost tens of thousands of dollars to add an EDI link and to mold one's own computer protocols to those used by the dominant customer. Such attributes mean that conventional EDI is best suited for linking the members of a relatively small, stable community—particularly a community in which one member is powerful enough to demand adherence to its communications standards. Conversely, it is ill suited for communities with a large number of transient members or members with limited IT resources. With traditional EDI, every time a new member is added to the existing system, a dedicated line—and in many cases, a special terminal on the member's premises—must be installed.

Conventional EDI has other limitations. It does not easily permit members of the community to exchange information with one another, because the system has to be specially configured to create each link between each pair of members that want to communicate. EDI networks tend to be used only to send information in batches and are awkward for creating real-time links between sites. Also, current EDI systems are not designed to allow members to operate a partner's computer from a remote location in order to use its applications software and computing power or to access its files.

Current EDI fills very little of the virtual factory's requirements. It provides only a low level of functionality and, because of its expense and fixed costs, is appropriate only for integrated partners. (See the diagram "Electronic Data Interchange and the Virtual Factory's Needs.")

Groupware. The class of software known as groupware addresses some of EDI's drawbacks and has become popular for building collaborative environments. Groupware applications help coordinate work in three ways. First, they make available a common body of information so that, for example, a salesperson on the road can check the in-stock status of an item for a customer. Second, they track work flows so that group members can—from a remote location—collaborate on documents and projects; all members of a design team, for example, can use proprietary groupware to make sure they are working with the most recent version of a drawing. Finally, the software provides a platform for communication and interactive discussions, from E-mail and bulletin boards to on-screen video. A major advantage of groupware is that all links do not need to be preestablished; authorized users can access and leave the system at will.

On the downside, groupware can be expensive. Each individual user must purchase a copy of the groupware application, and training and administration expenses for the new platform are high. Lotus Notes, for example, costs between $1,000 and $5,000 per user over a three-year period (*PC Week,* January 30, 1995).

A further drawback is that groupware cannot be used to gain access to remote computers that are not groupware servers. For example, it is not possible to use Lotus Notes to connect to another site's manufacturing information system to review inventory policies or to use its CAD software to work on the drawings of a part.

In summary, traditional groupware has many of the transmission and data access capabilities that an effective virtual factory needs. In addition, it requires a relatively low level of IT sophistication: people comfortable with PCs, for example, can use it without much difficulty. But groupware lacks adequate telepresence capabilities. Partners

Electronic Data Interchange and the Virtual Factory's Needs

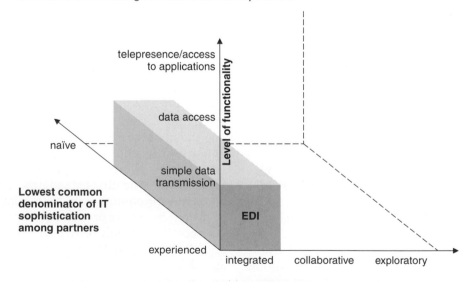

cannot use each other's applications. And because groupware entails a significant amount of administration and overhead, companies typically will not choose to use it to collaborate until it is clear that their relationship will continue. It will not be used by companies that are at the exploratory stage or anticipating a short relationship. If the community consists of a small number of partners that need to exchange only basic information such as orders, then EDI, because of its relative simplicity, is preferable to groupware. Although groupware is superior to traditional electronic data interchange in filling the requirements of a virtual factory, it nonetheless is far from perfect. (See the diagram "Groupware and the Virtual Factory's Needs.")

Wide-area Networks. This class of technology provides dedicated high-speed links that connect individual local-area networks. Unlike groupware links, wide-area networks are permanent and usually provide members with all the transmission, data-access, and telepresence capabilities that a real virtual factory requires. They provide universal access to all data and applications resident on members' local-area networks.

Membership in a wide-area network, however, is exclusive and expensive to obtain. The high-bandwidth telecommunications lines that make up their backbones, for example, typically cost more than $1,000 per month. In addition, administration of a dispersed network is complicated, and a group needs a relatively high degree of IT sophistication to participate. Consequently, wide-area networks usually exist only within a company and are rarely extended to other partners.

Because of those constraints, even large manufacturers build wide-area networks between only a few of their large sites and exclude smaller sites and smaller partner companies. Wide-area networks fill a tall but narrow slice of the total requirements of a virtual factory and cannot be extended to support companies that are at the cooperative or exploratory stages. (See the diagram "Wide-area Networks and the Virtual Factory's Needs.")

These limitations mean that proprietary wide-area networks are like an exclusive club. It is very difficult, for example, to use a wide-area network to share CAD data files with potential partners who might be interested in bidding for work. It also is difficult to add a new member to the system quickly to exploit a new opportunity to co-design a product—a severe limitation in this age of rapid product development.

Groupware and the Virtual Factory's Needs

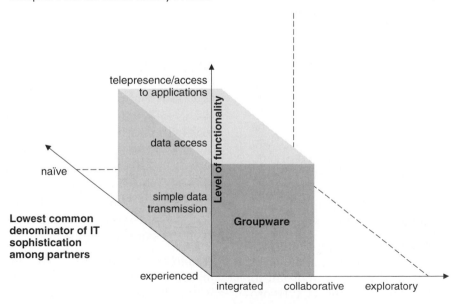

Stage of relationship between any two companies

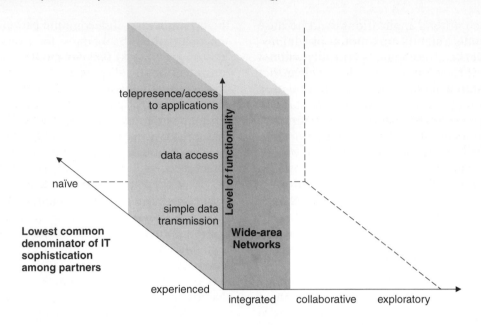

Wide-area Networks and the Virtual Factory's Needs

THE INFORMATION-BROKERED INTERNETWORK

Could someone patch together EDI, groupware, and wide-area networks to create a mosaic that would fill the needs of a full-fledged virtual factory? No. Proprietary and disparate standards make such a network extraordinarily expensive, complex, inelegant, and, in the long run, dysfunctional. Moreover, none of the three conventional technologies accommodate exploratory relationships.

But a more flexible and less expensive alternative for carrying out collaborative manufacturing has just emerged—the information-brokered internetwork. The confluence of several trends now makes this approach possible: the emergence of widely accepted, open standards; ever cheaper computing power; increasingly abundant bandwidth; the development of essentially unbreakable computer security; and accumulated expertise.

Open Standards. Standards among computers are simply agreements about how data should be formatted or transmitted. The most important for the emerging virtual factories are the TCP/IP protocols developed for the Internet, which standardize how dissimilar computers and networks pass data among themselves. The TCP/IP protocols

allow the three levels of functionality we have described: transmission, data access, and telepresence. As the unbelievable growth of the Internet attests, these increasingly dominant protocols have been helpful because they are comprehensive, open (published), and nonproprietary (free).

At the same time, standards for text files, spreadsheets, CAD drawings, and other electronic documents that make it easier for companies using different applications to exchange data also have emerged. Consequently, partners who share these standards on how to send information and what it should look like can communicate with confidence that nothing will be lost in the translation.

Cheap, Powerful Computing. Because of the phenomenal increase in computing power available per dollar, sufficient computing muscle for almost any information-sharing task in a virtual factory is now well within the financial reach of even the smallest companies.

Abundant Bandwidth. The information-carrying capacity of a communications link, or its bandwidth, has been increasing at least as fast as computing power. For example, standard modems today provide as much bandwidth as the highest-speed links did ten years ago, and dedicated links between two partners now provide enough bandwidth for full-motion video conferences, a very high bandwidth application. And several emerging technologies promise to increase bandwidth dramatically in the near future.

Security.   Information security is understandably a major concern for companies seeking to build virtual factories. But despite the continuing tales of break-ins and hacker exploits, tools such as network fire walls—computers that act as bouncers and check all incoming data—provide the means to keep outsiders out and to limit or customize each insider's access. In addition, essentially unbreakable data-encoding schemes now guarantee that information sent over the Internet or any other network remains unreadable until it reaches its destination.

Accumulated Expertise.   It takes time to master any emerging technology. But companies now are comfortably familiar with current open standards and the new technologies in computing, bandwidth, and security. Indeed, many businesses now have the skills required to innovate with these technologies and therefore the power to construct real virtual factories.

A network with the attributes listed above elegantly satisfies the demands of a virtual factory across all stages of relationships and all but the most naïve level of IT sophistication. (See the diagram "The Brokered Internetwork and the Virtual Factory's Needs.") Transient or prospective partners as well as small companies and unsophisticated IT users will be willing and able to join the community because the costs and overhead of membership are very low. Once all these companies are connected, each one can access a wider pool of computing power and information. For example:

- A large company can quickly and inexpensively send bid-request packages to a much wider range of potential subcontractors than it could before.
- People can access other companies' on-line catalogs, get all required product specifications, and place orders from their desktops.
- A machine shop can use the three-dimensional modeling software resident on a distant mainframe to place the part it plans to make within a digital mock-up of a larger assembly and check that it fits—before the first one is produced.

The Brokered Internetwork and the Virtual Factory's Needs

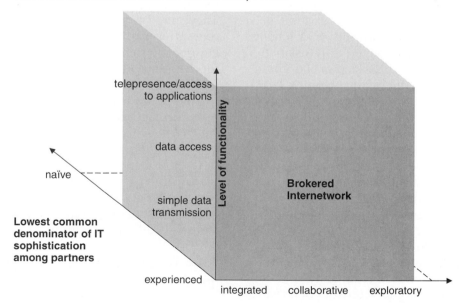

These examples represent only a tiny fraction of the total uses that members will find for a virtual factory. Robert Metcalfe, inventor of the widespread Ethernet networking standard, contends that the utility of a computer network increases exponentially, not linearly, as the number of users expands. We are confident that real virtual factories will provide solid support for Metcalfe's Law.

THE INFORMATION BROKER

Of course, it is one thing for a networked factory to be possible or desirable, and it is quite another to create and maintain it and help it evolve. Designing the system, administering it, updating its technology, maintaining security, and exploiting new opportunities as they arise are collectively a huge job—and one that most companies whose primary business is not IT will be loath to undertake. Indeed, McDonnell Douglas has turned to what we call an information broker to perform this function.

McDonnell Douglas's spin-off AeroTech developed the aero-space company's virtual factory and, in its role as information broker, keeps everything running smoothly. AeroTech maintains a database of all users and of all the information to which each is allowed access. It also has developed software packages and training manuals that allow small companies to join the community easily and quickly. For larger, more established partners, AeroTech builds gateways to their existing networks and establishes high-bandwidth links. Finally, AeroTech could eventually convert or translate the various data formats that exist across the virtual factory. For example, if one manufacturer's CAD data were written in Catia and another's is in Pro/Engineer, AeroTech could translate the data for them so that they could work together. More important, it could build a system that would perform this type of service automatically.

Potentially, an information broker can provide much more than the computer security, maintenance, and translation functions for the virtual factory. It can help the partners identify which information has value to particular constituents and how revenue might be generated from this information. For example, one company may have test data on the performance characteristics of its valve components, and that data might be tremendously useful to another company in its design process. Or the design department of a particular company might have ready-made CAD drawings of a wide range of electrical connectors and might choose to sell them to a partner that wanted to avoid drawing them from scratch. And a larger company might keep a list of suppliers that have been certified for meeting the ISO-9000 quality standards—a list that could be useful to others looking for such vendors.

Very few IT contractors presently have the kind of relationship that would allow them to explore and exploit opportunities like these jointly. Why? Identifying information-sharing opportunities on the network requires industry knowledge that is both broad and deep. Current systems integrators rarely have such knowledge.

The first generation of internetwork-building information brokers will probably be either spin-offs of larger companies, such as AeroTech, or completely new companies composed of computer networking experts and veterans of the particular industry who have a deep understanding of how the industry works. Real virtual factories are likely to proliferate first in environments where there is a large, dominant partner that can provide the impetus and the funding. McDonnell Douglas Aerospace, for example, had a clear idea of its requirements and was willing initially to assume all the costs of filling them, even though others also would reap benefits.

Eventually, however, many different models for building virtual factories are likely to arise. They may be star-like structures with dominant centers or manufacturing communities in which groups of small manufacturers band together for the same kinds of benefits available to large traditional factories with abundant resources for expanding information technology. The rigid formulation of traditional electronic data interchange will give way to a world of greater fluidity.

Once the benefits of the real virtual factory have been demonstrated, they will create a new manufacturing world. In this new world, companies that insist on remaining loners or that cling to today's closed, proprietary systems will find it increasingly difficult to survive.

THE REAL VIRTUAL FACTORY THAT AEROTECH BUILT

AeroTech Service Group, which is based in St. Louis, Missouri, has built a highly effective virtual factory with McDonnell Douglas Aerospace. The open and flexible network accommodates users whose IT sophistication and relationships with one another vary greatly. Moreover, it permits members to carry out a wide variety of collaborative tasks and is extremely secure.

Those attributes explain why the number of participants in this computer-linked manufacturing community has soared since mid-1993, when AeroTech, a McDonnell Douglas spin-off, began adding external suppliers to the network. Until then, the network had been limited to 50 or so McDonnell employees who used it to pass data between different computer systems within the organization. When external suppliers joined, they were so impressed with the way the network helped them work with McDonnell that they started to ask their suppliers and partners to join. By the fall of 1994, there were 400 internal and external users. There are now several thousand.

To accommodate a broad range of tasks and users, and to make the system as simple as possible to use, AeroTech employs protocols developed for the Internet, which itself is just an extra-large network that connects millions of dissimilar computers around the world. In addition, AeroTech permits members to choose from a wide assortment of telecommunication methods and speeds. Those members with minimal or sporadic needs access the system with modems, while more permanent participants, such as customers within other large aerospace companies or the U.S. government, use dedicated high-bandwidth links.

The network offers its members enormous advantages. Consider how McDonnell Douglas and UCAR Composites, a $12 million manufacturer of tooling for high-performance composite components based in Irvine, California, use the network to build prototypes of complex new parts rapidly. McDonnell wanted to send UCAR design updates electronically but could not allow UCAR to establish a direct link into its computers because of security concerns—namely, that an aggressive hacker might tap into such a link to access or modify data within McDonnell computers. (Although UCAR is a trusted supplier, McDonnell has a large number of suppliers of similar size and importance, and the cost of maintaining security if all had direct links would be prohibitive.)

AeroTech provided an alternative. At McDonnell, computer-aided design files are translated into the numerical-control machine code needed to operate UCAR's metal-cutting machines. Using standard Internet protocols over a dedicated high-speed link, McDonnell then transfers the CAD file and the metal-cutting program to AeroTech's secure network node. AeroTech's system then forwards them to UCAR on normal phone lines.

Once information on the job arrives in California, UCAR engineers can view it on their own CAD/CAM systems to make last-minute checks on the program. They then transfer the cutting program to their machines and begin manufacturing. The solution was particularly attractive for UCAR, which already had a paperless manufacturing operation. Now it could feed the data directly into its manufacturing and quality-assurance systems. As a result of the AeroTech system, the cost of these transfers has fallen from $400 per file (for tapes and express mail) to $4—and can be carried out in seconds rather than days.

This method of transferring cutting programs also is being used by hundreds of small machine shops, many of whose IT systems and expertise are much less sophisticated than UCAR's. These companies, which include many five- or six-person shops, can dial AeroTech using a regular modem, download a program or a drawing onto their PCs, and use the data to manufacture the parts.

This virtual factory also helps its members find the best suppliers much more quickly than before. In the past, McDonnell Douglas would invite representatives of qualified suppliers to come to St. Louis to view bid-request packages (containing engineering drawings and manufacturing-process specifications) so that they could decide whether and how much to bid for particular jobs. The groups would remain at the bidding table until all jobs were subcontracted—a process that often would take days.

Using the virtual factory's electronic bidding system, a McDonnell buyer now can E-mail qualified suppliers throughout the world that a job is available for bidding and let them access information about the job securely through the Internet. The suppliers then can use the system to return their bids to St. Louis. The system even ranks the bids for the buyer on the basis of cost. McDonnell estimates that the savings from electronic bidding alone pay for the operating costs of the entire system.

AeroTech also helps the electronic manufacturing community coordinate schedules better by allowing remote members to use scheduling software on one another's machines. A Department of Defense project manager in Washington, D.C., might use the system to access a McDonnell Douglas mainframe and run the graphics-based program that maintains a project's schedule. The manager then could get early warnings of time overruns by checking whether subcontractors were completing their subassemblies on time.

One of the most powerful functions that the AeroTech community provides is the ability to operate large, complex software programs securely from afar, without the need for sophisticated equipment on the local site. As a part of its contract with McDonnell Helicopter, for example, the U.S. Army periodically reviews engineering designs for the new Longbow helicopter. The army now can view these drawings by operating a McDonnell computer from a remote location, rather than by downloading the files, which would require the army to have the enormous CAD software systems on its own machines. The drawings and the graphics program to view them reside on a workstation in Phoenix, Arizona. AeroTech has configured the computer to serve this program to authorized clients, such as the army's reviewers. AeroTech maintains a database that constantly keeps track of which connections are allowed, by whom, into which computers, and with what level of functionality. All transmissions are routed in real time through AeroTech's watchdog computers to prevent Internet interlopers from breaking into the Phoenix computer or customers' computers on the network.

It's true that closed groups of technically sophisticated companies with long-standing partnerships carry out many of these same kinds of tasks. But, unlike them, AeroTech has made it possible for both longtime and casual partners to collaborate easily, securely, and cheaply, and without having to invest in new and proprietary information technology.

AeroTech and McDonnell are now exploring ways to generate even more value from this system. In particular, AeroTech is looking at how it might become an information broker for engineering data by providing a conduit through which McDonnell could sell and distribute drawings for the spare-parts business. Currently, spare parts are procured by the Defense Logistics Agency, which requests quotations for manufacturing them. Because many prospective manufacturers are unable to access the appropriate drawings quickly enough, a small number of companies, including McDonnell, end up with the business.

McDonnell, however, may choose to sell rapid access to the drawings and technical data so that a larger pool of qualified companies can bid on the jobs. By stimulating competition, this approach could improve the quality of its spares providers, allow McDonnell to manufacture only those spares that are most worth its while to make, and generate a higher return on the information systems that manage and store the technical data. AeroTech would help more producers of spares join the virtual factory, activate their access to the information required to make the spares, and bill the producer of the data, using whatever pricing model McDonnell Douglas chooses. Clearly, McDonnell Douglas, AeroTech, and the other members of this virtual factory have only begun to mine its vast potential.

VIRTUAL FACTORIES, THE WORLD WIDE WEB, AND JAVA

Advances in internetworking technologies are making virtual factories easier to build. First, there is the much vaunted explosive growth of the World Wide Web. The Web's primary importance, from a manufacturing point of view, is that it provides a common visual interface to connect to a computer network.

Growing numbers of companies are embracing these standard browsers and protocols as the way for sites in different organizations to communicate with one another. This broad acceptance makes the World Wide Web an immensely powerful tool for intercompany transactions. The power and ubiquity of these protocols and interfaces will make the Web one of the mainstays of virtual factories to come. Web sites already can help buyers of electronic components find what they're looking for on the Web (see http://centralres.com) or match buyers and sellers from more than 26,000 companies in the apparel and textile industry (see http://www.apparelex.com). And Netscape is teaming up with General Electric Information Services to offer EDI services through the Web.

A second development ultimately may prove to be at least as important as the Web: the advent of languages such as Sun's Java, which will allow a

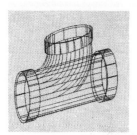

Applets let users work on distant CAD drawings.

user to connect to a remote site and grab tiny pieces of software (called applets) one at a time. Any computer that can run a Web browser can run this kind of software. Many people have speculated that this way of working will eventually challenge the existing methods of running programs on the desktop. Desktop users currently must buy increasingly large, complex program packages to perform tasks such as word processing or spreadsheet analysis. Those packages contain a vast array of functions that any individual user will never use. In contrast, Internet-based Java-like languages will allow customers to obtain modules for performing particular functions as they need them by downloading them across an increasingly fast and reliable Internet. Users will pay for the functions they need. For example, a customer purchasing a word-processing program will not have to buy a spelling checker as part of the package but, instead, can download an applet containing the checker from the Internet if and when needed. And Java was de-

veloped with security safeguards in place to foil viruses and other threats.

Consider what this capability will mean for the virtual factory. A company will be able to post work-sheet applets on its Web pages to allow customers to simulate the function of its products before buying them. For example, a valve manufacturer might supply an applet that allows engineers not only to see pictures and CAD drawings of the valves but also to use a working spreadsheet that would permit them to make key design calculations and show the results on-screen.

Such applets also will allow companies to deliver sophisticated bid requests over the Web. These requests could include a combination of moving diagrams of the product that they would like potential suppliers to bid on, along with bid forms and more traditional drawings.

A Java-based interface for a three-dimensional CAD system not only allows companies to put a catalog on the Web but also lets potential customers examine a three-dimensional representation of a product from any angle to see if it is right for their needs (see http://deneb.hbs.edu/public/javademo/viewer.html). If the user has to access a large legacy database at another company and doesn't happen to have the right kind of terminal, Java can even make a Web browser pretend to be that terminal by emulating it in software (see http://www.unige.ch/hotjava/Emulator3270.html). As network-based software becomes more and more sophisticated, it will present new opportunities to extract the power of the Web for manufacturing.

The Coordination of Global Manufacturing

Ramchandran Jaikumar and David M. Upton

Production capacity is now sufficiently flexible in some industries to be viewed as a commodity. Technological change has raised the prospect of global markets for a variety of types of flexible manufacturing capacity. This case outlines technological and commercial conditions under which markets for flexible manufacturing capacity are likely to arise, describes an industry in which a capacity market exists, and explores desiderata for such markets.

CONDITIONS FOR GLOBAL COMMODITY CAPACITY MARKETS

Important changes in manufacturing technology have occurred in many industries. Machines for many processes are now very flexible, in that they may be programmed to perform a wide variety of manufacturing tasks and are able to accommodate diverse product characteristics while providing both high quality and low cost. Although the products manufactured by such technology are highly differentiated, the broad diffusion and standardization of the technology has made productive capacity comparatively common and indistinguishable. Indeed, for many highly differentiated products (metal-machines parts or socks, for example), the precise source of the product is becoming much less relevant since the technology of production allows consistent quality and cost performance regardless of source. This suggests a novel situation—one in which flexible capacity may be seen as a commodity—inasmuch as units of flexible capacity are comparatively lacking in distinguishing qualities. The large number of product variations that such capacity may effectively produce means that the preliminary input for the process is information, in the form of well-codified, often computer-readable product descriptions. Advances in global telecommunications mean that such information may be effortlessly transmitted between customer and source, making the precise location of the manufacturer progressively less important.

Along with advances in telecommunications, diffusion of the supporting manufacturing technology to an ever-growing range of processes has had far-reaching consequences, from the shop floor to the global structure of industries. We are seeing fundamental change in such basic elements of production as firm size, the nature and form of product and process specification, transaction processing, and labor.

FACTORY SIZE

Why should factories be large? Companies have traditionally collected the machinery of production into large factories for two reasons:

- to gain economies of scale
- to share overhead costs, such as maintenance, quality assurance, materials tracking, and so forth.

Technological economies of scale have never been strong in industries that produce highly differentiated products: machines in such industries are gathered together primarily to share overhead costs. With the new technologies, even this source of pressure to aggregate has been greatly relieved. Today's machines are highly reliable and require very little maintenance. What little is needed may be performed by operators. Because machining processes are under programmable computer control and are, in general, well understood and predictable, machines produce good quality output time after time, eliminating the need for separate quality departments to weed out defects. Finally, technological solutions make overhead due to information and material flow very small, regardless of the size of the operation. Minimum efficient

Reprinted by permission of Harvard Business School Press. From *Globalization, Technology and Competition: The Fusion of Computers and Telecommunications in the 1990s* by S. P. Bradley, J. A. Hausman, and R. L. Nolan (editors). Boston, MA 1993, pp 169–183. Copyright © 1993 by the President and Fellows of Harvard College, all rights reserved.

scale for a modern manufacturing operation in many industries is a manufacturing cell of about six machines and fewer than a dozen people. Such a cell functions as a factory within a factory, effecting an entire production process under computer control, often including materials handling and inspection.

Product and Process Specifications

With computer-based manufacturing technologies, product and process specifications exist as computational procedures developed on specialized computer-aided design (CAD) systems. These procedures are transportable via standardized telecommunication links to the machine controllers that govern the manufacturing process. Moreover, to the extent that the people who write them are able to anticipate and solve every contingency, these procedures guarantee precise reproducibility, that is, every part made by any machine running a particular procedure will be exactly the same. The two characteristics of modern product and process descriptions—transportability and precise reproducibility—reduce the need in many industries to collocate engineering and design with manufacturing, except for pilot production. The standardization and predictability of the link between design and manufacturing weaken

traditional dogma, which insists that design engineers be on hand during volume manufacturing to make design trade-offs as manufacturing problems occur. Technologies in many industries now anticipate and eliminate such problems systematically rather than on an ad hoc basis, allowing engineers to be absent from volume production and rendering the location of volume manufacturing less relevant. Indeed, manufacturing units need not necessarily even have their own engineering functions; in the context that is evolving, engineering and design can be effectively supplied by physically and functionally distinct organizations.

Transaction Processing

One economy of scale to which firms in the new manufacturing context do have access is in sales and distribution. With the right communication links, one marketing department can today serve the world.

The traditional firm-to-market scenario is depicted in Figure 1, the electronic marketplace in Figure 2.

In the latter we envision direct links between individual facilities of a firm and the buyers of their products. Contracts in the electronic marketplace would likely be many and small, and the market system would learn through repeated

FIGURE I Traditional Firm-to-Market Scenario

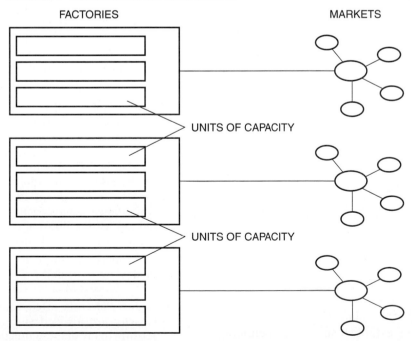

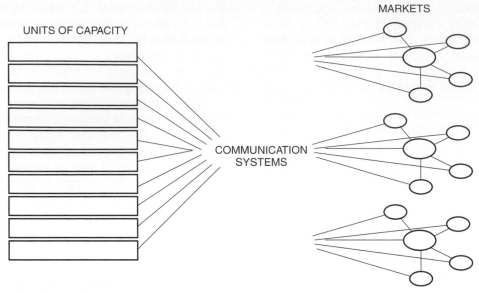

UNITS OF CAPACITY

MARKETS

COMMUNICATION SYSTEMS

FIGURE 2 Electronic Marketplace

transactions, enabling it, over time, to arrange almost universally ideal contracts. The speed of the system would be such that contracts would be renegotiated dynamically in the case of nonfulfillment, utilizing surge capacity among the manufacturers. Such a system minimizes transaction costs by effectively automating transactions. The telecommunications basis for such a system exists; all that is required is sufficient speed, memory, and reliability. If the memory is structured well, the market functions could be performed without human participation.

Labor

The existence of standard flexible technologies has decreased the need for firm-specific training. A number of industries may now draw from a pool of labor whose skill level is lower and more homogeneous. This, in turn, means lower costs for centralized training and personnel functions. For example, with a standardized computer numerical control (CNC) machine tool technology, a person trained in CNC milling may very quickly learn CNC turning.

Summary

Collectively, these factors serve to substantially de-emphasize economies of scale and reduce absolute cost outlay at the plant level. Manufacturing concerns can now establish small, independent

cells that operate effectively and economically with only a modest capital investment. Moreover, these small units of flexible capacity can be physically and organizationally separated from design, marketing, and engineering. Small minimum efficient scale, low capital requirement, and separability of volume manufacturing operations, by effectively lowering entry barriers, ensure the prospect of ample players in the market for flexible capacity.

Advantages of a capacity market. There are a number of distinct advantages to organizing an industry's manufacturing network so that providers of flexible capacity compete, among them:

- The pooling effect of the market better insulates capacity buyers from fluctuations in demand. Since products are diversified, it will often be the case that when one capacity purchaser's demand is high (for his/her particular product) another's may be low. The pooling effect enables capacity purchasers to take advantage of the disparate temporal requirement for flexible capacity and avoid the costs of capacity-constrained operation and low asset utilization that often face the firms to which capacity is dedicated.

- Poor capacity performance can be combated more quickly by switching suppliers than through the slower process of improving internal operations.

- Managerial costs of coordinating and balancing capacity are avoided since market mechanisms perform many of these functions. For example, the difficult task of assigning capacity to the highest priority task can be performed by the price mechanism—when industry capacity is tight, it goes to the highest bidder. This saves the cost of bureaucratic internal groups having to juggle jobs inefficiently in order of apparent priority, without information that would enable them to reflect priorities accurately.

- Capacity can be bought in the short term, providing the buyer faced with a high degree of uncertainty can access capacity without committing to its continued use.

Commercial conditions. The factors listed above will be most beneficial when demand is highly uncertain, the managerial costs of coordinating proprietary capacity are high, and transactions are small and great in number. Provided the technological conditions described above prevail, we would expect to see market for flexible capacity develop in industries that face such commercial conditions.

AN EXAMPLE: THE DISINTEGRATION OF THE TEXTILE INDUSTRY IN PRATO

Since the fourteenth century, the textile industry in Prato, Italy, has been the economic backbone of Florence and Pistoia regions. Once, armies of artisans carded and dyed, spun and weaved. But with the technological changes that precipitated the Industrial Revolution, which brought increased economies of scale, firms grew in size and vertically integrated so as to be able to schedule and balance capacity in these various process steps. Because starving assets of input materials incurred substantial penalties, given the heavy required investment in production technology, great advantage accrued to coordinating the process steps directly to avoid such circumstances. Production equipment for the various process steps was collocated to facilitate coordination and the quick resolution of interprocess problems, and central marketing and design departments were maintained on-site to work with production and match customers to production capacity and capabilities.

Rediscovery of Small Economic Scale

Most Prato mills were integrated in this way in the early 1970s, with fiber production, dyeing, spinning, and weaving performed in the same company. But many of these companies had progressively become unprofitable. Lower market prices, global competition, and rising internal costs had gnawed margins to the bone. Meanwhile, new dyeing and finishing techniques were becoming available and the market was demanding an ever-broader range of products from these new methods.

Some mill owners recognized that their integrated mills were an encumbrance in the new regime. The processes had become so well understood, and hence specifiable, that the various steps were largely independent of one another, yet the flexibility of the individual processes remained constrained by the particular output of the upstream, and requirements of the downstream steps. Capacity, such as weaving or spinning, had become cheaper and was now economical in much smaller units, eroding economies of scale. The increasing overhead burden and need to effectively coordinate production of the broader product ranges and take advantage of newfound flexibility in each of the process steps led firms to look very closely at the manufacturing structure that had been the industry paradigm for a century. In the face of extinction, firms began to change.

Many mills followed the example of the Menichetti family, which broke its mill into eight separate companies, one a realty company that leased space and services to the rest. As much as 50% of the stock in these companies, financed through profits, was transferred to employees. To ensure competitiveness, Menichetti insisted that each company find 50% of existing business outside the original business. At the same time, he established a New York-based marketing company to create new designs and match product with the best producer. This company was to provide no more than 30% of the business of any company in the Menichetti fold.

Within three years, all units of the disintegrated Menichetti mill were running at 90% utilization, product variety had increased tenfold, average in-process inventory was reduced from 4 months to 15 days, and attrition had reduced the labor force by a third while production had risen by 25% (largely because the satellite firms invested in new technology). By 1980, all but one of the Prato mills had undergone similar disintegration, turning a sluggish threatened industry into a thriving community of innovative flexible companies, each a world-class competitor. This process continued throughout the value chain (see Figure 3).

The predicament of the textile industry, which found itself on the brink of an important global change, is by no means unique. Disintegration may have progressed further in textiles than in other industries, but the conditions outlined at the beginning of this chapter apply to a growing enclave of industries. Very similar circumstances prevail in small-batch metal machining, for example, with the flexibility of the machining cell and its small economic scale.[1] But the lack of standardization of parts programs, the existence of some remaining machine-tool specializations, and the indifference of machine tool producers to small manufacturers have so far prevented the production of parts-programmed machine products from following the example of textiles.[2]

Network Coordination and the Modern Impannatori

The key to the success of the Prato system lies in the role of the modern impannatori.[3] A throwback to medieval times, these agents provide central brokerage for the firms in the network, of which there are now between 15,000 and 20,000, employing some 70,000 people. Today, several hundred such brokers draw from a hierarchical network of these thousands of suppliers. Brokers' thorough knowledge of the capacity, capability, and loading of each of the producers loosely collected in their folds enables them to source production for customers, find customers for spare production capacity, and intermediate in the negotiation process.

Effective management of this complex information set, coupled with trustworthiness and honesty, are the hallmarks of the successful impannatori. Indeed, it is this trustworthiness that prevents the problems often resulting from the contracts that are difficult to specify—the trust ensures that what is needed is provided without the constraint of legal specification. Many specifications are thus based on a tacit understanding of industry standards. The complexity of the capacity assignment problem is rendered manageable by the autonomy of the various actors in the system, who are able to concentrate on being effective in their specialties while contributing to the perfor-

Activity	Number of Firms
Wool scouring and combining	13
Spinning, twisting, winding, reeling	1,429
Weaving	7,013
Hosiery and knitwear	1,852
Waste reclaiming	491
Finishing	232
Total	11,030

FIGURE 3 Firms in the Prato Network by 1975

mance of the network as a whole. Assignments of capacity are made through the market mechanism and the impannatori, enabling the system to avail itself of the most appropriate vendor and thus the full flexibility of the market for each element in the value chain.

Globalization and Communication

Among the technological changes dramatically expanding and changing the textile industry is codification. Today, cloth required by the world market may be uniquely specified with a code of 50 digits. Computer-aided design systems permit rapid local prototyping of a fabric before sourcing to a volume producer. Most important, computers facilitate an electronic marketplace in which the complexity of the production hierarchy can be "managed." Global telecommunications and continued disintegration suggest the possibility of trading options on both products and production capacity. For example, a fashion manufacturer uncertain of the season's demand for a product that has not been precisely specified may insure against a lack of supply by buying an option on the use of flexible capacity. Today, at least toward the end of the value chain, it is capacity, not product, that is a commodity. Units of flexible capacity are now relatively indistinguishable from one another and have the capability of producing myriad products. The products themselves, characterized by variety and customization to a particular fashion, are not at all commodity-like.

Manufacturing and Negotiation

Integration of advanced telecommunications and information systems holds promise for more fully automating the negotiation process in the Prato textile industry by speeding information flows and allowing requirements to be matched more quickly to supply. The extreme complexity of information flows, given the plurality of operators acting at different hierarchical levels (the top level comprising hundreds of impannatori splitting control to thousands of suppliers and manufacturers), makes control of an automated negotiation system highly strategic. Such a system would be capable of integrating single elements of the network; it would support real-time monitoring of the entire negotiation process and its related services, and provide the necessary control to achieve optimization. It would also enable artisans and subcontractors, the largest group in the Prato system, to "see" the market, to discern market trends and review other suppliers' capacities in order to react quickly to market demands. Access to such information would greatly stabilize the activities of many of the small firms.

Conditions for the effective marshalling of resources in manufacturing systems that are coordinated using negotiation methods are currently of interest at many levels. As the flexibility of manufacturing elements increases and effective units become smaller and more independent, it becomes increasingly advantageous to permit entities to negotiate with one another.

Upton describes a negotiation system that functions within a plant.[4] In this system, the partly completed product (such as raw casting) is provided with a miniature manufacturing computer physically attached to it. This computer uses artificial intelligence techniques to negotiate the manufacture of the product (step by step) with the various processing entities in the system, such as transport vehicles and machine tools. Machines bid for the right to provide processing for the product and the product selects the best bid at each step.[5] Bidding machines take into account their prevailing workloads, commitments, and capabilities. After successfully visiting all the necessary stations, the semifinished product (which might be a component for a large earth-mover, say) relinquishes its computer so that subsequent products may avail themselves of its experience such as its knowledge about unreliable performers and optimistic bidders. Thus, the system slowly builds expertise about itself in the product stream. This system is able to adapt easily to the removal and addition of new machines, since removed machines stop bidding and new machines are simply told to start. The technique solves many of the problems of centralized computer control in dynamic manufacturing systems.

At the intracompany level, Jaikumar has considered the optimal behavior of users and providers of processing capabilities within the firm.[6] He describes a negotiation system in which a firm's sales agents are the buyers of capacity and the production resource managers are the providers. Jaikumar shows that such a decentralized system can both be optimal for the firm and provide an efficient incentive system. At the level of global coordination, we are most interested in exploring how a global, decentralized negotiation system might best be constructed for manufacturing.

ISSUES IN SYSTEMS DESIGN AND OBJECTIVES

A number of factors must be carefully considered in attempting to establish a structure for a Prato-like market, among them: reliability, management information, brokerage, and commodity-like transactions.

Reliability

Capacity must be reliable and there must be effective mechanisms for ensuring that unreliable suppliers discount appropriately. Information on the performance of previous contracts will enable the market to take into account both the quality and reliability of suppliers. The creditworthiness of buyers must similarly be assured. How might such information be promulgated and what recourse provided to suppliers and buyers for correcting inaccuracies? For example, suppliers might be required to specify the proportion of the last hundred contracts on which they were late, or in which there was a dispute concerning quality.

There will inevitably be transactions in which one party is aggrieved and assigns too much importance to one troublesome event. For example, a customer firm may suffer badly because of one instance of failure by its supplier and may feel the need to take some punitive measure. Of course, the consequences of a party's actions are not relevant in determining its ongoing performance, so the market should ensure that these kinds of occurrences are accommodated.

Management Information

What information does a supplier need in order to compete effectively in an automated market? Temporary differences in cost of capacity due to scheduling constraints are inevitable. Manufacturers currently making pink T-shirts, given sufficient demand, would very much like to continue doing so to avoid changeover costs; where should they seek buyers of such temporarily cheap capacity?

What internal information about changeover costs does a firm need? Decisions about what price to bid on a job rely on timely and accurate internal information. The advantage will go to players that are able to reliably predict their own performance for the purpose of determining their own bids as well as to ensure satisfactory acquittal of the contract.

Brokerage

Under what conditions is it advantageous to use brokers of capacity? Clearly if communications can be organized effectively in a distributed fashion, the need for a centralized hub is reduced. When information can be transmitted and received throughout a global network, the role of a central broker as a channel for information is less clear. Individual firms could begin to access the network to determine customer requirements and bid directly on jobs as they arise. Users of capacity could post requirements on the network (for products as well as for capacity options and futures).

Commodity-Like Transactions

Methods for limiting damage arising from nonperformance of contracts are essential. Some capacity providers will be able to provide insurance by maintaining spare capacity. A futures and options market in capacity would offer a hedge against increases in price, for example. Whereas product variety has previously limited such deals to commodity products, given the flexible capacity to produce commodity-traded products we expect to see commodity-like transactions.

Moreover, we need to explore the various methods by which different forms of capacity might be converted into financial instruments. Such forms would include futures and spot markets as well as options. The insurance of these instruments is also of interest, as is the entry and modus operandi of third parties in bilateral transactions, which might have a considerable effect.

THE GROWING ARENA

The application of programmable computer control is likely to continue to broaden and increase in sophistication. As we learn more about the physics of various processes, it is becoming possible to automate them and allow a computer to control precisely the variants of the items they produce. This is true even of processes that have traditionally been craft-based and required tremendous skill.

An example of such a process is sheet metal spinning, in which a flat plate of metal is rotated on a lathe-like machine and forced over a metal die using a mandrel. This operation can produce many different shapes (it is most often used for the production of shades for industrial lighting). Sheet metal spinning has traditionally required very high skill on the part of the operator, since it is easy to push too hard and tear the metal, or too softly and leave the metal too thick. But now this operation may be carried out automatically under computer numerical control. Operators complain that the quality of the product is "not what we can do," but it will not be long until control has been refined to such an extent that a computer program will be able to produce dies and spin customized products to order.

The foregoing is an example of a process in the early stages of programmability; other processes are much further advanced and have been reliably programmable for a number of years. The chief constraint in such processes is no longer the physical manufacturing process, but the information required to tell the machine what to produce. For example, in the manufacture of electronic circuit boards, all manufacturing instructions may be completely specified by a set of computer programs, from drilling holes in the boards to the exact placement of surface-mount and through-hole components before soldering. What is more, these operations may be affected reliably and consistently by programmable machines running standardized programs. Despite the tremendous variation in electronic devices, circuit board manufacturing capacity is becoming a commodity. Many firms now produce boards for products ranging from modems to fashionable electronic toys in small facilities with only one or two programmable machines. They are often in competition with a large number of similar subcontractors using identical machinery.

Spring making has traditionally involved the precise cutting of cams and gears to control an automatic spring-making machine. This was a task requiring high skill and years of experience. Some manufacturers were thus very much better than others and required substantial skilled machine shops to produce the appropriate cams. Today, springs can be produced under programmable computer control by small programmable machines that run a standardized program. Each machine is capable of interpreting the program and putting the appropriate kinks and hooks into any spring being produced. Such machines have dramatically changed the industry, and many small spring-making shops (often run by ex-employees of larger manufacturers) now bid readily on spring-making jobs for small electro-magnetic devices.

There are many other examples of industries in which the type of coordination described in this case is becoming practicable. Although the global computerization of such a market for flexible capacity is yet to be seen in practice, we believe that such markets will soon exist. As global telecom-

munications and information technology enable such manufacturers to compete efficiently, with standardized technology and minimal barriers to entry, sources of advantage for individual firms are hard to identify. This leaves small firms faced with the prospect of participating in such a global market for flexible capacity with a very important question: What is it now important to do well?

NOTES

1. R. Jaikumar, "Japanese Flexible Manufacturing Systems: Impact on the United States," *Japan and the World Economy*, 1, no. 2 (1987): 113–143.

2. R. Jaikumar, Statement before the Subcommittee on Innovation, Technology and Productivity of the Small Business Committee of the United States Senate, December 2, 1987.

3. The closest modern translation of this word is "rag-trader." Impannatori were coordinators of artisans during the Renaissance.

4. D. M. Upton, "The Operation of Large Computer-Controlled Manufacturing Systems," Ph.D. diss., Purdue University (1988); D. M. Upton, "A Flexible Architecture for a Computer-Controlled Manufacturing System," *Manufacturing Review* (March 1992): 58–72.

5. The question of why machines should "want" to bid for the right to work results only from the anthropomorphic analogy, and not because this causes any inherent functional problem.

6. R. Jaikumar, "Resource Allocation in Automated Flexible Manufacturing Systems," Harvard Business School Working Paper 88026 (1988).

MODULE 3

Designing and Implementing Operations Improvement Strategies

OVERVIEW

Few firms now view the activities of production only as costs to be minimized, and the value-generating possibilities of operations are becoming broadly understood. Managers accept that their operations, when managed well, can be powerful sources of competitive advantage. Toyota, Wal-Mart, and Southwest Airlines,[1] for example, have maintained industry leadership and profitability thanks largely to their operational excellence. In three very different industries, they show the sustained power of better processes and systems. They have each insulated themselves against their rivals by a relentless improvement in operations performance.

There are also many examples of leaders that slipped badly when their operations became ineffective through neglect or misguided improvement efforts. In late 1995, Hayes Microcomputer Inc., a leading manufacturer of personal computer modems, was forced to declare bankruptcy as a result of being unable to satisfy demand for its products. The company struggled to reconfigure its operations, and experienced a severe cash crunch when capacity, inventory, and procurement problems hobbled production.[2] While it was recovering from its problems, it fell behind upstarts like US Robotics. In the 1980s, General Motors responded to the threat posed by more efficient Japanese carmakers by automating its operations. Its Hamtramck, Michigan, plant opened in 1985 as the showcase of these efforts and contained a vast range of advanced technologies, including laser measurement systems, automated guided vehicles, and 260 robots.[3] This bold experiment was an unmitigated disaster—the result of an inappropriate and poorly developed operations improvement strategy. The automated plant could only produce cars at half the required rate, technical problems were continual, and quality plummeted. GM eventually removed much of the automation at Hamtramck, and lost 10 points of market share in North America during the 1980s.

As these examples suggest, when a significant operational performance gap appears between firms, it is exploited. The strongest performer presses its advantage, and the weaker players must respond or be forced from the game. Southwest, Wal-Mart, and Toyota have steadily captured territory from rivals, while Hayes and GM found themselves on the other side of increasingly large gaps and had to scramble to close them. If these gaps seldom appeared they would not be a major concern, and managers would need to worry only rarely about their operations becoming liabilities. If they appeared and disappeared randomly they would not warrant managers' attention, because it would be useless to anticipate or respond to them. A great deal of evidence, however, indicates that gaps in operational effectiveness among firms are neither rare nor random. Instead, they result directly from purposeful efforts to improve opera-

[1]Mishina, K. (1993), Toyota Motor Manufacturing, U.S.A., Inc., HBS Case (9-693-019); Bradley, S. P., and S. Foley (1994), Wal-Mart Stores, Inc., HBS Case (9-794-024); Heskett, J. L., and R. Hallowell (1993), Southwest Airlines—1993 (A), HBS Case (9-694-023).

[2]Pang, A., and E. Hausman (1994), "Hayes Files for Bankruptcy Protection." *Computer Reseller News,* November 21, 1994.

This note was prepared by David M. Upton. Copyright © 1997 by the President and Fellows of Harvard College. Harvard Business School Case 697-133.

[3]Anonymous (1991), "When GM's Robots Ran Amok." *The Economist,* August 10, 1991.

tional performance and, conversely, from failures to invest effort and creativity in managing operations effectively. Increasingly fierce competition means these efforts are becoming widespread and ongoing as firms look for ways to distinguish themselves. The result is heated competition among an industry's firms based on changing operations performance and innovative forms of operations. They strive to create gaps, and to close those that others have opened.

Operations improvement, of course, is nowhere near the whole story, and simply building operational effectiveness alone does not constitute a strategy. However, a company that fails to keep up and continually build its operational effectiveness may lose it, and find it very difficult to compensate in other areas. One school of thought holds that it is usually possible for a company to improve quickly, and so to close performance gaps soon after they open. Porter,[4] for example, suggests that operational effectiveness is a necessary but not sufficient condition for sustained competitive advantage, largely because the philosophies and tools for improvement are well understood, widely diffused, and readily available. All firms can thus get close to an optimal "productivity frontier."

There is ample empirical evidence, though, that competitors are not equally capable from an operations point of view. Nor do they find operations improvement an easy matter. Academic studies have delivered remarkably consistent conclusions on this point, regardless of the industry or operational characteristic studied.[5] They find that, instead of clustering on a frontier of roughly equivalent performance, companies demonstrate very different aggregate abilities in cost, quality, pro-

ductivity, flexibility, and product development performance. This is not surprising to companies that have attempted to benchmark their operations against competitors; results from these efforts often show very large and enduring performance gaps. If it were straightforward to close them, then laggards certainly would.

Even more surprising, perhaps, is the fact that this body of research finds large differences in performance among plants *within the same company* even after correcting for such factors as the age of equipment, the size of the operation, and other structural factors. One of the most important findings of the Hayes and Clark[6] work can be summed up as "operations management makes the difference," suggesting that there is considerable potential for the manager of an individual operation to improve its performance. Most operations managers appear to accept that significant gaps exist and are difficult to close, and that new ones continually appear. For operations managers, the primary problem is that it is difficult to know what to do next. In response to the widespread problems of lagging operations performance, a torrent of improvement tools and techniques has flooded the operations management world, each tool or approach promising to be the panacea.

It is easy to lump together all such new approaches—time-based competition, workforce empowerment, agile manufacturing, mass customization, business process re-engineering, "virtual factories," lean production, and so on—and dismiss them as management fads. This is especially true for companies that have adopted a succession of approaches to improvement but have not seen operational performance improve or de-

[4]Porter, M. E. (1996). "What is Strategy?" *Harvard Business Review*. November–December 1996.

[5]In the automobile industry, for example, Womack et al. examined manufacturing productivity, Clark and Fujimoto studied product development performance, and MacDuffie et al. assessed the impact of product variety on productivity and quality. All of these researchers found large variance across the world's auto manufacturers, with Japanese-owned plants, whether in Japan or elsewhere, typically the best performers. Away from automobiles, Chew, Bresnahan and Clark found large (2:1) differences in the productivity across forty operating units of a large commercial food service company, even after correcting for structural factors. Detailed cross-sectional studies of single performance characteristics within an industry, such as Garvin's research on quality in air conditioner manufacturing, Upton's study of flexibility among fine paper producers, and Iansiti's examination of workstation performance, also found wide variability in performance. See Womack, J. P., D. T. Jones and D. Roos (1990). *The Machine that Changed the World.*

Rawson Associates, New York; Clark, K. B., and T. Fujimoto (1991). *Product Development Performance: Strategy, Organization & Management in the World Auto Industry.* McGraw-Hill, New York; Chew, W. B., T. F. Bresnahan and K. B. Clark (1990). Measurement, Coordination and Learning in a Multiplant Network. *Measures for Manufacturing Excellence.* R. S. Kaplan, ed. Harvard Business School Press, Boston, MA. 129–162; Garvin, D. A. (1988). *Managing Quality.* Free Press, 49–68; Upton, D. M. (1995). "Flexibility as Process Mobility: The Management of Plant Capabilities for Quick Response Manufacturing. *Journal of Operations Management* 12: 205–224; Iansiti, M. (1995). "Technology Development and Integration: An Empirical Study of the Interaction Between Applied Science and Product Development." *IEEE Transactions on Engineering Management* 42 (3).

[6]Hayes, R. H., and K. B. Clark (1985). Exploring the Sources of Productivity Differences at the Factory Level. *The Uneasy Alliance: Managing the Productivity-Technology Dilemma.* K. B. Clark, R. H. Hayes and C. Lorenz, eds. Harvard Business School Press, Boston.

liver any competitive advantage. In these cases, there is a strong temptation to "stick with what works," or what has generated improvements in the past, and to give up on fads. It is dangerous to mistake operational innovations for fads, however. New approaches to operations and their improvement are not always the artificial creations of consultants and gurus; they may instead be powerful new techniques pioneered by rivals, capable of opening performance gaps on important competitive dimensions.[7] The activities of selecting and designing an improvement path from the many alternatives, separating fads from genuine innovations, creating new performance gaps and closing existing ones represent the most important functions of an operations manager. Operations managers can no longer simply be a caretakers of static plant and equipment.

In spite of the importance of these tasks, a general framework for making choices among the many performance improvement alternatives—to build a "strategy" for operations improvement at the plant level—has been lacking. There are many guides on how to manage and implement specific types of improvements, such as Total Quality Management (TQM) or self-directed workteams, but these do not alert managers to the full spectrum of

possibilities for changing their operations. Instead, they often promote the view that there is "one right way" to improve. As discussed above, this assumption can become a serious handicap if the competition finds a better way. There is also a wealth of work on effecting broad organizational change. This also provides some important and relevant lessons for operations managers but nevertheless fails to capture the kinds of *choices*, peculiar to operations, that need to be made by plant managers to provide ongoing improvement.

This module provides a framework for making decisions and taking action to improve a plant or operating unit's performance. It also explores a number of the practical challenges of implementing improvement strategies. The framework focuses on the kinds of improvement decisions made by plant managers, rather than more broadly in organizations as a whole. It builds on a number of the concepts introduced in the two previous modules in the book: operations processes and operations systems and information technology. This final part of the book integrates this material and looks at the improvement of the operation as a coherent unit.

MODULE STRUCTURE

The module comprises 10 cases, drawn from manufacturing, service, and non-commercial operations. Table 1 below shows the sequence of classes and the main teaching points of each case.

[7]Voss et al., for example, found a positive relationship between the adoption of various "world-class" manufacturing practices and operational performance. See Voss, C., K. Blackmon, P. Hanson and B. Oak (1995). "The Competitiveness of European Manufacturing." *Business Strategy Review* 6 (1). Spring, 1995. 1–25.

TABLE 1 Improvement Module Cases and Teaching Points

Cases	*Main Teaching Points*
Integron Incorporated	Benchmarking, direction setting
AT&T Universal Card Services	Selecting improvement focus and methods; combating scheme exhaustion
Daewoo Shipbuilding and Heavy Machinery	Multi-dimensional improvement; sustaining improvement; learning lock-in
Samsung Heavy Industries	Murphy's Law in capital investment; learning lock-in
HMS Thetis and Apollo XIII	Managing and preparing for operations crises. Complexity and coupling in complex systems; relative roles of planning and action; creativity in operations problem solving
PPG Berea	Implementing improvement strategies based on high-performance work systems
Vickers Inc.: Omaha Plant	Plant closure decisions; implementing plant turnarounds; improvement of aging plants
Deloitte and Touche	Implementing operations improvement as a consultant
Pacific Dunlop China (A): Beijing	Managing and improving internationally based operations
Micom Caribe	Role of the operations manager in strategy formulation; development and exploitation of new operations capabilities

The first part of the module focuses on the *design* of an operations improvement strategy: setting direction, determining the focus of an initiative, selecting appropriate tools and methods for improvement, and developing an improvement path that fits both the competitive and operations strategy for the operating unit. The second part concentrates on *managing and implementing* improvement of the operating unit: determining the relative roles of action and planning, implementing improvement in mature plants and international operations, using operations consultants, the challenges of improving operations *as* a consultant, and exploiting newly-developed operating capabilities.

MAJOR THEMES

1. Designing an Operations Improvement Path: The Concept of an Improvement Strategy

The primary goal of the module is to introduce a framework for designing an operations improvement path, and to apply it across a range of operations situations. This framework provides a starting point for analyzing plant improvement strategies and can be used to explore both the successes and the failed improvement efforts seen in the module's cases. The framework breaks an improve-

ment strategy into seven elements, as shown in Table 2.

This table and the discussions of each element that appear below describe a sequence. The various elements of the strategy are interdependent, and there is also an order in which they should be considered. Later, more detailed decisions build from earlier, broader ones. Decisions about the kind of techniques and methods to be used, for example, are made in light of the context and motivation for an improvement in performance. Similarly, an improvement effort's goals provide the foundation for deciding on appropriate resources and organization.

1. Developing the Motivation for Improvement

One clear motivation for improvement is an imperative. In a number of the cases in the course, a *crisis* provided the motivation for operational change. Lives were at risk during the Apollo XIII and Thetis recovery efforts. In John Crane (in Module 2), the fire in the Havant plant meant an immediate need to reorganize production in the remaining plants. The Vickers plant was threatened with closure, and Daewoo Shipbuilding saw one the worst industrial relations crises in Korean history. Crises and "galvanizing events," according to Kanter, Stein and Jick,[8] provide the impetus to

---

[8]Kanter, R. M., Stein, B. A., and T. D. Jick (1992). *The Challenge of Organizational Change.* Free Press, New York.

TABLE 2 Elements of an Improvement Strategy	
Element	*Questions addressed*
1. Context & Motivation	Why is the improvement initiative taking place? What is driving it? Why is the effort necessary?
2. Direction & Goals	On what dimensions is performance to be improved? How will this improvement be measured? What will be the *externally visible* results?
3. Focus	Where will we concentrate *internally* to achieve the desired goals? On what areas of the operation will the initiative focus?
4. Methods and Techniques	How will we achieve the desired results? What will our "toolkit" be for this improvement effort? How will we ensure the tools are available?
5. Resources	What financial and human resources will be required? To what extent will external resources be needed?
6. Organization and Phasing	How will the initiative be organized? What groups will it involve? Who will lead it? What will be the order of the projects tackled and when will each begin and end?
7. Learning Capture and Leverage	How will knowledge be brought into the operation? How will what is learned in the initiative be captured? How will the achievements of this initiative be leveraged into future projects?

break through the armor of the status quo.[9] They are broadly understood and palpable to everyone in the operation, and clearly require action.

Full-fledged operational crises are rare, however, and it is surely a bad idea to wait for one to compel an operation to change. In the majority of cases, an operation must make clear what the motivation for improvement is by deliberate action. The cases in the module describe a number of different methods by which operations managers create the motivating context for improvement. There are examples throughout the course that illustrate these methods. Motorola's benchmarking study, carried out on the basis of a suspicion of superior Japanese performance, provided the context for the Bandit Pager project. Integron also used a formal benchmarking effort, while Stermon brought in an external consultant to make it clear to all that it would no longer be able to compete on price, and had to become more flexible.

The Stermon example highlights one important consideration around providing the context for improvement. The motivation for performance improvement is often very clear to those in leadership positions, and not at all clear elsewhere in the operation. For example, it may be that without improvement, the five-year financial plan for the division will not be met, or the company will deliver an unimpressive return on investment. These consequences have meaning for corporate executives or plant managers, but not for most line workers. It is critical, however, that the reasons for improvement are evident to *everyone* who is to participate in the effort. Stermon's managers used an outsider to help with this.

For the operations manager embarking on an improvement initiative, the objective is to have a clear and compelling answer to the question: *why are we doing this?* Tom Moschetti tells a story of working late in the Micom Caribe plant in the depths of the 1987 quality crash. He went onto the shop floor, and found an assembly operator putting together a jig that would make it easier to assemble components without mistakes. "Why are you doing that?" asked Moschetti, inquiring about a detail. The operator, inferring a broader ques-

tion, said, "If I don't fix this, they'll send our work to Taiwan." At that point, said Moschetti, he knew the plant's performance would begin to improve.

2. Setting Goals and Direction

Often, when operations managers ask corporate managers questions like, "What shall we push hardest on: quality, cost, flexibility or innovation?" the answer is "yes." Similarly, the mission statements of many operations assert that they will be "The industry leader in quality, price and delivery performance, providing world-class customer service while generating superior return on investment." The problem with these statements is that they provide no direction to an operation; "get better at everything" is not helpful. To be useful instead of banal, the direction given to an operation as it begins or continues along an improvement path must accomplish three goals. It must be closely tied to the motivating context established for improvement; it must establish clear and concrete performance targets; and it must be concentrated, probably on no more than two or three dimensions of operations performance.

Direction for improvement should follow smoothly from the established motivation. Operations' mission statements often sound so empty because they aren't anchored to a compelling need. Tom Moschetti in the Micom Caribe case had done a great job of converting context to direction; his people knew why they had to reach the goals that he had set. Daewoo SHM explicitly focused on an ongoing improvement in the quality of its welding process, in spite of the fact that the customer cared much more about lead times and cost. Daewoo, however, had a widespread *architectural* understanding (in advance) of the way that improved welding quality contributed to these goals. If the welding quality was good enough, it would be possible to install propellers during the construction of the rest of the ship, instead of afterwards. Just as important, the welders understood this, and knew how working on the quality of their joints would contribute to broader company goals. Maria Chen at Deloitte & Touche, on the other hand, hadn't made clear to anyone working for her client that their efforts were important to reduce inventory, which was in turn important for the continued health of the operation. As this case shows, it is easy to skip the steps of establishing a broadly understood motivation and tying direction

---

[9]This does not always happen, however, as the Thetis tragedy shows. The British Navy was not spurred to effective action, and the contrast with the Apollo XIII crisis leads to valuable case discussions to determine the reasons for this.

to it. Many managers, in their haste to get started with a program, fly past these 'preliminaries,' and jump straight into ISO 9000 or just-in-time manufacturing.

A manager's other two principal direction-setting activities are ensuring that the improvement path is concentrated on a small number of performance dimensions, and providing targets for improvement on those dimensions. Skinner's idea that an operation should be focused around doing one or two things very well[10] also applies to the process of improvement. Except in unusual circumstances (which are discussed below), an improvement strategy that aims to improve everything at once is unlikely to succeed, for the same reasons that completely unfocused operations tend to fail. Without a parsimonious set of goals, there is no guide to emphasize the importance of one thing over another, no principle on which to base everyday decisions such as choice of machine or workgroup structure, and no simple, over-arching set of objectives to unify the community. These objectives should be stated in terms of quantified performance goals wherever possible.

It is true that operations improving on one dimension can improve on others, too. Reducing defect rates, for example, can often result in shorter lead times, since the lack of rework simplifies production flows. This does not, however, discount the importance of a primary objective for the improvement initiative; in fact, the "anticipated but not central" improvements might well blur the overall focus of the improvement initiative if they are included at the outset.

3. Selecting an Area of Focus

Having established *why* improvement is required and *what* should be improved, the next question for an operation is *where* the focus of improvement efforts should lie. Should it focus, for example, on the transformation processes discussed in Module 1 of the book (such as McDonald's initial focus on the replicability of its french-frying process)? Should it focus instead on the coordinative processes and associated information systems discussed in Module 2 (such as the efforts of EG&G Rotron to change its production control methods)? Table 3 shows some common areas of focus.

The focus of improvement activities is primarily determined by the goals of the initiative. For example, an operation might see that its lead-times had become much longer than those of its competitors and begin an improvement effort with the goal of cutting them by 50%. In this case, focusing the improvement on the introduction of new process technology would probably not make sense. Lead times are typically reduced through tighter coordination, not new machines, and the installation of the new equipment would possibly cause a "productivity dip" which, in the short term, could actually increase cycle times.[11]

An explicit evaluation of the primary areas on which the initiative will focus clarifies the effort to be undertaken and the people to be involved. There was little need to involve PPG's order fulfillment function in the improvement of its plant, for example, since the initiative was focused primarily on the shop floor. The focus of Deloitte &

---

[10]Skinner, C. W. (1969). "Manufacturing—Missing Link in Corporate Strategy." *Harvard Business Review* (May–June).

[11]Chew, W. B., Leonard-Barton, D., and R. E. Bohn (1991). "Beating Murphy's Law." *Sloan Management Review* 32 (3).

TABLE 3   Improvement Focus Areas and DMIO Case Examples

Primary Area of Focus	*DMIO Case Example*
Service/Manufacturing Process Level	Solagen, Stermon Mills, DAV, PPG Berea
Internal Coordinative Processes and Systems	EG&G Rotron
External Coordinative Processes and Systems	Kanebo
New Process Technology	Solagen, Cybertech
Distribution and Order-to-Delivery Processes	John Crane, DEC Endpoint
Sourcing Practices	AeroTech
Network Level Improvement	AeroTech

Touche's efforts with SKS, meanwhile, did not include network level improvements, and so did not need to include anyone outside the Pontiac Plant.

4. Choosing Methods and Techniques: the Toolkit of Improvement

The next questions to address concern *how* the improvement will actually be realized. To what extent will the goals be reached mainly through purchase and installation of new equipment, or through workforce training and education? Should an operation install a new IT system, or instill a new "philosophy" of improvement like Motorola's Six Sigma program? What combination of methods should be brought to bear?

One common mistake is to apply too many tools simultaneously to a problem. The tools and methods used also take time to learn, and it is useful to concentrate on a few methods or techniques. This does not mean that an improvement path focusing on new production technology should ignore operator training, or that an SPC-based initiative could not benefit from information technology. In each of these initiatives, however, it should be clear what the primary tools will be.

After selecting appropriate improvement tools, the next task is to get them into the hands of the right people and ensure that they know how to use them. In addition to their obvious usefulness toward the problem at hand, the methods used in an improvement initiative also provide an important unifying function. Since many people in the operation will need to understand the improvement method and its principles, they will often go through some form of training together, as in the DAV case in the first module. This provides a bedrock of common experience and vocabulary, and emphasizes the commitment of the operation to the goal. The Micom Caribe case illustrates how powerful and important it is to share a common understanding of the methods used for improvement throughout the operation. In the Vandelay case in the previous module, the consultants at ICS share a set of methods for "technology-enabled change" that helps them communicate goals and approaches to clients.

Methods for operations improvement can be broken down into the following four general categories. While they are neither mutually exclusive nor collectively exhaustive they are useful for understanding differences among the commonly used methods and techniques. Improvement efforts will generally include a combination of elements from these categories.

Equipment/Investment Based: FMS Systems, New Plants, New Production Lines, Machine Upgrade or Replacement. In earlier modules, Cybertech, Samsung, and Motorola each centered their improvement efforts on an investment in new plant and equipment. A new machine or a new facility often provides an outstanding opportunity to change the way the work gets done in an operation. For example, Motorola leveraged its investment in equipment to "break the mold" and even called the line "Bandit" to underscore the emphasis on finding a different way of operating. Cybertech was an extremely ambitious attempt to automate all the processes and systems of a slaughterhouse. Samsung's investments had traditionally been more incremental, but the new equipment and machines still entailed significant changes as they were brought into the shipyard. In all of these cases, the operation's improvement efforts centered on the introduction of equipment, and the challenge of bringing it online effectively.

Information Systems Based: MRP, ERP, Internetworking. The Vandelay Industries case shows how companies can use large-scale systems implementations to drive changes in their practices. Digital Equipment, Kanebo, and AeroTech also used these technologies for tighter integration with distant sites. As the cases show, however, the benefits promised to operations by information technology need careful attention in other areas, such as training and the reinvention of business practices if the advantages are to be realized. Information systems, in other words, are not improvements; they are tools to be used for improvement.

People/Community/Organization-Based: Employee Empowerment, High Commitment Work Systems, Pay for Performance. Most companies have recognized that equipment and computers by themselves rarely generate improvement, and stress that "people are our most important asset." To leverage this asset, they are trying to get their employees more involved in their jobs, by changing incentives, increasing decision-making authority, and creating a stronger sense of community.

In both the Daewoo and PPG Berea cases, operations managers use new work practices and training as the primary vehicles for change. Daewoo's meticulous emphasis on unity, training, and family involvement provides a foundation of trust and a common experience base for the initiatives to come. The PPG Berea case shows that "empowerment," while a powerful concept, is not a panacea; the company wrestles with several sensitive and difficult issues as it attempts to give workers more control over their jobs. AT&T UCS, meanwhile, uses employee incentives to drive improvements, and confronts a dilemma when it seeks to change the rules that set compensation levels.

Philosophy/Methodology Based: Total Quality Management; Value-Added Focus, Toyota Production System. Micom Caribe galvanizes its improvement path with a fundamental change in its "philosophy" of work. One feature of this kind of improvement is often an effective and charismatic leader, like Tom Moschetti. The much-maligned "vision thing" that they stress can be extraordinarily powerful, not only in developing goals and objectives, but also in communicating how they will be achieved. Motorola's ongoing Six Sigma initiative, Ford's 'Quality is Job 1' program in the 1980s, and the Toyota Production System are all more than slogans; they represent profound changes in the philosophy of their respective operations and the methods used for improvement.

When combining methods and techniques from these general categories, it is important to keep in mind that there are no magic bullets. No tool for improvement is effective for every situation, and none works well wherever it is used. Proponents of a particular philosophy may argue this point. An enthusiast for the Toyota Production System (TPS), for example, could claim with some justification that it is simply a superior method for producing most assembled goods. In the Pacific Dunlop case, however, it is clear that if Steve Littley had tried to use TPS as the primary vehicle for improvement, he would likely have been very disappointed in the results, and probably more exhausted than he already was. The facility would require much more organizational stability before it was ready for TPS, and the former Communists who made up the plant's management and staff might never be effective TPS team leaders. Appropriate methods and techniques for improvement, like the other elements of an operations improve-

ment strategy, are contingent on the situation at hand.

5. Selecting and Providing Resources

The next step in formulating the strategy is to assess the kinds of resources that are needed and to ensure that they are available. Among the most important resources for operations improvement are time, expertise, and money. Littley was unable to improve his operation because he was the only source of improvement expertise in the plant and because day-to-day operating pressure deprived him of the time he needed. John Weber, in the Vickers case, has both time and expertise, but may not have access to the financial resources he would need to upgrade and replace the plant's aging equipment.

After addressing the first four elements of the operations improvement strategy framework, it should become clear what expertise is needed to make an initiative work. The chosen focus and methods define what areas will be most affected, and highlight the kinds of expertise that will be required. To the extent that either time or expertise is lacking, the operation can look outside for additional help, either within the company itself—which Samsung Shipbuilding has regularly done—or to outside organizations such as vendors and consultants (as in the Deloitte case). Bringing in resources from outside, however, presents its own problems and often requires the operations manager to shift from managing people within the plant to managing the external consultants or engineers working on the project. The Deloitte case highlights some of these problems, which include managing the disparity between the goals of the consultants and those of the operation, ensuring adequate transfer of expertise to the plant, and mitigating the frequent lack of understanding of the culture, history, and peculiar circumstances of the operation. The Corning Z-Glass case from the first module also explores the difficulties that can occur when resources from different functions or locations are brought together.

6. Organization and Phasing

"Projects and teams," says Gerry Cusack of John Crane, "have been the lifeblood of our operations improvement." As the emphasis of operations management moves from caretaking to creating ongoing improvement, projects become part of the way the operation is run[12] instead of exceptions to "business as usual." While much of the work on project-management and team organization that has been carried out in recent years has focused on product and process development, the frameworks used in these contexts are extremely relevant and powerful in the broader context of operations improvement. Improvement projects often fail because too parochial a view is taken or because the organization and leadership of the various projects are not considered carefully. For example, a project to improve the delivery reliability of a fabrication shop would benefit greatly from the inclusion of the maintenance group and parts-procurement group, who might be unaware of how their current way of working is holding back performance.

Having decided who should participate in an improvement effort, the next question is how the team should be organized. "Teams" have become a ubiquitous feature of operations improvement. As Wheelwright and Clark point out, however, it is not the existence of a team, but the *type* of team that can make the difference between success and failure. "Organizing and Leading Heavyweight Development Teams"[13] provides some important background on the various ways of organizing the teams involved in projects. A brief summary of each type of team is described below.

Team Type	Cases
Functional	DEC Endpoint, DAV
Lightweight	John Crane (UK) Limited (initial projects), Micom Caribe
Heavyweight	Motorola Bandit, PPG Berea, Vickers Omaha
Autonomous	Cybertech, AeroTech

A *functional* team leaves its members in their existing departments, led by the manager of that group. Apart from initial meetings, members of the various departments meet only rarely, and coordination is carried out through the departmental managers, with little independent project oversight. Work is primarily performed "sequentially," with each group taking its turn at its part of the im-

provement initiative and then passing the baton to the next group. DEC Endpoint, in the last module, is an example of this kind of team coordination. Having finished its installation of the MRP system, the IT group handed the baton to Production. There appears to have been little ongoing coordination between the groups involved, and Production's task was then to make their part work.

A *lightweight* team assigns a member of the constituent group to coordinate the improvement project across functions. This person does not have the power to re-assign people or re-allocate resources, and the role is often offered to young managers as a "broadening" experience. The disparity between responsibility and authority in such situations can be large, placing the individual in a stressful situation, in which he or she is often forced to "beg" for resources and attention from departments who would much rather continue with their urgent business of the day. This book includes examples of how two "lightweight" managers dealt with the situation they were put in. Bob Gibbon, in the John Crane case in the last module, dealt with the problem by starting with small steps, which did not require substantial effort on the part of the departments with whom he worked. By providing evidence of the benefits of those past actions, he progressively gained credibility with the various groups, so that they were increasingly prepared to give him attention and resources. Tom Moschetti, in the Micom Case, was also a lightweight improvement manager in the sense that he had little influence over the design group in California, in spite of a clear need for improved quality through cooperation between the groups. Moschetti, rightly or wrongly, simply gave up on the uncooperative Californians, and compensated for the coordination problems within his own unit by building an operation that could manufacture anything that was designed. While we might see this as his failure to build the much needed coordination, his solution *did* work, at least in the short term.

A *heavyweight* team addresses many of the problems inherent in a lightweight team by using a powerful, senior manager as the leader of the improvement initiative. Heavyweight operations improvement leaders also supervise the work of those active on the various projects much more directly. In addition, team members spend a much larger proportion of their time on the improvement initiative, and are often dedicated to it. PPG

[12]Wheelwright, S. C., and K. B. Clark (1992). *Revolutionizing Product Development*. Free Press, New York 3–4.

[13]Clark, K. B., and S. C. Wheelwright (1992). "Organizing and Leading Heavyweight Development Teams." *California Management Review* 34 (3) 9–28.

Berea and Vickers Omaha each have powerful people running the projects, who have influence not only in their plants but also in the broader organization. Berea's John Povlik was able to command resources from PPG as a whole to facilitate the "empowerment" initiative, while Vickers' John Weber was also in a position to draw on a wide range of expertise (if not money), and to influence directly all activities associated with his proposed improvement initiative.

An *autonomous* organization removes all the participants from the existing organization, and gives them a "clean-sheet" from which to work. In many operations, this approach is simply impractical, since the equipment used for the operation and the organization surrounding it are inseparable. However, there are some circumstances where such an approach is possible. First is in a "demonstration" project, like the one described in the Cybertech case in the last module. Second is the case of a "greenfield" site, like PPG's Berea plant. An important advantage of such autonomy is that the improvement effort is unfettered by the ingrained custom-and-practice that trammels so many improvement initiatives. At the same time, the team can become a loose cannon—difficult to manage and direct, with objectives that are increasingly divergent from those of the parent organization, and which are subsequently difficult to rein in. AeroTech, for example, originally sanctioned by McDonnell Douglas and spun off to improve its inter-company coordination systems, is now looking at industries like textiles and automobiles to extend the application of its system—far from the original intent from McDonnell's point of view.

A common feature in the organization of successful operations improvement initiatives, as well as product and process development projects, is the existence of a *sponsor,* a *champion,* and a team of *implementers.* The **sponsor** of an initiative sets high level strategic objectives and protects the team working on the initiative from unproductive political "flak." We see the role of the sponsor in Paul Kahn (in AT&T UCS) or in Kim Woo-Choong (in the Daewoo case). Without an influential and inspired sponsor, an initiative can flail in political diversions, be pulled off track by tactical exigency, or be stonewalled by the proponents of the status quo. The **champion** is the person responsible for making the initiative work. Often described as "driven" and "obsessed," champions are the leaders of op-

erational change. Tom Moschetti in the Micom case and John Povlik in the Berea case were both champions of their causes. Without a clear champion, a project is leaderless and can easily founder. Without a set of effective **implementers,** there is no one to do the work of improvement. Steve Littley (in the Pacific Dunlop case) might well be an effective champion if there were anyone else around who could carry out the work necessary to get the plant back on track. Unfortunately for him, and Pacific Dunlop, there wasn't.

7. Learning from Others and Capturing Knowledge

The coda to the Solagen case in Module 1 underscores the importance of learning as one of the outcomes of an improvement effort. Because Kodak made no effort to capture what it had learned, the company had to re-start the Solagen pilot from scratch when competitive pressures made it a necessity. But what could they have done differently? More broadly, how can the learning and knowledge that result from an improvement effort, whether failed or successful, be captured? Garvin[14] suggests five mechanisms that create "learning organizations": systematic problem solving, experimentation, learning from the organization's own experiences, learning from the experiences of others, and transferring knowledge throughout the organization. When learning from operations improvement, this final capability is especially important. As Garvin points out, "Companies must review their successes and failures, assess them systematically, and record the lessons in a form that employees find open and accessible."

This last point is critical, but often overlooked. Since people switch jobs and companies relatively often, an operation cannot rely solely on its employees to be the repositories of accumulated knowledge. On the other hand, written project summaries and "lessons learned" documents are often thin references, capturing few of the facts and almost none of the organizational complexities of an initiative. The best approaches to learning capture combine both living and written records; they ensure that both the people and archives associated with an initiative will be available to others. They accomplish this by ensuring

---

[14]Garvin, D. A. (1993). "Building a Learning Organization." *Harvard Business Review.* July–August.

that people who want to know more about a particular effort or field have access to both colleagues and reference materials. This information (and the meta-information that captures where it resides) must be maintained, of course, so these approaches also require that people continually update their internal "resumes" and contribute to libraries. This can represent a significant amount of work, and the primary danger is that references become outdated. Organizations can fight these tendencies by scheduling special forums for information sharing, by building internal libraries or Web sites and making their maintenance a priority, and by insisting that a project is not complete until all the associated learning opportunities have been identified.

For the development of an operations improvement strategy, it is useful to look at the planned mechanisms for learning *before* the initiative begins, *during* the initiative itself, and *after* the execution of key milestones in the initiative. Integron is doing all it can to learn before the new improvement initiative is launched. By benchmarking competitors, it hopes to ensure that its improvement efforts set off in the right direction, armed with real data rather than hunches. If companies and managers address the need for learning before, during, and after projects—paying adequate attention to this final element of an improvement strategy—it is much less likely that an effort will finish as unproductively as the Solagen project.

2. Assessing Improvement Strategies

The various elements of the strategy outlined above, and the range of options within each of them, mean that there is a large set of possible strategies that might be employed by an operation facing the need to improve its performance. A critical issue, then, is how to select among various candidate strategies. Whether trying to design an improvement strategy herself or choose among proposals offered by others, the manager tasked with improving an operation needs some guidelines for evaluation and comparison. The five described below provide a starting point.

1. Completeness

An improvement strategy must address each of the seven elements discussed in the previous section. While this might seem to be an obvious quali-

fication, it is often overlooked. In many cases, individual projects are proposed as improvement measures. These projects may offer immediate and important benefits, but this is not enough. A project, even an excellent one, does not constitute a strategy. By the same token, a series of the "best available" projects provides no guarantee of a logical progression over time or across the seven elements. The shortcomings of this approach are discussed in greater detail below, in "Managing Improvement over Time." They are also exposed in the Deloitte & Touche case, where Maria Chen and the other consultants embarked on an important project but pay insufficient attention to some of the elements of the improvement strategy, such as providing a compelling motivation, establishing sustainable resources and developing an appropriate organization for the initiative. In contrast, Micom Caribe and Daewoo implemented improvement strategies that addressed all of the elements, and saw them work together to powerful effect.

Unfortunately, an ad hoc approach to improvement is the norm rather than the exception in operations. Large projects are often proposed as panaceas that will take care of all an organization's improvement needs. This is particularly common in technology implementation projects, such as the installation of information systems, robotics, or other advanced manufacturing technology (AMT). Several researchers have pointed out the shortcomings of this approach.[15] While improvement strategies that incorporate AMT may be effective if they address each of the elements of an improvement strategy, AMT implementations by themselves are not effective, since they represent only part of an overall strategy.

2. Coherence

The coherence, or "internal consistency" of an improvement strategy captures how well the elements within the strategy mesh with each other. For example, an improvement strategy with a focus on coordinative processes and a goal of

---

[15]See, for example, Adler, P. S., and T. A. Winograd, eds. (1992). *Usability: Turning Technologies into Tools.* Oxford University Press, New York; Majchrzak, A. (1988). *The Human Side of Factory Automation.* Jossey-Bass, San Francisco; Walton, R. E. (1989). *Up and Running: Integrating Information Technology and the Organization.* Harvard Business School Press, Boston, MA; and Upton, D. M. (1995). "What Really Makes Factories Flexible?" *Harvard Business Review.* July–August: 74–84.

decreasing lead times is less likely to benefit from the tools of TQM than it would from just-in-time methods. Similarly, an improvement path depending on the introduction of a radical new process technology will need to ensure that the appropriate expertise is available—possibly from a vendor or a consultant—if the expertise does not exist within the operation. The resources required for the strategy, in other words, need to fit with the methods employed.

The process outlined above for developing an improvement strategy aims to build coherence by proceeding sequentially through the seven elements. Later elements, such as focus and methods, follow directly from earlier ones like the motivating context and goals. In contrast, a strategy developed by combining the contributions of several people or functional areas may address all seven elements, but not weave them together in a coherent way. In the extreme, it may be a hydra made up of, for example, a lead time reduction goal proposed by corporate management, a method of installing a new distribution requirements planning (DRP) system led by the IS department, and a longstanding improvement organization based around teams of shop floor employees. This level of incoherence is a common feature of improvement strategies that are assembled, rather than formulated. When this is the case, the manager responsible for the operation and its improvement needs to bring the various efforts together as part of an integrated whole.

3. Fit with Competitive Goals

The improvement strategy should follow logically and clearly from the way the operation aims to compete. The AT&T Universal Card Services (UCS) case provides an example of a well-directed, powerful improvement strategy, designed to fit the organization's competitive strategy. AT&T decided to compete in the credit card business by delivering outstanding quality and customer service.[16] UCS's improvement strategy followed logically from this, and dictated virtually all the operation's improvement actions.

In contrast, many North American paper plants have for several years been following improvement strategies that are at odds with the competitive dynamics of their industry. For the past century, paper conversion machines have been steadily increasing in size, output rate, and investment requirements, because economies of scale have been significant and the industry has traditionally competed primarily on cost.[17] Larger machines, therefore, have continually been more efficient at producing standard paper grades. Many older, smaller plants have continued to try to compete directly with the giants, and have embarked on variable cost reduction measures (such as labor-removing automation) to maintain parity with their younger rivals. This has typically been an unsuccessful strategy, leaving plants less flexible than they were previously, but with costs that are still too high. A more effective improvement strategy for many of these might have been to work to increase responsiveness, or to expand the range of paper grades that they could produce. Such a strategy could have moved these plants into profitable niches, instead of placing them in the mainstream of a competition that they could not win.

Just as competitive strategy can be influenced by operations strategy,[18] so can a successful improvement strategy lead to a change in competitive dynamics. A company that greatly improves along important operational dimensions can use these new skills to change the "game" that is being played.[19] Atlas Doors, for example, progressively reconfigured its operations so that it could deliver customized industrial overhead doors with one-third the industry average leadtime. This allowed the company to charge a 20% price premium while growing three times faster and being five times more profitable than the industry average.[20] Atlas' competitors had little choice except to try to match these abilities through improvements of their own. In such cases, successful improvement strategies

---

[16]Even though UCS acquired customers with a low-APR, zero-fee strategy, it *retained* them through outstanding customer service. The operations were configured to provide this service rather than to be low cost. AT&T absorbed the additional costs through reduced profits, since the objective of the business was primarily to build customer contact to support its long-distance services.

[17]Upton, D. M. (1995). "Flexibility as Process Mobility: The Management of Plant Capabilities for Quick Response Manufacturing." *Journal of Operations Management* 12: 205–224.

[18]Hayes, R. H., Pisano, G. P., and D. M. Upton (1996). *Strategic Operations: Competing through Capabilities*. Free Press, New York.

[19]Nalebuff, B. J., and A. Brandenburger (1996). *Co-opetition*. Doubleday, New York.

[20]Stalk, G., and T. M. Hout (1990). *Competing Against Time: How Time-Based Competition is Reshaping Global Markets*. The Free Press, New York.

can shape competitive strategy in addition to serving it.

4. Fit with Operations Strategy

The improvement strategy should also fit the various elements of the company's operations strategy. These elements are described by Hayes and Wheelwright[21] and include structural elements such as capacity management, the number and focus of other operations facilities, the type of process technology being used, the degree and nature of sourcing arrangements, and infrastructural elements such as the makeup of the workforce, methods used for production planning and control, and the way the workforce is organized and compensated. An operations strategy describes and captures the essence of the existing "operations machine" that delivers the product or service.

Developing an improvement strategy that fits with the company's operations strategy is critical. Daewoo's operations strategy, for example, had traditionally been characterized by well-trained employees who developed process technology on the shop floor. An improvement strategy that focused on the installation of foolproof machinery developed in research labs (which would be in keeping with Samsung's operations strategy) would likely be rejected by the Daewoo plant because it would clash with the way the operation worked as a whole.

5. Speed and Efficiency

The final criteria for assessing improvement strategies are the time horizon and efficiency with which they deliver their performance results. If there is an externally dictated timeframe for performance improvement, such as a threatened plant closure (as in the Vickers case), a planned event (such as the launch date of a new product), or a move by a rival with a clear impact date, it is straightforward to compare various improvement strategies: those that won't meet the deadline can be rejected. Improvement strategies that consume immense resources without concomitant performance gains are inefficient by definition, and an assessment of the improvement strategy must obviously include determining whether the resources

required to make it work are worth the promised gains.

Even when time lines are relatively long it may be advisable to seek both immediate and long-term results from an effort. Even though a focus solely on immediate results can be very detrimental, some initial "quick-wins" can help fuel the credibility of the initiative and begin to test whether the promised long-term gains will materialize. In addition, a number of researchers have pointed out that a focus on action helps people make sense of their environments,[22] allows for a more adaptive strategy formulation process[23] and appears to explain the successes of some high-performing managers.[24] In contrast, a reliance on analysis or stage-setting over action can lead to further demonstrations of von Stauffenberg's principle[25]: "Any bureaucratic entity of forty or more people can stay busy ten hours a day, six days a week, with no inputs and no outputs." Given this, it is important to ask: Will the proposed efforts deliver quantifiable progress toward the goals of the improvement in a useful timeframe and with a level of resources that are appropriate given those gains?

3. Managing Operations Improvement over Time

The Role of an Improvement Strategy in Sustaining Improvement

Many operations managers have experienced the frustration that goes with trying to improve a plant that has been exhausted by previous improvement initiatives. In one British steel tube mill, for example, a new quality improvement program was launched to address a growing pool of customer complaints about poor surface finish and material condition. On the day that the new initiative was launched with a presentation to the

[21]Hayes, R. H., and S. C. Wheelwright (1984). *Restoring Our Competitive Edge: Competing through Manufacturing.* John Wiley and Sons, New York.

[22]Weick, K. E. (1995). *Sensemaking in Organizations.* Sage Publications, Thousand Oaks, CA.

[23]Mintzberg, H. (1988). Opening up the Definition of Strategy. *The Strategy Process: Concepts, Contexts, and Cases.* Quinn, J. B., H. Mintzberg, and R. M. James, eds. Prentice Hall, Englewood Cliffs, NJ.

[24]Nohria, N. and R. Eccles (1992). *Beyond the Hype: Rediscovering the Essence of Management.* McGraw-Hill, New York.

[25]Von Stauffenberg was a Prussian general and personnel specialist. He was executed in 1945 for his participation in the plot to assassinate Hitler, as described in Creech, B. (1994). *The Five Pillars of TQM: How to Make Total Quality Management Work for You.* Truman Talley Books / Dutton, New York.

workforce, the excitement of the managers was not shared at all by people on the line. "Here we go again!" was the common sentiment in the plant, which had seen a long series of such rollouts. Most operators considered the quality initiative to be yet another "flavor of the month." Problems like these result from the way an operations improvement path is managed over time. An explicit improvement strategy helps sustain the effectiveness of an operations improvement path by several mechanisms.

Guiding Project Selection. An improvement strategy gives direction and structure to operations initiatives. An unconnected string of projects asks people to chase changing goals, focus on various parts of the operation, and use a constantly changing toolkit of methods. An improvement strategy provides some guidelines for selecting projects from a large pool of candidates. Any operation has weak spots, areas that have been neglected for too long and other opportunities for development. A common method for selecting among these is simply to rank the projects according to an immediate cost-benefit estimate, then attack them in order. When viewed as part of an improvement strategy, however, the projects can be judged on the basis of their contribution to the overall path of the operation. The motivation and goals established, and the focus, methods, resources, and organization selected, help determine which candidate projects are suitable and which ones need to be modified or shelved. The role played by a strategy in winnowing projects should not be underestimated, because a common feature of improvement initiatives is the overabundance of candidate projects that they generate. When Ford announced its "Quality is Job 1" program in the 1980s, it was soon swamped with opportunities proposed by all levels. The company's strategy provided a means to select among them, and (just as important) a way to explain to people that their ideas, while good, were not going to be used immediately.

Providing Continuity. Management rotation also fuels haphazard improvement paths. In this module's cases, Pacific Dunlop's plant in Beijing and Vickers' Omaha plant have both experienced a series of short-term managers who changed the direction of the plant, then moved on. They did not provide any foundation for a long-term improvement, and shifted the course of the plant based on their own biases and predisposition. An explicit improvement strategy can help provide continuity between managers so that each plant manager can build on what has gone before and extend it, rather than automatically redirect it.

Building Predictability. Articulating a strategy, and demonstrating commitment to it, can be a powerful means of overcoming workforce hesitation. As Stevenson[26] points out, people crave predictability in many aspects of their lives and especially in their work, and any steps that managers can take to increase this predictability are both welcome and potent. Because improvement efforts are above all about change, they always threaten to reduce predictability; managers can mitigate this by showing how the efforts are part of a larger, more stable pattern. An improvement strategy, in other words, provides a road map for an operations so that the people working in it can see beyond the hills and curves that they are continually negotiating.

Allowing Changes in Direction To Be Made Explicit. A final benefit of an articulated improvement strategy is that it serves as a "straw man" for the organization; it can be discussed, debated, and compared to other possible approaches. Changes in customer needs or preferences, new capabilities demonstrated by competitors, and new operations management tools and technologies are constantly appearing, and it may be necessary for an operation to alter elements of its improvement path, or to redirect it entirely. It is much easier to do this in a directed and purposeful manner when the current path is widely understood.

Three Models of Operations Improvement over Time

While a clear improvement strategy plays an important role in sustaining an improvement path, there are still differences in fundamental philosophies of operations improvement that have a significant impact on the ability of the operation to sustain performance improvement over time. These approaches may be broken into three gen-

---

[26]Stevenson, H. (1997). *Do Lunch or Be Lunch: The Virtue of Predictability in a World of Corporate Chaos.* Harvard Business School Press, Boston.

eral groups. Each can be observed in the cases in the module.

Model I: Picking the Low-hanging Fruit.

This improvement model is based on the assumption that the opportunities for improvement in the plant are static, and that improvement involves picking the "lowest hanging fruit" first, and then progressively moving to the more difficult projects. Selection of sub-projects is thus based on how difficult they are to implement; easy ones get done first, difficult ones are deferred. Despite this model's being labeled "continuous improvement," both managers and employees assume that while the new initiative will show gains at first, over time the pool of easy wins will become exhausted. Eventually, it becomes so difficult to make improvements on the original dimensions of performance that opportunities to improve along other dimensions seem much more attractive and productive. It feels better to see something improve (even on a less important dimension), than to watch a tired initiative flounder as improvement becomes harder and harder.

It is in the "stalled" stages of old initiatives that new fashions like TQM and re-engineering find the most fertile ground. Quality Circles, an improvement fad in the late-1970s, provide a good example of this phenomenon. Many operations found the idea of cross-functional meetings to discuss how quality might be improved to be productive—at first. Over time, however, quality circles often degenerated as the easier sub-projects disappeared and it became harder and harder to produce noticeable results. The dispirited team would then become aimless and the initiative would be tagged "a waste of time." The scene would thus be set for the next scheme to take hold.

Model II: Linear, Focused Improvement.

Firms employing this model have an articulated improvement strategy. They also typically have a clear, long-lasting view of how they compete, and communicate it well to people through the operation. There is a shared understanding that improvement may become more difficult as time goes on, but that at each step on the path, new opportunities will show themselves (somehow) and fuel sustained improvement. The fact that the difficulties of sustaining improvement are generally understood guards against the disenchantment

that can quickly take the wind out of the initiative's sails. A faith in "getting better every day" and "stretch goals" keeps the improvement moving forward, for as long as people are prepared to put continued, focused effort into overcoming increasingly difficult obstacles.

While this approach represents a substantial improvement over picking the low-hanging fruit, it still faces diminishing returns over time. It forces an operation to deal with a series of progressively more difficult hurdles. Although the operation does not immediately jump to improve on another competitive dimension when things become difficult, it ultimately has to deal with a situation which has not been planned for or dealt with proactively. What happens to the operation's momentum and rhythm of improvement when it becomes exceptionally difficult to progress further?

AT&T's Universal Card Services operation provides an excellent example of such an initiative. After winning the Baldrige Award for quality in 1992, the operation found it progressively more difficult to improve. Indeed, there is evidence in the case that many people in the organization felt at odds with the zealots leading the quality campaign on the grounds that bonuses were becoming more and more difficult to achieve as they were pushed to continue improving quality. While such perseverance and focus is a marked improvement over Model I, it still does not plan for the day when the well of opportunity runs dry.

Model III: Planning for Ongoing Improvement.

The key feature of this approach to managing improvement over time is that improvement projects are selected based on two factors:

- The extent to which the project delivers direct improvement on the chosen dimension;
- The extent to which it generates future opportunities for improvement.

By using these selection criteria, firms ensure that improvement occurs continuously, but also proactively provides opportunities for further improvement. Teams working in this environment might spend an annual planning meeting discussing not only their overall improvement strategy, and their improvement plans for the year, but how to build a foundation for improvement in subsequent years. To do this, they might select projects with little immediate benefit, and even projects that appear to drag the operation on an improvement path headed in the wrong direction. But this is done carefully and judiciously, in order to build long-term capabilities that will provide opportunities for further improvement, on the appropriate dimension. This is very different from selecting a sub-project because it is an easy thing to do. The combination of progressive improvement and the provision of launch pads to provide future opportunities is very powerful, but very difficult to do well. However, this improvement mentality can provide an explosive, exponential performance improvement. The prime difficulty is that, because of the initial effort put into building long-term improvement opportunities, results may be slower at first. In the longer term, this approach will generate rapidly improving performance.

Daewoo's strict policy was that every improvement project should also provide a foundation for further improvement in productivity and lead-time. An example of such a project was the improvement of welding quality in the plant. While the quality of welding was not a primary goal of its improvement strategy, the progressive development of welding quality allowed the yard to install propellers in parallel with other components, rather than after distortion had settled down, saving valuable weeks of factory time.

The above models are archetypal, and most operations will fall between the lines, using a combination of each. However, the dominant philosophy is usually easy to recognize in an operation, and provides important clues about how the improvement process might itself be improved to build sustained improvement in the operation over time.

DESCRIPTION OF CASES

Integron Inc.: The Integrated Components Division (ICD) has recently been freed from its internal-sales-only relationship with Integron, Inc. and has assumed full profit and loss responsibility for the first time. It now has the opportunity to develop new businesses and customers in the external market. As it prepares to do so, however, it faces a serious problem. ICD's traditional business, hybrid integrated circuits, appears to be reaching maturity; its growth rate, already a slow 4%, is expected to slow even further. In search of

expanding markets, ICD is banking on a fledgling technology called Multi-Chip Modules, or MCMs, in which it has developed comparatively deep expertise. MCMs are used in four different market segments, each with different requirements. However, MCMs have been given highly variable growth forecasts—some analysts project rapid and sustained growth, while others forecast complete collapse of the market with the introduction of alternative technologies.

Gary Lloyd, who manages the business unit, is keen to consolidate and simplify the various manufacturing improvement schemes that have been instituted around the plant over the previous several years; he also wants to redirect these schemes to support the new MCM markets. To do so, he commissioned a benchmarking study using existing customers as his primary information source. The results of this study were informative, but brought him no closer to developing an improvement path for his operation. Lloyd is struggling to develop a strategy to accompany the operation's new charter, and is anxious to do well on all relevant performance dimensions. He knows, however, that trying to excel on everything at once is hazardous, and is trying to decide which measures are most important as he puts together a plan of action for his operation.

Integron is a case about direction setting, concentrating on the first two elements of the improvement strategy framework—*context* and *goals*. It first looks at the general issue of benchmarking as a means of establishing the motivation for improvement and the targets that an operation will shoot for. It also examines the practical difficulties of developing a competitive strategy based on operating capabilities. In circumstances where it is not clear which performance dimension of an operation to improve, what should be done? Should directions for improvement be based on the more certain needs of current customers or the more tenuous predictions of future requirements?

With **AT&T Universal Card Services Corporation (UCS),** the module moves from direction setting to the next improvement strategy elements of *focus* and *methods,* and poses the question of how to *sustain* a successful improvement path. In 1990, AT&T entered the credit card business with great fanfare. From the beginning, the company delivered outstanding quality and customer satisfaction. They did so by building an elaborate but effective customer-service organization that became the envy of the industry within three years. By focusing on the customer service associates, and employing an innovative method of compensating them, the new division grew quickly; by the summer of 1993, UCS had 12 million accounts.

But all is not well at UCS. As the organization strives for further improvement, tensions have begun to emerge. Much of the operation's success to this point has derived from the enthusiastic involvement of its service associates. This eagerness is largely a result of their compensation package, which ties bonuses to the performance gains achieved. The primary problem with this program, however, has been the "raising of the bar" in job performance required to qualify for the bonus payments. As UCS improved, what was once stellar performance has now become commonplace. This would be good news, except that UCS is worried that other credit card firms will be able to duplicate these improvements. To maintain its performance advantage, the company has required ever-better performance from its employees before they are eligible for the attractive bonuses.

This has caused resentment and disaffection among the staff, who have come to view the UCS slogan "Pleased but never satisfied" as a motto representing the futility of their actions. By 1993, they feel that continued performance improvement has become extremely difficult, but still expected. Also, there is (as seen later in the PPG Berea case) some concern about the "group" nature of the incentive program, and the difficulty of identifying associates who consistently deliver outstanding or below-par service. Finally, there are some suspicions among the management team that performing well *internally* on the particular measures used does not necessarily translate into good *external* performance in terms of customer satisfaction. In short, the wind has begun to leak from the sails of UCS' continuous improvement strategy.

Daewoo Shipbuilding and Heavy Machinery looks at a plant rescued from the brink of disaster. In doing so, it touches on all the elements of the improvement framework, especially *resources, organization,* and *learning capture.* In 1987, Daewoo's shipyard on Koje Island, just off the coast of South Korea, had been involved in a fiercely antagonistic labor dispute. This, combined with the depressed worldwide shipbuilding market, caused a loss of 42% of sales in 1988. Through the personal intervention of Kim Woo-Choong, the chairman of the Daewoo group (who actually came from Seoul to live on site as a demonstration of his commitment to the plant), Daewoo began a gradual, but powerful improvement program.

Daewoo's approach to improving the plant began at the community level, by focusing on training in both job-related and more generalizable skills. Next, it began sending operators (rather than managers) to observe how various manufacturing processes were carried out in Japanese shipyards. This had the effect not only of involving people in the improvement process, but also of exposing the industry's best practices and skills to the people that were best able to exploit them (the operators themselves). Over the following seven years, Daewoo gradually improved its performance until, by 1994, it was on a par with Japanese plants in terms of productivity and was continuing to improve rapidly. By developing new process and system technology on the shop floor, DSHM had improved on many dimensions at once: on quality, cost and lead-time.

At the time of the case, the rest of the industry, anticipating a boom, is planning to expand capacity through additional capital investment. Daewoo, however, is reluctant to invest in more plant and equipment in the highly cyclical shipbuilding industry. The danger is that if it does not have enough capacity to satisfy demand, the company might not make its target 10% share of the world market for supertankers, and could lose out on important orders. Daewoo's strategy is to continue to improve productivity and lead times to compensate for not installing new plant. "Productivity improvement," as one manager points out, "*is* capacity expansion."

A number of important questions arise in this case. First, there are many operations in which apparently exciting improvement initiatives fail dramatically or peter out (AT&T UCS, for example). What was it about Daewoo's operations improvement strategy that enabled it to improve so rapidly for so long? Second, many operations managers say that it is important to focus on one or two things to improve, whereas Daewoo seems to have improved its performance across the board. How did Daewoo manage to improve on so many dimensions at once? Finally, Daewoo is now placing a big bet on its ability to improve. It will not have access to new plant, but must ensure that it is able to satisfy demand in the upcoming boom. How can the plant, which has already shown exceptional performance, guarantee continued improvement and avoid the "brick wall" that seems to be looming in the AT&T case?

Samsung Shipbuilding and Heavy Industries' shipyard is located just a few miles from Daewoo's yard. It also faced the political turmoil of the 1980s and the depression in the shipbuilding industry. It is also looking at the same market upturn as Daewoo. Its improvement efforts, however, could not be more different, especially with regard to *methods, resources,* and *organization.* Whereas Daewoo has concentrated on shop-floor based improvement, Samsung has built its manufacturing prowess by developing new technologies away from the shop floor and then installing them once they are debugged. It is now installing a new dry dock and is very concerned that the process of *installing* the new dock may threaten the yard's ability to participate in the coming ship construction boom. Many operations managers assume a fairly simple and logical model for the installation of new equipment. The usual assumption is that the new machines will be put in place, and that there will then be some ramp-up time as people learn to use them. After this, the process will reach full output, as shown in Figure 1.

The reality of installing new equipment is often rather different. As illustrated by the Samsung case, the influx of plant and new people, the confusion and disruption caused by the project and the diversion of managerial resources away from "business as usual" makes such periodic improvements follow a very different path, as shown

in Figure 2. This effect has been called "Murphy's Law."[27] The challenge for Samsung's managers is to find ways of preventing or, at least, mitigating this effect. Evidence of performance deterioration has started to show itself around the plant, with existing operators worried about the new workers' ability to perform their jobs well. The question is, why exactly does the strong form of "Murphy's Law" apply to so many capital investment projects, and what can be done within an operation to avoid its effects?

Up to this point, the cases have focused on the design of an operations improvement strategy, and the questions that arise when setting direction for an operation and designing an effective and sustainable improvement strategy. The module now moves on to **implementation of improvement,** and begins with a case that underscores the dangers of not knowing when to stop analyzing and when to start taking action. **HMS Thetis and Apollo XIII** also provides some important lessons for operations managers on how to prepare for and deal with technical and operational crises. These are, unfortunately, not rare; a leak of hazardous chemicals from a plant, a dramatic increase in reject rates from a process, or the failure of a complex computer system are all examples of such crises. In all such cases, the ability to act quickly and effectively is critical.

At 3 p.m., on June 1, 1939, the submarine HMS Thetis, with 103 men on board, sank in Liverpool Bay while carrying out a diving trial. The next morning she was found with her stern jutting out of the water. Four men escaped, but at 3:10 p.m. she sank once more and disappeared. Ninety-nine men ultimately died.

As the subsequent inquiry discovered, Lieutenant F. G. Woods had read a poorly designed dial on a torpedo tube as meaning "closed" when it actually meant "open." In addition, the fail-safe device, a test cock on the rear of the tube, was blocked with a speck of paint.[28] Woods thus opened what he thought was an empty tube, only to have water flood into the vessel at a rate of two tons per minute. The bow of the submarine quickly

FIGURE 1 Predicted Performance of New Plant and Equipment

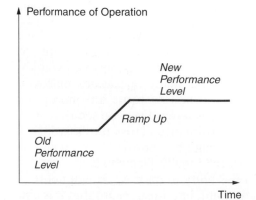

[27]Chew, W. B., D. Leonard-Barton, and R. E. Bohn (1991). "Beating Murphy's Law." *Sloan Management Review* 32 (3).

[28]Vat, D. v. d. (1994). *Stealth at Sea: A History of the Submarine.* Orion, London.

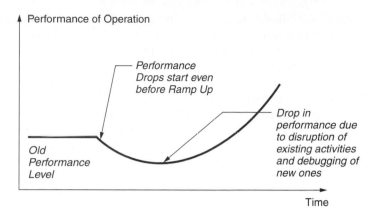

FIGURE 2 Actual Performance of New Plant and Equipment

sank until it came to rest on the seabed, leaving the air-filled stern poking out just above the water.

While Thetis was on the seabed, the Royal Navy and Cammell-Laird, the shipbuilder, scrambled to try either to help the men escape using the Davis escape apparatus or raise the boat from the bottom using cables. However, none of these efforts was successful, and lack of communication, unclear leadership and responsibility, and over-reliance on an "initial hypothesis" combined to doom the sailors. The initial hypothesis phenomenon is observed in a wide range of stressful and immediate technical problem-solving situations: people will take a first guess at the cause of the problem, and will cling to that explanation long after the objective evidence supports another, less obvious cause.[29] In the case of the Thetis, for example, the initial hypothesis was that the men *should* have been able to escape using the Davis apparatus at a rate of two men every five minutes. This, however, was the theoretical rate. In fact, because of lax drilling and the toxic and confusing effects of carbon dioxide, the rate was much slower. As it turned out, men were dying in their attempts to use the apparatus. Meanwhile, the Navy clung to what *should have been happening* for far too long, and did not pursue other rescue methods aggressively.

In Apollo XIII we see a much happier outcome from an equally grim situation. Three astronauts at the start of a moonshot, stranded in a spacecraft badly crippled by an explosion, their oxygen supply dwindling and becoming toxic, are trying to get home. In this case, the initial hypothesis of the NASA ground staff was that there had been an instrumentation failure, not an explosion. However, the evidence from astronauts was not only that they heard a bang, but also that they were venting fluid into space. Even more confusing, however, was that if the instruments *were* correct, the astronauts should already have been dead.

Over the following three days, however, rapid and effective technical problem solving, along with effective crisis management, saved the astronauts' lives. A number of questions arise from this case. First, how did the Apollo team members avoid being trapped in incorrect hypotheses, given that this phenomenon was so prevalent (and so deadly) during the Thetis disaster? Second, how much was pure luck responsible for the different outcomes in the two cases? Third, what principles can we develop about being prepared for such situations? Did it matter, for example, that the Apollo XIII team had never practiced or drilled for the *particular* crisis it faced? Finally, what can we learn from the two cases about general principles for managing such technical crises? This is an important skill since, according to Perrow,[30] failures in such complex systems are inevitable.

[29]Morrison, D. L., and D. M. Upton (1994). "Fault Diagnosis and Computer-Integrated Manufacturing Systems." *IEEE Transactions on Engineering Management* 41 (1) 69–83. See Torrey, L. (1979), "The Week They Almost Lost Pennsylvania," *New Scientist,* 174–178, for more information on diagnosing technical problems under stress. This was also a factor in the failed recovery during the Three Mile Island disaster (see Perrow, C. (1984). Complexity, Coupling and Catastrophe. *Normal Accidents: Living with High Risk Technologies,* Basic Books, pp. 62–110).

[30]Perrow, C. (1984). Complexity, Coupling and Catastrophe. *Normal Accidents: Living with High Risk Technologies,* Basic Books, pp. 62–110.

HMS Thetis and Apollo XIII allow students to examine the relative roles of planning and action in managing an operation. This focus continues in each of the improvement cases that follow, where there is a need for concerted action, rather than ongoing analysis. In each case, an individual protagonist (like Gene Krantz in Apollo) is clearly responsible for leading that action. In deciding what actions to take, these operations managers must consider the basic processes that change the nature of material or information (the theme of Module 1), the various systems that coordinate and marshall those processes (Module 2's emphasis), and—most important—the community formed by the people working in the operation.

PPG: Developing a Self-Directed Workforce looks at the improvement path taken by the manager of a small windshield plant in Berea, Kentucky, and the challenges that can arise when implementing broad programs of operator "empowerment." In 1989, the Berea plant was a greenfield site, constructed in part to escape from the labor relations problems that existed at other plants. The new site allowed PPG managers to combine tried-and-tested process technology with some very novel methods for managing the workforce at the plant. John Povlik, the Berea plant manager, set about building what was loosely described as a self-directed workforce.

After two years in which decision-making had been progressively moved from the "experts" who set up the plant to the people running and managing the equipment, some very thorny issues have begun to surface. First, even though only two grades, technician and operator, have been set up for people carrying out work on the floor, there is growing resentment among the operators that only technicians' advice is valued by managers. In addition, supervisors (or coordinators as they are called in the case) are becoming worried that they are managing themselves out of a job by delegating decisions downward. There are also problems with the methods available to reward individual performance. Povlik wants to find a way to reward individual initiative that is seen as equitable and beneficial in the plant. However, those rewarded are feeling as though they have been "patted on the head" by the management, and are often embarrassed by it. At the same time, peer review, in which the operators themselves appraise each other's performance, is being discussed. A sugges-

tion has been made to use these peer reviews to determine pay increases. Povlik is concerned that taking this radical step would open a Pandora's Box of problems in the plant and set it on a path from which it would be difficult to retreat.

The PPG case raises some very important issues around implementing the ideas of a "committed" workforce that were introduced in the first module. Many improvement initiatives focus on building new forms of workforce management. However, as we see in the Berea case, increasing employee involvement in decision making is a subtle and difficult challenge in which apparently small details can become very important over time.

Vickers Incorporated: Omaha Plant introduces the complication of entrenched custom-and-practice to implementing an improvement strategy. Unlike the greenfield Berea site, which PPG built to escape existing practices in its other plants, Vickers's Omaha factory, which makes hydraulic pumps, is run down in every sense of the word. It is a poorly performing jumble of aging, badly maintained equipment, dispirited operators, and very poor labor relations. The plant has been threatened with closure many times, leaving its people with an ongoing feeling of imminent dissolution. In addition, there has been a series of plant managers, each bringing their own flavor of improvement; workers have experienced this as a series of "waves" over the years and so expect future improvement efforts to wash over them, then dissipate.

Group Vice President John Weber has been given the task of figuring out what to do with the Omaha plant without—as the case says—spending a penny of TriNova's money (TriNova is Vickers's holding company). He sees three options. The first is to close the plant and build a greenfield site, like PPG Berea. However, the cost of closure and the cost of the new plant, which total $35 million, are unlikely to be justifiable. His second alternative is to close the plant but then transfer its product lines to other manufacturing units in the network. These units, though, are operating close to capacity, and would require further investment to accommodate the new processes. The third option is to keep the plant open and somehow improve its performance. Weber has a plan to keep the plant open. With a modest investment ($750,000), the introduction of mini "focused-factories," the establishment of self-directed teams, and a radical overhaul of the antiquated work rules, Weber feels he can turn the operation around. His first problem, before the details of implementation, is convincing all involved parties that he can do it, then securing their cooperation. He must first convince TriNova, whose tight purse strings might be loosened with a credible plan of action, but he must also talk the plant's union and the workforce into going along; they may prove a much tougher audience. In addition, Omaha is experiencing close to full employment, so employees know they can easily find work elsewhere if they don't like the changes at Vickers. Finally, Weber has to overcome years of antagonism and repeated breaches of trust. To make matters still worse, a strike over the current contract is imminent.

This factory is in a situation common even in the current age of "world-class manufacturing." There are tens of thousands of plants like Vickers Omaha dotted around the world. They are far from any frontier of optimal performance, yet are still in operation. They are protected by depreciated machines and plant that don't weigh heavily on a balance sheet, or are tolerated within a corporate philosophy that manufacturing is something that just "needs to be done" in the organization. Plants like Omaha are typically judged on their costs. Little attention is paid to the possibility that they might be able to create new sources of revenue, by becoming more responsive or producing higher quality products. This case explores the options available to managers of such facilities, and how to implement improvement strategies that draw on existing capabilities at the same time as building new ones.

Deloitte and Touche Consulting Group looks at problems that arise when trying to implement improvement as an outsider to the operation, and describes a predicament common to young consultants. Maria Chen is Deloitte's junior person on an engagement with SKS Manufacturing, an automotive component supplier. The project's goals are to improve cash flow, reduce inventories, and increase delivery reliability. A number of problems have arisen during the first six weeks of the project, not least of which is the fact that inventory levels in the plant have still not fallen. In fact, they have risen. Chen finds herself in the difficult position of having to explain to the client, and to her superiors, exactly why performance has not improved markedly, and has to develop a credible

plan for the remainder of the engagement (assuming it continues).

Despite her previous industrial experience, Chen is in unfamiliar territory and, has to some extent, "felt her way along" in the engagement. She has probably spent too much time on analysis and too little in taking action. Despite this, some progress has been made, and Chen feels that she has focused on steps that will provide a long-term solution rather than a quick fix to the numbers. She is under considerable pressure, however, to make more visible improvements. The question is what should Chen have done differently in tackling this engagement? Given that she may have made mistakes here and there, what should she now do to satisfy the needs of her company and the client? How should she balance her responsibility to provide a long-term solution for the operation with the client's immediate need for cash?

Pacific Dunlop Beijing adds a new twist to improvement strategy and implementation: managing an operation based in a foreign country. Having lost a series of ex-patriate managers from its Beijing sock factory, the Australian conglomerate Pacific Dunlop (PD) asked Steve Littley, one of its best young plant managers, to take it over. After 14 months in China, Littley is not finding things easy. In spite of a wealth of knowledge about managing operations in Australia, he finds that the systems, organization, and culture of his new environment are overwhelmingly different. First, he has a language problem, since he speaks no Mandarin and few people in the plant speak English. Second, he has to learn and adapt to the cultural norms of business in China (where, for example, the supplier, rather than the customer, is traditionally king). Third, he has been unsuccessful in his attempts to encourage Chinese managers to accept more responsibility. Fourth, his job involves not only running the plant, but also searching for new business to fill slack capacity when it appears; he has no experience at this. Finally, Littley's apartment is located in the plant, meaning that he is frequently awakened in the middle of the night with maintenance and production problems. The result of this litany of problems is that Littley has gone for too long without sleep, cannot leave the plant to rest, and is getting ill as a result. While it is very easy to point the finger at Pacific Dunlop as the cause for Littley's woes, the question is what should one *do* when faced with such circumstances?

Littley must decide not only what his priorities are, but also how to take action in a way that sets the plant on a path of ongoing improvement while alleviating his tremendously difficult personal situation.

Micom Caribe is the last case in the course, for reasons that become apparent during the class discussion. Tom Moschetti manages Micom Caribe, a small microelectronics plant in Puerto Rico that is the offshore manufacturing arm of Micom Communications Corporation (MCC), based in California. Moschetti's problems emerge when there is a quality problem with a new product, the Micom Box. Most of the quality issues are due to poor communication between the plant and headquarters. The California managers are primarily interested in inventing things, and see manufacturing simply as a subsidiary activity. This attitude is worsened by the cultural and geographic separation of the two entities. "MCC," said one Caribbean manager, "thinks Micom is second-class, third-world and fourth-rate." Moschetti, an ex-art professor from Berkeley, sets out to prove MCC wrong. Through a well-coordinated effort involving everyone from top management to line operators (each in different ways), he dramatically improves the flexibility and quality of the operation. In addition, he builds an organization that understands change as a matter of course, and is able to learn new things very quickly.

The question is: what is it that Moschetti *does* that makes this spark of improvement flare up so vigorously? None of his actions seem especially radical, brilliant, or even unusual. Yet Moschetti seems to have a magic ingredient, something about the way he *implements* things that makes them work! Micom ends the course with a challenge: to determine, beyond the rhetoric of empowerment and total quality, what exactly it is about a successful operations improvement implementation that makes it work, and allows it to continue to deliver new operating capabilities over time.

CASE 19

Integron Incorporated

The Integrated Components Division (ICD)

Gary Lloyd, vice president of the Integrated Components Division (ICD) of Integron Inc., pondered over his computer as he put together his slides summarizing the benchmarking study recently completed for his newly unleashed Multichip Module (MCM) manufacturing organization. In January 1994—two months previously—his division had assumed full profit and loss responsibility for the first time, and became able to compete for business outside the Integron group.

Lloyd had commissioned the study for two reasons. First, ICD had launched several improvement programs in an effort to boost competitiveness; and Lloyd wanted the benchmarking study to guide further initiatives and to determine which improvement steps should continue to be pursued. Second, he planned to use the results as a basis for setting a new strategic direction. Lloyd knew that his team of managers was technically skilled and excited about tackling the new challenges, but he was concerned about their lack of experience in external markets. This study would be an important step in building what had once been a manufacturing cost center into an organization that could exploit its capabilities to generate new commercial opportunities.

The results of the study, however, were worrisome. They implied that the MCM organization needed to make some radical changes in order to meet prevailing market needs. Although Lloyd agreed that the MCM group had to make some

fundamental changes, he had several nagging doubts and questions regarding the consultants' findings:

1. How well did benchmarking the current competition really help determine the path for developing new operations capabilities in the future? The MCM market was in its infancy, and the slate of competitors had by no means stabilized. Industry experts seemed unable to agree on an outlook; credible predictions ranged from explosive growth to complete dissolution. Lloyd worried that focusing on a goal based on current standards might leave them behind in this fast-paced, capricious industry.

2. How should ICD focus its marketing strategy? The MCM market comprised several diverse segments, and focusing on the development of one set of capabilities might preclude ICD from serving other segments as well as they could in the future.

3. Should ICD's manufacturing improvement plans focus on one element of performance, such as quality, to the exclusion of the others, such as quick-response and cost? ICD had embarked on a number of quality-improvement schemes over the years and last year had placed highest emphasis on customer-service improvement. This year ICD was implementing widespread cost-cutting initiatives.

Evolution of the Current Organization

Integron Inc. was the third largest telecommunications equipment supplier in the United States. The ICD division had its beginnings in the early 1960s when Integron developed technology for building hybrid integrated circuits. Internal demand for these circuits boomed and by the mid-1970s, five or six manufacturing plants had been built to provide much-needed capacity. At the same time, telecommunications became much more software intensive and demand for dedicated hardware slowed. Manufacturing of hybrid

This case was prepared as the basis for class discussion rather than to illustrate either effective or ineffective handling of an administrative situation. Names and data have been disguised.

This case was prepared by David M. Upton, Michelle Jarrad, and Laurie Thomas. Copyright © 1995 by the President and Fellows of Harvard College. Harvard Business School Case 695-060.

integrated circuits, (a technology combining digital and analog technologies) was consolidated into the single plant in Kincher Falls, Oregon. In 1990, with the formal integration of R&D and manufacturing organizations, the unit shifted from its functional reporting structure to a business unit structure as a self-contained cost center.

Because ICD had been a captive supplier to other groups within Integron, its organization was designed around the support of internal customers. Products were passed from unit to unit at cost, and the business was driven by research and the resulting technological needs in Integron as a whole. The $30 million business unit was organized on a product and customer basis, and even though R&D engineers had been integrated into the organization, there were lingering barriers between the functional areas. Demand for any given product usually evolved through informal channels of communication between the design engineers at Kincher Falls and design engineers at the "customers'" (other Integron) units. Such a customer would either approach ICD's design engineers with a technical problem or ICD's design engineers would call the downstream customers to discuss some new technological development or opportunity. If there was a match, design engineers from both units would team up to develop a product. While each new product was a result of a customized design, its technical characteristics did not change after entering production. A new product might be produced for years without significant modification. So, paradoxically, while the development group felt pressure to be agile and responsive, *manufacturing* at the Kincher Falls facility was organized for high-volumes with dedicated lines and a heavily specialized workforce.

STANDING ALONE

By the late 1980s, business units within Integron knew they would have to become independent and start to find external sources of business. In 1987, Henry Dornberg, Integron's CEO, let it be known that the 50-year-old company could no longer be managed as a hierarchical behemoth. His goal was to decentralize decision making so that operating units felt solely responsible for setting strategic direction, implementing competitive initiatives, and meeting financial hurdle rates. Although Dornberg did not specify required hurdle rates

publicly, unit managers knew they would be held responsible for attaining aggressive financial results very quickly.

With the chill winds of change blowing through the company, ICD initiated several improvement programs in an effort to become more competitive in the external market. Continuous quality improvement had long been a central theme at ICD. Indeed, the business unit was part of a group winning the prestigious Skinner Award[1] for Quality in 1993. Most employees in the plant were members of at least one quality team.

In January 1994, ICD was formally converted from a cost center to a profit center. At the time of the benchmarking study, the fledgling marketing department was six weeks old, and the unit still lacked a dedicated sales force. New marketing personnel were wrestling with novel and unfamiliar issues such as billing policy, pricing, segmentation analysis, and sales strategies for external customers, most of whom were original equipment manufacturers (OEMs).

This new responsibility came to ICD at a very difficult time. First, the hybrid integrated circuits product line, the majority of ICD's revenues, was reaching maturity. These products were used by telecommunications customers—primarily a captive market. The overall market was projected to grow at just 4% per year, and Lloyd knew his Integron customers were starting to seek out external suppliers in search of a better price for given levels of performance. Additionally, the most promising growth area, the emerging multichip module market, was so new that it was astonishingly difficult to predict how large it would grow, which market segments would grow the most, and which specific substrate technology would be in highest demand.

MULTICHIP MODULES

A multichip module (MCM) consisted of several microelectronic components bonded onto a common substrate. A module began life as a substrate onto which conductive material was patterned to form circuit interconnections. Different combinations of integrated circuits or "chips" placed on the substrate formed a hybrid circuit that was capable

---

[1] The Skinner Award was an internationally recognized award for quality.

of performing more complex functions than would be practicable on a single chip. The MCM itself consisted of several layers of hybrid integrated circuits separated by a thin-film polymer. The module incorporated passive components, such as resistors and capacitors, which provided it with functionality beyond that of existing integrated circuits.

MCMs provided cost-effective, custom solutions for technically advanced applications requiring high speeds in space-constrained systems. However, as speed requirements increased, the density of electrical components on the MCMs had also increased, causing routing problems that manifested themselves as signal delays and interference on the circuit.

There were three basic substrate types, which distinguished the various MCM families: MCM-C (Ceramic), MCM-L (Laminate) and MCM-D (Dielectric). Each family of MCM varied in terms of the solutions it offered. MCM-Cs were based on a thick-film technology substrate. The MCM-L technology was similar to surface mount technology (SMT), in that it achieved high densities and was the cheapest to produce. Finally, the MCM-D technology was the most technically advanced of the three product types. Based on a thin-film technology substrate, it was excellent for routing and density problems. MCM-Ds were also capable of working at very high frequencies, currently those above 100 MHz, as compared to printed circuit boards, which were limited to applications below 50 MHz. ICD offered products in the MCM-D class and was also working on an advanced technology product in the MCM-D category that would enable it to offer a much lower-cost dielectric solution.

THE DESIGN AND MANUFACTURING PROCESS

Product Realization

The creation of multichip modules at ICD was a process characterized by heavy early interaction between the customer and ICD applications engineers and designers. Prior to the actual bid, a team comprising customer engineers and ICD personnel determined whether there was a technical match and whether ICD had the operational capabilities to meet necessary lead times and produce the required volumes.

Next, the customers and ICD designers decided upon the technical specifications and layout of the module. Agreement regarding the specifications was acknowledged by a formal acceptance letter. This step ensured that all team members had clearly laid out their designs and product criteria. The team then embarked on a prototyping process to build and test the models and prototype batches. Throughout this process, (known to all as the product realization process, PRP), arduous functional testing was done to simulate the lot in full production with the highest possible fidelity. The customers checked the design of the sample product for their application after this first group of models had been built and tested within ICD. This step was documented with a customer model acceptance letter. The period from the original design acceptance letter until the model acceptance letter was typically four weeks.

During the final 10 week phase before volume production, the design team built an engineering pilot batch, usually a group of 10 to 20 modules that the customer would use in his or her design process (rather than simply check for functionality). This process was similar to the model process. Design changes were incorporated and the manufacturing process was fully documented to facilitate volume production. After completion of the lot, the customer again signed off with a product acceptance letter, indicating that she or he was ready to begin volume production (see Exhibit 1).

Volume Production

The volume production process at ICD began with either a forecasted order, generated in anticipation of a "win," or with a hard order. After the order was entered into the system, the material for the substrate was ordered. The lead time to receive the silicon was 16 weeks—a bottleneck for the entire process. The master scheduling system checked for bill of material availability and calculated available capacity in the factory. If material and capacity were available, the system automatically scheduled the build without the intervention of a planner.

Once scheduled, a route card and shop order were created and dispatched to the first step of the manufacturing process. A strong union ingrained custom-and-practice dictated very specific roles for each operator, necessitating a stable of material handlers, dispatchers, and "regular" operators.

EXHIBIT I Product Realization Process

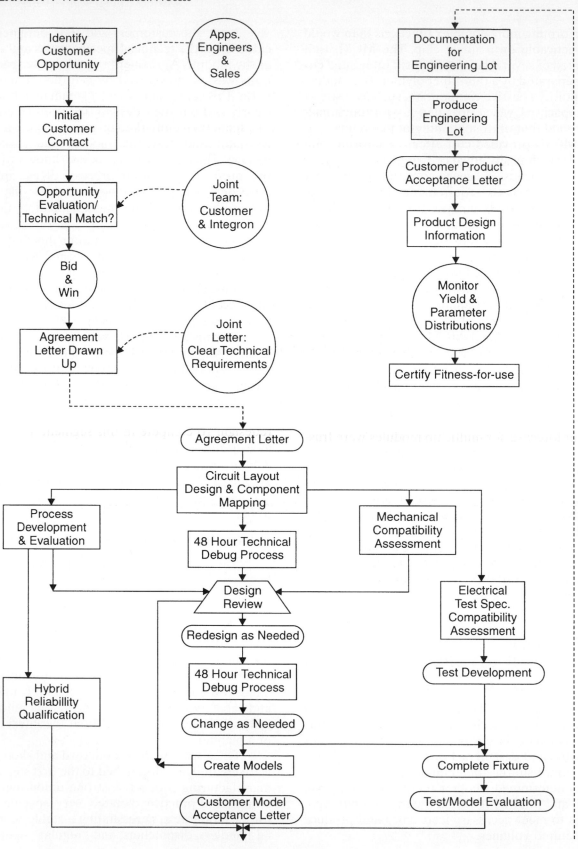

Each operator carefully documented, on the route card, his or her contribution to the process and moved the lot through the line. At the end of the process, the parts were entered via a bar code reader into the on-line tracking system, and in-process yield losses were calculated. The product was packed and shipped in a small room just next to the manufacturing area.

In the early 1990's, as part of ICD's commitment to improving its manufacturing abilities, the manufacturing area began transforming itself from a functional layout to three focused factories, each focusing on a different type of electronic packaging. Under the new system, all orders for a given product type would be produced on the same line. ICD's managers were sure this layout would help reduce manufacturing lead-times and increase flexibility to volume demands and design changes. The first line, for specialty products, was scheduled for completion in June 1994 (see Exhibit 2).

THE MARKET FOR MULTICHIP MODULES

Market forecasts for multichip modules were frustratingly varied and uncertain. One industry research organization, Dataquest, estimated the current market at $300 million and expected it to grow to $18 billion by the year 2000. However, these market size estimates had been decreasing substantially every year. Dataquest also estimated that 30% of all chips would be sold as part of a multichip module by that time. The federal government was supporting the growth of the market by deeming it a critical technology, and in late 1993 it appropriated $70 million in funding from the Defense Advanced Research Projects Agency (DARPA). There remained, however, other industry observers with less optimistic views. They believed that multichip modules would be confined to small niches, because current single-chip packaging techniques coupled with further shrinking of traditional microprocessors would offer the most cost-effective technical solution.

Not only was the overall growth of the multichip module market uncertain, but the *relative* growth of each of the highly diverse segments was also difficult to predict. There were three primary market segments: personal computers, wireless, and automated test equipment.

Personal Computers & Workstations. ICD projected this segment would grow from about $70 million in 1993 to about $1.1 billion in 1995. Although it was the largest single segment, it would most likely have the most stringent competitive requirements. Product life cycles were very short, customers demanded fast prototyping abilities, and cost pressures were tremendous. Also, most current multichip module competitors were focused on this segment. ICD had focused on the high-end workstation portion of this segment in order to leverage its leading-edge technology capabilities, but managers were certain of the need to develop a new, cheaper technology to remain a contender in this segment.

Wireless. Internal projections estimated this segment would grow from about $40 million in 1993 to $280 million by 1995. This segment currently had longer product life cycles than the PC market, and the required production runs were also longer. However, the wireless market was facing tough cost pressures and was moving to the use of "platform" products—base products that could be modified or upgraded over time without a full-scale redesign. To compete in this segment, ICD might have to reorient its whole "custom-design" process to shift from 100% custom to a much more incremental approach.

Automated Test Equipment and Instrumentation (ATE). The targeted areas of the ATE market included vision systems, high-speed instruments, integrated circuit testers, and circuit board testers. This market was expected to grow from $28 million in 1993 to $72 million by 1995. The high technical requirements in this segment fitted well with ICD's MCM-D technology. ICD had already acquired a prestigious external customer in this segment, and several others were in the pipeline.

THE COMPETITION

Because the multichip module market was so new, and might offer huge growth possibilities, a range of different types of competitor had been attracted, each trying to capture a piece of the market.

Vertically Integrated Systems Companies. Integron was a member of this category, along with companies such as IBM, AT&T, Fujitsu, and DEC. These companies originally developed multichip

EXHIBIT 2 Existing Internal Volume Production Process

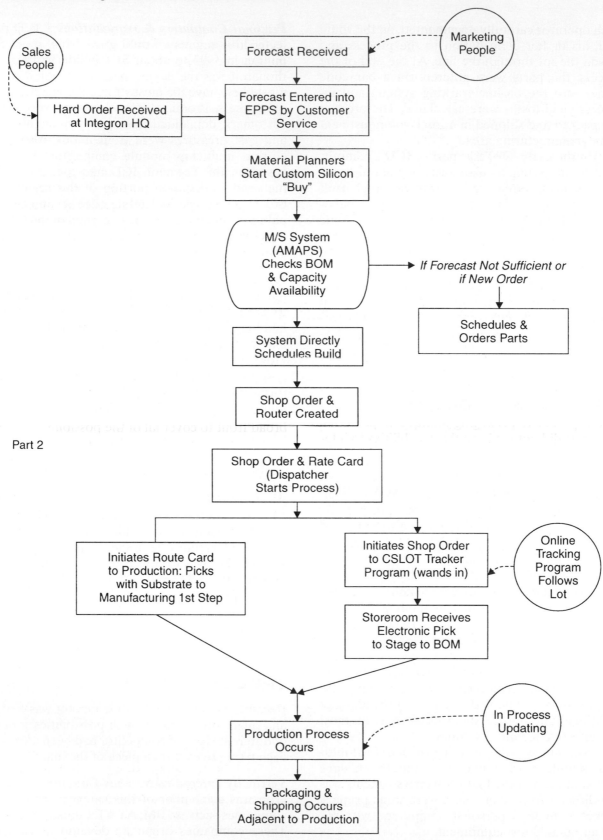

Sales People

Marketing People

Forecast Received

Hard Order Received at Integron HQ

Forecast Entered into EPPS by Customer Service

Material Planners Start Custom Silicon "Buy"

M/S System (AMAPS) Checks BOM & Capacity Availability

If Forecast Not Sufficient or if New Order

Schedules & Orders Parts

System Directly Schedules Build

Shop Order & Router Created

Part 2

Shop Order & Rate Card (Dispatcher Starts Process)

Initiates Route Card to Production: Picks with Substrate to Manufacturing 1st Step

Initiates Shop Order to CSLOT Tracker Program (wands in)

Online Tracking Program Follows Lot

Storeroom Receives Electronic Pick to Stage to BOM

Production Process Occurs

In Process Updating

Packaging & Shipping Occurs Adjacent to Production

module expertise to solve internal technical challenges and were now looking for external commercial opportunities to leverage their technical abilities. Each of these firms had substantial internal demand that could sustain them through early, uncertain external market developments. However, their specific market approach tactics were beginning to diverge. IBM, AT&T and Integron had kept MCM capabilities in-house, but recently, DEC had divested its capabilities into an independent company, Micro Module Systems (MMS).

Technological Competitors.   Potential competitors in this group included Cypress Semiconductor, Motorola, Harris Semiconductor, Pacific Microelectronics, and Texas Instruments. These players competed primarily through their abilities with monolithic silicon, but some were entering the MCM market. The market was attractive to these companies not only as a source of growth but also as an opportunity to offset the commoditization of their core products. Many of them hoped MCMs would provide price premiums and opportunities to differentiate on the basis of performance and service. While these competitors did have expertise in packaging multiple chips in one unit, most did not yet have the capabilities to integrate passive components (individual components that enabled increased functionality of MCMs such as capacitors and diodes) into products without the assistance of OEMs. These competitors had strong relationships with potential MCM customers through their other product offerings. Several of them were beginning to work with OEMs to build requisite skills.

Contract Assembly Houses.   Companies in this segment included nChip, Flextronix, and Promex. Historically, these competitors had lacked the high-performance multichip module design capabilities and were thus relegated to providing manufacturing outsourcing for chip makers and systems houses (e.g., Sun Microsystems). Additionally, the MCM industry lacked specific standards, making it difficult for assembly houses to replicate modules for appropriate specifications—many of the standards that did exist had done so only tacitly, among larger companies' engineers. However, with the development of third-party software-suites of standard design tools, contract assemblers were expected to acquire design capabilities quickly. In addition, the Microelectronics and Computer Consortium was developing industry-wide standards. If these competitors overcame their current obstacles, they would be in an excellent competitive position, because end users wanted the flexibility to use different companies' chips in any given design.

Within these competitive segments, the specific players were not solidly established and changed from week to week. At the time of the benchmarking study, several companies had exited the multichip module market while a number of others were just entering. Industry experts believed that the winning competitors would be those who had the most financial staying power and who bet upon the right technological option: either high-end, technically complex products or cheaper, standardized products. It seemed to Lloyd that everyone was simply gambling on their best hunch.

THE PROBLEM

Gambling, according to Lloyd, was not good enough for his manufacturing organization, and so he was determined to develop abilities across a broad front to cover all of the possibilities.

Lloyd knew ICD had to become externally competitive in order to grow, and the organization had developed a *to do* list to help boost its abilities (see Exhibit 3). He noted:

> I would love to think that there is some perfect, focused strategy out there that would ensure our success. But the fact of the matter is that we have to perform well in all aspects of our business. Specific strategic initiatives are typically the result of some personal vision. My old boss, Mike McManus, started to focus on quality. My current boss, Jenny Dudley, thinks we need to strengthen the voice of the customer; therefore, we have launched several customer service initiatives including a satisfaction survey.

Lloyd brought in two consultants from Hantwood Associates to conduct a benchmarking study of the manufacturing operation for two reasons. First, he wanted to assess the progress that had been made in the various, periodic improvement initiatives in the past. Second, he wanted a method by which the manufacturing group could set operational goals for itself. The consultants, Debra Spooner and Charlene Crandall, both recent graduates of a well-known Eastern business school, initially embarked on the generic steps of a

ME Initiatives	ME Objectives	Operational Programs
IMPROVE CUSTOMER SATISFACTION	CUSTOMER SATISFACTION	1. ISO9001 Certification 2. Customer Satisfaction Planning Organization 3. DQI Program 4. Customer Service and Quality Improvement Forums 5. Customer Removal Rate 6. Customer Change Notification & Acceptance Program 7. T2 Rating
	ORDER REALIZATION	1. Manufacturing and Order Management Systems 2. Service to Customer Improvements
	NEW PRODUCT INTRODUCTION	1. New Product Realization Improvements 2. MCM Product Realization Process 3. FCP Migration Program 4. FCP Product Realization Process
	SKINNER DISCIPLINE	1. Skinner Assessment
INCREASE PEOPLE INVOLVEMENT	PEOPLE INVOLVEMENT	1. Quality Improvement/Task Teams 2. Support Team 3. Employee Suggestion Program 4. Customer Focus
	LEADERSHIP	1. Leadership Training 2. Management Team Initiatives 3. Performance Appraisal 4. Skills Enhancement Program
COMPLETE TURNAROUND PLAN	PROFITABLE GROWTH	1. Microelectronics Transition 2. Domestic Sales Growth 3. International Sales Growth
	FINANCIAL COMMITMENT	1. ABC Implementation 2. MCM Focus Factories 3. FCP Focus Factories 4. Expense Reduction Initiatives
TECHNOLOGY		1. MCM-L Introduction 2. Low-cost Metallization Introduction 3. New Polymer Introduction 4. MIT Introduction 5. FCP Development (12 programs)
ENVIRONMENTAL		1. CFC/CHC Eliminations 2. SARA 313 (Air) 3. Paper Recycling and Reduction

EXHIBIT 3 Current List of Operations Development Programs

benchmarking study but quickly ran into problems as they thought about the design of this particular study.

What Attributes Should Be Benchmarked? The consultants wanted to benchmark a specific operational attribute as it applied to a single market segment. However, Lloyd had expressed strong feelings that his organization had to build a set of general capabilities that could serve all segments. He hoped that the study would help unearth this set of required skills; thus, he did not want the consultants to narrow the study in any way.

How Should Data Be Collected? Because there were no clear industry leaders, the consultants did not want to focus solely upon competitors' skills. They also suspected that if competitive plant tours were granted, they would be too general to be helpful. Talking to customers was a potential alternate source of information; however, ICD had very few OEM customers at the time of the study. Additionally, the consultants suspected that these OEMs had very little contact with other MCM producers. Thus, Spooner and Crandall were faced with the task of benchmarking a broad set of performance criteria across four market segments with little access to competitors.

They also recognized some risks associated with benchmarking in the multichip module industry:

- Should benchmarking be used *at all* to set long-term objectives in this fast-paced, new industry? If ICD set specific objectives based on the past performance of competitors, it ran the risk of focusing on achieving performance levels that those competitors might already have surpassed.

- Would the benchmarking process cause the firm to overreact in developing its strategy? For example, if technical capabilities were the current basis of competition and ICD focused on boosting those skills, would they be able to react if cost began to gain influence over the buying decision?

Initial Approach.   Because of the problems and risks, the consultants settled on an approach that deviated slightly from a traditional benchmarking study but would help set directional targets. They developed a questionnaire (Exhibit 4) designed to answer three broad questions:

- Which manufacturing performance criteria most influenced a customer's buying decision?

- How well did ICD perform against these criteria?

- How well were competitors performing?

The questionnaire was given to OEMs in each customer segment as well as ICD's applications engineers. Applications engineers served as the primary interface with OEM customers, solving their applications needs and generating sales for ICD. Indeed, as ICD had no sales force, they were the only day-to-day contacts for customers. Spooner and Crandall felt that the application engineers' contribution would help compensate for the small number of customers. The consultants also wanted to compare the internal perspective of

ICD people with customer evaluations. In this way, the study might reveal two types of gap: First the difference between ICD's self-assessment and customer evaluations; second, the difference between competitors' performance and ICD's performance, as reported by customers.

RESULTS OF THE STUDY

Exhibit 4 shows a typical response from the telephone survey conducted by the consultants. To assess the fit between ICD's manufacturing strengths and customers' buying criteria, they asked customers to rate ICD's performance on each of their criteria. Next, the consultants analyzed the differences between ICD's performance ratings and its competitors' ratings to determine the magnitude of any competitive gaps. Although ICD fared well in these comparisons, the analyses also highlighted a number of weaknesses (see Exhibit 5).

The consultants also made several observations based on comments that arose during the survey.

- Each market segment cited similar buying criteria but assigned different priorities to each (see Exhibit 6).

- While applications engineers also generated a similar list of criteria, they assigned relative importance quite differently from the customers (see Exhibit 7).

- The most serious disparity in perception concerned the importance of cost. Customers cited cost as only one of many barriers dissuading them from adopting MCMs—while applications engineers consistently saw it as the most critical element in the buying decision.

- The manufacturing organization, in choosing a general approach to all segments, might have been failing to meet the needs of any one segment (see Exhibit 8). For example, one customer who was willing to pay a high price required product characteristics that were too difficult to manufacture. Another customer felt that the costs required to produce a very simple product were too high.

- Applications engineers felt that ICD's approach was unfocused and that it inadequately met the specific needs of each segment. They also felt they were being asked to fill two different roles, one as a salesperson and one as a technical consultant (see Exhibit 9).

EXHIBIT 4   Benchmarking Questionnaire

INTEGRON BENCHMARKING QUESTIONNAIRE

Intent of Questionnaire

Our goal in analyzing this questionnaire is to gain an understanding of customers' needs, perceptions of Integron, and perceptions of the competition in the high-end multichip module market. The results will be compiled and used to help determine Integron's strengths and weaknesses. Please take a few minutes to look over the questions. We will call to discuss your responses.

A. Overall Perception of Integron

    1. Have they been, or are they now, a supplier to you?—if so, what do they supply?

    2. What is your general impression of their:

Criterion	Good	Average	Poor
Quality	/		
Delivery	/		
Technical Competency	/		
Price		/	
Other			

    3. What is Integron's strongest capability?

Engineering design talent and financial strength

B. Who makes the purchase decision regarding this type of technology?

    1. Is it the engineer/purchasing or a coalition? **Coalition**

    2. How long do you spend talking with the Integron sales rep prior to the buy decision?   **About 1 month**

    3. What is the critical factor needed to finalize a purchase from Integron?   **Ability to meet our design requirements**

C. What criteria are important to you when considering the purchase of MCMs? Please rank these on a scale of 1–7 (1 = not important, 3–4 of average importance, 7 critical). At the end, please rank your top five criteria by writing their rank next to them.

Rank	Criterion	1	2	3	4	5	6	7
5	Cost to you vs. other MCMs					X		
4	Cost to you vs. substitute technologies					X		
	Quality (adherence to spec.)					X		
1	Meet current technical requirements							X
	Degree of customization available				X			
	Difficulty and costs of changing from current tooling/designs: i.e. switching costs			X				
2	Length of time to get prototypes						X	
3	Length of time to get volume production						X	
	Adequate documentation of process specs.		X					
	Ability for supplier to be primary supplier		X					
	Continuing ability to offer leading-edge technical solutions		X					
	Reputation/longevity of supplier				X			
	Ability to order any lot size	X						
	Ability to produce at high volume		X					
	Other:							

EXHIBIT 4   *(cont.)*

D. Please rank how well you feel Integron performs on the same criteria below. (1 = poorly, 3–4 average, 7 excellently). Also, please rank Integron's five strongest characteristics.

Rank	Criterion	1	2	3	4	5	6	7
	Cost to you vs. other MCMs				X			
	Cost to you vs. substitute technologies			X				
	Quality (adherence to spec.)				X			
	Meet current technical requirements					X		
3	Degree of customization available						X	
	Difficulty and costs of changing from current tooling/designs: i.e. switching costs					X		
	Length of time to get prototypes			X				
	Length of time to get volume production			X				
	Adequate documentation of process specs.				X			
3	Ability for supplier to be primary supplier						X	
2	Continuing ability to offer leading-edge technical solutions						X	
1	Reputation/longevity of supplier							X
	Ability to order any lot size						X	
	Other:							
	Other:							

E. Please define what "flexibility" means to you.

1. If you had to choose, would you prefer more customization ability or shorter leadtimes to receive your prototype lots?

    shorter lead times—also engineer who returns calls promptly.

2. If you had to choose, would you prefer lower cost & limited Engineering Change Orders (ECOs) or higher cost and ECOs?

    lower cost & limited ECOs

F. What MCM alternatives to Integron do you know of? This can include substitute technologies as well as direct MCM competitors.

Competitor	Strengths	Weaknesses
MMS	Performance, cost	Financial stability
nChip	Marketing dept, Density, thermal performance	Financial stability
Fujitsu		Cost, flexibility
IBM	Process Staff	Cost, responsiveness
AT&T	Engineering, performance	
TI		
Kyocera	Quality	Cost

G. Is your physical proximity to a supplier important?

No.

H. For each criterion below, please determine Integron's strongest competitor and rank its performance on a scale of 1–7 (1 = poor, 3–4 average, 7 excellent)

Company	Criterion	1	2	3	4	5	6	7
MMS	Cost to you vs. other MCMs					/		
Kyocera	Cost to you vs. substitute technologies					/		
Kyocera	Quality (adherence to spec.)						/	
MMS	Meet current technical requirements					/		
MMS, nChip	Degree of customization available					/		
	Difficulty and costs of changing from current tooling/designs: i.e. switching costs					/		
	Length of time to get prototypes					/		
	Length of time to get volume production					/		
	Adequate documentation of process specs.?							
IBM, AT&T, Kyocera	Ability of supplier to be primary supplier						/	
IBM, AT&T	Continuing ability to offer leading-edge technical solutions					/		
Kyocera	Reputation/longevity of supplier						/	
MMS	Ability to order any lot size			/				
	Ability to produce at high volume						/	
	Other:							

I. What are the three most important things Integron could change to improve their relationship with you?

1. **Give me a single point of contact who can act as a liaison with all functional groups.**

2. **Lower your prices!**

J. Please add any other information that would help us assess Integron's relative competitiveness

Thanks for your help!

EXHIBIT 4 *(cont.)*

After hearing the consultants' findings, Lloyd realized there were some critical decisions to be made before charting ICD's future path. He left the presentation, went back to his office, and started to put together his recommendations.

LLOYD'S DILEMMA

The following Tuesday, Gary Lloyd looked down at the recommendations he had developed. They implied major changes for his organization, and he had several lingering doubts about the study.

First, the survey results were based on a very small number of respondents. Lloyd's feeling was that the results were generally accurate, but he had to admit they were by no means statistically significant. Second, ICD had plenty to do without the upheaval of the radical change implied by the findings of the survey, not the least of which was to continue serving internal customers. Other Inte-

Buying Criteria	Importance to Buying Decision (Customer Ave.)	ICD Performance		Competitor Performance	
		Customer Average	App. Eng. Average	Customer Average	App. Eng. Average
Cost to you vs. other MCM	5.25	4.60	2.50	5.75	7.00
Cost to you vs. substitute technologies	6.00	3.70	1.50	5.00	6.00
Quality (adherence to specifications)	6.40	6.00	5.00	5.75	5.00
Meet current technical requirements	6.80	6.00	5.00	5.50	5.00
Degree of customization available	5.10	6.25	4.50	5.00	4.50
Difficulty and costs of changing from current tooling/designs	4.50	5.00	3.50	7.00	4.50
Length of time to get prototypes	5.50	3.70	4.00	5.50	4.00
Length of time to get volume production	5.60	3.50	4.50	5.50	4.00
Adequate documentation of process and specs.	4.20	4.75	4.00	6.75	5.50
Ability for supplier to be primary supplier	3.20	6.00	6.50	6.00	4.50
Continuing ability to offer leading-edge technical solutions	5.20	6.75	5.00	7.00	5.50
Reputation/longevity of supplier	5.80	6.70	7.00	7.00	4.50
Ability to order any lot size	5.00	5.50	4.00	5.50	4.00

EXHIBIT 5   Survey Response Summary Data

Workstation	ATE	Wireless
1. Meet current technical reqs.	1. Service	1. Quality
2. Quality	2. Meet current technical reqs.	2. Meet current technical reqs.
3. Cost & ability to produce high volumes	3. Quality	3. Ability to test
4. Longevity/reputation	4. Cost	4. Cost
5. Length of time to get volume production	5. Continuing ability to offer technical solutions	5. Ability to produce at high volume

EXHIBIT 6   Comparison of Buying Criteria by Segment

Integron Applications Engineers	Workstation Customers
1. Cost	1. Meeting current technical requirements
2. Meeting current technical requirements	2. Quality
3. Longevity/reputation	3. Cost & ability to produce at high volume
4. Quality	4. Longevity/reputation
5. Continuing ability to offer technical solutions	5. Length of time to get volume production

EXHIBIT 7   Internal and External Rankings of Buying Criteria

gron units needed his organization to remain at the forefront of technological developments, and he did not want to do anything to put that capability at risk.

Lloyd was frustrated. He could not predict how the market would change, but the study had shown that each of the emergent lily pads was moving in a different direction, at unknown speed. Each needed different capabilities from its supplier. At the same time, his manufacturing people desperately needed to know if their improvement plans were headed in the right direction.

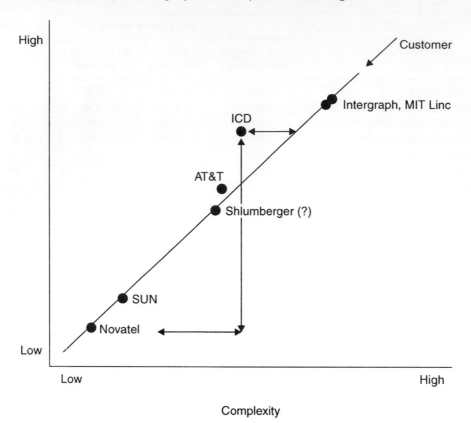

EXHIBIT 8 Market Positioning

EXHIBIT 9　Selected Applications Engineer Comments

> *"ICD either needs to find new niche markets for high-priced products or low-cost fabrication of MCMs."*
>
> *"I'm not sure if one organization can adequately address all four markets: I know our products can't."*
>
> *"Am I supposed to help customers solve problems or close deals? I feel like I'm asked to do two jobs."*

Lloyd could act now or wait and repeat the study when there were more customers available to participate, and the market had become more stable. Postponing action was very tempting. The MCM market was changing quickly, and he did not want to gamble on a strategy that could quickly become outdated.

Lloyd's direct reports were waiting to hear his recommendations and action plan in the conference room next door. "Okay," he thought as he got up from his desk, "let's see what I have to say . . . ".

A Measure of Delight: The Pursuit of Quality at AT&T Universal Card Services (A)

In the lobby of the headquarters building of AT&T Universal Card Services Corp., a crystal Malcolm Baldrige National Quality Award rotates silently on a pedestal within a glass case. On one marble wall, above a sheet of flowing water, are the words, "Customers are the center of our universe." The inscription on the opposite wall reads, "One world, one card." Despite a steady stream of visitors and employees, the lobby has the hushed and serene atmosphere of a shrine.

But on the upper floors of the building—in the heart of the operation that brought home the nation's top quality award—it is never silent. In a honeycomb of open and brightly lit cubicles, about 300 men and women are speaking intently but pleasantly into telephone headsets while deftly keying information and instructions into the computer terminals before them. In all directions, one phrase is repeated so often that it seems to hang in the air: "AT&T Universal Card, how may I help you?"

The workers appear private and autonomous, connected only to their customers on the other end of the line. Yet at any moment, day or night, there may be someone else listening. It may be a co-worker, monitoring the call in order to suggest how a request might be handled differently. It may be a team leader, gathering the information that will figure in next year's raises. It may be a senior manager, putting on a headset to listen to calls while working out in the company gym. Or it may be a quality monitor in another building, scribbling ratings and comments on a one-page sheet that will help determine whether everyone in the com-

pany gets a bonus for that day. And all the while, as the pleasant voices talk on, a computer tracks every call that comes in, continually measuring how long it takes to answer each call, how many seconds are spent on each conversation, and whether any customers hang up before their calls are answered. In the eyes of the executives who designed the company's operating philosophy and strategic plan, the monitored calls were an indispensable component in boosting AT&T Universal Card over its competitors, and making it a true quality company.

THE CHALLENGE

In the summer of 1993, Universal Card Services (UCS) was, by most standards, in an enviable position. The wholly owned AT&T subsidiary had broken into the highly competitive credit card business in 1990, determined to build on the AT&T name with a philosophy of "delighting" customers with unparalleled service. To help do that, the company had created an innovative measurement and compensation system to drive the pursuit of quality and customer satisfaction. Now just three years later, UCS, with nearly 12 million accounts, was the number-two credit card issuer in the industry. Not only that; in 1992, UCS was the youngest company ever—and one of just three service firms—to win the coveted Malcolm Baldrige National Quality Award.

But despite these successes, there was a sense within the Jacksonville, Florida–based company that some fundamental changes were in order. In particular, Rob Davis, vice president of Quality, was searching for ways to push UCS's quest for quality one step further. A number of factors triggered this critical self-examination. Competitors had begun to close the gap opened by UCS when it pioneered its innovative policies and practices three years earlier. The departure of two key

The case was prepared as the basis for class discussion rather than to illustrate either effective or ineffective handling of an administrative situation.

This case was prepared by Susan Rosegrant under the direction of Roy Shapiro and Michael Watkins. Copyright © 1993 by the President and Fellows of Harvard College. Harvard Business School case 694-047.

architects of company policy underscored the fact that now, with more than 2,700 employees and three new sites across the country, UCS was no longer in a start-up, entrepreneurial phase. Finally, Davis and other senior managers were questioning many of the basic concepts underlying the measurement system that had helped the company achieve so much. Nearly everyone agreed that changes were needed in what the company measured, how it measured, and what it did with the information. There was no consensus, however, on exactly what to do.

THE FOUNDING

When AT&T recruited Paul Kahn in 1989 to lead its foray into the credit card business as UCS's president and CEO, the information technology giant had two main goals. It wanted to offer a combined credit card and calling card that would bolster its long-distance-calling revenues. Perhaps more important, it wanted to regain the direct link to the customer that it had lost in 1984, when a court decision forced the spin-off of its regional Bell operating companies. With the backing of AT&T, Kahn, a 10-year veteran of First National Bank of Chicago and Wells Fargo Bank, developed a bold plan for breaking into the market, where unchallenged pricing practices and highly profitable operations were the norm. First, the new company did away with the annual membership fee, saving cardholders who signed up during the first year the $25 or more typically charged by issuing banks. Second, UCS set its interest rate on unpaid balances below what most bank issuers were charging, pegging it to the banking industry's prime lending rate.

In addition to such pricing strategies, AT&T and Kahn shared a vision of the kind of company they wanted to create: an organization where motivated and empowered employees would set new standards for quality in customer service. To achieve this ambitious goal, the new company set out to measure almost every process in sight. "We decided that we had to create an environment where the net take-away to both the parent company and to the consumer was an experience superior to anything they'd had before," explained Kahn.

On March 26, 1990, during the Academy Awards, UCS aired its first ad. The combination of the AT&T name and the waived annual fee proved more potent than anyone had imagined. In the first 24 hours, UCS's 185 employees received 270,000 requests for applications or information. The company opened its one-millionth account 78 days after launch.

PILLARS OF QUALITY

In contrast to many established companies that have struggled to superimpose "quality" on an existing corporate culture, UCS had the luxury of establishing quality as an overarching goal from the start. In fact, quality was less a goal than an obsession. The seven core company values—customer delight, continuous improvement, sense of urgency, commitment, trust and integrity, mutual respect, and teamwork—were emblazoned on everything from wall plaques to T-shirts and coasters. Senior management was convinced that quality processes—with the end result of superior customer service and efficiency—would give UCS a key competitive advantage in the crowded credit card marketplace. As a company brochure noted:

> Each time a customer contacts UCS, it's a moment of truth that can either strengthen our relationship with them or destroy it. Each call or letter is an opportunity to create a person-to-person contact that makes the Universal Card, and AT&T, something more than another anonymous piece of plastic lost in a billfold.

In order to provide such unprecedented customer service, the Business Team, an executive committee of a dozen top vice presidents headed by Kahn, took a number of steps (see organization chart, Exhibit 1). They made sure that the telephone associates—Universal's designation for its customer service representatives—were carefully selected and then trained to "delight" customers. They set up benchmarking studies, comparing UCS both with direct competitors and with other high-performing service companies. They conducted a Baldrige-based quality assessment in the very first year, as well as each successive year, and used the results as the basis for a companywide strategic improvement process.

But the most unusual mechanism built into the organizational pursuit of quality was a unique and multifaceted measurement system, designed to measure performance on a number of levels

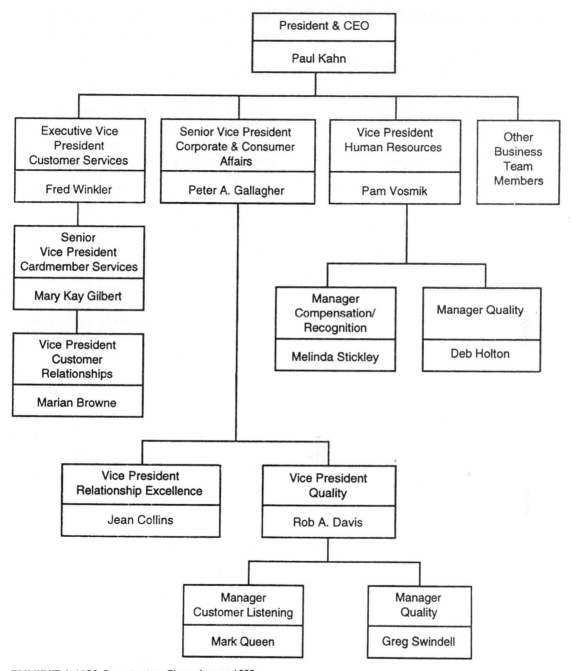

EXHIBIT 1 UCS Organization Chart, August 1992

both within the company and without. While it was not unusual for credit card issuers to monitor certain aspects of customer service, UCS's efforts went far beyond industry standards. Nor were most measurement systems designed to achieve so many purposes: to locate problem processes; to promptly address any problems discovered; to constantly assess how well customers were being served; and to reward exceptional performance. "We had an expression here, 'If you don't measure it, you can't move it,'" recalled Mary Kay Gilbert, a senior vice president who helped develop the original business plan for AT&T. "If you're not measuring a key process, you don't even know if you have a problem." UCS was determined not to let that happen.

THE QUALITY ORGANIZATION

As one of its first initiatives, Rob Davis and his Quality team developed two extensive surveys. The Customer Satisfier Survey was a questionnaire to gather market research data on what the company termed "customer satisfiers," the products, services, and treatment—including price and customer service—that cardholders cared about most. An outside market research firm conducted the survey, talking to 400 competitors' customers and 200 UCS customers each month. More unusual were the Customer Contactor Surveys, for which an internal team each month polled more than 3,000 randomly selected customers who had contacted the company, querying them within two or three days of their contact. UCS's survey team administered 10 to 15 different Contactor Surveys, depending on whether a customer had called or written, and on the customer's particular reason for contact, such as to get account information or to challenge a bill. Survey questions, such as "Did the associate answer the phone promptly?" and "Was the associate courteous?", were designed to gauge overall satisfaction as well as the quality of specific services.

But the effort most visible to telephone associates and other employees, and the one that had the most profound effect on the company's day-to-day operations, was the gathering of the daily process performance measures. Senior managers had debated every aspect of this so-called bucket of measures at the company's formation, and it was at the heart of how UCS operated.

The Business Team had agreed that the best way to drive quality service and continuous improvement was to measure the key processes that went into satisfying the consumer—*every single day*. Building on the experience of credit card industry veterans recruited at start-up, such as Fred Winkler, executive vice president for Customer Services, and adding information gleaned from the Customer Satisfier and Contactor Surveys as well as additional benchmarking studies, the Business Team assembled a list of more than 100 internal and supplier measures it felt had a critical impact on performance (see Exhibit 2 for an example of

EXHIBIT 2 Internal Process Measurement Linkages to Customer Satisfiers

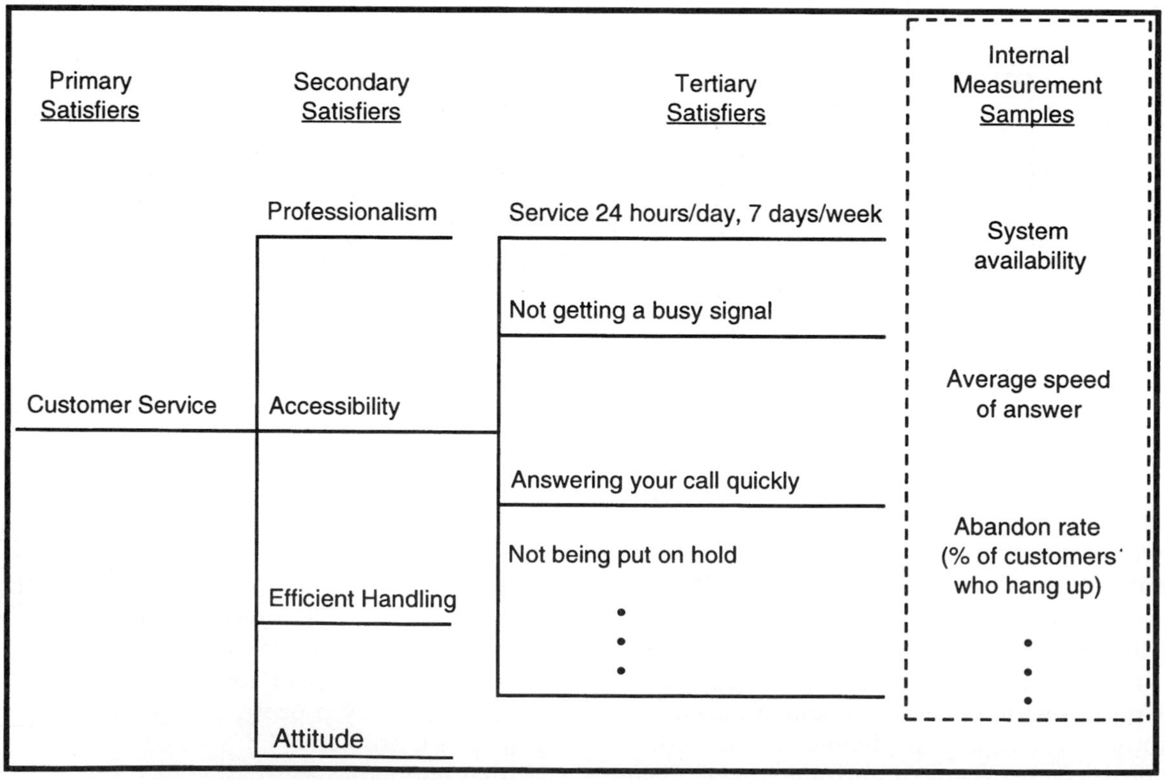

Source: Universal Card Services.

how UCS linked internal process measures with key satisfiers).

The original list was top-heavy with actions directly affecting cardholders—such as how soon customers received their credit cards after applying, and whether billing statements were accurate. But the list gradually expanded to include key production, service, and support processes from every functional area of the company, many of which were invisible to customers but which ultimately affected them (see Exhibit 3 for a list of such processes). By the middle of 1991, Vice President Jean Collins and her Relationship Excellence team, the independent monitoring group within UCS charged with collecting the measures, were tracking about 120 process measures, many considered confidential. Indicators ranged from the quality of the plastic used in the credit cards to how quickly Human Resources responded to job résumés and issued employee paychecks, and to how often the computer system went down.

UCS did more than measure, though; it set specific standards for each measure and rewarded every employee in the entire company when those standards were met on a daily basis. To make clear the importance of quality, the bucket of measures was linked directly to the company's compensation system: If the company as a whole achieved the quality standards on 95% of the indicators on a particular day, all the associates—or nonmanagerial employees—"earned quality" for the day, and each "quality day" meant a cash bonus, paid out on a quarterly basis.[1] Although some top managers questioned the compensation/quality link, arguing that, in essence, the achievement of quality should be its own reward, Kahn felt the tie to compensation was essential. "I think we ought to put our money where our mouth is," he declared. "We wanted quality, and we ought to pay for it." The financial incentives were not insignificant: The bonus system gave associates the ability to add more than $500 to their paycheck every quarter, and managers could earn 20% above base salary.

The daily push to earn quality—and to earn a bonus—was an omnipresent goal. Video monitors scattered around the building declared the previous day's quality results. Every morning at 8:00, Fred Winkler, in charge of operations, presided over a one-hour meeting of about a dozen senior managers to discuss the latest measures, identifying possible problems and proposing solutions. A summary of the "Fred meeting," as one manager dubbed it, could be dialed up on the phone later that morning. In each functional area, managers convened a similar quality meeting during the day, examining the measures for which they were responsible and, if they had failed to meet a particular indicator, trying to figure out what went wrong (see Exhibit 4 for a sample report showing telephone associate performance). Furthermore, the bucket of measures figured prominently in monthly business meetings, the Baldrige assessments, focus groups, and other regular process improvement meetings. According to Deb Holton,

EXHIBIT 3 Key UCS and Supplier Processes

Key Processes	UCS or Supplier
Business Processes	
Strategic and Business Planning	UCS
Total Quality Management	UCS
Support Services Processes	
Collections	UCS
Management of Key Constituencies	UCS
Customer Acquisition Management	UCS
Financial Management	UCS
Human Resource Management	UCS
Information and Technology Management	UCS
Product and Service Production and Delivery Processes	
Application Processing	Supplier
Authorizations Management	Supplier
Billing and Statement Processing	UCS
Credit Card Production	UCS
Credit Screening	Supplier
Customer Acquisition Process Management (Prospective Customer List Development and Management)	Supplier
Customer Inquiry Management	UCS
Payment Processing	UCS
Relationship Management (Service Management, Communications Management, Programs and Promotions, Brand Management)	UCS
Transaction Processing	Supplier

Source: Univeral Card Services.

---

[1]For managers to earn quality, they also had to meet standards on a separate set of indicators tied to vendors' products and services. Managers' bonuses were then based on three components: quality days, individual performance, and the company's financial performance.

Measure	Standard	Wednesday 06/30/93		Month-to-Date	
		Sampled	*Performance*	*Sampled*	*Performance*
Average Speed of Answer (ASA)	20 seconds	39,278	12.42 seconds	1,114,722	11.70 sec
Abandoned Rate	3%	39,278	1.24%	1,114,722	1.25%
Accuracy	96%	100	100%	2,400	98.58%
Professionalism	100%	100	100%	2,350	99.91%

EXHIBIT 4 Sample Daily Reliability Report—Telephone Associate Performance
Source: Universal Card Services.

manager of Quality, the daily measures were on everyone's minds: "It is virtually impossible to be in this building for 10 minutes without knowing how you did the day before."

THE EMPOWERED EMPLOYEE

At UCS, customers were referred to as "the center of our universe." At the center of the business, however, were the telephone associates who, although entry-level workers, had the highest pay and status among nonmanagerial employees. They, after all, were the front-line representatives who determined what impression customers took away from their dealings with UCS. Indeed, telephone associates were responsible for almost all customer contact—answering phones, taking applications, handling correspondence, and even collecting from overspenders and trying to intercept fraudulent card users.

To make sure that it had the right people for the job, UCS put applicants through a grueling hiring process: Only one in 10 applicants won an offer of employment after the two-part aptitude test, customer service role-playing, handling of simulated incoming and outgoing calls, credit check, and drug testing. Once hired, telephone associates received training for six weeks and two more weeks on the job. Instruction began with a two-day cultural indoctrination dubbed "Passport to Excellence," introducing concepts such as mission, vision, quality objectives, and empowerment. But the main purpose of the lengthy training was to give associates detailed coaching in telephone skills and the management of all phases of a customer inquiry, from initiation to conclusion.

UCS did not expect to get commitment and excellent customer service from the telephone associates, however, without giving them something in return. In fact, the company's vision of "delighting" customers rested on having "delighted" associates. Much of what the rest of the organization did—from Human Resources management to information support systems design and the measurement system itself—revolved around ensuring that telephone associates were able and motivated to provide the quality service that was the company's stated goal.

The Information Services group, for example, developed and continually upgraded U-WIN, an information management system tailored to the specific needs of the telephone associates. Drawing in part on the company's U-KNOW system—which gave managers on-line access to the customer, operational, and financial information in UCS's database, known as UNIVERSE—the U-WIN system allowed associates to pull up on their workstation screens information ranging from cardmember files to form letters to special product offers (see Exhibit 5 for an overview of the information management system). U-WIN even gave associates a head start on serving customers by automatically calling up cardmembers' accounts as their calls were being connected. "We're high touch, high tech," explained Marian Browne, vice president of Customer Relationships, the service area in which telephone associates handled general correspondence and responded to customer calls. "That means we work with our people and focus on our customers, but we can't do either unless we have leading-edge technology."

UCS top management was determined also to involve associates, listen to their ideas and concerns, and draw them into most facets of the business. Associates served side by side with senior managers on teams deciding issues ranging from what awards the company should bestow to how computer screens should be designed for maxi-

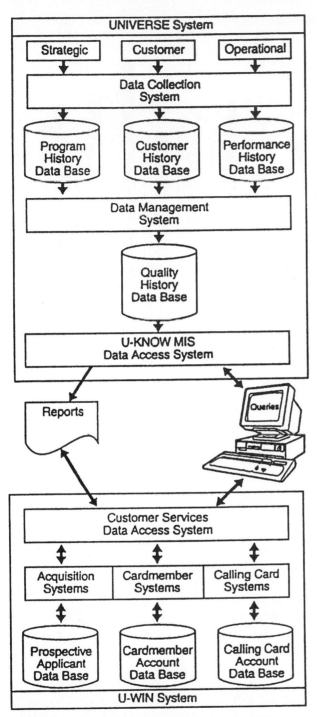

EXHIBIT 5 UCS's Integrated Data and Information Systems

gram, "Your Ideas . . . Your Universe," was broadly publicized, with impressive results: in 1991, more than half the work force participated, and management accepted and acted on almost half of the more than 5,000 suggestions.

In addition to these "empowerment"-oriented activities, the company looked for concrete ways to please associates. UCS provided generous fringe benefits, for example, a free on-site fitness center for employees and their spouses, and reimbursement for undergraduate and graduate courses. The company supported a substantial reward and recognition program, sponsoring six companywide awards, three companywide recognition programs, and more than 30 departmental awards. And the Business Team encouraged managers to look for reasons to celebrate. Indeed, boisterous ceremonies in the cafeteria marking such events as all-company achievements or the bestowal of specific awards were a regular occurrence. "The culture we've developed is very focused around rewards and celebration and success," said Melinda Stickley, compensation/recognition manager. "We've got more recognition programs here than any company I've ever heard of."

The far-ranging programs and activities appeared to be paying off. According to annual employee opinion surveys, associates rated the company significantly higher in such categories as job satisfaction, management leadership, and communication than was the norm for employees at high-performing companies. Not only that, absenteeism was low, and employee attrition was far below the average for financial services companies (see Exhibit 6 for selected employee opinion survey results and attrition and absenteeism rates).

Despite the efforts of senior managers to create a positive environment, however, the telephone associate's job was not easy. Many stresses arose simply from working for a 24-hour customer service operation—stresses that may have been particularly trying for UCS's well educated employees.[2] Telephone associates, organized in teams of about 20, spent long days and nights—as well as periodic weekends and holidays—on the phone, performing a largely repetitive task. There was often mandatory overtime, particularly during

mum efficiency. They were encouraged to ask questions at monthly business reviews and at "Lakeside Chats"—quarterly question-and-answer sessions held in the company cafeteria with Winkler. And the UCS employee suggestion pro-

---

[2]Because of underemployment in the Jacksonville area and the desirability of working for AT&T, UCS had been able to recruit a highly qualified work force: 65% of telephone associates had college degrees.

EXHIBIT 6   Employee Satisfaction Data

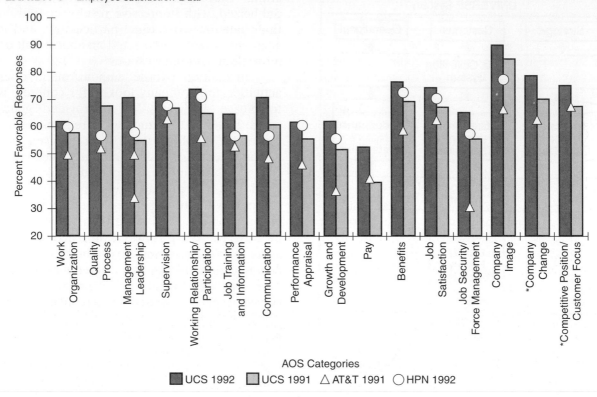

AOS Categories

■ UCS 1992   ▨ UCS 1991   △ AT&T 1991   ○ HPN 1992

Note: 1992 data for AT&T unavailable; AT&T conducts its AOS biannually.   *HPN not anailable

Note:

AOS = Annual Opinion Survey

HPN = High-Performing Norm (average response for a group of high-performing organizations that use the same survey)

Adverse Indicators	1990	1991	1992	Benchmark
Employee Turnover				
UCS Total	9.7%	10.1%	12.3%	N/A
Managers	8.7%	9.0%	7.2%	14%
Associates	10.1%	10.5%	14.1%	23%
Customer Contact Associates	10.2%	10.7%	13.5%	23%
*Absenteeism Rate**				
Managers	N/A	1.3%	1.1%	1.3%
Associates	N/A	2.2%	3.3%	1.9%

*includes pregnancy and disability

Source: Universal Card Services.

unexpectedly successful card promotions, and associates knew their schedules only two weeks in advance.

Along with these largely unavoidable downsides, the particular culture of UCS imposed its own stresses. The pressure to achieve quality every day was an ever-present goad. Furthermore, the company's determination to continuously improve—captured in an oft-used phrase of Fred Winkler, "pleased, but never satisfied"—frequently translated into increased performance expectations for the associates. As the telephone technology systems got better, for example, managers expected associates to take advantage of the increased efficiencies by lowering their "talk time," the average amount of time they spent on the phone with each customer.

Finally, there was the monitoring. About 17 process measures were gathered in Customer Relationships, the general customer service area. To begin with, the information technology system tracked the average speed of answer, the number of calls each associate handled, and how long each associate spent on the phone. As a result of their exposure to the daily printouts detailing these statistics, most associates could rattle off with deadly accuracy how many calls they handled in a day—typically about 120—as well as how many seconds they spent on an average call—in the range of 140 to 160.

Perhaps more daunting, telephone associates were directly monitored by a number of people both inside and outside of Customer Relationships. As part of the gathering of the daily measures, specially trained monitors in both the Relationship Excellence group and an internal

quality group listened in on a total of 100 customer calls a day.[3] The monitors—or quality associates—rated telephone associates on accuracy, efficiency, and professionalism, recording their comments on a one-page observation sheet (see Exhibit 7 for a description of these measures and how they were gathered).

Any "impacts"—UCS's term for a negative effect on a customer or the business—were reported at Customer Relationships's daily quality meeting, attended by representatives from both Relationship Excellence and the internal quality group.[4] Negative reports were then passed on to the team leaders of the associates involved to discuss and keep on file for performance reviews.

Other parts of the organization monitored calls as well, each with a slightly different purpose. Team leaders listened to 10 calls a month for each

---

[3]Relationship Excellence originally did the entire 100-call sample, but Customer Relationships began co-sampling when it created its internal quality department in November 1990.

[4]The ten areas in which impacts could occur had been identified as (1) telephone contact, (2) correspondence contact, (3) application contact, (4) change of address, (5) claims, (6) credit line increase, (7) payment receipt, (8) statements, (9) plastic card production accuracy/timeliness, and (10) authorization availability/accuracy.

EXHIBIT 7   Telephone Associates Measurement Regime

Measure	Description	Sampling and Scoring Regime	Performance Standard (1Q93)
Average Speed of Answer (ASA)	Average time between completion of customer connection and answer by telephone associate	100% sample by automated call management system (CMS)	20 seconds
Abandon Rate	Percentage of calls initiated by customers, but abandoned prior to being answered by telephone associate	100% sample by automated call management system (CMS)	3% of incoming calls
Accuracy	A qualitative measure of the level of accuracy of information given by associates to customers	Random sample of 100 calls per day evaluated by quality monitor	96%
		Scoring system includes predefined criteria for evaluating customer impacting errors, business impacting errors, and non-impacting errors	
Professionalism	Professionalism (courtesy, responsiveness) shown by telephone associate	Random sample of 100 calls per day evaluated by quality monitor	100%
		Scoring system includes predefined criteria for evaluating customer impacting errors, business impacting errors, and non-impacting errors	

Source: Universal Card Services.

of the approximately 20 associates in their groups, using the observations to review and "develop" the associates. And *all* managers at UCS, regardless of their function, were encouraged to monitor at least two hours of calls a month to stay in touch with services and practices. Rob Davis, vice president of Quality, for example, held a regular monthly listening session with all his staff, followed by a discussion period to analyze the quality implications of what they had heard. Finally, the results of the Customer Contactor Surveys, including verbatim remarks from cardholders about how associates treated them, were turned over to managers in Customer Relationships who could easily identify which associate handled a particular call if there was an "impact" or other problem to resolve.

The combination of high corporate expectations and these multiple forms of monitoring and feedback created considerable pressure at UCS not only to perform well, but to do so under intense scrutiny, at least for telephone associates. Some managers felt this took a toll. "The quality process, daily sampling, and feedback were not without pain," claimed Mary Kay Gilbert, who as senior vice president of Cardmember Services oversaw the Customer Relationships operation. "I had to stop people and say, 'Wait, we're here to make sure we're delivering the right service to customers. This isn't personal.'"

But others argued that the way the associates were monitored, and the way team leaders and managers delivered feedback, kept it from being a negative or stressful experience. Company policy dictated that all supervisors and managers were to treat associates with respect and to view mistakes as a learning opportunity. If an associate was overheard giving inaccurate information to a customer, for example, the team leader was not to rebuke the associate, but to explain the error and provide additional training, if necessary, so that the mistake would not occur again. "The positive stress for workers here is high risk, high demand, high reward," asserted Deb Holton, manager of Quality. "It is not the stress of coming in in the morning and checking their brains at the door."

RAISING THE BAR

Thanks in large part to the customer-pleasing work of the telephone associates, by the close of 1991, financial analysts had declared UCS a major success

for AT&T. During that year, holders of the UCS card had dramatically increased AT&T calling-card usage. And after less than two years in business, UCS ranked a stunning third in the dollar volume of charges on its card, with $3.8 billion in receivables, $17.2 billion in total sales volume, and 7.6 million accounts. Industry kudos included a "Top Banking Innovation" award from American Banker and "Best Product of 1990" from *Business Week*.

Despite this stellar performance, the Business Team was convinced that it was time to shake things up—that everyone could do better. Although some executives initially balked at the prospect of a change, after a series of debates, the Business Team agreed to "raise the bar" on the number of indicators the company had to achieve to earn quality. A compelling argument for the increase was that associates were meeting or exceeding standards so consistently. During 1991, associates had made quality at least 25 days out of every month, and in August they had earned quality every day, often achieving 97% or more of the indicators. Managers, too, were doing well. "We wanted to take it up," explained Davis, "because of our strong commitment to continuous improvement."[5] Added Marian Browne, vice president of Customer Relationships, "Everything was going fine, but if you look at perfect service every day, we weren't giving perfect service every day."

With the Business Team's blessing, Kahn sent the following letter to all employees on December 26, just five days before the change was to take effect:

Dear UCS Colleague,

In the spirit of continuous improvement, UCS will take another step in our never-ending commitment to customer delight. Beginning Jan. 1, 1992, the quality objective for associates will move from 95 percent to 96 percent. The quality objective for managers will move to 96 percent for the target goal and 97 percent to 100 percent for the maximum goal. UCS' Excellence Award program will continue to reward quality as it has in the past—the only difference will be that the objective will be moved up for both managers and associates.

---

[5]In fact, the threshold for managers had already changed: Since January 1991, managers had to achieve 96% of their quality indicators for full compensation, receiving only three-quarters of the bonus for 95%.

UCS people have demonstrated our value of customer delight since "day one." As we continue to improve our ability to delight customers, we'll also continue to evaluate and revise our quality standards and measurements. I'm extremely proud of the work each of you performs. Your dedication to our seven values continues to make UCS a leader in the industry.

What the letter did not mention was that the raising of the bar was actually a double challenge: Not only did employees have to achieve a higher percentage of measures, but individual standards had been raised on 47 of the indicators, making each of them harder to earn. In addition, Collins and her Relationship Excellence team took advantage of the start of the calendar year and the relative lull after the holiday season to retire and replace a substantial chunk of the measures. While only 15 indicators had been dropped in all of 1991 and 26 added, the monitoring group abruptly cut out 48 indicators, many of them among the most consistently achieved, and replaced them with 46 new ones. In effect, this meant that close to half of the measures by which associates judged their daily performance—and were judged—were now different.

The reaction to the change was immediate. Associates earned only 13 quality days in January and 16 in February, and managers fared even worse. Not only was the company failing to make the new goal of 96%, it was missing quality by as much as six percentage points on a given day, well below the worst daily performance of the previous month. "We fell flat on our faces as far as the number of days we were paying out as a business was concerned," Davis recalled. Added Collins, "For most of the days we were well below even the old standard."

The abrupt drop-off took management by surprise. According to Robert Inks, who started as a telephone associate in May 1990, associates were not so much angry as they were concerned—concerned that higher standards of efficiency might make it harder to deliver quality service, and concerned that regular bonuses might be a thing of the past. "The associates looked at it as, well, this is my money," explained Inks, "I'm not going to be getting my money." Added Pam Vosmik, vice president of Human Resources: "There was probably some grousing in the hallways."

It was no consolation that UCS was on the verge of logging its first profit. In fact, at a business meeting open to all employees, associates accused

management of having raised the bar as a cost-cutting measure to avoid paying compensation. Nor was the timing of the slump propitious. UCS was ready to make an all-out push to win the Baldrige award, and although the site examiners would not arrive until September, it was critical that employees be motivated and on board. "I went to the Business Team," recalled Gilbert, "and I said, 'Look, we raised all these indicators and measures and I don't think the people around this table understand the impact. But if we start beating people up as a result of this, you can kiss the Baldrige good-bye.' "

Senior managers took the performance plunge to heart. In fact, according to Davis, some managers were so concerned by the apparent associate disaffection that they were ready to lower the bar to its previous level. Instead of backing down, however, the Business Team concocted an alternate scheme to reignite associate enthusiasm. In March, the same month that UCS submitted its Baldrige application, the company announced the "Triple Quality Team Challenge." The special incentive program allowed associates and managers to earn triple bonuses that month for each quality day they achieved beyond a base of 20 quality days. If employees earned 22 quality days, for example, they would get credit for 26. A four-foot by 16-foot calendar board mounted in the cafeteria and small boards in each functional area displayed daily progress toward the goal. In explaining the incentive program, *HOTnews*, an internal publication reserved for important communiqués, noted:

> . . . quality results in January and through February 26 show UCS not doing as well as it did even before we raised our quality standards in 1992. Many of the current problems have nothing to do with our new standards or indicators, but are failures of basic courtesy and accuracy. "I know we can do better," says Kahn. "The results concern me and I know they concern you. It's important that we work together to meet our quality goals and delight our customers. The 'Triple Quality Team Challenge' must be a team effort—we need to help each other achieve our indicators, not look around for who's not making theirs and punish them."

SOFTENING THE SYSTEM

The Triple Quality Challenge was a rousing success. Associates' quality days spiked back up to 25 in March, and managers earned 19 days (see

Exhibit 8 for an overview of quality days achieved over time). But the organizational upset engendered by the raising of the bar, along with fears that telephone associates—on whose dedication the company's success depended—could become disillusioned, prompted a harder look at making both measures and feedback more participatory and more palatable. In the months that followed, UCS even abandoned the "pleased but never satisfied" expression because it gave associates a sense of inadequacy and futility.

Efforts to reach out to associates took a number of forms. Managers in Customer Relationships continued to coach team leaders, one-third of whom had been promoted from the associate level, to make sure they were comfortable and skilled at giving feedback. "We've got a lot of young, inexperienced team leaders, and what you have to teach your team leaders is that you can't use feedback as a club," noted Marian Browne. "You use it as a development tool. You don't do it to beat people up, or to catch people." Customer Relationships also began to experiment with peer monitoring, having telephone associates critique one another rather than relying solely on team leaders for developmental review.

Relationship Excellence, which had already been sharing the gathering of the daily measures with Customer Relationships since the end of 1990, helped other functional areas set up internal quality departments to co-sample, with the plan that they might eventually take over the measures entirely. Although some executives were concerned that this shift might hurt the integrity of the sample, Ron Shinall, a Relationship Excellence team leader, insisted it was a necessary evolution. "There's going to be a natural aversion to someone telling you how to make your process better if that person hasn't worked with you or been in that process," he declared.

Relationship Excellence also changed what it did with call observations. The daily Customer Relationships quality meeting, which had served largely as a chance for quality associates to report the mistakes they had caught, became, instead, a forum for discussion and learning. Telephone associates from the floor were invited to join the internal and external quality representatives, and the entire group debated whether negative impacts had occurred without ever identifying those who had handled the questionable calls. "It's helped get a lot of buy-in from the associates," remarked Darrin Graham, who had led Customer Relationships's internal quality department. "Back at the beginning, when you would hear that there is this group out there listening to my calls, you just naturally started to get an us/them mentality, and they're out to get us. Now that mentality is going away."

As part of this overhaul, Relationship Excellence experimented with no longer giving associates—or their team leaders—feedback on calls monitored for the daily measures. But although the experiment had been urged by an associate focus group, the so-called Nameless/Blameless program lasted only a few weeks. "The majority of the people wanted to know if they'd made a mistake," Browne explained. Feedback resumed, but with two important differences: negative impacts no longer went into associates' files, and team leaders received, and handed on, both good news and bad. The internal quality group also worked harder to stress the positive. "We used to walk up to people's desks and we'd have a piece of paper in our hand, and they'd be like, 'Oh no, here they come,'" recalled Paul Ferrando, team leader of

EXHIBIT 8   Quality Days Performance and Bonuses
Associate Quality Days and Bonus Performance

Quarter	# Quality Days as % of Total	Bonus as % of Salary
4Q90	76.1%	6.4%
1Q91	87.8%	11.4%
2Q91	92.3%	9.9%
3Q91	96.7%	12.0%
4Q91	95.7%	11.6%
1Q92	70.3%	10.6%
2Q92	75.8%	7.5%
3Q92	76.1%	7.9%
4Q92	95.7%	10.8%
1Q93	84.4%	9.4%

Management Quality Days and Bonus Performance

Period	# Quality Days as % of Total	Bonus as % of Salary
1991	87.9%	5.6%
1992	66.1%	4.7%
1Q93	76.7%	5.6%

Source: Universal Card Services.

Customer Relationships's first internal quality group. "And I'd say, 'Someone on your team had an excellent call.' When you bring good news, they don't grimace when you walk up to them anymore. People aren't afraid of quality, and they aren't afraid of this monitoring anymore."

The steady evolution of the system appeared to have increased associate acceptance of the measures. There would always, of course, be some employees who balked at being measured, as the following response to the June 1992 employee survey indicated:

> A big handicap is being monitored constantly. The people are not relaxed. They are under so much stress that they will get a variance, that they don't do their job as well as they could. Monitoring should be used as a learning tool—we're all human and sometimes forget things.

But most telephone associates professed their support. "The reason that we're measuring is to find out what we're capable of, and what we're doing right, and what we can improve on, and what we don't need to improve," declared Cheryl Bowie, who took a large pay cut from her former managerial position to become a telephone associate in 1992. "There is no problem here with the feedback. You're not branded or anything. It's just a learning experience."

On October 14, 1992, near the end of a challenging year of growth and change, Universal Card was awarded a Malcolm Baldrige National Quality Award. At a black-tie celebration party recognizing employees' part in the companywide effort, associates received a $250 after-tax bonus and a Tiffany pin, and a small group of associates, selected by lottery, traveled to Washington, D.C., for the actual Baldrige presentation. But the award did not lessen the sense of urgency at UCS. "When we learned we had won the Baldrige," recalled Quality manager Deb Holton, "our second breath was, 'But we will not be complacent.' "

In truth, UCS would have had to change, whether it sought to or not. Paul Kahn announced his resignation in February 1993 over differences within the company as to whether UCS should expand into new financial products, and Fred Winkler defected for archrival First Union Corp. in April. Although David Hunt, the banking industry executive who replaced Kahn, and Winkler's successor, AT&T veteran Gerald Hines, quickly won widespread acceptance, the departure of these two

critical and charismatic leaders created anxiety about the company's future direction.

The competitive landscape within which UCS operated also was changing. Although by early 1993, the company had captured the number-two ranking among the 6,000 issuers of credit cards, with almost 12 million accounts and 18 million cardholders, it was becoming increasingly difficult for UCS to make its product stand out. Competitors such as General Motors Corp. had introduced their own no-fee cards, and the variable interest rates pioneered by UCS had become common. "The sad part is, our competition is catching up with us," lamented Mark Queen, manager of Customer Listening and overseer of the Customer Contactor Surveys. "Where we need to continue to distinguish ourselves is in service."

But continuous improvement—finding ways to motivate associates beyond what they had already accomplished—was not an easy task. For one thing, with the company's growth slowing, it would no longer be possible for as many associates to quickly ascend the corporate ladder to team leader and other managerial positions. Moreover, the current measurements no longer seemed to be driving the quest for improvement, and Davis and others had become convinced that it was time to retool a system that no longer fit the needs of the company. Ironically, considering how much Universal Card had already done to create meaningful and effective measures, among the Business Team's top 10 goals for 1993 was the development of a world-class measurement system.

WEIGHING THE OPTIONS

By the summer of 1993, Davis's Quality organization was assessing a range of new approaches to measuring. In particular, a specially convened Measures Review Committee under Thedas Dukes, a senior manager now responsible for the daily measures, was taking a hard look at what to change.

Customer-Centered Measures

A project of particular interest to Davis was the company's early experimentation with customer-centered measures (CCM). While CCM might not change what UCS was measuring, advocates argued it would more concretely and powerfully express how the company was serving cardholders by stating this performance in terms of customer impacts.

Instead of reporting that 98% of cardholder bills were accurate on a given day, for example, a CCM report might state that 613 customers did *not* get a correct bill. "We are trying to change the language away from percentages and indexes to a language of customers," explained Davis. Added Ron Shinall, quality team leader, "It's hard to tell the difference between 99.8% and 99.9%, but in some of the high-volume areas, that can mean a tremendous number of people are actually affected. Fractions of a percent mean a lot when you're talking about 40,000 daily calls."

UCS had been considering customer-centered measures since visiting early Baldrige winner Federal Express Corp. in the summer of 1991. Unlike UCS, with its 100-plus measures, Federal Express had selected just 12 processes it deemed critical to serving customers and had based its reward system on that 12-component CCM index. In January 1993, Universal began a six-month test of CCM, reporting customer impacts on 13 existing process indicators that measured different aspects of accuracy and professionalism. The now 30-member Relationship Excellence group, which had changed its name to Quality Applications in December, sent out its first CCM report in March.

But the jury was still out on what impact CCM would have. Linda Plummer, a senior manager in Customer Relationships, applauded the idea of expressing error in human terms. Yet she found the initial reports, which simply listed the number of customers affected in each category along with the effects per thousand contacts, to be meaningless. "Someone needs to tell me at what point I have a concern," she complained. "Is it when 100 customers are affected, or 2,000 customers are affected? I don't even look at them anymore because I don't know how to interpret them." Jean Wentzel, another senior manager in Customer Relationships, agreed: "Until we've really communicated it effectively and tied it back to the compensation system, it's not going to have the same buy-in or impact."

But increasing the relevance of CCM by tying it to the compensation system would not be easy. In fact, the cross-functional CCM group responsible for the pilot project had recently agreed to shelve temporarily the issue of whether to create a compensation link, concluding that the points raised were too complicated to tackle all at once. Unresolved questions included how to set standards for customer impacts; whether the compensation system should include both business-centered measures reported the old way and customer-centered measures reported the new way; and whether UCS should retire its bucket of measures and move instead to a system more similar to that at Federal Express, with compensation based on just a dozen or so service measures, rather than on a broad range of company functions. This last possibility, which would result in many people and processes no longer being measured, fundamentally challenged the company's founding philosophy of having all employees work together, be measured together, and earn quality together.

Statistical Process Control

Statistical process control was another tool Quality Applications was examining. There was a growing conviction within UCS that the company needed to adopt a more long-term outlook in quality measurement. This belief was further fueled by feedback, late in 1992, from a committee that had evaluated UCS for AT&T's prestigious Chairman's Quality Award, noting that "there is no evidence of a statistical approach to data analysis, including determining out-of-control processes, identifying special and/or common causes, and the approach to prioritizing improvement opportunities."

In fact, the gathering of measures on a daily basis, as well as UCS's commitment to a "sense of urgency"—one of its seven values—had contributed to the focus on the short term. Only recently had Universal switched from monthly to quarterly business reviews, and the group that met every morning to discuss the daily measures, now headed by Fred Winkler's replacement, Jerry Hines, was for the first time adding a quarterly quality review. Remarked Davis, "With our daily focus on measurements and our fix-it-today mentality, the thing that sometimes suffers is looking at the long-term trends in the data."

Statistical process control (SPC) seemed to provide at least a partial answer to this shortcoming. The quality improvement methodology, developed at Bell Laboratories in the 1920s to chart manufacturing processes and identify events that affect product output, had been broadly defined in recent years to include such tools as cause-and-effect diagrams and Pareto charts, as well as control charts to statistically examine process capability and variation. But SPC had only rarely been applied in a service environment. The challenge at UCS, therefore, was to adapt the manufacturing tool to its customer service business.

Pete Ward, a process engineer within Quality Applications, was confident this could be done. He had already begun to prepare individualized reports for associates, allowing them to use SPC to chart and trend such daily productivity measures as talk time and number of calls handled. In contrast to mere daily statistics, Ward explained, the SPC charts would help telephone associates see the impact that one action—such as spending too much time on the phone with customers—had on another, as well as aid them in spotting cyclical patterns in their own performances.

But SPC, like CCM, raised questions about the existing measurement system. It was unclear, for example, whether it was valuable to apply statistical tools to something as ambiguous and subjective as deciding whether an associate had been courteous enough or had spent too much time with a customer. In addition, SPC charts, which allowed a more meaningful and long-term look at performance than the daily measures, presented ammunition for the argument that it was time for Universal Card to switch from its obsession with daily goals and rewards to a reliance on more statistically significant trends.

A Link to External Results

These and other questions had revived old complaints that the measures did not accurately reflect how customers actually viewed Universal, nor how the company was performing. Mark Queen, manager of Customer Listening and overseer of the Customer Contactor Surveys, acknowledged that although the internal measures were designed to measure processes important to customers, missing quality days internally did not necessarily show up in dissatisfied customers. When internal quality results took a nosedive after the bar was raised in early 1992, for example, the Customer Contactor Surveys indicated only a slight blip in customer satisfaction—a fact, Queen says, that "was driving everybody crazy."

Similarly, Queen noted that although recent customer feedback indicated that cardholders viewed associates as somewhat less courteous than before, the internal quality monitors listening in on phone calls had not logged an increase in negative impacts. "There is not a clear enough linkage," Davis admitted. "What people would really like would be for me to say, 'OK, if you can take this internal customer measure and raise it from 96% to 99%, I guarantee it will take customer satisfaction up by X amount.' But we can't say that, yet."

Linkage aside, on occasion, the internal measures seemed to be at cross-purposes with the company's financial goals. Greg Swindell, who in late 1992 became vice president of Customer Focused Quality Improvement, for example, described an unexpectedly successful marketing promotion for a new credit card product that left understaffed telephone associates unable to keep up with the rush of calls. Although the surge of new business was good for the company, the telephone associates were, in effect, doubly punished: first by having to frantically field additional calls, and second by missing their quality indicators and losing compensation. "The question is, is that high response rate a bad thing?" Swindell asked. "And my answer is no. We're here to bring on more customers, to become more profitable. So how do we balance this focus on these metrics and our business and strategic objectives? For me, this offers a very perplexing problem."

A NEW LOOK AT THE MEASURES

Spurred by these and other questions, there was talk at UCS of a radical rearrangement of the bucket of measures. Although it was not clear what would take the bucket's place, more and more managers were beginning to feel that UCS's drive for continuous improvement was being held hostage by the relentless and short-term push to bring home the daily bonus. What had originally been designed as a means for identifying and improving processes and as a motivational tool, critics charged, was now holding the company back rather than driving it forward.

Greg Swindell was one who questioned the status quo: "Perhaps it is a very good tool to help us *maintain* our performance, but I'm not sure it's the kind of tool that will help take us into the next century and really get a lot better at what we're doing." Swindell was particularly concerned about how inflexible the system had become in the wake of associates' intense reaction to the raising of the bar. Managers rarely suggested adding new measures, even when they spotted an area in need of improvement, he remarked, because they did not want to make the goals too challenging and jeopardize the all-important bonus. Mary Kay Gilbert agreed: "The more focus and pressure you put on your quality standards, the less people are willing to raise their hand and say, 'I think this process should be measured,'" she declared. "Tying compensation to it just kind of throws that out the window."

Similarly, associates had grown to resist having measures retired, not only because that usually meant the loss of an "easy win," but also because it required workers to realign their priorities and goals (see Exhibit 9 for charts illustrating the de-

cline in measurement system changes after 1992). In part to address the issue of stagnation in the system, Quality Applications, in a just-released draft on measurement methodology, urged managers to regularly review old measures and create new ones, noting particularly that "danger lies when the primary reason for a measurement is to adapt to the [compensation program] rather than to improve the performance of the team or process. . . . Our measures should be used to aid in our continuous improvement programs."

To keep the measures flexible, Davis was considering a "sunset law" on measures that required all indicators to be retired and replaced after one year. But although he had heard the com-

EXHIBIT 9 Changes in Standards and Measures

Number of Increases in Standards for Existing Measures

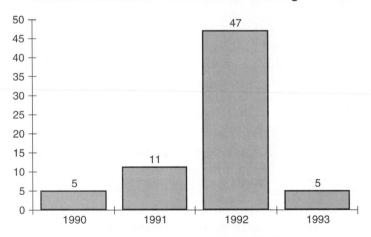

Note: Data for 1993 is year-to-date through June 30, 1993.

Number of Additions and Deletions of Measures

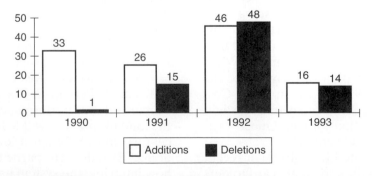

Note: Data for 1993 is year-to-date through June 30, 1993.

Source: Universal Card Services.

pensation plan referred to as "an entitlement," he remained a supporter of the basic concept. "Some people in our business believe that if we didn't have measurements tied to compensation, then people would be more willing to measure the right things," he mused. "My feeling, though, is that I'll take all the negatives that go with it any day in order to get the attention." Telephone associate Robert Inks agreed: "I don't think we would have gotten as far as we have today without it, because people can look at our monitors and say, 'We didn't do too well yesterday; we're not getting that money.' And then they look at the future and say, 'Well, we have eight more days in the quarter. We're going to really focus on quality and make it, because if we don't get those eight days, that's $100 I lose.' "

Although Davis was well aware of the measurement debates, he doubted that Universal would abandon its daily measures any time soon. In fact, he had more down-to-earth concerns: In January 1994, UCS was planning to raise the bar again, and Davis was already planning how to make the transition smoother this time around. Although he anticipated some resistance, Davis was convinced that the ongoing quest for continuous improvement was necessary. "We'll have to hit hard on the fact that we're going to keep raising the standards; it's not going to stop," he declared. "And if we think it is, we're just fooling ourselves."

But Pam Vosmik, vice president of Human Resources, voiced a separate concern. Recalling Winkler's "pleased but never satisfied" expression, she made a plea for balance. "You need to keep people focused," Vosmik asserted, "but by the same token, in the worst-case scenario, you can make an organization dysfunctional if there is never a hope that you're going to be satisfied."

CASE 21

Daewoo Shipbuilding and Heavy Machinery

With the sound of the waves of the East China Sea kissing the shore of Kŏje island, Park Dong-Kyu, executive vice-president and General Manager of Daewoo Shipbuilding and Heavy Machinery (DSHM), Ltd. looked out over the ocean and considered the course that lay ahead.

By 1994, DSHM had become one of the most efficient shipbuilding companies in the world. Probably more important, DSHM had recently benchmarked itself, and found its Okpo shipyard to be the fastest improving. Over the seven years between 1987 and 1994, Daewoo had built what many companies were still striving for: a plant that had learned how to learn—and was becoming better at it every day.

Despite DSHM's meteoric improvement path, there remained two driving goals which had eluded even the most inventive shipbuilding companies: speed and productivity. Construction lead time was becoming one of the key competitive elements in the industry. Daewoo's major competitors had each announced a major capital investment project to speed up their manufacturing process and become more productive. Daewoo had no such plans, relying instead on the promise of continued gains from its unique improvement methods, rather than further capital investment to maintain its targeted 10% share of the world shipbuilding industry.

It was a gamble. Could the shipyard continue to improve as it had over the past five years, and would this incremental path provide the needed capacity?

This case was prepared as the basis for class discussion rather than to illustrate either effective or ineffective handling of an administrative situation. Names and data have been disguised.

This case was prepared by David M. Upton and Bowon Kim. Copyright © 1994 by the President and Fellows of Harvard College. Harvard Business School Case 695-001.

DSHM

Daewoo's Okpo shipyard made a wide variety of vessel types, including crude oil carriers, gas carriers, chemical tankers and container ships. In 1992, DSHM built 1.7 million gross tonnes (GT)—about 10% of total world production of 18 million GT—and made a net profit of $280m. DSHM's quality and productivity were, by 1994, among the best in the world. Order books were full until 1995 and the yard was held up throughout Korea as a paragon of manufacturing performance.

Things had not always been so bright. Daewoo acquired the shipyard from the near-bankrupt Okpo Shipbuilding Company in 1978—primarily as a result of some government arm-twisting, as part of South Korea's industrial restructuring policy. At the time, the shipyard was only 25% complete. Daewoo completed construction of the yard and its first vessel floated into the East China Sea in 1982.

Upheval in 1987

It was not an easy year. In its first full year of operation, DSHM suffered a loss of $9 million on sales of $485 million, and for the next few years, Daewoo struggled with the challenges of building a new business in the face of a continuing world recession in shipbuilding.

As if these troubles were not enough, 1987 saw South Korea gripped by political unrest, and DSHM soon became part of a political firestorm that pulled even the healthiest Korean firms close to the flames. Throughout Korea, the democratic movement swept through workplaces, and newly organized labor unions demanded radical changes in the distribution of wealth and social status. The dispute at the Okpo shipyard was particularly harsh.

The labor dispute hewed deep wounds in the isolated community on the island of Kŏje. DSHM came close to total collapse, and many were concerned that the vitriolic battle was destroying any future chance the fledgling shipyard might have had to compete in the world market. Kim Woo-Choong, Chairman of the Daewoo group, was determined that the plant be saved, and in 1987 flew onto Kŏje island to personally supervise DSHM's rebirth.

DSHM: Tragic End to Violent Labor Demonstration: One Man Dead and 20 Injured

The bitter labor dispute between DSHM workers and management reached new depths yesterday, when workers responded to management's decision to close the yard by laying siege to the plant and its president. One worker died and 20 others were injured during the clash with riot police guarding the Okpo Tourist Hotel, where DSHM President Yoon was staying. Twelve companies of riot police blocked the road to the hotel, firing tear gas into the crowds of angry workers hurling stones. In the melee, Lee Suk-Kyu, an assembly worker, was hit in the chest by a tear-gas canister and was taken to hospital, where he died at 3:45 PM yesterday afternoon.

Source: Chosun Ilbo. August 23, 1987.

THE SHIPBUILDING INDUSTRY

The locus of power in the shipbuilding industry had traditionally been moved from region to region—as each region took advantage of particular skills or materials (see inset). By 1992, Japan and Korea had emerged as the world's shipbuilding giants, accounting for close to 42% and 25% of global production respectively (see Exhibit 1). Despite Japan's continued dominance, it was in Korea that the most dramatic changes had taken place. The 1980s saw explosive growth in Korean shipbuilding: In 1980, Korean companies had accounted for less than 4% of the world's output (versus the 47% for Japanese companies at that time). While the focus of the competitive war was Japan, Koreans were keenly aware of the possibility of new entrants from developing countries, such

---

"Until the first half of the nineteenth century, at a time when 90 percent of the world's merchant vessels were still made of wood, the United States was an undisputed leader in the shipbuilding industry with its abundant supply of cheap timber. With the advent of the steam-powered steel ship, however, the supremacy of the U.S. shipwright was quickly eroded by the British shipbuilders, who by 1882 captured 80 percent of the world's shipbuilding market. In the post-World War II period, the British shipbuilders succumbed to the other Western European shipbuilders who by then commanded the most sophisticated technologies. Before long, however, these Western European shipbuilders lost their market share leadership to the Japanese. By 1965, Japan firmly established its leadership and held on to it with about 50 percent of the world market. Today, a potent challenge to the indomitable Japanese shipbuilders is coming from Korea, and its prospect for overtaking the Japanese seems to be within reach. Toward the end of the twentieth century, however, China may well emerge as the industry leader."

Dong Sung Cho and Michael E. Porter in "Competition in Global Industries" p. 539 HBS Press 1986

as China, who might achieve the same kinds of success as they themselves had in the previous decade.

As well as fierce international competition with Japan, the Korean industry was also characterized by intense domestic competition among five Korean companies: Hyundai, Daewoo, Samsung, Hanjin, and Halla (see Exhibit 2). Domestic competition was becoming more of a concern for Daewoo, since it appeared that, despite industry over-capacity, a number of firms planned to increase their shipbuilding capacity in near future. While Daewoo had decided not to make such an expansion, it was not entering the fray unarmed. Its weapons were buried deep in the heart of its manufacturing process.

Building Ships at Daewoo SHM

The process of building a ship was primarily characterized by the huge scale on which manufacturing operations were carried out. The production process at DSHM is shown in Figure 1. First, raw materials (mainly steel sheet) transported by sea were discharged onto the Unloading Quay. The

Companies	# of Building Dry Docks	Total Capacity (DWT[a])	Construction in '92 (GT)
Hyundai	7	3,015,000	1,863,200
Daewoo	2	1,362,000	1,668,425
Samsung	2	315,000	712,417
Hanjin	2	210,000	104,220
Halla	—	—	141,000

EXHIBIT 2 Shipbuilding Facilities and Ship Construction of Korean Companies in 1992

[a]DWT stands for Dead Weight Tonnage, a vessel's carrying capacity.

incoming pieces of raw material then passed through the Treatment Line where they were blast-treated and physically re-arranged before passing to the Cutting Shop. While a small stamping shop might be able to juggle pieces of sheet steel in a simple stockroom, the sheer size of the slabs of steel coming into DSHM demanded careful thought about which sheet of steel should lie at the top of the pile to await cutting.

EXHIBIT 1 Ship Construction by Country (Unit: 1,000 GT)

	DSHM											
YEAR	Profit % of Sales	GT	Japan	Korea	Germany[a]	U.K.	China	France	Denmark	U.S.A.	World[b]
1980	10	1	6094	522	722	427	—	283	208	240	13101
1981	−1.7	80	8400	929	1061	213	30	502	352	311	16932
1982	10	400	8163	1401	958	435	135	265	451	459	16820
1983	10	350	6670	1539	1135	497	259	308	444	345	15911
1984	12	890	9711	1473	884	445	329	327	474	822	18434
1985	25	840	9503	2620	920	172	166	200	458	278	18157
1986	25	720	8178	3642	877	99	258	158	361	383	16845
1987	25	780	5708	2091	633	194	286	167	243	342	12259
1988	−42	300	4040	3174	813	60	254	72	377	453	10909
1989	−20	1000	5365	3102	718	102	325	160	343	405	13236
1990	10	980	6824	3460	857	131	367	60	395	15	15885
1991	20	1550	7193	3491	803	180	292	107	430	—	18254
1992	30	1668	7569	4502	882	228	346	131	534	54	18198
1993	35	920	7850	3382	NA	NA	NA	NA	NA	NA	17831
1994	35	1870	7106	5480	NA	NA	NA	NA	NA	NA	18700

[a] German data include West and East Germanies before 1990.

[b] The world total figures from 1976 to 1979 are 33906, 27532, 17594, and 13727, respectively.

In the Cutting Shop, the steel was cut by Computer Numerical Control (CNC) into appropriate shapes and sizes for the subsequent production steps. After preliminary assembly, flat steel components were sent to the Panel Block Shop— (a 300m long production line, with side wings for sub-assembly), while other components passed into the 3-Dimensional Shop. In the Panel Block shop (PBS), the large rectangular-shaped body parts of the ship were built. These blocks weighed between 200 and 400 tonnes. Steel stock passed through a frame planer (where additional surface treatment was applied), then through initial welding stages, sub-assembly and fitting through to final welding and outfitting. In the 3-D shop, plates and components needing complex curvature were bent, line-heated, sub-assembled and eventually welded together as a module. Blocks from the Panel Block Shop as well as modules from the 3-D Shop moved to the pre-outfitting Shop where unit and block outfitting was done (installing such parts as pipes, machinery and electric cables), and subsequently to the Painting Shop. These completed large blocks and curved modules were then put together to build gigantic pre-erection blocks. The use of these superblocks made DSHM unique.

A ship was usually built by laying a keel in a dry dock, and progressively building the ship from the keel up, using comparatively small and light pre-built subassemblies. DSHM's process was completely different. DSHM pre-erected enormous superblocks at the side of the dry dock which were then assembled in the dock like a giant Lego™ kit. Pre-erection was difficult: it required tremendous accuracy in manufacturing. Each of the blocks was a whole section through the ship, replete with pipes, wiring conduits, and occasionally half a room! These components had to fit perfectly together once built. While this would have been difficult even in a smaller scale assembly process, it was made much more challenging by the fact that many of the blocks were the size of office buildings. However, the advantages of overcoming this problem were also great. First, pre-erection required much less labor than dry-dock erection since welding and outfitting could be carried out at convenient angles and away from restrictive, inaccessible places. Second, a shipyard's primary bottleneck was usually its dry-dock, and pre-erection essentially rebalanced the line, and improved the output of the yard. Daewoo SHM also had the advantage of the world's largest dry-dock and—a necessity for building with the world's largest Lego set—the largest crane in the world.

By early 1994, DSHM was on track to achieve the annual sales goal of $2 billion by building 1.9 million Gross Tonnes, and had already filled 1995's order book. With 11,000 workers, DSHM operated in three major areas: Commercial Shipbuilding, Offshore and Plant Manufacturing, and

FIGURE 1 Ship Construction at Daewoo SHM

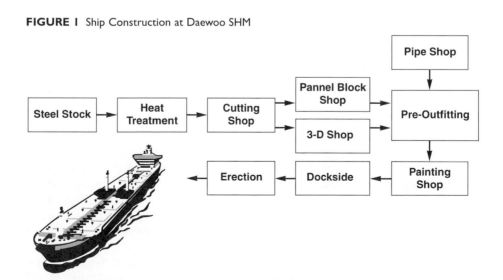

Special Shipbuilding. Exhibit 3 shows the layout of the shipyard. The commercial shipbuilding operation was hallmarked by vessels such as the Very Large Crude-oil Carrier (VLCC), and other large carriers for Liquid Natural Gas (LNG), automobiles, containers, and chemical products. Offshore and Plant Manufacturing involved the production of offshore drilling and exploration facilities, industrial plants, and industrial machinery. Finally, Special Shipbuilding focused on high-speed vessels and some military applications, and accounted for 7% of total dollar sales.

DSHM's productivity, quality, and delivery time had all improved so that by 1994 it was on a par with the best in the global industry. Even more impressive was that Daewoo SHM had made startling improvements without heavy capital outlay (see Exhibit 4). The number of labor-hours (LH) needed to build a VLCC had, for example, been reduced from 1.3 million in 1990 to about 0.65 million in 1993. The leadtime to build a VLCC had come down from 14 months in 1990 to 9 months in 1993. During the same period, the defect rate had shrunk from 20% to virtually 0.5%, and the accident rate from around 10% of the workforce per year to less than 1%. Not only had Daewoo SHM been saved from disaster in 1987, it had been set on a path which improved its performance—and for a number of years had improved the rate at which performance improvements were gained. While everyone remembered the bad times back in 1987, most often remembered were the experiences and actions that brought the plant back from the edge of the abyss.

BACK FROM THE BRINK

Family Values

Korea had historically been culturally distinct from neighboring countries such as China and Japan, and these roots, along with many periods of adversity, had fuelled a strong sense of collective identity among Koreans. The influence of Confucianism had contributed to the view that the family was the backbone of the nation as well as society as a whole.

The 1987 dispute had been painful and divisive for everyone and both management and the union knew that neither was likely to benefit from continued disruption. Yet resolution seemed diffi-cult to find. Daewoo management eventually took the initiative to resolve the crisis and Chairman Kim's personal action—to go and live with the plant—sent a strong signal of Daewoo's commitment to the shipyard to both union workers and field managers.

Kim's first step was to heal the deep wounds in the relationship between management and union, and to begin to build renewed trust between them. Kim started a "unity movement" which played on traditional Korean values and encouraged both sides to begin to act like members of the same family. The company sponsored a family training program which also included members of the community as a whole as well as its own workers' families. It also sponsored cultural events, and a variety of education programs. Many employees were single men so Daewoo sponsored opportunities for the single men to meet single women from other Daewoo affiliated companies (for example, in electronics and textiles).

Training and Education

The most important initiative addressed the training and educational needs of the hourly staff. First, the entire work force was divided into small groups, each comprising 10 to 15 members. This small group structure became the primary unit from which the on-going improvement endeavor was built. Education and training were based on this close-knit small group structure.

Training began with operators rather than supervisors. "A small group is like the roots of a tree. If these roots are healthy, the tree will flourish," observed Mr. Chung. The course addressed the following subjects:

1. Motivation for change and commitment
2. Technical knowledge of the job
3. Quality Improvement Techniques
4. Safety Improvement

Instructors were generally experienced Daewoo workers in the company rather than outside experts—though these new instructors attended external education centers to learn new and more efficient techniques. Having completed the external program, they came back to the company and taught their fellow workers.

Education and training were not just confined to directly applicable work skills. Daewoo

EXHIBIT 3 Shipyard Layout

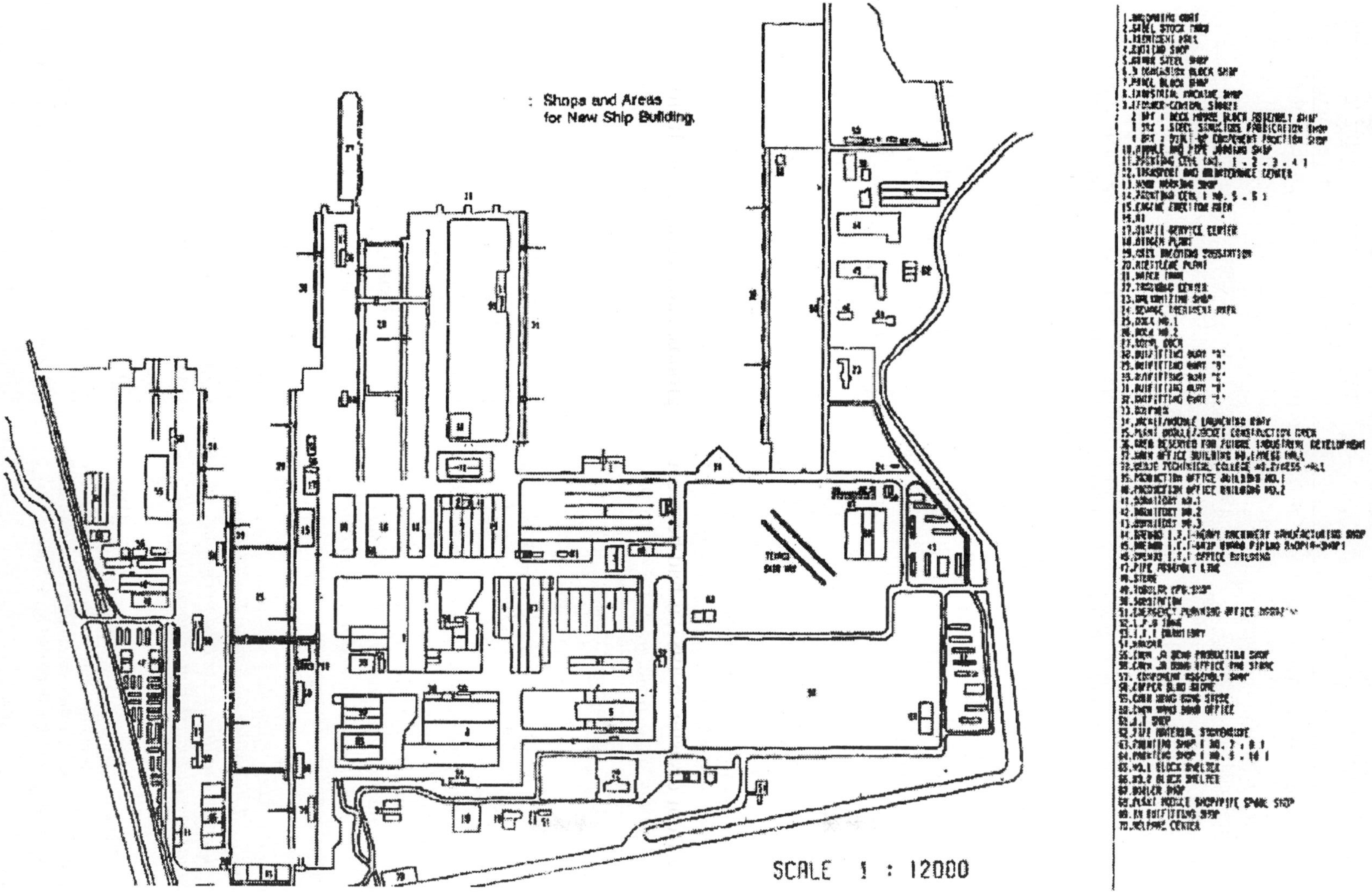

SCALE 1 : 12000

: Shops and Areas
for New Ship Building

399

	1990	*1991*	Δ	*1992*	Δ	*1993*	Δ
Total Sales (billion Won)	700	945	+35%	1195	+26%	1295	+8%
Production (000 Gross Tonnes)							
Commercial Shipbuilding	450	522	+16%	581	+11%	482	–17%
Offshore Plant	30	29	–3%	41	+41%	74	+80%
Ship Repair (billion Won)	3.8	12.5	+229%	23.9	+91%	91.5	+283%
Number of Employees	12,000	11,800	–2%	11,300	–4%	10,900	–4%
Overall Leadtime (months)	14	12.5	–11%	10.5	–16%	9	–14%
Labor Hours per Ship (million)	1.3	1	–23%	0.9	–10%	0.65	–28%
Overall First-Pass Defect Rate (%)	20	10	–50%	5	–50%	1	–80%
Panel Block Assembly							
Leadtime (Days)	24	19	–21%	14	–26%	11.3	–19%
Work-in-Progress (000 pieces)	100	40	–60%	25	–38%	18	–28%
First-Pass Defect Rate (%)	28	10.1	–64%	2.52	–75%	1.4	–44%
(Pre) Erection Timing (days relative to launch)							
Main Engine	–15	–20	–33%	–40	–100%	–55	–38%
Painting of Wing Water Ballast Tank	50	40	–20%	20	–50%	–10	–150%
Anchor Erection	50	35	–30%	–4	–111%	–10	–150%
Forebody Final Block Erection	–7	–10	–43%	–20	–100%	–35	–75%
Maintenance							
Mean Time Between Machine Breakdowns (hours)	54.7	65.2	+19%	72.5	+11%	83.4	+15%
Suggestions							
Employee Suggestions (#/yr.)	10,000	17,700	77%	26,700	51%	32,000	20%

EXHIBIT 4   Improvement Results

was keen to use training as part of a new benchmarking process:

> *"We sent our employees, both field workers and managers at all ranks, to the most efficient Japanese manufacturers[1] for benchmarking as well as education and training. We sent all employees, not just managers or a particular group of workers. The reason was that we believed workers could do the best job of benchmarking when they saw their best competitors doing their own jobs. For instance, a welder on the line is the best person to benchmark welding. He can compare his skill against that of the best welder in the world. Likewise, the welder himself is the one who can derive most benefit from observing the benchmarked welding process."*
>
> —SUH WAN-CHUL,
> EXECUTIVE MANAGING DIRECTOR

By 1994, more than half of the workforce had been through the education and training program.

An additional benefit of the small-group-based training scheme was that the members in a small group came to know one another extremely well. A production process based on the same small group structure was then a logical and effective work unit. Moreover, since managers had participated in the education program alongside operators, trust began to be rekindled between the two parties—and common goals again became clear. Once it became clear that each group's fate

[1]Group level corporate relationships were leveraged to allow this close observation. Japanese manufacturers were careful, however, to keep secret those processes they considered to be core technologies (such as parts of the design process).

was tightly intertwined, things began to change. Operators began to become active in making suggestions to improve inefficient operations or eliminate excessive consumption of resources. In turn, Daewoo management devised an incentive system to encourage and reward such suggestions, and also tried to build a process for more systematic learning and experimentation for those problems requiring higher levels of engineering expertise.

Dynamic Scheduling

This new way of working demanded radical changes in other areas of operations in the plant. An important change was the move away from tight command-and-control based scheduling. The old system had demanded workers simply "do the job"—in and at the allotted time, with very little flexibility. To fit and encourage the growing atmosphere of trust, a new dynamic scheduling system was devised, building on the strengths of the small group structure.

While aggregate project scheduling was still carried out centrally (though now by a computer-based Artificial Intelligence (AI) program), an important departure from tradition was made: The recognition that the most important events in any scheduling scheme were unexpected ones. Scheduling could never be perfect since such events were inevitable. In the past, schedule slippage in one part of the process affected all subsequent processes and resulted in disproportionately long leadtime increases, low productivity, and poor quality.

The dynamic scheduling system shifted the power to allocate short-term resources from the computer system to the people on the floor. Daewoo's new planning system was based on aggregation and disaggregation (see Exhibit 5). At the aggregation stage, the overall schedule was constructed using the AI system. This dealt with the problems of scheduling resources for the construction of multiple ships in the yard over the course of a year or so. A good aggregate schedule was vital to the plant, since level utilization of people, materials handling devices, and capital equipment throughout the year was critical for overall performance of any shipyard. At DSHM, there were often more than 10 vessels at various stages of production. With lead times of nine months or so, scheduling was a daunting task. Even though scheduling the yard was a complex matter, and re-

quired a high level of expertise, the harder problem had always been making the schedule happen, rather than the development of the plan.

Unless plans were effectively implemented at a detailed "blow-by-blow" level (the disaggregated level), the overall performance of the schedule would be unpredictably distant from the original projection. Such random schedule departures had been a common feature of operations in the past, and had become competitively unacceptable.

For this reason, a grand scheduling experiment was devised. Rather than trying to make a schedule happen by direct execution commands from the computer system, detailed planning at the disaggregate level was delegated to the foremen of the small groups.

All the monthly and some of weekly workforce allocation was carried out by the senior foremen, who were in charge of several of the small groups. These monthly and weekly plans were further refined by the foremen at the small group meetings each Monday. The products of these meetings were detailed weekly and daily plans (as well as the resolution of problems related to productivity, safety, quality and morale). On the Friday morning of the same week, the foreman had to evaluate the progress made during the week and determined whether the goal set up on Monday had been met or not. If the week's target had been met, then the following week's plan could be implemented according to the aggregate schedule. Otherwise, it had to be revised by the group to incorporate the remaining portion of the week's work into following week's workload. Slippage problems thus became the group's problems.

In most cases, the single small group could adjust its weekly workload to accommodate any minor scheduling slippage. Should it not be able to cope with a particularly severe or serious slippage, then the senior foreman in charge of that group could reallocate people among the groups he oversaw. If things became so difficult that even the senior foreman could not resolve things, then, and only then, did it become his responsibility to inform the management of the yard. Managers might then readjust the workload allocation among senior foremen, and (if absolutely necessary) revise the overall scheduling plan for the shipyard as a whole and promulgate it. Information thus flowed continuously in both directions: from the

EXHIBIT 5 Dynamic Scheduling

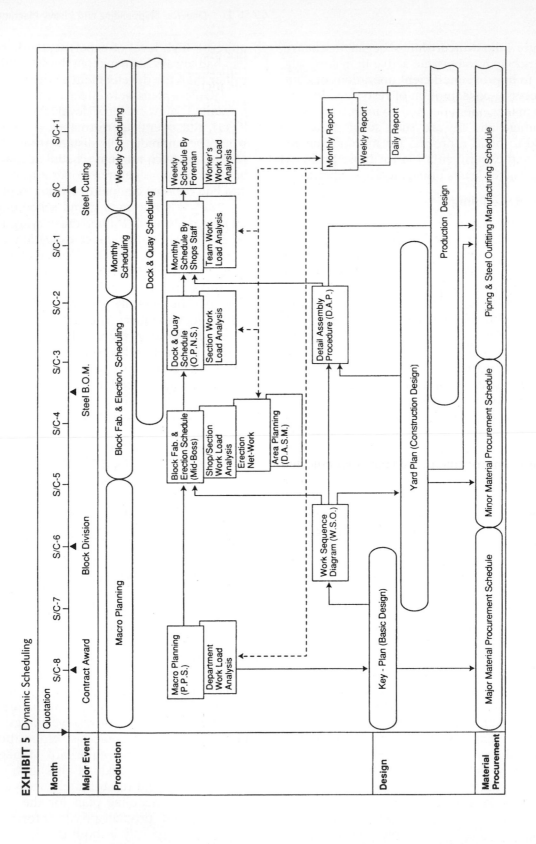

aggregate to the disaggregate level, and from the disaggregate to the aggregate.

Cutting Waste and Lost Time from the Manufacturing System

Over the next few years, as part of an ongoing policy of identifying opportunities for improvement without investing large sums of capital, Daewoo SHM began to develop methods for systematically reducing waste in materials and time from the plant. These methods again relied strongly on the educational foundations that had been laid, and encouraged people to recognize that the greatest gains were likely to result in a series of small improvements over time—each of which provided a platform for more improvement—rather than one or two immediate big hits. As the number of improvements made increased, people learned to look for prospective sources of waste reduction as a matter of course.

Cells in the Cutting Shop. A typical example of this philosophy translated into action was the layout change in the Cutting Shop. The Cutting Shop comprised seven bays, each of which operated as a separate processing line.

Before improvement, each bay was dedicated to a few particular types of steel stock, or particular processes. The components for each block were therefore cut in different bays, and considerable time was wasted in collecting together the exact set of components for a block. Moreover, the fact that each block made different demands on each of the processing bays meant that the allocation of work between them was often uneven. To address this problem, the cutting shop layout was changed so that each bay could cut a variety of shapes of steel stock, and be temporarily dedicated to the production of a particular module. In order to accommodate this, each bay had to be made much more flexible. However, this flexibility required little additional capital investment—though it did demand more careful sorting of raw materials before the Cutting Shop stage, more understanding of the production process by the operators, and dynamic allocation of labor.

Daewoo Specific Improvement

Although improvement programs like these were frequently seen in other manufacturing firms,

and seemed straightforward enough for other companies to emulate, most improvement steps were devised in a way that was unique and specific to DSHM's particular structure. Indeed, even those structural features which would have caused many firms to look to reconfiguring the system with new capital investment were turned to DSHM's advantage.

For example, the value of the huge investments in the Goliath crane and the Dry Dock hinged on Daewoo's ability to schedule these hungry overhead monsters effectively. As time went on, many shipbuilders had become skeptical about these investments, and saw them as albatrosses around Daewoo's neck, which they might well have become without some clever maneuvering in operations. Thus, a number of initiatives grew out of turning seemingly handicapping features to great advantage. Two such initiatives were **pre-erection** and the **dock operating** system.

Goliath and Pre-Erection. The shipyard had two dry docks. Dock 1 was 530m × 131m, and was served by the Goliath gantry crane—the largest in the world [see Exhibit 6]. Goliath was designed by Krupp with a width of 200m, and a capacity of 900 tonnes. Since Goliath spanned Dock 1, the difference between the width of the crane and the drydock, about 70m, was available for use as a pre-erection area. As described on page 397, there were great advantages in completing as much assembly as possible before the erection in the Dry Dock (provided, of course, that the work could be done with sufficient accuracy). However, in most shipyards, the proportion of work that could be done in pre-erection was limited by the capacity of the crane. For the Daewoo shipyard—with its huge crane—this was not a problem. DSHM could use Goliath for both pre-erection and erection in the dock. To build a VLCC, over 200 super blocks were needed. Without Goliath, most of the 200 blocks would have to have been assembled in the Dry Dock. By using Goliath, Daewoo could assemble super blocks in the Pre-Erection area, so that by 1992, only 80 super blocks were being assembled in the Dry Dock. DSHM could complete more than 85% of the shipbuilding operation before the Dry Dock (compared with 50% in 1990). The benefit of the increased pre-erection operation was dramatically reduced leadtime because of the simplicity of pre-erection compared to Dry Dock erection.

EXHIBIT 6 Goliath Crane

The Dock Operating System. In the past, the shipyard built several vessels in the Dry Dock simultaneously (Figure 2). The result was poorly balanced workload. Sometimes, everyone in the yard would be busy, at others, people would be waiting around. The busy, labor-constrained times resulted in poor dock utilization. To rectify the problem, DSHM changed the dock operating system so that Dock 1 was devoted to building only VLCCs.

After the change, Dock 1 built two full-VLCCs and two half-VLCCs concurrently. Once the two full-vessels were completed, the dock was filled with sea water to float them out of the dock, and the two half-sized VLCCs were moved to the dock door so that they could be built up to full-size. The result of this change was a well-balanced workload in the dry dock over the whole production cycle and an increase in dry dock utilization.

Continuous Improvement and Discrete Leaps

Paradoxically, the primary advantage of continuous improvement in quality for Daewoo was that it provided opportunities for step-improvement in lead times. Two conspicuous examples of this were the change from rigid matrix to in-line construction in the panel block shop and propeller

installation. Both operations required extremely accurate welding. The new levels of accuracy ultimately allowed DSHM to make step changes in the overall manufacturing process.

Step Change in the Panel Block Shop. Environmental concerns had meant that most new supertankers (VLCC) were double-hulled. If the outer hull became punctured, an inner hull would retain the contents of the vessel. A double hull was constructed from a criss-cross arrangement of T-beams sandwiched between two skin plates. The fabrication of these structures gave rise to one of the primary bottleneck operations. With the traditional levels of welding and marking accuracy, the design of the matrix structure had to provide large slack spaces when assembling T-bar frames onto the skin plates and accompanying web structures (see Figure 3).

In order to close the slack space accommodating jigging and cutting errors, operators had to patch it with a small collar plate. The need for this time-consuming operation was eventually removed by using a direct insertion method, which relied on making web-structures accurately enough to be inserted through the T-bar frames without any slack. This became possible only because of

FIGURE 2 New Dry-Dock Operating System

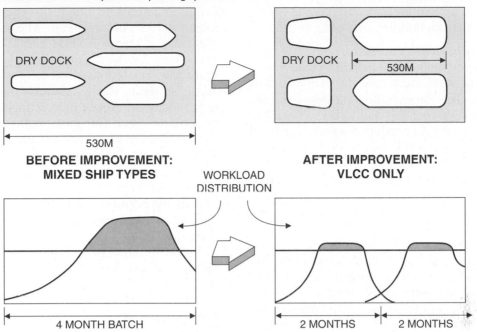

DRY DOCK

530M

**BEFORE IMPROVEMENT:
MIXED SHIP TYPES**

DRY DOCK

530M

**AFTER IMPROVEMENT:
VLCC ONLY**

WORKLOAD
DISTRIBUTION

4 MONTH BATCH

2 MONTHS   2 MONTHS

FIGURE 3 Collar Plate and Insertion

**DIAGRAMMATIC OF
LATTICE STRUCTURE FOR DOUBLE HULL**

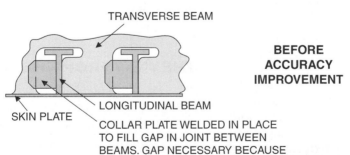

TRANSVERSE BEAM

**BEFORE
ACCURACY
IMPROVEMENT**

SKIN PLATE

LONGITUDINAL BEAM

COLLAR PLATE WELDED IN PLACE
TO FILL GAP IN JOINT BETWEEN
BEAMS. GAP NECESSARY BECAUSE
OF ERROR BUILD UP ALONG TRANSVERSE BEAM

**AFTER
ACCURACY
IMPROVEMENT**

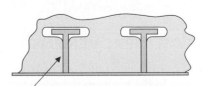

IMPROVED CUTTING ACCURACY
MAKES COLLAR PLATE UNNECESSARY,
REMOVING TIME AND LABOR
CONSUMING OPERATION

progressive improvement in accuracy of welding and marking, and completely eliminated a severe bottleneck in the shipbuilding process.

Propeller Installation. Another example of continuous improvement leading to step change was in propeller installation. Generally, the propeller was installed in the last stages building a ship. Conventional wisdom held that this had to be so since the installation of a propeller required a very high level of accuracy—the propeller had to be exactly centered with the rest of the ship. Unfortunately, the distortion of the hull caused by welding meant that it was unwise to install a propeller too soon—all relevant welding distortion had to be undergone before installing the propeller.

Because distortion precluded the parallel installation of a propeller with other parts of the ship, propeller installation time translated directly into lead time. It was also an unpredictable process and it could therefore prolong completion time without warning. However, the progressive improvement in control of the welding process had, by 1992, facilitated parallel propeller installation. This became possible because manufacturing engineers and operators could now predict the extent and direction of welding distortion accurately enough so that they could opportunistically select the best timing of propeller installation depending on how the hull was behaving from a distortion point of view, and how the schedule as a whole was playing out. This enhanced degree of control thus provided the flexibility to select from a range of (unprespecified) times for propeller installation. The benefits were twofold. First, DSHM gained a direct saving in lead time due to parallel operations. Second, they fitted the propeller at a convenient time for coordination with other operations. For example, installing the propeller at the end of the process was made more difficult by the fact that people had to work on both the inside and outside of the ship, in an awkward 3D space made more complex by fixtures and outfitting. Operators could now fit the propeller before such spatial impediments were fitted.

PHILOSOPHIES OF IMPROVEMENT

As the examples above show, each of the improvements made at Daewoo SHM built on foundations laid by previous improvements—step changes in operations permitted new forms of continuous improvement, and continuous improvement pro-

vided opportunities for step change. The identification and constant pursuit of such opportunities meant the rate of improvement on a number of dimensions at Daewoo SHM had initially increased over time. Daewoo operators' view of improvement had started to diverge from that of their Japanese rivals. Rather than seeing improvement as a process of slowly exhausting a static pool of possibilities (as a European competitor might see things), or even of continually drawing from a vast, apparently inexhaustible pool of improvement opportunities (as a Japanese firm might see things), Daewoo SHM began to see improvement as a way of providing opportunities for more improvement, and selected improvement projects by the same criterion.

At the core of this explosive improvement mentality had been a relentless learning capability nurtured and systematized by the education and training programs begun in 1988. At a deeper level, many saw the change of mindset as a result of a "spiritual endeavor" which bonded both management and workers. This spiritual unity (described by many people in the plant) powered the incessant drive for small improvements—which became the purpose of the plant. After a year or two, these improvements were flooding from virtually everywhere in the shipyard, as if the energy spent in conflict had only one place to go. Improvement and more improvement. Great pains were taken to harness this work, through careful integration and channeling of improvement, and the forging of new links between management and operators.

THE VIEW FROM THE BRIDGE

"Our biggest challenge for the coming years will be coping with the inherent uncertainty in the market for shipbuilding"

"While the recent focus has been speed, we cannot predict what the most important competitive dimensions will be in general, they will differ from customer to customer. We must manage the uncertainty by focusing on several strategic dimensions for improvement at once. Quality, productivity, lead-time, and product line mix may all *need to be improved."*

—Park Dong-Kyu, Executive Vice President and General Manager of the Daewoo SHM shipyard.

Although the outlook for the world shipbuilding industry as a whole had begun to look brighter by 1994, domestic competition among Korean shipbuilding companies was becoming fiercer. Some of the big players planned to further expand capacity, despite the prevailing excess (Exhibit 7). With regard to the escalating domestic and international competition, Chung Uee Dong, Director of the Management Strategy Center, pointed out:

> We do not have to meet the capacity increase in the industry by increasing capacity ourselves. Improvements in productivity have almost the same effect as increasing capacity. Moreover, we have options to utilize the increased productivity in ways our competitors don't. First, we may want to use the increased productivity [and thus capacity] in the shipbuilding operation. The second option is to shift the increased capacity to our other operations such as industrial machinery or heavy equipment. This option is based on the assumption that we do not grow our 10% target market share in the world shipbuilding industry, and will be necessary in any case when the industry dives into another cycle of recession.

> Although we believe we are among the best shipbuilders in the world, we know there is still ample opportunity to improve more. Recently, we completed an internal study to measure all of our processes to establish new standards. This helps us to re-benchmark. We know that we are achieving only 70% of the output that is theoretically possible from the way our current operations are configured. We will try to reach the 80% level early this year by eliminating all the losses that this new study helped us see. We believe we can achieve 100% level only if we can eliminate the less visible losses completely. In order to stay ahead, we have to reach that 100% target within a few years. However, the worrying thing is that we estimate the very best Japanese shipbuilding company would run at 120% *in our configuration*.

> Now admittedly, we have built this configuration as a result of our improvement program, and it's not clear that it could be emulated, but the difference in raw productivity is a concern. Our goal is to surpass their performance level by incrementally improving our productivity standards. Continuous improvement in the standards will lead us to a much stronger competitive position. We know from bitter experience that such improvement cannot be accomplished simply by pouring more money into the hardware. That is partly why we do not want to match our competitors' capacity expansion spree. Rather, we plan to spend efficiently in softer features which we know we can build on, using techniques we have proven will work.

EXHIBIT 7 Planned Capacity Increase among Korean Companies (as of late 1993)

Investment	Hyundai	Daewoo	Samsung	Hanjin	Halla
New Dock Size (L × W; meters)	#8 360 × 70 #9 366 × 70		650 × 97.5		#1 500 × 100 #2 400 × 65
New Crane	#8 900 (tonnes) #9 900 (tonnes)		700 (tonnes)		#1 600(tonnes) #2 600(tonnes)
Capacity Increase (#V.L.C.C./yr.)	6 units	?	6 units	?	6 units
Capacity Increase (GT/yr.)	1.5 Million	?	1.0 Million	?	0.5 Million
Construction Cost ($M)	500		500		440
# Employee Increase	2400		2200		2700
Other Investments in 1993	• Factory Building Renovation • Dry Dock Maintenance • Several Shops being Renovated	• Erection Painting Specialty Shop Building • Two 500t Transporter Purchase • Cutting Tools Change • CAD System Purchase	• Shot Blasting Expansion • Design Building Construction • 2000t Press Purchase	• LNG Factory Construction • Shot Blasting Shop Construction • N/C Cutting Machine Purchase	• 2000t Roll Press Purchase • Panel Line Expansion • Block Stock and Pre-Erection Space Expansion

This was a critical gamble for Daewoo. To eschew investment in capital equipment and rely on continued internal productivity improvement meant entrusting the future of the company to the culture that had been built since the 1987 conflagration. Echoes still resounded on the shop floor. A foreman voiced his concerns:

This year will be a crucial one. Ever since the big labor dispute back in 1987, management and union have been working together. But, now we face an even more intense environment and we need to reinforce our mutual trust firmly. Managers should spend more time on the shop floor, to communicate with the line workers, and get rid of any of the remaining barriers. They should not rely so much on the operators to look for improvements by themselves.

In the long run, Suh, Executive Managing Director, predicted:

Ten years from now, there will probably be very little change in the physical facilities in the shipyard. It will, however, become critical to speed up the entire shipbuilding process. This is the only way to continue to be superlatively productive and flexible, without committing ourselves to more capital investment. The key is building even more integration between functions and processes in the yard.

However, two mid-level managers were less sure of DSHM's strategy. Choi Dae-Soon, Deputy Manager of the NSC (New Shipbuilding Concept) Office made the following point:

I am convinced that the primary, untapped key to making the most of what we have is the progressive elimination of stochastic losses in the production process. For example, suppose the time needed to produce a panel block fluctuates between 30 and 40 days. The current scheduling mechanism would use 35 days as a standard for the formal production schedule. To be competitive, we want to move that standard towards 30 days, rather than leave it at 35. However, unless the new target is formally included in the schedule, line workers will not recognize the need to speed things up. It is up to us to find a solution to this problem—it's not easy when you look at how difficult it is to schedule in the first place. The speed-up must also be carried out in a consistent way across the whole of the process, not just part of it. A lot of the advantages we've achieved come from our ability to schedule our equipment better than our competitors. But we are also improving faster than they are, and want to improve even

faster. This makes the whole scheduling issue even more complex.

Jang Se-Jin was another Deputy Manager in the NSC Office. He sounded a related concern:

Although the engine of our improvement has been the workers on the floor, we are now faced with the limitations of that force. In other words—we have to acknowledge that we cannot continue to improve simply by relying on more and more hard work from the floor. This is why we have instituted this new project to better integrate the whole of shipbuilding procedure—from design to float-out. The project started three years ago, and we are now beginning implementation. We are trying to build a computer-integration system which builds on the expertise of our operators, rather than tries to automate it away. For example, we are currently trying to implement Computer Aided Process Planning at the production line level—which is an unheard-of idea. However, if we can pull it off, we will get a big advantage over the competition, who have just started to recognize the importance of integration.

Park Dong-Kyu agreed with many of these sentiments. Although the shop floor had indeed been the primary source of performance improvement over the previous few years, it was becoming clear that new paths for improvement also had to be found. Indeed, DSHM was relying on such improvement to carry the day in the face of daunting investment by competitors. Further manufacturing integration was a promising new source of opportunity.

First, Park wanted to know if productivity improvement effort would be enough to satisfy Daewoo's goal of maintaining 10% market share over the next five years. Park wondered how much of the wind was emptying from the sails of the shop floor improvement effort. While DSHM's improvements had originally been increasing in pace, recent results were more mixed (see Exhibit 4). What should be done to ensure its continued vitality and what dangers lay ahead? Second, what should 'integration' mean for DSHM and should integration projects be selected on the same basis as shop-floor projects? Finally, could DSHM continue to rely on generalized improvement, on multiple dimensions or was it now time to pick a more focused direction for improvement? While this would clearly focus attention and resources, the market was increasingly capricious, and there was great disparity between individual customers' re-

EXHIBIT 8 Workteam Practicing Safety Routines

quirements. In addition, there were many spillovers from one path to the next (say, in improved quality to improved lead times), many of which were not anticipated at the start of a project. Park also worried that constraining the plant to improve on one particular competitive dimension would itself begin to becalm the plant on its journey of improvement.

The questions ebbed and flowed from Park's mind has he watched the light flicking over the waves, as they kissed the shore of the East China Sea.

Samsung Heavy Industries: The Kŏje Shipyard

The newly built dry dock yawned like a mighty gash in the earth across Samsung's Kŏje shipyard close to Pusan in South Korea. From his office, high in the administration building, Hong Soon-Ick, Senior Executive General Manager of the shipyard, was carving out a new strategy.

The recent completion of the one-million gross tonne (GT) dry dock marked a significant change in direction for Samsung.

Samsung Kŏje Shipyard (SHIS) was, by 1995, a major participant in the international shipbuilding industry (see Exhibit 1). In particular, SHIS had developed a prominent reputation for outstanding quality in the Container Ship market. With four primary product lines (General Product Carrier Ships; Bulk Carriers; Container Ships; and Crude Oil Tankers), SHIS had thrived despite its two relatively small dry docks: Dock 1, able to make ships of up to 150,000 GT, completed in 1979, and the 300,000 GT Dock 2, completed in 1983. The sheer size of the new 1,000,000 GT Dock 3 would mean significant changes in the way in which Samsung's managers ran operations: if, indeed, they knew *how* to manage such a shipyard competitively (the structural changes were so radical that Hong was worried about the possibility of an extended hiatus in performance).

Managers at SHIS were anticipating at least a short-term deterioration of overall shipbuilding productivity. More worrying was the likely effect on the competitive hallmark of the yard: quality. Part of the drop in performance would result from the large influx of unskilled new employees (Exhibit 2), whose employment had doubled the total number of operators in the yard, and who would take time to train to the standards of their more experi-enced colleagues. In addition, the new dock would mean considerable disruption in the processes used to plan and balance production across the various elements of the shipbuilding process.

The goal was to fully recover pre-Dock 3 performance by early 1996. This, it seemed, was a formidable task: there was vast array of difficult-to-predict factors, any one of which could torpedo Samsung's efforts to achieve its goal. It was encouraging that an upswing was coming in the highly cyclical shipbuilding market, but without immediate, effective plant performance, Samsung would be prey to better-armed competition.

Samsung managers knew much less than its competitors about designing systems to manage a yard at this scale. All the experience and knowledge they had developed in managing to take advantage of medium-sized docks, it seemed, would be of little use as it developed methods to make the most of its new investment.

SAMSUNG HEAVY INDUSTRIES

Samsung was one of the largest business groups in Korea. By 1994, three business groups (or *chaebol*)—Daewoo, Hyundai, and Samsung—accounted for a sizable portion of the Korean economy. These three giants had each emphasized the critical importance of heavy industries, which they believed provided the fundamental base for growth. National success in "high-tech" industries, they believed, relied on the existence of a strong base in equally essential heavy industries.

In particular, each *chaebol* boasted a world-renowned shipbuilding business. By 1994, their combined ship production was over 5 million GT: 30% of the world total.

Starting from Scratch. In 1977, Samsung acquired the unfinished Kŏje shipyard from the Woojin Shipbuilding Company. Woojin had not completed construction of its first dry dock when the yard was acquired. In 1979, Samsung completed construc-

	'81	'82	'83	'84	'85	'86	'87	'88	'89	'90	'91	'92	'93
# Ships Built	5	4	3	7	7	6	3	6	6	7	8	10	10
Product Carrier	5	1	2	3	3	5	0	5	2	0	0	0	0
Bulk Carrier	0	3	0	2	2	1	2	0	3	2	0	4	2
Container Ship	0	0	1	2	2	0	1	1	1	5	7	0	3
Crude Oil Tanker	0	0	0	0	0	0	0	0	0	0	1	6	5
World Volume (Million GT)	16.9	16.8	15.9	18.4	18.2	16.8	12.3	10.9	13.2	15.9	18.3	18.2	17.8
Vol.(000) Gross Tonnes	60	151	99	233	310	313	234	246	437	383	394	761	580
Labor Hours/GT	54.9	26.6	34.5	27.2	29.8	22.6	12.1	15.5	9.5	12.5	12.6	6.2	8.5
Sales (Billion Won)	70.8	96.5	89.5	114	165	109	99.3	111	147	265	333	443	487
Sales/worker (Million Won)	40.0	30.1	27.5	30.0	30.9	25.4	36.8	35.6	46.4	78.6	94.8	129	127

EXHIBIT 1 Production Data

Item	'87	'88	'89	'90	'91	'92	'93	Feb '94	Apr '94	Jun '94	Aug '94	Oct '94	'94
Quality Rejections (%)	1.3	2.5	1.0	0.6	0.4	0.6	0.5	0.4	2.5	1.4	1.0	1.3	1.2
Welding Rejection rate (%) Ship Hull	6.0	10.9	7.7	4.3	2.1	2.5	2.4	3.1	2.4	2.7	2.8	2.9	2.9
Welding Rejection rate (%) Outfitting	0.4	1.7	1.0	0.0	3.2	2.5	2.5	n/a	n/a	n/a	n/a	n/a	14.3

New Dock Installation

EXHIBIT 2 Quality and Welding Data

tion of Dock 1 with a capacity of 150K GT. In the same year, Samsung received its first order: to build two oil supply vessels for the Australian carrier, Bulk Ship Pty.

As part of a continued effort to develop its shipbuilding operation, Samsung started construction of a second 300K GT dock, which it completed in 1983. In 1982, Samsung won its first container-ship order. Container ships had since become Samsung's focus. In 1983, Samsung Kŏje Shipyard became part of Samsung Heavy Industries Co., Ltd. (SHI). SHI was an integrated heavy industry firm which had already built some ships, constructed large plants and buildings, and produced heavy industrial machinery. This change gave SHIS access to broad-based engineering resources with a wealth of heavy industry experience.

SAMSUNG, DAEWOO AND KŎJE ISLAND

Although it was the second-largest island in Korea, Kŏje looked like many of the other islands scattered off the southern tip of the Korean penin-sula, with fishing and seaweed farming as its major industry. Kŏje, however, was also home to two of the world's largest shipbuilding firms, Daewoo and Samsung. The island, however, was probably one of the few things the two firms had in common: Each had followed very different developmental paths in terms of the way it had added capacity and developed its production technologies (see Exhibit 3).

Daewoo's Leviathan. The primary determinant of a shipyard's capacity was the size of its dry docks. While Daewoo had had physical capacity for ships of over 1 million GT since 1981, Samsung had competed with a much smaller capacity of 450K GT until late 1994.

The dry dock capacity of each firm played an important role in shaping the distinctive competitive and operations strategies for each firm.

Operations Structure and Market Selection. First of all, each firm's dry dock capacity dictated the kind of vessels for which each could develop a comparative advantage. Daewoo had competitive superiority for larger vessels such as *VLCCs* (Very

EXHIBIT 3 Comparison of Daewoo and Samsung Shipbuilding

	Samsung	*Daewoo*
Development History	–1977: acquisition of Woojin Ship-building (Shinhyun, Kŏje -do) –1979: Dock #1 (150K GT) –1983: Dock #2 (300K GT); merger with Samsung Heavy Industries –1994: Dock #3 (1 million GT)	–1978: acquisition of Okpo Ship-building (Okpo, Kŏje -do) –1981: Main Dock #1 (1 million GT) –1983: Dock #2 (350K GT) –1984: Dock #3 for ship repair –1994: merger with Daewoo Heavy Industries
Key Product Lines	–Container Ships, Tankers, Bulk Carriers: frequent product mix change; high-tech products	–Very Large Crude Carriers: few product lines; repeat produc-tion; relatively moderate (not so high-tech) technology
Technology Development Strategy	–R&D and Technology-Driven; - High Automation Levels - off shop-floor technology development	–Manufacturing System-Specific; - on shop-floor development/ learning

Large Crude-oil Carriers), whereas Samsung had traditionally built smaller vessels like container ships, bulk carriers, and product carriers. Although both firms had developed a global reputation for their product quality, they had relied on different technologies and improvement paths to deliver that quality. Despite their size, *VLCC*s by and large required less-sophisticated skills than the smaller container ships. Moreover, because the time needed to complete a container ship was much shorter, and the product mix more disparate, Samsung was able to experiment with diverse pro-duction technologies over a shorter period of time (see Exhibit 5).

SHIPBUILDING PROCESS AND TECHNOLOGY

Most shipbuilding firms used similar procedures for building commercial vessels (see Exhibit 4). The first step was to receive and treat the raw ma-terial, which was mainly steel stock. This treated steel stock passed into the fabrication stage where it was cut, heat-treated, and in some cases bent.

EXHIBIT 4 The Shipbuilding Process

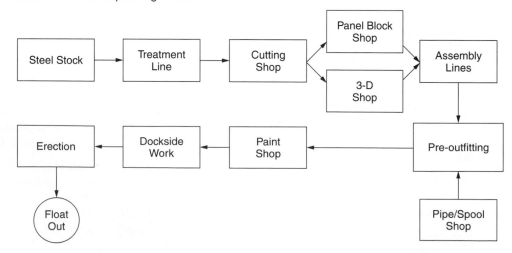

Fabricated structures then moved to small assembly lines where the structures were put together to form building elements, and afterward to large assembly lines which made *blocks* from these elements. In the pre-erection stage, some of these blocks were combined into *superblocks*. After pre-outfitting and painting, the superblocks were assembled in the dry dock (erection). Completed vessels were floated out from the dock, and were ready for delivery after final outfitting. Samsung's approach differed markedly from that of Daewoo, in that the latter firm constructed its ships almost entirely from superblocks, whereas Samsung used superblocks only for a few sections of a ship, relying much more heavily on in-dock fitting.

It took 7 to 12 months to build a commercial vessel. Because of the long production lead time and the large number of operations involved in the production process, the shipbuilding process presented an unusual set of challenges for operations management. Much of the effort in production went into problem solving of one sort or another.

> *Shipbuilding technology is all about how you manage your experience. The key engineering principles in shipbuilding are common across firms. But, since each shipbuilding firm's yards have very different configurations (like the capacity and structure of the dry dock, for example), each has to build its* own *production systems around that structural configuration unless it is willing to change the structure itself. The largest part of the effectiveness of any of the shipyards derives from its ability to manage its peculiar structure.*

—SUH JONG-OK, GENERAL MANAGER:
PRODUCTION CONTROL TEAM

The order-to-delivery process in shipbuilding comprised four major steps: product design, process design, scheduling, and production. The technology for each of these sub-processes came from two primary sources: process development carried out *during* the process itself, and *out-of-process* research and development in laboratories and prototype shops.

In product design, the primary source of technology was formal R&D (research and development), which developed automation, configured computer software and hardware and carried out joint projects with external experts and institutes.

Such work was therefore carried out "off-line" rather than as part of the process itself. The later stages of the process relied much more on development *during* and within the manufacturing process, and technology and expertise were more likely to be developed here through in-line learning, in-line experimentation and process-specific improvement, dependent on the peculiarities of the process on the floor. These two methods of developing expertise were highly dependent on one another.

MANUFACTURING TECHNOLOGY DEVELOPMENT AT SHIS

Importing Knowledge. From its early days, Samsung had focused on importing key production technologies from other shipbuilding firms and high-tech suppliers (Exhibit 5). In 1978, SHIS entered into a contractual agreement with B&W in Denmark to teach it about shipyard management systems and the technology used in the design process. Since then, SHIS had engaged in numerous efforts to "import" knowledge: outside sources continued to be used as sources of knowledge on such diverse subjects as shipyard management, ship design, manufacturing automation, and new vessel development.

Growing Independence in Product Development. SHIS passed through four key stages as it learned how to design ships. In the first stage (1979–83) Samsung developed an independent capability in *basic ship design*. During this stage, SHIS worked on the gross design of small vessels while subcontracting detail design. This was sufficient to complete the first few orders in small vessel shipbuilding. In the second stage (1984–86), Samsung brought detail design in-house. During this period SHIS developed the ability to design at a more detailed and fundamental level, as well as the ability to design and build much larger vessels. The next stage was termed "Independent Standard-Ship Development" (1987–1991): this period enabled SHIS to develop its own vessel models for more sophisticated ships such as container ships and Double-hull Crude-oil Carriers. The final and continuing stage of development was known as "High-tech High-value-added Vessel Development," from 1992 on: in this period SHIS launched a

Technology	Source	Period	Note
General Shipyard Management	B&W (Denmark)	3/78–12/84	- shipyard management system & basic shipbuilding technology
		3/81–12/87	- consulting and sub-contracting ship design
Design and Construction	IEC (Japan)	9/87–7/90	- production control
	MARCON (Germany)	4/83–8/89	- first extension ('86)
	NÖNNECKE (Germany)	3/83–1/92	- first extension ('88)
	B&W (Denmark)	5/85–5/88	- supporting construction technology
	IHI (Japan)	6/85–6/89	- first extension ('87)
	Sanoyath (Japan)	12/86–12/96	- first extension ('92)
Design Automation	AUTOKON (Norway)	10/82–11/90	- first extension ('87); ship-hull CAD design
	NKK (Japan)	12/87–12/88	- consulting 'outfitting CAD' development
	CADAM (USA)	8/89–12/93	- supporting 'outfitting CAD' design & development
New Ship Development	MARINTEK (Norway)	9/83–9/88	- prototype testing
	HSVA (Germany)	11/83–11/88	- prototype testing
	SSPA (Sweden)	4/85–11/95	- first extension ('88); prototype testing

EXHIBIT 5 SHIS Technology: Importing and Subcontracting

strategy focused on the high end of the market for such products as Crude Oil Tanker, Shuttle Tanker, Heavy Deck Cargo and Product Carrier (HDCPC), and Super-high Speed Ships.

CAD/CAM and Automation. While much of SHIS's technology was imported, SHIS became very sophisticated in finding new ways to apply that technology. It was in computer integrated manufacturing that SHIS derived strongest advantage from being part of the larger Samsung *chaebol*. From its early years, SHI (SHIS's immediate parent) had invested heavily in CAD/CAM/CAE[1] to provide a technological base from which it could build manufacturing systems able to deliver high quality products at a low cost.

The corporate-wide implementation of computer integration made it possible for SHIS to develop its own localized systems with fewer trial-and-error iterations, and it made heavy use of its access to development expertise and the experience accumulated in other parts of the *chaebol*.

Since its first use of CAD systems for basic vessel design in 1982, SHIS had steadily increased its commitment to the computerization of design and manufacturing processes (see Exhibit 6). While it expanded the use of CAD systems, SHIS automated many physical manufacturing tasks on the shop floor. By 1993, SHIS was ahead of its major domestic competitors, and within striking distance of Japanese competitors in terms of its overall level of automation (Exhibit 7).

The Skid-Conveyor System

In 1990, SHIS made a simple but significant breakthrough in assembly line technology. By working with the Samsung Corporate manufacturing group and running hundreds of experiments in production laboratories, SHIS developed a type of assembly line new to shipyards, by adapting existing technology from elsewhere in Samsung and from equipment suppliers. The new system promised more than just hardware. The system provided the right kind of hardware to implement a Samsung-tailored version of just-in-time production. It was a far-reaching project whose successful

---

[1]Computer Aided Design, Computer Aided Manufacturing and Computer Aided Engineering

Criterion	Unit	1987	1988	1989	1990	1991	1992	1993
Workstations	units	26	36	45	70	90	103	166
Density of Use	employees/workstation	14.4	7.4	5.3	3.4	2.6	2.3	2.2
Proportion of CAD-based Design	%	9.3	22.7	53.3	77.0	99.9	100.0	100.0
Investment	Won (million)	730	540	810	1320	1000	950	6120

EXHIBIT 6 Development of CAD/CAM
Note: In 1994, $1 = 800 Won.

	SHIS	Hyundai	Daewoo	Japan H	Japan N	Japan M
% of fully automated manufacturing tasks	22.3	16.8	12.8	27.1	25.8	25.1

EXHIBIT 7 Automation in Major Shipbuilding Firms

implementation would demand the coordination of all the improvement initiatives taking place in the yard.

Assembly Lines as a Bottleneck.   Before the skid system was developed, Samsung's assembly lines had been a sporadic bottleneck in the shipbuilding process. The bottleneck moved around the assembly shop and was unpredictably severe. Three factors contributed to its changeable nature:

(i)   Flow complexity

Many different types of components—panel blocks, three-dimensional blocks, bent steel plates and H-beams—all converged haphazardly onto the production lines. This complexity would slow up work in an unpredictable way, depending on the precise mix of components on the floor, and was a source of constant frustration for the line operators.

(ii)   Imbalance in production rates and poor coordination

Because of the poor synchronization between upstream and downstream processes, and temporary demand in excess of capacity for certain machines, many urgently needed parts could not be completed on time while non-critical parts were made too far ahead of time.

(iii)   Excessive changeovers

Since operators had to move back and forth between different product types frequently,

physical changeover costs and the psychological burden of switching were generating considerable productivity losses.

The Skid Conveyor Project.   The need for improvement in the assembly lines had been a gnawing irritation for many managers at the plant, and they had spent many long hours looking for solutions to the problem. However, on-shop, incremental improvement had not helped despite the best intentions and efforts of the operators, so in 1989 a concerted effort was instigated to re-think the architecture of the lines. Instead of looking around within the industry (where managers would have seen the same system as their own), they looked in other industries and worked with equipment suppliers to find a solution that could be adapted for Samsung. Managers developed a four-stage operations improvement project. After developing and pre-testing every stage in the production laboratory to iron out problems, the following steps were taken:

Stage 1 (1989–91): The block size was increased (from 12m × 16m to 16m × 16m) and the layout re-organized.

Stage 2 (1990–91): The skid-conveyor system was developed along with a central transporter and automatic overhead crane.

Stage 3 (1991–92): Welding machines were automated and made mobile around the shop floor.

Stage 4 (1992–): Standard procedures were developed for assembly process planning and block assembly, and the "Tact System" was implemented.

This system synchronized lots so that batches of components would arrive just-in-time to the next operation on the floor.

How the Skid System Worked. The skid-conveyor system was at the heart of the improvement project (Exhibit 8). Before the skid system, Samsung used a roller conveyor with fixed work tables along the length of the conveyor. Each fixed work table could process only one type of component (for example, either a panel block or three-dimensional block). This inflexibility was one of the main reasons for the complex production flow around the plant. This technology forced Samsung to

process the various products in an inconvenient order: Although a three-dimensional block might be available to be worked on, it had to wait until an empty, dedicated 3D workstation became available. Even the most sophisticated scheduling methods could not manage the complexity this caused on the lines.

The skid-conveyor system consisted of an H-beam rail and skids. A skid was a plate transporter of (L)15m × (W) 16m × (H) 0.3 m. Unlike the old fixed work table, a skid was buttressed by 24 rollers and had 225 pipe jigs on its surface. The pipe jigs made the skids very flexible in terms of the workpieces they could accommodate: by ad-

EXHIBIT 8 The Skid-Conveyor System

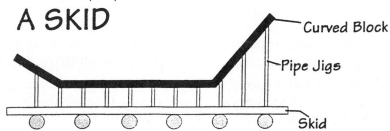

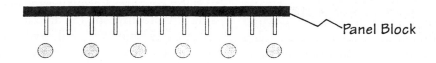

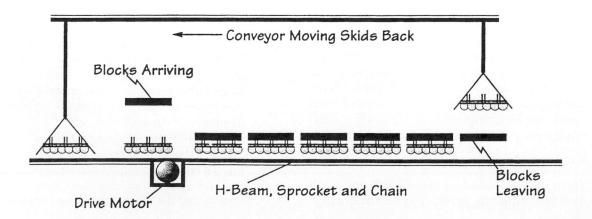

justing the height and angles of the pipe jigs, a skid could support any type of component, whether a flat panel or a three-dimensional part. For example, when processing a panel block, the pipe jigs were each adjusted to be the same height to support the panel structure. When processing a three-dimensional block, the skid would be arranged so the jigs supported the curved features of the block. Each skid was designed to hold two blocks at a time. This simple but effective method provided Samsung with much more flexibility in production, which in turn facilitated just-in-time manufactur-

ing: the blocks were processed when they arrived at the assembly lines without having to wait for the next appropriately configured work table.

Synchronizing Production with the Tact System. This new-found flexibility laid the foundation for full implementation of JIT production. The skids were not only small-sized transporters, but also became standard "units" of production for synchronized manufacturing: two skids constituted a production lot. The "Tact" system was used to synchronize the flow of the skids (Exhibit 9).

EXHIBIT 9 The Tact System

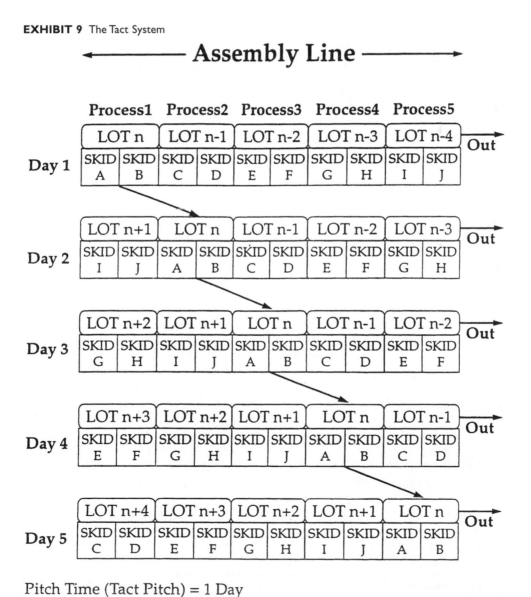

Pitch Time (Tact Pitch) = 1 Day

Each skid needed to pass through five processes in the assembly line. Each process station could hold one production lot, i.e. 2 skids (4 blocks) at a time. The Tact system demanded that each skid stay at its process station for exactly the same length of time. At a given moment, there would therefore be only 10 skids on an assembly line. The "Tact Time" was the time allotted for a production lot at each process. The Tact time might be one day or sometimes a few hours. SHIS was able to alter the Tact time to accommodate varying conditions in the yard. After each Tact period, the skids in an assembly line moved simultaneously: the entire assembly line thus became a *pull* system rather than a *push* system. Synchronized production flow reduced unnecessary work-in-process dramatically and facilitated the "visible management" of manufacturing. It slowly became much easier to identify the problems which had previously been hidden behind mounds of WIP.

Results of the Skid Project

The benefits of the skid-conveyor system were not solely philosophical. This simple new system generated huge tangible benefits for Samsung's business (Exhibit 10). The plant's material processing capacity shot from 7K ton/month to 10K ton/month, while productivity rose from 5.7 labor hours/ton to 4.8 labor hours/ton. It now took an average of 19 days (down from 25 days) to build a block. Most importantly, the skid project provided a clear communicable model for how Samsung improvement projects would work: research a new technique and develop the associated equipment *off* the shop-floor and make sure it was right before using the skills of the operators to tune it for real work.

Elimination of Slack: "No Margin" Engineering. A parallel improvement thrust at the process level was the managerial campaign to reduce and eventually eliminate the slack traditionally reserved for statistical variance in components. The primary areas targeted were the marking and welding tasks. Kim Hyun-Keun, Team Leader of the Production Engineering Team most closely involved in this managerial initiative, described the project:

In the past we produced blocks with huge margins for error, since we had never been able to predict the effect on downstream processes of unreliable marking and welding. Let me give you an example: in order to produce a 15m-long panel block in final assembly, we would have to cut steel panels with 25–40mm margins to allow room for unanticipated shrinkage and distortion. This had been causing way too much material waste as well as excessive processing times. While we middle managers saw an urgent need to fix the problem in 1987, it wasn't until 1989 that we attacked the problem in earnest. In 1989, we put together a formal task force and started statistical testing and experimentation using historical data from the shop floor. A substantial portion of actual data gathering and testing was done in collaboration with the shop-floor managers & operators as well as with the engineers in R&D. We tried some new systems in the lab and figured out how we might change things on the floor. The recommendations of the task force were finally put in place in the yard in 1991. We were all pretty pleased with ourselves when we started to see the results! Now we allow only ±6mm margin on a 15m × 15m block and we have built systems capable of highly accurate marking and welding, as well as an improved ability to predict the magnitudes and directions of welding distortion. Of course, we purchased more sophisticated cutting machines like Plasma Cutting machines (different from old N/C Chemical Cutting machines) and integrated

EXHIBIT 10 Analysis of Skid System Benefits

Category	1990	1991	1992	1993	1994
Sales (Billion Won)	230	335	438.5	468.7	490
Number of Ships Built	7.0	7.5	10.8	10.3	10.6
% of Skid Related Labor Hours[a]	21.4	21.4	21.4	21.4	21.4
Capital Investment (Million Won)		4888			
Fixed Cost (Mil. Won): Depreciation			550	550	550
Fixed Cost: Interest Expense			540	480	420
Fixed Cost: Operating Expense			150	130	120
Producer Price Index	100	104.7	107	108.7	110.65

[a]Implies that the labor hours associated with skid system constituted 21.4% of the total labor hours to build a vessel.

our experimental results into the CAD/CAM system. This all sounds very technical. Nevertheless, I believe the essence of this improvement success was that somebody cared enough about it to run some experiments in the lab. It was all about "managerial attention." It still is.

Suggestions from Operators and Group Compensation

SHIS used an incentive system to encourage operator participation. It assigned each operator to a group, and then measured and rewarded the group based on objective measures of the results of its participatory activity. A number of factors were taken into consideration in evaluating each group: (a) production output (±40%), (b) productivity (±30%), (c) equipment and human resources utilization (±20%), (d) suggestion activity (±10%), and (e) safety (±5%). SHIS rewarded high-performing work teams quarterly on the basis of this scheme, supplementing their base wages.

DOCK 3 AND THE NEED FOR BETTER INTEGRATION

The decision to build the third Dry Dock had triggered serious concerns and questions both inside and outside Samsung. The construction of the new dock was set to change not only the configuration and management of SHIS, but would also change the way in which it competed with other shipbuilders. Even though Samsung had become skilled at importing and implementing technology from outside (like the Skid system), the new dry dock meant a much more significant change.

When asked about the aggressive new expansion going on at Samsung, one senior manager in a neighboring shipyard was particularly harsh:

> Samsung's expansion will just drag down the market price for everyone. Our industry is already suffering from overcapacity, and now Samsung is building a one million GT Dry Dock? What can they be thinking?: "let's all die together"? It is an absurd move. Absurd.

Samsung managers' views were, predictably, less gloomy about the expansion. Middle managers' reactions were clearly, if not overly, optimistic.

> We're not worried about overcapacity in the industry. Most of the capacity is "capacity" in name only; much of it is old and inefficient. As long as we can stay highly productive, we will be able to keep a profitable share of the market. Suppose global demand is 20 million GT a year. The largest and most efficient shipyard will have 10–15% of it. We can have 10% of it as long as we are also among the best. Now consider what might happen when the total demand drops to 15 million GT. The best player will get 14–20% of it, and Samsung—if we are productive—will be able to grab 14% of it, too. The logic is that when the market is booming, less efficient players might obtain some orders, but when the market is down the best still get the same volume (in absolute volume) whereas the less-efficient ones just drop out of the bottom of the list. Why do we have to be overly concerned about the industry overcapacity? Only the poor performers need worry. [smiles] Having said that, we have to make absolutely sure we keep getting better, else we'll be hung by our own noose!
> —*Hwang Kyu-Ok*

EXHIBIT 11 Training and Employee Suggestions

Item	'87	'88	'89	'90	'91	'92	'93	'94
Benchmarking trips abroad (#/year)	41	87	175	190	222	86	69	15
Multi-function training sessions (#/year)	409	295	76	63	212	482	432	238
# Suggestions per employee	12.2	5.6	10.1	10.4	10.0	11.0	28.5	36.0
Suggestion acceptance rate (%)	16	30	47	43	46	49	63	80
Economic effect of suggestions (Bil. Won)	1.6	2.8	7.6	9.9	12.5	20.1	38.1	53.0

A SENIOR MANAGER'S VIEW

Senior management espoused a strategic vision in which the construction of gigantic Dock #3 was the centerpiece as Hong Soon-Ick described:

There were two compelling reasons for building the new dock. We clearly envisioned higher profitability as a result of it and we needed to meet the increased demand resulting from the coming expansion of world shipbuilding market (Exhibit 12). Despite chronic short-term market fluctuations the longer-term outlook was, and is, bright. The question was how to ride the tide of this golden opportunity. We had already become the quality leader in the container ship market, and we were making profit. But, that was not enough: the golden market is not in the product lines we have traditionally been good at. The lion's share of profit will go to those making larger ships. We have to be able to capitalize on that market opportunity. This does not imply we forego our high quality standards: we have to pursue the two rabbits at the same time, quantity and quality. Although our old docks were among the finest in the world from many aspects, they could not provide the kind of capacity with which take advantage of the new expansion in the world market. Dock #3 was the only option left to us. In effect, I believe the decision to build the new dock was primarily driven by the pursuit of profit. The second reason might sound a little idealistic. We felt we had a *responsibility* to become a world leader in the shipbuilding industry. Shipbuilding is a rare example of a successful Korean heavy industry. Shipbuilding is possibly the only area where Korean firms, if they want, can be completely independent of Japanese counterparts in terms of technology and engineering. We believe Koreans are becoming the world's finest shipbuilders and are surpassing their Japanese counterparts. SHIS felt responsible for contributing to that goal. Now is the time to do it, and the new dry dock is the vehicle with which we will achieve that goal.

A MIDDLE MANAGERS' VIEW

Sung Kun-Peo, Executive Director in the Production Engineering Department, was the key architect of the new dock:

When deciding to build the new dock, our primary concern was the effect it would have on our unit production costs. To compete in the expanding market, or any other market for that matter, we have got to be cost-competitive. Our old docks just didn't have the scale economies our competitors had. Although the sheer size of Dock #3 will provide such economies, we cannot rely on this alone to be competitive. We just need it to play in the game. Now, the real competitive focus is on technological efficiency. The new dock embodies not only the best technology from around the world, but also represents the cumulation of our own competence in technology and engineering over the past 15 years.

My most pressing worry is how we will integrate the operation of the new dock with the way we currently run the yard. We have to revamp the entire scheduling system to take into account the new capacity. We are, after all, *doubling* our total size. There are too many unanswered questions in my view. How, for example, will we schedule material and production flow among the three docks? How will we communicate between them? How will we take advantage of the newly developed marking and welding expertise in the new dock operation without severely disrupting the existing operation, and how will we train this army of new unskilled employees fast enough to be ready for the upsurge in demand? We need people to think about all these things, but there's only so much you can do.

The unprecedented challenges presented by the new dock along with ever-changing market was causing sleepless nights among all but the most senior managers at Samsung. There was little agreement about what the primary challenges

EXHIBIT 12 World Market Demand Forecast (1992–2000)

Product Line	Replacement Demand	New Ship Demand	Total Demand Million GT	%
Tankers	76.98	9.13	86.11	43.2
Bulk Carrier	51.10	21.00	72.10	36.1
Gas Carrier	1.08	4.37	5.45	2.7
Container Ship	6.13	8.76	14.89	7.5
Others	18.00	3.00	21.00	10.5
Total	153.29	46.26	199.55	100

would be, let alone the steps that needed to be taken to meet them. As always, it was in middle-management that these problems would be solved. Korean managers were well-known for their use of the "heated discussion" as a way of solving big problems, and this was a particularly big problem.

Suh Jong-Ok, General Manager in the Production Control Team, expressed no doubt about the most imminent task on his hands:

> Look. We are already seeing the signs of performance deterioration [points to Exhibit 2]. This bothers me a lot these days. The main problem is all of these new people around the place. They need experience. But, we don't have time to let them gradually learn for themselves. We are up against companies who are already up and running. Even though we believe our existing employees are the best in the world, we can't carry any passengers. You are either fuel or baggage, and we have no room for baggage. We must find new ways to help them to develop their own skills, but not by blundering their way through. We simply can't afford cycle after cycle of trial-and-error. We middle managers have to establish "harmony based on respect"[2] between old and new employees. The only teachers we have are our own operators. We have to find a way to encourage them to participate in the education process and train the new people. In turn, the new workers must respect and trust their senior colleagues. The question is, how should we do this?

Hwang Kyu-Ok   "Our ultimate success hinges on system integration," remarked Hwang Kyu-Ok, the key architect of CIM project.

> This is why we have initiated one of the most sophisticated computer-integration projects in the world, TOPCOS [Total Production Control System]. We started really getting rolling on the CIM project much later than our competitors, in November 1993. Nevertheless, we have worked really hard on it, with a number of truly dedicated people. It now looks like we are within a few months of implementation. TOPCOS is an ambitious project which aims to connect all shipbuilding processes (including order receiving, scheduling, cutting, assembly and delivery) across the entire plant. It will give us enhanced planning capability for material allocation, equipment assignment, operator allocation, and production scheduling for load leveling. TOPCOS will make it possible for us to transfer the knowledge we have accumulated from our experience with the old docks to the new dock without costly delay or disruption. Once it's in place,

the more we use TOPCOS, the better the system will be.

A FOREMAN'S VIEW

Few operators were prepared to comment on the changes. But one foreman's comment echoed the muttered views of many on the shop floor:

> There is an unbelievable confusion in the yard. First, there are hundreds of contractors still on site, and lots of things that still don't seem to work. Problem is, while we have our best people working on those jobs, they're not building ships. Second, the old standard times set up for operations in Dock #1 and #2 don't work on Dock #3. With all these new employees and new equipment, we can't build the blocks as fast as we did before unless we loosen the quality standards a bit. In my view, we went a bit too far on quality and we can afford a little here and there.

> The management is really going to have to take this into account somehow when it establishes the new standards. I know they are banking on the CIM project to help with this problem, but frankly, I don't think the men in my work group have a clue what the CIM project is all about. Although there is some communication between management and foremen, there has been little, if any, between management and yard workers.

> We've been used to having things work first time in this yard. We've never had much contact with the managers, but suddenly, they want us all to be involved making this new dock work.—*Anonymous foreman*

In spite of the many successes Samsung had achieved to date, Hong Soon-Ick recognized that he could not afford to be blindly optimistic as the operational fabric of his yard began to fray in front of him. The total capital investment in the dock would be well beyond W300 billion, and could reach W400 billion. It was critical for SHIS to recoup the investment before the end of the upswing in the highly cyclical shipbuilding industry. How long would the boom last? How many more ships needed to be built each year? Hong was not sure that the existing productivity could deliver that kind of output, let alone what it would be with all the disruption in the yard.

1995 would be a difficult year in Kŏje. Of course, experience told Hong that the performance crisis was only temporary, but then again, so was the market . . .

---

[2]This is the closest translation of the Korean phrase used by Mr. Suh.

Why (and How) to Take a Plant Tour

David M. Upton and Stephen E. Macadam

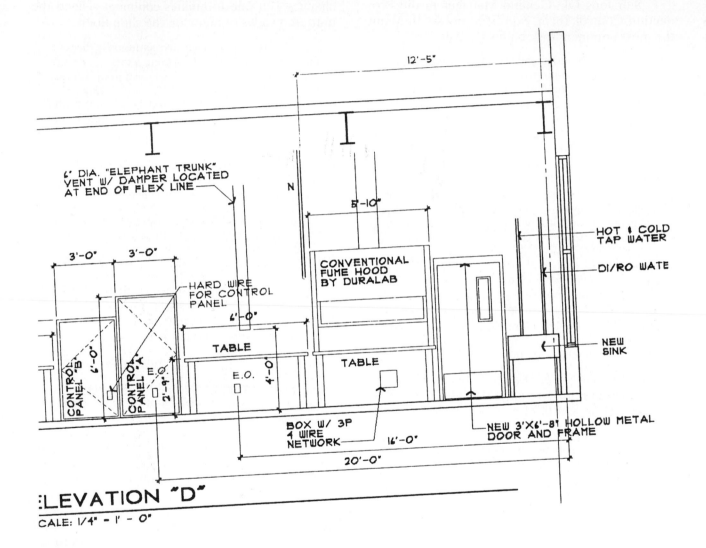

ELEVATION "D"

SCALE: 1/4" = 1' - 0"

In recent years, managers have recognized how manufacturing capabilities contribute to a company's overall strategic strength. The ability to respond quickly to customers' orders, to customize products to match customers' exact requirements,

or to ramp up production rapidly can be a powerful and difficult-to-imitate competitive weapon. But many corporate managers identify their plants' capabilities only by accident—as a result of chance conversations with plant managers or operations specialists. Consequently, many managers do not have the information necessary to cultivate, shape, and exploit their company's manufacturing capabilities. As plants develop, however, they need guidance to build capabilities that meet current and future needs. Plant tours can be a powerful way of providing factories with that kind of direction.

Almost everyone who leads, works for, or interacts with a manufacturing company can benefit from seeing a factory firsthand. Plant visits allow senior executives to build a better understanding of a site's performance potential; to assess a competitor; to rally the frontline workforce; and to communicate the company's performance, strategy, and current challenges. Plant visits allow managers to review a supplier's qualifications, to share best practices with a partner, or to benchmark performance and practices. Shop-floor operators can assess another plant's operations and apply what they've learned to their own factories. Consultants can benefit a great deal from tours, even of plants that are not part of their current assignment. Such tours allow them to amass knowledge about their clients quickly and to build a store of experience that will be useful on future assignments.

Managers often question the need to travel to remote locations to see a plant, particularly one in their own company. Even though management and financial reports are near at hand, factories are as difficult to understand solely by the numbers as they are to manage that way. Traditional reports rarely present an up-to-date, thorough picture of an operation's performance. Financial information tends to give an outdated picture of operational health: it will often reflect a plant's performance as it was a year or so ago. If a site has recently begun a comprehensive improvement effort, for example, the effects of the initiative may not yet be visible in any reports. And numbers rarely reflect a plant's revenue-generating potential, or the new capabilities it has developed. Finally, because financial and other conventional reports rarely indicate an explicit path for action, it is difficult to use them to learn how to improve performance.

Even people who know that plant tours are valuable can find it difficult to put them to effective use. First, unclear objectives often turn touring into tourism. If visitors don't know why they are taking a tour and what they hope to accomplish on it, they won't know where to focus their time and effort. Second, many people lack an organizing framework to structure observations and accelerate learning. Without such a framework, the myr-

iad observations made during a tour cannot easily be woven together and will not readily yield general conclusions. Third, information about plants and how to tour them is inevitably comparative; and those who have seen more, see more. Inexperience makes it difficult for younger, nonoperations-based managers in particular to make the most of a tour, since they are still building the knowledge base they need to draw comparisons. However, by setting clear objectives and applying an organizing framework to make sense of what they see and hear, visitors can make the most of plant tours—even if the industry, products, and processes are unfamiliar.

SETTING CLEAR OBJECTIVES

Unfortunately, most visitors don't begin thinking about the tour until they are in the plant's parking lot. The tour will be far more valuable if they spend time framing their objectives before the visit. There are three primary reasons for taking a tour: to learn, to assess, and to teach. Although those objectives overlap to some degree, they lead to very different types of tours. Learning tours are undertaken by people who believe that an operation has a feature or an ability that is valuable; they want to find out precisely what that ability is and how it works. Most often, the goal of a learning tour is to bring back the knowledge acquired on the tour to replicate the capability. Assessment tours are undertaken to determine how well a plant is doing either along an important dimension of performance or in terms of its ability to fulfill its role in the company's operations strategy. Teaching tours are undertaken to pass knowledge from the visitor to the plant being toured. The three types of tours demand different questions and focus on different parts of the site.

Learning Tours. The primary objective of most plant tours is to learn. There are a few general principles that can help increase how much visitors learn during a tour.

The first way to enhance learning is to focus on practices rather than on numbers. A plant tour provides an opportunity to observe how work actually gets done. Even the most lucid description of how work flows are managed around a shop or how operators use charts and diagrams to solve problems is no substitute for seeing things happen in practice. For example, managers at John Crane Limited, a mechanical seal company in the United Kingdom, often spoke of using "squares on the floor" to control work-in-process levels. A yellow square was painted on the floor at each station's input and output locations. When either square was full, the operator stopped work and coordinated with downstream and upstream operations to solve the work-flow problems. In effect, Crane had built a simple, visible shop-floor control system similar to the Japanese kanban system. By actually seeing such a system, visitors are able to develop a clear mental picture of it. They can then answer questions such as, How far apart are the squares, and how many are there? and Which processes use this system, and why? And they are better able to envision how a shop-level innovation might be introduced into another environment.

The second way to enhance learning is to make sure the right people are on the tour: different people will focus on and have insights into different aspects of a work setting. In the late 1980s, for example, Daewoo, a Korean shipbuilder, began a program of visiting Japanese and European shipyards to learn about new methods of constructing ships. The people on the tours included some senior managers, but most were welding operators—which made a profound difference. The operators were able to relate the various practices they saw at the Japanese and European shipyards to their own jobs. They were able to see more clearly how new operating practices might be replicated in their own plant. The welders also were able to identify for senior managers real innovations and merely incidental differences. Finally, they were able to communicate credibly and effectively what they learned to their shop-floor peers at Daewoo.

The third way to enhance learning is to keep an open mind. Much of the learning that occurs on a plant tour is unexpected. It is not unusual for a visitor to go to a site intent on observing one process or operation and to end up picking up excellent ideas in a completely different area. Visitors should take care not to home in too exclusively either on their own areas of expertise or on those aspects of the plant that the host is most proud of. Similarly, practices that might seem commonplace to the host may strike others as important innovations. For example, managers at the

Cummins Engine plant in San Luis Potosí, Mexico, painted milling and grinding machines different colors based on their statistical capability to perform their designated operations: green for a machine that could do the job easily, yellow for a machine that had more difficulty performing the job, and red for a machine that had great difficulty holding the required tolerances. The simple innovation of color-coded machines directed workers' attention to where it was most needed. This tool was particularly powerful in a multilingual environment in which communication can be a source of confusion, and it could be just as powerful in many other environments. But few people in the plant considered this basic innovation remarkable.

One must resist the temptation to be too judgmental. It does not pay to judge the effectiveness of a practice or to compare that practice with one's own operation before finding out why the operation is run as it is and what might be learned from that information. For example, at one paper plant in Ohio, the crew that managed changeovers of the main machine from one paper grade to the next was organized according to a very rigid hierarchy. The foreman had a nonrotating crew of people, each dedicated to one job. Everyone simply obeyed orders during changeovers. Many observers remarked on how old-fashioned this practice seemed in an industry that was increasingly embracing empowerment and rotating teams of operators. The fact was that this crew could change over a machine from one grade to another faster than almost any other crew in the industry. Each person knew his or her job, could do it better than anyone else on the crew, and was perfectly content to be part of a group of people that worked like a well-oiled machine. Even if a practice seems at first glance to be inferior, look for the rationale behind it.

The fourth way to enhance learning is to visit plants in different industries and to resist the immediate temptation to visit only plants "like ours." Almost all operations confront some of the same problems—for instance, how to marshal the flow of work through a facility, to translate customers' demands into products or services as quickly as possible, or to involve operators in process improvements. When touring outside their home industry, visitors often can witness completely new ways of accomplishing familiar tasks. In contrast, when they stay closer to home, visitors typically do not encounter new methods or practices. People tend to carry customs and practices with them when they move from job to job in a particular industry, making much of any given industry homogeneous. To see something different, it is valuable to travel far from home.

Assessment Tours. The main purpose of assessment tours is not to acquire new knowledge. Rather, it is to use what visitors already know to evaluate a plant. There are a number of different types of assessment tours. Some aim to determine whether a plant can fill a particular role. For example, a customer may visit a potential supplier to assess quality, or a corporate planner may visit a plant to decide if it could develop the ability to fill orders quickly enough to support the company's new strategy. Other assessment tours focus less on a plant's existing capabilities and more on how that plant might be changed to perform better or differently in the future. For example, a tour can provide a much deeper understanding of the potential value of acquiring a plant or making a capital investment in it. Visiting a site also is essential for assessing what is needed in a turnaround. Only with sufficient direct observation is it possible to develop the right prescription for improving the operation—whether it be capital for reconfiguring a plant, new management, or different improvement techniques.

Before embarking on an assessment tour, decide which elements of the operation are to be assessed and how they will be judged. One particularly useful technique is to divide a group of visitors into subunits, each of which focuses on a particular aspect of the operation. For instance, one group might concentrate on material flows, another on quality, and a third on human resources management, training, and compensation.

Regardless of the approach used to make the assessment, it pays to be on the lookout for problem areas. For example, the chief operating officer of an office equipment company was assessing one of his plants to determine if it could supply parts to another operation that was developing a promising stream of new products. The plant's managers had assured the company's management that it was well positioned to fulfill this new role. The plant, they reasoned, had recently made significant capital investments in modern, state-of-the-art component-placement equipment. But during a visit to the plant, the COO noticed some important features of the operation that the plant's managers had overlooked. Those features suggested that the plant would have difficulty doing the work. First, the material-transfer-and-handling systems were too rigid to accommodate new, unanticipated products. Second, the conveyor system prevented the plant from taking on new tasks because it fenced off a large amount of floor space. Finally, the plant's material-control policies, which made sense for long runs of comparatively stable products, would have collapsed in the face of a rapidly changing production schedule. The COO had to observe only a few production runs and change-overs to uncover those facts. As a result of the tour, the company was able to avoid a logjam in the new product stream by devoting renewed attention and resources to reconfiguring the plant.

Teaching Tours. Plant tours are important vehicles for bringing new knowledge to the tour's host. An expert's insights are much more powerful and credible when shared in person on the plant floor than they are when submitted to the plant's staff in the form of a written report. For example, a plant network manager can add tremendous value by transporting the best practices of one plant to another and demonstrating how those practices might be applied on the floor. Without regular visits, it is difficult to transfer this knowledge effectively.

There is, however, an art to such teaching. Simply ordering people to perform a task in a different way—without helping them understand why performing the task differently might be better—is an ineffective method of teaching. One excellent teacher is Chris Evans, the chief executive officer of North End Composites, a 90-person subsidiary of the Sabre Yachts Company in Rockland, Maine. Founded in 1970, North End started out making composite marine hulls and built a reputation for outstanding quality and customer service. By the time Evans took over managing the company in 1995, however, North End was in decline. The company still made only marine-related products and was in danger of being marginalized by competitors with a broader product range. Evans realized that the company needed to broaden its product line but immediately ran into a problem: plant workers knew how the manufacturing processes worked to make standard marine composite parts, but they didn't always know exactly why the processes worked. "Some people on the floor had great expertise, but there was a lot of black magic in the manufacturing processes," Evans says.

Evans began methodically asking people questions such as, "Why do you leave this piece to cure for three hours but the other pieces for only one hour?" and "Why do you use this kind of material?" In this manner, he encouraged people on the shop floor to think about the manufacturing processes and how they could be applied to making other products such as ultralight carbon-fiber hulls or enclosures for magnetic-resonance-imaging machines. By probing in this manner, Evans was able to help workers acquire the knowledge and skills they needed to make new products—without years of trial and error.

"Posing the right questions is a great way to instruct people," Evans says. "It's far less threatening than just telling them. In any case, you often don't have all the answers. Having people teach something to you is a great way of teaching them."

In addition to sharing knowledge, senior managers can have a tremendously positive impact on the morale of a plant's workforce when they conduct teaching tours. By asking the right questions, they send a powerful message about their commitment to superior performance. When a senior manager asks the right questions, the plant's employees learn that what they do matters. Taking an unscheduled side trip or speaking to operators who are not part of the official tour strengthens that message still more. Employees who see that senior managers notice and care about what is happening on the floor are much more likely to become involved in the process of improvement.

APPLYING AN ORGANIZING FRAMEWORK

No matter how clear their objectives, many visitors come away with only a vague understanding of what they have observed on their tours. Visitors rarely have a conceptual framework for understanding and organizing what they see and hear on the factory floor. Such a framework would help visitors ask better questions, gather more helpful information, and make more informed decisions.

We recommend a four-part framework: identifying a plant's strategic role, structural alignment, day-to-day management, and improvement path.

Strategic Role. It is vitally important for a visitor at the outset to understand what role the plant plays in the company as a whole and whether the plant's managers know what that role is. One way to find that out is to ask, What does this plant aim to do exceptionally well? Does it aim for low cost? High quality? Quick response? Many plant managers will use such phrases as "world class" and "best practice," but they often do so to cover a multitude of strategic sins—not the least of which is an inability to accept the fact that having a strategy means not doing certain things. It is simply impossible to excel at everything.

For example, large, diversified paper companies might have two kinds of facilities: those that produce large orders of low-cost commodity goods and those that produce small orders of high-margin specialty value-added goods with short lead times. Each type of operation requires a different plant configuration and different skills and practices.

Although it is vitally important that a plant understand its strategic purpose, the fact of the matter is that many do not. Often, managers do not establish clear priorities. Consider how many shop floors and reception desks have banners displayed above them that read:

> This operation will be a high-quality, low-cost facility providing outstanding flexibility, reliability, and customer service. We commit to generating the most innovative products at the leading edge of technology. We pride ourselves on safety and care for the environment. We will strive to be world class on every dimension, while providing a rewarding work environment for our people—who are our most important asset.

Such well-meaning, but fundamentally muddled, objectives are often the result of design by committee. One can imagine the circumstances that give rise to them. A meeting is held in which someone proposes that low cost be the most important dimension of improvement for the plant. "But what about quality?" asks another member of the team (1990s' code for committee). "What about flexibility?" asks yet another. Soon the plant's mission statement includes everything and says nothing.

Try to ascertain during the tour if the plant's managers really do have priorities and have made decisions that reflect them. One can uncover important clues by talking to people on the floor. Plants rely more and more on operators to be a source of new capabilities rather than simple machine tenders, and a visitor needs to find out if operators understand the plant's strategic priorities. Find out whether their perception of the plant's role matches that described by managers. Do frontline personnel know whether cost, quality, or flexibility is the highest priority? If they refer only to the particular product they are working on, they may not understand the strategic role of the operation as a whole. How is information concerning the plant's strategic role shared and used in the plant? Who gets this information? Does it drive action? Does each individual understand his or her role in executing the plant's strategy? By answering these questions, visitors can determine whether a company's strategy has truly been woven into the fabric of the plant's day-to-day operations.

Key performance indicators for the operators themselves provide another valuable clue to how broadly the plant's role is understood. Do the operators focus on performance measures that are clearly tied to the plant's mission? For example, management's goal may be to change a plant so that it competes on its ability to provide customized products. But if people on the shop floor are focusing on maximizing the utilization of equipment, the plant is unlikely to meet that goal.

If it becomes clear during the tour that a plant does not have a clearly defined strategic role, visitors should try to find out why. Often, a lack of focus can be traced to senior managers, who in turn may be giving plant managers conflicting objectives. For example, a business unit manager urged one textile plant to become more responsive to its customers. A memorandum from headquarters stated, "Responsiveness to customer needs through quick response and reduced order quantities is now the primary objective for the South Falls operation." The performance of the plant and its managers, however, was still measured in terms of tons of fiber produced. Such miscues by top management can be a recipe for confusion and disaster.

Structural Alignment.   Once visitors have identified a plant's strategic purpose, they then must ask, Does the plant have the right equipment for the job? This question addresses the plant's structural alignment, or how well its physical equipment and

systems fit its strategic role. Without the proper tools, even the best managers cannot make a plant function well.

During the tour, look for distinctive elements that might contribute to (or diminish) the operation's competitive effectiveness. Are there characteristics of the hardware that would make it particularly easy or difficult to perform the job expected of the plant? For example, in an electronic assembly plant, rapidly programmable machines allow for fast changeovers, which are particularly important if the plant is moving to quick-response manufacturing. Don't limit your focus to things that work well. Look for evidence of excessive investments in huge or extremely complex "monument" systems that, once implemented, are expected to solve the plant's problems. Talking to people about such investments can reveal a great deal about how a plant is run. Why was the new degreasing machine put in? How was it justified? Why was the money spent here and not in the worn-out machine shop? How did the last few investments in capital equipment turn out? If you had to pick a white elephant in the plant, what would it be? Why was the project so disappointing? A pattern of poor capital investments typically indicates a mismatch between a plant's structure and its strategic role: the plant needs to do one thing but buys equipment or systems to do another.

Structure refers to more than just "hardware," however. Visitors also should examine "software": the manual and computer-based systems and processes that run the plant. Physical information flows—in the form of routing cards and stock tags—are becoming much less common as computer-based systems replace them. It is considerably more difficult to assess computer-automated systems during a tour, however, because they are opaque to the casual observer.

Still, there are ways of collecting some clues about an operation's information systems. Rather than asking about the particular hardware or software used to run the plant, ask operators how they access the day-to-day information they need to carry out their jobs. What do they think of the computer system? People often are very complimentary about systems that help them do a better job. Is the system designed to exclude them from the decision-making process? Or does it give them information to make better decisions? How would they improve the system if they had the chance? How often is the system changed to meet the needs of the plant better? How often is the system down?

Visitors also should try to determine how well integrated the information systems are. Because they often interact with a physical environment, manufacturing-based computer systems are notoriously complex. Subsystems are added over time, and, as a result, systems often cannot communicate well with one another. Do people have to take information out of one system and reenter it into another? Do people understand why the information is needed and who uses it once it is entered? Find out how easy it has been to adapt systems as requirements have changed. The prefix soft in software can be misleading. Software for manufacturing is so complicated and interdependent that it often is just as difficult to change as the plant's physical equipment.

Of course, much more detailed analyses of a plant's hardware and systems can be made. But for the purposes of a plant tour, in which rapid assessments must be made, one's own eyes and ears—along with the people who actually use the equipment—are the best guides. A few complaints and grumbles should be taken with a grain of salt, but widespread dissatisfaction with a plant's equipment and systems is an important clue that something is amiss.

Day-to-Day Management.   Having determined the plant's direction and whether it has the right equipment, the next question to ask is, How well is it being managed on a day-to-day basis? To assess day-to-day management, visitors must consider a plant on three levels. At the first level, a plant is a set of processes: it comprises the physical methods used to transform material and information from one form into another. At the next level, a plant is a set of systems—computer-based and manual—that facilitate and coordinate those processes. At the third level, a plant is a community of people. A plant can have all manner of processes and systems; yet absent a common sense of purpose, it can flounder competitively.

Consider first how well a plant's processes are being managed. Excessive scrap and product-and-process variability are signs of poor process management. Product variability is fairly easy to observe, because it usually is carefully tracked and

historical data are usually available. Process variability is much more difficult to determine during a short tour because the right measures are not always tracked. When observing overall production quality, try to look beyond the degree of variability to determine whether the plant's personnel understand its underlying causes. Do operators systematically identify sources of variability? Does one machine frequently fail to produce to specification, and what causes it to do so? Do operators know which variables to monitor? Is the manufacturing process more like a science or an art? Is it the kind of process that varies regardless of the particular operator? Are there standard procedures to follow when the process fails? Keep in mind that acceptable levels of scrap or variability are determined by a plant's strategic role. For instance, a plant intended to provide a very broad range of products will usually generate a larger amount of scrap than will a low-cost plant.

When a process fails, managers and operators in plants that manage processes well are like good detectives on the trail for clues. They insist on knowing why a failure occurred and are not satisfied if it seems to be "all right" for the moment. More important, they find novel ways of transmitting that zeal for knowledge throughout the operation. To learn about machine uptime, look for evidence of a rigorous review of the causes for downtime. Is the typical response to breakdowns fire-fighting heroics or proactive problem solving?

When considering how well existing systems are being managed, one should look at work-in-process levels, lost items, the frequency of mistakes, and the availability of machines. Ask for or calculate some simple ratios: How many days of work-in-process inventory are there? How many man-hours per unit are required? How often does the customer-request date match the actual delivery date? What is the ratio of the time the product is actually being processed to the total throughput time? People on the shop floor are a good source of anecdotes regarding lost materials or products. It is worth asking for stories of both typical and exceptional mistakes. Ask plant personnel to identify who really runs the shop, decides what to make and when, and deals with such problems as late or missing orders. Typically, people will praise a person who knows how to handle a crisis (a sign that crises are common) or one who finds solutions to problems before they arise (a sign that they are not).

To assess the plant as a community, make a point of gathering as much information as possible by talking to people not on the tour schedule. As you walk around the plant, see if employees are merely caretakers of equipment or if they are more like craftspeople involved in improving the overall process. Caretakers watch the production process and hope that nothing will happen that requires them to act. They feel entitled to their jobs and want to be paid for their time and experience rather than for actual action or progress. In a plant full of caretakers, challenges will likely be met with such excuses as, "We don't do it that way" or "It's the other shift's fault." Caretakers frequently use the word they when referring to management, another function, or another shift as the source of problems. They do not believe the plant is improving and do not feel that they play a meaningful role in the improvement process. In contrast, craftspeople are actively engaged in both production and the improvement process. They grasp the entire, integrated production process, not just their piece of it. Their thirst for facts, insight, and feedback compels them to challenge established methods and to conduct experiments on how to improve the operation. They know they play an important part in improving performance and are committed to doing so.

Plants usually are composed of a mixture of caretakers and craftspeople. Look for patterns within the plant. Are the caretakers primarily in one area, function, or shift? If so, how does the current mix affect performance? Are managers aware of any problems, and are they addressing them? Is there an aggressive program in place to build a higher number and proportion of involved and committed craftspeople within the plant, particularly in critical areas?

Managers constantly nurture the processes, systems, and community of their plants to ensure that the overall operation runs smoothly. Broader strategic thinking may be increasingly important in a plant manager, but managers who can't run a plant on a day-to-day basis are in trouble—regardless of strategy. A plant tour offers an opportunity to gather clues at each of these levels about how well the plant is being run.

Improvement Path. The final element of the conceptual framework consists of determining whether managers have identified and articulated a path of improvement for the plant. If managers and employees are aware of the strategy that the plant has in place to improve its performance and can describe it conceptually, that strategy is much more likely to be successful. Visitors first should find out if there is a clear improvement strategy in place. Although it is difficult to make a full diagnosis on a single plant tour, a few visible signs often attest to the overall strength of the improvement process. (See Exhibit A.) This chart provides

EXHIBIT A   The Elements of an Improvement Strategy

1. Context	Why does this operation need to improve?
	What are the primary changes in the competitive environment?
2. Goals	What are the objectives of the improvement effort?
	Lower cost? Faster response?
3. Focus	What areas of the operation are currently the primary focus of the improvement effort?
4. Methods and Techniques	What techniques are being used to build improvement—for example, statistical process control or total quality management?
5. Resources	Where are the resources for the improvement coming from?
	Are they internal to the plant?
	Do they come from elsewhere in the organization?
	Are they consultants?
	How many people are actively involved in the improvement process?
6. Organization and Timing	How many improvement projects are there?
	How are the teams involved with those projects organized?
	Are they cross-functional teams?
	Do their members span different production departments and organizational levels?
	What will the sequence of projects be?
	Over what time frame will they take place?
7. Learning	How is new knowledge captured and used in future projects?
	How does the plant ensure that it doesn't have to learn the same lesson over and over again?
	Does it carry out postproject audits?
	How does each team involve others that may have similar, relevant experience?

a general framework for analyzing any operation's improvement strategy. Visitors can examine each of the elements described in the chart by asking the right kinds of probing questions.

First, a visitor should find out if management understands the context for improvement. Why is there a need to improve in the first place? Within what kind of competitive environment does the organization operate, and what demands for improvement are being placed on the organization by the environment?

Second, the visitor should try to identify what the goals of the improvement process are. Look for specific goals with specific time frames. For example, "Reduce the defect rate to 1% by August 1997" is a more effective goal than "Improve quality." On what dimensions of performance does the plant aim to improve? An answer of "everything" is evidence of an unclear improvement strategy. When companies strive to improve everything at once, they rarely see significant improvements on any dimension. For example, a manufacturer with a fierce new competitor that is offering consistently shorter lead times should decide either to meet that competitor head-on or to pursue, for example, a low-cost strategy. Trying to tackle both at the same time would be a mistake because the two goals are likely to conflict.

Third, the visitor should ask whether the improvement effort has a clear focus. The focus may be on particular departments or functions, on cross-plant processes, or on relationships with suppliers and customers. Does the focus fit the objectives of the improvement strategy? For example, a plant struggling to build its ability to respond quickly to customers' orders might focus on material and information flows across different departments. In contrast, a plant concerned about improving the quality of a product might focus on individual departments in which there are problems.

Fourth, having determined why the plant needs to improve, what dimensions of performance it aims to improve on, and where the focus of the improvement effort is, visitors next need to address how it will improve performance. What methods does the plant use? For example, a plantwide effort to improve responsiveness will benefit from reengineering the order-to-delivery process, whereas a plant with nagging quality problems might benefit from a total-quality-management approach. Is the

plant using techniques and tools—such as statistical process control or self-directed work teams—that will deliver the required improvements?

Fifth, the visitor should find out what resources are being pulled together to work on the improvement project. A lack of vital resources can be a sign that management is not committed to the improvement process. Where are the resources coming from? How many people are actively involved in the process?

Sixth, the visitor should look for clearly defined organization and timing. Whether improvement teams follow the existing organizational structure or are staffed cross functionally, the number of team members and the frequency of team meetings should be clearly specified. Look at the staffing of improvement initiatives. Are they staffed with people who have not only the right skills but also the ability, authority, and will to implement solutions? Look also for reinforcing mechanisms that maintain the energy behind the process and keep it on track, such as scheduled status reports and regular process reviews.

Seventh, the visitor should examine the plant's learning processes. It is important to look for signs that management is improving the improvement process itself through a concerted effort to learn from other operations and to make the most of what has been learned along its own improvement path. See if management is following the improvement process closely in order to apply the lessons it learns in later projects.

Even the best-designed improvement strategy can be hampered by "scheme burnout." Too often, plant managers latch onto the flavor of the month—some new management theory they pick up in an airport bookstore. A given plant may have been exposed to a long series of managers bringing with them an equally large collection of improvement philosophies. When one new initiative after another is launched, long-serving people in the plant will discount the latest one with a sigh of "Here we go again!" Listen for clues that belie an excessive number of prior campaigns that might take the wind out of the sails of the latest initiative. Managers must be committed not only to change but also to a particular approach to change. By keeping an eye out for scheme burnout during the plant tour and by tracking the seven elements of improvement strategies, visitors will be able to determine whether a plant's improvement strategy has been well conceived and is being implemented effectively.

People going on plant tours will benefit greatly from setting clear objectives and applying a conceptual framework to structure what they see and hear. But there is one final prescription for making the most of plant tours: take lots of them. As people see more plants, they develop a more practiced eye and build a richer base of comparison for subsequent tours. Even a plant that seems to be of no direct interest can help build that base. The essence of successful manufacturing organizations is their ability to do things of value for their customers that their competitors cannot. A plant tour is a powerful way of developing a deep understanding of what those capabilities are and how they might be exploited.

CASE 23

HMS Thetis and Apollo XIII

HMS THETIS

Disaster

In June, 1938, Cammell Laird Ltd, the Liverpool, England, shipbuilders, launched His Majesty's Submarine Thetis from their shipyard at Birkenhead. HMS Thetis, constructed at a cost of £350,000, belonged to the new "15 Triton" class of submarine. She weighed 1200 tons, measured 265 feet long and could attain a speed of up to 15¼ knots. Intended to serve as a general patrol submarine, Thetis possessed one four-inch gun and six 21-inch torpedo tubes. Her normal complement of men would number five naval officers and 46 ratings (non-officers).

The Thetis, like all submarines, could not be turned over by her builders to the Admiralty until her safety and effectiveness were proven by a series of trials. Technically, she remained entirely the responsibility of Cammell Laird until completion of these tests. In reality, however, the Admiralty became increasingly involved in Thetis's superintendence and welfare as her inspections progressed. By mid-1939, Thetis had passed most of the required tests and, with full naval participation, was engaged on her final diving trials.

At 10 a.m. on June 1, 1939, Thetis left Birkenhead and headed into Liverpool Bay for a diving test. Unusually warm sun, good visibility, a light breeze and a tugboat, the Grebe Cock, accompanied the submarine on her 50 mile journey to the location where she would begin her trial maneuvers. 103 people crowded Thetis to twice her intended capacity. This was not unusual, though, as many observers customarily attended diving trials. Most of the ship's occupants were naval officers

This case was prepared as the basis for class discussion rather than to illustrate either effective or ineffective handling of an administrative situation.

This case was prepared by David M. Upton and Sari Carp. Copyright © 1996 by the President and Fellows of Harvard College. Harvard Business School case 696-097.

and men, but 26 members of Cammell Laird's staff and two caterers were also present. Captain H. P. K. Oram led the naval contingent. Capt. Oram had served on submarines since 1917. The other senior officers also enjoyed significant submarine experience, while most of the Cammell Laird employees were highly trained engineers and submarine experts.

At 2 p.m., Thetis dove for her first exercise. Minutes earlier, she had radioed to the Grebe Cock that she would not, as she had been expected to, be disembarking some of the excess passengers. Those witnessing the Thetis's dive from the tug thought the submarine dove rather unevenly. Inside the ship, Lt. Commander Guy Bolus, Thetis's captain, was also slightly unnerved by his craft's behavior. Bolus ordered Lt. H. G. Woods to ensure that torpedo tubes #5 and #6 had been filled with water. Because no torpedoes were carried during trials, two tubes were usually flooded to compensate for the missing weight. Lt. Woods opened the test cock of tube #5. If the tube contained water, this procedure should have discharged a slight, easily stemmed stream of liquid. Unbeknownst to the lieutenant, however, the test cock had been painted shut. No water could emerge. Woods naturally assumed that tube #5 must be empty. He ordered the cap on the portion of the tube connecting with the sea to be shut (later examination revealed, though, that this valve was only partially closed) and opened the tube's door to see what was inside. The sea poured into HMS Thetis at a rate of two tons/second.

Recovery: The Submariners

Woods and other sailors rushed to close the watertight door of the compartment. However, the door was latched open, and they could not free it and fasten its eight bolts before the water began flooding the next compartment as well. The sailors succeeded in closing the second door, but two compartments were already full of seawater and weighing down the nose of the vessel. Thetis sank nose first, hitting bottom at a 35 degree angle and eventually coming to rest on an even keel at 130 feet. The impact destroyed the submarine's signaling apparatus.

The submariners made several attempts to enter the flooded forward compartments through a connecting escape hatch and close the open torpedo tube valve. The water pressure proved overwhelming, though, and the crew members could not reach the valve. Eventually, they did manage to lighten the ship by emptying the main ballast tanks with compressed air. This induced 18 feet of Thetis's stern to surface sometime during Thursday night.

Although they had immediately floated vividly painted marker buoys containing telephones with direct lines to the submarine, the men trapped in Thetis knew their ship would be difficult to detect. Under normal conditions, the submarine's air supply could be expected to last 48 hours. However, the presence of additional passengers shortened this period dramatically. The submariners could not afford idly to await deliverance. They decided to attempt escape via the Davis apparatus.

Pioneered in 1930, the Davis apparatus had enabled the rescue the following year of the only six survivors of the Poseidon[1] disaster. Since then, the Admiralty had ordered the apparatus installed in all new British submarines, designated it as the preferred method of saving lives in submarine crises, and trained all submariners in its use. According to individuals involved in Davis apparatus training, though, many trainees considered this instruction a waste of time, believing that they were unlikely ever to require it. Unremarkably, then, the Admiralty feared that trapped sailors would ignore the Davis apparatus and anticipate rescue by salvage. Hence, the official announcement promoting the apparatus emphasized that "escape by the Davis gear is an act which demands coolness and determination and which must not be delayed longer than absolutely necessary if it is to be successful."

Each submarine contained escape chambers fore and aft. These chambers extended from the ship's floor to its hull, opened into the sea and were fitted with watertight doors. The Davis procedure obliged two men to enter a chamber wearing bags filled with oxygen and with a carbon dioxide absorbing chemical. The men would secure the doors of the chamber and flood it with seawater. Once the water had risen sufficiently, they would open the upper hatch and rise to the surface of the sea. The oxygen apparatus permitted its wearer to breathe underwater for 35–40 minutes. The bag, whose pressure could be equalized with surrounding water pressure, would both help him float to the surface and serve eventually as a lifebelt. Men remaining in the submarine would close the escape hatch, drain the chamber and begin again. In theory, two men every five minutes could escape by the Davis mechanism.

The submariners selected Oram and Woods as the first pair using the Davis apparatus. They chose Oram because he had developed a plan for pumping air into the submarine from outside and thus would be the most useful to the rescue effort, and Woods because he could offer a firsthand account of how the disaster occurred. Since the soggy prisoners did not know if the submarine had been located, Oram and Woods were unsure whether they themselves would be discovered by rescuers once they reached the surface of the sea. Oram bound messages detailing the Thetis's location to his wrists in case he was recovered unconscious or dead.

Before leaving the ship around 8 a.m. on Friday morning, Oram instructed the remaining men to come up in pairs of one trained seaman and one civilian. Oxygen was becoming scarce, however, and the trapped submariners feared that they could never save everyone if only two escaped at a time. Contrary to theory, it appeared that each exit cycle from the Davis escape chamber would last at least 30 minutes. Consequently, four men entered the chamber. These men were certainly enfeebled by lack of oxygen and may not have been sufficiently alert to remember the instructions they had received. They never exited the chamber to the sea and were hauled back into the submarine one halfhour later. Three were dead; the fourth perished soon after. Because the men remaining in the ship were also extremely debilitated, the task of

---

[1] HMS Poseidon sank upon collision with a Chinese steamer off Wei-hai-wei on the Chinese coast. Two of her six survivors died shortly after being pulled from the sea.

removing the bodies and preparing the escape chamber for another effort consumed almost two hours.

The next pair to essay escape by the Davis apparatus included a Cammell Laird engineer, F. Shaw. Shaw later described his experience: "The first thing I saw when the escape hatch opened was the sun shining through the water. It was one of the finest sights I've ever seen." He also characterized the air when he left the submarine at 10 a.m. as "foul, and getting dreadful" and confided to his employer, the Managing Director of Cammell Laird, that he "didn't think he'd have lasted another half-hour if he'd stayed."

Recovery: The Rescuers

After observing Thetis dive, the crew of her accompanying tug, the Grebe Cock, prepared to witness signs of her specifically detailed test program. The watchers became increasingly distressed as no smoke candles, periscope or indicator buoys appeared on schedule. At 4:45 p.m., 15 minutes before Thetis should have surfaced, Grebe Cock's captain telegraphed to Fort Blockhouse, the submarine base coordinating Thetis's dive. The telegram merely requested confirmation of the dive's planned duration: its innocuous wording was "intended to convey anxiety without raising alarm."

Fort Blockhouse was located on England's southern coast, more than 200 miles from Liverpool Bay. This distance conspired with unfortunate incidents (most notably the puncture of a telegraph boy's bicycle wheel) along the missive's circuitous path to prevent the Grebe Cock's telegram from reaching the submarine base before 6:15 p.m. Meanwhile, Fort Blockhouse had dispatched a routine summons of its own to the Thetis at 4:45, reminding her that she was due to surface shortly. The submarine never responded. However, those at the base did not "wish to imagine trouble because of lack of news of Thetis," and raised no alarm until the Grebe Cock's telegram arrived at 6:15.

At 6:22 p.m., the destroyer HMS Brazen, passing along the west coast to Plymouth, received orders to divert and search Liverpool Bay for the Thetis. At 7:25, eight R.A.F. planes joined the quest. At 9:40, a flotilla of eight destroyers departed Portsmouth, on the south coast, for the half-day's journey to Liverpool. Five minutes later, the salvage vessel Vigilant set out from Liverpool. Many other ships, including warships equipped with modern submarine-detection apparatus and towing camels designed to right capsized vessels, enlisted in the search during the night. The rescue ships' crews were informed of the emergency and recalled to service through a variety of means, including messages flashed on cinema screens.

Throughout Thursday night, the R.A.F. planes reported sightings of marker buoys, oil bubbles and other potential indications of Thetis's location in the bay. The Brazen investigated all of these reports, but uncovered nothing related to the missing submarine. At 7:50 a.m. on Friday, however, the dumbfounded crew of the destroyer distinguished Thetis's rudder and rear fins protruding from the water. The wounded submarine lay 14 miles north-west of Llandudno, on Great Orme's Head in North Wales.

The Brazen's crew immediately commenced rescue efforts. Suspecting that the nose of the submarine was lodged in sea mud, they dropped depth charges to disturb the seabed and free the ship. The irrelevance of these activities was soon made clear by the testimony of the first pair of survivors, who surfaced near the Brazen around 8 a.m. Cheered by Oram's and Woods's escapes, those above water seized on the hope that all the Thetis's occupants could be retrieved by the Davis apparatus. Although they persevered in halfhearted attempts to right the submerged ship, the rescuers were quite confident that the submariners would be able to save themselves. While divers banged cheerful encouragement on the submarine's hull to those within, the Admiralty proudly informed anxious wives and the public that history's first mass escape from a submarine disaster was about to occur.

The news brought by the second pair of survivors was rather dampening. It now seemed that Thetis's prisoners might need to be rescued by means beyond the Davis apparatus. This suspicion was reinforced as hours passed with no evidence of a further exodus. The rescuers developed alternative plans. They had hoped to attach an oxygen line to the submarine, but the angle of her position rendered her air connections inaccessible to divers. So, the Admiralty determined to slice a hole in Thetis's stern with oxy-acetelyne tools. The hole could then be employed both as a conduit for air entering the submarine and as an exit for the sailors. A team at Cammell Laird's works hastily crafted a 12 foot steel cylinder to be used as a caisson over the hole.

For the rescuers to open a hole in the stern and allow for exit without risk of flooding the ship, Thetis would have to be lifted. Shortly after noon on Friday, Vigilant and two towing camels managed to fasten steel lines around the submarine and elevate her slightly. The lines then slipped off. Another attempt was made, but at 3:10 p.m., the tow ropes snapped and Thetis's stern plunged out of sight. Severe cold on the sea floor hampered the efforts of divers laboring to attach salvage ropes to the ship. Powerful seasonal tides also cursed the frogmen, sweeping them away from the vessel. The currents eventually became so ferocious that the divers could work only at slack tide, one hour in every six. Meanwhile, the tides forced the Thetis to cant even more unhelpfully.

At 6:00 p.m., slack tide, the Thetis's stern failed to reappear as had been hoped. By this point, the trapped sailors were almost certainly too weak to drag themselves through an opening in the ship's hull. The only hope was to bore an aperture large enough to pump oxygen into the submarine while the rescuers developed another strategy for freeing its occupants. The Thetis was finally relocated at 11:00 p.m. The rescuers endeavored to lift her stern with pontoons (portable floats) and to avert further sinking by lashing cylinders of air to her hull. At 1:00 a.m. on Saturday, specially-trained deep-sea divers arrived from the Orkney Islands, north of Scotland. The divers tried to cut two holes in the ship's stern, one to force in air and the other to pump out water, but this too failed. Around 2:00, the divers hammered on the hull of the submarine and were rewarded by faint taps from within. These were the last sounds heard from inside the Thetis.

At 4:10 that afternoon, the Admiralty regretfully announced that all hope of rescuing the doomed submariners would have to be abandoned. All the remaining 99 lives were lost.

APOLLO 13

Disaster

At 1:13 p.m. Houston time on April 11, 1970, three men left Earth for the moon. The trio was captained by Commander Jim Lovell. At 42, Lovell was already an accomplished astronaut: he had traveled on the Apollo 8 mission, the first to see the far side of the moon, and been an alternate

for Apollo 11, the original moon-walking expedition. The other two astronauts, lunar module pilot Fred Haise and command module pilot Jack Swigert, were both experienced test pilots but had yet to venture beyond their native planet. Lovell and Haise planned to land and walk on the moon; Swigert would remain behind to safeguard the non-lunar portions of the spaceship.

The astronauts would travel in Apollo 13, a rocket of the "Saturn 5" variety. Apollo was comprised of three components: the command module, in which the crew would spend most of the voyage, the lunar module, which would convey Lovell and Haise to the moon, and the service module, which supplied the command module with electrical power and oxygen. The service module contained 5.5 million pounds of explosives and two tanks of liquid oxygen. NASA remained unaware that oxygen tank #2, 10 feet below the crew's couches, suffered from a crack in its wiring.

Six hours before liftoff, the crew drove in a van to the launch site. They were unaccompanied; all service personnel were kept at least three miles from the explosive Apollo. The astronauts climbed into the rocket and familiarized themselves with its interior. Apollo's launch proceeded smoothly. The ship orbited the earth for several hours, then fired the rockets which would propel her towards the moon. Apollo's speed in earth orbit was five miles/second, increasing to seven miles as she headed moonwards.

For the first day, nothing diverged from plan. The astronauts were relaxed and even somewhat bored. Haise entertained himself by depressing the rocket's repressurization valve at intervals, thereby emitting a resounding boom and terrifying his spaceshipmates! Since the beginning of the flight, the crew had been drawing on the flawed oxygen tank. Nonetheless, the cracked wire remained submerged in liquid.

Fifteen hours after departing Earth, the astronauts reconfigured the rocket. In preparation for their journey to the moon, they reversed the command module and docked it into the lunar module, creating a tunnel between the two components. Forty hours later, on April 13, Apollo had completed four-fifths of her outward voyage. Two hundred thousand miles from Earth, the cracked wire in tank #2 was finally exposed. Before turning in for the night, the crew obeyed a routine request from mission control: turn on the fans in the oxygen tanks. The fans' operation produced a spark between the cracked wires, igniting a fire. The spacecraft rocked as a massive bang ensued.

Recovery

Silence followed the explosion. This serenity was punctuated only by what Haise described as "a metallic, tinny noise" emanating from the tunnel between the command and lunar modules. At first, Lovell suspected Haise of responsibility for the noise. He realized quickly, though, that his jokester colleague was mystified by the blast. A carmine warning gleamed from the control panel, signaling the failure of part of Apollo's electrical system. Then, with "a sinking feeling," the astronauts noted a gaseous substance streaming from the service module. Haise declared later: "I knew then that we'd lost the mission. We weren't going to land on the moon."

The astronauts understood that their mission would have to be aborted; mission control, however, was less enlightened. The ground crew's indicators showed a loss of both oxygen tanks, the electrical system and fuel. NASA was incredulous. Sy Liebergot, the Command Module Systems Controller, recalled that he and his associates thought "there was no possible way this could happen in this spacecraft, the way it was designed." Mission control reasoned that if the indicators were correct, the crew would already have perished. Hence, the ground staff assumed they were experiencing an instrument failure. Once they identified the defective instrument, Apollo could still land on the moon.

Twenty minutes into the crisis and unable to distinguish a faulty instrument, Liebergot acknowledged that his indicators were telling the truth. Less than two hours' worth of oxygen were left to nourish the fuel cells and the crew of Apollo 13.

As 15 minutes of oxygen remained in the command module, mission control reached a decision. The astronauts were ordered to move into the lunar module, which enjoyed its own supply of oxygen and electricity. Lovell and Haise activated the limb's power and life support. Before joining them, Swigert shut down the systems in the command module. Among these systems were the spacecraft's thrusters, which kept the ship on course and within reach of NASA's guidance equipment. Apollo drifted neurotically for an agonizing 2.5 minutes, then stabilized.

Although it represented the only viable alternative, relocation to the lunar module carried considerable risks. The lunar module contained two days' supply of oxygen for two people. It was improbable that Apollo's three passengers could be returned to Earth that soon. The cramped, seatless lunar module was also extremely thin-skinned: its walls were the density of a triple layer of aluminum foil. A boot in the wrong place could easily knock a hole through which the astronauts would be sucked into space. Most importantly, though, the move to the lunar module meant suspension of all the command module's systems. These systems would need to be reactivated before entering the earth's atmosphere, as the command module was the only portion of the ship which could survive reentry. Once frozen in the bitter cold of outer space, though, the systems and their batteries might cease to be functional. No tests of the guidance equipment had ever been performed in freezing conditions.

After the astronauts had safely migrated into the lunar module, mission control turned its attention to Apollo's course home. The rocket was still heading towards the moon. Taking the most direct path back to Earth would entail burning fuel to turn Apollo around. Mission control opted for a less risky strategy: continue on a free return trajectory around the moon, allowing gravitational pull to return the ship home along a figure-eight-shaped path. NASA estimated that the oxygen used by the astronauts during the additional 24–48 hours they spent circling the moon would be less than the amount required to rotate Apollo.

Apollo's crew was pleased by mission control's decision. Lovell said, "at least we'd be on a course which had some intercept with the Earth. It might not be survivable, but it was better than being a permanent monument to the space program, going back and forth for eons." Also, though Lovell and Haise could not realize their dreams of becoming the third and fourth men to moonwalk, it was some consolation to know that they would at least see the Earth's satellite at close range. As Apollo glided by the far side of the moon, rookies Haise and Swigert "played tourist," snapping photographs and craning for better views from the spacecraft's windows. Lovell, meanwhile, searched for a small mountain he had identified during the Apollo 8 mission and named after his wife.

Soon, miserable reality intruded. The lunar module had not been designed to operate with the other modules attached. Its center of gravity had shifted, rendering Apollo difficult to control. The astronauts tried to adjust, "essentially learning to fly all over again." Meanwhile, mission control fretted over the ship's dwindling power. The hungriest power consumer was the guidance system, but interest groups within mission control disagreed on whether to turn it off. Six hours after the accident, crew and mission control realized that, at her present speed, Apollo would run out of power and water before returning to Earth. Hence, the astronauts prepared to increase the craft's speed, lopping 24 hours from the ship's travel time through a final, terrific rocket burn. Houston's warring factions finally compromised on leaving the guidance system on through the burn, so that Apollo would be properly positioned at that crucial moment. Then, however, the crew would be required to extinguish all systems and complete the journey in darkness and cold.

The lunar module's temperature rapidly declined below freezing. Lovell and Haise donned their lunar boots, but decided not to put on the rest of their moon suits, as their perspiration might freeze inside the heavy casing. The astronauts' dehydrated food did not mix well with cold water, and their misery was compounded when mission control requested that they cease dumping urine overboard, since it interfered with analysis of Apollo's trajectory. The crew members began drinking less water, both to conserve that precious resource and to limit the urine they produced. Haise developed a bladder infection and chills. At one point, the chills became so violent that Lovell wrapped his body around his friend in an effort to warm the ailing astronaut. Twenty-four hours before Apollo was expected to reenter Earth's atmosphere, the ground crew recognized that the spacebound trio's energy was "flagging quickly."

Yet another problem soon developed: carbon dioxide was accumulating inside Apollo, threatening to poison the astronauts. The lunar module had run out of carbon dioxide filters. The command module still had many filters, but these were round and would not fit the square apertures of the lunar limb. Mission control constructed a prototype filter from materials available to Apollo's crew, such as cardboard, plastic bags and duct tape. Describing this creation to the stranded astronauts was a complicated process. Actually locating the materials and assembling the filter took two hours. How-

ever, once the makeshift masterpiece was in place, the crew breathed more easily.

With less than a day before scheduled splashdown, mission control noticed that Apollo was slightly off course. To return to Earth, the spacecraft would need to hit the planet's atmosphere at a precise, two degree wide angle. Apollo's approach, however, was too shallow: she would enter below this angle and fail to reach the planet's surface. Course correction without guidance equipment was fraught with peril, but the crew managed to determine the correct direction by precisely centering the Earth in the window of the module. Meanwhile, mission control strove frantically to construct a plan for restarting the frozen command module. The principal dilemma was allocation of the module's limited power. Of course, each interest group lobbied for maximum power to the system in which it specialized. Arguments and repeated computer simulations delayed the plan's finalization. Ten hours before they were expected to land, the astronauts were becoming frantic. Swigert, the novice command module pilot, needed time to test his instructions. One hour later, mission control finally began radioing the complicated strategy to the crew. Transcription of the instructions occupied two hours and every scrap of paper the astronauts could locate. As Apollo hurtled toward Earth at 20,000 miles/hour, Swigert performed a dry run in the command module.

Before reentry, the crew had to amputate the lunar module from the service module. While still inhabiting the lunar module, they jettisoned the service module. As the service module spun into space, Apollo's crew had their only opportunity to determine the cause of its demise several days ago. They recognized the enormity of the explosion they had survived only upon seeing that an entire side panel had been blown away from the module. Fifteen minutes before splashdown, Lovell and Haise joined Swigert in the command module, locking the tunnel door behind them. Mission control instructed them to discard the lunar module. Years later, Haise remarked nostalgically, "I was sad to see the lunar module go. If I could have brought it back, I'd have liked to put it up in my backyard."

For the past three days, the recovery team had been preparing for the spaceship's landing in the Pacific Ocean. The ground staff knew that this preparation could prove futile, though, as Apollo might land anywhere within a 500 by 250 foot area. If she landed upside down, the spacecraft would be nearly invisible and entirely undetectable by the radar of the ships, helicopters and air squadrons massed in the world's largest ocean.

With minutes to go, Apollo was still drifting slightly off course. Mission control ordered a minor correction, and crew and ground staff exchanged thanks and compliments. Nineteen seconds after penetrating the atmosphere, Apollo, as expected, entered a period of maximum heat and lost contact with her earthly mentors. Radio blackout should have endured for three minutes; at the end of this time, there was still no word. The rescuers resumed breathing only after sighting Apollo and her parachutes breaking through the cloud barrier. More than twenty years later, Gene Krantz, mission control's flight director, fought to describe that moment: "it was neat."

EXHIBIT 1   1938 Vintage Submarine (The USS Croaker)

EXHIBIT 2 *The Times*—June 2, 1939

THE TIMES FRIDAY JUNE 2 1939

SUBMARINE MISSING

SILENCE AFTER DIVING

MANY EXPERTS ON BOARD

MINESWEEPERS TO THE RESCUE

There was growing anxiety last night concerning the new British submarine Thetis which, after diving during trials off Birkenhead, was not seen again. She is believed to have 79 men on board.

The Admiralty, in an official statement at 11 p.m., said:

"The Admiralty regrets to announce that H.M. Submarine Thetis, which was carrying out acceptance trials in Liverpool Bay, dived at 13.40 hours [1.40 p.m.] and has failed to surface at the time she intended, which was three hours after diving.

"The Thetis was built by Cammell Laird, Limited, and was manned by a naval crew of five officers and 48 ratings. There were also four other naval officers on board and certain of the builders' technicians, the exact number of whom is not yet known.

"H.M.S. Brazen is now in the position in which the submarine was last reported. Air patrols organized by the R.A.F. were carried out before dark and will resume operations at daylight to-morrow.

"The Sixth Destroyer Flotilla, the First Minesweeper Flotilla, the submarines Cachalot and Porpoise, and H.M.S. Belfast are proceeding at full speed to render all assistance possible.

"Captain J. A. P. MacIntyre, chief of staff to Rear-Admiral Submarines, has proceeded in H.M.S. Winchelsea to take charge of the operations.

It was stated at the Admiralty shortly after 3 o'clock this morning that no news had been received of definite location of the submarine, and that any reports indicating or suggesting her location are entirely without official confirmation.

NAMES OF OFFICERS AND CREW

At 2.15 this morning the Admiralty announced:—

The following are known to have been on board the Thetis, and all next of kin have been informed:—

Captain H. P. K. Oram, Engineer Captain S. Jackson, Commander R. G. B. Hayter, Commander (E) L. G. Pennington, Lieutenant (E) C. M. H. Henderson, Lieutenant-Commander G. H. Dolus, Lieutenant H. Chapman, Lieutenant F. G. Woods, Lieutenant W. A. W. Poland, Commissioned Engineer R. D. Glenn.

Chief E.R.A. W. C. Ormes, P/M 14525; Chief Stoker H. J. Dillon Shallard, P/K 58669; P.O. T. T/Goad, C/J 108933; E.R.A. A. W. Byrne, P/MX 47269; Chief E.R.A. P. F. Jackson, P/MX 46112.

P.O. E. Mitchell, P/J 102658; P.O. (Tel.) J. A. Hope, D/J 81414; C.P.O. G. P. Cornish, C/J 71379; E.R.A. J. C. Creasy, D/MX 47651; A.B. J. Wilson, C/JX 138072; E.R.A. H. W. E. French, D/MX 49582; E.R.A. H. G. Howells, D/MX 50785; S.P.O. J. W. Wells, D/KX 76558; Cook J. C. Hughes, P/MX 48198; P.O. C. E. Smithers, C/JX 129326; Leading Stoker W. C. Arnold, P/KX 78879.

L. Stoker R. S. Brooke, D/KX 81583; L. Tel. W. E. Allen, D/JX 135513; L. Stoker J. S. Feeney, C/KX 81225; L. Stoker T. W. Kenney, C/KX 82462; Stoker W. Orrock, D/KX 85667; Stoker T. Bambrick, D/KX 86327; L. Stoker D. Cunningham, C/KX 80547; L. Stoker E. J. Youels, D/KX 80198; Stoker J. Craig, D/KX 77855; Stoker A. G. Hills, P/K 61207; Stoker L. E. Green, P/KX 80815; Stoker A. E. Yates, D/KX 81352; Stoker W. A. Matthews, C/KX 87674; Stoker W. T. Hole, D/KX 80876; Stoker A. H. Dunn, D/KX 86322.

L. Sig. F. B. Batten, D/JX 129058; A.B. N. Longstaff, P/JX 132478; A.B. J. H. Turner, D/JX 134566; L.S. W. A. Lock, C/JX 134188; Tel. C. T. W. Graham, P/J 112924; A.B. J. A. Morgans, P/JX 132797; A.B. S. Crombleholme, D/SSX 17810; L. Tel. G. A. Harwood, C/JX 134789; A.B. S. W. G. Stevens, P/JX 135921; A.B. F. Rogers, D/JX 13735; L.S.A. H. Smith, D/J 80062. A.B. E. A. Kendrick, D/JX 157904; A.B. J. Costley, P/J 84330; L.S. W. L. Hambrook, P/J 115289; Tel. T. W. Mortimer, D/JX 138326; L.S. J. R. Read, C/J 107220; L. Steward F. N. Stock, C/LX 21640.

20 TECHNICIANS

Mr. S. Woodward, secretary of Messrs. Cammell Laird, said that on board the submarine, in addition to the naval men, were 20 Cammell Laird technicians and a pilot. He added that it was not expected that it would be possible to announce any of the names of the Cammell Laird men until to-day.

It is computed that the submarine has sufficient air to last for 36 hours. No messages have been received from her, and every effort is being made to locate the vessel, which is somewhere on the sandy and muddy bottom of Liverpool Bay, probably in about 132ft. of water.

Soon after 10 p.m. the Mersey Docks and Harbour Board's salvage vessel Vigilant left the Princess landing stage, Liverpool, to search for the sunken submarine, which is believed to be lying some miles from the Mersey Bar lightship. Another salvage vessel, the Salvor, left later.

EXHIBIT 2 *Cont.*

THE TIMES FRIDAY, JUNE 2 1939

COMPANY'S STATEMENT

In a statement last night Messrs. Cammell Laird declared:—

"We are absolutely in the dark at the moment as to what has happened. The submarine, carrying 20 men of our staff in charge of Mr. Crout and a number of Admiralty experts, left our yard at high water, about 10 a.m., to-day. She was accompanied by a tug, and it is from the tug, we understand, that the Admiralty received a message that something is amiss.

"As far as we know the submarine was last heard of in Mersey Bay, and we cannot yet make any definite statement as to what has happened. Following messages between the firm and the Admiralty one of our officials, Mr. J. Watters, left the yard to-night in the Vigilant.

"The Vigilant is one of the vessels of the Mersey Docks and Harbour Board, and when she reaches Mersey Bay we expect a full account of what has occurred."

It was not a part of the exercise for the submarine to send signals during the time she was submerged, and nothing was thought amiss until she did not come to the surface. A Cammell Laird tug with a submarine officer on board was standing by during the exercise, and is still standing by in the hope of giving assistance.

The pilot in the Thetis is 25-year-old Mr. N. D. Wilcox, of Carlaw Road, Trenton, Birkenhead. His father and brother are also Mersey pilots. There are several wrecks in the vicinity of the spot outside the bar where the submarine dived, and officials fear that she may have struck a submerged object which put her electrical equipment out of action.

From wireless messages received by the Dock Board, it is understood that when the submarine failed to reappear the charter tug wirelessed a message to the pilot-boat at Point Lynas, off the Anglesey coast, and this was relayed to Liverpool. It was from this message that the Admiralty sent out their S O S.

Mist prevailed over the sea in Liverpool Bay last night. From the north Welsh coast visibility was only about five miles.

MESSAGE TO CINEMAS

There was intense activity in the Home Fleet at Portland last night. The Commander-in-Chief Home Fleet, Admiral Sir Charles M. Forbes, ordered telephone messages to be sent to all cinemas and theatres in Weymouth and Portland recalling men serving in the 1st Anti-Submarine Flotilla and the 6th Destroyer Flotilla.

The notice which was flashed on the screens in each place read:—

"Service notice.—S.O.S.—All ratings of the 1st Anti-Submarine Flotilla and 6th Destroyer Flotilla must return to their ships immediately."

The managers in each case also posted notices outside and many ratings were prevented from going into the theatres and told to go back to their ships.

Eight destroyers of the Tribal class left Portland for Birkenhead at 10 p.m., and the ships of the 1st Anti-Submarine Flotilla, the Achates, Walpole, Vanquisher, Widgeon, and Bittern, were also getting ready to sail during the night. These ships, as well as the destroyers, are all fitted with the latest and secret detector devices used in under-water operations for locating submerged craft.

Two sister ships of the Thetis, the Triumph and the Titan, are at present carrying out trials at Portland, and the Thetis would have gone there in the ordinary course to carry out her trials.

MINESWEEPERS SAIL

The 1st Minesweeper Flotilla, comprising the Hebe, Niger, Speedy, Sharpshooter, Salamander, Hazard, and Seagull, left Brixham shortly after 10 p.m. and proceeded to Birkenhead. All the officers and men who were on leave at Brixham were recalled, and there was a very speedy response.

EXHIBIT 3 *The Times*—June 3, 1939

LITTLE HOPE FOR MEN IN SUBMARINE

DAY AND NIGHT RESCUE EFFORTS

FOUR SAVED BY ESCAPE APPARATUS

NO REAPPEARANCE OF STERN AT LOW WATER

Little hope was held out early to-day of saving any more lives from the submarine Thetis, which has been lying on the sea bottom off Llandudno since Thursday afternoon, although the Admiralty stated that at 2 o'clock divers reported faint tappings.

Yesterday morning four men had come safely to the surface by means of the Davis escape apparatus.

At 10 o'clock last night the Admiralty announced that it had not been possible to resume efforts to cut a hole in the hull of the Thetis through which to extricate survivors. The tail of the submarine, which had been protruding from the water in the morning, was submerged by the tide during the afternoon. It had been hoped that it would reappear when the tide slackened about 6 p.m., but that hope proved vain. This seems to indicate that more water may have found its way into the boat.

It was officially stated at Cammell Laird's shortly before midnight that an attempt was then being made to lift the Thetis with camels, but soon afterwards they announced that there was little hope left for the men remaining in the ship.

Submarines carry large stores of compressed air in reservoirs, but much of that was no doubt used in the attempt to bring her to the surface when the accident first occurred. It is unlikely that even with that aid there could be any survivors this morning.

EXHIBIT 3 *Cont.*

FOUND AFTER 18 HOURS

VESSEL'S BOW IN 130 FEET OF WATER

From Our Special Correspondent

LIVERPOOL, JUNE 3

Early to-day it was stated that little hope could be held out of saving the 86 men left in the submarine Thetis, which is lying on the sea bottom in Liverpool Bay. Four men had been rescued yesterday morning by means of the Davis Escape Apparatus.

At Cammell Lairds' yard at Birkenhead last night some of the relatives were allowed to go through into the yard and there was a feeling of deepest anxiety. Among those who had gathered was the

wife of the commander of the Thetis, Mrs. Bolus. She talked to many of the wives and mothers of the men on board and urged some of them to go home and rest.

At 2 a.m. the destroyer Eskimo arrived at Liverpool from the scene of the disaster, bringing Lieutenant Woods, one of the survivors, who was then taken by ambulance to the Southern Hospital. He is stated to be suffering from shock. It is understood that two other survivors will be landed later, either here or at Portland.

The locating of the submarine off Llandudno and the attempts to rescue the men on board have been a grim race against time. It was on Thursday that the vessel went on her acceptance trials from the Mersey, and it was at 8.45 this morning that it was officially announced that half an hour earlier, or 18½ hours after she had made her last dive, she had been located.

FOUR MEN SAVED

The Admiralty issued the following announcement shortly after 10 a.m.:—

"H.M. submarine Thetis has been located in a position 14 miles from Great Ormes Head. Her bow is in 130ft. of water and her stern is on the surface. Captain Oram, Lieutenant Woods, Leading Stoker Arnold, and Mr. F. Shaw, of Cammell Lairds, have escaped by Davis escape apparatus."

Captain Oram escaped to direct the salvage operations and to make a full report on the state of the submarine. The commanding officer and all the remainder of the crew were alive at 10 o'clock, and salvage equipment was being rushed to the spot. The Thetis was first sighted by the destroyer Brazen at 7.50 a.m., and it was two and a half hours later that the Admiralty announced the rescue of the four men.

By daylight there was an anxious crowd at the Birkenhead shipyard gates of Cammell Laird, Limited, where the Thetis had been built. Many of the wives, mothers, and other relatives of the men in the submarine had gathered, and their faces bore the marks of the strain through which they had been passing.

The full resources of the Services were mobilized in the search for the Thetis. Eight R.A.F. aeroplanes scoured the sea, and more than 20 warships steamed throughout the night to the rescue. It was an airman who yesterday first saw the marker buoys released by the Thetis, and a destroyer at once made for the spot. The water was about 132ft. deep at the point in Liverpool Bay where the Thetis descended.

As the day wore on and no further rescues were announced there was a return of the anxiety of the early morning. Communication with the submarine crew was maintained by divers tapping on the hull, and oxy-acetylene apparatus, it was thought, might be used to cut a hole in the stern in order to release the men. Air in the vessel was estimated to be sufficient to last until 1.40 a.m. to-day.

At first it was thought there were 79 men in the vessel, but the names given this afternoon by Cammell Laird's of their staff on board the submarine show, however, that there are at least 90 men in the vessel. These included, in addition to the crew of 58, 29 members of Cammell Laird's staff and three employees of Vickers-Armstrong. With the four rescued this leaves at least 86 men still in the submarine.

The following is an official list of the employees of Cammell Laird's in the submarine:—

Mr. R. W. Crout, assistant shipyard manager; Mr. A. S. Watkinson, assistant engineer manager; Mr. Roberson, assistant engineer manager; Mr. Armstrong, assistant electrical engineer manager; Mr. Kipling, foreman caulker; Mr. Owen, foreman electrician; Mr. A. Robinson, foreman engineer; and G. Scarth, A. Craven, and Watterson, ship's fitters; Beatty, caulker; E. Lewis, S. Broad, C. Hamilton, A. Chinn, W. Smith (apprentice), and G. Somers, electricians; F. Shaw, W. Brown, Griffith, Smith, Quinn, Eccleston, Homer, Page, and Gresner, engineer fitters.

Rear-Admiral B. C. Watson, commanding submarines, arrived in Liverpool during the evening to direct rescue operations; a destroyer was waiting to take him to the scene.

EXHIBIT 3 *Cont.*

DIVERS FROM SCAPA

The War-time salvage boat, Ranger, of the Liverpool and Glasgow Salvage Association, has been at the spot since the morning. The Ranger, carrying oxy-acetylene equipment, two experienced divers, air compressors, and a pipe through which it was thought a connexion might be made through the hull giving an air supply to the men, reported at about 6 p.m. that it had got a lift rod under the submarine, but the effort was unsuccessful.

A party of Admiralty divers who were flown to Speke Airport, Liverpool, from Scapa Flow were taken aboard the destroyer Matabele, which left immediately for the scene of the wreck.

AT THE SCENE OF THE WRECK

TWO VAIN ATTEMPTS TO RAISE THETIS

FROM OUR CORRESPONDENT

LLANDUDNO, JUNE 3

About 2 o'clock this morning the tug Stormcock arrived at Llandudno carrying an official who, after consultation with the pier authorities, was driven away in the pier manager's car. The squad of St. John ambulance workers, who had been waiting all last evening, were then informed that their services would not be needed. Their dismissal was taken to imply that there was no longer hope of saving more men from the Thetis.

At 10 o'clock last night the Llandudno motor-lifeboat returned home after an absence of about nine hours, several of which it spent alongside the salvage ship which was working over the lost submarine.

Shortly after 1 o'clock in the afternoon the lifeboat set out with Dr. A. Maddock Jones, a local surgeon, carrying medical equipment. The sea was moderately choppy and the voyage took 2½ hours. Dr. Jones was first put aboard the destroyer Somali and later in the salvage ship Vigilant, where the rescued men had been removed.

Another doctor had meanwhile been flown from Holyhead by seaplane, and Dr. Jones remained on board to go back to Holyhead by the seaplane. At 8 o'clock the lifeboat left for home.

The coxswain of the lifeboat, Mr. Robin Williams, of Llandudno, said there were six destroyers, six tugs, a minesweeper, and several salvage vessels anchored in a circle around the spot where the submarine had sunk.

A number of divers had been down, experts who had worked on the salvaging of the German fleet at Scapa Flow. Two attempts had been made to bring the submarine to the surface. When he left, the vessels were getting their searchlights ready with the intention of working all night, and he formed the impression that they had hoped to get the submarine to the surface during the hours of darkness. Their plan apparently was to run it ashore on the nearest shelving beach, probably at the mouth of the Menai Straits, near Beaumaris.

So far as he could tell the submarine was lying nearly flat on the bed of the sea and apparently they had hoped at the rising tide to bring her to the surface by means of camels and hawsers. There seemed little hope that the remaining men would be alive.

At midnight it was stated at the Admiralty that four men only had been saved from the submarine. They were picked up by the destroyer Brazen and all survive. "There are unconfirmed reports that two others were drowned in trying to escape," it was added.

STERN SWEPT UNDER BY TIDE

DIVERS BAFFLED BY CURRENT

FROM OUR NAVAL CORRESPONDENT

The sequence of events leading up to the accident to the submarine was as follows. The Thetis, laid down in December, 1936, and launched 18 months later from the Birkenhead yard of Messrs. Cammell Laird, was on the point of completion. It is the practice for the officers and men of a new submarine to be attached to her for some months before completion, not only that they may be fully acquainted with all the intricate mechanism of their ship, but also because the trials of a submarine call for a fully trained crew, expert in the highly specialized art of working a submersible vessel. It is not possible for the builders to carry out the trials themselves before handing the craft over to the Navy.

The preliminary trials, including diving trials, of the Thetis had all been carried out successfully without a hitch. On Thursday she put to sea from Liverpool, attended by a tug, to carry out diving trials at sea, culminating in a three-hour dive.

The details of the trials carried out have not been made public by the Admiralty, but they probably included surface running under the Diesel engines, together with preliminary "trimming for diving," and shorter dives before the official three-hour trial was begun.

90 PERSONS ON BOARD

As always on such occasions, there were many people on board beside the boat's own crew. Captain Oram, in command of the flotilla which the Thetis was to join on completion, and which already contains one boat of the same class, was on board with some of his expert staff officers, 26 from Messrs. Cammell Laird, the builders, officials and workmen, and three from Messrs. Vickers-Armstrongs, makers of the gun armament, were on board to turn over their handiwork to the naval ship's company as soon as the trials should be completed. There were also the pilot, who had brought the ship down river, and two caterers. Together with the ship's own naval complement, there were thus about 90 persons on board.

This is no excessive number. One thinks, perhaps, of a submarine as a small craft, but actually the Thetis displaces some 1,090 tons in surface trim, and is 265ft. long. Moreover, it is an invariable practice for submarines going to sea to carry a set of Davis submarine-escape apparatus for every person on board; no exception to that rule was made in this case.

The Thetis submerged for her three-hour dive in the early afternoon of Thursday. It was only when she failed to surface at the appointed time that anxiety was aroused. Assistance was at once summoned to search for and locate her, and various ships of the Home Fleet were ordered to the spot. Machines of the Royal Air Force joined in the search, and it was actually one of them which, early yesterday morning, located the mark buoy which had been released from the submarine when she failed to return to the surface by her own efforts. She was found some 40 miles from the mouth of the Mersey, 14 miles north from Great Orme Head, Llandudno.

EXHIBIT 4 *The Times*—June 4, 1939

THE KING'S DEEP SYMPATHY

GREATLY DISTRESSED

ROYAL FAMILY AND THE RELATIVES

The First Lord of the Admiralty has received the following message from the King:—

" The Queen and I are greatly distressed to hear of the disaster to Thetis, which has been attended by the sad loss of so many lives. Please convey our deep sympathy to the relatives of those on board.—GEORGE, R.I."

The First Lord has sent the following reply :—

With humble duty I beg to tender thanks to your Majesty for your gracious and most sympathetic message, which will be sent to the relatives of all those who have lost their lives in the disaster to H.M.S. Thetis.

The First Lord has also received the following message from Queen Mary:—

" I am deeply distressed to learn of the tragic disaster to H.M.S. Thetis. Please convey my heartfelt sympathy to the wives and families of all those who have lost their lives.-- MARY, R."

SYMPATHY ABROAD

FRENCH MESSAGE OF REGRET

FROM OUR OWN CORRESPONDENT

PARIS, JUNE 4

The disaster to the Thetis has aroused deep and sincere regret in France, and everywhere spontaneous expressions of sympathy make it clear that the loss of so many brave men could hardly have been more deplored if they had belonged to this country.

M. Campinchi, the Minister of Marine, has sent the following telegram to the French Naval Attaché in London : —

Kindly convey to the First Lord of the Admiralty my regretful condolences for the tragic accident of the Thetis, the attempts to save which we had been following with fraternal anxiety. The entire French Navy joins in mourning with the British Navy, and the families of our crews express an affectionate compassion which unites them to the families of the brave men lost in the Thetis.

HERR HITLER'S TELEGRAM

FROM OUR CORRESPONDENT

BERLIN, JUNE 4

Herr Hitler, in a telegram to King George VI expresses his own and the German nation's sympathy over the disaster which has befallen the submarine Thetis. The sympathy finds a warm echo in the German Press. The *Völkischer Beobachter* writes to-day : —

It is not too much to say that not only Britons but also countless newspaper readers in Germany followed the rescue attempts, which at first appeared so promising, with growing anxiety. Such events unite all-- beyond political and other divisions--in a communal hope. To-day, when hopes are lost, our warm sympathy goes out not only to the relatives of the dead but also to the nation in whose service the lives were lost.

EXHIBIT 5 *The Times*—June 5, 1939

THE TIMES MONDAY JUNE 5 1939

99 LIVES LOST IN THE THETIS

STATEMENT IN PARLIAMENT TO-DAY

MESSAGE OF SYMPATHY FROM THE KING

A MANSION HOUSE FUND

The submarine Thetis lies at the bottom of Liverpool Bay, with 99 men dead inside her, only four having escaped. All doubt about the fate of the others was dispelled on Saturday afternoon by the following official announcement:—

"The Admiralty regret that there is no longer justification for hope that any further lives can be saved from Thetis. Salvage work proceeds."

The Admiralty announced last night that "some little time" might elapse before the Thetis was brought to the surface.

The King has sent the following message to the First Lord of the Admiralty:—

"The Queen and I are greatly distressed to hear of the disaster to Thetis, which has been attended by the sad loss of so many lives. Please convey our deep sympathy to the relatives of those on board."

The Lord Mayor of London will open to-morrow a Mansion House Fund on behalf of the dependents of those who have lost their lives in the disaster.

HOPE GIVEN UP

END OF AN ANXIOUS WAIT

FROM OUR SPECIAL CORRESPONDENT

BIRKENHEAD, June.

A telegram from the Admiralty stating that "hope of saving lives in the Thetis must now be abandoned" was posted late yesterday afternoon at the entrance gate to Messrs. Cammell Laird's yard, through which the men of the Thetis passed to their last duties four days ago. The dreaded notice had long been awaited, for hope was slight on Friday night, and, except for a misconceived rumour, had dwindled with each succeeding hour. Indeed, there was but a small cluster of people round the gate when the official statement was made: overnight there had been a crowd of 2,000 waiting, harrowed, but hoping.

They had a desperately anxious wait. Unlike crowds which gather at the pithead after a mining disaster, they were set far removed from the scene in point of time as well as distance; four hours elapsed between one message and the next. Rumours sprang up quickly in such circumstances, and there was no information by which to check them. This lack of news was disconcerting, and those on the spot were perhaps two and a half between three and a half and five hours, according to the tide, to return from the scene of operations. Once the destroyer Ashanti called at the Princes Landing Stage to embark important officials, but it brought no message of real hope.

CHLORINE GAS POISONING

Actually it was later apparent that the wait was vain long before it was actually abandoned, because an official of Cammell Laird's announced to the journalists in the early afternoon that the men in the Thetis must have died about midnight: from chlorine gas poisoning. Submarines carry storage batteries to provide power for the electric motors which are used to drive the boat when submerged, and it is assumed that water got to the batteries and caused them to give off the gas. There is evidence in support of this, because one of the rescued men—the second in fact to be released by the Davis apparatus—had to be treated for chlorine gas poisoning, and two of the three other survivors are Captain Oram, was the first to escape and, though he reported that the air was fairly he appeared so little affected that it is thought possible that the gas had not formed in any great quantity before he left the ship. Unfortunately it is not possible to make contact with him. The man treated for gas was Frank Shaw, of Ivydale Road, Tranmere. When I called at his house I was told that he was in bed, and his doctor had forbidden discussion of the disaster even with members of his own family. At the Royal Southern Hospital, Liverpool, there was equally no hope of asking any questions of Lieutenant F. G. Woods, the only other survivor, brought ashore; a naval doctor is watching by his bedside.

SOME CONJECTURES

In all probability it was this escape of gas which limited the rescue to four. Captain Oram has stated that, when he left, the others were preparing to leave in their turn. Something stopped them. That something, later on, was possibly the new position of the ship after she was moved and wholly immersed by the high tide on Friday evening, because the David apparatus cannot be used if a ship has turned turtle. But nine hours elapsed between the escape and the final sinking. One conjecture is that the apparatus jammed in the magazine, but the more likely explanation seems to be that the men left in the submarine were overcome by gas. Against this are to be set the Admiralty statements that tapping from within announced that some of the men at least were still alive, but it has not been possible here to establish whether these tappings were in fact Morse messages or whether they were accidental noises, or, as suggested by the general manager of Cammell Laird's, an odd release by a compressor valve still functioning automatically in the flooded part of the ship. But conjecture gets us nowhere, and clearly more definite information must await the beaching of the Thetis, which is now engaging the attention of the salvage vessels.

A LONG RAISING PROCESS

Late last night one learned that one of the camels had been connected to the sunken submarine, and that at subsequent slack tides two other, waiting near by, would if possible be secured in the same way. Then, having between them raised the vessel a few feet, they would be towed landwards. If the submarine should be stopped by a sandbank or other obstruction it would be raised still higher, and the towing would begin again. This would be a long operation. It might take days, or even weeks, if conditions were adverse. Fortunately the sea is calm, but even so it takes a long time to lift the dead weight of a waterlogged submarine. The method is to sink the camels about 40, by admitting water to them, and, as the water is pumped out of the camels, air takes its place; they rise and bring the submarine with them. As they do so the chains are taken in by the obstruction through which the vessel rises. Thus if the whole of this lifting only a few feet are taken up. The practical plan is to perform a few of these operations as necessary; and once the ship is clear of the bottom lowing will begin somewhere on the north Wales coast, which is the nearest land.

EXHIBIT 5 *Cont.*

THE TIMES MONDAY JUNE 5 1939

CAUSE OF DISASTER

STATEMENT BY BUILDERS' SPOKESMAN

When this has been done answers will be found for many questions which have been raised in Birkenhead. The first obviously is the cause of the mishap. Mr. R. S. Johnson, managing director of Cammell Laird's, announced yesterday afternoon that it was water entering the first and second compartments of the submarine which put her nose down at so sharp an angle that the ship struck at 45deg. in water of a depth only half her own length. This presumably is Captain Oram's explanation. The second question is unanswerable now—Why did not the remaining men use the Davis apparatus? Another question which people who have not visited the scene may ask is why it was not found possible to cut a way through the stern while it was sticking out of the water. They have read that the sea was calm, and so it was—comparatively. But the rowing boats from which the work was operated bobbed about on the swell, and the submarine herself, with her nose stuck in the sea bottom, was pivoting and rocking because of the under-currents pressing on her sides. To work at all on a smooth surface in these conditions was extremely hazardous, and the men who attempted it are in no way to blame. From the start the task was probably beyond them, given even the best of conditions, because they had little time in which to cut through the outer shell, get through a watertight manhole, and, all the time working in a very restricted space, cut through a further watertight door. With the ship on a steep slope, with no means of supporting the tail of the submarine, the work was beyond human contrivance.

One more question is being asked here, and will certainly be raised at the official inquiry. Why were not salvage vessels stationed near the testing grounds as a precaution against accident? Apparently this has not been the practice, and Cammell Laird's have built and tested many submarines before this. It has even been suggested that two of the three camels now at the wreck were high and dry and had to wait priceless hours for a tide to float them, but Sir Lionel Warner, managing director of the Mersey Docks and Harbour Board, scouted this when I spoke to him on the telephone. He said they were in the dock, and were ready to go out when requisitioned by the Admiralty, who were in control of the salvage operations. He added that the salvage vessels Vigilant and Salvor put the necessary gear on board and were ready to leave within an hour of being summoned. This raises the question why all salvage vessels were not summoned earlier. The answer given is that it was hoped that the Thetis would extricate herself under her own power, but the facts remain that her propeller was above water at 7.50 a.m. on Friday, that one camel arrived in the evening, and that the others were much later on the spot. It is unfortunate that all these queries should arise, but there has been no official pronouncement on the matter to answer them at once.

MIDNIGHT CONFERENCE

Last night a conference was held on board the Somali. It was conducted by the Third Sea Lord, Rear-Admiral B. A. Fraser, and was attended by Admiral Sir Martin Dunbar-Nasmith, V.C., Commander-in-Chief at Plymouth, who had come by flying-boat, and Rear-Admiral B. C. Watson (Rear-Admiral, Submarines), by Mr. R. S. Johnson, managing director of Messrs. Cammell Laird, and by the captains of the destroyers at the scene of the disaster. The conference lasted until 3 o'clock this morning, when Mr. Johnson returned to Liverpool.

This afternoon Sir Martin Dunbar-Nasmith took off by air to return to Plymouth, and the destroyer Winchelsea brought ashore the Third Sea Lord, Rear-Admiral Watson, Captain Oram, the first man who escaped from the Thetis, and also the divers from Scapa Flow, who are going back to-day. The Third Sea Lord was in a hurry to catch a train to London at 4 o'clock. Captain Oram was in the car with him. In the second car were Rear-Admiral Watson and Mr. Johnson. Rear-Admiral Watson stated: " We have to refer you to the Admiralty for any information. Salvage work has been started, and is proceeding satisfactorily. We are hoping to bring her here."

EXHIBIT 5 *Cont.*

THE TIMES MONDAY JUNE 5 1939

THE DIVERS' TASK

WORK HINDERED BY STRONG TIDE

One of the divers stated that they arrived from Scapa Flow on Friday night, and got to the scene shortly after midnight. It was easy for people not there to make criticisms, but the work was conducted in the dark with a strong tide running, and the divers could remain under for only an hour.

Another diver said that he went down to the submarine at 1 o'clock, and while he was there heard faint tappings some distance away from where he was. There was no regular Morse communication. He could not hang on any longer, and had to come away because the tide was so strong. He never got near the hatch through which the four men escaped, so he could not say whether it was damaged. The submarine is lying on her keel on a firm, hard shingle bed, but has a list of about 30deg. He was down this morning trying to put a mark buoy on the wreck. There is a wreck buoy marking the position, but they wanted a buoy made fast to the wreck so that they could know where she was lying. They had almost succeeded when they were called to the surface again because of the tide. This morning the submarine was not much embedded, because of the hard bottom. The nose was more down than the tail, because of the water which she had taken in.

Mr. Johnson told the Press representatives that the eight destroyers are leaving to-morrow for their normal cruise, but the camels and two sloops are standing by. Captain Oram has gone to the Submarine School at Gosport. Mr. Johnson stated that the ship was now being salved by workers commissioned by Cammell Laird's on behalf of the underwriters. The operations were no longer being directed by the Admiralty. So long as life existed, the Admiralty actually did all they could to save their men, but now they are known to be dead and the matter is one of salvage. His firm take charge, as the ship is theirs, the contract with the Admiralty not having been completed. He could not say how long the salvage operations would take. They might take two days, or two weeks.

Mr. Johnson told the Press representatives that the eight destroyers are leaving to-morrow for their normal cruise, but the camels and two sloops are standing by. Captain Oram has gone to the Submarine School at Gosport. Mr. Johnson stated that the ship was now being salved by workers commissioned by Cammell Laird's on behalf of the underwriters. The operations were no longer being directed by the Admiralty. So long as life existed, the Admiralty actually did all they could to save their men, but now they are known to be dead and the matter is one of salvage. His firm take charge, as the ship is theirs, the contract with the Admiralty not having been completed. He could not say how long the salvage operations would take. They might take two days, or two weeks.

SALVAGE WORK

NAVAL HELP FOR BUILDERS

The Admiralty issued the following statement at 11.15 a.m. yesterday:—

"Salvage work on H.M.S. Thetis is proceeding, but it may be some little time before the vessel can be brought to the surface. Messrs. Cammell Laird and Co. will be responsible for the work from now onwards, but H.M.S. Tedworth, diving school tender, H.M.S. Hebe, and H.M.S. Seagull, with officers of the Submarine Service, will remain on the spot to render any assistance or advice required by the firm.

"A full inquiry is being held as soon as practicable."

The Hebe and Seagull are minesweepers.

MINISTER TO REPORT TO COMMONS

FROM OUR PARLIAMENTARY CORRESPONDENT

An official statement on the submarine disaster is to be made this afternoon in the House of Commons by Mr. Geoffrey Shakespeare, Parliamentary Secretary to the Admiralty.

Public feeling has been deeply stirred by the heavy loss of life in circumstances which at first raised hopes that the men in the Thetis might be saved, and M.P.s will be anxious to have the fullest information available. But much relevant information must still be lacking. The whole matter will have to be investigated by a naval Court of Inquiry before the Admiralty are in possession of the full facts. It is quite likely that M.P.s will press for the investigation by the Court of Inquiry to be held in public.

LORD STANHOPE

Lord Stanhope, First Lord of the Admiralty, has been away from London since May 26 on a visit to the Home Fleet and various naval establishments in the Admiralty yacht H.M.S. Enchantress. When the accident to the Thetis was reported he was at Plymouth, and he at once conferred with the Commander-in-Chief there, Admiral Sir Martin Dunbar-Nasmith, V.C., under whose command the submarine would have come when she had finished her acceptance trials. The First Lord remained in close consultation with the responsible Commander-in-Chief, and all the information coming to the Admiralty was sent to him at Plymouth. Lord Stanhope will return to London to-day.

EXHIBIT 6 Apollo XIII Service Module after Jettison

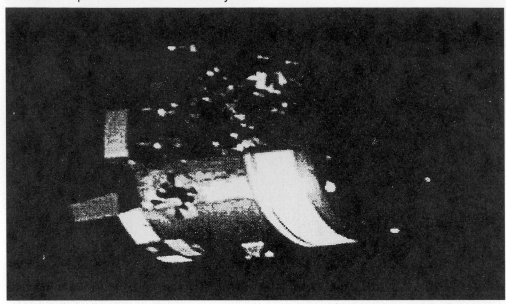

EXHIBIT 7 Mission Control Center During Apollo XIII Oxygen Cell Failure

EXHIBIT 8 Makeshift CO2 Filter

PPG: Developing a Self-Directed Work Force (A)

*(handwritten margin note, rotated): How are peer reviews & accepted by * *they should be anonymity reviews ?*

In December 1991 John Povlik, manager of PPG's Berea, Kentucky, windshield plant, and Don Stine, the plant's manager of employee services, sat down to take another look at peer review, a system in which fellow workers, rather than management, would be responsible for assessing an employee's job performance. As Stine pulled out his files on the subject, Povlik recalled the recent advice of a shop floor employee:

> Better not do it. You have people out there with totally clashing personalities. There is no way anyone's comments should go in anyone else's record.

Yet the first workers at Berea, hired in January 1990, had been told that they would eventually have the opportunity to evaluate their peers. Moreover, Povlik hoped to develop a fully self-directed work force at the plant, and peer review seemed like the logical next step. But many employees were against the idea. They had repeatedly told management that they were not interested in evaluating one another—although they had expressed a willingness to evaluate team coordinators and management staff.

COMPANY BACKGROUND

PPG Industries, with fifty production facilities in the United States and one hundred worldwide, was a global producer of flat glass, fiberglass, coatings and resins, chemicals, and medical electronics. In 1990 its sales totaled $6 billion, with $2.38 billion contributed by the Glass Group. Glass Group earnings were $332 million, and both sales and earnings were little changed from the previous year.

This case was prepared as the basis for class discussion rather than to illustrate either effective or ineffective handling of an administrative situation.

This case was prepared by Norman Klein and David A Garvin. Copyright © 1992 by the President and Fellows of Harvard College. Harvard Business School case 693-020.

The Glass Group made flat glass products for industrial, commercial and residential uses, and was also an original-market and replacement-market supplier of auto glass. Six of its seven U.S. float glass plants made standard flat glass from raw materials, while the latest float plant, in Perry, Georgia, produced new compositions of energy-saving glass for specialized applications. The auto glass plants, like the one in Berea, Kentucky, did not actually make glass; their manufacturing processes began with blanks of glass, made elsewhere, which were then cut, shaped, and processed further.

THE GLASS GROUP'S EVOLVING PLANT STRATEGY

Between 1958 and 1990 PPG built twelve new glass plants in the United States. Each contributed to an evolving plant strategy that focused on new approaches to managing the work force.

Union-free Plants

In 1957 all of the Glass Group's U.S. plants were under contract with the International Glass Workers Union or other unions. All contracts divided workers into two categories, production and maintenance, with work assignments further determined by job classifications and seniority. These categories meant that plant managers had little discretion in assigning work. Labor relations were often adversarial. After a particularly damaging strike, PPG management decided to pursue a "union-free" strategy for its new plants. In 1958 the first such plant was opened in Crestline, Ohio, and its workers were promised everything that a union could give them, except dues and strikes, if they would forgo representation. The issue eventually came to a vote, and Crestline workers elected not to have a union.

PPG later established union-free glass plants in several other locations, using the same model.

Further advances came in 1966–1968, when the company built plants in Tipton, Pennsylvania, and Meadville, Pennsylvania. Both continued the trend toward more cooperative labor relations and a more flexible work force. Meadville, for example, eliminated time clocks and placed all workers on salary. The company also strove to give management more flexibility in assigning work by creating fewer job levels and grades. Meadville operated with only 14 job levels; in contrast, the unionized plant in Crystal City, Missouri, had 67 job levels in the wareroom department alone.

Chehalis

A further step in the evolution came in 1986, with the opening of a new float glass plant in Chehalis, Washington. The plant was viewed by Gene Mosier, group vice president of the Glass Group, as a test bed for new ideas, and he asked that it be designed accordingly. Chehalis was the first PPG glass plant to serve a narrow geographic region, and the first to have a sales person stationed at the plant. It was also expected to make new formulations of glass, using a radically new technology. Mosier instructed his start-up team to "break the mold" of previous efforts. The chief engineer, for example, was told to be "as innovative and risk-taking as possible"; the plant manager, Larry McGee, recalled being instructed to:

> . . . try a different accounting system and different management organizations. In fact, at one point we were told that if we were one hundred percent successful we hadn't tried hard enough.

Because of its innovative, proprietary technology, Chehalis was expected to propel the company onto an entirely new learning curve for the making of glass. Technology and engineering concerns were therefore the overwhelming priority of the start-up team, and experts in technical design worked on a separate track from those, like McGee, who had been asked to develop new approaches to the work force. McGee recalled the irony of a visit he had paid to a Rohm and Haas plant the week before Chehalis's startup, where he had listened intently as he was advised, "Whatever you do, don't try to implement new technology and a new approach to managing people at the same time."

The advice came too late. McGee and his team had chosen a work system that represented a leap ahead in PPG's evolving plant strategy. Old job distinctions and roles were pushed aside, and six semi-autonomous work teams were created in their place. Each work area was to function as a separate team, as were department heads and clerical employees, and each team was encouraged to organize itself and find the best ways to assign and perform its work. Team members were encouraged to learn about costs, scrap ratios, and budgeting, and to take on responsibilities usually reserved for management. They were expected to become increasingly adept at day-to-day problem solving. Workers were also to rotate to new positions periodically; as they gained skills, their teams would acquire additional flexibility.

Despite these advances, Chehalis encountered severe problems. Its new technology took months to debug, and profit projections were never met. In 1989 McGee was promoted to director of technology transfer for the Glass Group; a year later he became director of human resources for the group. He soon learned of a corporate decision to mothball Chehalis. A downturn in the economy, the need to reline the melting furnace, and the desire to focus further technology development at the Perry, Georgia, plant were the primary causes.

Reactions to the closing varied. Some managers viewed Chehalis as an investment in the company's future and were unhappy about its closing. To them, it was a model of the technological strength and work force practices that would carry PPG into the twenty-first century. Others viewed the plant less favorably. They felt that it had absorbed more than its share of capital and human resources. The fact that it was four years old and still operating in the red was, in their eyes, reason enough to close it.

Looking back, McGee believed that the technology had progressed further because of the use of work teams, although some teams needed more direction than others. He also felt that the plant's customer service, regional sales, and lean staffing concepts had been a success. Overall, McGee credited Chehalis's workers with remarkable cohesion, initiative, and willingness to contribute, and regretted that the continuing sense of crisis, brought on by technical problems, never gave them a chance to show everything they could do. He also faulted himself:

> I pushed all kinds of decisions downward at Chehalis, and realized later that this created some confusion. In retrospect, I should have made clear which decisions were to be shared with workers and which were not, and should have been more attentive to the kind of consultive support the teams needed. Peer review, for example, didn't work.

From Chehalis to Perry

The float glass plant that opened in Perry, Georgia, in 1989 was a direct descendant of Chehalis. Perry was to produce some of the same specialized glass formulations that had been developed at Chehalis, using the same technology, although it was not designed to serve a distinct geographical region. Instead, Perry supplied a niche market that valued the unique properties of its glass.

Technology transfer was carefully staged from Chehalis to Perry, with months spent in planning to avoid past mistakes. Here again, the new production process was the primary focus, and McGee, who was by then the Glass Group's director of technology transfer, played a major role in ensuring a smooth transition. Perry was also intended to be the logical next step in the group's approach to work practices. It pioneered an innovative approach to employee selection, while further refining the power of work teams. Many of these same ideas were later incorporated at Berea.

PLANNING FOR BEREA

Rationale

In May 1988 the Auto Replacement Glass Division was at capacity and buying significant amounts of product from competitors. Senior management considered adding capacity at an existing plant in Greensburg, Pennsylvania, but opted instead for a new facility, capable of producing 600,000 windshields per year. The decision was made, in part, because of the traditional union-management relationship that had long existed at Greensburg.

PPG management approved a site in Berea, Kentucky, in November 1988. Robert Duncan, who had replaced Gene Mosier as group vice president, described three goals for the plant. Berea was to be a low-cost producer, provide needed capacity, and serve as the work force model that would point the way for changes at unionized plants like Greensburg. Duncan observed:

> My conviction is that we have to start improving existing plants, and making that a higher priority, as opposed to shutting down old plants and building new ones.

Implementation

John Povlik, the designated plant manager; John Kelleher, director of production and distribution; and several members of division engineering became the implementation team for Berea. Design and start up were expected to be much less demanding than at Chehalis, because Berea, while highly automated, was based on current, off-the-shelf technology. With the exception of one operation, proven processes and manufacturing methods were involved. Like Greensburg, Berea would also ship virtually all production to the division's distribution center in Chillicothe, Ohio, rather than dealing directly with customers.

When Povlik and Kelleher started to design the work system, they began with the strong belief that it should be the antithesis of Greensburg. Both men had managed at Greensburg at one time. It was in many ways a typical union plant, with two job categories, production and maintenance, and multiple job levels. Povlik recalled his frustration at seeing production workers being prohibited from making even minor repairs to their machines, and who then had to stand around while maintenance workers made the repairs. He was determined that Berea have only one job description for the entire plant. With one job, he reasoned, there would be complete flexibility in assigning work, fewer employees, and lower costs. For similar reasons, Povlik wanted Berea to have minimal supervision, supported by teamwork, and no physical division between the office and the plant. But a complete vision proved difficult to develop, as Kerry Rowles, the division manager, recalled:

> We wanted to go along the lines of Chehalis, but there was no clear picture of the endpoint, or sense of how to measure our progress. We just knew that at Berea we were counting on the ingenuity of workers on the floor to give us continuous improvement.

THE HIRING PROCESS

Chehalis, Perry, and Berea all required new skills of employees because of their innovative work systems. In particular, Povlik's plan to have flexible job assignments at Berea meant that every worker had to learn every job in the plant. Jeff Gilbert, director of human resources policy and practice, recalled:

> As we began to think about staffing Perry and Berea, one thing became clear: we didn't really have a way to select for those things which would be different from our traditional plants . . . things such as the ability to be a good team member, to communicate, and teach people how to do other jobs. Perry and Berea also required a greater emphasis on problem-solving skills and initiative, and you had to be able to organize work, because it wasn't going to be organized for you.

These needs soon led to the idea of using an assessment center to screen potential employees.

THE PERRY/BEREA ASSESSMENT CENTER

Assessment centers are an approach to screening employees that relies heavily on "live" behavior. Typically, they involve a simulation, or series of simulations, that mimic the demands of the job and require applicants to demonstrate their ability while trained evaluators observe their performance. Centers were first used in the early 1900s to select German military officers; during World War II they were used by the U.S. Office of Strategic Services to select agents. Programs to select, evaluate, and promote managers began to appear at companies like AT&T, General Electric, and Sears in the 1950s and 1960s, and most early efforts focused on first-level supervisors or middle managers.

In 1989 an assessment center was developed to select the first Perry employees. It was prompted, in part, by dissatisfaction with Chehalis's selection process, which lacked a systematic approach to identifying employees who best fit the proposed work system. The effort was spearheaded by Cheryl Schoenfeld, a human resources specialist at corporate headquarters. In partnership with Personnel Decisions, Inc., a leading consulting firm in designing selection processes, she began by developing a list of key dimensions of effective performance for Perry employees (see Exhibit 1). These were based on discussions with plant management about the critical job responsibilities and tasks of the plant's hourly jobs, and the skills, abilities and characteristics needed in employees. The resulting dimensions

EXHIBIT 1 Dimensions of Employee Performance

1. *Communication Skills*—the ability to speak and write clearly, understandably, and concisely, listen attentively to others, and inform others of important information.
2. *Judgment*—the ability to develop alternative courses of action and make decisions that are based on logical assumptions and that reflect factual information.
3. *Problem Solving*—the ability to seek and use information, understand and develop unique solutions to problems, learn new information, and anticipate and identify problems.
4. *Organizing Skills*—the ability to develop efficient strategies and procedures for accomplishing tasks, sequence tasks according to priority, and make efficient use of own time.
5. *Thoroughness and Accuracy*—the ability to follow tasks through to completion, check work for errors and ensure accuracy, keep track of important details, and not take short cuts.
6. *Initiative*—the ability to come up with ideas for improvement, show consistent energy, start work quickly, stay busy, take initiative to correct problems without being told, show pride in high quality work, and work well without direction.
7. *Performance Reliability and Adaptability*—the ability to maintain a good attendance record, come to work on time, consistently complete assigned tasks, easily adapt to changes in policies, procedures, or directions, and handle constructive criticism nondefensively.
8. *Interpersonal Skills*—the ability to get along with others, work together and help others when needed, and work through problems and disagreements with co-workers.

included the ability to establish sequences and procedures; to identify, weigh, and solve problems; to collaborate and resolve conflicts; and to show initiative and take pride in quality work. All were thought to be desirable for a self-directed work force organized in teams. From this list, interview questions and simulations were developed and used to select Perry employees.

Berea plant management completed the same questionnaire used for job analysis at Perry. Because the analysis identified the same dimensions of effective job performance at the two plants, management elected to use the same hiring process as Perry, with the same performance measures, interview questions, and simulations. This meant that all candidates would have to pass four written tests assessing their cognitive ability, respond successfully in interviews to questions about their past job behavior and its fit with the eight performance measures, and perform well on the Assessment Center simulations. Only candidates who survived the first two requirements would be asked to participate in the Assessment Center.

THE ASSESSMENT CENTER SIMULATIONS

The Assessment Center consisted of three simulations that required 2½ to 3 hours to complete. In all three, candidates were asked to play the role of a worker in a box-building simulation, and were informed that they would be evaluated by trained assessors.[1] They were also told: "This process provides a well-rounded view of your job-relevant skills." But they were *not* informed of the eight performance measures that would be used for evaluation.

The simulations began by telling candidates to assume they had been hired into a hypothetical company; their first step was to learn the job. The initial simulation asked candidates to construct a product—in this case, a paper box—by following a multi-step process and detailed instructions. At the same time, they were expected to adhere to quality

standards, conform to safety procedures, and make accurate measurements. (See Exhibit 2 for excerpts from the instructions for each of the Assessment Center simulations.) Because the product was one with which no candidate was likely to have had production experience, this simulation was expected to assess candidates' ability to learn new tasks.

The second simulation asked candidates to train another person to construct the same product. This simulation was used because employees at the plant would be involved in cross-training their peers. Several steps were involved. First, each candidate had to create training materials, including detailed written instructions. They were also given the opportunity to suggest improvements to the construction process they had originally followed. Then each candidate had to teach and coach a trainee through the box-building process. This part of the simulation was particularly challenging because, unknown to the candidates, the trainees, who were played by assessors, had been instructed to be slow and contrary, to resist instruction, and to make frequent mistakes.

In the third simulation, candidates were brought together in small groups to determine how best to construct the product as a team. Each group was responsible for planning their work, sequencing tasks, allocating tasks to members of the team, and setting production goals for a simulated production period. Any approach was permissible, with one exception: a team could not have each of its members produce boxes individually. A production session then ran for several minutes immediately after the planning session.

Each simulation had a slightly different purpose. The first simulation was designed to determine how well candidates followed instructions and used the information and resources available to them. In addition, assessors looked for good work habits: candidates who kept their work areas clean, avoided waste, used their safety gloves, and were responsive to critical comments about quality. The second simulation focused more on interpersonal and coaching skills, as well as the ability to improve processes. Because assessors were playing the role of a slow and resistant trainee, candidates were also judged on their ability to patiently offer clear instructions, remain supportive, and at the same time hold firm on quality and safety standards. In the final simulation, assessors

---

[1]The assessors consisted of Povlik, his 12-member staff, and 9 human relations experts from other PPG plants. All were trained before the sessions began.

The Box Building Exercise

1. Cut a sheet of 8½ by 11 paper in half, and then fold the half into thirds lengthwise.
2. Fold the paper twice widthwise so that you have perfect squares in all four corners, and then cut the paper along the lengthwise folds down to the widthwise folds.
3. Glue one of the model number labels to the outside bottom of the box.
4. Fold the end folds up so that one side flap goes outside of the middle flap, and the other goes inside.
5. All folds must be neat; the end flaps must match evenly; and the box labels must be properly centered on the outside bottom of the box.

The Training Exercise

1. Take 15 minutes to decide how you will train your new employee. Do everything you can to improve on the methods used to train you, including rewriting the instructions if you like.
2. Do whatever coaching is necessary to get the new employee to construct one box that meets the quality standards.
3. Next, urge the new employee to produce as many boxes as possible in ten minutes, and explain that you will reject any boxes that do not meet quality standards.

The Group Exercise

1. Working with the members of your team, decide how to best produce boxes as a group. Agree on a division of tasks, and decide who will play each role.
2. Agree on specific production goals.
3. When told to begin, your group should produce as many boxes as it can in the ten-minute production phase.

EXHIBIT 2   Excerpts from the Instructions for the Assessment Center Exercises

were looking for people who listened well and made good suggestions, and were both contributors and facilitators. Schoenfeld observed:

> We wanted to see how people interacted in a group, and to see who exhibited behavior that promoted the group's completion of its task—and conversely who might lead the group away from its mission.

These objectives were not always apparent to the individuals participating in the exercises. One Berea employee, who was one of the first new hires, recalled: "We didn't know what to expect, or what they were looking for." Another employee recalled showing up to participate in the exercise, only to find no one there. He eventually contacted a member of the plant staff, was told that there had been a mix up, and was directed to a different location. Management had, in fact, made a scheduling error, but the employee, who had no way of knowing, long suspected that sending him to the wrong location was part of the test.

The first candidates to successfully complete the assessment center were hired in January 1990. Because Povlik had been rethinking the original idea of a "one job" plant, two levels of workers were actually hired. The first level, called "support workers," had relatively little technical experience, while the second level, called "technicians," had demonstrated strong technical skills in previous jobs and would initially be assigned to the more technically demanding work stations. Of the original group hired, 35 were support workers and 5 were technicians. The job descriptions of the two groups were quite similar, although technicians were expected to take the lead in technical problem solving. They were also responsible for keeping track of the information at each of the "Sun stations" (the Sun computers that contained the data and diagnostics for each work area) and for logging significant events at the end of each shift.

All of the first hires lacked experience making windshields. None had worked before in a glass plant; some had never worked in a factory. To begin, they visited another PPG plant to see how windshields were made, and then spent several weeks receiving training, cleaning the plant, and installing equipment. During the training, each worker was assigned to one of five work areas in the plant, and was trained by the engineer temporarily overseeing that area. Production began late in April 1990 with a single shift.

THE PLANT IN OPERATION

Organization

The plant opened with a management team of 12; as second and third shifts were added, the number eventually grew to 20. By late 1991 the organization included a superintendent of operations, managers of employee services and plant services, coordinators of employee services and maintenance services, four team coordinators, five operations engineers, and several assistants. (See Exhibit 3 for an organization chart.) Of these, the team coordinators had the least traditional role. Most had formerly been first-level supervisors; here they were expected to support and facilitate the teams, but with little formal direction. When all three shifts were in operation, each coordinator was assigned a single shift, and the plant employed just over a hundred people.

The Production Process

The process began at the "cold end," so called because all of the steps at this work area were performed on glass that had yet to be heated. For each windshield, two blanks of glass were cut, one for the inner piece and one for the outer. Computer-controlled equipment cut the blanks, and then a robot smoothed the edges. Black borders and trademarks were silkscreened onto the windshield.

The next area consisted of the two furnaces, or lehrs. Here, the inner and outer pieces from the cold end were placed one on top of the other onto a "bending iron," an iron frame shaped to the exact contour of the windshield. When placed in the lehr, the flat pieces of glass were bent by the heat so that they conformed to the shape of the iron, and the silkscreen paint hardened.

At the next station, called "vinyl," the cooled pieces of glass were separated and a sheet of vinyl was placed between the inner and outer pieces. It was then cut to the exact size of the windshield. Next, windshields moved to the lamination area, where a machine joined the two pieces into one windshield and removed most of the air bubbles trapped between vinyl and glass.

In the "final" area, windshields were placed in a large football-shaped vessel called an autoclave, which removed the remaining air bubbles and completed the lamination process. They were then inspected, packed and prepared for shipment.

The Role of Teams

At Berea the word "team" had several meanings, which continued to evolve. The first workers were trained in areas, and therefore thought in terms of area teams. Several workers, for example, stayed together as they learned to cut, trim, and test vinyl; another group worked together to master the lehrs. During this period, there was strong team awareness in each area—and some unhappiness when the teams were broken up by the hiring of a second shift in June 1990. To facilitate the training of new employees, experienced crews were divided up and spread across the shifts. For example, half of the experienced workers in the vinyl area stayed on the first shift, where they were joined by new hires, while half went to the second shift. When a third shift was added a month later, the original experienced team was spread across all three shifts.

Once the third shift was added, employees began to think of the shift, rather than the area, as the primary team. Many learned new jobs and developed a deeper understanding of the production process; they soon saw that the work areas were interdependent and that it was the shift that actually made windshields. Povlik took an even broader view: he began to use the word team to describe the entire plant work force.

There were two additional types of teams: ad-hoc teams, which had a limited life and were disbanded after addressing a single issue or problem, and standing teams, which tackled long-term concerns such as ergonomics and quality improvement. Members volunteered to participate on these teams, and all work was done on company time.

Pay and Promotion

All plant employees were paid weekly salaries, based on hourly rates of $8.00 for support workers and $9.00 for technicians. These rates were about average for workers in the area. Because of the difference in hourly rates, many support workers strove for promotion to technician. In fact, support workers from the first and second group of hires recalled being told that they could expect to become technicians within six months—that it was automatic, "a done deal." Many believed that there were only minor skill differences

EXHIBIT 3 Partial Organizational Chart, the Glass Group, December 1991

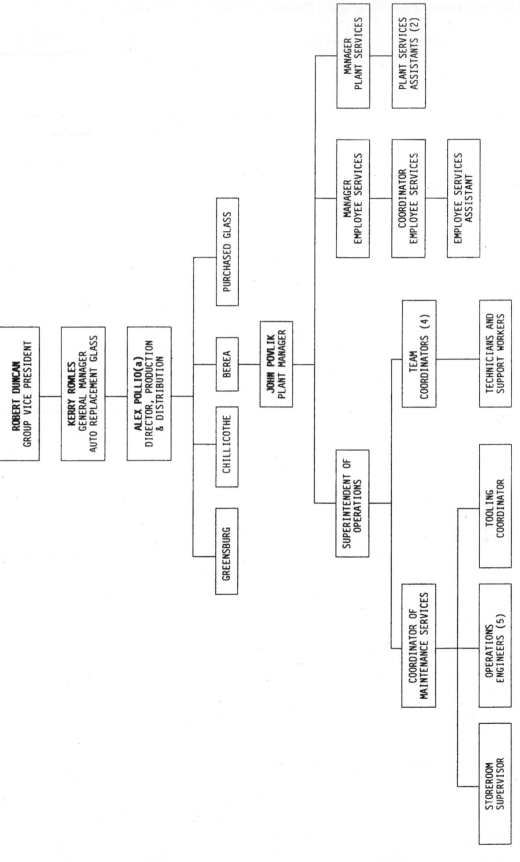

(a)Appointed June 1990, replacing John Kelleher.

between themselves and technicians, and that they would readily acquire the needed skills. Of the first group of support workers, sixty percent later became technicians. But because there was little need for additional technicians in 1991, few of the later hires were promoted.

Job Rotation

In the first year of operation, workers in a given area, sometimes with the input of a team coordinator, decided how they would rotate through the jobs in their area. But in spring 1991 the standing team on ergonomics presented a report on several critical jobs that involved repetitive motion. The team informed management that the "off-loading" jobs, which required lifting glass by hand and moving it from one work station to the next, and the vinyl trim job were more threatening than had been suspected. The team recommended shorter, uninterrupted work periods at these stations, coupled with shorter work assignments. This, in turn, led to a second recommendation—the scheduled rotation of support workers. Over a 36-week period each support worker would work all of the support jobs in the plant, with equal time in every position. After 36 weeks, workers would begin the same rotation on the next shift. (These recommendations did not apply to technicians, who were expected to develop deep technical knowledge in two or three work areas and therefore rotated to a new area only once per quarter.) Both recommendations were quickly implemented.

TOWARD A SELF-DIRECTED WORK FORCE

Start Up

All Berea employees had been exposed to the idea of a self-directed work force when they were screened and hired, and knew that it was a long-term goal. But because workers lacked experience, Povlik believed that, at start up, the vision had to be put aside temporarily while he and his staff taught employees how to make windshields. Six months were budgeted for the process. Only then would self-direction be pursued. During the plant's first few months, Povlik and his staff were constantly on the shop floor performing jobs, issuing instructions, and training workers. One team coordinator described the

process as "do it for them; do it with them; let them do it." Later, when the second shift was hired in June and the third shift in July, the first group of workers assisted in the training. But it remained, in Povlik's words, a "directive approach," and when Robert Duncan, group vice president of the Glass Group, toured Berea in November 1990, he did not like what he saw and heard. Duncan did not find the self-directed work force he had envisioned, nor did he find a model for PPG's traditional plants.

Refining the Model

Stirred by Duncan's visit, Povlik began to orchestrate a shift toward greater self-direction. His first step, in February 1991, was to confer with corporate human resource specialists; his second, in March, was to launch the plant staff on an assessment of progress to date. In each case the guiding question was the same: "What do we mean by a self-directed work force, and how will we know when we get there?"

This question proved to be extremely difficult to answer, for there were few companies with fully self-directed work forces that could serve as models. Povlik elected to proceed incrementally: even though the endpoint was a "moving target," he would make changes that met obvious needs. As an initial step, he invited Harold Shafer, a corporate training expert, to work with Berea for several months. In addition to training, Shafer would help improve plant communications, the recognition and reward system, and the work climate.

Shafer soon made an invaluable contribution. He presented Povlik and his staff with a framework, called situational leadership, that fit well with their initial directive approach. Situational leadership suggested that no single approach to leadership was best; it depended on the competence and commitment of followers.[2] A directing style fit well with beginners, who were enthusiastic about the task but lacked skill. Coaching styles were necessary when employees had some experience but remained uncertain about their skills and needed help making decisions. With high levels of skill and commitment, management would provide neither

---

[2]More complete explanations of situational leadership can be found in Paul Hersey and Kenneth H. Blanchard, *Management of Organizational Behavior*, Fifth Edition (Englewood Cliffs, NJ: Prentice Hall, 1988), ch. 5, 8.

direction nor support; both would come from the employees themselves. In total, this approach proposed four distinct leadership styles (see Exhibit 4). Berea management quickly saw the relevance of the framework to their own activities and began to talk about changes in their own leadership styles as an evolutionary process. They even created diagrams to illustrate the transition to self-direction (see Exhibit 5).

Self-direction in Action

By December 1991 there was definite progress toward the ideal of a self-directed work force. At start up engineers and team coordinators had worked alongside technicians and support workers; now they were much less visible on the shop floor. A systems engineer might still be needed to program a new robot, but day-to-day problem solving was increasingly the job of technicians and support workers. Technicians were now qualified to play their roles in two, and in a few cases, three areas; support workers were on a rotation that would introduce them to all jobs within the next few months. One technician observed:

> It's very rare for the coordinator to know more than I do. When I do deal with him, I'm just making him aware of the problem. If I can't do it myself, I'll call the engineer. But ninety percent of the time I can.

Material movement and supply were employees' responsibility. Every morning the technician in the vinyl area met with the furnace technicians; sometimes the cold end was brought in as well. Together, they checked the production

EXHIBIT 4 Situational Leadership: Four Leadership Styles

Each leadership style combines varying amounts of directive and supportive behavior. Directive behavior typically involves one-way communication. The leader spells out the follower's role; clearly tells the follower what to do, where to do it, how to do it, and when to do it; and closely supervises performance. Supportive behavior is more collaborative. The leader engages in two-way communication, listens, provides support and encouragement, facilitates interaction, and involves the follower in decision making. When both types of behavior are represented in a matrix according to their relative use, four leadership styles emerge. No one style is best in all situations; each is preferred for followers at a different level of development.

		Directive behavior	
		low	high
Supportive behavior	high	Supporting	Coaching
	low	Delegating	Directing

The four leadership styles are defined as follows:
1. *Directing*—Leader provides specific instructions (roles and goals) for followers and closely supervises task accomplishment.
2. *Coaching*—Leader explains decisions and solicits suggestions from followers but continues to direct task accomplishment.
3. *Supporting*—Leader makes decisions together with the followers and supports efforts toward task accomplishment.
4. *Delegating*—Leader turns over decisions and responsibility for implementation to followers.

Source: Adapted from Blanchard Training and Development, Inc., "SLIITM: A Definition," 1985.

EXHIBIT 5 Self-Directed Work Force Model

LEADERSHIP STYLE	EMPLOYEE DEVELOPMENT	LEADERSHIP ROLE	TASK SITUATION
HIGH DIRECTIVE LOW SUPPORTIVE			
	ENTHUSIASTIC BEGINNER	FOREMAN	"I'LL DECIDE."
DIRECTING	HIGH COMMITMENT LOW COMPETENCE		SPECIFIC DIRECTION
HIGH DIRECTIVE HIGH SUPPORTIVE			
	DISILLUSIONED LEARNER	SUPERVISOR	"LET'S TALK, I'LL DECIDE."
COACHING	LOW COMMITMENT SOME COMPETENCE		LISTENS TO IDEAS
LOW DIRECTIVE HIGH SUPPORTIVE			
	EMERGING CONTRIBUTOR	FACILITATOR	"LET'S TALK, YOU DECIDE."
SUPPORTING	MODERATE COMMITMENT HIGH COMPETENCE		SHARES DECISION MAKING
LOW DIRECTIVE LOW SUPPORTIVE			
	PEAK PERFORMER	COORDINATOR	"YOU DECIDE."
DELEGATING	HIGH COMMITMENT HIGH COMPETENCE		ACCEPTS DECISION

PROGRESSION

REGRESSION

SELF-DIRECTED WORKFORCE

schedule and arranged to cut the right kind of vinyl and use the right silkscreens. Without supervision, workers wheeled the required racks of bending irons into place, and made sure that the cold end was cutting the same windshield that was specified for the irons. If they found that the necessary silkscreens were not available, as they did one day in December, they came up with a way to juggle the production schedule, and then arranged to have replacement silkscreens shipped quickly to the plant. On their own, workers ordered rolls of vinyl and followed up with vinyl suppliers if they experienced quality problems. They also phoned in requests for slight modifications in the boxes used to ship product. Workers also designed new tool racks and tables, and continually came up with ideas to improve productivity and safety.

Team coordinators acknowledged that while they still walked the floor every hour, they very seldom directed work. One coordinator commented:

> Most technical things we can't do. We don't know how. Today the workers think they know more than the coordinators—and it's true.

Another coordinator observed:

> Gone are the days when the supervisor was expected to see the flaws and tell the workers how to fix them. That has implications for accountability, too. Now they are the experts, and they are accountable to each other.

Roles began to change throughout the plant. As the coordinators became less directive, they took on more plant projects. Engineers also reported that for the first time they had completed their "catch up" lists of needed repairs and were able to work on plant improvements. Even Povlik saw himself in a new light. In his new role, he was much more involved in leadership and employee development—as he put it, "looking ahead, trying to assess where we are, and then mapping a path"—and far less focused on day-to-day operations. Povlik estimated that at start up he spent virtually every minute on the shop floor; now only 50% of his time was devoted to operating issues.

By December 1991 Berea could boast of a number of successes. It had an admirable safety record, was meeting and in some cases exceeding quality goals, and was meeting production targets. Its target yield, a critical measure of productivity,

was set four percentage points higher than Greensburg's, yet it had been exceeded four months in a row. Moreover, Berea was accomplishing these goals with plant workers, rather than management, responsible for daily operations.

UNRESOLVED ISSUES

With success came growing pains. Roles continued to evolve, and responsibilities remained in flux. Two of the thorniest issues involved support workers and team coordinators.

Shifting Roles

Many support workers felt that they lacked status when compared with technicians. Subtle distinctions, they believed, had crept into the plant culture. "The technicians are being used more and more like foremen," one observed, "and they are not supposed to be." Another support worker added:

> They say there is no seniority system here, but there is. When the coordinator comes by, he will ask, "Where's the technician? Let me talk to the technician." He doesn't value our opinions as much.

Support workers also saw technicians as obstacles to their own chances of promotion, because some would not take the time to train them. One worker commented:

> If we are supposed to be a total team, everybody has to be given the time and opportunity to learn everything. But when I started out on the cold end and something broke down, I wasn't allowed to figure out how to fix it. Instead, someone who knew the answer jumped in, fixed it, and then told me that the idea was to get the glass out—and that later on he would try to show me what was going on. But if I can't learn, where's my opportunity?

Technicians were aware of the resentment. One recalled that when he had started on the job, production pressures and the need to learn the equipment had led to the same goal: rapid problem solving and increased knowledge for all. But today, with technicians from the first group of hires possessing superior knowledge, pressure to meet production goals meant that the team coordinator would come straight to an experienced technician when the line went down.

This same technician noted that the current 36-week job rotation, established at the suggestion of the ergonomics team, made training even more difficult. "If you rotate 50 people through the cold end in a year, they are going to leave knowing very little," he said. Longer job assignments meant greater learning, yet ergonomic concerns demanded shorter assignments.

The changing role of team coordinators posed an equally difficult challenge. If coordinators were effective in encouraging employee self-direction, they would soon be out of a job. One coordinator observed:

> We're training people to take over our jobs so we'll be unnecessary. That must be addressed with coordinators at the outset, as well as what they'll do next, because coordinators could make the system fail if they wanted to.

The next step for coordinators was not yet defined, although one argued that the traditional supervisory role would always be needed "as a kind of eye in the sky."

Recognition and Rewards

Recognition was a third unresolved issue. Support workers knew that if they hoped to be promoted to technician they needed to be recognized as individuals who performed superior work. Yet many did not want to be praised or publicly applauded. One support worker observed:

> I don't want to be singled out, because everyone else is working too. Besides, it's like a teacher patting the head of just one kid—if you're singled out, it's assumed you've been kissing up.

A team coordinator added:

> We're successful at group recognition. But individual recognition is a Pandora's box. When we posted individual successes [a list of outstanding performers], people on the list didn't like it and asked that it be taken down.

Other coordinators added that it was increasingly difficult to assess the work of individuals. They observed:

> We tend to grade on a curve, and try to create distinctions, but the work team as a whole is strong. . . . There are no low-lifers at Berea. The worst worker here would be an average worker anywhere else.

A support worker drew a similar conclusion, but from a different vantage point:

> They'll tell you as a team when you've done a good job, but as far as individual recognition is concerned, there isn't any. Because they don't know. They know your name, but they have no idea what you do.

This perception of management's lack of awareness of individual performance spilled over into concerns about how decisions were made about who would be promoted to technician. As one worker put it, "I know for a fact that they drew names out of a hat."

Setting Plant Policy

A final unresolved issue concerned policy-setting at Berea and the relative responsibilities of management and the work force. The boundary between the two was ill-defined and was continually being redrawn. One coordinator observed, "It's still not clear. Each person has a different idea of where the line should be." The start of shift rotations brought the problem into sharp relief.

When Berea added second and third shifts in June and July 1990, workers were assigned to a fixed shift crew, and each crew rotated to a new shift time each week. Employees soon questioned the arrangement, even though all prospective hires had been told in orientation sessions that shift rotations were planned. It was, in fact, company policy, in place at all PPG plants because of the high turnover that had been experienced when employees were assigned permanently to night shifts.

Over time dissatisfaction with shift rotation grew. Management first allowed a worker team to tackle the issue, then hired a consulting group to pursue it. Eventually, management presented employees with two alternative approaches and asked for a survey of employees' views. Neither involved fixed shift assignments. Later, in spring 1991, when the ergonomics team recommended a 36-week job rotation, employees were assigned to a single shift for the entire 36-week period. But dissatisfaction with the earlier policy never disappeared completely. One worker summarized the issue by calling it

> . . . a thorn in our side. The option the majority wanted was thrown out. Thrown out by someone, I don't know who. But I'd sure like to talk to him. We voted, and 70% wanted steady shifts.

Management was aware of these feelings and understood their impact on the plant culture. Don Stine observed: "We need to get beyond the shift issue and the we/they problem." There were similar disagreements about overtime and vacation policy. Employees, for example, wanted more control over how much overtime they worked, and when they worked it. But management believed that these and other policy choices were management's responsibility. Employees, predictably, felt differently. They knew that production goals, pay, and benefits were out of bounds, but questioned why they were not allowed to make choices in other areas. One worker commented: "We were given the impression when we came here that majority rules, and that's not the way it is."

Peer Review

Peer review was one area where employees could begin to exercise their collective voice. Yet many seemed resistant to the idea of evaluating one another. Coordinators observed that while employees generally got along well together, the few difficulties involved strong, assertive technicians. Support workers were loathe to confront them directly; typically, they first took their complaints to coordinators. Other workers seemed, on occasion, to be carrying heavier work loads to cover for their less effective peers, yet little action was taken.

Management wondered if some form of peer review would be a step forward, helping to resolve these problems, or a barrier to further self-direction. There were several options. Alex Pollio, who had replaced Kelleher as the division's director of production and distribution, observed:

> Peer appraisal raises some interesting questions. How do you use the results? To determine pay? Just to encourage individual performance improvement? Or for something else?

Whatever the decision, management knew there was no turning back. As Shafer put it:

> A plant can't change its mind on having a self-directed work force. It's like teaching a bear to dance. Once you and the bear start dancing, you don't get to say when it's time to stop.

A Note on High-Commitment Work Systems

This note describes the history, theory, and practice of high-commitment work systems.[1] Such systems are designed to produce high levels of employee involvement and motivation through enriched jobs, shared authority and decision making, team-based organization structures, and open communications. They are of interest for two reasons: (1) they represent a fundamental shift away from the narrowly defined tasks and control-oriented management approaches that have long dominated the work place, and (2) companies that have successfully introduced these systems report dramatic improvements in quality, productivity, and overall operating performance.

HISTORY

The Classical School

For much of the twentieth century business organizations have been modeled on the principles of the classical school.[2] The original ideas can be traced to the late 1800s and early 1900s, when Frederick Taylor, the father of scientific management, and Max Weber, the father of organizational bureaucracy, published major works. Together, their views produced organizations with multiple levels and functions, extensive division of labor, hierarchical chains of command, and exacting rules, procedures, and policies for guiding behavior. Employees were given limited opportunities to contribute ideas, and decision making was largely the province of management.

Managers were also responsible for the design and specification of jobs. Typically, time and motion studies or other industrial engineering techniques were used to divide work into narrow specialized tasks; after further analysis of fatigue, effort, and output workers were instructed in the "one best way" of performing their jobs.

Human Relations and Human Resources

For many years these principles shaped efforts to improve productivity and enhance corporate performance. Then, in the 1920s and 1930s, a new perspective emerged, triggered by the now famous Hawthorne Experiments.[3] Working with a group of assemblers at Western Electric, the Hawthorne researchers found that the theories of the classical school could not explain the patterns they observed. In one well known experiment, illumination in the work area was increased, leading to increased output; yet when illumination was decreased, output rose again. Changes in the length and spacing of rest breaks were equally difficult to correlate with improved productivity. Clearly, forces other than fatigue and objective job characteristics were at work.

The Hawthorne researchers concluded that organizations were in fact complex social systems. Output was affected not only by a job's scientific design, but also by social norms, informal groupings, management-employee communications, and the intensity of employee involvement. Superior performance was linked to high levels of employee satisfaction; satisfaction, in turn, was tied to such non-economic factors as a sense of belonging and participation in decision making.

---

[1]These systems go by various names, including high-performance work systems, high-involvement systems, semi-autonomous work groups, and self-managing teams. Their primary distinction is level of analysis. Systems are larger, multi-group entities that constitute a whole organization or unit, while groups and teams are smaller, less complex entities that perform shared, interdependent tasks.

[2]Amitai Etzioni, *Modern Organizations* (Englewood Cliffs, NJ: Prentice-Hall, Inc., 1964), ch. 3, 5.

This note was prepared by Norman Klein and David A Garvin. Copyright © 1993 by the President and Fellows of Harvard College. Harvard Business School case 693–080.

[3]The Hawthorne Experiments are described at length in Elton Mayo, *The Human Problems of an Industrial Civilization* (New York: Viking, 1933), and F. J. Roethlisberger and W. J. Dickson, *Management and the Worker* (Cambridge: Harvard University Press, 1939).

These findings helped launch the human relations movement, which flourished in the 1950s and 1960s. It was soon followed by the human resources approach, which reinforced the idea that employees were capable, intelligent actors and further specified management's role in leading and directing them. Here, however, the focus was not on achieving high levels of employee satisfaction, which was often associated with permissiveness and loose control, but on "the creation of conditions such that the members of the organization can achieve their own goals *best* by directing their efforts toward the success of the enterprise."[4] Followers of the human resources approach developed a number of ideas that today shape high-commitment work systems. Two of the most important involve the sources of employee motivation and the principles of job redesign.

Motivation and Job Redesign

The pioneering research on motivation was conducted by Frederick Herzberg.[5] In a series of studies, he distinguished the sources of job satisfaction from the sources of dissatisfaction. The former he called "motivators"; they included achievement, recognition, the work itself, responsibility, and growth or advancement. The latter he called "hygiene factors"; they included company policy and administration, supervision, interpersonal relationships, working conditions, salary, status, and security. These distinctions led to an important conclusion. Job satisfaction and dissatisfaction were not opposites, as conventionally assumed, but distinctly different phenomena with their own roots. At best, hygiene factors could explain the presence or absence of employee dissatisfaction; only motivators could contribute to higher levels of satisfaction.

Herzberg then proposed an approach to job enrichment that drew on these distinctions. He called it vertical loading, to distinguish it from traditional, horizontal approaches in which jobs were broadened by imposing more demanding targets or assigning a larger number of unfulfilling tasks.

Vertical loading was designed to provide employees with additional opportunities for growth and personal achievement—in other words, to increase the presence of motivators. Employees might, for example, be given more authority to make decisions, granted further accountability for their work, or introduced to new and more challenging tasks.

Later scholars refined this approach and expanded it in new directions. The most important research was by Hackman and Oldham, who identified five core functions of a job that were linked directly to motivation: skill variety (the range of skills that the job required), task identity (the extent that the job involved completion of a whole task or an identifiable piece of work), task significance (the importance of the task, including its impact on other people and its links to organizational performance), autonomy (the amount of freedom, independence, and discretion that the job permitted), and job feedback (the amount of information provided directly to employees about their effectiveness).[6] These concepts provided a scientific basis for expanding jobs and further weakened the influence of the classical school.

Sociotechnical Systems Theory

Meanwhile, a group of British researchers at the Tavistock Institute of Human Relations were developing an even broader approach.[7] Rather than studying individual jobs, they were focusing on entire work systems. Special attention was paid to work groups and their contribution to increased productivity and job satisfaction. Today these ideas go by the name of sociotechnical systems (STS) theory; they mark the true beginnings of the high-commitment systems approach.

The initial application of STS came in the British coal mines. New working arrangements were introduced in the 1950s through the combined efforts of scholars, management, and the union. They were quite different from the usual practices of strict supervision and simplified tasks that characterized modern longwall mining. Instead, the new approaches involved autonomous work groups

[4]Douglas McGregor, *The Human Side of Enterprise* (New York: McGraw-Hill, 1960), p. 49.

[5]Frederick Herzberg et al., *The Motivation to Work,* 2nd edition (New York: John Wiley and Sons, 1959), and Frederick Herzberg, "One More Time: How Do You Motivate Employees?" *Harvard Business Review,* September-October 1987, pp. 109–120.

[6]J. Richard Hackman and Greg R. Oldham, *Work Redesign* (Reading, MA: Addison-Wesley, 1980).

[7]Eric L. Trist, "The Sociotechnical Perspective," in Andrew H. Van de Ven and William F. Joyce, eds., *Perspectives on Organization Design and Behavior* (NY: John Wiley & Sons, 1981), ch. 2.

responsible for small portions of the coal face, with group members able to interchange roles and regulate their affairs with minimal supervision. Surprisingly, these groups were more productive than longwall miners, even though they were less mechanized and did not use assembly-line techniques. They also incurred fewer absences and accidents and reported greater personal commitment.

Armed with the coal mine study, the Tavistock researchers began to develop a more comprehensive framework. Their goal was to integrate human and technological perspectives and deal holistically with the work place. Throughout, the emphasis was on large-scale, systemic change and the best way to introduce it:

> When redesigned in accord with the sociotechnical approach, work systems are never changed in piecemeal fashion. Although jobs, rewards, physical equipment, spatial arrangements, work schedules, and more may be altered in sociotechnical interventions, none of these is taken as the primary focus of change activities. Instead organization members, often including rank and file employees and representatives of organized labor as well as managers, examine all aspects of organization members' experiences.[8]

These, and other principles of STS, are discussed at length later in the note.

Recent Developments

Sociotechnical approaches arrived in the United States in the 1960s and 1970s. Early experiments were conducted at General Foods (Topeka, Kansas), Cummins Engine (Jamestown, New York), and Procter & Gamble (Lima, Ohio). Despite their success, further adoption was slow. Few companies chose to experiment with more than one site, and most efforts were confined to newly constructed plants. But the concepts and philosophy stuck. Over time, they began to spread, as employers became more comfortable with high levels of employee involvement and the use of self-directed teams. Two factors were primarily responsible: the growing realization that a committed work force could be a competitive strength, and the burgeoning quality movement.

During the 1960s and 1970s, many companies began to revamp their human resource strategies under the banner of "quality of work life." Employees were increasingly seen as valuable assets, to be cultivated and developed over time, rather than interchangeable, easily replaceable parts. There was progress on many fronts: tasks were broadened, compensation systems were redesigned, job security was enhanced, communication was improved, and decision making was shared. "At the center of this philosophy," one scholar has observed, "is a belief that eliciting employee commitment will lead to enhanced performance."[9] Initially, unions resisted the approach, fearing that it would undermine their role. But early experiments at General Motors, supported by the United Auto Workers (UAW), led to broader acceptance, and today a wide range of unions support quality-of-work-life and participation programs.

Meanwhile, the U.S. quality movement was gaining strength and taking firm hold in the 1970s and 1980s. It was initially driven by the success of Japanese manufacturers in such diverse industries as automobiles, consumer electronics, and machine tools. Later, the underlying principles were codified in the Malcolm Baldrige National Quality Award, open to all American manufacturing and service companies. In both cases, success was linked to problem-solving teams and employee decision making, often at low levels of the organization. Today these efforts are usually termed empowerment.

The high-commitment systems approach continues this evolution. No single event or publication marks its birth. Instead, it is the culmination of earlier trends, a weaving together of the best thinking on employee involvement, shared decision making, and worker self-management. The seeds were planted by the human relations and human resources movements, and the conceptual foundations were provided by sociotechnical systems theory. All three were rebellions against the classical school, which flourished in the early 1900s. Recent research on employee motivation, job enrichment, quality of work life, and empowerment have elaborated and refined the underly-

---

[8]J. Richard Hackman, "Work Redesign for Organizational Development," in Michael Beer and Bert Spector, eds., *Readings in Human Resource Management* (New York: Free Press, 1985), pp. 532–533.

[9]Richard E. Walton, "From Control to Commitment in the Workplace," *Harvard Business Review,* March-April 1985, p. 79.

ing themes. The result is a core set of principles, drawn from diverse sources, that together describe an innovative approach to work systems design and management.

THEORY

The theory of high-commitment work systems is broad and prescriptive, yet surprisingly open ended. There is room for considerable tailoring of individual designs, and systems seldom operate in precisely the same way. Nevertheless, most designs can be traced to the same small set of ideas. They specify both the process of design (the first three items below) and the desired characteristics of work systems, teams, and individual jobs.

Joint optimization of social and technical systems According to this principle, the best results are obtained when social and technical aspects of work are designed together. People and equipment, after all, are linked by the structure of work; they are parts of a single, cohesive system. Compatibility is therefore crucial. To ensure "a structure that is both productive and humanly satisfying," designers must create the best possible fit between employees, tasks, and technology.[10]

Participative design The design process too must be framed with compatibility in mind. Because "a participative social system cannot be created by fiat," high levels of operating involvement require broad participation in design.[11] Employees must have some responsibility for shaping their own jobs, and some say in the design of the overall system.

Minimal, rather than complete, design This principle makes a virtue of incompleteness. It suggests that only the essentials of the work system be defined up front. Once minimal conditions for effective operation have been established (what sociotechnical theorists call "minimum critical specification"), the remainder of the design is allowed to emerge over time. Tasks, roles, methods, and policies are left deliberately broad and open ended, to be sharpened and refined later. The work system that results is shaped by experience, and employees take an active role in creating the final, tightly specified design. Learning and continuous improvement are thus built into the fabric of the organization.

Open systems To ensure adaptability and responsiveness, operations must be linked closely to the environment. They should be designed as open systems, with direct ties to customers and suppliers, rather than isolated groups pursuing their own ends. Buffers are to be avoided, so that any environmental changes will be felt immediately by the operating unit.

Autonomous work groups Teams are the building blocks of high-commitment work systems. They are expected to be autonomous and self-managing, with responsibility for assigning tasks within the group, scheduling rest breaks, monitoring performance, and selecting and improving work practices. Typically, teams are assigned a whole task—manufacturing a piston, for example, or processing an insurance claim—and individuals' jobs are closely linked. To further ensure autonomy, teams are often given responsibility for support activities, like materials management and employee selection, that accompany their work.

Boundary location and control Self-managing groups require clear, well chosen boundaries to function effectively. The scope of their work must first be defined; boundaries should then be drawn to place all necessary activities within the group's control. Interdependent tasks, in particular, must be grouped together; otherwise, teams will be unable to complete their assignments without intruding on others and disrupting their work.

Control variances at the source Variances, in sociotechnical terms, are unexpected or unprogrammed events. Quality problems are an obvious example. If they are controlled close to their point of origin, the autonomy and responsibility of the work group increases. The group controls its boundaries, solves its own problems, and learns from the experience. If variances are exported to other groups, however, problems of coordination and fingerpointing often emerge. Additional levels of management may be required to allocate responsibility, and groups quickly lose the ability to regulate themselves.

Enriched jobs Enriched jobs are the norm in high-commitment work systems. Enrichment may take any of several forms; they appear separately and in combination. The first is multiskilling—providing employees with diverse skills so they can handle more than one job. The second is vertical loading—adding support activities, like materials management, scheduling, employee selection, and peer evaluation, to normal operating tasks. The third is responsibility for problem solving—teaching techniques of data collection, problem diagnosis, and corrective action so employees can address problems in their work areas and the operation as a whole.

---

[10]Thomas C. Cummings, "Self-Regulating Work-Groups: A Socio-Technical Synthesis," *Academy of Management Review,* July 1978, p. 626.
[11]Albert Cherns, "The Principles of Sociotechnical Design," *Human Relations,* vol. 29, no. 8 (1976), p. 785.

Shared power, information, and rewards This principle strongly rejects classical notions of hierarchy and control. It suggests that power, information, and rewards should be where the action is—at the lowest levels of the organization. Decision-making should rest with those personally involved in making a product or delivering a service, not with senior managers. Information should be widely dispersed and easily accessible, available where and when it is needed. And rewards for improved organizational performance should be shared through profit-sharing or gainsharing plans.

Egalitarian and humanitarian values Most high-commitment work systems embrace a common set of values. Equity and equality are at the core. Together, they have had a pronounced impact on design, leading to flat organizations, with few levels, that blur the lines between management and the work force and keep status differences at bay. Trust is equally valued. It has led to the elimination of most traditional supervisory and policing roles. Perhaps most important, work is viewed in broad human terms—as an opportunity for growth and personal learning—and employee satisfaction and development are regarded as vital ends.

Together, these ten principles provide the foundation for most high-commitment work systems. They are an eclectic mix, rooted in sociotechnical systems theory but combining ideas from human relations and human resources, quality of work life, motivational theory, and empowerment. Because of their scope, they are best viewed as guidelines or maps of general direction, rather than detailed design rules. They are thus more of an approach to management than a fully specified model or a clearly defined set of techniques.

PRACTICE

There are at least several hundred high-commitment work systems in the U.S. today, and possibly as many as a thousand.[12] Many are less than five years old. The number outside the country is un-

known, although examples are readily found. Overall, the performance of these units has been impressive. General Mills, Corning, and Procter & Gamble, for example, have reported productivity and quality advantages of 30 to 40 percent over traditional facilities. A recent study of nearly one hundred high-commitment work systems found even more dramatic differences: a return on investment over three times the industry average and a return on sales more than five times the norm.[13]

Similarities

A number of common practices, in addition to those cited above, have emerged over time. One is the careful screening of new employees. High-commitment work systems are not for everyone; they require a special type of employee with compatible goals, values, and work habits. Prospective hires normally undergo a battery of interviews and tests, including simulations and group exercises, to assess their ability to function well in these environments. Manual dexterity is far less important than problem-solving skills, personal initiative, commitment to continued learning, and the ability to work in groups.

Other common practices involve pay, supervision, job design, and training. Compensation systems, for example, have moved slowly toward pay-for-knowledge or skills. In traditional organizations employees are paid according to their job classification, individual merit, or seniority; in these new systems they are paid according to the number of tasks or skills that they have mastered. Greater knowledge means greater pay, and the organization gains flexibility as skills increase. Approximately 40 percent of high-commitment work systems now use this approach.

Most systems have eliminated traditional supervisors, replacing them with team coordinators or facilitators. Their primary task is to assist employees and teams, not direct them. Commands and instructions are avoided whenever possible, and the goal is to foster employees' capacity for self-management. As one expert has observed, this requires a new set of skills:

> The leader [coordinator, facilitator] attempts to invoke subordinate self-management through a se-

[12]Unless otherwise noted, all material in this section is drawn from the following sources: Edward E. Lawler III, "The New Plant Revolution," *Organizational Dynamics,* Winter 1978, pp. 3–12; Lawler, "The New Plant Revolution Revisited," *Organizational Dynamics,* Winter 1990, pp. 5–14; Lawler, "The New Plant Revolution: A Second Generation Approach," *Organizational Dynamics,* Winter 1991, pp. 5–14; Richard S. Wellins et al., *Self-Directed Teams: A Study of Current Practice* (Pittsburgh: Development Dimensions International, 1990); and "New Work Systems, New Choices," *Labor Relations Today,* March/April 1991, pp. 1–2.

[13]G. Ledford, T. G. Cummings, and R. Wright, "The Design and Functioning of High-Involvement Organizations," mimeographed, June 1992, p. 17.

ries of directed questions. First, self-observation: "Do you know how well you are doing right now?" "How about keeping a record of how many times that happens?" Second, self-goal setting: "How many will you shoot for?" "When do you want to have it finished?" "What will your target be?" Then, self-evaluation leading to self-reinforcement: "How do you think you did?" "Are you pleased with the way it went?" Finally, rehearsals: "Why don't we try it out?" "Let's practice that." The aim, of course, is to give the employee practice in self-management behaviors.[14]

Job rotation has also become increasingly popular. It offers varied work, produces a broader mix of skills, and leads to effective problem solving. Over 60 percent of high-commitment work system rotate jobs to some extent. Training has broadened as well, because it is essential for supporting the above practices. Today training includes such topics as understanding technical and financial information, problem solving, using computers, and social and group dynamics. It is normally extensive and continuous, with some systems

---

[14]Charles C. Manz and Henry P. Sims, Jr., "Self-Management as a Substitute for Leadership: A Social Learning Theory Perspective," *Academy of Management Review*, vol. 5, no. 3 (1980), p. 365.

reporting training investments as high as $10,000 per employee. During peak periods, training can amount to as much as 10 to 15 percent of employees' time.

Differences

Despite these similarities, high-commitment work systems are not all alike. Many are at vastly different levels of maturity and employ quite different designs. Team sizes, for example, range from fewer than five people to more than twenty, with an average of six to ten. Some teams select their own leaders, others do not. Perhaps most important, teams vary widely in their autonomy and range of responsibilities (see Exhibits 1 and 2). Tasks such as house-keeping, maintaining safety, daily work assignments, and vacation scheduling are routinely vested in teams; they are operational matters that require few new skills. Preparing and managing cost budgets, performance appraisals, and compensation decisions, on the other hand, are less frequently seen; they involve managerial decisions and delicate comparisons that can undercut fragile relationships. The latter activities are normally limited to mature, well-established teams.

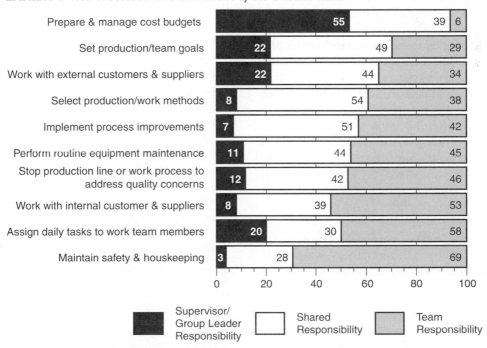

EXHIBIT 1 How Production Tasks are Handled by Self-Directed Teams

Task	Supervisor/Group Leader Responsibility	Shared Responsibility	Team Responsibility
Prepare & manage cost budgets	55	39	6
Set production/team goals	22	49	29
Work with external customers & suppliers	22	44	34
Select production/work methods	8	54	38
Implement process improvements	7	51	42
Perform routine equipment maintenance	11	44	45
Stop production line or work process to address quality concerns	12	42	46
Work with internal customer & suppliers	8	39	53
Assign daily tasks to work team members	20	30	58
Maintain safety & housekeeping	3	28	69

Source: Richard S. Wellins et al., *Self-Directed Teams: A Study of Current Practice*, p. 23

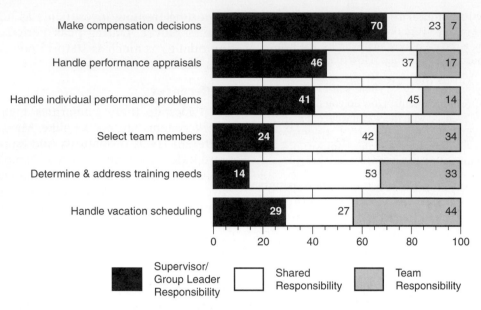

EXHIBIT 2 How Personnel Functions Are Handled by Self-Directed Teams

Source: Richard S. Wellins et al., *Self-Directed Teams: A Study of Current Practice,* p. 24

Problems and Concerns

High-commitment work systems are not without problems. Many result from the systems' distinctive cultures and underlying values. Unrealistic expectations, for example, are common. Many employees begin their jobs with unbounded enthusiasm and utopian visions. Reality usually comes as something of a shock. According to one expert: "They expect their work to be interesting all the time, and they expect to be in total control of their work lives. When these expectations are not met, problems are created."[15]

Problems of inequity have similar roots. Because high-commitment work systems are based on norms of equality, employees are extremely sensitive to variations in status and pay. Individual differences, however, are a fact of life, making it virtually impossible to create a completely egalitarian work place or develop a perfectly fair wage system. Inevitably, some employees are more skilled or knowledgeable than others; they must usually be paid commensurately, creating a world of "winners and losers" and the perception, in at least a few minds, that inequity exists.[16]

The role and functioning of coordinators has remained a problem.[17] Many coordinators were previously supervisors at traditional facilities, yet have been assigned to their new positions after receiving only limited training. The transition has usually been difficult. In most high-commitment work systems the coordinator's job is ambiguous and ill-defined. There are few clear guidelines, other than to be non-directive and help employees master their jobs. The future is especially troubling, because career paths are seldom clear. Many coordinators wonder: once employees have mastered their jobs and teams are managing themselves, what are we supposed to do?

Finally, high-commitment work systems suffer from problems of regression and topping out. The first problem arises when production pres-

[15]Edward E. Lawler III, *High-Involvement Management* (San Francisco: Jossey-Bass, 1986), p. 182.

[16]Charles C. Manz and John W. Newstrom, "Self-Managing Teams in a Paper Mill: Success Factors, Problems, and Lessons Learned," in Albert Nedd, ed., *International Human Resource Management Review,* vol. I (1990), pp. 55–56.

[17]Richard E. Walton and Leonard A. Schlesinger, "Do Supervisors Thrive in Participative Work Systems?" *Organizational Dynamics,* vol. 8, no. 3 (1979), pp. 24–39.

sures intensify and managers respond by adopting traditional, directive behavior. Instructions and commands begin to replace norms of participation; eventually, workers may question management's dedication to the new model. Returning to a high-commitment approach is difficult and, at times, impossible.

Topping out occurs under different circumstances: long-term success of the system, but fuzziness about future goals and direction. Employees may have mastered all posted job skills and reached the top of their pay ladders; where are the next challenges, and what will be their sources of additional income? The unit may have institutionalized high-commitment values and reached its initial productivity and quality goals; how should the system evolve in the future, and what new goals should it pursue? These are the challenges of maturity, incurred five to ten years after founding. They raise a fundamental question: how does an established high-commitment work system renew itself? To date, the challenge has been faced by only a handful of systems, and the next generation model is still emerging.

Vickers Incorporated: Omaha Plant

John Weber was just about to birdie the fifth hole when his cellular phone rang. Knowing it must be bad news, Weber motioned for his wife and two children to play on without him. Since becoming Vice President of the Industrial Group at Vickers six months earlier, Weber had been working non-stop to create a plan that would justify continued investment in the Omaha plant. The outcome of this work was a turnaround strategy which hinged upon obtaining several union concessions. During this late-August weekend in 1994, the seventh round of negotiations between plant management and the United Paperworkers International Union was occurring. The bargaining was taking much longer than anticipated due to staunch resistance to certain key features of management's plan. Steve Whitworth, the Operations Director at the Omaha plant, had been instructed not to call unless the talks had reached an impasse. As Weber retrieved the cellular phone from his golf bag, he thought maybe it was time to reconsider the alternative options, one of which was to close down the Omaha plant.

VICKERS, INCORPORATED

The predecessor of Vickers, Incorporated, Vickers Manufacturing Company, was formed in 1921 by Harry Franklin Vickers. In the beginning, with only one part-time employee, the company focused on designing and building hydraulic machinery. A gifted engineer, Harry Vickers used his knowledge of fluid dynamics to develop the vane pump, a high pressure piston pump, and a vehicular power steering system. In 1937, through an exchange of stock, Vickers, Incorporated became a subsidiary of

This case was prepared as the basis for class discussion rather than to illustrate either effective or ineffective handling of an administrative situation. Data in this case have been disguised.

This case was prepared by Helen N. Han. Copyright © 1995 by the President and Fellows of Harvard College. Harvard Business School case 696-052.

Sperry Corporation and Harry Vickers became the Executive Vice President of Sperry. With a 115,000 square foot plant in Detroit, Michigan, Vickers had become a leading manufacturer of hydraulic variable-speed transmissions, pumps, valves, and controls.

The plant in Omaha, Nebraska, originally the Omaha Production Company, was acquired in 1947. Five years later, after Harry Vickers became President of Sperry, Vickers built another hydraulic equipment manufacturing plant in Joplin, Missouri. In 1955, the merger of Remington Rand, Incorporated and Sperry Corporation made Vickers a wholly owned subsidiary of the newly formed Sperry Rand Corporation, whose President and Chief Executive Officer was Harry Vickers.

Over the next fifteen years, Vickers built five manufacturing plants in three countries while establishing manufacturing presences in twelve other countries. The company also constructed an Engineering Center in Troy, Michigan, to concentrate on product refinements and innovations. Harry Vickers retired as Chairman of the Board at Sperry Rand in 1968, just as the existing Omaha plant was razed to provide room for new construction. Along with its manufacturing capabilities, this plant would also have a research and development laboratory. At 456,000 square feet, the plant would be the world's largest manufacturing facility expressly devoted to the production of hydraulic components.

In 1984, Libbey-Owens-Ford Company (LOFC) acquired Vickers from Sperry Corporation. At the time, LOFC consisted of three separate entities: Vickers, Incorporated, Aeroquip Corporation, and Sterling Engineered Products. With distinct product lines and few overlapping capabilities, little technological cross-pollination occurred amongst these three companies. Aeroquip manufactured fluid connectors along with a wide assortment of customized molded automotive and industrial plastic components, while Sterling manufactured automotive and commercial glass products. After several years of disappointing financial performance, Sterling was sold to Pilkington Brothers in the United Kingdom in 1987 and LOFC changed its name to TRINOVA. Exhibit 1 shows the Income Statement for TRINOVA. Between 1990 and 1994, Vicker's contribution to TRINOVA's net sales declined from 56% to 51%.

Around the same time, Vickers' Product Engineering and Product Management groups, previously based in the Engineering Center in Troy, Michigan, were relocated to the Omaha plant. To accommodate these extra functions, a 30,000 square foot Engineering Laboratory was added to the Omaha facility. Over the years, the plants in Joplin; Havant, England; Bad Homburg, Germany; and Searcy, Arkansas, had also been expanded to support new and/or transferred functions. Vickers' product line now included pumps, hydraulic and electric motors, electric drives, hydraulic and electronic controls, and remanufacturing services.

THE OMAHA PLANT

The Products

The field of hydraulics is based upon a principle discovered by Blaise Pascal, a 17th century physicist. He found that, due to the incompressibility of liquids, pressure (force per unit area) applied to an enclosed liquid is transmitted undiminished to every portion of the liquid and the walls of the containing vessel.[1] Thus, a small force applied to a small area can create a proportionally larger force on a larger area. Hydraulics is defined as the branch of physics which is concerned with the mechanical properties of liquids in motion. A force pushing on an area of confined liquid causes the liquid to flow, transmitting pressure which can be used to create hydraulic power (work per unit time). Pumps are devices which convert mechanical pressure and motion into hydraulic power. The Omaha plant, which manufactured and rebuilt hydraulic pumps, comprised three businesses: vane pumps, piston pumps, and remanufacturing services. Each of the vane and piston businesses could be broken down further into pump components and completed pump units. The plant was organized by manufacturing process and, with the exception of heat treating ovens, each product type had dedicated equipment (Exhibit 2).

Vane Pumps. Exhibit 3 illustrates the operating principle behind the vane pump.[2] A rotor on the

---

[1]Resnick, R., and Halliday, D., *Physics: Part One,* John Wiley and Sons: New York, NY, 1977, p. 376.
[2]*Vickers Industrial Hydraulics Manual,* Vickers, Incorporated, Rochester Hills, MI, 1992, p. 17–6, 17–8.

EXHIBIT I TRINOVA Statement of Income *(in thousands)*

	1994	1993	1992	1991	1990
Net sales	$1,794,695	$1,643,841	$1,695,512	$1,681,212	$1,955,424
Costs of products sold	1,351,403	1,247,414	1,307,357	1,309,094	1,477,676
Manufacturing Income	443,292	396,427	388,155	372,118	477,748
Selling and general administrative expenses	246,758	246,221	263,863	286,727	289,530
Engineering, research and development expenses	55,465	55,314	65,312	74,867	75,413
Special charge	—	26,000	—	166,400	—
Operating Income (Loss)	141,069	68,892	58,980	(155,876)	112,805
Interest expense	(21,060)	(25,516)	(26,313)	(26,453)	(31,698)
Other—net	(18,754)	(26,265)	(8,625)	(12,950)	(6,042)
Income (Loss) before Income Taxes	101,255	17,111	24,042	(195,279)	75,065
Income taxes (credit)	35,400	6,600	9,600	(11,200)	29,600
Income before Cumulative Effect of Accounting Change	68,855	10,511	14,442	(184,079)	45,465
Cumulative effect of accounting change, net of income tax benefit	—	(70,229)	—	—	—
Net Income (Loss)	$65,855	(59,718)	14,442	(184,079)	45,465

EXHIBIT 2 Omaha Plant Manufacturing Layout

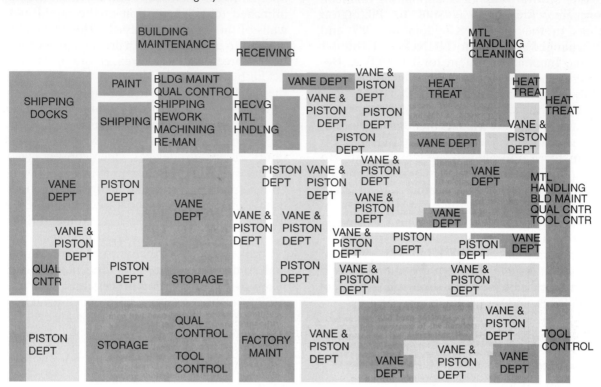

EXHIBIT 3 Vane Pump Schematic

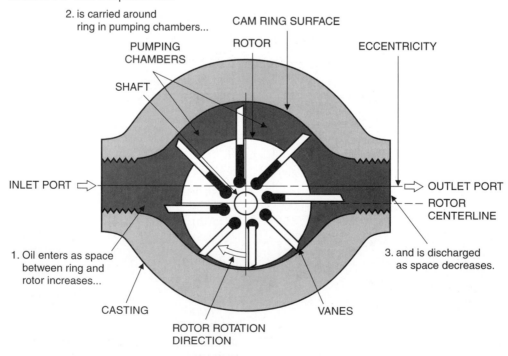

drive shaft turns inside a cam ring. During the turning, the vanes, fitted loosely into the rotor's slots, are thrown out against the cam ring where they are held by centripetal force and fluid pressure. As the rotor turns in a clockwise direction, the vane tips follow the inner surface of the cam ring. Pumping chambers are formed by the vanes, rotor, cam ring, and two side plates (not shown in Exhibit 3). Because the drive shaft is not centered in the cam ring, the chamber size increases above the centerline, creating a partial vacuum that collects liquid entering the inlet port. As the vanes cross over into the region below the centerline, the chambers become progressively smaller, forcing the liquid to be expelled through the outlet port. The flow capacity of the pump depends upon the diameters of the cam ring and rotor, and on the distance from the rotor surface to the cam ring surface. The displacement (volume of liquid transferred in one revolution) determines the hydraulic horsepower[3] of the pump.

The typical vane pump produced in Omaha contained approximately 65 parts, with all the key components as well as those with the most value-added being manufactured on site. The ring, rotor, vanes, cover, inlet support plate, outlet support plate, shaft, and body were all manufactured simultaneously in the Omaha plant (Exhibit 4). The finished parts were stored in the assembly area where they would eventually be combined with a number of outsourced standard parts (e.g. bearings, screws, nuts, and gaskets) to construct a completed pump. The ring, rotor, and vanes were the most critical to the proper operation of a vane pump (Exhibit 5).

---

[3]One unit of horsepower equals the power required to raise 550 pounds one foot in one second.

EXHIBIT 4 Vane Pump Construction

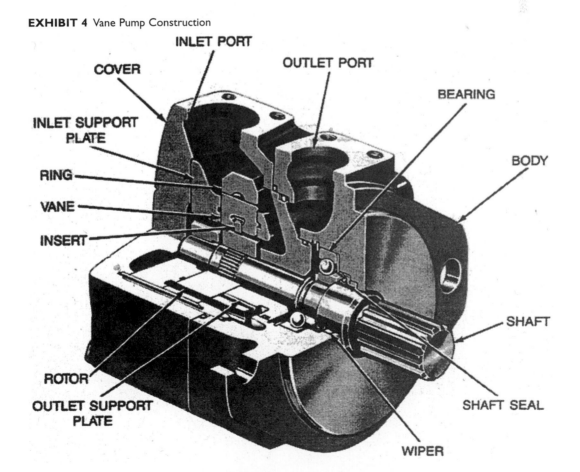

EXHIBIT 5 Vane Pump Manufacturing Process

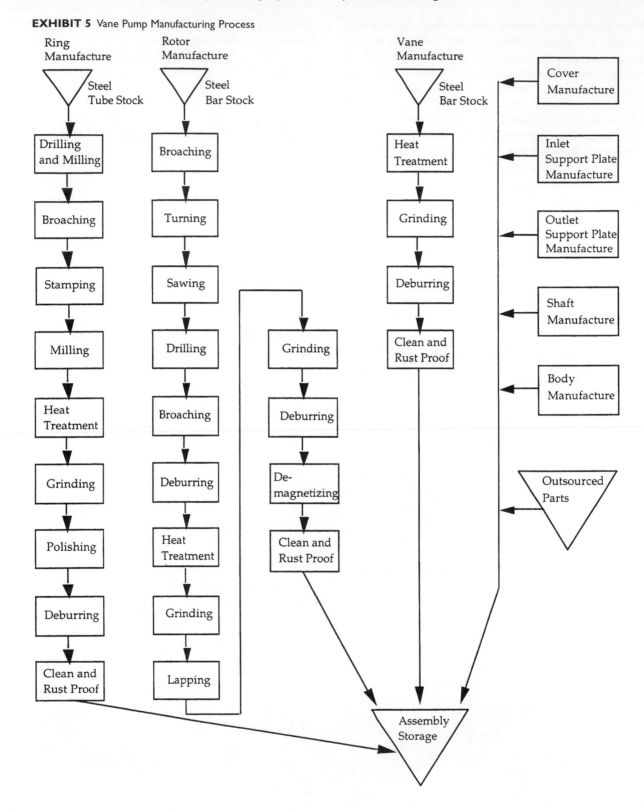

Piston Pumps. Piston pump technology is based on the fact that a piston alternately draws in and expels liquid as the piston moves back and forth in a bore.[4] There are two fundamental piston pump designs: radial and axial. Radial pumps have pistons arranged like wheel spokes in the cylinder block while axial pumps have pistons arranged parallel to each other and to the radial axis of the cylinder block. The operation of a radial piston pump (Exhibit 6a) is similar to that of a vane pump. A cylinder block rotates around a central tube (pintle) inside a circular reaction ring. The rotation of the cylinder block and the fluid pressure cause the pistons to extend from their bores, producing a partial vacuum within the bore. As the pistons move outward, they take in liquid from holes in the pintle. Since the cylinder block is offset from the centerline of the reaction ring, as the pistons follow the inner surface of the ring the proximity of the cylinder block to the reaction ring changes. This distance determines whether the piston is moving outward and taking in liquid from, or moving inward and discharging liquid into, the pintle ports.

In axial pumps (Exhibit 6b), the pistons move back and forth parallel to the axis of rotation of the cylinder block. The cylinder block is turned by the drive shaft. Pistons in the cylinder block are connected via piston shoes inserted into a shoe plate. This plate is attached to an angled swash plate which oscillates as the cylinder block turns. The piston shoes follow the motion of the swash plate, causing the pistons to move back and forth. The holes in the valve plate are arranged so that the pistons pass the inlet hole as they are pulled out and the outlet hole as they are pushed back in their bores. The displacement of both radial and axial piston pumps is determined by the size and number of pistons, as well as their stroke length.

Omaha's most common piston pump product was an axial pump consisting of over 100 parts. Again, the core components as well as those with the most value-added were manufactured at the Omaha facility. The manufacture of the housing, yoke, cylinder block, valve block, shaft, piston, shoe, shoe plate, valve plate, and compensator[5]

body occurred simultaneously in the plant (Exhibit 7). At the conclusion of their manufacturing processes, all the finished parts were stored in the assembly area, where they would be combined with a number of purchased parts (e.g. springs, bearings, screws, washers, and gaskets) to construct the completed pump. Of the components manufactured in Omaha, the housing, yoke, cylinder block, and valve block were the most critical (Exhibit 8).

Remanufacturing Services. Remanufacturing consisted of servicing and rebuilding used equipment. Remanufacturing services and remanufactured products were often less expensive than purchasing a comparable piece of new equipment. In general, an individual worker performed all of the operations required to remanufacture a particular pump.

The Market

Hydraulic pumps were used in mobile applications such as truck, bus, and tractor transmissions as well as forklift and bulldozer implements. Non-mobile applications included industrial equipment such as machine tools, injection molders, and presses. While either vane or piston pumps could be used for most applications, the final pump choice usually depended upon the design of the operation and the requirements of the operator. Each pump type possessed certain inherent advantages. Vane pumps generally had lower manufacturing costs and thus lower prices than piston pumps of comparable displacement. Vane pumps were technically less complex, making them simpler to apply and service in the field, and also tended to be more forgiving of fluid contaminants and other environmental variations. They often were quieter, with typical operating noise levels around 63 decibels as compared to approximately 80 decibels for the typical piston pump. In contrast, piston pumps usually were capable of higher pressure and permitted easier control of fluid flows. Higher energy efficiencies translated into lower operating costs when compared to a vane pump generating the same power.

Since 1970, forecasters had been predicting a general decline in the market for new vane pumps due to a gradual switchover to piston pumps. However, the annual global market for vane pumps had remained relatively uniform at approximately 780,000 units. In 1994, the Omaha plant sold

---

[4]*Vickers Industrial Hydraulics Manual,* Vickers, Incorporated, Rochester Hills, MI, 1992, p. 17–15, 17–18, 17–20.

[5]The compensator adjusted the fluid output of the pump to the level required to develop and maintain the preset pressure. This adjustment was achieved by changing the angle of the yoke which changed the swash plate angle, thus changing the displacement of the pistons.

EXHIBIT 6 Piston Pump Schematics

EXHIBIT 6A Radial Piston Pump

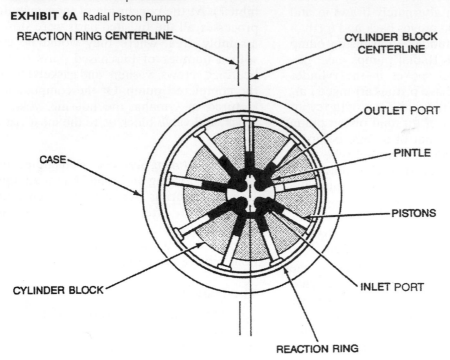

EXHIBIT 6B Axial Piston Pump

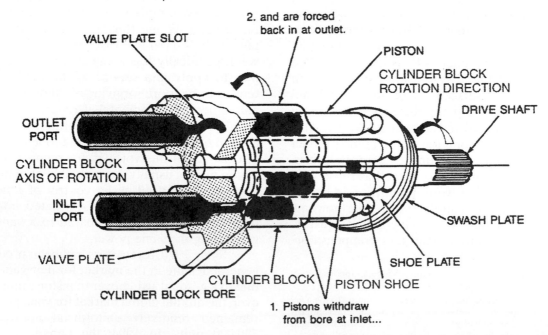

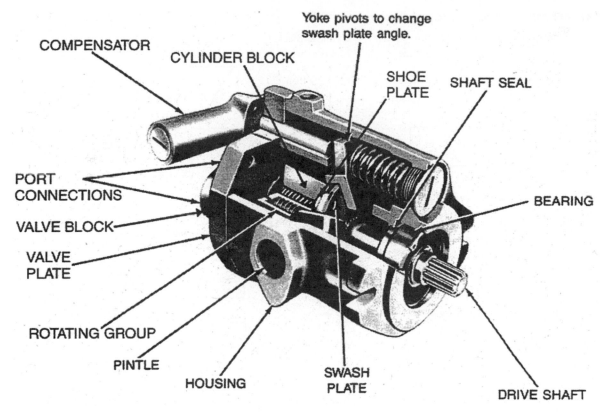

EXHIBIT 7 Piston Pump Construction

275,000 vane pumps worldwide, down significantly over the previous five years. In contrast, the plant's vane parts sales continued to increase.

Customers frequently preferred to rebuild an old vane pump or replace it with an identical pump rather than install a comparably priced, alternative style of pump, even if it meant foregoing improved performance. Unless customers were specifically intent upon upgrading their operations, they were often uninterested in introducing perturbations into their operating system. Their existing systems had been painstakingly optimized with the older style pump and introducing a newer style pump with potentially different operating characteristics would mean undergoing a costly re-optimization process. Additionally, workers would have to be re-trained to understand the particulars of the new pump's operation, maintenance, and repair. The sale of a new pump often generated 25–35 years of follow-up component sales and remanufacturing services, which could add up to several times the cost of the pump itself. While major maintenance and repairs were executed by the pump supplier, routine work was usually performed by the workers.

Piston pumps were preferred in new installations with high power requirements. These units now comprised over 50% of the world pump market, up from 25% ten years earlier, and had exhibited an annual growth of 15%, with 1,085,000 units sold in 1994. While Omaha's piston pump sales had remained relatively steady at around 95,000 per year over the past five years, sales of piston pump parts had increased steadily. The plant's piston product line primarily served the North American market, which represented approximately one third of the world sales volume. Since North American users tended to employ pumping systems which lacked computer control and complex circuitry loops, their needs were generally less demanding. Vickers' piston products, geared toward the less stringent requirements of this market, were unsuitable for the more sophisticated European user. With their limited electronic control capabilities, they also had higher operating noise

EXHIBIT 8 Piston Pump Manufacturing Process

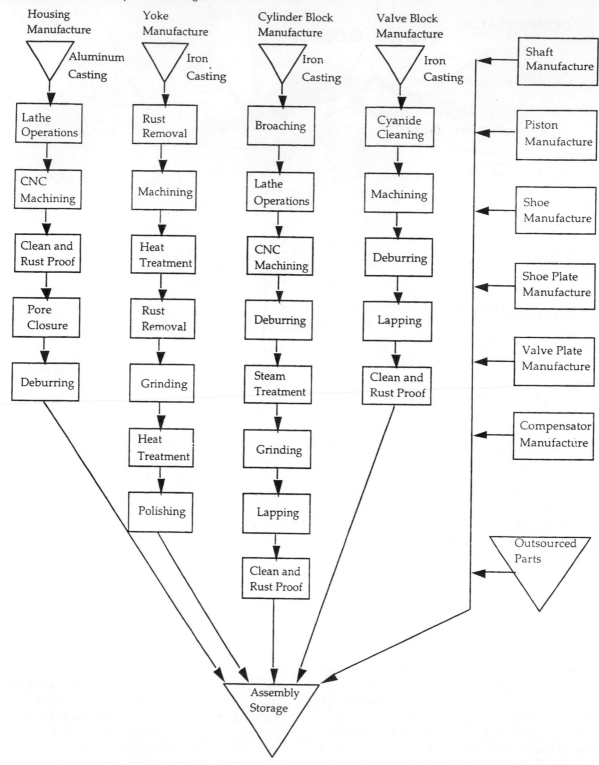

levels and lower pressure transmission capacities than the comparable offerings of Vickers' competitors. Exhibit 9 shows the product revenue trends for the Omaha plant.

The latest entry into the power generation arena was the electric pump. While these were the focus of much research and development, their reliability and operating cost were yet to be determined. Experts generally believed that the hydraulic power industry would make a gradual transition from vane to piston technology, with electrics as a potential future alternative. There were no "leapfrog" technologies seen on the horizon.

The most recent market trend was for customers, who were eager to reduce costs, to shift ever-greater portions of their pump manufacturing responsibilities to the pump supplier. As the customers' needs became increasingly complex, the pump supplier had to be prepared to accommodate these demands. In their drive to outsource more of their pump requirements, customers were searching for suppliers who had the manufacturing experience to build to specifications as well as the engineering expertise to help solve difficult hydraulic power problems. Suppliers who provided more comprehensive product lines and services could achieve higher profit margins.

In Weber's review of the Omaha operation, he concluded that new product development in the plant had been haphazard and reactionary. While Omaha's engineering facility was state-of-the-art and its employees were quite knowledgeable

technically, there was insufficient communication among groups working on different projects. Therefore, while the engineering services were being heavily utilized, there was much redundancy in the work, especially with the piston products. In addition, management had spent little time developing the comprehensive product line necessary for Vickers to be a full line supplier of hydraulic pumps. The rate of new product introductions had declined sharply, with recent introductions being driven by the desire to match competitor offerings rather than to strengthen the company's long-term strategic position. Furthermore, new products were often designed with little consideration given to minimizing plant engineering and manufacturing costs (Exhibit 10). For instance, the plant currently manufactured 17 products using 147 different components. The engineers on Weber's management team estimated that Vickers would need 49 products to cover the complete vane and piston pump market. By designing for manufacturability and interchangeability, all of these products could be completed using only 197 components. With part commonality, these 49 products could all be manufactured in the Omaha facility.

The Competition

The Omaha operation had two primary sources of competition. The first and less obvious source was composed of small pump shops who reverse engineered standard items from larger manufacturers and then sold these pirated products at much lower prices. These family-owned shops

EXHIBIT 9 1990–1994 Omaha Plant Revenues

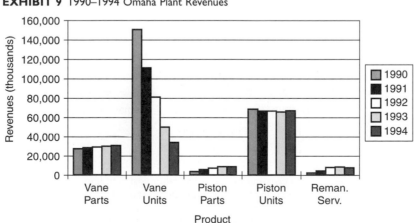

EXHIBIT 10 1990–1994 Omaha Plant Costs

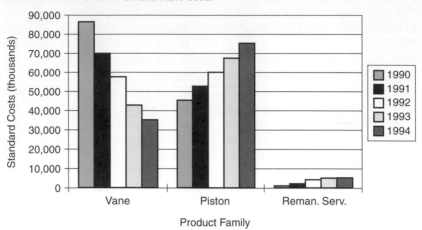

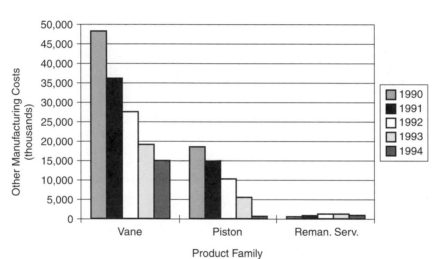

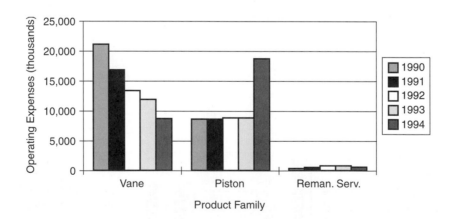

Definitions
Standard Costs = material cost, material burden, labor cost, and labor burden
Other Manufacturing Costs = maintenance, variance, scrap, shipping, inventory, and warranty costs
Operating Expenses = sales, general administrative, engineering, and research and development costs

required only a modest capital investment and had very low overhead costs, operating out of makeshift storefronts and employing few workers. While they sold pump units, the preponderance of the revenues for these "will-fitters"[6] derived from the sale of replacement parts for OEM[7] pumps. Compared to OEM replacement parts, these pirate parts were less expensive but provided measurably lower performance and reliability. Often located near their customers, these "will-fitters" were easily accessible and their technicians could arrive quickly in case of emergencies. Specializing in rapid, personalized, low cost service, these shops catered to start-up or smaller companies who had little credit and limited working capital. These constraints made the cost-performance trade-offs of these pirate products acceptable. Extremely rare a decade ago, these small "knock-off" shops were thriving and their numbers were fast growing in North America, stealing an estimated 20% of Omaha's "aftermarket" part sales in 1994.

The second and more threatening source of competition came from hydraulic equipment divisions within large multi-national corporations such as Mannesmann AG, Parker Hannifin, and Robert Bosch GmbH. These major corporations provided a full spectrum of product lines manufactured at cutting-edge production facilities. Along with high quality products, they also possessed the technical expertise to develop innovative solutions to the most advanced customer problems. These companies had manufacturing plants, administrative and sales offices, stores, and warehouses around the world, as well as thousands of distributors who attended quickly to customer needs. However, as these vendors expanded and increased their productivity, their product offerings became indistinguishable from competitor units and their service began to suffer.

The Plan

When John Weber became Vice President of the Industrial Group in February, he assumed responsibility for six North American, one Latin American, and three European operations along with joint ventures in Japan and India. Additionally, besides overseeing all Vickers' sales and service locations, Weber was leading the advance into China and the expansion in India. Gregarious and direct by nature, Weber was born in Calgary, Alberta, and was trained as a mechanical engineer at the University of Toronto. After working for three years as a Facilities Engineer at Shell Canada, he enrolled at the Harvard Business School. In the ten years after graduation, Weber worked at McKinsey & Company, Baxter Healthcare, and General Electric. Each consecutive appointment entailed greater challenge and authority. In spite of his success at General Electric, Weber had readily accepted TRINOVA's job offer, eagerly anticipating its rigors and potential rewards. In their first meeting, TRINOVA's CEO, Darryl Allen, informed him that, despite being headquartered in Maumee, Ohio, his first responsibility was to address the situation at the Omaha plant. Weber recalled Allen's exact words, "Whatever you decide to do with that facility, do it without spending a nickel of TRINOVA's money."

During his first tour of the Omaha plant, Weber noticed some obvious signs of trouble. Much of the equipment was over forty years old and had been poorly maintained. On those machines still in use, operators had become skilled at making minute readjustments in the control settings in order to produce output which met design specifications. There were also numerous pieces of antiquated equipment which appeared to have been untouched for many years. Indeed, a significant portion of the floorspace was occupied by unused, obsolete machinery which no one had bothered to remove. In addition, the morale of the work-force seemed to be low. After multiple visits and many group sessions with hourly workers, who were initially wary and reticent, Weber gained some insight into their apparent apathy. The plant, which had seen a series of plant managers, was generally acknowledged to be unprofitable and workers felt that their jobs were in jeopardy either through imminent layoffs or plant shutdown.

After a series of strained meetings with plant management, Weber decided that the organization focused much of its energies on crisis control, leaving limited time for business planning. Despite having installed an activity-based accounting system in late 1989, management had yet to close the feedback loop. Little time was devoted to analyzing and

[6]These pirate shops were often called "will-fitters" because their parts "will fit" OEM pumps despite being made with significantly looser tolerances than OEM replacement parts. The Omaha plant maintained strict tolerances of ±0.0002 inches on all of its manufactured parts.

[7]Original equipment manufacturer, such as Vickers, Incorporated.

interpreting the collected data. Thus, valuable cost information was not being used to help improve the plant's manufacturing or product development performance.

Initially, Weber felt there were three equally viable alternatives. First, he could keep the Omaha plant open and try to make it profitable again. Weber was drawn to this option, feeling that the plant had been neglected and with some investment could be transformed into a world-class manufacturing operation. While overcoming the restrictive work rules at Vickers' only unionized facility would be difficult, this type of challenge was also a once-in-a-lifetime opportunity.

Second, he could shut down the Omaha plant and build a brand new facility in another state with lower wage rates. In exploring this option, Weber had quietly contacted various state governments to inquire about possible relocation. The governor of Oklahoma expressed an interest in possibly siting a new plant in Vinita, close to the Oklahoma-Missouri border and approximately fifty miles from the existing Joplin plant. With Oklahoma offering generous financial incentives and an inviting location, close to one of Vickers' other plants as well as to an iron foundry, this option was highly tempting. However, building and furnishing a new plant would cost an estimated $35 million. Additionally, in the event of a closure, the National Labor Review Board required the plant's management to negotiate the "effects of the decision." A settlement must be reached on elements such as worker severance pay, benefits, transfers, and relocation. Weber realized that the combination of closing the Omaha facility and building a greenfield plant would be extremely expensive.

Third, he could close the Omaha plant and disperse its products to existing plants in Joplin and Searcy. Since these two plants had little spare capacity, this option would require expanding Joplin and Searcys' present operations to accommodate the new product influx. An estimated $18 million of new equipment purchases would be necessary. Moreover, the productivity of the Joplin and Searcy plants would suffer during the initial stages of the transition as existing operations were rearranged to create space to manufacture the additional products. These product transfer costs along with the closing costs for the Omaha facility made this third alternative only slightly less expensive than the second option.

Weber, along with a small group of advisors which eventually included plant management personnel, spent two months of fourteen hour days examining Omaha's operations, product lines, finances, and competitors as well as forecasts about the future trends in the pump market. From their analysis, this management team devised a plan to keep the Omaha facility open. To excel in the oncoming competitive environment, the plant needed to become more aligned with customer demands. Weber envisioned this realignment along three dimensions: product scope, product quality, and service performance. An aggressive improvement agenda was crafted for each dimension, to be pursued simultaneously.

The Engineering Laboratory was to begin developing a series of products to cover the entire vane and piston pump market. To reduce risk and uncertainty, customers were consolidating. In this vein, they wanted to deal with fewer vendors. To be one of those selected, suppliers had to be able to satisfy all the customer's product needs. However, the goal was not only to have a full line of offerings, but also to create distinctive products which would be difficult to copy, thus creating switching costs for the customer and a barrier against competitors. This strategy would stimulate the sale of new pumps while helping the Omaha plant capture the more lucrative "after market" sales of replacement parts.

To achieve world-class quality, the plant needed to upgrade its manufacturing equipment and reconfigure its operating system. Improvements were divided into two sections: manufacturing apparatus and process, and employee mindset. The plant required a new set of testing equipment, at an estimated cost of $400,000. This purchase was of top priority since the existing system was outdated and could only detect gross malfunctions and defects. To reduce process variability and eliminate unnecessary rework costs, management wanted to introduce Statistical Process Control techniques. To reduce material handling costs and batch cycle times, the current manufacturing layout was to be rearranged into sets of work cells, called "focus factories," organized by product type or design (Exhibit 11). The individual cells would manufacture separate components, while a set of linked cells would produce a specific pump. Converting to multi-functional manufacturing teams was intended to increase productivity and flexibil-

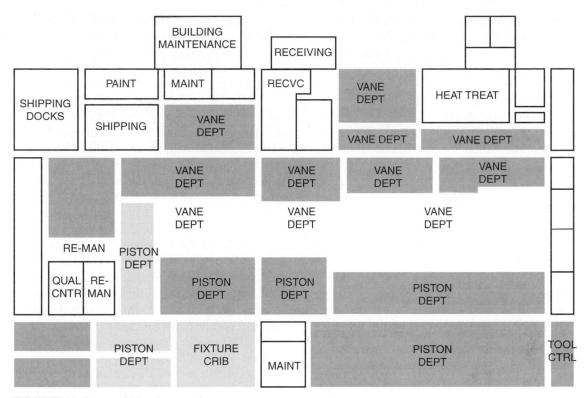

EXHIBIT 11 Proposed Manufacturing Layout

ity. With the exception of heat treatment, pumps were to be produced from raw material through assembly by the workers within a focus factory.

It was recognized that these manufacturing improvements could only be achieved by changing the employee mindset. This aspect of the proposed plan was by far the most challenging. In order to group equipment and workers into flexible, multi-functional cells, workers needed to be trained in a diverse array of skills, from operating to conducting mundane maintenance activities on numerous different types of equipment. To improve and better control the part quality within these cells, workers also needed to be instructed in the fundamentals of self-inspection. Initial training costs were calculated to be in the range of $350,000. For cellular manufacturing to succeed, workers had to become accustomed to functioning in self-directed teams, without an official reporting hierarchy. Many of these changes in worker responsibilities were not allowed under the current labor contract.

The changes to be implemented in the new product development and manufacturing processes would have immediate effects upon customer ser-

vice. Streamlining the component demands would lower the manufacturing costs, allowing the Omaha plant to offer competitively priced products. Restructuring the manufacturing process would increase the plant's flexibility, allowing it to lower its lead times and meet a higher percentage of its delivery commitments. With improved product quality, the Omaha plant could expand and extend its product warranties. Management also intended to exploit Omaha's vast technical resources, from its Engineering Laboratory to its remanufacturing division. Groups of engineers were to be assigned to work exclusively with individual companies in order to develop trust and a service history. This program would lay the groundwork for eventually siting technical teams at the customer's plant. These resident engineers would provide the latest product information and help anticipate the direction of the customer's future needs.

Weber realized that the proposed plan was extremely ambitious and controversial. To combat large competitors, the Omaha plant needed to provide a comprehensive array of products and services. Attempts to halt the encroachment of small "will-fitter" shops with legal actions had proven ineffective and uneconomical, so the plant needed to make pirating its products unprofitable. Weber felt the plan emphasized the Omaha facility's strengths while remedying its weaknesses. To its advantage, the plant already had a few of the key ingredients. The work-force, though specialized, was highly trained and the remanufacturing service was well-established. The advanced Engineering Laboratory was capable of developing new products and solving complicated hydraulic problems. The plant also had access to TRINOVA's extensive, highly efficient network of distribution channels to facilitate rapid customer service. However, the plan also required the cooperation of both TRINOVA's CEO and the union. Weber was confident that he could convince Darryl Allen to infuse the necessary $750,000. Weber was far less certain that he and his management team could overcome the objections of the workers' union.

The Employees

The plant operated with three, 8-hour shifts/day, 5 days/week, and employed 1,173 workers, 960 of whom were hourly and 213 of whom were salaried. Approximately 95% of the hourly workers, with average age and service of 43 and 14 years respectively, were members of the United Paperworkers International Union. The relationship between the plant's management and the workers' union had not always been cordial. Since its certification in 1952, the union had staged six work stoppages in Omaha. The longest strike was 13 weeks in 1970 and the most recent strike was a 2 week walk-out during 1979.

Management considered the current contract to be unsupportive of the proposed turnaround strategy. The most contentious issues centered around work rules and pay rates. The existing work rules were highly restrictive, with 35 different, narrowly defined job classifications. For instance, material handling and part inspection duties were separate classifications, idling machine operators when inventory buffers emptied and preventing them from inspecting their own work, thus, creating bottlenecks in the manufacturing process. In addition, the temporary assignment of workers to different job classifications was limited to 10 regular work days out of 50, restricting management's ability to respond to both expected and unexpected manpower imbalances. The cap on tempo-

rary assignment time also reduced the availability of on-the-job cross-training experience for workers. These types of constraints on duty overlap and worker mobility were completely incompatible with the proposed cellular manufacturing scheme.

In the new contract, management wanted to reduce the number of classifications to 10 by combining job functions and permitting shared duties. This restructuring would relieve certain bottlenecks and allow management greater freedom to allocate workers where they were needed in the manufacturing process. However, the workers had two related concerns. First, they feared that reallocating workers would lead to reductions in the overall labor-force. Second, if this event occurred, the workers feared that management would be tempted to overload the remaining workers with additional responsibilities, making promotions and raises based upon the mastery of ever more duties, thus eroding seniority rights.

The existing compensation scheme promised a base wage of $15.15 per hour, with premium pay for weekend work. The Omaha plant's pay scale was the highest in the region. Management wanted to negotiate less ambitious wage increase guarantees and the elimination of premium rates for weekend work. In return, management offered an expanded profit-sharing plan, with year-end bonuses tied to the financial performance of the plant. The workers, being risk averse, were opposed to any proposal which did not ensure a continuing annual increase in their total take-home pay. Most workers were part of a two-income family and, due to the region's rapidly expanding business sector, Omaha's unemployment rate was only 3%.

In two weeks, the current labor contract would expire. A senior manager at the plant expressed the general sentiment of management personnel: "While I sympathize with the workers' predicament, I still think they are not looking at the big picture. We need to implement this plan to turn Omaha's operations around. Otherwise, there won't be any jobs for the union to fight for." However, one of the younger plant workers had a different view: "I've worked at this plant for five years and my father has worked here for 28 years. During that time, we've seen plans and managers come and go. The workers are the ones who will make this plant successful again. The only way this plant will have a future is if management plays fair with the workers."

There was little hope that the workers would continue to work beyond the expiration date without a ratified contract. There had been previous strikes over less substantial contract changes. It was clear to both sides that if a new contract had not been approved by the negotiation deadline, the workers would strike. Management was willing to compromise on the cross-training issue. Initially workers would only be required to perform their own quality inspections and material handling, with operators gradually expected to develop maintenance and additional machine skills. As September approached and the union deliberated over this concession, management began to analyze the impact of different scenarios (Exhibit 12).

Weber ended the phone call with his mind far away from his abandoned golf game. He had just asked Whitworth to convene an emergency meeting of the management team. As he hurried to catch up to his family, Weber wondered what course of action he should recommend at tomorrow's early morning session.

EXHIBIT 12   Strike Impacts and Contingency Actions

Strike Duration	Impact	Contingency Actions
1 week	$1.5 million loss in profit	Increase utilization of subcontract suppliers for work which can be outsourced
4 weeks	$5 million loss in profit $13 million non-recoverable loss in sales	Utilize excess capacity at other Vickers manufacturing plants for work which can be relocated Utilize salaried work-force and Engineering Laboratory for assembly and testing respectively, both of which cannot be subcontracted or relocated Monitor order backlog and have communication plan ready to manage customer reaction to work stoppage Define clear responsibilities for all inexperienced plant personnel to prevent work-related accidents Contact local authorities and media to ensure security for continuing workers and production facility
> 5 weeks	Cripples Omaha business forever	

Deloitte & Touche Consulting Group

June 14, 1995, was unseasonably warm and humid. Maria Chen, a senior consultant at Deloitte & Touche Consulting Group (Consulting Group), was half way through a twelve-week engagement with SKS Manufacturing, a Pontiac, Michigan based auto supplier. SKS had engaged the Consulting Group to reduce inventory levels in its main plant. After six weeks, however, work-in-process inventory had actually increased by 13%.

Early that afternoon, Chen had retreated from the shop floor to the relative calm of the second-floor conference room to pick-up her messages and to briefly escape the stifling heat and throbbing noise from the floor below. She fell into the first available chair, leaned back, breathed in the coolness and tried to relax, but her concerns about the engagement interfered. To make things worse, she had been stopped on her way up by Jack Skidmore, the SKS president. He had tersely requested an explanation for the plant's lackluster inventory improvements. She had no solid answer. She took a deep breath, picked up the phone, punched in her password, and felt her stomach tighten as she listened to not one but two urgent voice messages from, David Hendry, the partner leading the project. She dialed the number he had left, and listened to him say:

> Maria, I talked to some folks at SKS this morning and they are not at all pleased with the way this thing is going. Listen, I know you're doing your best there, but next Monday at the steering committee meeting—we *have* to make them understand we're moving in the right direction. I'll be out there tomorrow. Let's get together with Annette and Ben to decide what you might do.

As she dropped the phone into its cradle, she realized she wasn't certain about what to do, but thought there were probably two options. She could either build a presentation for the steering committee based on all the positive changes that occurred over the past six weeks (however, most of the evidence would be qualitative) or she could focus the next couple of days on trying to produce a noticeable reduction in inventory, which would be a long shot at best.

DELOITTE & TOUCHE CONSULTING GROUP

In 1995, Deloitte & Touche Consulting Group was officially designated a wholly owned subsidiary of Deloitte & Touche LLP. Deloitte & Touche LLP, known as one of the "big six" accounting firms, was formed in December 1989 by a merger between Deloitte, Haskins & Sells and Touche Ross.[1] Traditionally Deloitte & Touche had been thought of as an audit and tax service firm, but at year end 1993, the Consulting Group, which had a client base significantly different than the audit and tax practices, comprised 28% of the firm's total revenue. In the United States, the Consulting Group was comprised of 2,700 professionals (including 250 partners) and 5,600 consulting professionals worldwide.

The Consulting Group focused on delivering services in four main areas: operations, information technology, financial management and strategy development in a broad set of industries, including manufacturing, healthcare and financial services. In addition to the core, the Consulting Group teamed with its wholly-owned subsidiaries to deliver services. Those organizations included Braxton Associates, a Boston-based strategy consulting firm; DRT International and CMD Systems, application and systems development firms.

[1]*Professional Service Trends: Deloitte & Touche,* Dataquest ® report, Dun & Bradstreet Corporation, February 25, 1994, was referenced for this section.

In 1995, the Consulting Group merged with ICS, a firm specializing in the implementation of large scale SAP projects.

The Consulting Group's primary competitors included Andersen Consulting, Price Waterhouse, Ernst & Young, as well as McKinsey, BCG, Booz Allen and CSC Index. Industry-wide, the range of management consulting services could be described as a spectrum with strategy consulting on one end and systems implementation on the other. The Consulting Group viewed its strength and position in the market as an "implementation" consulting firm. The firm's ability to offer a fully integrated solution of strategy, operations, and information technology was key to its success.

The Consulting Industry

Since the early 1990s, considerable transformation had occurred within the consulting services industry. Due to a number of factors, clients had become much more informed and demanding, which had resulted in the following:

- **Integrated teams** As late as the early 1990s, consultants often worked alone. Now, work teams almost always included key client employees as well as consultants. This arrangement usually allowed both parties to learn from the other more effectively, as well as help the client to participate more fully in defining and implementing business solutions. At the same time, the breadth of personalities involved, their disparate backgrounds and a lack of common understanding of approaches could often add additional complexity to the situation.

- **Knowledge transfer** In the past, the norm had been to perform the agreed upon services and then to move on, once the consulting assignment was complete. However, clients began to realize that the benefits from their consulting investment were very short lived unless its employees could carry on effectively where consultants had left off. Clients expected critical knowledge to be transferred from the consultants to key employees. *Teaching* had became an integral part of successful consulting.

- **Third party ratings** The proliferation of consulting firms had fueled increased scrutiny and the birth of independent organizations which compiled evaluative reports and cross-industry ratings. The Gartner Group, for example, evaluated a range of factors, from success of implementations to "completeness of vision."

- **Integration of approaches** Clients were beginning to require consultants to have the ability and resources to develop and implement solutions that linked strategy to operations and technology more closely than they had in the past. Additionally, clients increasingly expected consultants to have industry-specific knowledge and an ability to provide solutions world-wide.

Career Progression

A new professional at the Consulting Group could expect his or her career to progress through the following levels, with a partner being the most senior position:

- **Consultant/Analyst** While consultants performed many of the same tasks as the senior consultants, they generally lacked the experience level of their senior colleagues. Consultants were typically hired as undergraduates fresh from college. Although some consultants made their way through the ranks, many in this position chose to return to graduate school. Analysts were also hired straight from undergraduate programs, and were expected to provide the analytical support needed to make informed decisions during the engagement process. In addition, the Consulting Group hired Summer Associates, usually MBAs between the first and second year of their coursework. Summer associates' responsibilities were similar to the senior consultants.

- **Senior Consultant** Senior consultants were usually hired from MBA programs, often with two or three years of industry experience. Major tasks included collecting and analyzing data, focusing and taking responsibility for particular sub-projects and presentations, facilitating and managing client teams and helping to prepare proposals to clients. They were often supported by an analyst.

- **Senior Manager/Manager** Senior managers dealt with the upper levels of client management, particularly with issues and problems that arose during the course of an engagement, and sometimes worked with multiple clients at one time. They also handled proposal presentations to prospective clients. Managers supervised several senior consultants on a single client engagement.

- **Partner** Just under 10% of the firm's consulting professionals earned this title, which generally took six to eleven years to achieve. As senior managers became partners, their focus shifted from the work involved in engagements to managing the client relationship. Partners typically handled two or three clients at one time, and focused on applying their experience to finding solutions and making sure the client remained satisfied with the Consulting Group. Partners were also responsible for selling consulting group services, and usually developed specialization in a particular industry or service line.

No fixed rules existed regarding progression up the ladder, but a framework of "expectations" outlined what professionals were expected to master in order to proceed. Professionals received appraisals at the end of each engagement. In general, new hires with undergraduate degrees entered at the analyst or consultant level, and could expect to be promoted to senior consultant within approximately three years. New hires with graduate degrees or a minimum of five years of work experience were given the senior consultant title. Training for the new consultant was a combination of new hire/new position retreats and on-the-job training. The Consulting Group put a great deal of emphasis on learning from doing.

Roughly two-thirds of new hires came from industry, with the remainder coming from universities like Harvard, Wharton, Chicago and Kellogg. About 75% of the latter category had advanced degrees (primarily MBAs) and therefore also had some prior work experience. Turnover at the Consulting Group was between 15 and 20% annually. The consultants that decided to leave the firm often cited a desire for a change in lifestyle or decided to join a client in management and executive positions. Additionally, some consultants left to apply their "implementation" skills in start-up businesses.

SKS MANUFACTURING— THE CLIENT

The Company

SKS Manufacturing, a metal stamping manufacturer, was founded in 1959 by two General Motors trained engineers, Allen Kramer and John Stefanski. SKS supplied a variety of exhaust system components to Tier I and Tier II suppliers, as well as after-market distributors. Since its founding, SKS had been, for better and for worse, completely tied to the automobile industry.

In the beginning, Kramer and Stefanski made the most of their "big three" connections and translated them into a solid and steadily growing business. In the early 1960s, a third partner, Robert Skidmore, came aboard. Skidmore, a renowned charmer, was able to win new contracts quickly and ultimately set the company on its current trajectory. Still privately held, Kramer's eldest son, Jack was named president in 1989. Ownership was split between the Kramer and Skidmore families; Stefanski was bought out in 1977. Since those early days, SKS had grown into an formidable competitor and a leader within its industry; 1995 year end sales were projected to be just under $570 million, and SKS now employed over 5700 people.

The elder Skidmore had brought a vision to the company of industry leadership and sales figures that were far beyond his partners' original conservative projections and careful cash flow analysis. He firmly believed sales focus was the vehicle with which long term success would be attained, and instituted a sales structure that had remained intact. SKS salespeople focused on direct sales and kept existing customers happy within Region I (Michigan—especially Metro Detroit, Ohio, and western Indiana). Manufacturing representatives were used to cover the rest of the United States and to a small, but growing, degree Mexico and Canada. Sales were heavily concentrated with three major customers, which comprised 65% of the total. SKS had only begun exporting in the last five years, and consequently only 3% of sales were outside of the U.S. The current generation of managers realized this would have to be changed to ensure ongoing viability.

SKS's main plant was located in Pontiac, Michigan, an industrial suburb north of Detroit. The facility was 450,000 square feet, which gave the company ample capacity for current volume plus a little room to grow. Most of the manufacturing processes were performed at this location. Some items required special coatings, and were shipped out to one or two nearby suppliers. One warehouse was also located on the premises, but a second was inconveniently located six miles to the south of this facility.

The SKS shop-floor was a dingy, noisy place—smelling of the lubricating oil used to coat the metal to help it flow in the presses. In the press section, brake-presses, making between 20 and 60 blows per minute, stamped out metal parts from raw sheet metal, then spat the newly trimmed components into a chute, which emptied into a wire-cage bin on a pallet. The presses were drawn from a variety of vintages—from new, automatic presses with computer control to a few battered old WWII-vintage presses, with automatic guards incongruously retro-fitted. Testament to the bad old days of press-work were the occasional old-timers who would shake one's hand absent a full complement of digits. In general, press work involved some vigilance for safety's sake, but was primarily a machine-tending job. Over the previous few years, SKS had seen more pressure to change between components more quickly as their product range grew and customer demands for responsiveness became stronger. As a result of this, runs had become shorter and die-changes more frequent. Operators had become involved in this activity, but press-*setting* was still, primarily, a job for a skilled setter. Most people on the floor agreed that it was now a much better place to work than it had been, but that it was still a little chaotic on occasion, with many components sitting between presses and "split-batches" making the job of keeping the production shop orderly very difficult.

SKS's new products were conceptualized and, for the most part, designed in-house. SKS had a full-time engineer pool of nine, with an average experience level of twelve years. The in-house design engineers used manual drawings and CAD applications. On occasion, for specialized applications, SKS would seek the help of an outside engineering and design firm.

Key Personnel

The majority of the SKS management had been with the company for most of their respective careers, and had fairly homogeneous backgrounds. SKS management stated that employees were treated "like family." From the Consulting Group's perspective, it was important to work well with the following people.

Jack Skidmore had been the SKS president since 1989. The eldest son of Robert Skidmore, he was, they said, "molded in his father's image." So, quite naturally, he began a career in sales after he graduated from Central Michigan University in 1972 with a BA in history. He successfully worked for a few firms outside the family business (including starting his own insurance agency), and then moved into the business thirteen years ago. Within SKS, he proved himself as a sales manager, tightening long term relationships that had begun to unravel with escalating industry competitiveness.

Skidmore was known to "promise the world" and then somehow find a way to deliver. This behavior solidified several teetering customer relationships, but made his sales trips dreaded among the core group of workers that could be counted on to, in Jack's own words, "make things shake." Often out of the plant on customer visits, Skidmore relied heavily on David Fletcher to run the day-to-day operations.

David Fletcher had been the SKS plant manager for the last eight years. Fletcher, with an engineering background and twenty two years experience in the automotive industry, had joined SKS about fourteen years previously. Since then he had held a variety of positions, including material manager, production control manager, chief engineer and assistant plant manager. Fletcher was known as a hard working and fair person, and although his temper could flare unexpectedly, he had won the respect of many SKS employees. He knew the plant inside and out, and tolerated little less from his core management staff.

Stan Janovich was the first shift supervisor, and had been for nearly nineteen years. Janovich was just a few years from retirement, and, although he was looking forward to spending time at his northern Michigan cabin, he wondered aloud how things would continue to work without him around. He took a great deal of pride in his contributions to SKS, and felt things were "pretty much in place." Janovich had been with SKS almost since its beginning, and had seen the ebbs and flows of the auto industry, so, as he explained at the last staff meeting, things will "work themselves out."

The Engagement

SKS had sought out the help of a third party several months earlier. The company was experiencing a critical cash flow shortage and had delayed payment to several suppliers in order to service its payroll obligations. Additionally, SKS was unable to maintain acceptable customer service levels, shipping only 77% of customer orders in time to make required delivery dates. By April 1995, SKS management realized it no longer had the luxury of time, or the internal capability and focus to turn around the situation; they interviewed several consulting firms before ultimately engaging the services of the Deloitte & Touche Consulting Group.

The Consulting Group initially considered a longer term "reengineering" approach that would focus on redesigning cross-functional business processes. This approach would be a radical change from the "functional silos" from which SKS currently performed business tasks. However, to begin with, the Consulting Group proposed a shorter, and more focused, twelve week engagement that would stabilize the current cash position. The consultants advised that a radical "reengineering" approach, with the company in a cash crunch, might introduce a level of risk that the firm might not recover from. The Consulting Group viewed the twelve week engagement as a necessary foundation to start the longer term project, and SKS, with little previous experience with consultants, thought this would be a good time to "test drive" the firm.

The SKS project fell onto David Hendry's line of responsibility, and Annette Wattley-Davis, a senior manager, would be second in command. Together, they selected a team of three consultants and two business analysts for the first 12 week project to stabilize operations. Additionally, they obtained commitment from Jack Skidmore, David Fletcher, and Stan Janovich that they would spend at least 25% of their time working with the team.

The engagement began in early May 1995.

The Engagement Team

A typical Consulting Group engagement of this scope involved four to five professionals: a partner, a manager or senior manager, two to three senior consultants, as well as a couple of analysts. The team for the SKS engagement included the following people:

David Hendry was a partner based in the Detroit office. Hendry had spent the last eighteen years heavily involved in the automotive industry. He had worked with the three major automotive manufacturers and many of the major automotive part suppliers around the world. An MIT-trained engineer, Hendry began his career as a design engineer at Ford Motor Company, and after several years and an MBA from the University of Chicago moved into the consulting world. He had been a partner for seven years, and his concentration in this industry made him one of the Consulting Group's automotive "gurus." Hendry had recently taken on even greater responsibility for bringing in new business, and was successfully shouldering his

new load. Over the years he had acquired a reputation for results in the industry, which was a source of personal pride and continued motivation.

Annette Wattley-Davis joined the Consulting Group as a senior consultant eight years ago, fresh from an MBA at Wharton. Based in Cleveland, she had focused, for most of her Consulting Group tenure, on business process reengineering for manufacturing firms. As a manager, she was nominated by her local office to participate in a six-month national effort to develop the Consulting Group's next generation Reengineering for Results™ methodology. Since Wattley-Davis became a senior manager last year, she had focused almost exclusively on the automotive industry.

In addition to the SKS engagement, she was finishing up another project in Dallas that required between 2–3 days of her time over the first six weeks of this engagement.

Maria Chen worked for three years after finishing her BA in economics (Amherst '89) for General Electric as an associate in their management training program. In this program she was exposed to many different areas of operations including finance, internal audit, manufacturing, and engineering. At the Harvard Business School (MBA '94), Chen performed well academically, and had a knack for quantitative analysis. After her arrival at the Consulting Group in August 1994, Chen reflected, "I came to this firm to get some diversified hands-on operations experience." Since that time, she had been undergoing training and assisting with various projects. SKS, although her second direct manufacturing experience, would be the first project where she had direct responsibility for significant pieces of the work.

Ben Rohan and **Ramesh Patel** were the other two consultants on the engagement team. Rohan was an experienced senior consultant based in the Detroit office. He had a BS in computer science from the University of Illinois and an MBA from Dartmouth, and a number of years of procurement and manufacturing experience. Since he joined the Consulting Group last year, he had been on three different engagements, one in health care, one in financial services, and the last one in manufacturing. Patel joined the Consulting Group as a summer associate. A Cornell-trained engineer, his objectives were to gain some practical client experience and to evaluate the Consulting Group as a future employer. The firm looked for Patel to be an active team member and to provide analytical support. The Consulting Group also wanted to recruit him for the following year.

The Planning Meeting

Wattley-Davis recognized that a multiple pronged approach would be required to address the SKS short term business and manufacturing problems. A quick analysis of the company's cost structure and inventory levels indicated that an effort to both reduce cash investment in raw material and to synchronize production and procurement would alleviate the immediate problems.

About a week before the start date, she brought the team together to discuss the preliminary issues and to make sure everyone knew what they were expected to accomplish and were comfortable in their roles. One team would be led by the industry-hire Ben Rohan. His job was to attack the material procurement processes and raw material levels. The second team was led by Maria Chen. She would address the production scheduling processes and synchronize production operations with purchasing. They were expected to work together on this "quick hit" opportunity to reduce inventory.

Chen walked away from the meeting excited and was eager to begin the project. When she returned to her office, she reviewed her notes to make sure she knew exactly what she needed to accomplish over the next twelve weeks. As she saw it, her main goals were:

- To develop production scheduling rules and processes that would smooth production, relieve the most severe bottlenecks and reduce the number of crises the plant was experiencing, which would decrease the need for "buffer" inventory;
- To design and implement a pilot of a pull-based synchronous manufacturing cell in twelve weeks, as well as a new factory layout design and roll-out plan;
- To work with Ben Rohan to reduce overall inventory levels by $10M within twelve weeks.

Additionally, the Consulting Group wanted to position itself for the larger reengineering opportunity, and identify any further add-on work.

Time Zero

Chen was very anxious to make a good first impression with the client. She had spent the weekend before reading up on synchronous manufac-

turing techniques, and had placed a few calls to a few Consulting Group colleagues that she had heard worked on similar engagements. She flew into Detroit Metropolitan airport the night before and was the first to arrive at the plant.

Upon arriving, Chen notified the receptionist that she was with the Deloitte & Touche Consulting Group reengineering team, and, although early, asked to see the plant manager, David Fletcher. In a few minutes, Fletcher came into the lobby, and approached Chen. She expected a warm welcome, but realized immediately that either Fletcher was not pleased she was there or hadn't had his requisite caffeine intake that morning. After a perfunctory handshake, Fletcher wanted to know "What exactly did she think she was doing there?" Chen was shocked with the cold reception and Fletcher's lack of information, and did not understand why Jack Skidmore had not informed Fletcher about the start of the engagement, the use of consultants, and the scope of the project. Fletcher suggested Chen leave the plant site until he had time to sort the whole thing out.

Soon the rest of the consulting team arrived in the lobby, and Chen relayed her story to Hendry and Wattley-Davis. Hendry phoned Skidmore, catching him on his way to the airport, and found Fletcher had just that day returned from a ten-day vacation. Skidmore agreed to smooth everything over, and the consulting group team entered the plant an hour and a half later. The engagement had begun, but Chen could not imagine a rockier beginning.

Ramp Up

Annette Wattley-Davis recognized that Chen, as a fairly new consultant, was taking on a lot of responsibility and was being thrown into a difficult and vague situation with this engagement. She spent some extra time with Chen talking her through some of the issues she would likely run into in the next few weeks. Wattley-Davis relayed lessons she had learned the hard way, for example, the importance of gaining consensus around new ideas and the difficulty of making changes on the factory floor. She also worked with Chen to develop a detailed work plan for her part of the project, and suggested ways to integrate the work into the team's overall work plan.

The first week was hard but after the second week, Chen had started to settle into the SKS culture. The team had made a spartan but comfortable conference room on the second floor their headquarters They spent the first few weeks there collecting data, creating a spreadsheet model of material flow, and eating late night pizzas. The team had begun to work well together, and although Jack Skidmore and David Fletcher only spent parts of their work day with the consultants, they had begun to spend more time with them after hours. Chen was working at full speed on a complex spreadsheet model that she believed would "knock the socks off" both Wattley-Davis and their client. Because the spreadsheet turned out to be a bit more complex than she had first designed, she ended up having to sacrifice some of the other items on her list of things to do.

At the end of the third week, the team members, including client team members, prepared summaries of their analysis and previewed them with selected members of the plant staff. In a group of eighteen, the team members individually presented their overheads. Chen's presentation on her material flow simulation did not go nearly as well as she had anticipated. Stan Janovich, whom she had wanted to talk with earlier in the week (but had run out of time), pointed out many issues that had not been accounted for in the model. She grudgingly realized Janovich was completely on target with his criticisms, and jotted some notes for the simulation revisions.

After the meeting, Wattley-Davis took Chen aside and quizzed her about how much of the modeling effort had been reviewed with Janovich and other key people on the floor prior to the meeting. She also asked how much time she had actually spent on the factory floor and with the other team led by Rohan over the last few weeks. Wattley-Davis's displeasure was obvious as she suggested Chen move her work space from the conference room to the factory floor. Chen dejectedly agreed and as she turned away, the senior manager continued, "And, pull the plug on that spreadsheet for a while."

Phase Two

By the end of the fourth week, Chen began to realize the value of her manager's mandate to move down to the shop floor. After staining and nearly ruining her new Donna Karan suit, she wore jeans and an equally replaceable shirt. Her first encounters with Janovich left her with the dis-

tinct impression that he was gruff, unapproachable, and not at all interested in the Consulting Group's work, but as she came to know him, she realized that was not completely true. She began to have casual conversations with him about his twin grandchildren (Nicole and Nicholas), the history of the plant, and eventually how scheduling work was really done outside of the computerized program which she had been briefed on.

She gradually learned that there were two sets of procedures being followed on a daily basis—a formal documented process and the way work was really done. Alterations from the formal process were sometimes for the sake of a short cut and other times to avoid the computerized system which many folks on the floor felt was basically useless. Chen also found that Janovich's opinion carried a lot of weight in the SKS world even though he only held the title of day shift supervisor.

As she spent more and more time with Janovich, she realized he consistently "bad mouthed" the sales group for dumping orders at the end of the quarter and changing priorities of jobs once they had been launched. He also explained his computer mistrust; the bills of material and parts lists developed by engineering were always out-of-date. He pointed to a dented gray (and "rust") filing cabinet that contained marked-up parts lists and prints that were the plant's "true" records. Janovich also admitted that inventory accuracy had always been a problem. Chen also discovered that in addition to poor data in the system, most of the applications were not integrated. Much of the basic data for an order had to be reentered when moving from order entry to the manufacturing system. Betty Ranowski, a long time SKS clerk, was responsible for re-keying the orders into the manufacturing system every Monday.

Chen mentioned this new information to some of her team mates. They suggested she meet with the sales, engineering, and information technology managers to contrast their points-of-view with Janovich's. This made sense to Chen, but she decided to stick closely to the directives given by Wattley-Davis—stay on the floor until you fully understand the production system. The memories of the first-day and her sinking spreadsheet model seemed very fresh, and she was intent on redeeming herself as quickly as possible. She did, however, talk to the clerk, Betty Ranowski, about the time and effort required to re-enter all of the manufacturing orders.

During the fifth week, Wattley-Davis evaluated Chen's progress (versus her original work plan), and asked again that she spend more time working with Rohan and key information technology people at SKS. By the end of the week, Chen began to feel like things were back on track. She had started to make some changes in the floor layout with Janovich's input. One of the major bottlenecks in material flow started to ease, and jobs seemed to be moving much faster. She began collecting data and posting the performance trends by stamping line in a location where they couldn't be missed. The trend lines looked unchanged, and Skidmore had the charts showing poor on-time deliveries taken down just before a major customer was scheduled to tour the facility.

After the customer meeting and tour, Skidmore found Chen and asked for a quick update on the progress that was being made. He also expressed his concern that Chen was giving his employees the impression that the consulting group work at SKS meant some people were going to be fired. Chen was shocked to hear this, fumbled with her response, and ultimately promised to look into it. Skidmore, not seeming overly pleased, dismissed her and walked away. Chen was stunned, and had no idea how something she had done could have resulted in such a conclusion. She later learned that her chat with Ranowski had been interpreted, by Ranowski, as "the beginning of the end."

"White Knuckle" Time

Chen sat tensely at the conference table, and considered her options. She knew progress was being made, but not at the accelerated pace that she had initially envisioned. She also knew the steering committee meeting would be a showdown if she had no substantive improvements to show. She wanted desperately to show a major improvement in inventory reduction for her first six weeks of effort.

The performance metrics she had just graphed showed that although on-time delivery had improved slightly from 77% to 79%, total work-in-process inventory had actually increased by 13%. She heard the warning words of Janovich ringing in her head. Maybe he was right. Maybe this business was unique, and inventory levels needed to be at a higher level, especially at the end of a quarter, to buffer the poor forecasts generated by sales.

Chen also reflected on Hendry's counsel two weeks earlier to start a formal change management and communications process, even during this first phase of the project. She had that on her work plan, but she wondered if that would have really helped calm Ranowski's fears. How could she have jumped to the conclusion that she was going to get fired?

Deep down, Chen knew that she had made progress, even if the numbers didn't reflect the results. For the first time in the company history the individual managers were starting to act as a team, and were taking a cross functional view of their business. She had raised their level of awareness above the finger pointing between functions for problems, and complaints of the "stupid mainframe system" to really focusing on the underlying problems. Fletcher, who had nearly thrown her out of the plant the first day, was now spending more time with her testing different plant floor layouts and trying to reduce work-in-process inventory.

Chen feared that if she didn't have the hard numbers, the project would be shut down before it could be successful. She also worried that the early termination of a strategically important engagement would virtually eliminate her firm's ability to sell the larger reengineering engagement to this client. And finally, she believed that she had been placed in a very difficult position, and that her evaluation would not accurately reflect the degree of difficulty of this situation, and what she had accomplished.

EXHIBIT I   Selected Operating Results and Balance Sheet (SKS)

	1995	1994	1993	1992	1991
Operating Results					
Sales	567	536	482	464	397
Gross Profit	88	90	86	83	71
Sales and Administrative Expense	56	60	58	60	52
Depreciation	5	4	3	7	5
Earnings before interest and taxes	11	19	23	17	14
Net Income/(Loss)	(4)	14	16	9	4
Assets					
Cash	0.4	4	9	0.7	2
Receivables	112	79	61	94	73
Inventory	126	117	82	67	78
Net Property, Plant and Equipment	115	107	97	101	86
Other	20	7	59	27	33
Total Assets	373	314	308	290	272
Liabilities & Net Worth					
Accounts Payable	73	51	33	37	30
Long Term Debt	123	108	112	98	86
Other	80	56	57	58	54
Net Worth	97	99	106	97	102
Total Liabilities and Net Worth	373	314	308	290	272

EXHIBIT 2 Selected SKS Products[a]

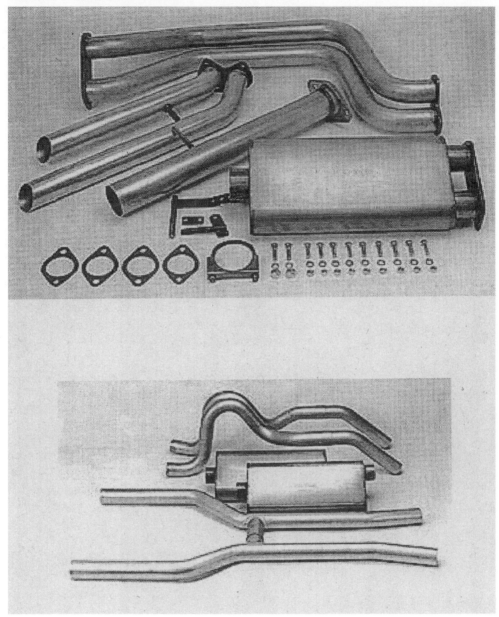

[a]http://www.edelbrock.com/catback.html

Pacific Dunlop China (A): Beijing

太平洋鄧祿普(亞洲)紡織集團

What Was Said	Ideal Translation	Actually Translated As
Littley: Madam Li, could you tell us what engineering has done about making the list of equipment for the container that's waiting in Australia. They can't send it half-empty.	**Littley:** 工程部門能否把在大利亞要裝箱的設犕列個清單出來？	**Littley:** Madam Li, where is the list of equipment from engineering? People are waiting for you in Australia because you haven't done it. They can't send it half empty you know.
Li: 我可不能肯定這是工程部門的事情。	**Li:** Well, I'm not sure that that is really an engineering problem.	**Li:** That's not my job!
Littley: What do you mean not your job! I don't want everyone to think the engineers just spend their days sitting smoking cigarettes!	**Littley:** 但那是你工作的一部份。	**Littley:** But everyone knows your engineers do nothing but sit around smoking cigarettes!
Li: 甚麼？你怎麼能這樣說呢，我們都要忙死了。	**Li:** What! How can you say that. We've been working like crazy!	**Li:** I don't understand what you mean. We work hard!
Littley: Ok! - it was a joke!	**Littley:** 我只是開個玩笑而已。	**Littley:** Joke! Joke!
Li: 你的玩笑一點兒也不好笑。	**Li:** Your joke was too serious!	**Li:** You are too serious!

Patience, especially in China it seemed, was a virtue. Steve Littley had discovered this in his 14 months as divisional manager of Beijing Pacific Dunlop Textiles Ltd. in the Shi Jing Shan district of

Beijing. It was November 11, 1994 at 5:18 pm, and Littley did not have *time* to gaze thoughtfully out of the window musing over abstract business problems. He had a plant to run.

It was a frustrating meeting. The heated exchange was just one of many between Littley and Madame Li, the Chinese manager of the engineering department. Littley had organized these weekly caucuses to gather information essential for running Pacific Dunlop's Beijing sock and underwear factory, such as the status of late orders,

This case was prepared as a basis for class discussion rather than to illustrate either effective or ineffective handling of an administrative situation. Some facts have been disguised.

This case was prepared by Richard Scct under the direction of David M. Upton. Copyright © 1995 by the President and Fellows of Harvard College. Harvard Business School case 695-029.

the progress on maintenance problems and equipment requirements. But as usual, even such simple tasks were proving extraordinarily difficult. What in Australia would normally have been a 20-minute exercise dragged into two hours.

Other Agendas

Littley had had an ancillary agenda for the meetings: to take his Chinese managers, by example, through the step-by-step process of analysis, diagnosis, and solution of the everyday problems that would face any textile factory. His responsibilities had shifted from overseeing three plants in Australia to micro-managing department managers in their duties in China. What he had taken for granted back home—independent problem solving—seemed rare to him in China, or at least in Beijing. The obvious solution was to provide even more training in plant management. But the problem seemed to be one of attitude as much as skill. Dispositions towards work were deeply ingrained in Beijing. The Maoist old guard, raised at a time when pronouncements flowed only from the top down, could not seem to learn any other way of working fast enough. While there *were* young people willing to accept responsibility for getting a job done, their prime advantage, their youth, which had prevented them from being steeped in Maoist doctrine—and the hangover left throughout China from the Cultural Revolution—was also their Achilles' heel. To promote the young based on their merit was still unacceptable in a society where rankings were slated by age. He had tried once and the older workers revolted—making management impossible for their underaged overlings.

The difficulties of delegation meant that Littley was permanently occupied with the minutiæ of running a plant. Seven days a week. Twenty-four hours a day. Littley's apartment was situated in the plant, and it was quite common for him to be woken at four in the morning with problems in the plant. Vacations, it now seemed, were not a good solution to the continual stress. Every time Littley left, he returned only to find another crisis which people had procrastinated in solving—no one wanting to take the initiative without his oversight. It seemed like there was never enough time to get everything done. No time to reflect, no time to train, no time to breathe. No time.

Computers and Production Control

Exacerbating the organizational problem was the lack of an automated system for production management. Information on stock levels and production plans were generated and maintained by hand, because of the plethora of problems associated with running computers in China. This, in concert with the already tenuous managerial structure, had made running the plant unusually challenging to say the least.

Attacking the Problems

Despite the tremendous time pressure, and life pressure, Littley remained upbeat—but realistic. The plant had come a long way since he had taken over but he knew that there were two critical things to do to make the plant manageable in the long term: First, he had to find or build managers to whom he could delegate. This would relieve him of tasks like making sure that the maintenance man had checked that the water supply had sufficient pressure for the toilets to flush, or haranguing an operator to put oil in a noisy machine.

Second, he needed to build systems that would provide the information that Western plant managers took for granted. While a good production management system would not be a panacæa, it would make the factory controllable and allow him to concentrate on readying it for the forthcoming capacity expansion.

PACIFIC DUNLOP AND CLOTHING AND TEXTILES

Pacific Dunlop Limited (PD), founded in 1893, was a firm built upon its stated philosophical lynch-pins of "people, ideas, and technology." PD's strength had grown from its combination of "innovative products, creative marketing, and cost competitive sourcing," and in nurturing "world-class technology." An international marketing company with sales to more than 80 countries, as well as global procurement and distribution capabilities, PD was an Australian-based conglomerate with 1994 sales of A $7.0 billion and A $6.8 billion in world-wide assets (see Exhibit 1). Employing more than 49,000 employees world-wide, Pacific Dunlop had over 12,000 employees, 38 factories and over A $700 million invested in Asia (see Exhibit 2). PD comprised five core business groups:

consumer products; healthcare; automotive products; building and construction; and distribution. The consumer products group, with revenues of A $1.8 billion, marketed and manufactured clothing, footwear, sporting goods and packaged food products (see Exhibit 3). Pacific Brands, the clothing and textiles, footwear, and sporting goods division of the consumer products group, generated 1994 revenues of A $874 million (see Exhibit 4), of which clothing and textiles contributed 55%.

By November, 1994, four joint venture plants were manufacturing clothing and textiles both for export and for the Chinese domestic market:

- Beijing Pacific Dunlop Textiles Ltd. produced socks and ladies' underwear;
- Shanghai Holeproof Garments Ltd. produced underwear and Ping Hu Ausbrands Knitting Co. Ltd. made socks. Both were in Shanghai.
- Taiping Pacific Dunlop Garments Ltd. in Guangdong produced underwear, babywear, polo shirts, and bras.

Using less expensive Chinese labor, the production facilities served primarily as export manufacturing centers for the Australian market. All of the joint ventures operated under the Chinese 70/30 rule: a minimum of 70% of manufactured product was to be exported in order to receive tax relief under Chinese law.

CLOTHING AND TEXTILES: LOOKING TO THE FUTURE

The free market reforms introduced by Deng Xiaoping had helped stimulate China's economy to grow at an average of 9.5% real GDP annually from 1978 to 1994. In this environment, China saw the beginnings of a new middle class. This new tier was, however, not evenly distributed throughout China. Industrial development was concentrated along China's eastern seaboard. The new middle class was gathered in an area less than one-third of the Chinese geographical land mass and was

EXHIBIT 1   1994 Pacific Dunlop Operating Results and Balance Sheet

(in A $m)

	1994	1993	1992	1991	1990
Operating Profit					
Group Sales	6,967	6,305	5,806	4,922	5,048
Earnings before Interest and Tax	546	493	448	449	501
Operating Profit after Tax	312	266	220	244	306
Dividends	240	213	190	154	142
Cash Flow from Operating Activities	484	446	474	310	488
Assets					
Cash	1,012	1,207	1,003	965	793
Receivables	1,125	1,040	1,036	756	778
Inventories	1,253	1,156	1,066	890	859
Property, Plant and Equipment	1,571	1,497	1,349	1,062	1,008
Investments	207	174	289	156	152
Prepayments and Future Income Tax Benefits	424	408	363	241	196
Intangibles	1,153	968	878	575	465
Total Assets	6,745	6,450	5,984	4,645	4,251
Liabilities					
Borrowings	1,872	1,947	1,712	1,535	1,386
Creditors	1,821	1,620	1,527	1,214	1,017
Provisions	670	646	604	386	429
Other Liabilities	13	46	89	125	141
Total Liabilities	4,376	4,259	3,932	3,260	2,973
Net Assets	2,369	2,191	2,052	1,385	1,278
Less Outside Interests	31	31	27	20	19
Shareholders Equity	2,338	2,160	2,025	1,365	1,259

EXHIBIT 2 Pacific Dunlop Locations in Asia

Japan

	Plants	Offices	People
GNB	-	1	6
Ansell	1	1	5
Nucleus	-	1	9
Brands	-	1	1
Food	-	1	5
Total	1	5	26

New Zealand

	Plants	Offices	People
GNB	2	11	181
SPT	2	115	1,021
Ansell	-	1	3
Nucleus	-	1	9
IFF	11	18	433
Cables	1	6	153
Brands	-	-	22
Food	1	5	55
Distribution	-	107	911
PDL	-	-	2
Total	17	264	2,790

China & Hong Kong

	Plants	Offices	People
GNB	1	-	2
Ansell	-	2	8
Nucleus	-	3	29
IFF	1	-	20
Cables	3	2	466
Brands	6	4	2,490
Food	11	1	1,703
PDL	-	2	28
Total	22	14	4,746

South East Asia

	Plants	Offices	People
GNB	-	-	4
SPT	-	1	84
Ansell	3	3	4,047
IFF	5	3	278
Cables	1	1	25
Brands	2	-	4
Food	1	1	4
PDL	-	1	2
Total	12	10	4,448

Europe

	Plants	Offices	People
GNB	-	1	7
Ansell	1	8	379
Nucleus	-	7	210
IFF	-	2	3
Brands	-	1	30
PDL	-	1	2
Total	1	20	631

India, Pakistan & Sri Lanka

	Plants	Offices	People
Ansell	1	2	2,477
IFF	1	-	30
Cables	1	2	408
Total	3	4	2,915

Australia

	Plants	Offices	People
GNB	2	47	750
SPT	25	439	5,100
Ansell	-	7	73
Nucleus	3	6	589
IFF	54	44	3,282
Cables	10	30	1,667
Brands	20	44	4,587
Food	16	58	4,909
Distribution	-	581	5,475
PDL/Other	1	12	336
Total	131	1,268	26,768

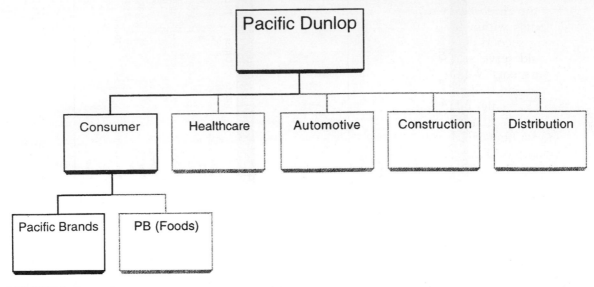

EXHIBIT 3 Group Organization

	1994	1993	1992	1991	1990
Sales (A $m)	874	809	777	759	850
EBIT (A $m)	73	61	72	77	69
% of Sales	8.4	7.5	9.3	10.1	8.1
Total Assets (A $m)	525	456	409	409	414
Capital Expenditure (A $m)	19	17	25	14	37
Depreciation (A $m)	15	14	13	14	16
Factories	28	26	29	35	43
Other Establishments	50	44	44	42	60
Employees (000s)	7.1	7.6	7.5	5.7	6.6

EXHIBIT 4 Pacific Brands: Financial Summary (A$m)

concentrated in three epicenters: Guangzhou, Shanghai, and Beijing. It was estimated that by the year 2010, China would become the largest economy in the world, with rising affluence among the 375 million urban residents of the coastal cities. Market analyses projected that by the year 2000, 45 million Chinese would have the purchasing power of the average Singaporean of 1994.

A Strategy for China

PD's Clothing and Textiles group was well positioned to take advantage of this new source of growth. With joint ventures already operating in China's three largest consumer markets, Robert Hershan, Managing Director of Pacific Brands;

Alan Goodfellow, Group Director, Clothing and Textiles; and David Lau, Group Director of PD's Clothing and Textiles operations in China, had devised and begun the execution of an aggressive strategy to capture the evolving Chinese market, while maintaining enough productive capacity to supply the comparatively stagnant Australian home market.

The cities of Beijing, Shanghai, and Guangzhou would serve as production and distribution centers to feed the market on the eastern seaboard. Products would be shipped among the three cities to supply a complete range of Chinese manufactured PD goods (each plant was focussed on different products and brands). Stocked with a full range, the three cities would serve as distribution capitals within their municipalities and for developing second cities close to them. Thus, Shanghai would serve as the distribution center to supply garments within its city limits and into Hangzhou, and Beijing would supply the capital city and Shenyang. Freight shipments among the various market cities would be performed by local carriers within their "areas of influence" (it was not uncommon for freight to be lost or hijacked if a freighter without influence was contracted).

This Asian strategy required an aggressive ramp-up of production in the Chinese plants to build a visible presence in the growing local market. The projections suggested that unit capacity would have to be grown by 190% between 1995 and 2001. This expansion would initially be fueled by investments in the latest high-speed production equipment along with complementary manufac-

turing information management systems within the next two years.

Preparing for Growth

"We know it's aggressive," said Lau, *"but we've learned a lot from being here for longer than most people. We believe it's the right strategy—and we're pretty sure we can do it."* PD's history in textiles in China passed through three distinct phases. Ten years previously, the company had begun to build a manufacturing base to supply the home market, shipping old machines made too expensive by Australian labor costs from Melbourne, and at the same time, investing in new equipment in Australia. Initial manufacturing problems of poor delivery and quality slowly began to be solved. Next, PD began to develop international markets for its Chinese products, such as Canada and Switzerland. Having cut its teeth on these challenging markets, the company again began to look

EXHIBIT 5 Locations in China

for opportunities for growth. The solution quickly became clear: China itself. Lau described the experience of building the Chinese operations:

> I've learned so much since we began. The first thing I learned was not to underestimate how much managerial time doing business in China consumes. You can't take anything for granted. We were saddled with a horrible managerial structure at first [in 1987]. I was running the Melbourne operation and running China part time. It nearly killed Alan Goodfellow and me!

> Second, we now know how important it is to assess your joint venture partner's powerbase effectively. If they don't have enough pull, they won't be able to grow the business with you later. They won't give up equity, but they'll be unable to raise any capital. Influence and connections mean a lot in China. On the subject of joint ventures, I can't emphasize enough how important it is to ensure that the articles of association are really specific and not left vague. The Chinese language is very ambiguous at the best of times—and if you leave things vague, you can be sure it'll hurt later.

> Third, if I had to do it again, I would start building local managers earlier. Ex-pats bring a fresh mind and don't accept local standards—but they wear out really quickly, even the tough ones. They have to learn a lot of new skills. They kind of go through stages: in the first six months, they learn not to shout! Things in China are done gently, by gradual persuasion. Over the next 18 months, they start to become productive. After this, the environment can start to really wear them down. It can be very destructive of families. We have to remember, that wives and husbands in China are part of the business. Without them being able to deal with it, you are lost. China is a much more hostile environment than people think! I would use ex-pats as consultants if I did it all again.

> Finally, you need to plan a future for the manager you bring in—you can't just say "Here's a great opportunity—but when your spouse has had enough and wants to come home, we won't tell you what's going to happen to you."

Lau's upbeat outlook had been a great advantage in building PD's manufacturing base. But now he had to consider how he would make the new growth plan happen. Like many manufacturing people, he knew that most operations plans failed in execution rather than conception and that this new plan was critically dependent on the growth in capabilities and capacity of the existing manufacturing plants. Each plant and area of the country had its own problems, and new challenges appeared with each stage of the growth.

The Beijing plant provided a prime example of how processes, people and systems were constantly being challenged by the environment and by the continued expansion. While Lau faced challenges at the network level, very different challenges were being handled by people managing the plants.

THE BEIJING PLANT

The Beijing plant was on the outskirts of the city, 45 minutes by car from the center. The plant was close to an old steel mill, and the skies rained ash and sulphur dioxide occasionally. While the plant was amongst the best textile plants in Beijing, the working environment was not comparable to what one might see in Australia or the US. The more relaxed local standards made housekeeping extraordinarily difficult.

Making Socks

The plant's budgeted capacity was 580,000 dozen pairs of socks per annum, though in November 1994, it was making socks at a rate of 620,000. The plant also made 260,000 units of women's underwear. The materials for the plant's products were cotton, Spandex, nylon and Elastane (a rubber material for the welt of the sock). Cotton purchasing had originally been carried out at group level and sourced through Beijing or Shanghai, but as local relationships strengthened, cotton was being sourced locally from the state-run Beijing Mill #1 and Mill #2. Spandex, Nylon, and Elastane had all been originally sourced outside China, but lately good quality indigenous sources had been found, by knowing someone, who knew someone else, who knew someone else . . .

Finding good quality indigenous material sources was important because they could then be paid for in local currency rather than Australian dollars. In 1994, the *renminbi* (RMB) remained a troublesome currency to convert.

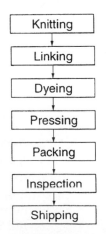

Sock manufacturing could be broken into five process steps:

Knitting

The first process step was knitting the sock. The four yarns were placed on the wide variety of knitting machines in the operation. The plant used 45 brand-new electronic Lonati machines, alongside 27 30-year old German Esta machines retired from the Australian operation. The remaining 255 were English Komet machines which were between 40–50 years old.

Linking

The next step was to close the toe of the sock. Three different technologies were used for this operation, which was carried out in the next shop. The slowest, and highest quality, was hand-linking, which demanded high dexterity and entailed considerable labor content. The Merrow overlocking machines provided automated closing, but produced at a lower quality than the three Rossi machines, which incorporated state-of-the-art closing technology.

Dyeing

Socks were then batched into a 40–45 kilo batch for a dyed color or a 60 kilo batch for bleached white or black. 40–45 kilo production went into the three P&L dyeing machines. A dye batch would normally take 4–5 hours for cotton. Older technology was used for the 60 kilo batches (the Smith drum), which used hydrogen peroxide for the bleaching process. Each of the P&Ls had a built in spinning program which extracted the excess water.

Pressing

The socks were then tumbled in a dryer to a set moisture level, then were set to shape on one of two shaping machines. Each was run by a crew of four people, one loading, one straightening, one unloading and one examining. This was a 24-hour operation, with 6 teams.

Examining, Pairing and Packing

The socks were then put into cartons of 240 pairs which went into rack stock. Packaging and presentation variety was then produced by drawing from this inventory, making multiple consumer-packaged SKUs from common manufacturing numbers. Thirty people worked in the packing area, working on one shift.

Capacity

Total production was between 2400 and 2500 dozen pairs per day. The new 44-hour working week had recently been mandated by the Government, and an announcement had just been made that there would be a further reduction in the maximum working week, possibly to 40 hours a week by January, 1996.

The process was characterized by a very diverse set of production technologies, qualities, and output rates, even for similar operations. This diversity brought with it its own set of problems, though it reflected the overall PD operations strategy: to start with older machines from Australian plants, then upgrade to the latest technology over time.

The plant rated an average of 60 to 80 defects per 1000 items, which was similar to what was achieved in Australia. Young women aged mostly between 17 to 21 staffed the labor intensive knitting, dyeing processes, pressing, and sorting activities of the plant. The women were recruited from the local district and most had not completed their secondary school education. The Chinese government's methods of allocating labor occasionally suggested a view that "labor" was more or less a fungible commodity. It was not uncommon, for example, for a state run factory to be closed, and the employees sent off to work in a department store at very short notice. Of the 350 employees, indirect workers numbered 75 of the total. If supervisors were counted in the indirect pool, the total reached 84, resulting in an almost one to three indirect to direct employee ratio: unusually high for such an operation. In Australia the ratio was closer to one indirect for every eight direct employees.

MANAGING THE BEIJING PLANT

The plant's organization chart is shown in Exhibit 6. Littley described his experience as he started to manage the plant 14 months previously:

The first three months when I arrived—I didn't know what had hit me. You feel like you're Robinson Crusoe with 350 Man Fridays. And like Robinson Crusoe, you have to find a way of communicating. I was running around trying to work out why things happened a certain way and why I couldn't change them. I didn't understand them, they

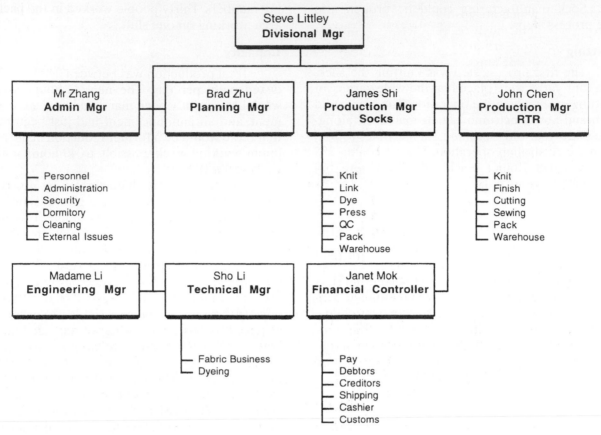

EXHIBIT 6 Beijing Plant Organization Chart

didn't understand me. They find it very hard to come to grips with the change. Anyone who's coming to China really has to make a commitment to come for longer than two years. Two years is too short. It's too long from the Westerner's point of view, but it's too short from the business point of view. I'm going through the learning curve even now. I wish I had learned more about China before I had come.

Managing Managers

One of the primary problems, Littley found, was the lack of qualified and independently-acting middle managers. This meant important changes in the way he had traditionally worked. Because information had traditionally only travelled down the organization, any information received upwards could be highly suspect. Managers would often just say yes—that they understood a problem—when they did not. They would then procrastinate on it, until it was too late to solve.

More important was the lack of the checks and balances on his own decisions. Like most good managers, Littley had relied strongly in the past on people prepared to tell him that he was wrong, and that there might be another way of doing things. This never happened in the Beijing plant.

You have to tell them how to do everything at first, but then you're very quickly in a position where you are relied on for everything. People would *never* come to me and say they think I'm making a mistake. My style had become quite autocratic in some ways. But I need to be autocratic to get things done, but then that stifles responsibility. It's a Catch-22.

Meetings

To counter the problems, Littley held meetings every week with every department, from basic design to services, to engineering. While the meetings generated action plans, and a commitment from people to execute their plans, the following meeting generally showed that the tasks were not complete, for one reason or another. Meetings were characterized by long periods waiting for translation, which meant that both Littley and his managers spent much of the meeting waiting. In addition, there were inevitably untranslated side-discussions, in one language or the other, leaving at least someone isolated from the group. Mistranslation was common, even if only in tone, and much time was spent clearing up such misunderstandings.

Reports

Littley asked for daily reports from every department. Each manager was required to fill out a report detailing what progress had been made, along with specific information that Littley had asked for from each group. Every day, by every machine in the company, he received a report of everything that had been produced, what seconds had been made and what the problems were—to ensure that corrective action had been taken, though it rarely had. Then, by machine group, output was compared against what would normally be expected and reasons for discrepancies identified; then by style level—why deliveries weren't being met, what would be done about overtime, whether work would be subcontracted, whether machines might be sped up or whether alternative materials had been considered.

Finding People

One larger plant management problem loomed on the horizon. Young Chinese graduates were becoming increasingly reluctant to work on the floor where they could gain the experience vital to be a manager:

> One person came back to me and said 'I didn't get a university education to go on the factory floor!' They are often just looking for a springboard—to get you on their resume, even though they are paid 30–50% higher than base [500 RMB per month on the shop floor]. Of 18 graduates we had come in here, there are only 3 left.

This difficulty in retaining educated university graduates forced Pacific Dunlop to focus hard on training from within for day-to-day plant management:

> What this means then is that you cannot attract the type of people you want—those out of the university. You now have to hire middle school graduates and train them as if they'd never had a job before. But that takes time and money. You need to take them through the ranks. And when you are try-

ing to grow the business like we are, then it becomes hard to achieve that and get the management training as well.

Custom and Practice: China and Australia

A willingness and ability to solve minor, tactical problems seemed to be almost completely absent in the plant at first—this again meant huge demands on Littley's time. Even the most minor problem would be deferred up the chain of command, and very often, just "sat on." While Littley had worked to try to cultivate some self-reliance, by holding weekend training sessions, so far, his attempts had not really borne much fruit. An acceptance of the need for autonomous action was simply not common practice in state-run industries.

In addition, even when problems were solved independently, there was a wide disparity in Australian and Chinese views of what constituted a "good" solution to a problem. An example was the loading of the dyeing machines. These machines comprised axially-horizontal, rotating drums, rather like a big spin-dryer and indeed, this was part of their function, to spin-dry after the dyeing operation. However, the drums were split into three compartments. Each compartment should have been loaded with 15kg of material. To try to be more "efficient," the operators frequently loaded one drum with 15kg, one with 17kg and another with 20kg. Despite being told many times not to do this, operators continued with the practice, which meant that the loaded assembly was dynamically unbalanced, and led to the bearings in one of the new machines burning out (bearings are rarely good at handling an oscillating load).

Chinese Solutions on Western Equipment

To fix the problem, the shop-floor people, for once, acted independently, and ordered bearings from a supplier, which they could only get in the wrong size. The engineering department therefore bought a smaller diameter and used metal shims to jam the bearing into its housing. While few Western technicians would have even considered such a makeshift solution, in China—it seemed like the right thing to do, even though this new bearing wore out much more quickly than the first, and probably damaged the rear bearing as well.

This example was just one of the myriad of problems in the plant, which would not arise in the West but which, in their multiplicity, were an incessant drain on time. The inevitable therefore happened—some things just had to be allowed to slide.

Building Guanxi

The Chinese concept of *guanxi* (roughly translated as "connections or "relationships") was an important aspect of managing a plant in China, and one which was usually dismissed as trivial by plant managers when they arrived, then emphasized by them incessantly after their "burning-in" period. While in Western plants, authority and prestige tended to be carried much more by the formal position, in China, such formal authority meant very little. Much more important, as Littley quickly found out, was a person's *guanxi*. While the plant in Beijing had three Western managers, each took his *guanxi* with him when he left, leaving the new manager to start over.

> This is much more important than I ever, ever thought it would be, especially when dealing with people outside the firm. If you don't have the right relationship with people, it doesn't mean anything that you are prepared to pay a lot to buy something. The customer is not King in China—the supplier is. They will often refuse to sell to you at any price. Most often, they will smile and nod. Then nothing will happen.

Like many Western managers Littley was originally frustrated by these tiny things that seemed so inconsequential. Since he had realized that running a plant in China *was* dependent on such things as who one meets, and how one meets them—even what one eats, he had put many precious hours into building *guanxi* with the critical suppliers and government officials.

> I realized, it was kind of like a test. We would go out to dinner, and I would have a few drinks with them, and eat a couple of things from the dishes they set in front of me. Hardly anything to do with business seemed to get done at these meetings. Then I realized—business was being done—I was under test. The first few times we went out, they would bring an army of people, each of whom would drink a toast to me—I would end up plastered! Then they'd talk business. I realized what was happening. Now, I always take a load of my key guys, and insist that they each take a turn to be toasted.

> The food is another thing. This is also a series of tests—to see how tough you are and how serious you are about doing business and working with the Chinese. Now, I eat just about anything—and I do mean anything. Of course, you can try any excuse you like to avoid doing this stuff—religion, vegetarianism, health. It doesn't matter. If you do, they'll think you're not willing to adapt. You won't get the supplies or permits your plant needs to keep running. The deal just won't happen without doing this kind of thing—or if it does, you'll be compromised as a short-term hit, rather than seen as worthy of a long-term relationship.

Living on Site

Littley lived in a one bedroom apartment above his office. It was his place to eat, sleep, and think. He had tried commuting to work and living away from the office, but the time and, more importantly, the constant attention required by the factory forced him to live at work.

> Living on site, all you do is work and you do not get away from it. You are here everyday, you hear the shift changes. They come and knock on your door and you end up working 24 hours a day.

Such demands took a toll on his personal life, as it did on many Western plant managers in Beijing. Littley knew of several other ex-patriate Australians within the vicinity but had not found time to meet with them. Moreover, his health had begun to suffer, partly as a result of the high level of pollution. He was battling a cold that had lasted two weeks and only recently he had suffered what he thought was a heart attack:

> It was a real scare. I went down with some excruciating chest pains. I have never felt anything like it in my life. It was too late to go to the embassy hospital so I had to see one of the local chinese doctors, a witch doctor really. He gave me some heart massages and declared everything clear. I went for a full medical for two days at the Chinese hospital specially for Westerners. They gave me all kinds of tests and declared me okay, except for the stress.

BEIJING'S PERFORMANCE

While the plant had improved dramatically in the previous 14 months, Littley knew there was still a long way to go. The poor management system and discipline problems meant that 25% of orders were still running late. There was also a variance in lateness of six weeks across the outstanding jobs. One person, it seemed, could only do so much. In stasis, such problems might gradually have been solved—but the strategy of aggressive growth in

China meant that soon, new challenges would face the plant and its creaking systems. Something had to be done to ready the operation for the explosive growth and new manufacturing technology to come. And it had to be done now.

Building a Production Management System

The information systems needed to run the plant were sorely lacking. There had been a rudimentary production control system, brought up by the previous manager from Australia. For one reason or another, Littley found, on his arrival, that the hard disk on the PC running the planning software had been erased. Even if the disk had been saved, it would have helped very little, since no one else understood it. And despite its existence, the plant had had much poorer delivery performance at the time it was used. Few people questioned the output of the computer, so errors would snowball as a result of poorly entered information, sometimes with fairly dramatic results. For the previous 18 months, the plant had run on a manual or semi-manual system.

While 90% of output was destined for Australia, Littley was also responsible for selling spare capacity onto the market, often in Switzerland, Canada, Denmark or Bulgaria, which required careful planning to ensure that capacity was available to fill the current orders.

> I have a good young guy in the planning department. If I had another 300 of him, I'd be happy, I can tell you! Brad Zhou is the youngest manager we have and he controls the planning and purchasing for the whole factory. Before he took it on we had only 40% of our deliveries on time, with some jobs over a year late, and average lateness running at 3 months. Now we're up to 75% on time, with an average lateness of about 6 weeks on the rest. He's done a great job, but it's taken a lot of training and a lot of sitting down on Sundays after work. I got him to do it manually at first, then adapt it to simple programs on the computer.

Planning Production

Production planning was carried out by three mechanisms:

For each machine in the plant, by month, Brad Zhou produced a simple Lotus 1-2-3 spreadsheet, showing the number of days available and the specification of output, thus providing a rudimentary capacity analysis. This provided the abil-

ity to know what could be sold. Second, on the same spreadsheet, the orders, by customer, were blocked in. The value of each order was also recorded. This enabled Zhou to ensure the plant was on target for sales value as well as unit volume. Third was an exception report which showed up the "holes." Littley would then go out and find business to fill the holes.

This was the full extent of the production control system. There was no system, for example, to explode production projections into bills of materials. This had to be done manually—a clerk would sit down with the specification and calculate through.

Shop-floor Control

But generating schedules was only part of the problem. Operators would often ignore the schedule entirely, and produce the orders-on-hand in the sequence in which they had arrived at the plant (First-Come-First-Served), in keeping with the way lines were serviced in shops and markets. Littley was convinced this was causing an excessive number of late deliveries and was making poor use of the available capacity. The inability to work around scheduled downtime, for example, could often mean setting up a machine two or three times for the same order (see Exhibit 7 for an example of Zhou's spreadsheets).

In addition, production controllers would frequently order far more material than the plans advised, to provide safety stock for the plant. Inventory levels were becoming excessive. The warehouse contained piles of boxes full of unneeded labels, for example. [Exhibit 8]

Preparing for Growth

The 50% growth in sales and 25% growth in volume projected for the plant over the next year would mean a severe test for the already creaking production control system. Something had to be done to control the way things were currently done, but care had to be taken.

The last system that was used had been a failure in terms of delivery performance because no one was able to maintain the integrity of the data it held or the hardware on which it ran.

There was an existing base of six unconnected Personal Computers in the plant: Janet Mok used one to keep track of financial data, and Zhou used one to generate the Lotus production control spreadsheets described above. At the end of the month, Mok and Zhou would get together to resolve discrepancies between their machines. They never agreed.

Australian Plants' Manufacturing Information System

In Australia, Littley had had a system which produced the kind of reports he needed for running the plant, including:(1) Sales from the previous day and sales from month to date; (2) orders outstanding for the month and the month before; (3) orders on hand; (4) production plans; (5) delivery schedules; and (6) inventory levels and allocation; all of which were available with the stroke of a key.

Viruses

Littley was cautious about the introduction of such a system in Beijing. Over-reliance on computer systems was dangerous in part because of an endemic problem that would be relatively easily cured in the west: computer viruses. Only a few months previously, a virus attacked the system

used by Mok for financial accounting and crippled it. The problem took so long to correct that Mok was forced to resort to pen and paper to maintain the financial system.

We were dead for a week. The virus went through the plant like wildfire. Everyone says this is a big problem in China and it is. Another one of those things that sounds completely trivial when you're at home, but here it stops the operation dead. Western virus protection does not work against Chinese viruses and they are everywhere, on every disk it seems. Even the CAD systems controlling the knitting machines were affected, meaning we couldn't produce anything. We managed to get some IBM people out here, but it took them almost a week to clean the plant. The machines aren't even on a network! and they were dying left, right and centre. It was unbelievable!

The virus problem was widespread throughout China for two reasons. First, virus transmission was facilitated by the relatively liberal interpretation of copyright law in China concerning the duplication of software (see Exhibit 9). While all

EXHIBIT 7 Patterning Esta Machines: Capacity Projection—January 1995

Day	1	2	3	4	5	6	7	8	9	10	11	12	13	14	15	16	17	18	19	20
Esta 1	Down until Thurs.																			
Esta 2	Previously Scheduled																			
Esta 3					Refitters from Australia working (machine to be stripped down)															

EXHIBIT 8 Patterning Esta Machines: Orders on Hand—January 1995

Order (in arrival sequence)	Number of Days Processing Time	Set up Time (days) (additional)*	Finish Date to Meet Promise Date	Feasible Machines	Estimated Contribution of Order
A	5	1	7	1, 2, 3	$900
B	2	1	10	1, 2, 3	$300
C	3	1	13	1, 2	$600
D	6	1	14	2, 3	$900
E	8	1	18	1, 2, 3	$1200
F	1	1	19	2	$300
G	2	1	9	1	$600
Total	27	7			$4800

*Jobs could be split between machines, but would then need set up time on both machines

†There was a 50% probability that a late order would not be accepted by the customer (resulting in having to sell the inventory at cost), independent of how late it was.

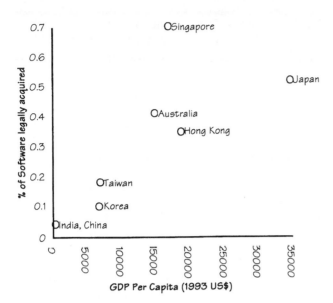

EXHIBIT 9 Software Copying

software used in the plant was legal, people would bring disks to work to try out "borrowed" software, and use advance copies of newly released versions. The disks inevitably contained viruses. Even repeated proscription by Littley had not stopped the practice. Second, the viruses that existed were "Chinese" strains, mostly invented by hackers with a lot of time and inventiveness on their hands. Many Chinese viruses were unknown in the West and were often immune to Western virus-killing programs.

BUILDING A SYSTEM

The Electronic Data Processing (EDP) group in Melbourne had looked at three options for automating production control at the Beijing plant:

The first option was to install a mainframe computer in Beijing. While mainframe computing was past its heyday in the West, it did provide some advantages over a distributed system. It would be straightforward to protect as a whole entity and would run software that was well-tested and not dependent on a continuously effective network. The drawback though was the maintenance and operation of such a computer. It was hard to think of anyone who could run it. Second, a mainframe

or even a minicomputer would be "overkill" for a plant the size of PD Beijing.

The second possibility was to install a PC network with ready built software. Backup and recovery routines could be built into the network architecture. However, if a PC network was installed, the plant would have to wait at least six months (and probably a year) for the development of appropriate software. On the other, hand, it might be able to use the system which had been developed in the Taiping plant (which made bras and polo shirts) though this catered to a very different type of production. Bras and polo shirts exhibited much more variety, and were manufactured by a very different process—with much more focus on assembly than primary processing.

The third possibility was to rent a land-line from Beijing to Hong Kong (which could then connect with an AS-400 minicomputer in Melbourne). A variation on this was to use a satellite link to connect the plant with Australia. While such a method would be very expensive, it would solve the problem, but realistically would probably be very inflexible to any changes needed in the system.

Something had to be decided soon. While it had worked as a stop-gap solution, the existing way of coordinating production needed to be improved if the plant was to continue to prosper as the market grew.

Building Improvement

The challenges were clear and urgent. While the production management system was a thorn in the side, the dilemma eating into Littley's already minimal sleep time persisted: what should be done to build a culture of self-reliance in such a reluctant environment? And how could such self-reliance be vindicated in peoples' eyes when even their best guess provided what would have been considered in the West a "wrong" solution, potentially damaging to both the plant's performance and its equipment? With so little time for training (even if it were available), it seemed inevitable that Littley would have to continue to intervene, especially as the technology became more sophisticated.

The problems danced around in Littley's head as he tried to sleep amidst the clatter of the machinery.

It was going to be a short night.

Micom Caribe (A)

*"You'll never be where you think you
are if you stay where you are."*
—TOM MOSCHETTI[1],
Micom Caribe[2] Plant Manager

"We have a quality problem with the Micom Box," came the accusatory voice from corporate offices in California.

"What's the problem?" asked Tom Moschetti.

"It's a quality problem," the voice responded tautly, "you people down there just need to get it fixed!"

Though only a memory by January 1991, calls like these had so bombarded Micom Caribe (Caribe), the Puerto Rican manufacturing facility for Micom Communications Corporation (MCC), that their echoes still resounded in Moschetti's ears. Quality problems had plagued the 1987 introduction of the Micom Box, and the tantalizing ambiguity of these "quality problems" had compelled Caribe to develop an entirely different manufacturing operation.

This new structure had been a great success. The latest MCC product introduction—perhaps the most important in company history—would finally give Caribe the chance to demonstrate its newfound quality and flexibility.

While the plant was consumed with the new product launch, Moschetti and the rest of the steering committee debated how Caribe should chart a strategy to build on its emerging capabilities—and at last weld manufacturing firmly into MCC's competitive strategy.

---

[1]Pronounced *Mosketti.*
[2]Pronounced *Kah-rēē-bay.*

This case was prepared as the basis for class discussion rather than to illustrate either effective or ineffective handling of an administrative situation.

This case was prepared by Joshua Margolis under the direction of David M. Upton. Copyright © 1991 by the President and Fellows of Harvard College. Harvard Business School case 692-002.

MICOM CARIBE

Micom Caribe, the only manufacturing facility of Micom Communications Corporation, bought components, assembled them into circuit boards, and manufactured MCC products using those boards and other purchased components (power sources and outer casings, for example).

Caribe first began operating in 1981 when the plant opened fittingly in April, Puerto Rico's Month of Industry. As sales grew from $1.5 million in 1982 to $23.6 million in 1990, Caribe moved from an original space of 11,000 square feet to a 75,000 square-foot facility, both provided by Puerto Rico's Economic Development Administration. Located in the town of Cayey, 45 minutes from San Juan, the plant employed 214 people. (See Exhibit 1 for map of Puerto Rico.)

Micom Communications Corporation (MCC)

Although based in Simi Valley, California, Micom Communications Corporation could have come straight from the pages of a Silicon Valley success story. Founded in 1973, MCC had been a world pioneer in the data communications industry. Its products connected many different types of data and communications equipment using one "box" rather than a complex system, which reduced communications costs. This box, filled with circuit boards, took information and concentrated it so it could travel easily between pieces of equipment. The Micro800 Data Concentrator, for example, connected remote users to a host computer, creating wide-area networks (WAN); MCC's other major product, INSTANET, created local-area networks (LAN) by connecting personal computers, work stations, data terminals, and mainframe computers located within a building or campus.

MCC made its first public stock offering in 1981, the same year it moved manufacturing to Puerto Rico. In 1988 Odyssey Partners, a private investment firm, acquired the company in a leveraged buy-out (LBO). Through three sets of own-

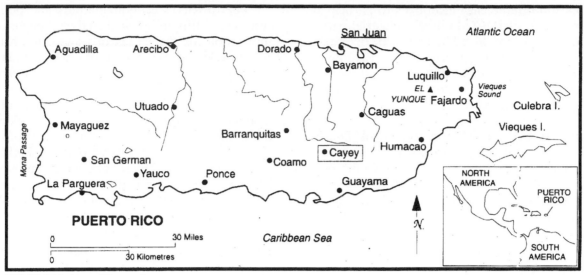

EXHIBIT I   Map of Puerto Rico

ership, MCC continued to concentrate on simple, full-featured products in a market dominated by expensive, complicated equipment.

Customers and Competitors   MCC had over 400 customers. Sixty percent of sales came from independent distributors and 40% from original equipment manufacturers (OEMs) who incorporated MCC products into equipment that they assembled and sold. IBM and AT&T were MCC's two largest OEM customers, but others included Digital Equipment Corporation, Prime Computer, Sun, and Hewlett-Packard.

In August 1989 MCC shipped its 200,000th multiplexor, a total that surpassed all competitors' sales combined.[3] But constant innovation and rapid change characterized the entire computer and communications industry—and change was coming faster as time went on. Fleeting market dominance would not secure MCC's future.

PUERTO RICO, MCC AND MANUFACTURING

Since 1898, Puerto Rico had been affiliated with the United States, first as a colony and then as a free associated commonwealth. Situated in the Caribbean Sea, Puerto Rico covered 3,435 square miles,[4] roughly two-thirds the size of Connecticut. With a population of 3.3 million in 1988, Puerto Rico had a density of 951 people per square mile, compared to 70 for the United States mainland.[5]

Operation Bootstrap   When Spanish forces conquered Puerto Rico in the early 1500s, they introduced sugar cane and used African slaves and native Taino Indians to work the fields. Until the 1940s, sugar remained the island's main economic product. But in 1942 the government of Puerto Rico initiated "Operation Bootstrap," a self-help program designed to improve the standard of living by attracting industrial development to the island. By 1985 manufacturing comprised 39% of the gross domestic product, making it the single largest sector, while agriculture comprised just 2%. The administrative body known as Fomento ("development") managed the industrialization effort and included two organizations. The Economic Development Administration (EDA) promoted industrial projects, reaching out to foreign investors and coordinating all necessary activity and resources. The Puerto Rico Industrial Development Company (PRIDCO) actually constructed physical

---

[3]Richard S. Borden, "Micom Communications Corporation: Corporate Backgrounder."

[4]8,897 square kilometers.
[5]Puerto Rico's population density: 1,531 per square kilometer. U.S. population density: 111 per square kilometer.

facilities and offered cash incentives to participating companies. PRIDCO built 99 industrial parks, including the one in which Micom Caribe operated. PRIDCO provided inexpensive leases (as low as $0.25 per square foot in 1990) and offered cash incentives for leasehold improvements, employee training, and start up costs.[6]

Section 936 A second component of Puerto Rico's rapid development revolved around Section 936 of the U.S. Internal Revenue Code: with certain stipulations, all profits earned in Puerto Rico were not subject to federal tax. The government of Puerto Rico supplemented those tax incentives with its own exemptions from commonwealth and local taxes.[7]

Progress and Potential

From a one-crop economy at mid-century, Puerto Rico emerged to become the hub of industrial activity in the Caribbean Basin. Life expectancy in the 1940s was just 46, but by the mid-1970s it reached 72, on a par with that of the U.S. mainland. Net income per capita had grown from $121 in 1940 to $4,200 in 1985. Although that paled in comparison to the U.S. figure of $14,565, Puerto Rico's cumulative economic growth between 1985 and 1989 (16.4%) surpassed that of the United States (14.5%). Gross domestic product hit $30 billion in 1990 and gross national product reached $21 billion.[8]

---

[6]Jonathan Goldman, "Puerto Rico," *Institutional Investor,* December 1990. Government Development Bank for Puerto Rico, 1990 Annual Report. Puerto Rico Industrial Development Company, 1987 Annual Report and 1990 Annual Report.

[7]Jonathan Goldman, "Puerto Rico," *Institutional Investor,* December 1990.

[8]Gross domestic product (GDP) calculates the output of production attributable to all labor and property located in the commonwealth. Gross national product (GNP) calculates the output of production attributable to entities owned by citizens of the commonwealth. Because U.S. companies owned many of the businesses on Puerto Rico, GDP for Puerto Rico was higher than GNP. Earl Parker Hanson, Puerto Rico, *Encyclopedia Americana,* 1990 ed. The Economist Intelligence Unit, Cuba, Dominican Republic, Haiti, Puerto Rico: Country Report (London, England: Economist Intelligence Unit, 1990), No. 1. Jonathan Goldman, "Puerto Rico," *Institutional Investor,* December 1990. *Information Please Almanac, Atlas, and Yearbook* (Boston, MA: Houghton, Mifflin Company, 1991). Bureau of the Census, *Statistical Abstract of the United States,* 1990 (Washington, D.C.: U.S. Department of Commerce, 1990), 110th edition. *The Economist,* The World in Figures (London, England: The Economist Publications, Ltd., 1987). Commonwealth of Puerto Rico, Public Improvement Bonds of 1991.

Puerto Rico's economic affairs and political status were intimately connected well beyond the ramifications of special tax privileges, and Micom Caribe reflected their relationship. Just as the economy as a whole depended largely on exports to the U.S. and on tax privileges accorded by the U.S. government, individual firms recapitulated this relationship. MCC initially situated a plant on Puerto Rico as a tax haven for its most profitable products. MCC leased a plant built by PRIDCO and enjoyed reduced leases and handsome tax exemptions. But Caribe had developed into an expert manufacturing facility, one whose products generated 95% of the parent company's revenues.

Despite all of Micom Caribe's advantages and accomplishments, like Puerto Rico itself the plant still labored under a disparity in status, only part of which could be attributed to the very real facts of economic dependency. It was a widely held view that culturally ingrained attitudes on both sides of the ocean had to be considered significant. One manager at Micom Caribe, a native of Puerto Rico and a long-time veteran of Micom Caribe, echoed the views of many at the plant:

> Most Puerto Rican plants are treated like subcontractors of U.S. firms, and they see themselves that way. There's a mentality of colonialism. "The gringos arrived, and we must bow to them." U.S. firms are the fathers, the only people with right and reason, no one else.
>
> Micom Caribe began as a child to MCC. The message was clear from California: "We are to teach. You are to follow." We've done something different than the parent company, though. We joke that we decolonized the island.
>
> We may never be free of the U.S. belief that we have not advanced. Any little thing that happens between MCC corporate and Micom Caribe gets exaggerated. Our doubt is always there that they will not see we have made a lot of progress. Bleeding was there—their approach left wounds—so any time a problem arises, it bleeds a little.

Puerto Ricans filled over 90% of all management positions within the U.S., European, and Japanese factories on the island,[9] and all managers and directors at Micom Caribe except Moschetti were native Puerto Ricans. Nonetheless, industry

---

[9]Jonathan Goldman, "Puerto Rico," *Institutional Investor,* December 1990.

as a whole in Puerto Rico, and Micom Caribe as one example, struggled with the legacy of what Puerto Rico continued to confront politically: making real the 1953 ruling by the United Nations that Puerto Rico was no longer a colony.

Manufacturing Operations At first, MCC intended to produce only high-volume, stable products in its Caribe facility—that is, those products simple to manufacture. But like the historical evolution of Puerto Rican industry, Caribe became a highly skilled plant, gradually supplanting other MCC facilities in the United States, Mexico, and Singapore—each originally vaunted for its superior technology, worker training, and/or lower wages. Caribe proved itself more effective and more profitable, before taxes, than any of the other MCC plants. MCC had initially wanted Caribe to account for no more than 30% of gross revenues, but by 1990 Caribe products generated 95% of MCC revenues. Plant Manager Tom Moschetti underscored the significance of the plant's accomplishments: "MCC is now in Puerto Rico not because of taxes but because we at Caribe are the most efficient and effective organization."

UNDERSTANDING, LEARNING, AND QUALITY

"We have to ensure that operators do not see themselves as victims of the factory."
—TOM MOSCHETTI

Accusatory phone calls and customer complaints had made the Micom Box problem the critical turning point in the plant's development. Until 1987, Micom Caribe had operated more or less as a manufacturing service to the California-based engineering and marketing groups. MCC designed the products and provided the stream of innovations which had been the traditional source of its competitive edge. Caribe's job was simply to manufacture the product—to take the specifications and to build in quantity. MCC saw manufacturing as a matter of simply keeping machines running and meeting delivery dates. There was little dialogue between design engineers and the plant.

The structure of MCC's Puerto Rican manufacturing facility had reflected the subsidiary role of manufacturing in MCC's competitive strategy. Like many similar plants in Puerto Rico, Caribe

had been set up to hit budgets and deadlines by tightly controlling costs and schedules. This had been achieved through an infrastructure based on a strictly hierarchical organization and through a direct labor force trained to do only one task well. Coordination and scheduling were carried out by "pushing" work onto the floor, while quality systems relied on traditional techniques such as Acceptable Quality Levels (AQL) and inspection. Caribe was little different from hundreds of other plants in Puerto Rico: traditional, static and hierarchical—designed to provide low cost over a stable range of products. Then, in 1987, came the Micom Box.

The Micom Box

The Micom Box differed from the manufacturing Caribe had been accustomed to: it was much more exacting of the manufacturing process. In addition, the schedule for introducing the Micom Box was more aggressive than Caribe was used to—reflecting the need of MCC to serve the quickening pace of innovation in the industry. While its function was very similar to the previous generation of devices, the Micom Box was based on a novel modular electronic design, which made it easy to configure to a wide variety of applications. To distinguish the Micom Box from the products of its increasingly innovative competitors, MCC's new managers focused on its quality, touting the product as the company's best ever—as the one device that would satisfy all customer needs for connecting computer and communication equipment. MCC promoted the Micom Box as "*the* quality product."

Customers awaited the "quality" product they had heard so much about, yet what they received instead, they told sales representatives, was not quality. Complaints deluged MCC. Moschetti recalled the confusion and frustration Caribe experienced. "Customers were using the language MCC had given them. They expected quality, and they were telling the company, 'This isn't a quality product.' But that was a marketing term, not an operations term." Accusations within MCC amplified intense customer complaints as all fingers pointed to the plant. It took Caribe six months to locate the origin of the problem. "We realized then that none of us—engineering, marketing or manufacturing—knew what quality meant," recalled Moschetti.

As MCC lost market share, Caribe scrambled to fix the problem. MCC's new president and his management team knew little about manufacturing and provided no guidance. Edwin Franceschi, Caribe's director of technical services, commented: "The information being provided by Marketing wasn't any use. They didn't know how to communicate in a way that would help us pin-point the manufacturing problems. By the time we had figured out what the problem was, a new one had appeared. We just couldn't seem to get feedback fast enough, or in the right form."

The plant was running out of fingers to put in the dike. It was time for a radical change of approach. Although Moschetti had worked under six different vice presidents in six years, he realized this situation was different. "I always expected corporate to provide leadership. It's easy to do what others tell you to do. But now the people above me knew nothing about manufacturing and assumed it was just about 'running the equipment,' so I had to go out and learn what we should do." Caribe could no longer survive by fighting intermittent fires without ever really tracking down their sources; it had to learn more about its own manufacturing operation and *why* things went awry.

Zen and the Art of Operations Strategy

From his days as a student, Moschetti had been fascinated by eastern philosophy and, in particular, by Zen Buddhism. As Caribe delved beneath the symptoms of its manufacturing ignorance, Moschetti drew on the Zen notion of Ka, acceptance of the unknown. He explained the orientation it suggested: "The relationship of the things I know is a tiny piece of the universe. The relationship of things I don't know is Ka. Knowing and respecting what you don't know is an asset."

As Caribe concentrated on improving production of the Micom Box, Moschetti also mapped out a long-term plan to change the plant's fundamental approach to manufacturing. He wanted to remove the mystery behind quality and provide people with the knowledge they would need to manufacture flawless products. He wanted employees to concentrate on how they were doing what they were doing rather than on a particular goal they were trying to achieve, and to realize that it was good to negotiate and experiment; that it was good to ask questions and not just blindly follow standard procedures; that it was even OK to fail.

Participation and democracy lay at the heart of his plans to manufacture better products. Operators had to contribute (see Exhibit 2). Employees had long been told, at least tacitly, that they were incapable of making decisions on their own; Moschetti even wondered whether they would have sufficient confidence in their own abilities. Managers had to accept participation and needed to share authority and responsibility. Caribe's metamorphosis would require managers to encourage non-managers to offer ideas for improvement. The people actually putting the products together knew the most about the process; they therefore were most likely to have the best ideas for improvement, reasoned Moschetti, and it was management's responsibility to elicit contributions.

Moschetti had a strong belief in the plant, but knew he would have to take specific actions to put in place an infrastructure in which improvement could flourish and become the natural way of doing things. To set up an environment conducive to this he initially set about making changes in the following areas:

- Encouraging senior managers to concentrate on developing a manufacturing strategy
- Increasing middle management responsibility
- Providing tools for quality improvement
- Installing manufacturing cells and teams, and
- Introducing cross-training of direct labor.

Getting middle managers to take responsibility would be difficult, since they tended to rely on the directors to guide them in running the plant. The directors were equally loath to give up their perceived responsibility of managing the plant, despite the need for them to be free to concentrate on longer-term strategic issues. While a firm believer in direct, honest approaches to management, this problem forced Moschetti to resort to subterfuge.

Managing Middle Management

Efforts to expand involvement began in early 1987 with the second tier of managers: ten people who comprised the plant's operating committee and reported to the directors of each function (see Exhibit 3). This operating committee was set up to manage the day-to-day running of the plant. However, it soon became clear that the steering committee, composed of the functional directors, had

EXHIBIT 2   Carmen Olmeda—An Assembly Operator

either refused or were finding it difficult to relinquish *de facto* control. The plant's directors were called to a conference in New Orleans with MCC management, and Moschetti deviously asked his directors who would run the plant, since they had previously insisted that the managers were not qualified. Everyone involved knew they had only one option: leave the plant in the managers' hands. With daily telephone conversations between New Orleans and Cayey, managers proved more than capable. From then on the operating committee took control of daily operations, freeing the steering committee to chart policy and attend to the plant's strategy for the future.

By 1990 the ten members of the Operating Committee met every day from 3:30 until 5:00 to discuss issues of mutual concern—everything from unexpected surges in orders to equipment assessment. "We came with the impression," one member commented, "of 'why waste an hour and a half when we have better things to do?' But we learned that only by extending our view of what a company does could we broaden our abilities to perform in our function." Their knowledge had broadened to such an extent—in part because committee leadership rotated—that Gonzalo Cordova, accounting manager in finance, had accepted additional responsibility as a manager of production control in the operations department.

Each manager on the operating committee had been accustomed to making decisions on his or her own, based only on his or her expertise. Although it had taken the group several years to coalesce, they did indeed feel comfortable working together to run the plant. One member commented, "Divergent views rather than convergent views bring us together." Another member put it simply, "We fight a lot." Noted one member, "It's more natural to ask your people to work in teams if you set the example. You're more familiar with the conflicts and pressures."

Tools for Quality Improvement

To weave quality into the fabric of the plant's ongoing operation, Moschetti, Manuel Morales, director of human resources, and Ramon Rivera, director of quality assurance, investigated quality programs and chose Philip Crosby's Quality Improvement Process (QIP). Although only one of many quality schemes popular among corporations, and though criticized by some, the Crosby approach appealed to Caribe because it was easy to understand, fitting, and came in the form of a product on which everyone could be trained.

EXHIBIT 3 Organization Chart

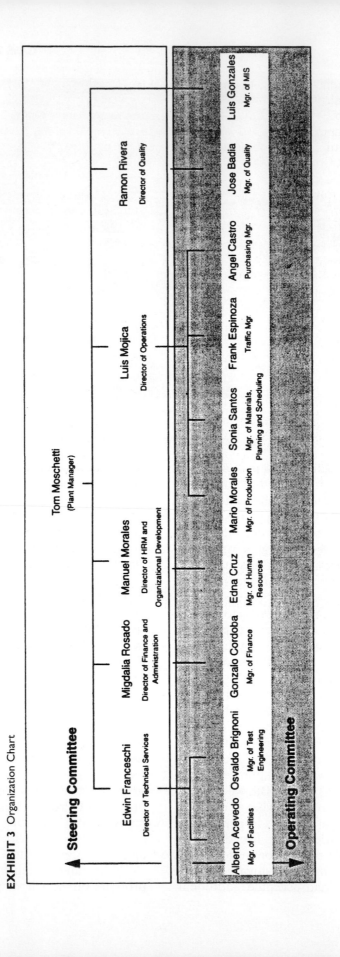

Steering Committee

Tom Moschetti
(Plant Manager)

Edwin Franceschi
Director of Technical Services

Migdalia Rosado
Director of Finance and Administration

Manuel Morales
Director of HRM and Organizational Development

Luis Mojica
Director of Operations

Ramon Rivera
Director of Quality

Operating Committee

Alberto Acevedo
Mgr. of Facilities

Osvaldo Brignoni
Mgr. of Test Engineering

Gonzalo Cordoba
Mgr. of Finance

Edna Cruz
Mgr. of Human Resources

Mario Morales
Mgr. of Production

Sonia Santos
Mgr. of Materials, Planning and Scheduling

Frank Espinoza
Traffic Mgr.

Angel Castro
Purchasing Mgr.

Jose Badia
Mgr. of Quality

Luis Gonzales
Mgr. of MIS

Crosby's system featured a gradual process for imparting sensitivity to quality, with 14 steps carefully mapped out. (See Exhibit 4 for Crosby's 14 steps.) Crosby stressed the importance of fundamental changes in a plant's culture, which coincided with Caribe's own intentions. Crosby's QIP aimed at involving everyone at the plant—just what Moschetti sought—but followed traditional paths of authority to get there, which conformed with Caribe's culture at the time.

Crosby preached that quality could not be described in relative terms: quality standards had to reflect market requirements; either a product conformed to those standards or it did not; either the product had quality, or it did not; products could not be said to be better or worse in quality. In Crosby's system, quality could be measured by adding up the costs of all activities that could be eliminated if products were produced without problems. By using zero defects as a principle, rather than a slogan, Crosby believed people would see the folly of tolerating a percentage of errors. Instead they would search for ways to make products correctly to begin with. Just as people do not expect doctors and nurses to drop a certain percentage of babies delivered, neither should they expect a certain percentage of products to be damaged. Companies, he argued, should find ways to make the manufacturing process work correctly.[10]

Caribe followed Crosby's approach, first eliciting senior plant management's commitment to quality, then establishing an infrastructure for recognizing problems with quality, and finally imparting techniques and mechanisms for identifying and solving problems. Directors and managers formed the Quality Improvement Team (QIT), which set and managed a master plan. The QIT appointed a chairperson for each of Crosby's steps, and that person would then recruit a team to implement the step. Quality assurance engineers at the plant trained production operators in the fundamental steps and tools of collecting information about problems, using statistical process control, and taking corrective action.

For the first time in Caribe's history, directors alone were not setting policy. Even more important, the QIP embraced every layer of the organization; everyone from floor workers to Moschetti became equipped with skills and mechanisms for introducing changes. The QIP sanctioned any change, suggested by anyone, if it improved quality. Process performance measures were developed to monitor each change and provide evidence for the value of a changed process. This reinforced the importance of contributions from anyone at the plant, finally making real Moschetti's aim of worker involvement.

Manufacturing Cells

Caribe had initially configured manufacturing in a rigid line and relied on automatic conveyors to transport material from station to station. But in 1987 Caribe swapped automated sizzle for flexible cells and cross-training. The plant was reorganized into 15 cells: 2 sequential cells for subassembly, 12 product-oriented cells for assembly and 1 cell for special testing. Each cell had from

[10]Philip B. Crosby, *Quality Is Free: The Art of Making Quality Certain* (New York: McGraw-Hill Book Company, 1979). Philip B. Crosby, *Quality Without Tears: The Art of Hassle-Free Management* (New York: McGraw-Hill Book Company, 1984).

EXHIBIT 4 Steps of the Crosby Quality Improvement Process

1. Management Commitment
2. Quality Improvement Team
3. Quality Measurement
4. Cost of Quality Evaluation
5. Quality Awareness
6. Corrective Action
7. Committee on the Zero Defects Program
8. Supervisor Training
9. Zero Defects Day
10. Goal Setting
11. Error Cause Removal
12. Recognition
13. Quality Councils
14. Do It Over Again*

*Philip B. Crosby, *Quality Is Free: The Art of Making Quality Certain* (New York: McGraw-Hill Book Company, 1979). Philip B. Crosby, *Quality Without Tears: The Art of Hassle-Free Management* (New York: McGraw-Hill Book Company, 1984).

five to eight people, who worked together as a team—rather than as peas in a pod, as they had previously. (See Exhibit 5 for the revised plant layout.)

For sub-assembly, workers in the insertion cell inserted components into circuit boards. Then the boards moved to the soldering cell, where they went through the wave-soldering machine.[11]

Members of the soldering cell then cut the circuit boards into the different shapes needed for MCC products and prepared the boards for further assembly.

In the 12 assembly cells, completed circuit boards were made into MCC's finished products. When the boards came out of sub-assembly, they went to a U-shaped cell dedicated to one particular type of product. All other parts peculiar to the cell's products were gathered from the stockroom as needed.

Once in a cell, circuit boards went through an initial functional test. From there they moved to

---

[11]In a wave soldering machine, the circuit board traveled above a bath of molten metal about 6 inches long and 18 inches wide. A paddle pushed waves of the metal down the bath, lightly soaking the board and thereby soldering the inserted components in place.

EXHIBIT 5 Micom Caribe Plant Layout in 1990

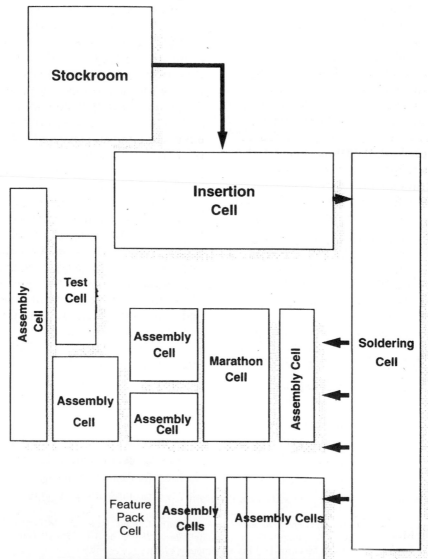

the burn-in section of the cell.[12] Caribe engineers and operators had devised their own burn-in machines that detected failures more quickly and cut total burn-in time from three days to two—and to 12 hours in some cases. Problems unearthed in testing or burn-in would be addressed by the technicians in each cell. Cell members then assembled the circuit boards and additional components into a completed MCC product, packed it, and sent it to the shipping area.

Cross-Training and Flexibility

The plant condensed nine classifications of employees down to one, Operator 1. From that entry-level position, workers were trained in 12 key skills (Exhibit 6). Once they received certification in those different areas within their cells, they could be promoted to Operator 2. To qualify for merit increases in their wages, workers had to be certified in 80% of all skills within a cell—their own cell the first year, and a different one every year thereafter. Caribe spent 7,000 hours on training, and all but one of the 90 production operators had been certified as Operator 2. With that number of employees cross-trained, the plant had become agile. People could shift easily between tasks, and their understanding of multiple aspects of the manufacturing process made attention to constant improvement a fact of operation. Carmen Rodríguez, an Operator 2, explained:

> Because we've been trained in all areas, we understand how what we do here will affect the step further down the process. It used to be, assemble, assemble, assemble—don't think about it, just do it. If you put something in the wrong direction, you would-

n't know it was a problem. The person doing testing would find it inserted wrong, but he or she wouldn't know what to do to prevent it happening again because testers were unfamiliar with prior processes.

Under a traditional manufacturing system, such as an assembly line, the absence of one person could disrupt the entire line. Because Caribe workers were trained in many processes, workers could easily be shifted among tasks to accommodate the most subtle of changes and thereby balance all steps of the process. Although this also made Caribe workers attractive to other firms, Caribe enjoyed a 4% turnover rate, 2% below the industry standard in Puerto Rico. By 1989, Caribe had built one of the most agile plants on the island.

Hurricane Hugo   Hurricane Hugo lashed Puerto Rico at the most inopportune time for Micom Caribe. Under new ownership, MCC was rebounding from several disappointing years. To reinforce the company's renewed vigor, management offered a gain-sharing program that depended upon meeting certain revenue and profit goals. Initial distributions were to come in October 1989. The expected bonuses had created a sense of euphoria throughout the company.

MCC was on the verge of achieving the prescribed goal, and pressure was mounting on the plant. The sales had been made, and the orders were set to hit Caribe during the final week of September. But Hurricane Hugo hit first. The factory was completely disabled. Some MCC managers in California had all along doubted that Caribe could achieve the target. "We've done our jobs," Moschetti recalled hearing, "they won't do theirs." Even those who had faith in the plant now knew the hurricane would impede its efforts.

Communication lines were all down, and a week's delay existed in relaying information. Sales orders could not reach the plant. Raw materials

---

[12]Circuit boards experienced a high rate of failure in the initial hours and days of their use. Manufacturers of any equipment involving circuit boards therefore ran their products for several days in a process known as "burn-in," which eliminated all faulty units and moved the products past the initial period of high failure.

EXHIBIT 6 Components of Operator Certification

1. Material Handling
2. Mechanical Skills
3. Document Interpretation
4. Packing Skills
5. Quality Criteria in Metal Parts
6. Soldering Skills
7. Testing and Procedure Interpretation
8. Machine Operator Skills
9. Group Concept Training and Problem Solving Skills
10. Quality Awareness
11. Self Inspection
12. Safety Awareness

could not be delivered because the airport had been closed. When Caribe finally received the sales orders, the plant faced a stack of orders for the Micom Box. The cell that assembled the Micom Box simply lacked the capacity to meet the orders.

Spontaneously, operators from other cells designed a second Micom Box cell. That same afternoon, the new cell—staffed by engineers, secretaries, maintenance technicians, and manufacturing operators from other cells—began producing Micom Boxes. Caribe made its shipments, MCC achieved its targets, and everyone in the company received the promised bonus. Caribe had proven itself capable, building credibility and trust with corporate management. In addition, operators had built confidence in the system and a deeper trust began to develop between workers and managers. With the tools to improve quality and the confidence and desire to do so, quality began to spread through the plant like a flame in a tinder box. The Process Improvement Teams were the spark to the flame.

IMPROVEMENT SPREADS: THE PROCESS IMPROVEMENT TEAMS

Caribe continued to move methodically through the 14 steps of Crosby's system, and in the autumn of 1989 every cell formed its own Process Improvement Team (PIT), the fundamental rubric of the quality improvement process. Cell members would meet to identify problems, discuss ways to solve them, and track their progress. Gerardo Batista, an Operator 2 certified in two different cells, described the radical change PITs and the whole quality process had made: "Before, employees couldn't have insights. They did not matter to Micom. But now I know that if my idea is good, it will be adopted." Rafael Rios, a manager for human resources, commented on the metamorphosis he had witnessed.

People in manufacturing used to be treated like children. They were given everything in their hand, and they expected everything. Caribe used to go out of its way to be parental: "Let me make the decision for you." Now people are solving problems on their own.

Every cell had a simple chart printed on an 8 ½ x 11 sheet of paper: the corrective action sheet. Cell members kept track of every problem they encountered as soon as it arose. Six columns detailed the status of each problem. The first column named the problem; the second defined the problem; the third listed the quick-fix (the temporary solution); the fourth listed the cause, once discovered; the fifth column gave the corrective action (the solution addressing the underlying cause); and the final column detailed any later follow-up (see Exhibit 7).

EXHIBIT 7 Corrective Action Report

Customer	Sales Order	Problem Definition	Quick Fix	Root Cause
MST	68252	Customer received incorrect product	Packer w/o training was replaced. Shipping audit was performed	Lack of awareness in some personnel Part numbers stocked in the same location
BLACK BOX	65893	Customer received incomplete order	Personnel awareness	Shipping audit not performed in some cases. Lack of awareness in some personnel
BLACK BOX	65893	Customer received correct product with incorrect label.	New personnel were trained for rush periods. Shipping audit was performed.	Not trained personnel at assembly area in rush periods. Inspection and sampling plans not followed by production personnel.
HEWLETT PACKARD	58736	Customer received incorrect product	Shipping audit was performed.	Shipping inspection not performed in some cases.
AQUILA	67568	Customer received incomplete order	Audit at shipping area. Physical inventory performed in the cell for this part number.	Lack of awareness in some personnel Some doubts due to new product

Prepared by Lucy Guerrero.

Negotiation and Experimentation

Moschetti succinctly characterized the plant's approach to quality: "While we have learned that quality for us is 'conformance to requirements,' we have also realized that the goal of quality is customer satisfaction, and the customer is the next operation." Every step in the manufacturing process was defined as a customer of prior steps and a supplier for future steps. Whoever found a problem had to take responsibility for solving it, which meant finding the source of the problem, physically getting together with the people responsible for that process, and solving the problem. Whenever an operator learned of a problem, he or she had to address the problem, just as a supplier would.

Caribe employees were encouraged to look for solutions through knowledge, negotiation, and experimentation. When a quality problem arose, those affected by it in the downstream step had to be precise about their problem. Operators had to define precisely what they needed from their "supplier" and why, so their suppliers could meet those needs. Once the objectives were understood, both supplier and customer had to work together to determine together whether they had the technical knowledge necessary to reach the objective. If they lacked knowledge, they both had to experiment until they found a solution.

Negotiation and experimentation formed the plant's common language, replacing traditional talk of action items and results. "When most people face a problem, they think they know where they're going and exactly how to get there," Moschetti observed. "But we learned you cannot do that with quality—so much of the difficulty is a result of the absence of knowledge." Improving quality meant accepting that absence and working through it. If people encountered a problem with quality, they had to explore why it arose: What did they not know about "customer" needs? What requirements had to be clarified for "suppliers"? What technical knowledge did they lack that caused the problem to arise? How could they acquire that knowledge? Only by engaging these questions could they actually move to a point of knowing what they wanted to do and how to do it. People began to accept that questioning, learning and changing were a normal part of their job. As Moschetti put it, "The only way to get there is to get out of thinking you're there."

An Example of the Quality Improvement Process: The Feature Pack Cell

MCC's Feature Pack was a small rectangular device the size of a candy bar that enhanced the capabilities of MCC's multiplexors. The Feature Pack production cell looked like every other cell in the plant—except for the blue and silver Micom Caribe banner hanging overhead. The U-shaped cell area had a corrective action sheet and two flip charts (giant pads of paper on easels): one tracing the ongoing work done by the cell's PIT; the other, hanging at the cell's entrance, listing the questions the cell had for engineers—a list engineers roaming through the plant would check.

Like all other PITs in the plant, when the Feature Pack team held their first meeting, cell members listed all of the problems that prevented them from doing their jobs effectively or resulted in defective products. These were listed on a flip chart, and then each team member assigned a rating, from one to five, to each problem. The team tallied scores and ranked the 19 major problems they had identified. The team chose 12 problems to address first, from a lack of tools to inadequate visual aids—problems common to many PIT lists.

After culling these "vital few" impediments most responsible for their quality problems, the team gathered data about each impediment: how it hindered them, how it affected their work, how often it occurred. They probed for the root cause, experimented with solutions, and sought support from the plant's engineers when necessary. For example, the team worked with the manufacturing engineers to develop succinct, clear visual aids (diagrams) in color for any of the cell members to follow when assembling the Feature Pack. When asked what people did before the visual aids had been available, the only operator formerly responsible for assembly pointed to her head and remarked, "If I wasn't here, no one could do the work." Now the five members of the cell produced 1,500 Feature Packs every month, and as the PIT leader remarked, "We all know the same essential things." Like all others in the plant, the cell used Pareto charts to determine which defects in the Feature Pack they should focus on most intently (see Exhibit 8). They also drew on Caribe's unique model for negotiating better quality.

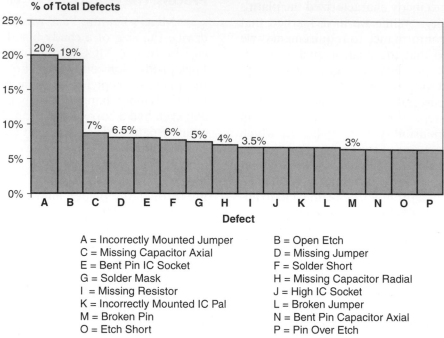

EXHIBIT 8 Feature Pack Pareto Chart (December 1989–May 1990)

In May 1990 the Feature Pack cell had been receiving faulty circuit boards. The cell kept track of the rejected boards for two weeks, and then cell members arranged a meeting with the insertion cell. The Feature Pack PIT presented the data it had collected, showed some of the faulty boards, and discussed the consequences for Feature Pack assembly. Once the people from insertion understood the problem and its ramifications, they understood the need to address it. The Feature Pack PIT then posted a graph in the middle of the plant to show the percentage of errors coming from the insertion cell. The graph called attention to the problem and traced the progress made by the insertion cell as it addressed and corrected the error.

Hanging overhead, the Micom Caribe banner testified to the cell's remarkable efforts. Eight consecutive months without a single defect in the Feature Pack had earned the cell the highest honor bestowed within the plant. Every quarter the 15 cells selected the one that had proven itself most dedicated to quality, and the banner celebrated that distinction. (See Exhibit 9 for the results of Feature Pack's quality improvement.)

INSPECTION, DESIGN AND QUALITY IMPROVEMENT

"Quality should be like breathing. You just do it."

—RAMON RIVERA,
DIRECTOR OF QUALITY ASSURANCE

To check for errors, Caribe had once needed as many as 30 quality inspectors. By mid-1990 it had none. The number of circuit boards that required trouble-shooting dropped by 82%. The plant had cut inventory by 68% and could respond to customer requests from 25% to 50% faster. Caribe cut throughput time from 18 days to fewer than 8. On-time delivery improved by 21%. Warranty returns dropped by 30%. (Exhibits 10, 11 and 12 show summary data on quality improvement.) "Most people get high on the results of our quality process," Moschetti concluded. "But even more significant, it relaxed our resistance to change."

The personal efforts behind the statistics underscored Caribe's accomplishments. Members of the soldering cell, for example, typified the plant's dedication to quality. Production operators would

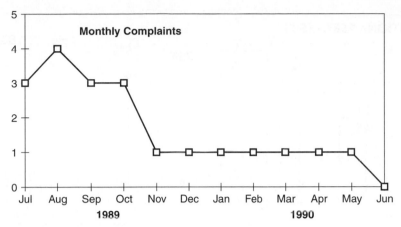

EXHIBIT 9 Feature Pack: Customer Complaints

Indicator	1988	1990	% Reduction
Work-in-Process Inventory	$3.97m	$1.27m	68
Total Inventory	$10.85m	$7.56m	30
Scrap (Annualized)	$700k	$175k	75
Manufacturing Lead Time (Days)	18	6	66
Internal Rejections (%)	1.86%	1.1%	41
Printed Circuit Boards Requiring Trouble Shooting	1602	288	82
Warranty Returns (Units)	189	132	30

EXHIBIT 10 Manufacturing Improvements Micom Caribe, 1988–1990

take boards from the wave soldering machine, and using a fixture—a frame that fastened the circuit board in place and served as something like a stencil—they would maneuver a router to create the appropriate shape. Caribe had traditionally ordered fixtures from professional manufacturers specializing in them. Each fixture cost between $400 and $600 and took a month or more to make. Not only did operators have difficulty using the professional fixtures, which never seemed perfectly tailored when they arrived, but there were never enough fixtures to match the different boards Caribe manufactured each day. Worse yet, some ordered fixtures would simply never arrive.

By the spring of 1990, just six months after workers in the soldering cell had formed their process improvement team, they had eliminated those problems. Whenever the cell needed a new fixture, one of the operators, Carlos Torres, would make a finely tailored fixture from otherwise discarded materials—scrap circuit boards and wood panels from incoming shipping crates. In about 30

minutes, Torres could produce a superior fixture, all for a cost of $2 in materials. Perhaps as important as the savings and better fit, the home-made fixtures reduced the time it took to perform the cutting task from 1 minute 58 seconds to just 48 seconds. Because he worked in the cell itself and understood the processes involved, Torres made fixtures that produced more reliable products. In addition, problems and urgent demands could be addressed immediately within the cell.

Design for Manufacturability As an extension of its quality effort, Caribe established a Design For Manufacturability plan. It provided a structured way of linking the plant with corporate design teams in California. Caribe had pursued a closer relationship with California, and despite considerable skepticism from the U.S. engineers, Caribe finally convinced designers to visit the plant. As Edwin Franceschi, director of technical services, commented, "We wanted to show them that we don't have monkeys in the trees around

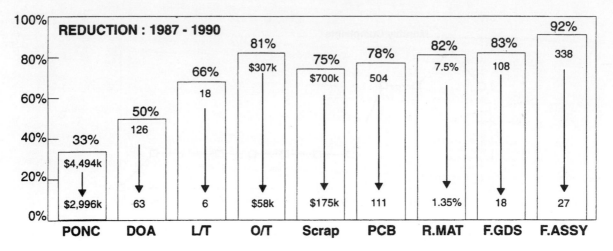

PONC = Price of Non-Conformance (costs associated with correcting errors)
DOA = Dead On Arrival (units that fail at customer sites within first three months)
L/T = Lead Time, Days
O/T = Overtime, Annualized
PCB = Printed Circuit Boards (sub-assembly failures), units monthly
R.MAT = Raw Material (rejection rate of materials received from suppliers)
F.GDS = Finished Goods (shipment verified to contain exactly what customer ordered), units/monthly
F.ASSY = Final Assembly failures, units/monthly

EXHIBIT 11 Quality Improvement at Micom Caribe, 1987–1990

here. We wanted to give them some idea of our new capabilities." A formal channel now existed to relate suggestions from factory workers on this team to the corporate development group. In its first nine months, the first product designed with Caribe's input recorded no failures in the field, and the streak had yet to be broken. Micom Caribe had passed down an average of 250 engineering change orders[13] per month in 1988, but by the end of 1990 that figure had dropped to just 40.

Breathing

In June 1990, Caribe detected a recurring problem in one particular circuit board. A teleconference between engineers in California and operators and engineers at Caribe clarified the problem and the flaw was eliminated. Later that month, a manager from MCC's California offices called Moschetti and asked him for samples of the

bad circuit boards. Moschetti went to a test engineer and asked him if he was aware of the request. The test engineer candidly responded, "We don't build bad boards. Do you want me to make some fail?" Caribe was breathing.

MARATHON

In the summer of 1990, MCC again revolutionized the industry when it announced its Marathon series of data/voice network servers (DVNS). MCC would be the first company to link voice and data communication on a data line. Because voice could not tolerate transmission delays acceptable for data, voice could not be carried along with data and fax transmissions, except on special lines (called T1) too expensive for all but the largest companies. Like MCC's other products, the Marathon 5K was a box containing numerous circuit boards with communication chips. A digital signal processor lay at its core, allowing the Marathon 5K to take voice, break it into digital packets, nestle them among normal computer traffic on the leased data line, and process those packets so fast the conversation sounded like any

---

[13]An engineering change order (ECO) informed design engineers of a problem encountered in manufacturing and attributable to design of the product or process. The ECO requested a change to rectify the problem.

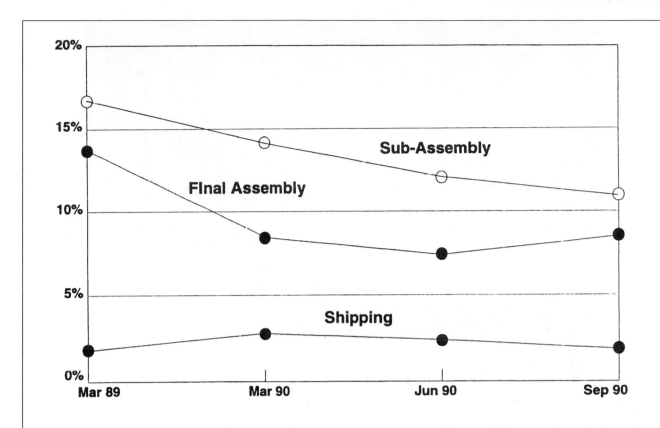

EXHIBIT 12 Manufacturing Quality Indicators: Non-Conformance

	% Items Non-Conforming		
	Sub-Assembly	Final Assembly	Shipping
March 1989	16.6	13.2	1.8
March 1990	13.9	8.8	2.4
June 1990	12.3	6.1	2.3
September 1990	11.5	8.9	1.7

normal phone conversation.[14] (See Exhibits 13 and 14).

The Marathon products were expected to range in price from $2,750 to $9,900, depending on the features chosen, so MCC would once again pro-

vide a critical product accessible to medium-sized companies. As Ken Guy, vice president for corporate strategy and business development, explained, "The T1 companies are aimed at the Fortune 500. We are aimed at the Unfortunate 500,000."[15]

To make room for production of the Marathon series, Caribe needed to clear 20% of

[14]Micom Communications Corporation, news release: "New Product Developed to Curb Office Communications Costs," November 2, 1990. Audio Video Reporting Services, "Chip Talk," KNX Radio, December 12, 1990. Harry Newton, "Every Man's Network," *DataCommunications,* supplement to November 1990, p. 4.

[15]John T. Mulqueen, "Micom Integrates Voice, Data, and Fax at Low Speeds," *DataCommunications,* November 1990.

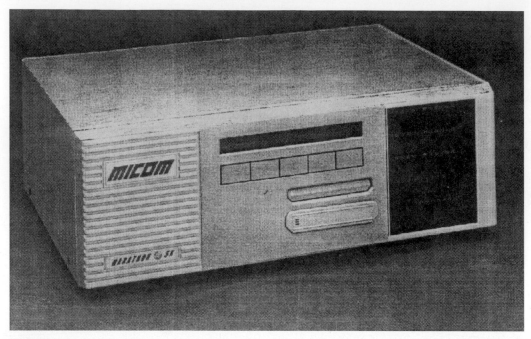

EXHIBIT 13 Marathon 5K

floor space. The plant's engineers usually rearranged plant layout, spending a tremendous amount of time and effort to complete work-flow and work-space analyses. Luis Mojica, director of operations, went to the PITs instead. "You have complained about your work space in the past," each cell was told, "and now you have permission to rearrange your area in a way that's best for you. But can you create a 20% savings in space?" Within five days, the PITs had created a 30% reduction in space.

Marathon provided a special opportunity for Caribe. The Marathon product development team had asked Edwin Franceschi to join them, and in addition to Franceschi's frequent visits to California, two manufacturing engineers from Caribe spent six months in Simi Valley. Even more important, Marathon promised to compensate for declining sales of other MCC products.

CHARTING A COURSE

Caribe was now a plant to be proud of. Marathon would finally provide it with an opportunity to demonstrate that its new way of running operations could provide a clear, competitive advantage to its parent: world-class quality—with enough flexibility to beat the competition to the marketplace. While the Marathon launch had the plant enthusiastically consumed—with everyone intent on showing MCC the plant's new mettle, Moschetti was more reflective:

"When we set out on this journey, we wanted to know how to improve quality. But we have learned more than that. Much more. We can now do things which we would never have thought possible before 1987. I am sure we have capabilities that none of us are aware of. As managers, we are less involved in fire-fighting now—we have time to think more strategically about manufacturing.

"We know we can't sit still," said Moschetti, "We have to develop a lot of our long-range plans on our own. We often sit and wonder: 'What do we really know now, and what should we be doing and learning next? What should *our* strategy be, as a manufacturing operation, if we are to continue to build on our successes, and provide a lasting competitive advantage to MCC as a whole?' "

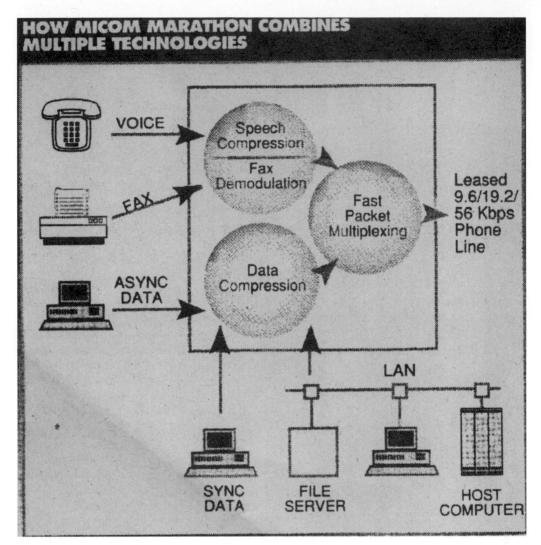

EXHIBIT 14 Data Voice Networking

Micom's Marathon uses two basic methods to pump information through leased analog or leased digital lines. The first method is compression. It compresses data and voice into more economical streams. The second method is fast packet multiplexing, which should be called "intelligent" fast packet multiplexing. It does three things: it sends information only if there is information to send. Second, it can start sending a packet of information before it has completely received the packet. Third, fast packet multiplexing can interrupt delivery of one packet in favor of sending another. Typically, it would interrupt (delay) a data packet in favor of sending a more urgent "voice" one.

Source: *Data Communications,* November 1990.